A DISARMING SPIRIT

A DISARMING SPIRIT

The Life of
Archbishop Raymond Hunthausen

Frank Fromherz

Foreword by Rev. Michael G. Ryan
Tribute to a Colleague by Bishop Thomas Gumbleton

A Disarming Spirit: The Life of Archbishop Raymond Hunthausen

Paperback ISBN: 978-1-941392-12-6
Hardcover ISBN: 978-1-941392-13-3

A Disarming Spirit: The Life of Archbishop Raymond Hunthausen is published by Marymount Institute Press and TSEHAI Publishers Loyola Marymount University, One LMU Drive, Suite 3012, Los Angeles, CA 90045

www.marymountinstitutepress.org
www.tsehaipublishers.com

First Edition: Summer 2018

Publisher: Elias Wondimu

Editor: Theresia de Vroom

Typesetting and Design: Sara Martinez

Cover Photograph: "Janice Duffell, 10, left, and Archbishop Hunthauesen, right, at Good Friday nuclear demonstration at Bangor Naval Submarine Base, Friday, April 1, 1988" by Mike Siegel. Copyright © 1988, *The Seattle Times*. Used with permission.

Copy Editors: William Gish, Sofia Leggio, Alyssa Venezia, and Rozella Apel

In loving celebration of and aspiration for my sons,
their Bolivian spouses, and our five grandchildren.

“Neither the life of an individual nor the history of a society can be understood without understanding both.”

C. Wright Mills, *The Sociological Imagination*

CONTENTS

PUBLISHER'S NOTE

When we accepted this manuscript for publication, we wanted to publish it immediately. However, due to Archbishop Hunthausen's personal request and the author's commitment to members of the Hunthausen family we did not publish this book until the Archbishop had died. We stood by the author and have respected the wishes of Archbishop Hunthausen and his family. Now, since the time has come, it gives us great pleasure to share this authorized biography of Archbishop Hunthausen with the world.

The photograph on the cover of this book was taken by Mike Siegel on Good Friday April 1, 1988 and appeared in the *Seattle Times* the day afterward. At the time there were two simultaneous demonstrations against nuclear proliferation; one in New York City and the other at the Bangor Naval Submarine Base near Seattle, Washington. The photograph depicts the subject of this book exactly.

In a modern-day reenactment of the passion play, Archbishop Raymond Hunthausen walks behind a young and contemporary incarnation of Jesus. As the ten-year old Janice Duffell carries her cross, the Archbishop follows her. He is ever in the background; an observer, a seer, a participant in the enfolding events, as well as a prophet whose call for resistance and disarmament would send shock waves through the US government and the Vatican.

Just as the photograph depicts him on that day, the Archbishop's life's work was to follow Jesus. In doing so he would pit the way of the cross against the way of the missile; in doing so he would try to ensure the future for generations to come by simply, quietly, and heroically standing behind them.

Theresia de Vroom
Editor
Marymount Institute Press

Elias Wondimu
Publisher and Manager
Marymount Institute Press

ACKNOWLEDGEMENTS

Key supporters Nancy Nordhoff, Jim and Becky Burns, Bishop Tom Gumbleton, Fr. Mike Ryan, Elise DeGooyer and Bernie McDonough, Conley Lynch, Jack and Carol Lynch, Neil and Charlotte Lynch, Fr. Mike McDermott, Shelley and Jim Douglass, Kim and Bill Wahl, J.L. Drouhard, Don Hopps and Pam Piering, Kirby Brown, Fr. John Heagle and Sr. Fran Ferder, and Con Kelly (who worked with me in a chapter by chapter editing process)—thank you! Special thanks also to Archbishop Hunthausen's kin—members of the Hunthausen, Stergar, and Walsh families who shared stories about "Uncle Dutch"—and to all the people who have backgrounds with Archbishop Hunthausen and gave of their time for personal interviews.

So many have assisted in one way or another as this book has developed, including the Graduate Theological Union faculty (John Coleman, Karen Lebacqz, Eldon Ernst) who worked with me on the original dissertation, *Archbishop Raymond Hunthausen's Thought and Practice in Society and Church: A Socio-Historical and Ethical Case Study of Nonviolence*, completed in 1990. In that early period, I benefited greatly from the assistance of various staff members of the Archdiocese of Seattle, including Archbishop Hunthausen's secretary, the late Marilyn Maddeford, and the head of Public Affairs, the late Kay Lagreid. University of California at Berkeley-based mentor, the late Robert Bellah, greatly influenced my thinking in general and this book in particular. During these past few years while I've been researching and writing this book, various colleagues, staff, students, and social science reference librarians at Portland State University—and my good friend and sociologist Peter Callero of Western Oregon University—have been so helpful. Thanks also to the staff at the Carroll College alumni office and at the libraries of Carroll College, the University of Portland, and Seattle University, along with the archivists and others at the Archdiocese of Seattle, the Diocese of Helena, the University of Washington, Pacific Lutheran University, and the Montana Historical Society.

I have been delighted and honored to work with Theresia de Vroom, this book's editor, and Elias Wondimu, publisher, and their team at Marymount Institute Press at Loyola Marymount University: Sara Martinez, graphic designer; Ryan Beitz, graduate assistant; William Gish, graduate assistant; Sofia Leggio, Alyssa Venezia and Rozella Apel, student interns; and cartographer, Ellen White.

All profit made from the sale of *A Disarming Spirit* will be given to the Ground Zero Community, a nonprofit organization established for the educational work related to the Ground Zero Center for Nonviolent Action. Established in 1977, just as Bangor Naval Base was being built, Ground Zero set forth on a mission "which seeks the goal of a world free from nuclear destruction and unjust division of humanity." That mission continues today. (See www.gzcenter.org). Those who founded this community inspired Raymond Hunthausen and encouraged his witness for justice and peace.

It has been said that gratitude is the heart of prayer. I want to especially thank Bridget Cooke, my beloved spouse, who has been with me each step of the way.

Frank Fromherz

FOREWORD

by Reverend Michael G. Ryan

If I were to write a book about my friend and mentor, Archbishop Raymond G. Hunthausen, I would center my thoughts on his conscience, his courage, and his character. And that's exactly what Frank Fromherz has done in this homage to a truly remarkable man and leader. But it's more than a homage. It's the story of a bishop who got his on-the-job training at the Second Vatican Council and who devoted his life and ministry to making the great vision of that Council come alive in a local church. In telling the story, Fromherz brings together some of the major players in the archbishop's life and ministry—family members, friends, colleagues, associates—and allows them to share their perspective on this remarkable man. He even gives some of the archbishop's critics and opponents their day in court and, in doing so, sheds light on why the archbishop's ministry came under investigation by the highest authorities of the Church he loved and served.

To anyone who had the privilege of knowing him, Archbishop Hunthausen was a hero, but a very unlikely hero. With the archbishop, it was never about him; it was always about you, and about the world, and the Church, and the great issues of the day. But for all his humility, his personal diffidence, his quiet, unassuming ways, he made his mark, a mark that sunk deep into the very soul of the Church of Seattle that he led during the years following the Second Vatican Council, years that were sometimes heady and exhilarating, and at other times trying and turbulent. And even when the storms of controversy swirled around him—as they inevitably do for any prophet—the archbishop remained steady and calm, rooted in God, rooted in family, rooted in a conviction that was God-driven and God-centered. That's why conscience, courage, and character belong at the heart of any attempt to tell the Hunthausen story.

And Frank Fromherz has done a fine job in telling important parts of the story. His own personal fondness and abiding respect for the archbishop and for all he stood for make his telling of the story credible and compelling. Without a doubt, he makes an important contribution to a significant chapter in American Catholic Church history which needs to be told.

During the days, weeks, and months when his name was in the headlines, I remember telling the archbishop more than once that he was going to be an important footnote in the history of the Church in this country. In typical fashion, he dismissed the thought and quietly went about his work. But over time he proved me wrong. He was not a footnote. He was a whole chapter.

And what was his work? Preaching and teaching, listening and learning, inspiring and instructing, all the while never compromising principle, never striking back, never losing faith. "The Lord is in charge," he would remind me time and again. "We just need to listen to the Spirit and to follow the Spirit's lead."

And that is what he did. In season and out of season. In parish churches, and far-flung missions, around conference tables and at committee meetings, at military bases and gatherings of nuns, at prayer services and protests, on university campuses and at ecumenical meetings, before crowds large and small, friendly and hostile, he listened and he led. And in the process, the Church of Seattle became the Church envisioned by the Second Vatican Council—strong, holy, more grass-roots than top-down, more consultative, more compassionate, more courageous. Just like its leader.

If you knew Archbishop Hunthausen, reading this book will remind you why you loved and respected him, why you were convinced that he was exactly what a bishop should be. And if you didn't know him, be prepared to meet a giant of the late-twentieth century Church. An unassuming giant, but a giant nonetheless and, yes, "a disarming spirit."

Father Michael G. Ryan
Seattle, Washington

TRIBUTE TO A COLLEAGUE

by Bishop Thomas Gumbleton

To write a book giving the facts of a person's life is important. But to write a book that brings out the depth of a person's character is a true achievement. Even the title of Frank Fromherz's book, *A Disarming Spirit*, begins to give you a sense of the type of person Ray Hunthausen was.

The first time I laid eyes on Ray Hunthausen was when I was a student-priest in Rome. He came over as a newly ordained bishop for the first session of Vatican Council II. I heard from a fellow student that there was an American bishop who was looking to buy a car. I had one that I used for a year and I no longer wanted it. It was not very practical to have a car in Rome and I was anxious to sell it. I managed to make contact with Ray and he arranged to purchase the car. In that brief encounter I was impressed with the kind of eagerness which he so clearly brought to everything he did. Participating in the Council was no exception. Ray wanted to become as deeply involved in the learning process as possible. He was the youngest in seniority at the Council, having been ordained a bishop only a few weeks before the Council began. I learned from his friends how he tried to be involved in the Council itself and also in the informal gatherings of bishops so he could participate in this historic event as much as possible.

Years later, after I had been ordained a bishop and became a member of the United States Conference of Catholic Bishops (USCCB), I came to know him as a colleague. Even though we were from different parts of the country and did not have frequent contact other than at the semi-annual national meetings of the bishops, I became impressed with his thoughtfulness, his clarity of thought and his ability to express his ideas. When you got to know Ray Hunthausen, there was never a doubt about who he was. The integrity with which he lived his life was always very clear.

Both of us became deeply involved in the peace movement, especially the effort to abolish nuclear weapons from the world. In fact, he made a dramatic change in his life. He became one of the strongest voices against nuclear weapons in the United States, even going so far as refusing to pay half his income taxes as a protest against the constant development and commitment of our country to use these weapons of mass destruction. He did not come to this position easily. As a loyal citizen of the US, he was always ready to give government policies the benefit of the doubt. But once he began to be aware of the destructive capability of our arsenal and the United States government's commitment to use the weapons, he never wavered in his conviction that the government policy was wrong. Nor did he ever waver in his determination that in conscience he must work to bring about a change in the policy.

In the early 1980s the USCCB undertook an effort to develop a pastoral letter regarding the possession and use of nuclear weapons. I was named to the committee charged with the development of this pastoral letter. We came quite quickly to the judgment that any use of such weapons could never be justified. However, a secondary question concerned the United State's policy regarding the possession of such weapons as a strategy of deterrence. This policy meant that we would maintain a nuclear arsenal to be used in the event that we were ever attacked with nuclear weapons. After lengthy discussions our Committee concluded that a strategy of deterrence could be justified as long as our policy included continuing steps toward disarmament leading, ultimately, to the abolition of all such weapons. Obviously, if that condition were not met, the possession of such weapons would be immoral. With some reluctance, I accepted this judgment of the Committee. When the draft was presented to the whole Conference Ray Hunthausen saw clearly that our government's policy would not be one of moving toward disarmament. For this reason he continued to press for an outright condemnation of the strategy of deterrence.

And in fact, over the years his judgment has proven to be correct. The United States has continued to maintain its full nuclear war-making capacity. In the face of this, the USCCB has never been willing to call the government to account for not meeting the condition we had stated as necessary to justify a strategy of deterrence. I look back with regret that I was not more adamant in following the policy that Ray advocated.

He did all of this as a leader of the Archdiocese of Seattle where, obviously, many people would not agree with him. But he always maintained an openness and a willingness to listen to people and engage in dialogue over the issue. Very often, there were disagreements, but because his conviction came from his deep and informed decisions, and because he was able to listen to other viewpoints without anger or malice, people respected him and he was able to maintain good relationships even with those who disagreed with him. However, besides the issue of nuclear weapons, he was also confronted by members of the Church who disagreed with him regarding other areas of implementing Vatican Council teachings.

Among other issues, his detractors objected to the changes he promoted in the liturgy, his openness to gay and lesbian people, going so far as to allow Dignity to hold their meetings and celebrate liturgy at the Cathedral. He also made great strides in easing the attainment of annulments for people in broken marriages. It was on the basis of these issues that the Vatican investigated and ultimately imposed on him an "auxiliary" bishop with authority in those specific areas. In effect the Vatican was removing him from those areas of diocesan leadership and administration. Ray's integrity compelled him to bring this decision into the open. He was willing to be transparent because he felt the people had the right to know who was making decisions in these areas. When this became known, huge controversy developed in the diocese. A great majority of people supported his leadership and wanted his full authority restored. The controversy was only resolved when he reluctantly accepted a co-adjutor archbishop appointed by the Pope. But this "two-headed" leadership was not workable. Ultimately, he found it best to resign. Archbishop Hunthausen lived through that demeaning experience without developing any kind of hatred or resentment for what was being done to him. He never exhibited any hostility toward those who were deeply critical of what he was doing. He never wavered in his commitment to implement what he saw as Vatican Council directives.

As a bishop, I have great admiration for this—he was very committed to drawing the people of the diocese into the decision making process. He was doing for the Archdiocese of Seattle what we see Pope Francis is now doing for the whole Church—devising ways for the voice of the people to be heard and to share in the decision making process.

Ray also had a fantastic ability to interact with people of other faiths and denominations. He was far ahead of other dioceses in that regard. Some of his closest friends were rabbis and ministers.

Ray drew strength to act with integrity and compassion from a deep prayer life which he nurtured. He was part of a small group of bishops who prayed together on a regular basis and even made retreats together. I believe that as a result of his deep prayer life he was able to act with extraordinary courage and integrity as Archbishop of Seattle and also became an outstanding leader for Catholics throughout the whole country.

Ray Hunthausen is a role model and hero for me because of his integrity and total commitment to leading the Church in its mission to transform our world into as close an image of the Reign of God as possible. I am a better person and bishop because I knew him.

Bishop Thomas J. Gumbleton
Detroit, Michigan

NOTE FROM THE AUTHOR

I first met Archbishop Raymond Hunthausen in the early 1980s just after he decided to do conscientious war tax resistance. Hunthausen inspired me just as he has so many others. How can each of us try to become a just person while living in an unjust society and in an unjust church, and how can we help to transform both religion and society? By how he lived, Raymond Hunthausen offers some answers. Grounded in numerous interviews with him directly and with people close to him (colleagues, friends, and family), this book also includes the voices of critics. My research has included a trove of historical records—local, regional, national, and international newspaper articles, as well as dissertations and other sources. This book includes the complete text of Archbishop Hunthausen's watershed "Faith and Disarmament" speech, Cardinal Ratzinger's 1985 confidential letter, and the two contrasting chronologies of the Seattle-Rome conflict: Rome's version and Hunthausen's.

I have tried to let various voices speak for themselves—supporters, as well as detractors of Hunthausen. I set out to convey in rich social context a blend of personal biography and public history. The central objective has been to do justice to a complex biographical and sociological study involving a religious leader, accounting for the milieu within which he lived his life. I have many people and many research sources to credit, as will be seen in the extensive endnotes of each chapter. I have made conscientious efforts to provide attribution for all the diverse sources informing this work, for in so many ways the book is more a carefully researched compilation and contextualization of many voices and perspectives rather than an original thought-construction of my own perspective--which I have not ignored but have downplayed. To be sure, my own background has influenced the research approach I have adopted. I cannot claim to be value-free. I warmly welcome constructive critiques. Do please let me know if you see errors I may have made. Contact me via email: frankfromherz@gmail.com and thank you.

As to what has motivated me to pursue this study, over the course of twenty-five years in Catholic social justice and peace work, I had the experience of meeting several Latin American bishops involved in liberation theology. I also had the experience of working with various U.S. bishops—on economic justice, the environment, and peace. I have seen up close the oppressive power structures of their religion and society, which U.S. bishops sometimes challenge but too often reinforce. In this context, Archbishop Hunthausen's integrity and prophetic witness have been both humbling and fortifying. He did not pay the same price as Archbishop Oscar Romero of El Salvador, but Hunthausen was inspired, like Romero, to speak truth to power.

Frank Fromherz

Part I

CONSCIENCE

"Conscience is the most secret core and sanctuary of a man. There he is alone with God, whose voice echoes in his depths."—*Pastoral Constitution on the Church in the Modern World* (paragraph #16), Second Vatican Council, 1965

Chapter One

FAITH AND DISARMAMENT

Like a stream in a mountain meadow, his gentle demeanor and calm voice put the audience at ease. A close friend and fellow bishop once said, "I don't think he has a mean bone in his body."[1] Seattle's Archbishop Raymond Hunthausen, who would turn sixty later that summer, had no desire to threaten anyone. What he said that day, however, angered some folks out in the wider community once they got wind of its content. "Faith and Disarmament," delivered at Pacific Lutheran University in Tacoma, Washington on June 12, 1981, roiled deep waters.

Archbishop Hunthausen's message that day was a prayerful invitation to examine personal and collective conscience on great moral questions regarding nuclear arms. Still, even the receptive audience was caught a little off guard to hear a radical gospel call to disarmament coming from a Roman Catholic archbishop. Lutheran pastor and old friend Rev. Jon Nelson, along with the Lutheran bishop of the region, had invited Hunthausen. In a retrospective interview, Nelson recalled:

> "We had decided to ask him to speak on the issue of Christian faith and its relation to the nuclear arms race. It really startled us when Hunthausen came out that way. I remember sitting there; I couldn't believe what I was hearing. I knew by the speech that he had moved from political critique to resistance, and there's quite a line of demarcation between political critique, and finding yourself at such odds with the culture that you are willing to go against the prevailing law."[2]

A single speech might not change the world, but "Faith and Disarmament" changed the life of Raymond Hunthausen. News coverage spread quickly. Some critics, reacting to provocative headlines, branded him a traitor. President Reagan's navy secretary, John Lehman, would soon denounce the whole "ignorant and repugnant" trajectory of Hunthausen's ideas and actions. Defenders and decriers agreed on one thing: the speech and the speaker would not be ignored. Fr. Michael G. Ryan, Hunthausen's closest associate in those years, described with irony the archbishop's discourse as "the shot heard 'round the world."[3] Like the deadly shot in Sarajevo that sparked World War I or the rifle fire at Concord that inspired Emerson's hymn about the American revolutionary war, Hunthausen's plea for U.S.

nuclear disarmament took the media and the public by storm. Prior to giving the speech, he wrote a letter to all the priests of Western Washington:

> "I am enclosing for your information the text of an address I am giving today at the Pacific Northwest Synod of the Lutheran Church in America. Many of the thoughts expressed in it will not be new ones for you since you have known my convictions in this area for a long time. When asked by a major Christian Denomination to address their Synod on the subject of Peace and Disarmament, I realized that this was the right time to express, once again, these convictions and to attempt to draw from them some possible implications. As I do so, I realize that I am putting myself and the Church in a difficult position. This is not something I do lightly. I am convinced, however, that not to do so would be to treat lightly a matter that is of life and death importance for all of us."[4]

By that time, the peace movement in the region was gaining momentum and more people of faith were getting involved. Communities such as the Ground Zero Center for Nonviolent Action had formed to protest the Trident nuclear submarine base Bangor on the Hood Canal. Such activists were elated by Hunthausen's talk. Not so those who disparaged peace activism in general during the Cold War era; they believed Archbishop Hunthausen's disarmament proposals would make America defenseless against Godless Soviet communism. Moreover, if subversive ideas like Hunthausen's were to spread this could affect the defense industry and thereby cost the region plenty of jobs.

Hunthausen believed that faith ought to make a difference in the world—and in the church itself—on a range of issues. He had been entering the fray on several fronts and now his heightened prominence from the Tacoma speech put more attention on other aspects of his public life. As we will see, he got involved in Central American concerns, supporting sanctuary for refugees. He encouraged gender equality in the church. He opened St. James Cathedral to the gay Catholic group Dignity. Ecumenical and interfaith collaboration mattered to him greatly and helped him engage many social issues. Overall, his way of being a rather egalitarian-minded bishop and his vision of a church of widely shared responsibility did not curry favor, especially once Pope John Paul II had taken the helm at St. Peter's.

On issues of war and peace, economic disparity, women's empowerment and equality, respect for sexual differences, and other struggles for social justice, Archbishop Hunthausen met with people and listened and learned. He did not chart a progressive journey with a grand strategy in mind. The communal practices of his vibrant and evolving faith tradition, personal encounters with folks, and deep prayer guided him. He tried to be transparent about his own "learning curve" in discerning what to say and do. This humble style endeared him to many. Others fiercely opposed the course they thought he was on. In the late 1970s and into the 1980s, certain individuals and social movements buoyed him with courage to speak his mind and heart. Others sought to sink him and the entire fleet of ideas he came to represent.

Hunthausen—in the public mind of the 1980s—came to personify large social and sacred causes. Icon status was never his ambition. Not once did he seek to be a representative character, yet he became one. In the 1980s bestseller *Habits of the Heart: Individualism and Commitment in American Life*, Robert Bellah and co-authors discussed this idea:

> "A representative character is a kind of symbol. It is a way by which we can bring together in one concentrated image the way people in a given social environment organize and give meaning and direction to their lives. In fact, a representative character is more than a collection of individual traits or personalities. It is rather a public image that helps define, for a given group of people, just what kinds of personality traits it is good and legitimate to develop. A representative character provides an ideal, a point of reference and focus, that gives living expression to a vision of life."[5]

To many people engaged in the struggle for a progressive society and church, Hunthausen was an authentic prophet who suffered for speaking truth to both secular and ecclesiastical powers. On the other hand, to others he represented and personified a social threat to both the Catholic Church and the United States. The Tacoma address lifted him into prominence and it therefore must be heard in full if we are to appreciate why it did so, but a range of issues would drive him into the Vatican's dog house before long.

"FAITH AND DISARMAMENT" SPEECH

June 12, 1981, Tacoma, Washington. It was the beginning of the final decade of the Cold War, though few people could have known this. The United States and the Soviet Union had a devil's accord called MAD—mutually assured destruction. There was widespread worry that nuclear war could be unleashed and many were troubled by the massive investments going into the arms race. Imagine yourself there in the conference room, gathered with others at Pacific Lutheran University on that day to hear Seattle's Catholic Archbishop Raymond Hunthausen share a personal story of awakening. He looked and sounded calm and centered, but you could tell in short order that he was calling you, the country, his church—and himself—to a serious examination of conscience and to corresponding action:

I am grateful for having been invited to speak to you on disarmament because it forces me to a kind of personal disarmament. This is a subject I have thought about and prayed over for many years. I can recall vividly hearing the news of the atomic bombing of Hiroshima in 1945. I was deeply shocked. I could not then put into words the shock I felt from the news that a city of hundreds of thousands of people had been devastated by a single bomb. Hiroshima challenged my faith as a Christian in a way I am only now beginning to understand. That awful event and its successor at Nagasaki sank into my soul, as they have in fact sunk into the souls of all of us, whether we recognize it or not.

I am sorry to say that I did not speak out against the evil of nuclear weapons until many years later. I was especially challenged on the issue by an article I read in 1976 by Jesuit Father Richard McSorley, titled "It's a Sin to Build a Nuclear Weapon." Father McSorley wrote: "The taproot of violence in our society today is our intention to use nuclear weapons. Once we have agreed to that, all other evil is minor in comparison. Until we squarely face the question of our consent to use nuclear weapons, any hope of large scale improvement of public morality is doomed to failure." I agree. Our willingness to destroy life everywhere on this earth, for the sake of our security as Americans, is at the root of many other terrible events in our country.

I was also challenged to speak out against nuclear armament by the nearby construction of the Trident submarine base and by the first-strike nuclear doctrine which Trident represents. The nuclear warheads fired from one Trident submarine will be able to destroy as many as 408 separate areas, each with a bomb five times more powerful than the one used at Hiroshima. One Trident submarine has the destructive equivalent of 2,040 Hiroshima bombs. Trident and other new weapons systems such as the MX and cruise missile have such extraordinary accuracy and explosive power that they can only be understood as a build-up to a first-strike capability. First-strike nuclear weapons are immoral and criminal. They benefit only arms corporations and the insane dreams of those who wish to "win" a nuclear holocaust.

I was also moved to speak out against Trident because it is being based here. We must take special responsibility for what is in our own backyard. And when crimes are being prepared in our name, we must speak plainly. I say with a deep consciousness of these words that Trident is the Auschwitz of Puget Sound.

Father McSorley's article and the local basing of Trident are what awakened me to a new sense of the Gospel call to peacemaking in the nuclear age. They brought back the shock of Hiroshima. Since that re-awakening five years ago, I have tried to respond in both a more prayerful and more vocal way than I did in 1945. I feel the need to respond by prayer because our present crisis goes far deeper than politics. I have heard many perceptive political analyses of the nuclear situation, but their common element is despair. It is no wonder. The nuclear arms race can sum up in a few final moments the violence of tens of thousands of years, raised to an almost infinite power—a demonic reversal of the Creator's power of giving life. But politics is itself powerless to overcome the demonic in its midst. It needs another dimension. I am convinced that a way out of this terrible crisis can be discovered by our deepening in faith and prayer so that we learn to rely not on missiles for our security but on the loving care of that One who gives and sustains life. We need to return to the Gospel with open hearts to learn once again what it is to have faith.

We are told there by Our Lord: "Blessed are the peacemakers. They shall be called children of God." The Gospel calls us to be peacemakers, to practice a divine way of reconciliation. But the next beatitude in Matthew's sequence implies that peacemaking may also be blessed because the persecution which it provokes is the further way into the kingdom: "Blessed are those who are persecuted in the cause of right. Theirs is the kingdom of heaven."

To understand today the Gospel call to peacemaking, and its consequence, persecution, I want to refer especially to these words of Our Lord in Mark: "If anyone wants to be a follower of mine, let that person renounce self and take up the cross and follow me. For anyone who wants to save one's own life will lose it; but anyone who loses one's life for my sake, and for the sake of the gospel, will save it." (Mark 8:34-35)

Scripture scholars tell us that these words lie at the very heart of Mark's Gospel, in his watershed passage on the meaning of faith in Christ. The point of Jesus' teaching here is inescapable: As his followers, we cannot avoid the cross given to each one of us. I am sorry to have to remind myself and each one of you that by "the cross" Jesus was referring to the means by which the Roman Empire executed those whom it considered revolutionaries. Jesus' first call in the Gospel is to love of God and one's neighbor. But when He gives flesh to that commandment by the more specific call to the cross, I am afraid that like most of you I prefer to think in abstract terms, not in the specific context in which Our Lord lived and died. Jesus' call to the cross was a call to love God and one's neighbor in so direct a way that the authorities in power could only regard it as subversive and revolutionary. "Taking up the cross," "losing one's life," meant being willing to die at the hands of political authorities for the truth of the Gospel, for that love of God in which we are all one.

As followers of Christ, we need to take up our cross in the nuclear age. I believe that one obvious meaning of the cross is unilateral disarmament. Jesus' acceptance of the cross rather than the sword raised in his defense is the Gospel's statement of unilateral disarmament. We are called to follow. Our security as people of faith lies not in demonic weapons which threaten all life on earth. Our security is in a loving, caring God. We must dismantle our weapons of terror and place our reliance on God.

I am told by some that unilateral disarmament in the face of atheistic communism is insane. I find myself observing that nuclear armament by anyone is itself atheistic, and anything but sane. I am also told that the choice of unilateral disarmament is a political impossibility in this country. If so, perhaps the reason is that we have forgotten what it would be like to act out of faith. But I speak here of that choice not as a political platform—it might not win elections—but as a moral imperative for followers of Christ. A choice has been put before us: anyone who wants to save one's own life by nuclear arms will lose it; but anyone who loses one's life by giving up those arms for Jesus' sake, and for the sake of the Gospel of love, will save it.

To ask one's country to relinquish its security in arms is to encourage risk—a more reasonable risk than constant nuclear escalation, but a risk nevertheless. I am struck by how much more terrified we Americans often are by talk of disarmament than by the march to nuclear war. We whose nuclear arms terrify millions around the globe are terrified by the thought of being without them. The thought of our nation without such power feels naked. Propaganda and a particular way of life have clothed us to death. To relinquish our hold on global destruction feels like risking everything, and it is risking everything—but in a direction opposite to the way in which we now risk everything. Nuclear arms protect privilege and exploitation. Giving them up would mean our having to give up economic power over other peoples. Peace and justice go together. On the path we now follow, our economic policies toward other countries require nuclear weapons. Giving up the weapons would mean giving up more than our means of global terror. It would mean giving up the reason for such terror—our privileged place in the world.

How can such a process, of taking up the cross of nonviolence, happen in a country where our government seems paralyzed by arms corporations? In a country where many of the citizens, perhaps most of the citizens, are numbed into passivity by the very magnitude and complexity of the issue while being horrified by the prospect of nuclear holocaust? Clearly some action is demanded—some form of nonviolent resistance. Some people may choose to write to their elected representatives at the national and state level, others may choose to take part in marches, demonstrations or similar forms of protest. Obviously there are many ways that action can be taken.

I would like to share a vision of still another action that could be taken: simply this—a sizable number of people in the State of Washington, 5,000, 10,000, ½ million people refusing to pay 50% of their taxes in nonviolent resistance to nuclear murder and suicide. I think that would be a definite step toward disarmament. Our paralyzed political process needs that catalyst of nonviolent action based on faith. We have to refuse to give incense—in our day, tax dollars—to our nuclear idol. On April 15 we can vote for unilateral disarmament with our lives. Form 1040 is the place where the Pentagon enters all of our lives, and asks our unthinking cooperation with the idol of nuclear destruction. I think the teaching of Jesus tells us to render to a nuclear-armed Caesar what that Caesar deserves—tax resistance. And to begin to render to God alone that complete trust which we now give, through our tax dollars, to a demonic form of power. Some would call what I am urging "civil disobedience." I prefer to see it as obedience to God.

I must say in all honesty that my vision of a sizeable number of tax resisters is not yet one which I have tried to realize in the most obvious way–by becoming one of the number. I have never refused to pay war taxes. And I recognize that there will never be such a number unless there are first a few to give the example. But I share the vision with you as part of my own struggle to realize the implications of the Gospel of Peace given us by Our Lord. It is not the way of the cross which is in question in the nuclear age but our willingness to follow it.

I fully realize that many will disagree with my position on unilateral disarmament and tax resistance. I also realize that one can argue endlessly about specific tactics, but no matter how we differ on specific tactics, one thing at least is certain. We must demand over and over again that our political leaders make peace and disarmament, and not war and increased armaments, their first priority. We must demand that time and effort and money be placed first of all toward efforts to let everyone know that the United States is NOT primarily interested in being the strongest military nation on earth but in being the strongest peace advocate. We must challenge every politician who talks endlessly about building up our arms and never about efforts for peace. We must ask our people to question their government when it concentrates its efforts on shipping arms to countries which need food, when it accords the military an open checkbook while claiming that the assistance to the poor must be slashed in the name of balancing the budget, when it devotes most of its time and energy and money to developing war strategy and not peace strategy.

Creativity is always in short supply. This means that it must be used for the most valuable purposes. Yet it seems evident that most of our creative efforts are not going into peace but into war. We have too many people who begin with the premise that little can be done to arrange for a decrease in arms spending since the Soviet Union is bent on bankrupting itself on armaments no matter what we do. We have too few people who are willing to explore every possible path to decreasing armaments.

In our Catholic Archdiocese of Seattle, I have recommended to our people that we all turn more intently to the Lord this year in response to the escalation of nuclear arms, and that we do so especially by fasting and prayer on Monday of each week. That is the way, I believe, to depend on a power far greater than the hydrogen bomb. I believe that only by turning our lives around in the most fundamental ways, submitting ourselves to the infinite love of God, will we be given the vision and strength to take up the cross of nonviolence.

The nuclear arms race can be stopped. Nuclear weapons can be abolished. That I believe with all my heart and faith, my sisters and brothers. The key to that nuclear-free world is the cross at the center of the Gospel, and our response to it. The terrible responsibility which you and I have in this nuclear age is that we profess a faith whose God has transformed death into life in the person of Jesus Christ. We must make that faith real. Life itself depends on it. Our faith sees

> the transformation of death, through the cross of suffering love, as an ongoing process. That process is our way into hope of a new world. Jesus made it clear that the cross and empty tomb didn't end with Him. Thank God they didn't. We are living in a time when new miracles are needed, when a history threatened by overwhelming death needs resurrection by Almighty God. God alone is our salvation, through the acceptance in each of our lives of a nonviolent cross of suffering love. Let us call on the Holy Spirit to move us all into that nonviolent action which will take us to our own cross, and to the new earth beyond.[6]

Something irreversible but long latent had begun in Hunthausen's own psyche, emotionally and spiritually, in the mid-1940s, when he heard about Hiroshima and Nagasaki. And something like a reawakening of conscience became manifest soon after his arrival in the Seattle area, brought on by his awareness of the Trident submarine base and first-strike nuclear weapons. Let us try now to begin to appreciate the personal and social impact of the "Faith and Disarmament" speech. The Roman Empire used the cross to execute those it deemed revolutionaries. Hunthausen was following Jesus and the cross as "a call to love God and one's neighbor in so direct a way that the authorities in power could only regard" his own words and actions as subversive and revolutionary. He voiced a personal need to take up his cross in the nuclear age. He felt he had to take risks, including civil disobedience, for personal conversion. Yet the speech was not only a call for a kind of personal disarmament. He prodded the collective conscience by asking people to grapple with the moral implications of America—the American Empire—relying on a credible threat to use such horrific weapons. The American Empire might well deem Hunthausen a revolutionary.

He was asking about the social psychological state of U.S. society. "I am struck by how much more terrified we Americans often are by talk of disarmament than by the march to nuclear war." He called into question power and privilege. "Nuclear arms protect privilege and exploitation." Could Americans—privileged and wealthy Americans especially—give up their special status? Arms corporations had inordinate influence. Monstrous weaponry went hand in hand with the concentration of wealth and power.

He would have to take some form of personal action. He shared a vision of a sizable number of people doing tax resistance. He had never before refused to pay war taxes. This was a radical idea coming from a person in such a religious office. An American Catholic archbishop was now openly considering civil disobedience on the fundamental matter of American military might. The argument was not just a self-challenge. He appreciated the potential social power of the resistance action. If enough people would take this action, he said it "would be a definite step toward disarmament." Here was radical talk, law-breaking as collective nonviolent action, coming from a person of high office in a religion perceived widely to be politically and theologically conservative.

Fr. Jack Morris, a Jesuit priest from Anaconda, the southwestern Montana copper smelter town where Hunthausen was born, spoke briefly with his fellow Montanan at St. James Cathedral in Seattle a day or two after the speech. Familiar with down-to-earth "Dutch" from their childhood days back in the 1920s and 1930s in Anaconda, Morris knew that the archbishop was not grandstanding. Yet news about the "Faith and Disarmament" speech was taking off like a wildfire in dry tinder. Morris told Hunthausen that what he had said in Tacoma was truly prophetic utterance. Hunthausen did not think himself to be prophetic so he told Morris, "I shouldn't have used the word 'vision' because this cast what I was saying into a kind of fundamentalism, as if I was saying I had a vision directly from God."[7]

Hunthausen did receive a vision directly from another human being a few days before the Tacoma speech. Personal encounters affected him and his way of approaching most issues. In this case, Charlie Meconis, a laicized priest and long-time scholar-activist and organizer working on justice and peace issues for the Church Council of Greater Seattle, provided a trenchant analysis of nuclear arms at a special retreat held at St. Thomas Seminary in Kenmore, on the north shore of Lake Washington. George Weigel of the World Without War Council provided the group of ecumenical religious leaders with a perspective much less critical of U.S. nuclear policy. Meconis and Weigel had been invited to make presentations for the various executives of the denominations making up the Church Council and the Washington Association of Churches. When Meconis delivered his impassioned talk on the dangers of the nuclear arms race, he explained how it was in his estimation contrary to Christian conscience. He argued that because activist efforts to prevent the building of the Trident submarine base Bangor on the Hood Canal had failed, the religious leaders should join efforts to prepare to blockade the arrival of the first Trident submarine. And he wanted them to know there was one place "where the nuclear arms race reaches everyone of us in this room and makes us complicit." We all, or most of us, pay taxes. He urged them to seriously consider conscientious war tax resistance, which he himself had been doing for some time.[8]

Hunthausen came over to Meconis and said something to the effect of "my car broke down on the way over here, I don't think it's anything serious but I dropped it off, so could you give me a lift over to the garage?" Charlie Meconis was thinking to himself, "not only is this archbishop driving his own car, something not every high prelate might do, but he is driving a clunker!" He gave the archbishop a lift. Driving to the garage he discovered that the archbishop had another agenda. Raymond Hunthausen could have asked almost anyone else at the retreat to help retrieve the car, but he wanted to talk with Meconis. He had a feeling that perhaps tax resistance could be one way to take action. "That was a really powerful presentation and you have given me a lot to think about," Hunthausen said as they headed for the mechanic shop.[9]

He reflected back on this some months later at Catholic University:

> "I was invited by a Lutheran bishop to speak on war and peace at the Lutheran Synod. I planned to say something about unilateral disarmament. But a day or two before the speech, I met a young man working for the Seattle Church Council. He had been withholding taxes for some time and is really very conscientious and prayerful about it. It seemed to me that if he is willing to do that, it is a feasible strategy. And people are looking for a way of doing something about this horrendous danger, but seem unable to oppose it. It seemed to me that war-tax resistance was a way of doing something about it. That example, plus the presence of the Trident submarine base in Seattle, and agreeing with the statement that 'The taproot of violence in our society is our intent to build nuclear weapons,' all of this moved me to speak out."[10]

Charlie Meconis had no idea what would transpire when Hunthausen went to Tacoma on June 12. He did not know what Hunthausen would say. Meconis recalls what happened when he arrived at Pacific Lutheran University. He got there too late to be in the audience for the shot that would be heard around the world. Raymond Hunthausen's talk was one in a series of presentations scheduled in the Friday program and Meconis was booked to speak right afterward, so he arrived just in time to deliver his own talk. The young activist pulled in, found a parking spot, and headed into the conference center. Hunthausen had just stepped away from the podium. There was commotion, Meconis recalls, "a hubbub, people commenting, with reporters all running and fighting in that benighted era over pay phones." Meconis heard repeatedly "Archbishop Hunthausen, Archbishop Hunthausen" across the large room. War tax resistance, Trident as the "Auschwitz of Puget Sound," and unilateral disarmament—language like this coming from an American Catholic archbishop was sure to spur the media and provoke vigorous debate. Charlie thought to himself, "Oh my, oh my," he recounted. "I had to sit down. Because I immediately had not the slightest doubt about what the blowback would be of his taking that kind of position publicly. I was excited, uplifted, but I also thought, oh my."[11]

THE PRESS BARRAGE

Hunthausen faced significant blowback. The *Seattle Times* on Saturday, the day after the speech, ran this headline: "Archbishop Hunthausen urges taxpayer revolt against N-arms." One journalist described Archbishop Hunthausen's address as "the strongest anti-nuclear-arms statement yet by a Pacific Northwest church leader as the archbishop called on up to 250,000 taxpayers to participate."[12] A negative editorial days later stated: "The Most Rev. Raymond G. Hunthausen's suggestion to refuse to pay 50 per cent of federal income taxes to protest nuclear escalation is bound to cause sharp divisions within his own church—even though he chose to make it before a gathering of Lutherans in Tacoma." Hunthausen had encouraged "an illegal action, carrying serious threat of imprisonment, with no assurance it might produce the desired result."[13] A self-described "practicing American Catholic" from Seattle wrote, "To urge, via credence placed in his office, Americans not to pay taxes in protest of the Trident nuclear project smacks of treason. The Archbishop should be chastised, defrocked and released to civilian life to protest all he pleases."[14]

Catholic peace activists along with other peace communities celebrated Hunthausen's bold stand. The *Seattle Post-Intelligencer*'s Evelyn Iritani reported that Hunthausen's call for tax resistance "has given a big boost to local pacifist and religious groups whose members have long practiced and urged a tax protest as a way to end the arms race."[15] That newspaper ran a headline, "Archbishop's war tax stand gains support" and began the story this way: "After recovering from the initial shock, Seattle's religious community has begun drumming up support for Roman Catholic Archbishop Raymond Hunthausen's call for a taxpayer revolt to protest the U.S. nuclear arms buildup."[16] In another piece, Iritani reported that then U.S. Senator Slade Gorton's spokesperson Anna Perez indicated that the senator "just can't imagine why the archbishop would be advocating something that is illegal."[17] Yet a state senator, James McDermott, called Hunthausen's "Faith and Disarmament" speech "the most courageous public statement he'd heard in a long time."[18] On Sunday, June 21, the *Seattle Post-Intelligencer* ran its own editorial, which did not have the negative edge found in the *Seattle Times* editorial noted above. The archbishop was calling for tax resistance. "What the archbishop advocates is, obviously, illegal." Even so, the newspaper praised him. This was a time when military leaders of both the United States and the Soviet Union were discussing the possibility or even the probability of nuclear war. "The full horror of nuclear warfare must be understood; the steps toward disarmament must be taken; the initiative must be ours. To bring this message to our leaders may require something as alien to the law-abiding as Archbishop Hunthausen's crusade. The archbishop's courage is considerable. He has put the focus where it belongs."[19]

The Tacoma speech soon became national and international news. In mid-July, a *New York Times* story reported that "Archbishop Hunthausen's proposal has led to intense debate in his archdiocese, which encompasses the headquarters of the Boeing Company, a military supplier; the Bangor nuclear submarine base, which soon will be home port to 10 Trident submarines; the Fort Lewis Army post, and

McCord Air Force Base." The story noted that Rev. Joseph Erny, in a sermon to his parishioners at Bremerton's Holy Trinity Catholic Church, said "In principle, we agree with the moral question of disarmament. But I say if you disagree with his political action of I.R.S. withholding, then you have the responsibility to come up with alternatives." Many parishioners had jobs either at the Bremerton naval shipyard or at the Bangor base. "They have their conflicts of conscience," Erny said. "I know of one man who has retired from the Navy and was working for a weaponry company but has decided to give that job up." Rev. Gerald Moffat, of Our Lady of Sorrows in Snoqualmie, said folks "are on one side of the fence or the other." Some people "feel no one should withhold taxes and break the law. They feel we need a stronger America and support the arms race. The other side is ideologically opposed to nuclear arms and want to destroy all our weapons and bombs."[20]

In early August, United Press International's John Long wrote a piece entitled "Archbishop attacks arms race." Hunthausen was asked why he had said, "I think the teaching of Jesus tells us to render to a nuclear armed Caesar what that Caesar deserves—tax resistance." This was his way of expressing profound concern, Hunthausen explained. "I did this to show how truly serious this matter is. If I hadn't said that about taxes, nobody would have heard about the speech. This is the most important issue before the American people and the human family." Why did he call for unilateral disarmament? "Somebody ought to take the first step and perhaps the United States is the only one which can do it, given our form of government. We're beginning to think the unthinkable, talking about first strike capability and limited nuclear war. The limited nuclear warfare idea is ridiculous."[21]

An Associated Press article in early August showcased some of the emergent energies of the peace movement. "In a time of military buildup, the 'peace' people are marching, praying, fasting and signing petitions. Several denominations have made 'peacemaking' a current priority. And some church leaders, including a bold bishop, have advised refusing to pay the portion of taxes that goes for arms." Reporter George Cornell used "bold bishop" to describe Hunthausen. "Archbishop Raymond G. Hunthausen of Seattle, in a mid-June speech that has since evoked wide and varying reactions, suggested Christians refuse to pay the half of their federal income taxes going for armament."[22]

In early September, Kenneth Briggs with the *New York Times* documented the new anti-nuclear movement and how faith communities were becoming more engaged: "The movement has been spurred in the past few months by a number of dramatic actions." One of those actions was Hunthausen's Tacoma speech, which had "aroused controversy earlier this summer by suggesting that Christians withhold 50 percent of their Federal income tax as a form of nonviolent resistance" to nuclear murder and suicide.[23] David Anderson with United Press International underscored the breadth of the coverage: "It was his call to tax resistance, believed to be the first such endorsement by a ranking Catholic official, that stirred the brief flurry of publicity surrounding Hunthausen's June 12 speech to the Pacific Synod Convention of the Lutheran Church in America." Hunthausen's speech should be seen as part of a larger pattern, as "a growing number of mainline religious leaders and church bodies are becoming alarmed at the nuclear arms race." There were conversations between church leaders in the U.S. and church leaders in Russia "to explore ways the churches in each country might aid the cause of disarmament."[24]

The Tacoma speech was a significant moment within a growing role being played by religion in the peace movement. A *Washington Post* headline in mid-September read: "Render Not Unto Caesar…Outcry From the Pulpit Against Nuclear Armaments Grows More Intense." In the *Washington Post* story, Marjorie Hyer traced the emerging influence of the religious community: "Criticism of the escalating arms race, and particularly the amassing of nuclear weapons, is a theme that is being sounded with increasing frequency by religious leaders throughout the nation." During the summer, the United Church of Christ and the Christian Church (Disciples of Christ) had "overwhelmingly voted to make peace and peacemaking institutional priorities for their denominations for the coming years." In August, "the Leadership Conference of Women Religious approved unanimously a resolution opposing production and deployment of the MX missile, the neutron bomb and nuclear weapons generally." Hunthausen was not alone. "In Texas, Hunthausen's fellow Catholic bishop, the Most Rev. Leroy T. Matthiessen of Amarillo, issued an appeal to workers in the local Pantex plant to give up their jobs rather than work on the neutron bomb, scheduled to be manufactured there." Though the neutron bomb program was eventually cancelled, Pantex, a major employer in the region, assembled the triggers onto the nuclear warheads and put them on the "white trains" lined up outside the plant. Many of those warheads would be delivered to the Bangor base of the Trident submarine. Just as with Hunthausen in the Seattle region, so too Matthiessen's "proposal has touched off a major controversy, fueled by economic arguments as well as differences of opinion over both the morality and political wisdom of the nation's nuclear arms policy."

The "New Abolitionists" included the Fellowship of Reconciliation, Sojourners, New Call to Peacemaking, Pax Christi and World Peacemakers, and Roman Catholic bishops such as Hunthausen, Matthiessen, and others. This movement included a "New Abolitionist Covenant," which expressed profound concern that "the growing prospect of nuclear war presents us with more than a test of survival; it confronts us with a test of faith." This was not simply a matter of public policy, but in essence a matter of faith. "We believe that the wholesale destruction threatened by these weapons makes their possession and planned use an offense against God and humanity, no matter what the provocation or political justification." Hyer noted the gap between the stand of some religious leaders and the views of vocal critics in their congregations. "Hunthausen and Matthiessen and others have been sharply criticized by their own laity for the stands they have taken." Still, she observed that "church historians would have to note that a generation ago a similar gap existed over the question of racial equality, when only the visionaries advocated legislation to put an end to discrimination based on race."[25]

IT'S A SIN TO BUILD A NUCLEAR WEAPON

Richard McSorley, a Jesuit priest and scholar, had written "It's a Sin to Build a Nuclear Weapon" in 1976. McSorley's argument had a substantial impact on Hunthausen and therefore deserves close attention as we continue to consider Hunthausen's "Faith and Disarmament" speech. McSorley began with this question: "Does God approve of our intent to use nuclear weapons?"[26] United States policy was indeed to intend to use nuclear weapons in the hopes that a sincere intention to use them would make for a credible deterrent. McSorley moved directly to the message of the *Pastoral Constitution on the Church in the Modern World*, from Vatican II: "The danger of world suicide through nuclear war 'compels us to undertake an evaluation of war with an entirely new attitude,'...."[27] Hunthausen was affected by his personal experience of the Second Vatican Council, since he attended the very first session just a short time after he was first made a bishop in 1962, during the Cuban Missile Crisis. He was one of the youngest bishops to attend the Council. And now the nuclear situation, especially the plans for the stationing of Trident in Seattle's backyard, compelled him to reawaken his conscience and undertake an evaluation of war with an entirely new attitude. Hunthausen first read McSorley's article at the very time when he was just beginning to awaken to the meaning of Trident in 1976.

McSorley posed mind-boggling questions and nightmare answers. What would happen if a 20-megaton nuclear weapon were to be detonated in New York City? The first result would be horrible death: "Ten times as many deaths as all the battle deaths that occurred in all the wars of U.S. history—from the Revolution up to and including the 55,000 battle deaths in the Vietnam War. Seven million people would die from blast, firestorm, and radiation."[28] Above the blast area there would be a ball of fire four miles wide and 20,000 feet high. "Within a thirty-nine mile radius a sea of fire would roll and boil fanned by the winds of the shock wave." Destruction would not stop there. "From the huge cavern dug by the blast, vaporized material pulled up into the air by the fireball would form a radioactive cloud of death."[29] Hunthausen held in his memory a deeply unsettling nightmare image of Hiroshima and Nagasaki as he read McSorley.

McSorley asked: "How many bombs do we really need?" Even if it were not sinful to make a nuclear weapon, he wrote, we could surely get by with far fewer. Secretary of Defense Robert McNamara had told Congress that "we won't need any more than 200 to 400 weapons delivered on target." We could wipe out the 200 cities in the Soviet Union that have populations of over 100,000 people, with just that many nuclear weapons. The United States had in its stockpile, at the time McSorley wrote, over 30,000 nuclear weapons. "We are making one new nuclear weapon every eight hours. We have enough weapons in our arsenal to deliver over 615,000 Hiroshima bombs. We can destroy every Soviet city of 100,000 or more forty-five times over. The Soviet Union can destroy every American city of 100,000 or more thirteen times over."[30]

Then the Jesuit moral theologian asked questions that Hunthausen grappled with in prayer: "Can the use of these weapons be reconciled with the Gospel? Can even their existence be reconciled with the command 'Love your enemies'?" McSorley was crystal clear about the nature of actual U.S. policy. "The United States policy is that we will retaliate with massive nuclear destruction if we are attacked. This is the very heart of our nuclear-deterrence policy. This is what we mean by deterrence." Deterrence, McSorley added, meant we were prepared to kill every human being in every Soviet city of 100,000 or more. If their government were to attack us with nuclear weapons, at any scale, we would retaliate with a massive nuclear obliteration.[31] "Is there any way that the Christian conscience can accept this policy of nuclear deterrence?" Christians have tried two ways to reconcile war with their faith, he noted. "One is the way practiced by the Christians in the first three centuries. During the first three centuries Christians considered joining the army incompatible with the following of Christ. The other is the just/unjust-war theory of St. Augustine of the fourth century. This theory holds among other conditions that in any war there be a proportionality between the evil done and the good to be hoped for, and that there be no direct killing of the innocent." He asked, "Have we in the nuclear-war age reached the point where we finally must say that war is incompatible with the Christian conscience?"[32]

HUNTHAUSEN ON THE "FAITH & DISARMAMENT" SPEECH

One week after the Tacoma address, Archbishop Hunthausen admitted he was surprised by all the attention the speech—but especially the call for tax resistance—was generating. "Humanly speaking, I'd probably be more comfortable today if I hadn't made that suggestion about taxes and avoided all the fuss that has arisen," he told the *Seattle Post-Intelligencer*'s Evelyn Iritani. "But if I look at it in a spiritual sense, I'd have to say my convictions are that strong and I am absolutely at peace with the fact that this is the direction we should move." People were beginning to react to his call for civil disobedience. "Some people would interpret this as treasonous, disloyal or unpatriotic," he lamented. "Quite frankly, the reason I am concerned is out of my great love for the country. I'm proposing something that's very radical, I don't deny.... But it's something which I believe has more chance—

although it's risky—than what we're doing now." Why did he speak out? "I'm no different than anybody else.... I don't particularly want to be in the middle of a fight." He could not have known how far into the middle of a fight he would find himself drawn in the near future. "The gospel isn't all that popular. It's not that easy to live what we believe."[33]

A few priests in the archdiocese were upset that he had not briefed them before he made the speech. Yet he had sent that brief letter, cited earlier, to all the priests the day before he spoke in Tacoma. Some of the older priests who were much more comfortable with predecessor Archbishop Connolly's leadership style—not to mention his much less critical attitude toward U.S. foreign policy—were upset, according to Jim Burns, who worked as Hunthausen's development director and would hear what priests thought as he approached them annually for the archdiocesan financial appeal.[34]

When Hunthausen was in Washington, D.C. in November of 1981 for a meeting of the U.S. Catholic bishops, he and his colleagues, Bishops Thomas Gumbleton of Detroit, Leroy Matthiessen of Amarillo, Texas, and Walter Sullivan of Richmond, Virginia were asked about their stands. Hunthausen recollected the Tacoma address:

> "So I spoke about withholding war taxes as a feasible strategy. I thought maybe my remarks would create a stir, rattle around Seattle for a couple of days, and go away. But they didn't. They stayed around. I must say it bothered me that the media picked up on the issue of taxes and lost the crux of what I really wanted to say, which was that the issue of nuclear weapons is one that prompts us to be men and women of faith and ask if we have put our security in our weaponry rather than in God."[35]

In the early July 1981 edition of *The Catholic Northwest Progress*, the official newspaper of the Archdiocese of Seattle, Hunthausen wrote to the Catholic people of Western Washington. Because the June 12 speech has "provoked interest, discussion, and some distortion," he wanted to clarify and amplify what he had said. "My basic position was that all nuclear war is immoral because there is no conceivable proportionate reason which could justify the immense destruction of life and resources which such a war would bring about." If continued, the arms race would make war inevitable, and thus participating in it was immoral. He believed his position was consistent with the stands already taken by both Popes Paul VI and John Paul II in addresses made at the full assembly of the United Nations. Because mutual disarmament was not happening, we were left "with only one moral position in this tragic situation, the position of unilateral disarmament with trust and reliance on the Lord for our security."[36]

He acknowledged that some people thought his call for unilateral disarmament was naïve, but he argued that it was even more naïve to think that we could continue a nuclear arms race and not risk a devastating nuclear war. He could "hear the pain and struggles of conscience" his words had caused. "Some feel that the position I advocate can only lead to the destruction of the free world by the Soviet Union. Others, especially those in our area of the United States, are so dependent on jobs in the nuclear armaments industry that what I have said can only be interpreted as an attack on the means by which they live and support their families." Others would claim that his stand reflected disloyalty toward the country. "Rather, I believe that a stand like mine reflects a love of our country because it reflects a belief that it is responsive to challenge for moral growth."[37]

As bishop he "not only had the right but the duty to speak out on the concrete issues of the day as they affect the values of the Gospel tradition." A bishop should not hide safely behind the rhetoric of general principles, but "must also take the risk of applying them in the best way he knows how to the actual life situations he and his people must face." He had spoken about war and peace in his own backyard and now he was facing trouble there. But he did not claim to speak for every Catholic. "Rather, I have called all to consider this issue and have given my own response. I invite all to examine the situation in the light of Gospel values." In all the reactions to the June 12 speech, some people argued that a bishop may not speak out on issues that involve the political realm. This argument was false, he insisted. Though the disarmament issue had a political dimension it also had a moral dimension "that I as a Christian leader must address." If a bishop were to have no right to speak on such matters, he would be relegated solely to the realm of personal morality. Such would be "to declare with the secularist mentality of recent centuries that religion is to be locked up in the sacristy and the home."[38]

What about the call for war tax resistance? It was "a quite secondary aspect of my talk; it is a tactic that may or may not be used by persons who agree with the main points I made on disarmament." He would not push it on anyone. However, he was concerned about the view some people held, namely, "that it is utterly immoral to disobey a law of the state for a good end." In general, according to the Roman Catholic tradition, the laws of the state ought to be obeyed. "However, we may peacefully disobey certain laws under serious conditions. There may even be times when disobedience may be an obligation of conscience." Christians of the first three centuries "disobeyed the laws of the Roman Empire and often went to their death because of their stands." Rev. Dr. Martin Luther King Jr. was fully within his rights when he "engaged in demonstrations that broke the laws of the state" in order to call attention to injustice. Hunthausen would not let civil law be an absolute "god that must be obeyed under any and all conditions."[39]

Any "nation which makes as first priority the building up of armaments and not the creative work of peace and disarmament is immoral." Hunthausen, however, did not assert that his views constituted the last word. "We do not live in a world in which absolute pronouncements about complex social situations can be made." He asked the Catholic community of Western Washington to join him "in applying the principles we know to circumstances that are always too complex to be seen totally and with perfect clarity." The absence of complete certainty could be no excuse for inaction. "You may disagree with the concrete actions and tactics I suggest. What no good Catholic may do is to continue to live without thought as if the arms race is not a problem, as if huge buildups of nuclear weapons are justified without examination, as if there are not principles and assessments of facts which challenge us all to rethink what we are doing as a nation in this matter."[40]

In August 1981, the journal *Christianity and Crisis* (*C&C*) highlighted two approaches to nuclear weapons. One was Hunthausen's. The other was a mid-July address before the Foreign Policy Association by the Reagan Administration's new secretary of state, Alexander Haig, a Catholic. Haig set forth the so-called arms control policy of the new administration, which was then embarking on a huge military buildup. The U.S. must take seriously the nature of power and the potential consequences of powerlessness, Haig claimed. *C&C* editors published the two perspectives side by side, stating: "Because they start from such radically different premises, the two speeches cast light on each other. They bring us back to basics." To these editors, Haig's position could not be lightly dismissed, "not even when there is reason to suspect that our policymakers lack the will to engage in serious negotiations toward reduction of nuclear arsenals. Of course it is insane to contemplate the waging of nuclear war. Of course the world in the nuclear era needs another way, other than war, to resolve its conflicts. But what follows?" Citing the influential Christian realist theologian Reinhold Niebuhr, *C&C* suggested that "the flaw in the reasoning of antiwar idealists is to assume that what is necessary is therefore feasible."[41] Had Hunthausen made this idealist mistake? Or was there a flaw in the reasoning of Haig that Hunthausen was trying to point out? The editors wrote that Hunthausen's address included "passages suggesting that our leaders and we ourselves insist on maintaining a nuclear capacity only for the sake of retaining our position of global power and privilege."[42]

A few months after the Tacoma speech Hunthausen traced the early period in the evolution of his thinking:

> "I was in college when World War II erupted, and I saw many of my closest friends go into the military. I struggled to decide whether to go to seminary or into the military. I was involved in a civilian pilot training program, and I was excited about the prospect of moving into what the government called the secondary program. I wanted

> to do aerobatics, but it was clear that if one was in the program and the United States entered the war, one would automatically be in the Air Force.
>
> My spiritual director helped me to see that I had to give my call and vocation to the priesthood a chance, so I opted for the seminary; but I would have to say that at the time I certainly felt keenly about going into the military.
>
> I was in the seminary in 1945 when the atomic bombs hit Hiroshima and Nagasaki. I'll never forget that day, because I was appalled; I just could not believe what had happened, that there was an instrument of destruction as awesome as this bomb. I was caught up in a great turmoil wondering, worrying, praying about this, and I could not grasp that our world had totally changed.
>
> Well, I was ordained and lived with this reality just like the rest of the world, and though I wondered about much of the upheaval in our world, I didn't do anything about it.
>
> I was appointed bishop in 1962. Another bishop was working with the synod on a statement about the ICBMs [Intercontinental Ballistic Missiles] being deployed in Montana. We made a number of such statements, the first public witnesses that I, with others, was willing to take. It frightened me to death. I wasn't sure of my position, and I had that sense of being unpatriotic. I also got involved in a counseling service for conscientious objectors."[43]

I asked Hunthausen's closest associate in Seattle, Fr. Michael G. Ryan, about Hunthausen's recollections of Hiroshima when he was in the seminary. "He was very close to ordination during the summer, August 1945, when Hiroshima happened. He once told me about it. He said there was great jubilation in the place. The war was over. The place was flying high, people were dancing in the streets, so to speak, literally, I guess in many places. He went off, I don't know if it was to a chapel or to the woods, but he went off by himself, and tried to understand the enormity of what had happened, and it was just more than he could take. He grieved deeply, in the core of his person. So that's who he was. It wasn't that he was a pacifist at that point, in fact, he had told me more than once he had thought of going into the service.... But this is when he first started to think deeply about just war in this time and in this place, how can this be."[44]

The moral implications of the atomic age—and America's role in the Cold War—would return to the foreground of his consciousness after he came to Seattle in 1975. A reawakening found prophetic expression as he learned of the planned deployment of the first-strike Trident nuclear weapon system. We shall see what led to "Faith and Disarmament."

ENDNOTES

1 Skylstad, William. Personal interview, Portland, Oregon. 2 April 2013.

2 Sanger, S.L. "A bishop 'converts' to peace activism." *Seattle Post-Intelligencer* 19 Feb. 1987, D1,11.

3 Ryan, Michael G. Personal interview, Seattle, Washington. 2 Dec. 2011. In the Archdiocese of Seattle in those years there were two Ryans serving as priests: Rev. Michael G. Ryan and Rev. Michael J. Ryan. Their common network of friends and associates had good-natured "pious fun" distinguishing them as "G" for God and "J" for Jesus. The "shot heard round the world" was Ralph Waldo Emerson's line in his Concord Hymn about the start of the American revolutionary war but has also been linked to the Sarajevo assassination of the archduke and his spouse.

4 Hunthausen, Raymond. Letter. 12 June 1981. Catholic Archdiocese of Seattle Archives.

5 Bellah, Robert, Richard Madsen, William Sullivan, Ann Swidler, and Steven Tipton. *Habits of the Heart: Individualism and Commitment in American Life*. Updated ed. Berkeley and Los Angeles: U of California P, 1996. 39.

6 Hunthausen, Raymond. Speech. "Faith and Disarmament." 12 June 1981. Catholic Archdiocese of Seattle Archives.

7 Morris, Jack. Personal interview, Portland, Oregon. 5 July 2011.

8 Meconis, Charles. Personal interview, Seattle, Washington. 27 Mar. 2013.

9 Meconis, Charles.

10 Quoted by Richard McSorley. McSorley, Richard, and John Dear. *It's a Sin to Build a Nuclear Weapon: The Collected Works on War and Christian Peacemaking of Richard McSorley, S.J.* Baltimore: Fortkamp Publishing, 1991. 240-241.

11 Meconis.

12 Ruppert, Ray. "Archbishop Hunthausen urges taxpayer revolt against N-arms." *Seattle Times* 13 June 1981. *Historic Seattle Times, 1900–1984*, 1. (With the help of reference librarians at the main library in downtown Seattle I was able to access online *Historic Seattle Times, 1900–1984*; this I did in September 2012, for all of the citations from *Historic Seattle Times* hereafter noted.)

13 "Breaking the law in the name of 'morality'." Editorial. *Seattle Times* 17 June 1981. *Historic Seattle Times, 1900–1984*, 12.

14 Delane, John. Letter. *Seattle Times* 18 June 1981. *Historic Seattle Times, 1900–1984*, 15.

15 Iritani, Evelyn. "Protesting Catholics gratified by archbishop's war tax stand." *Seattle Post-Intelligencer* 18 June 1981.

16 Iritani, Evelyn and Joe Frisino. "Archbishop's war tax stand gains support." *Seattle Post-Intelligencer* 17 June 1981.

17 Iritani, Evelyn. "Politicians criticize archbishop's stand against military spending." *Seattle Post-Intelligencer* 19 June 1981.

18 Iritani, Evelyn.

19 "Breaking laws for defense?" Editorial. *Seattle Post-Intelligencer* 21 June 1981, B8.

20 "Seattle Clergy Support Tax Protest Against Nuclear Weapons." *New York Times* 13 July 1981, A8. Lexisnexis.com. Web. 7 Aug. 2012.

21 Long, John. "Archbishop attacks arms race." United Press International 2 Aug. 1981. *Lexisnexis.com.* Web. 14 Aug. 2012.

22 Cornell, George. N. title. Associated Press. 7 Aug. 1981. *Lexisnexis.com*. Web. 14 Aug. 2012.

23 Briggs, Kenneth. "Religious Leaders Objecting to Nuclear Arms." *New York Times* 8 Sept. 1981, A1. Lexisnexis.com. Web. 7 Aug. 2012.

24 Anderson, David. "Underlying Archbishop's Church leaders' new push." United Press International 6 Sept. 1981. *Lexisnexis.com*. Web. 14 Aug. 2012.

25 Hyer, Marjorie. "Render Not Unto Caesar…Outcry From the Pulpit Against Nuclear Armaments Grows More Intense." *Washington Post* 11 Sept. 1981. Final edition, F14. *Lexisnexis.com*. Web. 14 Aug. 2012.

26 McSorley, Richard, and John Dear. *It's a Sin to Build a Nuclear Weapon: The Collected Works on War and Christian Peacemaking of Richard McSorley, S.J.* Baltimore: Fortkamp Publishing 1991, 93.

27 McSorley. 93.

28 McSorley. 94.

29 McSorley. 95.

30 McSorley. 95-96.

31 McSorley. 95-96.

32 McSorley. 96.

33 Iritani, Evelyn. "Archbishop surprised." *Seattle Post-Intelligencer* 20 June 1981.

34 Burns, Jim. Personal interview. Edmonds, Washington 17 Sept. 2012.

35 Wallis, Jim, ed. *Peace-Makers: Christian Voices from the New Abolitionist Movement.* Harper & Row, 1983, 30.

36 Hunthausen, Raymond. "Archbishop Reiterates Speech in *Catholic Northwest Progress*." 2 July 1981. Catholic Archdiocese of Seattle Archives.

37 Hunthausen. 2 July 1981.

38 Hunthausen.

39 Hunthausen.

40 Hunthausen.

41 *Christianity and Crisis*. 17 Aug. 1981.

42 *Christianity and Crisis.*

43 Hunthausen, Raymond. From his statement at the Catholic University conference in Nov. 1981. See Jim Wallis, ed. *Peace-Makers: Christian Voices from the New Abolitionist Movement.* Harper & Row, 1983, 30-31.

44 Ryan, Michael. Personal interview. Seattle, Washington 2 Dec. 2011.

Chapter Two

SENT TO SEATTLE

The style of Seattle Catholic leadership changed when Raymond Hunthausen arrived. In some ways, nevertheless, there was continuity. His predecessor, Archbishop Thomas Connolly, had been progressive on labor issues. In keeping with Catholic social teaching, Connolly backed collective bargaining. But at one point in his tenure, the region was faced with the question of whether there would be jobs at all—unionized or not. In the early 1970s, Boeing underwent a downturn, and since the regional economy depended so heavily on this single corporation, the effect of layoffs was amplified across numerous sectors. Foreclosures followed and families were hurting. The pain was not confined to "the usual victims." Hundreds of Boeing engineers were suddenly standing in the unemployment lines. The company had been highly invested in contracts that flopped, including that of the Supersonic Transport aircraft. By 1975, the year Hunthausen was sent to Seattle, the dire situation was beginning to improve. New defense contracts were among the reasons for Boeing's resurgence. Jobs were reappearing.[1] In addition to being a strong advocate for worker rights, Connolly had joined in ecumenical efforts and in civil rights issues, criticizing school segregation. On the one hand he and Hunthausen shared a concern for social justice in a number of aspects. On the other hand, in his mode of leadership, Connolly was a classic "top-down" authority figure. He was chief pastor, public relations director, builder of schools, banker, financier, real estate broker, architect, and contractor. While he adopted some of the reform spirit of the Second Vatican Council, his governance of the archdiocese differed dramatically from the method Hunthausen brought to the office.[2]

On war and peace, Connolly never seriously questioned the region's military-industrial complex. Indeed, his frequent stop-over guest in the years of American involvement in Southeast Asia was the pre-eminent American Catholic churchman, Cardinal Spellman of New York, Vicar to the U.S. Armed Forces. Spellman gave his blessing to U.S. foreign policy—and literally blessed new ships and tanks. Some of that holy water was probably sprinkled on American tanks that rolled into the jungles of Vietnam. Spellman and Connolly were ardent anti-communist hawks. At a spring 1969 Seattle University graduation ceremony, Connolly surprised the assembly when he began by saying the U.S. had to end this war. Students started clapping. Then he completed his line of thought; the only way to do this was to bomb Hanoi. Long-time justice and peace organizer Don Hopps recalls, "Everybody started heading for the exits."[3] Connolly advocated the bombing of Hanoi and the mining of the Haiphong harbor. Dresden, Hiroshima, and Nagasaki helped bring about peace, he asserted. His speech did not go down well on the Jesuit campus. Connolly's hawkish stand was criticized in an open letter by professors who referenced the Second Vatican Council's statement: "Any act of war aimed indiscriminately at the destruction of entire cities or of extensive areas with their population is a crime against God and man himself. It merits unequivocal and unhesitating condemnation."[4]

Connolly, in both how he practiced ecclesiastical authority and in the stand he took on U.S. foreign policy, was bound to be challenged in the late years of his tenure. Seattle University, to be sure, was not the only hotbed incubating dissent in that intensely rebellious era. During the Vietnam War and the years leading up to Hunthausen's arrival, women religious were trailblazers in social change efforts in both church and society. By the mid-1970s, many were determined to live out these words: "We religious have a leadership role to play by living the Gospel radically and thereby denouncing all injustice."[5] Ninety-five sisters from the Pacific Northwest participated in a national meeting of women religious which, according to Sister Diane Bader, O.P., at the time the chair of the Sister's Council of the archdiocese, called for the ordination of women and for solidarity with Pacific-nations women then seeking a Nuclear Free Pacific.[6] Sisters pushed the church toward a stand against the war-making system and for much greater participation by women in church leadership. We will see much more on the theme of gender at different points in the book.

FROM MONTANA WITH THE SPIRIT OF VATICAN II

Just before the Second Vatican Council commenced in October 1962, Hunthausen was appointed Bishop of Helena, Montana. The Council "called us back to the primacy of love in our lives," he said often over the years ever since. Vatican II was not so much a new direction as a confirmation of his own vision. "I try to live out my ministry as a bishop in the spirit of the Second Vatican Council," he told me in one of our interviews. "I was liberated by that spirit. It said so much to me just in itself. It resonated with where I felt the church and Christianity ought to be moving. I was elated by it." For "what the Council was saying was an affirmation of my own sense of church, my own sense of spirituality, my own sense of justice, which made me feel much more comfortable in going home and being a bishop of this church."[7]

In Helena, Hunthausen ushered in new structures of church reform such as a priests' senate, sisters council, pastoral council, and parish councils. Ecumenism came alive. Initially, he did not pursue issues of war and peace to any great degree.

"I went home after the Council and made no statements, little or nothing relative to the Vietnam War. Although on one or two occasions with the priests senate in the Helena diocese we did together make a statement about the ICBMs that were being deployed in the Plains area of Montana, protesting, trying to make our voices heard, to sensitize the people of Montana."[8] Most American Catholic bishops in those days still felt ill at ease taking on the issue of American militarism. "Again, extremely conscious of the fact that to say anything that might be interpreted as disloyal or unpatriotic, I was not that willing to place myself in that position of jeopardy, to be somehow criticized or even taken seriously."[9] When he got to Seattle, this would change.

In March 1975, two months before he became Seattle's new archbishop, he spoke at a press conference held at the Seattle-Tacoma airport. He had reason to feel reluctance about the move. He would be leaving behind a Catholic population of less than 48,000 and taking on an archdiocese numbering close to 344,000. He felt that he should get to know the needs and the problems of the people in Western Washington. There would be challenges. The Catholic Church had already gone through disruptive innovations in the ten years since Vatican II. "We've got to find a way to live with the changes which have taken place." He called for reconciliation. "I truly feel there is a need for this throughout all society," he said.[10]

He loved the Montana outdoors. As in Norman MacLean's *A River Runs Through It*, the mountains and valleys and waters of western Montana had helped shape him. Western Montana, after all, was his home. His character was formed in small-town Anaconda, in small-capital Helena, and in rustic and wild places. Even after moving to Seattle he tried to spend every August back in Montana. The *Seattle Times* profiled the new archbishop. "A genial, approachable man, Archbishop Hunthausen has about him the air of old-shoe simplicity, perhaps engendered by his upbringing as a grocer's son in small-town America." Hunthausen talked about the move. "Humanly speaking, I wouldn't hesitate very long to say I'd much rather stay where I am (Helena). Yet I somehow sense—and I've analyzed this in prayer—that this is God speaking to me in a new and different and strange way…."[11]

Archbishop Hunthausen's public ministry in "The Evergreen State" began with the installation ceremony at the Seattle Center Arena. On May 22, 1975, he stood before 5,000 people. One reporter described it this way:

> "Someone began to clap—a tiny, almost lonely sound in the Arena which had become, for a time, a cathedral. Others picked up the applause. Soon the great hall was alive with a loud, long, standing ovation. Archbishop Hunthausen stood there, a calm, smiling man who may have been surprised by the joy of the spontaneous outpouring of affection from the people whom he is pledged to serve. He quickly

captivated the friendly crowd. Archbishop Hunthausen began his first sermon to his new flock with a long litany of acknowledgements of the cardinal, archbishops, abbots, priests, sisters, civic dignitaries and leaders of other churches who were there. Then he smiled at the people and said quietly, 'Good evening.' The people answered with laughter and more applause. 'I've been wanting to say that for some time,' he said."

Those first soft spoken words, Hunthausen's "good evening," were the very same first words that Pope Francis expressed in a similar tone decades later from the balcony above St. Peter's Square, "buona sera." Hunthausen told the crowd that when he first became a bishop he adopted as his motto, "'Thy Will Be Done,' not realizing, he grinned, what that might get him into."[12] Hunthausen said, "I would pray that we might truly be a loving people who recognize that if peace is to come into our world it must begin first with us, a people who strive to be at peace with themselves, at peace with God, and at peace with one another."[13]

To gain a sense of the impression Hunthausen made upon his arrival as the new archbishop, I interviewed some folks who came to know him early in his Seattle years. Sr. Kathleen Pruitt, a member of the Sisters of St. Joseph of Peace, collaborated with Hunthausen on many issues. One moment in the Seattle Center Arena ceremony stood out in the memory of this veteran health care professional and peace and justice activist. What happened in that moment gave her an immediate feel for Hunthausen's character. Pansy and George Kotolaris, a mother-and-son team who would become known as "legendary gate-crashers" because they invited themselves to public events all around town, sure enough were there. George invariably took pictures. "So George and his mother were there for this big event, the installation of the new archbishop, and George naturally came across during the ceremonial procession to take a picture. The new archbishop-to-be stepped out of the line to greet him." Sr. Kathleen thought, "This guy is going to be okay. Hunthausen had that gospel sense that the least among us is also the greatest. He didn't stand on pomp."[14]

Fr. Paul Magnano, a priest in the Archdiocese of Seattle who worked with both Connolly and Hunthausen, drew a comparison between Hunthausen and his predecessor. "Connolly did not like the idea of Hunthausen taking his place. He once called Hunthausen 'the Teutonic plague'. Under Connolly we called the diocesan paper, which was officially *The Progress*, the *Regress*." Magnano recalled the installation. "All the priests who came from Helena for the event were wearing suits and ties. We were in clerics, by contrast." It was a clear indication of a different model of church. Hunthausen was driving a VW Rabbit, whereas Connolly always had a driver for his fancy car. "I watched Hunthausen put his own gas into his car at the local station there by the seminary in Kenmore."[15] If Magnano was excited by

Hunthausen, the same could not be said for one older and very angry pastor who a few years later told Hunthausen's development director, Jim Burns, that "one day they will undo everything he has done to the church."[16]

While a student at Seattle University in the late 1970s, Hunthausen's nephew Denny Hunthausen now and then stopped in at St. James Cathedral where Uncle "Dutch" had simple quarters. Like Pope Francis, who has opted for a modest residence instead of the elaborate papal apartments, Hunthausen never lived in the archbishop's mansion. "I would go into his residence, wait for him and look at a book. He had lots of them. I remember *Call to Conversion*, by Jim Wallis. I would ask him about a given book, and he would talk about it and then just give it to me."[17] Denny says "Dutch would literally give you the shirt off his back. If you expressed admiration for some material thing in his room when you were visiting, he more often than not would say, 'oh, you like that, you have it.' He would just have you take it. He really was not attached in that way."[18]

Once, when Uncle Dutch was living on the grounds of the seminary in Kenmore (located on the north shore of Lake Washington, before the archbishop moved to the residence at St. James Cathedral a few blocks up the hill from downtown Seattle), Denny went to see him. The seminary had groundskeepers. Archbishop Hunthausen nonetheless always had some outdoor project in the works. "I remember coming out there one time and he's coming in all sweaty and had some type of lawn maintenance instruments and he says, 'Oh yeah, I'm trying to make a trail, there's this place outback here that's just been overgrown and I'm trying to clear it out and make this trail.' So the next day he took me out there and it's this huge undertaking. And I'm thinking, what are you out here doing this for? He's always had those kinds of things as outlets, the physicality of him, the hand labor, always being connected in that way."[19]

I asked Denny what he thought about his uncle's movement into the war and peace issue. His uncle's engagement in the disarmament cause was a response to a spiritual call, Denny felt. "Following that calling, you don't know what it's going to require of you until you take that step, each step of the way. What is this going to mean?" Uncle Dutch just wanted to be present to the spiritual call. He could not control what the media would do, or how other elements in the church would react. "He wasn't making move three while anticipating move two or four from someone else. It wasn't that kind of thing. He would have said, 'Well, I feel compelled, I've reflected on it, thought about what those in the peace movement, let's say, at Ground Zero, are doing. I've reflected on it, I've prayed on it, and I felt I needed to do something more. I was being called to do something more, so I did.'"[20]

TO LIVE WITHOUT TRIDENT

Both preparations for war and protests against war have long shaped the social character of the Seattle region. Joel Connelly, a writer for the *Seattle Post-Intelligencer*, described the region on March 19, 2003 as the U.S. military was unleashing 'Shock and Awe' over Baghdad. "This corner of the country is famous as a manufacturer and repair center for weapons of war, and a training and staging area for its troops. Hanford manufactured plutonium for the atomic bomb dropped on Nagasaki. It was carried to target by a B-29 assembled in Seattle. We have, at the same time, been an epicenter for dissent against the Vietnam War, Cold War, Gulf War and all-but-certain war on Iraq. Crowds of as many as 10,000 people have marched for peace in downtown Seattle, and between the city's Catholic and Episcopal cathedrals."[21]

The area's rise as a military-industrial powerhouse could be traced to the Second World War. The economic development impact of the war on the region was breath-taking. In 1939, Boeing Corporation employed just 4,000 people. By 1944, 50,000 worked at its Seattle area plant alone, with new branches spreading up and down Puget Sound. The war effort established a strong nexus of elevated military spending, prosperity, and optimism. After those years, the region's economy remained tethered to military spending.[22] Besides the major contractors such as Boeing and Lockheed, educational centers such as the University of Washington participated in the militarized economy. Five counties—King, Pierce, Kitsap, Island, and Benton—were steeped in defense contracts, four surrounding Puget Sound and Benton, down along the Columbia, hosting the Hanford Nuclear Range. A veritable litany of military installations included McChord Air Force Base, Fort Lewis Army Base (later they became a joint air force-army base), the Puget Sound Naval Shipyards, the Whidbey Island Naval Air Station, and others too numerous to cite. Trident and its Bangor base, perhaps as much as anything else, illustrated the concentration of lethal power and financial incentive. In May 1974, the Seattle Chamber of Commerce put forth a resolution to support the U.S. Navy's plans for the base. The resolution was shaped in part by economics. Other chambers of commerce lent their support. A year earlier, U.S. Senator Henry "Scoop" Jackson had announced the Bangor site selection for the world's single most expensive military project to date. "The Navy and Kitsap County have had a happy marriage for most of this century, and we want it to stay that way."[23]

Federal military spending, though used to construct potentially lethal machinery, was the seemingly indispensable lifeblood for the state's economy. This was certainly the case when Archbishop Hunthausen began to find his public voice on the issue. The arms industry growth rate shot up in the early years of the Reagan administration.[24] Trident became a galvanizing focus of opposition. Slightly more than one year after Hunthausen spoke at Pacific Lutheran University, the first

Trident submarine made its way into the Hood Canal. By the late 1980s, the Bangor base housed eight Tridents. The base had been purchased by the Navy in 1944 to serve as an ammunition shipment point for the war in the Pacific. Since the early 1960s, attack submarines had docked at the site, and Trident was the latest version.[25]

In "Confronting the U.S. Navy at Bangor, 1973–1982," Brian Casserly analyzed the tension between those who saw Trident as an economic boom and those who questioned the planned development. "The navy's Trident program consisted of a new fleet of nuclear-powered submarines equipped with Trident nuclear missiles. At 560 feet long, the new vessel was almost twice as large as its predecessor…the Trident missile had longer range and greater accuracy than previous models, and each of the 24 missiles carried by the submarine had 17 separate, independently targetable nuclear warheads." The navy promoted the idea that the Trident was a defensive weapon crucial to national security. But anti-nuclear protesters pegged Trident as a "first-strike" behemoth.[26]

A local civic-military partnership favored the submarine. Chambers of commerce from all around Puget Sound coalesced to form the Puget Sound Trident Task Force, building public affirmation. At the same time, the opposition to Trident made its debut. When the members of the Pacific Life Community planted a cross at the Trident site in March 1975 and demonstrated outside the Bangor base that summer, they saw themselves as "following in a tradition of protest against the Bangor facility begun in 1972, when a group called the People's Blockade tried to block the transshipments of ammunition to Southeast Asia by lying on the railroad tracks leading into the base and by preventing ships from leaving the facility."[27]

The historic peace churches, along with the Fellowship of Reconciliation and the American Friends Service Committee, resisted Trident even when it was still only on Lockheed blueprints. By the summer of 1975, several organizations turned their attention to Trident, joining with members of Concerned About Trident, a Kitsap County association of residents anxious about the impact of the proposed Trident base on their local community.[28] Among these groups was Pacem in Terris (the Seattle chapter of the Catholic Worker, who chose their name to honor Pope John XXIII's encyclical on peace). As Larry Keil, one of the participants from the outset, tells the story, the Catholic Worker started a community kitchen to serve daily meals to those in need in the area, and with the receptiveness of the pastor they based their operation at St. James Cathedral in Seattle.[29] These Catholic Workers joined with a group of Canadian-based peace activists to form the Pacific Life Community. Sixteen people from Seattle and Vancouver B.C. came together for a weekend meeting in January 1975, and the Pacific Life Community was born. Their backgrounds ranged from Catholic to Quaker to anti-organized religion.[30]

Jim and Shelley Douglass were part of the Pacific Life Community. When they were living in British Columbia, a former Lockheed engineer by the name of Robert Aldridge told them about Trident. His conscience led him to resign from work on the Trident nuclear missile. Shelley Douglass recounts the reaction of the Pacific Life Community to Aldridge. "Our response was to bring together a group of people to experiment in a nonviolent response to the nuclear arms race, and particularly to Trident."[31] For the next two years, members of the Pacific Life Community got together each month either in Canada or in the United States. There were weekly meetings on both sides of the border. The agenda was to craft a nonviolent campaign against Trident. Shelley Douglass recalls, "Small-group civil disobedience at the Trident base, initiated by Pacific Life Community and the Fellowship of Reconciliation on July 4, 1975 had helped create this awareness."[32]

Early on, Seattle's new archbishop lacked a clear grasp of the region's militarized matrix. "I was not that aware of the Bangor missile base or the Trident submarine. Had I stopped to think of it I would have been more aware of the involvement of Boeing in war efforts, and so on, but that was not part of my consciousness at all when I came to Seattle and it was not for many months."[33] At the time Pacific Life Community members were reading Congressional records, arms industry reports, and analyses of the arms race. As Shelley Douglass puts it, they were trying "to reach out and share that knowledge with anyone interested enough to listen."[34] Writing from his birthplace in British Columbia, Jim Douglass exchanged correspondence with the new archbishop. Pacific Life had already found a kindred spirit in Bishop Remi De Roo of Victoria, B.C. just across the Strait of Juan de Fuca, through which Trident submarines pass, who spoke out against the impending Trident base. Subsequent to his correspondence with Hunthausen, Douglass sought a meeting. They met at some point in late September or early October 1976 at the diocesan seminary alongside Lake Washington in Kenmore, where Hunthausen lived. He told the archbishop that he and two others were going to Washington, D.C. for a thirty day fast. The U.S. presidential election was imminent. Both Jimmy Carter and Gerald Ford were supporting what to Douglass and others amounted to a first-strike nuclear technology.[35] Jim Douglass and others entered into the fast for peace to make a dramatic appeal to both presidential candidates and the wider public to renounce any first use of nuclear weapons.

Hunthausen once told me what he thought about folks such as Jim and Shelley Douglass and their peace community: "These are people who live a life freely chosen in a commitment to nonviolence and world peace. They have done it at great cost to themselves but I have no hesitation in saying that they are a peace-filled and happy people. They have great trust in the Lord. It is that kind of influence. They are genuine."[36]

It was in October 1976 that Hunthausen first read Jesuit Richard McSorley's article, "It's a Sin to Build a Nuclear Weapon."[37] As we know, the article later influenced the June 12, 1981 speech that would put Hunthausen on the national and international stage. While Jim Douglass was fasting in the nation's capital and other members of the Pacific Life and Catholic Worker communities were fasting in the Seattle area, Hunthausen wrote to the priests of the archdiocese telling them what he had learned from the visit with Jim and from the McSorley article:

> "By the time this letter reaches you *The Progress* will have published an article about several men and women who are engaging in a 30 day period of prayer and fasting October 3-November 2 in Washington, D.C. They are representatives of the Pacific Life Community. I know one of them personally, Mr. Jim Douglass, author of the book 'The Non-Violent Cross'. I have found him to be a serious and Christian gentleman. During this period of prayer and fasting appeals will be made to the leading Presidential candidates against first use of nuclear weapons.... My own personal prayer and reflection has led me to support these men and women in whatever way I can, especially by my prayer. I have a deep conviction that they and their cause deserve my encouragement and cooperation. I say this because the nuclear first use policy has been described by them as 'the most dangerous military policy in history, which cannot be justified before the human family.' I agree. As a teacher and preacher of Christ's gospel message of peace, I have a deep conviction that silence and inaction at this time is nothing less than the betrayal of the charge given to 'preach the gospel in season and out of season.'"[38]

Later that same year, Jim and Shelley Douglass were in King County Jail for acts of nonviolent civil disobedience at the Trident base. Hunthausen intended to visit them both in early December. However, he couldn't get in to see Jim. Ironically, because he was practicing the classic civil disobedience mode of noncooperation with the authorities, and therefore did not respond when he was asked by the guards to do so, Douglass did not know that Archbishop Hunthausen was trying to meet with him. "I remained in the cell. The guards came into the cell. They rolled me (by wheelchair) through the jail and out into the street. They put me in a car and took me to the King County Courthouse. I said, 'What on earth is going on here?' They said to me, 'you've got a visitor.'" The visitor, to the joyous surprise of Jim, was Ray Hunthausen. Then, on Christmas Eve, December 24, 1976, Hunthausen and Jesuit Fr. Pat Hurley went to visit him again. At that time Jim Douglass had been moved to the Public Health Hospital in Seattle.[39]

Seattle Times religion reporter Ray Ruppert wrote about this resolute peace activist and his influence on Hunthausen: "Who is Jim Douglass? He can be categorized in various ways: as a white male 39 years old, a Canadian citizen, an author, a theologian, a Roman Catholic, a layman, a law breaker, a former university professor, a husband, a father." Douglass was in jail along with John Williams, another member of the Pacific Life Community. "They passed out leaflets at Bangor, a technique Douglass found effective at Hickam Air Force Base." Douglass had done civil disobedience at Hickam Air Force Base in Hawaii during the Vietnam War, managing to pour blood on classified files before being arrested.

> "Douglass and Williams also dug a hole at the Bangor main gate in which to bury a replica of the Trident submarine. Douglass drew 90 days for property damage and 60 days for trespassing. Williams got 90 days. Douglass and Williams are in the second week of a water-only fast as another form of protest. Douglass has just come off a 30-day fast in Washington, D.C., as an appeal to the American and Canadian people to oppose first use of nuclear weapons."[40]

The *Seattle Times*' Ruppert also described the October 20 letter Hunthausen had sent to all the priests.

> "One of the most widely circulated personal documents in Seattle in years is the now famous 'archbishop's letter.' Because it expresses an influential church leader's forthright stand against nuclear weapons right here in the birthing place of Trident, the letter has enheartened many of those active in the peace movement. For that reason, the letter has been copied and recopied, circulated and recirculated, read and re-read, almost like a modern-day epistle from Seattle."

It was, Ruppert opined, a strong piece of writing. "No wonder the people who have been snipping wire fences at Bangor, carrying signs and otherwise protesting the Trident missile system are encouraged."[41] Hunthausen's stand against Trident and the U.S. first strike doctrine had found regional expression only a year into his tenure. Because of this stand, he faced criticism long before he made the Tacoma speech in 1981. It was not easy trying to live out the call of active nonviolence in its full implications while being in the role of an American Catholic bishop, no matter how small or large a stage.

Was Raymond Hunthausen ready for civil disobedience? What was going through his mind while he thought of those putting their bodies on the line? I once asked him about this. "In one sense, gratitude that there are people so deeply committed that they will help the rest of us see the importance of this issue." They were risking jail. How could he live out the call to resist Trident precisely at the same time that he was a bishop, a symbol of unity? He really did not want to go to jail. Yet, in a way, he wished that within himself he could muster the courage so "that the thought of jail wouldn't bother me."[42]

Douglass was, in Hunthausen's judgment, "a very deeply spiritual man, a man who has chosen poverty and all that means to somehow in his efforts bring to his fellow men and women a sense of what we are about as human family."[43] Spokane's Bishop Topel, Hunthausen's spiritual mentor as far back as 1939 when Dutch enrolled as a student at Carroll College in Helena, was another major influence. Topel lived in voluntary poverty. He called the church to be with the poor. Topel, in Hunthausen's estimation, walked a sacred path. "I saw him living the life, I saw him committed to God's will and holiness in his own life. I recognized that I was not Bishop Topel and I was not being asked to do exactly what he was doing, but I was taken up with the realization that we are all called to holiness."[44] A bishop living in voluntary poverty and a theologian living in voluntary incarceration impressed Raymond Hunthausen. The new archbishop felt troubled by the impact of the expensive arms race on so many people facing involuntary poverty. "Here as a church leader I began to sense my responsibility to at least speak out, the sense of evil that this (militarization) represented in my life and had to represent in the life of the world."[45]

As he searched his own conscience, Hunthausen sought to create greater awareness in the Catholic community. In the spring of 1977 he sent the clergy a resource booklet, "Repent Trident," suggesting they preach on the theme.[46] The *Seattle Times* reported on his letter.

> "Opposition in the religious community to the 'first strike' capability of the Trident nuclear-submarine base at Bangor on the Olympic Peninsula became stronger this week with a statement from the Roman Catholic archbishop of Seattle and announcement of an interdenominational evening of prayer and testimony against Trident. In a letter to priests of the archdiocese, the Most. Rev. Raymond G. Hunthausen said the time seemed right to support nuclear disarmament and continuation of the Strategic Arms Limitation Talks."

He feared that the United States was shifting to a first-strike posture.[47] In one passage Hunthausen wrote: "Thought is trigger to our actions. An aggressive intention to use a weapon will surely lead to active use of it." He asked priests to search their own consciences, and to consider preaching on the Trident issue and inviting their congregations to participate in an ecumenical service for Trident Concern Week.

Around this time, a broad-based anti-Trident organizing effort was in the works. Joe Ratstatter, a tenacious activist with a farm worker organizing resume, brought his skills to Live Without Trident (which would later take the name Armistice). Live Without Trident (LWT), though not explicitly religious, had gained the support of the Church Council of Greater Seattle. Together with other executives of various denominations, Hunthausen participated regularly in the Church Council. LWT organizing efforts had a direct impact on him and on other religious leaders. Study action groups were started, campus ministries got involved, and significant numbers of people came out for demonstrations. LWT was the broad civic organizing base, while the Pacific Life Community was in some ways the more spiritual and 'pure principles' effort of the two. They often worked together. As a matter of fact, Trident Concern Week was a collaboration of many groups.[48]

Knowledge and energy were coalescing to try to stop Trident. Among those involved were Rev. Jon Nelson, who had been the Lutheran campus minister at the University of Montana in Missoula when Hunthausen was the bishop of Helena, and Charlie Meconis, who was active through the Seattle Religious Peace Action Coalition (SERPAC). SERPAC had begun back in 1971 with a focus on the Vietnam War issue. Years challenging U.S. policy in Southeast Asia fed into the anti-Trident campaign, as many of the activists who organized against the Vietnam War jumped into the Trident resistance movement. Meconis, like others, thought the faith communities could be instrumental. The goal was to produce broad public participation across the religious and secular spectrum. Other key organizations were Puget Sound Sane and Physicians for Social Responsibility.[49]

Trident Week was designed to reach the public imagination. The image of a nuclear Leviathan loomed in the consciousness of the dean of St. Mark's Episcopal Cathedral, the Very Rev. Cabell Tennis, who delivered a sermon as part of the May 1977 Trident Week observance. "I become aware from time to time that you and I sitting here, right now, are hostages…. We are targeted by the Soviet Union and probably China soon because of the base at Bangor, because of the silos in Montana." Tennis said "The holiness of God, the unity and wonder of all being is defiled by even the presence of a Trident submarine and all the other brutal instrumentalities of nuclear arms, but what can I do?" He hoped that the church would speak up. So many other institutions—labor, universities, and businesses—have jobs, grants, and sales that limit their voice and tie them to the military-industrial patronage system. Perhaps only the churches "are free enough to speak the truth." A *Seattle Times* story contrasted Tennis' perspective with that of a retired rear admiral who saw things quite differently. Rear Adm. J.A. Jaap reportedly expressed his views, reacting to all the anti-Trident rhetoric, in a letter to Hunthausen. In it, he rejected the view that Trident could be judged a "first strike" weapon. He had served with the Atomic Energy Division of the Office of Naval Operations and as the Pacific commander in chief's representative to the director of the joint strategic (nuclear) target planning staff. "Our national leadership has opted for Trident as one element of a system to deter any hostile power from attacking the United States with nuclear weapons…. But without that deterrence a hostile power would be much freer to launch an attack on the United States whenever it decided that such attack would be to its advantage."[50]

Jaap may have aimed his hard-hitting words at Hunthausen in particular but he was no doubt concerned about the collective potential of the organizations, secular and religious, then finding ways to work together in the anti-Trident campaign. Collaborative efforts were not uncommon on numerous issues, hardly just Trident. Western Washington, indeed the Pacific Northwest as a region, represented one of the nation's most "unchurched" or unaffiliated areas. For some time, Washington state ranked as the lowest in percentage of church membership of all the states. Because religious bodies did not have the numbers to be strong opinion drivers, coalitions across faith traditions and the secular continuum were thought to be crucial. Yet there were contrary impulses within some religious groups. One tendency was to separate from society so as to insulate one's faith community from the dominant secular atmosphere. The other approach, adopted by Hunthausen, was to link together faith communities in a concerted attempt to transform society on key issues.[51] They also reached across to join with people not affiliated with religion, focusing on human solidarity in pursuit of common peace and justice goals. But this "reach" made the insular-thinkers more than a little nervous.

Rev. William "Bill" Cate, who directed the Church Council of Greater Seattle, felt that the contrary impulses within religious bodies in relation to society could help explain some of the tensions that arose around Hunthausen's involvement. As did other leaders in their respective denominations, Hunthausen had to contend with these contrary impulses going on within his own church.[52] His participation in interfaith and religious-secular coalitions on numerous social justice and peace issues was of concern to those Catholics who wanted their Catholicism to be insulated from all of these pluralistic influences. Yet like many other religious leaders, Hunthausen felt the church must build alliances in order to seek the good in common.

While many of the people who focused on the Trident issue were also active on other peace and justice issues, a particular form of Trident resistance, which became known as the Ground Zero community, was primarily centered on the Bangor Naval Base on the Hood Canal. Ground Zero was inspired in no small part by the people involved in the Pacific Life Community mentioned earlier. Shelley and Jim Douglass and others organized what they called "Bangor Summer workshops" to examine violence and nonviolence in personal life, while at the same time people conducted acts of civil disobedience actions at the base. Shelley recounted the origins of Ground Zero: "The experience of Bangor Summer [1977] was one of building contacts and sympathy. People involved in that project began to gain a sense of the possibilities in Kitsap County, and of the violence implicit in a campaign where people came from outside to protest the Trident base without knowing those who were economically dependent on it."

In the autumn of 1977 a parcel of land, 3.8 acres right next to the base, was purchased as a nonprofit land trust with nine people incorporating themselves and adopting the name Ground Zero Center for Nonviolent Action. In the fall of 1978, she writes, "we moved to Kitsap, and in concert with other Ground Zero folks, began to plan programs at the Center. Ground Zero began a tradition of Wednesday night meetings for clarification of thought, and of Thursday morning leafleting of workers entering the Trident base." Their goal was to be "a community of people working to change a violent world through a commitment to nonviolence." Over the next three years, Ground Zero slowly became accepted by many local residents—but not all, to be sure—in Kitsap County.[53] Reaction to the antinuclear drive was documented by Brian Casserly. "Part of the hostility undoubtedly grew out of a sense of economic self-preservation: the protesters opposed the navy, which was the source of employment and economic security for many locals. Some Kitsap citizens saw criticism of the military as a sign of protesters' naiveté or even disloyalty to the United States during a time of cold war tensions."[54]

As he became more and more conscious of what Trident signified, Hunthausen came to share the Ground Zero community's intensity of focus, though as a bishop he stayed involved in many other social justice concerns affecting people in the region. Something influential was coming his way from the witness of peace activists by the Bangor base. He read works by Jim Douglass, including *The Nonviolent Cross* and *Resistance and Contemplation*. The theologian-activist made this paradoxical observation about self and U.S. society: "The risk of prison in America is the condition of my deepest freedom because without that risk of truthful living I am already in a prison of my own making."[55] Prophetic thoughts in solitude from a Cistercian monk in Kentucky, Thomas Merton, affected both Douglass and Hunthausen. Merton's accidental death in 1968 could not keep his eloquent "contemplation in a world of action" from reaching countless people who loved his writings, which, especially in the 1960s, combined spirituality and a passion for peace. In "The Christian Roots of Nonviolence" Merton wrote something that Hunthausen kept close to his heart when he began to face opposition to his controversial stands. "Instead of trying to use the adversary as leverage for one's own effort to realize an ideal, nonviolence seeks to enter into dialogue with him in order to attain, together with him, the common good.... The key to nonviolence is the willingness of the nonviolent resister to suffer a certain amount of accidental evil in order to bring a change of mind in the oppressor and awaken him to personal openness and to dialogue."[56] In his Easter homily of 1977, Hunthausen invoked the poet-monk: "Thomas Merton writes 'to be risen with Christ means not only that one has a choice and that one may live by a higher law—the law of grace and love—but that one must do so.'" The Christian, Hunthausen believed, "must have the courage to follow Christ...dare to be like Christ...dare to follow conscience even in unpopular causes."[57]

By May 1978, some 3,000 people converged next to the Bangor base for a rally and march. Ten percent of them climbed over the fence in acts of nonviolent civil disobedience. Hunthausen manifested a style of learning and leadership that brought him near the prophetic edge with people like Douglass. Some thought this to be dangerous and subversive, because in Douglass they saw represented not just a lone individual but the kind of social momentum exemplified by the May 1978 rally and march. So, when, in the fall of 1978, Jim Douglass started contributing an opinion column to the archdiocesan weekly, the reactions could be predicted—and some of them were printed in the same paper. One 'letter to the editor' writer, after Douglass wrote about nuclear idolatry, wondered: "How could the *Progress* hire a 'traitor'? How can this man profess to love God and demonstrate against his country?"[58] Such attacks on Douglass had implications for Hunthausen. This was the official diocesan paper, after all. The weekly had by then been carrying several stories about the Trident base protests. Letters to the editor in response ran the gamut from paeans to harsh criticism. One individual, outraged that some Catholic leaders were supporting troublemakers such as Jim Douglass, thought it preposterous that clergy should repudiate laws.[59]

On the occasion in the late 1970s, when Hunthausen came to the Bangor base for the first time, more than 1,000 people attended the demonstration co-sponsored by Ground Zero Center for Nonviolent Action and Live Without Trident. Hunthausen did not speak. The way Jim Douglass remembers, "He just showed up."[60] He made himself one of the throng, not trying to stand out or take charge. He simply listened and took it all in.

Daniel Berrigan, the Jesuit peace activist, paid Hunthausen a visit in August 1979. Berrigan had been active in civil disobedience since the Vietnam War era, and now he sat down with an archbishop openly struggling to discern how to live the courage of his convictions. "We talked about Bangor," said Berrigan, "and his part in it as spiritual leader of this very large diocese.... I find him very, very troubled and sympathetic and open to having some larger part in speaking out."[61] When Hunthausen shared his thoughts with a large resistance community gathered at the entrance to the submarine base on October 29, 1979, he wondered out loud about the meaning of patriotism. "I love my country and I love the human family. I recognize that the issue is complex. But while I may be criticized, I think that to do nothing is to open myself to deeper criticism." He was there with some 2,000 protestors. Catholic peace action was on the rise. Sisters, priests, archdiocesan officers in education, business, finance, and development, and others were there. Hunthausen told the crowd that they were "doing the country a great service" by expressing their convictions.[62]

BICENTENNIAL PROCESS, SHARING RESPONSIBILITY

As resistance to Trident was expanding, Archbishop Hunthausen was also working to transform the church. Many people wanted change in the church. All of this church reform talk and action was stirring up fears among some church members and priests, as we will soon see. In March 1977, referencing the national Call to Action meeting for church reform and social justice held in Detroit in 1976, Hunthausen said: "We have enough documents and studies appealing to our heads. The pains and joys shared in Detroit touched our hearts."[63] He believed the spirit of the Second Vatican Council needed to take specific shape in each local region, and he spoke of this time and again, as in his May 1978 Pentecost pastoral statement: "Although we are in union with the Church around the world, no other church can answer for us, whether it be in Calcutta or the other Washington or Rome. The Church of Western Washington—our Church—is a mix of peoples with a unique heritage and a unique mix of questions."[64]

One noteworthy push for church reform had begun as the nation prepared to celebrate its two-hundredth birthday. The Archdiocese of Seattle participated in a bicentennial project happening in dioceses all across the nation. Fr. James Dunning, the coordinator of Seattle's effort, was versed in adult education and in the liturgical reforms coming out of Vatican II. Dunning's vision was like Hunthausen's. "He was," says Fr. Michael G. Ryan, "a cutting edge guy." Hunthausen, being predisposed to listening and learning, saw real merit in the plan to get a good sense of the views of all the people, so a questionnaire went out to the whole archdiocese. One question taken up in small-group discussions in the parishes in the fall of 1975 and in the beginning of 1976 was: "Should Catholics work together in a more visible way to bring about political and social change?" A statement prepared for small group discussions read: "We need more sermons on social justice and political issues."[65] From 1976 onward, the whole bicentennial process in the archdiocese generated a series of task forces to take up various justice and peace concerns raised by the people. This included task forces on everything from issues of hunger to the problems in Northern Ireland, and as all this developed, there gradually emerged the idea of creating an archdiocesan justice and peace center.[66] We will look more closely at some of the work of that center, including its focus on Central American issues, in a later chapter.

This bicentennial process took place in the context of a nation trying to recover from the tragic war in Vietnam and in a church struggling with its own deep tensions just a few years after Vatican II. Questionnaires asked such things as: What do people believe? Where are they in their faith life? What are people's hopes and dreams? Of course these sorts of questions, not to mention ones about justice and peace in society, would be welcome by many, but not by all Catholics. Some would see such surveys as portending trouble. "Even then we were on the radar of disgruntled nervous people who already were focusing on reacting to Hunthausen. They were concerned that his approach to governing was democratic," Fr. Ryan says.[67]

An "unexcitable archbishop was generating excitement," wrote Ray Ruppert in the spring of 1976. The calm Montanan was unleashing a spirit of freedom, "getting away from the old Catholic concept of the ruler and the ruled." Yet some Catholics were frightened. "They see the new attitude not as encouraging freedom but as encouraging laxity which could weaken, even destroy the church." Tensions and distrust were brewing. "One vignette which illustrated this fear came when Archbishop Hunthausen told a lay-clergy gathering, that 'I am not saying doctrine is up for grabs.' This brought some applause and a quick, happy rejoinder from a priest who was 'glad to hear you say that.'" One dismayed priest wrote: "I, myself, have arrived at a point where I have asked to be considered for re-assignment outside this area.... Not only do we have a leadership vacuum but such an erosion of Catholic faith and practice that, not only laity but priests as well are dumbfounded."[68]

Others were pleased that Hunthausen shared power. Hunthausen himself was reflective and hopeful: "Overall, I would judge there is a sense of excitement about the church, generated by a number of things. Primarily by the bicentennial program."[69] Fr. Michael McDermott was one of those people guiding the bicentennial process. He developed the questionnaires and organized listening sessions throughout the archdiocese in 1976 and 1977, so McDermott came to know Hunthausen's way of operating. "He would be there, listen to all, give people in each department the room to move ahead with their areas of responsibility, let them carry it out and encourage them." McDermott shared with me two vintage tales from Hunthausen's days as a coach at Carroll College. The first story comes via Tom Vandenberg's experience when he was a student at Carroll College in Helena. Vandenberg later became a priest. Carroll College was in a baseball tournament in Billings. Rocky Mountain was the opposing team, and Vandenberg could not forget the critical moment. Vandenberg:

> "It was the first game of the day and frost was still on the grass. I was the starting pitcher and proceeded to walk the first three batters for Rocky Mountain. The bases were loaded with no one out. Father Hunthausen called time-out and came to the mound to settle me down. In effect, what he said was this. 'Tom, you're the best pitcher we have out here right now. Relax and just give it your best.' With that simple, verbal sleight of hand he must have boosted my confidence because it worked. We got out of the inning without giving up a run, although we ended up losing the game by the score of 1 to 0."

McDermott related another tale, when Carroll was playing a basketball game against the University of Montana in Missoula. Carroll was getting stomped. The score was something like 93 to 54. The Missoula home crowd started chanting '100!'

> "Not only were the Carroll players losing, they were demoralized and feared humiliation. Coach Hunthausen, sensing the seriousness of the situation, called a time-out. It seemed a bit strange because there is nothing anyone could do to save the evening, or so everyone thought…except Father Hunthausen. As his players gathered around him, he laid out his plan, saying in so many words, 'Guys, we can't win this game. So let's have some fun anyway. Everyone is chanting for Missoula to score a hundred points. Our objective, for the rest of the game, is to keep them from doing it. Go into a stall!' The team did just that. (This was before the current-day shot clock rules.) The crowd pushed even harder when they realized what Carroll was trying to do. When the final buzzer went off, it wasn't at all clear who had won the game, as the Carroll players jumped up and down in triumph. The scoreboard no longer mattered because they felt like winners…thanks to an astute coach."[70]

Just as he did as a coach with the team, as a bishop, Hunthausen encouraged the whole community. McDermott observed, "You see, the paradigm of a coach fit in with his understanding of collegiality. And so when you bring people together and you start talking with them instead of telling them what to do, you say, this is where we need to go, and you listen then to the people and their responsibility, well?" The point was to combine teaching and empowerment centered on an image of the church as the people themselves. "He really was formed as a bishop at the Second Vatican Council those four years. When he came to Seattle he was able to build a team, treat people as adults, and work with people. He was very clear about what the Church taught. It was a question of how to best make it a reality in the lives of people."[71]

Another Hunthausen cabinet member, Fr. Jack Walmsley, says Hunthausen would always take days off with priests. He would meet up with some of them at Enumclaw and they would head up to Crystal Mountain in the Cascades to ski. It was, Walmsley says, "like he just knew a group of priests would be going skiing, and he would just show up. He felt comfortable enough to call priests and meet them at the restaurant in Enumclaw and carpool up there." In the summer he would do the same, this time when it came to golfing and the South Tacoma public golf course. "He was not a country club guy."[72] This was not just about Hunthausen's capacity to enjoy sports. It was about his way of being with people, whether in work or play.

Hunthausen saw the church as a guide, not an institution that controls lives, and talked about this in a 1977 interview. "The church has got to be a celebrating, joyful, loving entity in our lives." Shared responsibility was the watchword. "I would like to see a growing awareness of our call as Christian people to be more and more responsible to the Gospel message. To me, this means growth in our personal responsibility before Almighty God, to know his will in our lives, guided by the church, guided by one another, but to live in a spirit of joy and love and charity toward one another." Another key theme for Hunthausen was respect for diversity. "We have a hard time accepting the fact that it's possible to be united in our loyalty to Jesus Christ and our commitments to faith while, maybe, disciplines and modes and methods we use to live out that commitment might be different.... I don't think we have become comfortable with this (diversity in the church) but I think it is something we are going to have to learn really to live with and pray through.... I would hope we could manage this with charity.... On the part of some, though, you get the impression that if you don't do it my way, we won't do it at all. It's reflected in great measure by some of the letters I get from people, anonymously and otherwise."[73]

In the same interview, Hunthausen was asked about the closing of St. Edwards and St. Thomas seminaries. The context was that of an evolving church, the downturn in priestly vocations, and how Hunthausen handled all this. A meeting with priests took place in the spring of 1977. "Underlying it all was, obviously, a deep-seated anger over the whole situation of the seminary," Hunthausen said. "I just laid before them, point by point, moment by moment, going way into last fall, how all of this began to move in the direction it did." It was not an easy issue. For Hunthausen the decision, though painful, came, as "the result of prayerful examination of what seems to be God's will in the matter." Hunthausen told the interviewer: "Seminarians of the archdiocese are being sent to other seminaries around the country. A task force is studying the whole matter of preparing men for the priesthood. Some are asking very seriously if there is a new and different approach to training for priesthood.... Given the changes in the church, is there a better way?" He reflected on the meeting with the priests. "Some of the guys referred to it as Black Thursday. It was black only in that it was hard. It was hard on all of us. Myself, I would call it White Thursday. It was a step ahead." A priests' institute, held a few months later, gave the archbishop a sense that there was a growth in mutual understanding. "There were men (at the institute) at odds with one another about where we should go and how we ought to get there. But the fact we were really able to talk about it in a systematic fashion and hold together I felt was a tremendously important time for us."[74]

Hunthausen closed St. Edward's, the minor seminary program in Kenmore, and a year later closed the theologate, St. Thomas Seminary, named for Archbishop

Thomas Connolly who built it. The buildings were no longer needed, given the presence of other places of formation in the Pacific Northwest region and the financial pressure to consolidate resources. The decision to close the seminaries came about through a process of discernment and consultation involving the bishops of the whole region. However, St. Thomas represented the crown jewel of all the brick and mortar accomplishments of Hunthausen's predecessor. So this episode, according to Fr. Mike Ryan, was the "final nail in the coffin" for Connolly. From that decision time in 1977, Ryan believes Connolly worked against Hunthausen.[75] Fr. Paul Magnano could recall Connolly once saying of Hunthausen, "he threw me out into the garbage dump." The then editor of the archdiocesan newspaper, a Connolly appointee, repeatedly published critical comments about Hunthausen. As to what became of the seminary property, when Hunthausen authorized the sale of a large portion of the land, it went to the state of Washington and became St. Edward's State Park.[76]

If there were already tensions locally, the situation of the church globally was about to enter a new phase, which would have a major impact in Seattle. In August 1978, Pope Paul VI died. At a memorial mass at St. James' Cathedral, Hunthausen interpreted the significance of the fifteen year papacy. He highlighted Paul VI's commitment to solidarity with the poor, his passion for social justice, his cry for peace at the United Nations, and his leadership in morality and doctrine.[77] Ray Ruppert wrote about it: "In a simple but powerful homily in a cathedral packed with Protestant and Jewish leaders as well as Catholic priests, nuns and lay people, the archbishop noted that Pope Paul in his turn had carried on the work of Pope John XXIII, his predecessor." Hunthausen said Pope John XXIII had faced a church where unity was experienced through predictable custom and practice, and his tenure saw big changes in liturgy and authority in the church. Such changes produced confusion for many. Hunthausen described Pope Paul's efforts following the papacy of Pope John as an attempt to find a middle course between continuity and change. The price of unity often is pain and suffering, the archbishop said, and Pope Paul was willing to pay that price.[78]

Hunthausen enacted the type of change—especially in the model of authority—embodied in Pope John XXIII, and just like Pope John, Archbishop Hunthausen encountered the painful confusion of many people as they reacted to his approach. Hunthausen lived out the kind of experience that he, in this homily, saw embodied in Pope Paul VI, trying to adopt a pluralism that could usher ahead the prophetic spirit and yet keep people united. Hunthausen in the homily said, "This work of integration (the old with the new) was the work Pope Paul set for himself."[79] Hunthausen set this same work for himself, trying to find the best processes to share responsibility, to change the old pattern of authority, and to move at a pace that would integrate good customs with new dimensions.

ECUMENICAL APPROACH

As Archbishop Hunthausen and the Archdiocese of Seattle became involved in a broad range of justice and peace issues, he made the connections in an ecumenical and interfaith context. Rev. William "Bill" Cate, the executive director of the Church Council of Greater Seattle (CCGS) when Archbishop Hunthausen arrived, recalled with affection their first encounter. Church executives from across several denominations that formed the Church Council and the Washington Association of Churches had the custom of meeting for breakfast every Thursday morning. "When he came to our breakfast meeting, Wayne Roberts, the Baptist executive, asked him, 'how do we address you?' And he said, 'Ray, just call me Ray.' And Roberts said, 'we never could call your predecessor, Archbishop Connolly, Tom,' and Hunthausen said, 'neither could I'." Hunthausen began attending the weekly breakfast meetings shortly after his arrival in Seattle.[80] In Cate's view, Hunthausen became a liberalizing force in the Catholic Church and beyond. He was "an honest man who went through the Second Vatican Council and came out with a much more ecumenical and human rights and social justice view, and what happened here is that a lot of the more conservative Catholics resented it, did not like it."[81]

Rev. Loren Arnett served as the executive director of the Washington Association of Churches. Like Cate, Arnett recollected his first meeting with Hunthausen and remembered what it was like working with him in the years that followed. "Ray had a firm commitment to ecumenism that he brought with him from Montana. He had been very active in the Montana Association of Churches."[82] As of January 1, 1978, the Archdiocese of Seattle became a full member of the Washington Association of Churches, which had replaced the Washington Council of Churches two years earlier. Full participation followed a careful study process by the Archdiocesan Commission on Ecumenical and Inter-religious Affairs. Announcing the decision, Hunthausen said: "This is only the beginning.... We must back our sentiments with strong participation in the association's programs and with strong support for its services.... We must feel free always to speak our own position and to voice our concerns."[83]

In late summer of 1978, the Church Council caught the spotlight. One major issue in that time period was Seattle school desegregation, reported Ray Ruppert. CCGS and the religious community in the region were taking an active role. The larger reality of racial injustice in education was a focus for ecumenical work. Other issues were Native American concerns, urban development, housing and homelessness, police and community relations, energy and ecology, women and religion, gay and lesbian issues, and mental health concerns. The Church Council had a series of luncheons with members of the business community. "Generally speaking, the Church Council is playing a role of mediation between a particular body out there—like the gay community and the more conservative, middle-class aspects of the community." Rev. Cate noted that the religious community in the region, though only one third of the population, could do something significant by working together as one religious voice. "We can become a very strong pressure group if we want to pull ourselves together on an issue. You get one third of the population, especially the leadership, moving on an issue and you've got some real strength." In an expression of his appreciation, Cate spoke of "the excellent caliber of ecumenical relationships among our leaders, like Archbishop Hunthausen who is a real jewel." [84]

The Church Council was of course also involved with events around Trident. Rev. Jon Nelson, at one of these Trident-awareness/resistance gatherings, described Trident as "the beast of the Apocalypse who rises out of the sea." Floyd Schmoe, a Quaker and long-time peace activist, equated Trident with Hiroshima. Hunthausen attended the event where both Nelson and Schmoe spoke. He too spoke up, recalling the feeling of horror over Hiroshima still haunting him from his days when he was in seminary along Lake Washington's north shore. At one point during this conference an individual who worked for the Trident program stood up and said that it was not until that evening that he had become fully aware of the destructive capacity of Trident. In front of everyone there he burned his last paycheck.[85]

THE SUCCESSION OF THREE POPES AND THE DEATH OF ARCHBISHOP ROMERO

After the death of Pope Paul VI, the cardinals elected a man who remained in the papal office for one of the shortest tenures in church history. Hunthausen saw in John Paul I the same spirit manifested in Pope John XXIII. People the world over saw in that 34-day papacy in late summer and early fall of 1978 a person "full of love and good will," as Rajashree Deri, a Hindu from India described him. Laughs and simple words were his trademarks.[86] Hunthausen felt deeply moved. He had just spent time with John Paul I a week earlier when he and other Northwest bishops were at the Vatican on September 21. There was a peacefulness and depth of faith, Hunthausen said. "He actually seemed comfortable with the huge responsibility which had become so unexpectedly his and I can only attribute this to his strong faith in the Lord's love for him and in His presence in his life."

Hunthausen said that the "death of any public figure makes us pause and ponder ultimate things such as the meaning of life and death. This is particularly so in the case of this good, simple, humorous and profoundly holy man who captured the hearts of people the world over in the all-too-brief days of his pontificate." Another observer speculated about just what might happen in the wake of this "all-too-brief" papacy. The president of Seattle University, Jesuit Rev. William Sullivan, said: "His death raises real concern about his successor and the question whether we will find someone with the kind of balance which he already demonstrated.... That is a major concern of mine."[87] The concern would prove prescient. At a press conference held on September 29, Hunthausen said he hoped the College of Cardinals would "elect someone with the same pastoral feel and concern as the simple Italian the world now mourns." Hunthausen said that John Paul had "touched many hearts and given a great deal of hope." Hunthausen saw in him "a man of deep compassion."[88] A near reincarnation of Pope John XXIII, Pope John Paul I was quickly replaced by someone with great charisma. Such charisma, however, would soon unleash a distinct approach to papal authority.

On March 24, 1980, a year and a half later, in another part of the globe, a prophetic religious leader was shot to death while celebrating Mass with fellow El Salvadorans in a small chapel in San Salvador, the capital of El Salvador. Hunthausen had been to Latin America—Guatemala, where the diocese of Helena had a mission, and Peru, but not to El Salvador—but he had never met Archbishop Oscar Romero. Romero was truly one of the giants of prophetic Christianity in Latin America in that era. He underwent a profound transformation as he saw injustices all around him. Romero broke with the conservative members of the El Salvadoran hierarchy, who had ties to the repressive regime. The witness of his own priests, sisters, and lay people had called the reluctant and bookish Romero into the liberation struggle. He became a powerful voice for social justice and active nonviolence. And as would be the case for Hunthausen as time went on, Romero never received strong support from the highest echelons of the Catholic Church when he took a prophetic stand. Hunthausen eulogized him. "The death of this good man is a tragic end for a man whose ministry as a bishop was directed toward social reform for his people with frequent warnings against extremism both to the right and the left. His death is a sign."[89] Just as the Vatican of John Paul II would come down on Hunthausen, it was also critical of Romero in the late days of the 1970s, concerned that he was becoming too radicalized.

Hundreds of church workers in El Salvador were being killed. Any efforts at raising consciousness and organizing people would be met with severe repression by the oligarchy in power. The situation in that country had become brutal and deeply divided. And as noted in the case of Romero, those in the church who chose to stand in solidarity with the poor and the oppressed were not likely to get much backing from a Vatican wary of anything that looked to it like a Marxist-influenced liberation theology. In one shocking case that caught the media's attention in the United States, four women, Ita Ford, Maura Clark, Dorothy Kazel, all nuns, and Jean Donovan, a lay missioner, were raped and killed in early December 1980 in El Salvador. El Salvador was already at that time a task force focus in the Seattle Archdiocese. Things in that country were only going to get worse with a huge infusion of U.S. military "aid" by the new Reagan administration. These women, like Archbishop Romero and countless Salvadorans, paid the ultimate price of discipleship. That is how Archbishop Hunthausen reflected on the horrible injustice inflicted on these four women. He denounced his own country's role in the Central American conflict. "They were drinking from the chalice that Jesus drank from before them. Their blood mingled with his and with Archbishop Oscar Romero's and with the more than 9,000 others who have died in El Salvador this year." Hunthausen called for an end to all U.S. military aid to El Salvador.[90]

WELCOMING TO THE GAY AND LESBIAN COMMUNITY

In early November 1978, Seattle was caught up in a highly charged issue involving an anti-gay measure put before voters. Initiative 13 would remove the words "sexual orientation" from city housing and employment ordinances providing legal protection from discrimination. A broad base of women and men in the faith community urged religious leaders to speak out against the initiative. Represented by Archbishop Hunthausen, nine Seattle religious leaders made a joint statement at a press conference. "In response to these individual Christians and because of our personal commitment to a Christian ethic which calls for fair and equal treatment of all citizens, we make public our personal opposition to this initiative, and we urge this city's religious community and all citizens to do the same," Hunthausen said on behalf of the group. Other signers of the statement included Casper Glenn of the United Presbyterian synod, William Ritchey of the United Methodist, United Church of Christ minister James Halfaker, Episcopal bishop Robert Cochrane, Christian Church (Disciples of Christ) minister Wesley Ford, American Baptist minister Wayne Roberts, A.G. Fjellman of the Lutheran Church in America, and Loren Arnett of the Washington Association of Churches. As Ray Ruppert reported for the *Seattle Times*, "Evangelical and fundamentalist churches back the measure and have quoted from both the Old and New Testaments to support their position. Archbishop Hunthausen, responding to a question, said those people were reading the Scriptures selectively while the entirety of the gospel 'urges us to see other values' accepting other people."[91]

Seattle's mayor, Charles Royer, and Rabbi Earl Starr of Seattle's Temple De Hirsch, also spoke out against the initiative. When Hunthausen spoke, he indicated that he, as well as other religious leaders, had received letters from people in support of the initiative, but he said no large petition drive on that side of the highly emotional issue had taken place. By contrast, people opposed to the measure had developed a strong social voice. By standing prominently against the anti-gay initiative of 1978, Hunthausen stirred up the wrath of socially conservative Roman Catholics who then began to raise their collective voice against him. After all, he not only signed the statement of the church leaders but was a spokesperson on their behalf.[92] Why did Hunthausen put himself out there, knowing it would not sit well with socially conservative people in his Catholic community? When I posed this question to Rev. Loren Arnett, key organizer of the statewide Washington

Association of Churches engagement of the issue, he said: "I always remember Archbishop Hunthausen saying, after we'd had a great deal of group discussion, 'If we don't do this, who will?'" The religious leaders held meetings all across the state, had 'back and forth' discussions in the board of the Washington Association of Churches, and Hunthausen vigorously called for nondiscrimination.[93] To this issue as well we must return later in the narrative, for Hunthausen's public support of people facing discrimination because of their sexual orientation was not limited to a single moment in time. His stand was certainly going to provoke antagonism not only from some social conservatives in church pews, but also from certain guardians of moral doctrine working at the headquarters on the Italian peninsula.

WOMEN AND GENDER EQUALITY

In the long run, Hunthausen's support for gender equality in society—but especially in the church—was not going to curry favor in the Vatican. But what we ought to note at this early juncture is the fact that during the very first years of his tenure in Seattle, he was paying attention, learning, and thinking about how to foster equality of voice. Women religious in the archdiocese pioneered church renewal and social justice. In May 1976, the Sisters' Council Social Action Task Force opposed the construction of the Trident nuclear submarine and missile system at Bangor. This same task force, supported by Hunthausen, pushed the local church toward structural change.[94] The sisters found a receptive listener in the new archbishop. One of his friends, fellow Anaconda native Jack Morris, told me years ago: "It's going to be the Sisters who drive the Church into the twenty-first century!"[95] Raymond Hunthausen's own sibling, Sister Edna Hunthausen back in Browning, Montana, and many women religious and lay women in the archdiocese found in him a sincere openness. Nonetheless, sincere listening would not be enough. It would be an understatement to say that the male-controlled Catholic Church was not making the kinds of strides in cultural and structural reform that were needed. Women religious posed this challenge to Catholicism when the National Assembly of Women Religious met near Spokane in 1976. That same year, the Archdiocesan Council of Women expressed their belief that the Vatican II notion of shared responsibility meant that a predominantly male-dominated system needed fundamental change.[96]

"Are Roman Catholics ready for women in ministry?" asked religion writer Ruppert in a May 1979 *Seattle Times* story. "Those who urge an answer of yes, contend the question should not be asked within the narrow limits of ordination of women in the priesthood. Rather, they contend, the question should address the renewal of the entire church, liberating it from forms and structures of the past—including an all-male priesthood." He interviewed women then quite active in the church in Seattle, including Sisters Diana Bader and Margaret Casey. Bader told him, "We're talking about the total renewal of the institution. And with that renewal of the institution will come renewal of everything that is in it." Sr. Margaret Casey felt that "If anything is going to happen...it will happen in this archdiocese. I really believe that.... There is an atmosphere for open discussion in spite of some of the things we have run into...." Sr. Bader commented, "We have an archdiocese where there is an archbishop who believes in collegiality...and acts accordingly.... I wouldn't say the same for all dioceses throughout the country."[97]

In autumn of 1980, Hunthausen issued a pastoral statement on the subject of women and their role in the church. One sister said, "I really respect him.... I think he'll be hurting (from criticism)." Hunthausen encouraged the people of the Catholic community of Western Washington to "continue to look critically at existing structures to discern whether they foster or hinder full personhood of women and men in the church."[98] The statement came from a long process of dialogue. Hunthausen invoked the example of St. Catherine of Siena: "This laywoman and doctor of the church was known to have urged obedience to legal church authority, while at the same time challenging popes to face the structural issues of their day." Hunthausen added his voice to the movement calling on the pope and Catholicism as a whole to face and overcome structural sexism.

Among the first such letters by a Catholic bishop in the United States, the pastoral on the role of women in the church arose—like almost everything Hunthausen wrote or said—through a careful period of listening and discussion. He acknowledged the social and cultural oppression of women in the history of church and society. Women's personal experiences, he wrote, had revealed "inconsistencies in the religious doctrine of universal salvation when set against the realities of exclusion and discrimination." He asked: "What does a Church look like that is whole, just, and moving toward full incarnation of the Kingdom?"[99]

He asked questions which had arisen in all the dialogues preceding the letter:

> "What opportunities for responsibility and authority do women have in the Church? What avenues of influence, of leadership, are open to them? What inequities exist in the discharge of menial tasks in our Churches? Do women, in truth, as full members of the faith community have access to all ministries according to their gifts, the needs of the community, and their generosity in responding with the full impetus of their baptismal commitment? Is the Church drawing, to the fullest degree possible, on the distinct human qualities of the feminine person in the exercise of its ministry, by integrating women in an official, public way in all forms of service and mediation, especially in the uniquely ecclesial areas of Word and Sacrament?"

He spelled out actions that should be incorporated in the life of the Catholic Church—specifically, in the Archdiocese of Seattle, including equal access for women and men to theological and pastoral education; elimination of sexist language; equal employment opportunities and equal compensation for qualified women and men; and active recruitment of qualified women to serve in full professional capacity in leadership positions.[100]

I asked Sister Kathleen Pruitt, long active in a host of social and religious concerns during the Hunthausen years in Seattle, what she thought about the archbishop's approach to women and their concerns for justice. "He opened doors for women in the church. He was a tremendous inspiration." He was born as a bishop "out of the experience of Vatican II, but he did not need mentoring around the role of women in the church. His opening space for women's empowerment was really out of his own sense of what church is. The rest of us helped to nurture this, but not as mentors. It was already his own vision of the church."[101]

Sr. Carol Ann McMullen, who also worked very closely with Hunthausen, remembered how he first went around to the various deaneries and regularly met with sisters as well as with priests. He always treated people equally. She told me a story she said he would often tell about what happened when he first came to Seattle and met Archbishop Connolly. Connolly had not made any arrangement for where Hunthausen would stay. "So Hunthausen went down, used a pay phone and called a priest friend and stayed there. He loved being a priest."[102] He was more at home with this basic vocation than ever with the role of a prelate, she thought, and moreover he felt equality between brother priest and sister religious.

When I sat down with two other women religious, Srs. Chauncey Boyle and Mary Grondin, these feisty veterans of many social justice struggles in both religion and society remembered the Seattle Center Arena installation. What stood out was how down to earth Hunthausen was. Chauncey said that right from the beginning he came across very differently from Connolly. "Connolly had an ornate crosier. Hunthausen had a simple wooden one. It symbolized so much about the difference in these two men. His whole approach to everyone was so different."[103]

Victoria Ries, among the first lay women during Hunthausen's Seattle years to be leading a parish, came to the Seattle area in 1979 from St. Louis, Missouri to serve as campus minister at Pacific Lutheran University and the University of Puget Sound. With a Ph.D. from the University of Chicago, where she studied with theologians David Tracy and Anne Carr, she was asked by Hunthausen to provide theological perspective on work and a just wage for employees working in the church. "I always felt he was open, prayerful, discerning." He was, however, operating out of a male-dominated hierarchical system. So that was the bind he experienced. "He took bold stands." The pastoral statement on women expressed the openness he had for all areas of ministry. "His wholeness was so clear. When you were in his presence you knew you were in the presence of a holy and centered person. People felt his simple holiness." Ries herself was bold. It was the spring of 1979 that she said to herself, "I think I should be preaching, since I am leading these students." So she did, there on the two campuses. On one occasion she was asked to preach at a parish, St. George. She read the gospel that day. She preached. Not long after that, she got called in. The pastor, telling her that she could not read the gospel, was simply expressing the official position of the hierarchy. So she boldly called for a meeting with Archbishop Hunthausen to let him know face to face that it would have been much better if she could have heard this from him directly. She challenged him on the point. One thing she remembered so clearly from that episode: "He listened."[104]

Patty Repikoff, like Victoria Ries, brought a passion for gender equality to her work. She was actively involved at St. Leo's in Tacoma. Her earliest memories of Hunthausen involved a school closing. She was teaching there in the school at St. Leo's Parish. Hunthausen had a bit of a bad reputation for having already closed schools in Helena. He was reported to be much more in favor of faith formation programs than in the continuation of Catholic schools. The high school at St. Leo's was in fact closed in 1976. People who came to respect and love Hunthausen did not always agree with him. Still she found him to be genuine and always ready to learn. "That man has a connection with Jesus that is so simple. The Gospel is the center of his heart; it is the measure of his life." Years later, through the Viable Faith Communities project, people like Repikoff became the officially recognized leaders of their parishes. She said that Hunthausen supported women through the years, always seeking ways to foster equality.[105]

A TAPESTRY OF SEVERAL STRANDS

By July 1980, many strands were weaving their way through the tapestry of religion and society and the life of Seattle's Archbishop Raymond Hunthausen. Ruppert wrote of Hunthausen's willingness to "put himself on public display by marching at Bangor against the Trident submarine." Hunthausen explained how he had decided to engage in public protest on this issue:

> "I guess I did it because my own deep conviction is that nuclear armaments and the horribly destructive nature of armaments generally, but especially nuclear armaments, is something which as a human family we just don't seem willing to address.... When I was invited to take part in that march, I prayed and thought about it long and hard. I came to the conclusion it was a much more positive witness for me to do it than not to do it. I felt that even if there were those who would judge it negatively, maybe it would spur them to

> reevaluate and to rethink the matter.... I just think in some instances actions are demanded."

Hunthausen had recently returned from a two-week stay in Peru. Maryknoll priests there put him in touch with poverty unlike anything he had ever encountered before in his life. On hunger in Peru, and on nukes in the Pacific Northwest, Hunthausen spoke from his heart:

> "I don't think most of the people in our country see nuclear weapons as a conscience matter for them personally to grapple with. They're leaving it to someone else and it's too horrendous. One has to come to a position on something that is so all-encompassing. One has to. Most of our people have not been confronted with it. They haven't dealt with it in their own minds. I'm not saying I'm right and they are wrong. I am simply saying many people have not even looked at it. And that I think is the evil." (He saw "structural evil" in Peru.) "That's true about so many issues where you can't reach out and point at an individual or even one group. But the evil is there and people are suffering."

Hunthausen addressed polarization in the church. He had the pattern of visiting parishes. "I don't run into that when I am visiting weekends. But I do sense it through letter writing and a whole series of things that we've been caught up in here." *The Wanderer*, a right-wing Catholic paper with a national audience, had been attacking him on whatever front it could. One issue was altar breads. *The Wanderer* focused on what it felt were unacceptable practices such as the use of something other than unleavened bread. Ruppert ascertained that for Hunthausen such a concern was "being like the fellow on the Titanic who just moves his chair around to get a better view of the disaster." Still, Hunthausen could also appreciate that the matter might point to deeper issues. For some, he said, "it is an issue of authority and my willingness to submit to the word of Rome or whatever." Already the Vatican was stating the rule about unleavened bread in an authoritarian manner he found troubling: "the way this was coming down to us; we really weren't being consulted."[106]

During those early years in Seattle, Hunthausen fostered a wide consultative process all across Western Washington, inviting the opinions of the Catholic community on a whole host of questions. This process led to a series of goal statements for the church. Hunthausen said that the goals—such as moving the church more effectively into ecumenical and interreligious activity, or raising the level of consciousness and a commitment to social and economic justice as a constitutive part of the Gospel—resulted from "a lot of people, a lot of time, a lot of prayer, a lot of effort." Hunthausen had an abiding commitment to listening and consulting. "I really feel that Christianity, discipleship of the Lord, means personal investment.... I don't think personal investment, in most instances, is as real when one is responding to a directive or edict without internalizing it.... Not that we don't give directions and give guidelines. But we do try, more and more, to get people to, well, be the church...."[107]

If a friendly narrative described Hunthausen in a "tapestry of several strands," a hostile one depicted him in "a tangled web" of left-leaning liberalism requiring Roman oversight and correction. Hunthausen's critics were only becoming more vocal. Dolores Cullinane wrote a letter to the *Seattle Times*, commenting on the July 12, 1980 article Ray Ruppert had written about Hunthausen. Cullinane, a Catholic and a resident of Seattle, was not happy with Hunthausen in the least.

> "I feel we...find ourselves alienated in some parishes and while reading *The Catholic Northwest Progress*.... Many Catholic parishes are still allowing children to receive the Eucharist, I am told, without first receiving the sacrament of penance.... It seems Archbishop Hunthausen has lost credibility with many of his flock.... Pope John Paul has provided us with hope and comfort from afar. We pray that his courage and strong spiritual leadership will inspire Archbishop Hunthausen to reconsider the needs of all of us, those who love to experiment, and the silent majority."[108]

Hunthausen had described the subject of altar breads as a "non-issue." For her, this was an example of the general climate of "experimentation" in the church of Hunthausen. A few days later Ruppert received a note from Phoebe O'Neill, a Seattle Catholic, who thanked him for publishing Cullinane's letter:

> "The lady's serious letter to a public newspaper appears to be a necessary rebuttal in view of a 'lightweight' reply to a serious Catholic concern—invalid altar breads—that was made by His Excellency in a recent expression of your column (July 12). When considering petitions made to His Excellency by Catholics who remain faithful to the teachings of the Catholic Church, inevitably His Excellency's attitude seems to be, 'My way is best.'... His Excellency, in consistently requiring that his personal way become dominating, should, in justice to his episcopal responsibilities in the Catholic Church, establish a church of his own to become head of."[109]

The merits of such criticisms could be debated. More importantly, the attacks on Hunthausen were not happening simply in a secular forum. Pope John Paul II was hearing such voices through organized letter-writing campaigns designed to persuade the Vatican to take action in Seattle.

Certainly Hunthausen thought other matters were more important than arguments over what to use for altar bread. In late July 1980 he signed a Pax Christi statement which challenged young Americans "to consider conscientious-objector status to the draft, should it be re-instituted."[110] Thirty-six national religious leaders issued a "Religious Call to Conscience" and criticized both the resumption of draft registration and increased military spending. "America has lost God's view of history and replaced it with the idolatry of violence." Massive military spending undercut pressing economic needs. For here was an issue of "bread" worth debating. "We call upon all Americans, especially upon those in positions of power, to reflect upon whether true national security can be accomplished through preparations for war or rather through God's command to act justly."[111]

An assassination attempt was made on the life of Pope John Paul II on the 13th day of May 1981. Shortly after, Archbishop Hunthausen spoke at a news conference. He believed this shooting as well as the earlier attack (weeks before) on President Reagan, "could be a moment for people to take stock of where we are going as a human family."[112] The *Seattle Times* reported on a special noon hour liturgy held at St. James Cathedral. Archbishop Hunthausen reflected on the Gospel of St. Matthew and the Sermon on the Mount, recalling how Jesus gathered with his disciples on a hillside and spoke of the merciful, the persecuted, and the peacemaker. And Hunthausen said, "The pope has chosen for his hillside the entire world."[113]

John Paul, like Ronald Reagan, recovered. Both believed their recoveries from near fatal assassination attempts were providential. One question that would arise in the years ahead had everything to do with how open—or not—Pope John Paul II could be to Hunthausen's way of being a bishop. In Penny Lernoux's introduction to *The People of God: The Struggle for World Catholicism*, she wrote that, since the Second Vatican Council, the Catholic Church had changed radically in many parts of the world.

> "No longer identified with the rich and powerful, it has become a force for democracy, justice, and peace. The reforms spawned by Vatican II have not gone unchallenged, however. Since 1978, when John Paul II became pope, a counterreformation, known as the Restoration, has been in progress. Were it to succeed, Catholicism would revert to the narrowness and authoritarianism of the pre-Vatican II church.... At stake are two different visions of faith; the church of Caesar, powerful and rich, and the church of Christ—loving, poor, and spiritually rich."[114]

Perhaps the contrast was not quite so stark. John Paul II developed a strong theme of social justice and made a trenchant critique of capitalism. Yet with respect to equality and justice within the Catholic Church itself, by 1989 Lernoux saw with clear eyes a sharp divide. The story of the 1980s, including Rome's treatment of Hunthausen, was by then part of her evidence. As Seattle's archbishop spread by example a more egalitarian ethos, John Paul II concentrated on restoring a model of leadership from above. The Vatican hammer came down on Seattle just a few years after Hunthausen's Tacoma speech, where he explained why he felt compelled to resist Trident.

ENDNOTES

1 Hopps, Don and Pam Piering. Personal interview. Seattle, Washington 25 Mar. 2013. I also learned much about the background of Catholic engagement in labor concerns and related social justice struggles from Roger Yockey, long active in many aspects of Catholic social justice, when we met in Lynnwood, Washington on December 13, 2012.

2 Gandrau, James. "Worth Raising." *The Catholic Northwest Progress* (will refer to henceforth simply as *Progress*) 26 Aug. 1964, 29. See also: Schoenberg, William. *A History of the Catholic Church in the Pacific Northwest, 1743-1983*, 671. Washington, D.C.: Pastoral Press, 1987.

3 Hopps, Don. Personal interview. Seattle, Washington 25 Mar. 2013.

4 Kearney, John. "Incident at Seattle University." *Continuum*. Summer 1969, 377.

5 Schafer, Dolores. "Sisters Program goal Social Justice." *Progress* 10 Jan. 1975.

6 "95 Sisters from Northwest Attend NAWR Conclave." *Progress* 5 Sept. 1975, 5.

7 Hunthausen, Raymond. Personal interview. Seattle, Washington 16 Dec. 1988.

8 Hunthausen, Raymond. "Coming to a Position on the Global Arms Race: A Personal Journey." Speech given at a Consultation on Justice and Peace conference, Mt. Angel Seminary, St. Benedict, Oregon. 22 Feb. 1982. Archdiocese of Seattle Archives.

9 Hunthausen, Raymond.

10 Ruppert, Ray. "Future archbishop needs time 'to adjust'." *Seattle Times* 11 Mar. 1975. *Historic Seattle Times, 1900–1984*, 22.

11 Ruppert, Ray. "New archbishop is offspring of Vatican II." *Seattle Times* 18 May 1975. *Historic Seattle Times, 1900–1984,* 15.

12 Ruppert, Ray. "New archbishop installed at Center." *Seattle Times* 23 May 1975. *Historic Seattle Times, 1900–1984,* 61.

13 "Thousands Welcome Our New Archbishop." *Progress* 30 May 1975, 1.

14 Pruitt, Kathleen. Personal interview. Seattle, Washington 3 Dec. 2011.

15 Magnano, Paul. Personal interview, Seattle, Washington 10 Dec. 2012.

16 Burns, Jim. Personal interview and review of draft manuscript. Lafayette, Oregon 20 May 2014.

17 Hunthausen, Denny. Personal interview. Tacoma, Washington 14 Dec. 2012.

18 Hunthausen, Denny. Personal interview. Tacoma, Washington 25 Mar. 2013.

19 Hunthausen, Denny.

20 Hunthausen, Denny.

21 Connelly, Joel. "War-And Protest-Have Shaped This Region." *Seattle Post-Intelligencer* 19 Mar. 2003, A2. *Lexisnexis.com*. Web. 6 Sept. 2012.

22 Nash, Gerald. *The American West Transformed: The Impact of the Second World War*. Bloomington: Indiana Univ. Press, 1985, 28, 79.

23 "Navy's Mighty Trident Takes Aim at Kitsap County." *Argus* 16 Nov. 1973.

24 Holland, David and Phil Wandschneider. "U.S. Military Expenditures: Their Impact on the Washington Economy." March 1989. Washington State Institute for Public Policy, Evergreen State College, Olympia.

25 Arkin, William and Richard Fieldhouse. *Nuclear Battlefields: Global Links In the Arms Race.*

Cambridge: Ballinger, 1985.

26 Casserly, Brian. "Confronting the U.S. Navy at Bangor, 1973-1982." *The Pacific Northwest Quarterly*. Summer 2004, 130. *Jstor.org*. Web. 21 Oct. 2011.

27 Casserly, Brian. 135.

28 Meconis, Charles. Personal interview, Seattle, Washington 22 December 1988.

29 Keil, Larry. Personal interview. Seattle, Washington 27 March 2013.

30 Williams, John, ed. *Seattle Catholic Worker: A Scrapbook History 1974-?*. Pacem in Terris, Seattle, Washington. 1990, 19. (Personal copy loaned to me by Larry Keil.)

31 Douglass, Shelley. "Trident Campaign in the Northwest: An Historical Overview." *Ground Zero* March/April 1982, 4.

32 Douglass, Shelley. "Trident Campaign in the Northwest: An Historical Overview." *Ground Zero* March/April 1982, 5.

33 Hunthausen, Raymond. "Coming to a Position on the Global Arms Race: A Personal Journey."

34 Douglass, Shelley. "Trident Campaign in the Northwest: An Historical Overview." *Ground Zero* March/April 1982, 4.

35 Douglass, James. Personal (telephone) interview. Birmingham, Alabama. 26 April 2013.

36 Hunthausen, Raymond. Personal interview. Seattle, Washington. 16 Sept. 1988.

37 McSorley, Richard. "It's a Sin to Build a Nuclear Weapon." *U.S. Catholic* October 1976, 12-13.

38 Hunthausen, Raymond. Letter to priests of the Archdiocese of Seattle. 20 Oct. 1976. Catholic Archdiocese of Seattle Archives.

39 Douglass, James. Personal (telephone) interview, Birmingham, Alabama. 26 April 2013.

40 Ruppert, Ray. "Changing times bring mixed blessings." *Seattle Times* 11 Dec. 1976. *Historic Seattle Times, 1900–1984*, 26.

41 Ruppert, Ray. "Scannings from a notebook." *Seattle Times* 18 Dec. 1976. *Historic Seattle Times, 1900–1984*, 8.

42 Hunthausen, Raymond. Personal interview. Seattle, Washington 16 Sept. 1988.

43 Hunthausen, Raymond. "Coming to a Position on the Global Arms Race: A Personal Journey."

44 Hunthausen, Raymond. Personal interview. Seattle, Washington 16 Sept. 1988.

45 Hunthausen, Raymond. "Coming to a Position on the Global Arms Race: A Personal Journey."

46 Douglass, James. *Lightning East to West: Jesus, Gandhi, and the Nuclear Age*. New York: Crossroad, 1983, 85.

47 "Archbishop outlines opposition to Trident." *Seattle Times* 30 Apr. 1977. *Historic Seattle Times, 1900–1984*, 6.

48 Ratstatter, Joe. Personal interview. Portland, Oregon 23 Jan. 2013.

49 Meconis, Charles. Personal interview. Seattle, Washington 27 Mar. 2013.

50 Ruppert, Ray. "Church dean: Trident holds us hostage." *Seattle Times* 18 May 1977. *Historic Seattle Times, 1900–1984*, 40.

51 Buerge, David and Junius Rochester. *Roots and Branches: The Religious Heritage of Washington State*. Seattle: Church Council of Greater Seattle, 1988, 139. See also Rodney Stark and William Sims Bainbridge. *The Future of Religion: Secularization, Revival and Cult Formation*. Berkeley: Univ. of California Press, 1975, 70-71. See also Patricia O'Connell Killen and Mark Silk. *Pacific Northwest: The None Zone*. Walnut Creek: AltaMira Press, 2004.

52 Cate, William. "God's Resisting Community: A New Ecumenical Phenomenon." Unpublished manuscript, Church Council of Greater Seattle.

53 Douglass, Shelley. "Trident Campaign in the Northwest: An Historical Overview." *Ground Zero* March/April 1982, 9.

54 Casserly, Brian. "Confronting the U.S. Navy at Bangor, 1973-1982." *Pacific Northwest Quarterly*. Summer 2004, 137. *Jstor.org*. Web. 21 Oct. 2011.

55 Douglass, James. *Resistance and Contemplation: The Way of Liberation*. New York: Dell, 1972, 174.

56 Merton, Thomas. "*Blessed Are the Meek: The Christian Roots of Nonviolence*." See in Gordon Zahn, ed. *The Nonviolent Alternative*, New York: Farrar, Strauss and Giroux, 1980, 208-218.

57 Hunthausen, Raymond. Easter Sunday homily. *Progress* 8 April 1977, 6.

58 "New Columnist draws comment." Letter. *Progress* 13 Oct. 1978, 5.

59 See letters to the editor, *Progress* 19 Jan. 1979.

60 Douglass, Jim. Personal (telephone) interview. Birmingham, Alabama 26 April 2013.

61 Miller, Tom. "Nuclear Weaponry Seared." *Progress* 24 Aug. 1979, 1.

62 Miller, Tom. "Catholic presence in anti-Trident protest grows." *Progress* 2 Nov. 1979, 6.

63 "Call to Action motivated response on many levels." *Progress* 18 Mar. 1977, 3.

64 Hunthausen, Raymond. "Shared Gifts, Shared Responsibility, Shared Spirit." May 1978. Archdiocese of Seattle Archives.

65 Ruppert, Ray. "Catholics have the chance to face tough questions." *Seattle Times* 13 Sept. 1975. *Historic Seattle Times, 1900–1984*, 8.

66 Hopps, Don. Correspondence comments on draft of manuscript. May 2014.

67 Ryan, Michael. Personal interview. Seattle, Washington 13 Dec. 2012.

68 Ruppert, Ray. "'Unexcitable guy' generates excitement." *Seattle Times* 27 Mar. 1976. *Historic Seattle Times, 1900–1984*, 6.

69 Ruppert, Ray.

70 McDermott, Michael. Personal interview. Tacoma, Washington 14 Dec. 2012.

71 McDermott, Michael. Personal interview. Tacoma, Washington 25 Mar. 2013.

72 Walmsley, Jack. Personal interview, West Seattle, Washington 8 Dec. 2012.

73 Ruppert, Ray. "Views of the archbishop." *Seattle Times* 24 Sept. 1977. *Historic Seattle Times, 1900–1984*, 6.

74 Ruppert, Ray.

75 Ryan, Michael. Personal interview. Seattle, Washington 13 Dec. 2012.

76 Magnano, Paul. Personal interview, Seattle, Washington 10 Dec. 2012.

77 "Clergy leaders join to mourn Pope." *Seattle Times* 7 Aug. 1978. *Historic Seattle Times, 1900–1984*, 15.

78 Ruppert, Ray. "'Unfinished work' left for new Pope." *Seattle Times* 11 Aug. 1978. *Historic Seattle Times, 1900–1984*, 10.

79 Ruppert, Ray.

80 Cate, William. Personal interview. Bellevue, Washington 28 Mar. 2013

81 Cate, William.

82 Arnett, Loren. Personal interview. Bothell, Washington 28 Mar. 2013.

83 No specific author noted. "Catholic Archdiocese takes ecumenical step." *Seattle Times* 10 Dec. 1977. *Historic Seattle Times, 1900–1984*, 16.

84 Ruppert, Ray. "Ecumenicism: reconciling the communities." *Seattle Times* 26 Aug. 1978. *Historic Seattle Times, 1900–1984*, 6.

85 "God pray to halt nuclear race." *Progress* 20 May 1977, 1.

86 "Pope's final audience filled with laughs, simple words." *Seattle Times* 19 Sept. 1978. *Historic Seattle Times, 1900–1984*, 19.

87 "Archbishop talks of Pope, 'A good, simple, humorous man'." *Seattle Times* 29 Sept. 1978.

Historic Seattle Times, 1900–1984, 19.

88 Emery, Julie. "Archbishop mourns death of 'a man who touched many'." *Seattle Times* 30 Sept. 1978. *Historic Seattle Times, 1900–1984*, 5.

89 Hunthausen, Raymond. "No Matter what the tragedy or cross, Easter comes." *Progress* 14 Apr. 1980, 1.

90 Hunthausen, Raymond. "Archbishop calls for end to US aid to El Salvador." *Progress* 25 Dec. 1980, 3.

91 Ruppert, Ray. "Church leaders ask defeat of 13." *Seattle Times* 4 Nov. 1978. *Historic Seattle Times, 1900–1984*, 7.

92 Broom, Jack. "Final furor over anti-gay measure." *Seattle Times* 4 Nov. 1978. *Historic Seattle Times, 1900–1984*, 7.

93 Arnett, Loren. Personal interview. Bothell, Washington 28 Mar. 2013.

94 "Sisters Against Trident." *Progress* 14 May 1976, 5.

95 Morris, Jack. Personal interview. Seattle, Washington 1 Sept. 1988.

96 "Post-Conciliar Strides slow, Archbishop says." *Progress* 15 Oct. 1976, 5.

97 Ruppert, Ray. "Women in Catholic ministry—not so far away?" *Seattle Times* 12 May 1979. *Historic Seattle Times, 1900–1984*, 8.

98 Ruppert, Ray. "'Statement on Women' can be read in different ways." *Seattle Times* 18 Oct. 1980. *Historic Seattle Times, 1900–1984*, 10.

99 Hunthausen, Raymond. "Pastoral Statement on Women." 30 April 1980. Archdiocese of Seattle Archives.

100 Hunthausen, Raymond. "Pastoral Statement on Women."

101 Pruitt, Kathleen. Personal interview. Seattle, Washington 3 Dec 2011.

102 McMullen, Carol Ann. Personal interview. Seattle, Washington 11 Dec. 2012.

103 Boyle, Chauncey and Mary Grondin. Personal interview. West Seattle, Washington 12 Dec. 2012.

104 Ries, Victora. Personal interview. Seattle, Washington 11 Dec. 2012

105 Repikoff, Patty. Personal interview. Seattle, Washington 13 Dec. 2012.

106 Ruppert, Ray. "Archbishop's concerns go far beyond a Sunday smile." *Seattle Times* 12 July 1980. *Historic Seattle Times, 1900–1984*, 8.

107 Ruppert, Ray.

108 Culinane, Dorothy. Letter. *Seattle Times* 2 Aug. 1980. *Historic Seattle Times, 1900–1984*, 9.

109 O'Neill, Pheobe. Letter. *Seattle Times* 16 Aug. 1980. *Historic Seattle Times, 1900–1984*, 4.

110 No specific author noted. "Archbishop signs paper against draft registration." *Seattle Times* 26 July 1980. *Historic Seattle Times, 1900–1984*, 61.

111 Cornell, George. "Clergy Criticize Draft Registration, Military Spending." Associated Press 19 July 1980. *Lexisnexis.com*. Web. 14 Aug. 2012.

112 Ruppert, Ray. "Senseless: Pope's shooting called shocking act of insane violence." *Seattle Times* 13 May 1981. *Historic Seattle Times, 1900–1984*, 2.

113 Ruppert, Ray and Peter Rinearson. "Shocked Seattleites pray...." *Seattle Times* 14 May 1981. *Historic Seattle Times, 1900–1984*, 15.

114 Lernoux, Penny. *The People of God: The Struggle for World Catholicism*. New York: Viking Penguin, 1989.

Chapter Three

RESISTING TRIDENT

> "I need not tell you, my friends that you and I, we are wonderfully privileged to live here in the Northwest; one of the most strikingly beautiful portions of God's creation—forested hills and mountains reflected in clear, still water and so much more. But there is one disturbing sound, at least, among others, the waters are disturbed by a slight ripple—the periscope of a nuclear submarine. On the surface everything is orderly, beautiful, attractive. But under the surface lurks a destructive force capable of destroying the whole area, killing millions, maiming millions, deforming future generations."[1]
> —Archbishop Raymond G. Hunthausen

Hunthausen had already been perceived in some quarters as a contentious figure—and not only on Trident—well before he delivered the "Faith and Disarmament" speech in Tacoma. And yet, the June 1981 "Faith and Disarmament" talk catapulted him into controversy unlike anything before it. As we shall see, in the wake of the Tacoma address, he moved forward on many fronts—in society but also in the church. While staying in touch with the larger socio-historical context, this chapter focuses special attention on Archbishop Hunthausen's emerging commitment to conscientious war tax resistance and his participation in the peace movement, including the collective effort to nonviolently resist the first Trident submarine as it entered the Hood Canal headed for the Bangor base.

Just two weeks after that milestone speech in Tacoma, Hunthausen sat down for an interview with religion writer Ray Ruppert. "I think you know me well enough to know I don't want to be at the center of a boiling pot. That's not my nature." But if "it's going to bring people to think more about this and take some responsibility, then I guess I will have to say that's what I was hoping for—whatever it means to me.... Obviously, I do not feel I have the right answers. I am simply saying this is how I view it.... If people disagree with me, I would hope they have at least formed their conscience prayerfully and come to a conviction about the matter." The Reagan administration was escalating the arms race and claimed popular support. "I am not of that opinion," Hunthausen said, yet "I do think if there is going to be any change in our country it has to come from a response by the people. I think somehow the people don't know how to do that.... We are confused and frustrated and overwhelmed and frightened by the complexity and horrendous nature of the arms race. Somehow we have to take responsibility for it." He had a duty, he said, "to relate what's happening in the world to the life of the people and there's nothing affecting the lives of our people more dramatically than the arms race."[2]

An anonymous petition called "Catholic Parishioner's Pledge to the I.R.S." went to the *Seattle Times* shortly after the Tacoma speech. "We Northwest Roman Catholics recognize the fact that Archbishop Hunthausen's activities are not religious but political left-wing socialism. Catholics recognize him only as our titular head, and we will respond only to Archbishop Connolly as our Roman Catholic leader."[3] If Hunthausen was fiercely criticized by some, he was robustly supported by others. Eight leaders, members of the Washington Association of Churches, stated: "We understand your position to be consonant with the great roots of our faith and tradition that our trust must be in the acts and reality of God's love in the midst of the human community rather than in the implements of fear and violence that our skill and technology can devise."[4] The council of the Episcopal Diocese of Olympia (Western Washington) also lent its solidarity: "Archbishop Hunthausen's witness raises to public debate the whole question of nuclear war and its importance as a prime issue, if not the issue, for the world today in hopes that there will be a world tomorrow."[5]

"We've been waiting for someone in our group to have the courage to forthrightly state the commitments that the Archbishop declared that day in Tacoma," said Rev. William Cate.[6] In late August, Cate, chief staff of the Church Council of Greater Seattle, and Rev. Loren Arnett, executive minister of the Washington Association of Churches, convened a meeting in Olympia of leaders of mainline churches and ecumenical bodies in the state to decide how they would respond to Hunthausen's June 12 speech. Hunthausen had created what he called "a tense situation in their lives." Ray Ruppert conducted a mail poll of leaders in the mainline churches across the state. Bishop A.G. Fjellman, Pacific Northwest Synod, Lutheran Church in America, said the speech spurred him "to become more actively involved in doing what I can to support nuclear disarmament." Rev. Cate was thinking about doing tax resistance. He welcomed the Tacoma speech "as a prophetic utterance by the most influential Christian leader in our area." The Rt. Rev. Robert Cochrane, bishop of the Episcopal Diocese of Olympia, believed Hunthausen "so eloquently thrust into the public forum...the moral issue of nuclear weapons." Cochrane did not plan to do tax resistance. "Any punitive reactions aside, the response of an 'unconverted' government to reduced national income could well be to continue the arms buildup at the same level while decreasing even more drastically expenditures for essential human needs," Cochrane felt. Nevertheless, the nuclear-arms race needed to be halted.

"The archbishop has made a start. I am willing to work with him in the task of 'conversion'." United Church of Christ conference minister Rev. James Halfaker felt "He has helped us see the danger of massive military armaments at Trident (submarine base at Bangor, Kitsap County) in our backyard. He has helped us see the main issue that, if our wills come toward accepting the possibility of using limited nuclear force, we have already gone too far." Arnett deemed the Tacoma talk "a courageous call for peace deeply rooted in the biblical faith." Rev. E. Wayne Roberts, executive minister of the American Baptist Churches of the Northwest, cheered. "Bravo! Thank God one of us had the courage to make a challenge to the on-rushing, unchecked preparation for holocaust.... It's time we put on the brakes in the masterminding of carnage." Bishop Melvin Talbert, Seattle Area leader, United Methodist Church, was not sure "that withholding income taxes is the only response one can and should take.... However, every concerned person should be willing to take the risk of doing something to oppose proliferation of nuclear arms."[7]

Ruppert assessed the Olympia meeting: "Almost every major denomination in the Northwest was represented at yesterday's gathering. Bishops and regional church executives cut vacations short in order to be present and show solidarity with Archbishop Hunthausen. This in itself was a remarkable public display, considering that some of the regional church leaders could face criticism and anger from their members." The June 12 oration had "become a kind of scripture for an emerging anti-nuclear-arms movement" and church leaders united "to find ways to keep the issues raised by Archbishop Hunthausen alive and growing, becoming perhaps a national and even international movement against nuclear weapons." They pledged to meet with their congressional representatives to urge an end to the arms race, create a common statement opposing nuclear proliferation, encourage their own clergy on the issue, and invite their congregations to join in the region's Catholic practice of setting aside each Monday for fasting and praying for peace.[8]

What kind of influence could be expected from the religious community? Only about 30 percent of the state's population had any faith affiliation compared with about 60 percent nationally. Even so, the leaders of mainline Northwest church bodies made their concerns public, and even some people within the evangelical community, including Rev. Billy Graham on the national level, were starting to take a strong stand against nuclear arms. What would occur going forward, asked Ruppert? "The real test of what may happen as a result of the Hunthausen Manifesto may depend upon how quickly the pulpit and the pew heal their differences." How did Hunthausen handle differences? He always said he honored the conscience and responsibility of each person. He would not force his views on others.

> "Since he came here as archbishop six years ago, Archbishop Hunthausen has hammered at the theme of shared responsibility, a message sometimes hard to grasp. It calls for individuals, whether lay or ordained, to respond to such issues out of their informed, personal consciences rather than being told to do so by a clergyman. Because of this diffused life-style, it could be difficult to form any kind of structure around which to rally opposition to nuclear weapons."

Hunthausen never wanted people to do something simply because he had done it. He would not dictate. He prized personal relationship-building. This was behind the strong support Hunthausen received from the church leaders. "Those church leaders have been meeting on Thursdays for an informal breakfast for several years. They've gotten to know each other and regard each other as brothers. This makes it much easier for them to agree on the nuclear-arms issue."[9] He could not sit down for a "Thursday morning breakfast" with everyone in the region, however. Most faultfinders reacted to the archbishop's stand without knowing him personally.

In early October 1981, the *Seattle Times* noted that "the imbroglio stirred up by the anti-nuclear, pro-peace statement" of Hunthausen was "showing no signs of abating," as evidenced by a newsletter of a group called the Christian Anti-Communism Crusade. The newsletter's front-page read: "An Archbishop Seeks Surrender to Communism." Commenting on a U.S. Communist Party report in early September, the Crusade alleged that "the message of Archbishop Hunthausen was a clarion call to surrender to communism. Combined with repetition of Communist slanders of the U.S.A., the enthusiasm of a devout Communist for the message of a leading Catholic is understandable." The "devout Communist" Herbert Aptheker referenced here had written: "It is impossible to believe that the archbishop's speech reflects only personal convictions of the speaker.... His position, occasion and audience indicate that his quite radical views really are widely held throughout our land." Aptheker argued that this "consideration should embolden all who strive to reverse the catastrophic foreign policy of the Reagan administration. A splendid tool to assist in that effort is this speech by Roman Catholic Archbishop Raymond Hunthausen." The *Seattle Times* commented:

> "The archbishop's views continue to be kicked around from pillar to post.... There seemed to be nothing new or surprising in the commentary by either the Left or the Right in this exchange between The Daily Worker and the newsletter of the Christian Anti-Communism Crusade. But the imbroglio is spreading."[10]

To members of a local group calling itself Catholics Against Marxist Theology (CAMT), the archbishop's thinking was communist influenced. Danny Barrett, a Boeing employee and an organizer of CAMT, set out to expose any religious figure who would "go on a liberation binge and distort the Magisterium of the Church to promote their liberation thinking." Hunthausen was a prime target.[11] Hunthausen came under fire from a nationally organized effort headed up by Paul Weyrich, a political activist whose New Right organization put together workshops throughout the country in the early 1980s to discredit any bishop who took an outspoken disarmament stand. Weyrich had close ties with Al Matt, editor of the Minnesota-based archconservative Catholic "watchdog" paper, *The Wanderer*. Matt attacked "peace bishops" at every turn. *The Wanderer* ridiculed Hunthausen's anti-Trident stand. Not long after the "Faith and Disarmament" speech *The Wanderer*'s Frank Morriss called for an anti-Hunthausen campaign. This helped generate a flurry of letters to Rome from Catholics decrying the "irresponsible" actions of this "so-called religious leader." "If a revolt is needed in the Archdiocese of Seattle," Morriss asserted, "it is not against paying for arms to match those of an avowed and evil enemy."[12]

For the 800th anniversary of the birth of St. Francis of Assisi, John Quinn, the archbishop of San Francisco, said the enormous poverty suffered by so many in the world is "in large part a direct by-product of the arms race out of control." St. Francis was "a prophet of poverty and peace" whose example "reminds us of our critical need for a clear moral perspective on what is unquestionably one of the greatest life and death issues threatening us today." Quinn tied his moral view to concrete action. Catholic hospitals ought to reject a government plan that would set up a Civilian-Military Contingency Hospital System. Participation in such a system would help support "the illusion that there can be an effective medical response" to nuclear war.[13]

With Quinn and others speaking up, Hunthausen was not a lone voice crying in the wilderness. *Washington Post* columnist Colman McCarthy wrote about "Brave Bishops" Hunthausen and Amarillo's Leroy Matthiessen.

> "In Seattle, the bishop is saying that it is time to go beyond mere sermonizing against the Reagan campaign to seek 'nuclear superiority'. Deeper, what is accomplished by praying for peace while paying for weapons? In Amarillo, the bishop is arguing that individuals can't build peace by building bombs. The source of these messages is as startling as the bluntness. These are centrists, not cutting-edge leaders like Daniel Berrigan or William Sloane Coffin. Hunthausen was once a college president in Montana. Matthiessen performed routine parish duties for much of his 35 years in west Texas."

These two bishops were trying to "de-radicalize what is radical.... Hunthausen challenges the power of the state, Matthiessen of the corporate arms-maker."[14]

On October 8, 1981, those denominational executives who had met in Olympia issued a statement. "The spectre of a Communist threat does not, in our view, justify building such nuclear weapons." They echoed Hunthausen. "A willingness on the part of some to destroy life everywhere on this earth for the sake of our security as Americans is at the root of many other terrible events in our country." Were they not concerned about Soviet arms buildup? "We do not see this as sufficient justification to continue to build new nuclear-arms systems. We need to risk some de-escalation initiatives, and to publicize those limitations as a way of announcing our intentions and as a challenge to the Soviet Union to similar steps. Such unilateral initiatives are not nearly so risky as maintaining the present initiative to increase our weaponry."[15]

This only stoked the fire for the wary. *The Wanderer* editor in chief, A.J. Matt Jr., charged that bishops like Hunthausen and Matthiessen had fundamentally compromised their moral leadership. Frank Morriss added gender equality to the indictment, warning that Hunthausen was lending his full institutional support to the ordination of women. Other "doctrinal and liturgical" allegations would come up as watchdogs went after him in the ensuing years, but in 1981 the publication relentlessly attacked Hunthausen for his disarmament stand.[16]

Hunthausen had numerous defenders. "The churches are out of step with the militaristic mood of the nation in two main ways," said Rev. Jay Lintner, peace priority coordinator for the United Church of Christ. "One is that the church is a global institution. We are not just Americans. We look out for the whole world." And secondly, "the nation is now saying that weaponry is the best way to achieve security; the churches have thousands of years of history that is exactly opposite from that." Linter had worked on social issues, including peace, in the Seattle area for many years before taking the post in New York City. "The churches can be very powerful. It is difficult to overstate how important, for example, Archbishop Hunthausen's statement was—and the statements of Catholic bishops." Speaking of the Reagan administration premise "that war is complex and peace is simple or naïve," Lintner countered, "None of us in the peace movement ever thought we were simple or naïve. We know that peacemaking is always harder than war...."[17]

In late October 1981, the Nuclear Weapons Freeze Campaign sponsored a "Call to Halt the Nuclear Arms Race" rally at Seattle's Garfield High School. Related events included "Networking for Peace" featuring keynote Major Gen. (U.S.M.C. Ret.) William Fairbourne, formerly senior strategic planner for the Joint Chiefs of Staff. Rosemary Powers, a former Roman Catholic nun who went to jail for her own stand on war and peace issues, spoke at forums held at the Epiphany Episcopal Church in Seattle.[18] Carey Quan Gelernter reported from the Garfield High School event. Two thousand people filling the bleachers in the Garfield High School gym "exuded an aura of energy and mission which recalled the anti-Vietnam-war movement." The True Experience Choir, composed of members of seven local denominations, sang "Ain't Gonna Study War No More" as "the crowd clapped and shouted as though it was a revival meeting—as it almost was." Hunthausen spoke: "Our race for nuclear dominance is making us a godless and lawless force in the world.... I hope we can learn to make peace through nonviolence with the same depth of sacrifice as those who willingly and at great risk have sought peace through war.... Nonviolence requires at least as much of our lives as war does." He added, "I do not feel the need for a nuclear arsenal to protect us. I am not secretly glad that I can go to bed at night knowing that nuclear weapons are there to protect me. Their presence makes it harder, not easier to sleep." He declared, "As our nation prepares for nuclear war, we must allow God to cast out that evil by offering our lives through prayer, fasting and civil disobedience based on higher laws." Representative Mike Lowry, Seventh District Democrat, Dr. Judith Lipton, University of Washington psychiatrist and president of Washington Physicians for Social Responsibility, Rev. Dr. Samuel McKinney, pastor of Mount Zion Baptist Church, and Dr. Giovanni Costigan, University of Washington professor emeritus, also spoke. The peace movement was gaining considerable leverage by the growing participation and leadership of the churches, and the Garfield rally was broad based. The Freeze Campaign held the rally as its first major public event in the region. Participants included the Church Council of Greater Seattle, Armistice, Greenpeace, the Washington Democratic Council, and the local chapter of the National Organization for Women. Among the banners being waved were "Live without Trident" and "Sisters of St. Joseph of Peace Support the Nuclear Freeze."[19]

Hunthausen wanted the audience to know that his stance was primarily a faith position:

> "I am challenged increasingly by the nonviolent truth of the cross, by the calling of the God of Love to lose our lives for peace. What further steps that will mean in my life, I hope to leave to God's will, as that will is revealed in response to prayer. Whatever it is, I am certain it will be harder than anything I have in mind today. I think one consequence of praying our way into nonviolence is that God takes us more seriously than we wish. A prayerful nonviolence is dangerous to our lives. But Trident is dangerous to everyone's life. I hope I can persevere, with all of you, in choosing...the life-giving danger of nonviolence."[20]

The nuclear freeze campaign was spreading into many segments of society. But the Garfield event was mostly white. The Rev. Dr. Samuel McKinney, African-American pastor of Mount Zion Baptist Church, said that "this issue unfortunately is seen as a middle-upper-class elitist issue for those who can afford to think about it." But it mattered to all, he argued. Problems facing the poor were inextricably tied to the massive investment going into military spending. Roberto Maestas, director of El Centro de la Raza, thought the nuclear issue was "particularly relevant" to Indians and Chicanos, because uranium was being mined in the Southwest. Navajos were seeking compensation for ill health or death "brought on by dust or polluted mine water." According to reporter Lee Moriwaki, the most noteworthy feature of the newly emerging peace movement was the growing participation of the religious communities. "The peace movement has endured mostly in quiet since the turbulent Vietnam-war era on the campuses and in the streets. Now it is from the churches that the movement seems to be emerging again most strongly. And in the state of Washington the most visible representative character from the religious community was Archbishop Hunthausen." Hunthausen said he would back a proposal by Ground Zero Center for Nonviolent Action for a year-long presence next to the Trident submarine base. This, Hunthausen said, "would involve growing numbers of our church people."[21]

The Garfield High rally happened during the United Nations' Disarmament Week, with simultaneous actions afoot in many cities across the country. Disarmament demonstrations were reported in London, Rome, Paris, Brussels, and beyond.[22] Just days later, the bishop of the Episcopal diocese, Rt. Rev. Robert Cochrane, spoke before the 71st annual diocesan convention held at Seattle's St. Mark's Cathedral. "I am not a pacifist, although that is a highly acceptable and respectable position sincerely held by many deeply committed Christians.... In a sinful world there will always be the need for some armed forces fully equipped with conventional weapons to guard and protect against the maniac leader or the outlaw group." He took a position in some ways different from Hunthausen. But Cochrane, like Hunthausen, spoke up. "I join now that company of fools (he referred to Christian leaders across the world, including Rev. Billy Graham and Pope John Paul II) and add my voice to the growing chorus." He would continue to pay his taxes, "but at the same time every penny that I save under our President's new tax plan I shall give away to meet the needs of the poor and uncared for. I invite all of you to do the same."[23]

In November 1981, a contradiction came to light. The *National Catholic Reporter* ran a story on the investments in military stocks by various dioceses. The investment practices of the Archdiocese of Seattle were not in keeping with Hunthausen's peace stand. It held stock in companies that manufactured military weapons. Hunthausen acted to address the discrepancy. "It has never been our intention to support such enterprises." The archdiocese, according to the *Seattle Times*, had "$25,908 worth of stock in the F.M.C. Corp. which had $500 million in United States military contracts last year. Until a week ago, the archdiocese also owned $43,665 worth of stock in Tenneco, Inc., a firm that had nearly $800 million in 1980 military contracts." The archdiocese pulled its shares from Tenneco. Hunthausen noted that the amount of stock in the two firms was a very small percentage of archdiocesan investments, but it "has certainly caused some embarrassment…and has taught us a valuable lesson on the need to monitor all of our investments more closely and to develop policies which are clearly consistent with our church's position in these matters." The archdiocese, moreover, would henceforth avoid investments in any company with ties to South Africa. "A similar sensitivity and consistency will be brought to bear on all investment decisions in the future."[24]

It must be stressed that Hunthausen was not alone in his questioning of U.S. posture at that point in the Cold War. Many bishops were criticizing the nation's nuclear war policy. Bishop Leroy Matthiessen told an Air Force hearing on the MX intercontinental missile to "forget it entirely." A United Press International story reported on bishops such as Elden Curtiss of Helena and Thomas Murphy of Great Falls being against the MX; Thomas Grady of Orlando and Raymond Lucker of New Ulm being critical of nukes; Anthony Pila of Cleveland publishing a pastoral study critical of nuclear proliferation; Michael Kenny of Juneau speaking out against the use and the possession of nuclear arms; Ignatius Strecker of Kansas City asking that moral issues be part of U.S. debate on nuclear weapons and strategy; Walter Sullivan of Richmond telling a "largely military audience that it is immoral to be associated with the production or use of nuclear weapons"; John Quinn of San Francisco saying that a "just nuclear war" is a contradiction in terms; John May of St. Louis saying there is no way to win a nuclear war; John Roach of St. Paul-Minneapolis criticizing the Reagan administration's plan to stockpile neutron warheads; Thomas Gumbleton of Detroit encouraging study of the idea of unilateral disarmament; and Edward O'Rourke of Peoria saying that the urgency of the crisis required a change from the status quo. To be sure, even if many prelates were speaking up in one way or another, Hunthausen's particular views were not shared by every bishop. Bishop Edward O'Rourke of Peoria, for example, claimed unilateral disarmament was inconsistent with papal teaching. Archbishop Philip Hannan of New Orleans argued that the possession of nuclear weapons, not their use, could be justified as a deterrent. So even if they did not all agree, many bishops were engaged in the issue. They were embarking on voyages—bold, nuanced, or cautious. Their stands may have been influenced in part by how they understood their authority in relation to U.S. power—and to the power of the Vatican.[25]

Some critics of Hunthausen claimed that he and other prelates should stay out of politics. He was disloyal to the nation. Wrote one such critic, "I believe the archbishop should guide us in matters of faith to follow the teachings of Christ but in matters of politics related to the well-being of our country he should not interfere."[26] Hunthausen thought he was following the teachings of Christ and that doing so had political implications, just as it did in the times of the Roman Empire.

A CATHOLIC REVOLUTION

In mid-November 1981, Monsignor Vincent Yzermans, a priest of the Diocese of St. Cloud, Minnesota, envisioned the Catholic Church in the United States fast becoming a "peace" church. "This revolution is being waged in the hearts and minds of Catholic thinkers and leaders. Thank God, the American bishops are shouldering the responsibility of leading this revolution, at times to the chagrined and vocal opposition of their flocks. They are emerging more and more as worthy successor of Thomas a Becket. Their words and actions are not in any sense pious rhetoric." Archbishop Hunthausen and Bishop Leroy Matthiessen "have spoken out boldly and courageously, emphasizing that unilateral disarmament is the only Catholic position to take." Yzermans thought that the bishops as a national body would adopt this call for unilateral disarmament. Though too hasty in that prediction, he got it right to suggest that some people in power might be worried about the possibility of a Catholic revolution.[27]

When the U.S. bishops met in Washington, D.C. in late November 1981, the auxiliary bishop of Seattle, Nicolas Walsh, had something to say about the archbishop. Too many people just reacted to "startling headlines" or to Hunthausen's specifics of tax resistance and unilateral disarmament rather than paying attention to the archbishop's faith foundations. "Archbishop Hunthausen comes through as a very prayerful man," Walsh said. The faith dimension of Hunthausen's statements "has been neglected by the media (in Washington, D.C.). People don't understand it." Each bishop received a copy of the full text of Hunthausen's "Faith and Disarmament" address.[28]

Catholic peace movement participation was on the upswing. The Leadership Conference of Women Religious went on record unanimously against the production and deployment of nuclear weapons. Pax Christi, the Catholic peace group, could count over 50 of the approximately 300 U.S. bishops as members. Peoria Bishop O'Rourke, however, was not one of them. According to a Canadian paper, *Globe and Mail*, O'Rourke warned that unilateral disarmament could lead to Soviet domination, something worse than nuclear war. "We are talking about a dark age if we have a wholly Communist world." The Canadian publication painted the canvas backdrop:

> "Roman Catholics in the United States, with some exceptions such as the pacifist Catholic Worker movement and anti-Vietnam war activists, have historically supported a strong military. Millions of Catholics have and continue to serve in the U.S. military and are active in traditionally pro-defense veterans organizations. Until the Vietnam War, only a handful of Catholics refused combat service on religious grounds. In the 1980 election, President Ronald Reagan,

whose campaign stressed the need for a military build-up, increased the Republican vote among rural and blue-collar Catholics."

In this social context, channeling the entire legacy of Catholic just war theory, O'Rourke announced: "A strict pacifist position is not part of our church history. When people declare all possible use (of nuclear weapons) immoral, I simply do not agree."[29] There was, within the ranks of the hierarchy, push back against Hunthausen and the basic shift on war and peace he and like-minded bishops represented. Some Catholic prelates maintained the just war argument for the military defense of the common good, particularly in the context of the Cold War and concern about the intentions of the Soviet Union. Many Catholics were attached psychologically to a strong U.S. military.

Colman McCarthy, columnist for the *Washington Post*, attended that November 1981 conference of Catholic bishops, and shed light on the divisive scene surrounding Hunthausen. "Among the rulers in black, Hunthausen, a priest for 35 years who was elevated to the episcopacy in 1962 by Pope John XXIII, was as unlikely a celebrity as he is a leader of what is fast becoming an opposition church." In the vexed minds of some people, Hunthausen had become the icon of an opposition church. "Is this a revolutionary moment for the bishops or are they merely a slow-moving patriarchal group lurching to a position they might have taken long ago? Is the American Catholic church becoming a peace church, or are a few of its leaders catching up to Pope Paul VI's 1965 cry of 'No more war, never war again'?" Hunthausen's "opposition church" was already facing significant push-back. McCarthy asked him about this. Hunthausen said, "I have some indication both ways. There have been people who have responded positively. They feel that the church is now more relevant in their lives. But there have also been people who have been frightened by it. People feel that this is not the role of the bishop."[30]

U.S. Navy Secretary John Lehman was one of these people who felt Hunthausen was out of line. Lehman faced some rough waters of his own from the National Conference of Catholic Bishops. Bishop Thomas Drury of the diocese of Corpus Christi, Texas, objected to the name that had been given to a nuclear attack submarine. Senator John Tower, Republican from Texas, at the behest of Lehman, had christened one as "Corpus Christi." The bishops rallied around Drury. Tower was then chairman of the Senate Armed Services Committee, and his assistant, Linda Hill, reportedly said, "The intention was to name the submarine after the city in Texas that has a long tradition of connection with the Navy. It has a naval air station and it is an honor for the city.... Actually the senator was a little taken aback when the controversy first erupted." Drury had written to Lehman in October 1981, suggesting "you take steps to transfer the name Corpus Christi to another type of sea craft, one, perhaps, that cares for the sick."[31]

All of this helps depict the wider drama playing out as Archbishop Hunthausen came on the public stage. One Associated Press account, from December 8, 1981, illustrated the context. "Spurred by fear that nuclear war somehow has become an acceptable option in Washington, an anti-nuclear movement is developing grassroots strength across America." Twenty-four New England towns voted for a nuclear freeze; Physicians for Social Responsibility organized well attended seminars in many cities, focusing on the threat of nuclear war as a monumental medical problem; the Journal of the American Medical Association called on doctors the world over to help alert humanity to the great dangers of nuclear war; the National Freeze Clearinghouse, based in St. Louis, reported that "its campaign for a halt to the arms buildup has been endorsed by 46 national organizations, including the National Council of Churches, SANE, the Roman Catholic Pax Christi, and the Young Women's Christian Association." As social protest theater, a band of 40 people was traveling from Bangor, Washington to Moscow to stir interest in nuclear disengagement. At the same time, the Reagan White House was claiming that a nuclear war in Europe could happen without escalating into a world war. Reagan was pushing for deployment of the new MX missile system. He was building B1 bombers and Trident nuclear submarines.[32]

Hunthausen would have to challenge not only the Reagan administration, but also influential Catholics who supported Reagan. In December 1981, the editor of *The Christian Century*, James Wall, described Hunthausen as a "sincerely dedicated man…passionately worried about nuclear weapons." Hunthausen was not the classic radical. "I [Wall] am accustomed to social activists chaining themselves to the fences of nuclear installations. He [Hunthausen] is not that type of man. He is the respected head of a major Roman Catholic diocese. But he is grieved by this whole thing. Therefore, he is trying to raise the consciousness of the public through rather drastic methods." Wall tried to paraphrase Hunthausen's inner voice on the whole matter: "I am not sure how this is to be done. I am not sure that withholding my personal taxes should be one way. But I am sure it is a moral wrong to have hanging over our heads the possibility of blowing up the entire world."[33]

What type of man was he? Would he do conscientious war tax resistance, and not just talk about it? On December 16, William Strong, the executive director of the National Council for a World Peace Tax Fund, wrote to Hunthausen: "Just want to express our hearty thanks for your tangible support and encouragement in the check which we have just received." Seattle's archbishop was already supporting a peace tax as an alternative to paying for war even before the announcement he would make a couple months later that he would start doing war tax resistance himself.[34]

On December 21, 1981, Rev. Neil McCaulley, president of the National Federation of Priests' Councils, wrote to Hunthausen on behalf of the Federation's board "to extend our congratulations to you on your public stand concerning the arms race." McCaulley also wrote to Cardinal Terence Cooke of New York, Spellman's successor heading up the pastoral care of Catholics in the armed forces. Cooke had just sent a letter to military chaplains, in which he upheld the principle of nuclear deterrence. Cooke asserted that "nuclear deterrence can be morally tolerated if a nation is sincerely trying to come up with a rational alternative." McCaulley respectfully disagreed.

> "It does not seem fitting that the chief shepherd of those in the armed forces would merely repeat a defense of American governmental policy and would not also encourage legitimate conscientious objection and challenge the arms race and nuclear weapons.... We are in a new age, and the church is raising a prophetic voice against the instruments of death. May I humbly ask you to reconsider your defense of the present policies of our government on nuclear weapons."[35]

The Priests' Councils hoped the cardinal would add his voice to those bishops like Hunthausen who directly confronted U.S. nuclear policy.

According to the *Wall Street Journal*'s Christmas Eve story, Cooke found himself in confrontation with priests, brothers, sisters, and lay people in his own archdiocese over the letter he had written to the military chaplains.[36] Catholic conservative thinker William Buckley, Jr. heralded Cooke. Buckley surmised that the cardinal may well have cast his disapproving eye on some brother bishops such as Hunthausen when Cooke wrote: "The Church does not require, nor have the Popes of the nuclear age or the Second Vatican Council recommended, unilateral disarmament." Cardinal Cooke was in line with John Paul II, while those whom Buckley labeled "militant unilateralists" were "fond of quoting this or that pronouncement of the bishops or Vatican II, suggesting that inherent in such pronouncements is the straightforward theological disavowal of the nuclear bomb, even as a deterrent instrument." They might imagine that John Paul II agreed with them, but to date the Holy Father had not.[37]

On Christmas Day, *Washington Post*'s Marjorie Hyer presented a more nuanced view of the diversity of outlooks in the Catholic hierarchy. "Through most of the nation's history, the Roman Catholic Church could be counted on to bless without reservation almost any military venture the country embarked on. But a movement developing in the highest levels of the church within the past year is changing that." During 1981, more than 40 U.S. Catholic bishops made public statements criticizing U.S. nuclear policy. Hyer continued,

> "Nowhere is the church's attitude toward war and patriotism more dramatically illustrated than in New York City, where only a little

more than a dozen years ago, Cardinal Francis J. Spellman responded to criticism of the United States' military involvement in Vietnam with 'My country right or wrong–my country.' Only a handful of antiwar activists in the church registered outrage over that attitude at the time. Today, Spellman's hand-picked successor, Cardinal Terence Cooke, is under fire from priests, nuns and lay members for a letter he wrote to chaplains in which he called for nuclear de-escalation but said that 'a stratcgy of nuclear deterrence can be morally tolerated if a nation is sincerely trying to come up with a rational alternative.' Two days after Cooke's letter to the chaplains was made public, groups of clergy, nuns and lay persons—including some officials of the archdiocese—accused the cardinal of providing the theological rationale for the Reagan administration's increased military spending and nuclear policy."

Hyer described a controversy that broke out earlier in heavily Navy-oriented Norfolk, Virginia:

"Speaking in a church there, Bishop John J. O'Connor, a former Navy chaplain and now auxiliary to Cooke in the Military Vicariate—the ministry to Catholics in the armed forces—took sharp issue with the local Bishop Walter Sullivan, one of the most peace-oriented members of the hierarchy. In October, Sullivan had declared that it is 'immoral to be associated with the production or use of nuclear weapons' and that nuclear bombs are 'absolutely incompatible' with the Gospel of Jesus Christ. O'Connor disagreed. 'I know nothing in official church teaching that suggests that our military people are engaged in immoral activity in carrying out their military responsibilities,' even if their duties involve nuclear weaponry, he said. Two days later, the diocesan priests' council weighed into the debate with its own statement, coming down unanimously on the side of Sullivan. 'The teaching of the church is clear; nuclear war and the arms race are immoral,' it said."[38]

But in the same vein as Buckley, James Huntley, a fellow at the Battelle Memorial Institute in Seattle, upbraided the peace movement, writing "if we, as Seattle's Archbishop Hunthausen proposes, unlawfully withhold taxes in protest at the decisions of those whom a majority of us have elected to conduct the affairs of our country; if our steadfastness disintegrates in the face of our enemies—then we shall indeed enjoy, paradoxically, a good chance of having the world nuclear holocaust that they so rightly fear." The arms buildup was essential to ensure that the Russians know "we will not allow them to attain a marginal superiority of force, which they could use to work their will in the world diplomatically and politically…." Nuclear deterrence must be maintained. Those critical of the deterrence strategy, such as Archbishop Hunthausen, "have an obligation to tell us how they would like our government and its allies to pursue the strategy, with safety, of disarming unilaterally." Unilateral disarmament would leave us and our allies "subject to Soviet political and diplomatic blackmail."[39]

Another critic, later an official biographer of Pope John Paul II, was George Weigel. In the late 1970s, Weigel taught theology at St. Thomas Seminary in Kenmore. He got involved with the World Without War Council, which espoused peace through strength in the mode of Senator Henry "Scoop" Jackson. Weigel saw Hunthausen as well-intentioned but unrealistic. "Adversary power is a fact of the contemporary world; to deny this suggests to me a misinformed position."[40] For several years he made a series of criticisms of the archbishop in a regular column in the archdiocesan newspaper. In December 1981, the *Progress* published Weigel's four-part essay, "The 'Peace bishops' and the arms race." Four problems plagued the views of bishops such as Hunthausen, he argued. They often confuse moral witness and prudent political decision-making. They put too much emphasis on the actual weapons and their destructive potential, failing to address the fact that war can arise regardless of which weapons are involved. They also fail to give adequate attention to the complexities of international relations. And finally, their stand would lead to divisiveness within the faith community and would foster a dangerous ambiguity about the role the U.S. should play in global affairs.[41] The archbishop's sincere moral witness would nevertheless challenge people to think through their convictions on war and peace issues, Weigel acknowledged.

In that aforementioned interview, which took place in November 1981, Colman McCarthy asked both Archbishop Hunthausen and Bishop Leroy Matthiessen of Amarillo why the teaching of the church on nuclear war had seemingly not reached the larger Catholic community. Hunthausen:

> "We're not saying at the moment anything that wasn't said by the Vatican Council or the Holy Fathers along the way. But most of us have felt that somebody else will do something about it.... At one time I thought it was total apathy. But I don't really feel it's that. I just think that people are overwhelmed and they can't quite find a handle.... That's essentially what I've been trying to do: bring people to awareness that they have a responsibility to come to a position."

Hunthausen, questioning his own approach, thought about how to try to reach people.

> "The tax issue, I've discovered, while it is a strategy to indicate the depths of one's conviction on this matter, can also tend to be divisive. It so touches at the roots of who we are as people that some don't get beyond that loyalty and patriotic issue. So they stop listening. They

> feel that you have gone too far and you've touched a raw nerve that they can't live with. That's a reality, and you've got to have a listening audience out there. That doesn't mean that (tax resistance) isn't still a viable strategy that one has to, almost in conscience, identify as usable."

Matthiessen was prescient about the trouble they were getting themselves into. "I do think that we are on a collision course with some forces in this country, and within our own church." Could they see themselves bringing their boldness on issues of war and peace into other areas of church policy? Archbishop Hunthausen: "This past year, I wrote a pastoral (letter) on women which is designed for our own archdiocese. It seemed to attract the attention of the women. At the moment, we're finalizing the establishment of a women's commission which will help us carry out the recommendations in the pastoral about the equality of women in church affairs." McCarthy reminded the two bishops that powerful players in the Reagan administration at that time were Catholics, such as Alexander Haig, Reagan's secretary of state, and Richard Allen, serving on the National Security Council. What about their influence? Bishop Matthiessen:

> "Mr. Haig and Mr. Allen represent that element within our church which is strongly allied with the stance that God and country are equal, that waving the flag is tantamount to being a Catholic. That's a very strong strain in our Catholic people. I've got a letter in my files from a serviceman who's really shaken by all of this. He said, 'My gosh, you've just shattered my whole life. I've spent 30 years doing this and now you're pulling the rug out.' I say, 'Hey, wait a minute, we're not questioning the defense of our country or our free way of life. We're challenging the way in which it's being done.'"

Hunthausen thought part of the problem lay in the Just War theory.

> "We have to abandon that. Wasn't it Einstein who made the observation that everything has changed with the advent of atomic explosions, everything except our way of thinking. I don't know that we have adjusted to that. The church has got to indicate that the principles that govern the Just War theory are shattered, and that there is no way we can accommodate ourselves to that, given the weapons of destruction now available to us. I don't know Haig, but I would guess that he's working out of a stance that he felt was in keeping with his church's teaching, and he has not been able to adjust."[42]

THE MOVEMENT GROWS

In Seattle, the Thursday morning breakfast group of denominational leaders, and others with them, decided they would encourage the people of their churches to join in a presence at the Bangor base each Sunday beginning in January 1982, as an ongoing silent vigil to continue each week until the arrival of the first Trident submarine. In the wider context, as the Reagan administration sharpened its militaristic rhetoric and the nuclear freeze effort advanced, regional plans were underway for a major Puget Sound peace and education debate project. In early January, Rev. John Conner, campus minister at Oregon State University, spoke at a peace conference held at Seattle's Woodland Park United Presbyterian Church. The churches need to do much more. "It takes the courage and charismatic leadership of Archbishop Hunthausen and others across the church to give the rest of us encouragement." The *Seattle Times* described Hunthausen as "a national leader on the peace issue."[43] Ruppert opened a Sunday, January 17, 1982 story in this way:

> "Waves of reaction are continuing to spread, generated last June by the Most Rev. Raymond G. Hunthausen when he made his statement against nuclear weapons. That now includes the announcement that, as a proponent of unilateral disarmament, the Roman Catholic archbishop of Seattle has been invited to speak January 29 at the University of Notre Dame."

Nearly two dozen members of the Lutheran Peace Fellowship in New York had signed a statement making a commitment to do conscientious war tax resistance. Their decision to do so, they said, was inspired by Hunthausen. The widely read *Sojourners* magazine's January 1982 issue featured Hunthausen.[44] It was partly because he was a chief official in a large social institution that Hunthausen's call for unilateral nuclear disarmament stirred such great tumult. Other social institutions also entered the fray. There were voices, such as the Southern Baptist Convention, that expressed peace pronouncements, though they steered clear of unilateral disarmament and war tax resistance.[45]

Archbishop Hunthausen and the newly formed Justice and Peace Center of the Archdiocese of Seattle sponsored a day long retreat at the Ground Zero Center for Nonviolent Action, adjacent to the Trident submarine base Bangor. It was a classic Pacific Northwest winter day on the west side of the Cascade Range. Dozens of people on staff at the archdiocese, and folks from parishes, participated. One skeptical participant was George Weigel, who wrote about the episode in his book, *Tranquilitas Ordinis*. About one hundred people crossed Puget Sound on a Washington State ferry for Kitsap Peninsula to attend a retreat led by Jim and Shelley Douglass.

> "On arriving at Ground Zero, we trudged through ankle-deep mud to a semi-finished wooden geodesic dome, under which the retreat would be conducted. Once inside the dome, after our eyes adjusted to the dim light provided by a creaking electric generator outside the door, we could see a gigantic golden Buddha, before whom was laid a basket of oranges, and in whose honor joss sticks burned, adding to the dimness and fragrance of our surround. We were led in an opening prayer by the archbishop of Seattle, and then told by the Douglasses that the purpose of our time together was not to think analytically about the arms race, or the varieties of Catholic moral response to it, but, rather, to 'get in touch with our feelings.'" Weigel was not impressed. "On the ferry ride back, I noticed, hunched over a table with two large plastic glasses of beer in front of him, a leading Catholic educator who had listened quietly to the Douglasses. Staring into his beer, he mused on how the Church had probably invested half a million dollars in his education—and now he was being told not to think, but to 'get in touch with his feelings.'"[46]

The Catholic educator happened to be the President of Seattle University, Rev. William Sullivan S.J.

Others were far more enthusiastic. Kim Wahl, at the time a parishioner from a parish in Bellevue, remembers: "It proved to be one of the most powerful influences on my life. I learned about Trident, saw the Bangor base, and heard about the Peace Blockade that was planned for that summer when the first Trident was due to arrive."[47] In her recollection, there were probably about 90 to 100 people there, sisters, priests, educators, staff from the archdiocese, folks from parishes. "The speakers were powerful. This was the Archdiocese of Seattle at Ground Zero. It was an amazing day." Kim also remembers hearing Bill Sullivan, the Seattle University president, saying, "I don't know what we are doing out here, this is disgusting." It was damp, to be sure. Perhaps everyone was uncomfortable in some way. After all, they were being invited to get in touch with their feelings next to what would likely be ground zero. But for Kim, the experience of being next to the Hood Canal home of a first-strike system, and spending the day learning about Trident, was personally transformative. "We drove the perimeter of the Bangor base."[48] The key thing to remember about that day, she felt, was that it involved a commitment from the social institution—not just individuals. The Archdiocese of Seattle was well represented.

The *Seattle Times* front page headline, January 28, 1982, announced: "Arms protest: Prelate to withhold tax." Hunthausen said that he had, "after much prayer, thought and personal struggle," come to the personal decision to withhold half of his income tax. "I am not suggesting that all who agree with my peace and disarmament views should imitate my action.... I prefer that each individual come to his or her own decision on what should be done to meet the nuclear-arms challenge."[49] In a pastoral letter to the people of the archdiocese, he wrote that some folks would back him up while others "will be puzzled, uncomprehending, resentful and even angry." He was taking personal action consistent with the vision of war tax resistance he had imagined. The Associated Press covered the breaking news.[50] Hunthausen explained his decision. "I believe that as Christians imbued with the spirit of peacemaking expressed by the Lord in the Sermon on the Mount, we must find ways to make known our objection to the present concentration on further nuclear arms buildup. Accordingly, after much prayer, thought, and personal struggle, I have decided to withhold fifty percent of my income taxes as a means of protesting our nation's continuing involvement in the race for nuclear arms supremacy."[51]

"Strong winds from a midwinter storm are testing and buffeting the Roman Catholic Church in the Pacific Northwest. The forecast is that the storm will continue and may intensify. But then, the forecasters could be wrong, and the winds might ease to a breeze," wrote Ruppert. The storm would intensify in the coming months and years, but at that moment Ruppert speculated on the possible effects of Archbishop Hunthausen's tax stand. "At the storm's center is a quiet, introspective archbishop who has spoken out against the proliferation of nuclear weapons." What would be the effect of Hunthausen's stand? It might end up making little, if any, difference. It could cause some to leave the church, reacting angrily to Hunthausen. It could make the church stronger, leading some to come back to the church. Or those people who think that the church ought not to be involved in political issues might simply withhold their financial support. Back on September 27, 1981, Hunthausen spoke about his decision-making process on an ABC TV program: "I haven't made a final decision, but I suppose I would have to say that if the mood doesn't change, if there's no indication that the trend is changing, in honesty to myself, I would have to take some kind of action next April.... I am willing to take this kind of drastic action in order to indicate my own conviction, my own conscientious position." Ruppert recalled another moment. "One description of the travail of Archbishop Hunthausen as he struggled in his own conscience was given in a sermon last June in St. Mark's Episcopal Cathedral by Dean Cabell Tennis. He told about a meeting in which Archbishop Hunthausen spoke 'quite openly and frankly about matters that were on his heart and mind.'" Dean Tennis said that Hunthausen "was clearly troubled by the buildup of nuclear armaments in general and the presence in our community of the Trident base at Bangor.... I think I can honestly describe him as a man, deeply troubled. One could say a sword had pierced his heart." Ruppert wrote that "Archbishop Hunthausen has embarked upon a lonely, risky course which many people may not understand and which can result in pain, anguish and division. He is motivated by his fear of man's capability of total self-destruction. The least that can be done is to debate the issues without rancor. Otherwise the storm will rage on."[52] The rancor would grow in the years ahead. Hunthausen and the Catholic Church would experience pain, anguish, and division.

The *Seattle Times* introduced Hunthausen's pastoral statement:

> "What soon may become one of the most debated documents in the Pacific Northwest and perhaps the nation is being circulated throughout Western Washington and beyond.... In the interest of encouraging fair and open debate on an issue in which, in the archbishop's words, 'the very existence of humanity is at stake,' The Times is publishing here the text of the archbishop's message. It is done not to endorse the stand taken by the archbishop but with the hope that many different views on tax resistance and nuclear war can be aired and explored."

Ever since that Tacoma speech, Hunthausen was a media phenomenon. Whenever he made a statement or wrote a pastoral letter to his own Catholic community, he ended up reaching wider society. Hunthausen closed with these words, "I cannot make your decision for you. I can and do challenge you to make a decision."[53] These words were probably read by thousands of people beyond the Catholic community.

FINDING OUR WAY BACK

At Notre Dame University, on January 29, 1982, Archbishop Hunthausen delivered an address entitled "Finding Our Way Back: A Christian Response to Nuclear Weapons." That same day Hunthausen received a confidential "Dear Dutch" letter from Notre Dame's dean of students, James Roemer. Roemer wanted Hunthausen to be careful. "Apparently you have decided to withhold half of your federal income tax as a protest against the Government position on nuclear weapons. I would hope that you would do this in such a way as to avoid any criminal sanctions, and my concern is for you personally." Filing no income tax return at all could be viewed as tax evasion and the result could be criminal penalties and imprisonment. Tax resistance, even when one was open about it and included a statement of conscience with one's tax return, could be counter-productive, Roemer argued. Through interest and penalties, "your protest can be self-defeating because it results in a total payment by you to the Government higher than the amount you originally owed. In my opinion, the Government cannot afford to ignore a person who is a prominent Archbishop in a prominent sector of the United States." Roemer did not hold back from expressing some anxiety. "You must be careful to make sure that these issues involve only your personal income tax and your personal property so as to avoid involving the property of the Archdiocese in this protest."[54]

When he spoke at Notre Dame, Hunthausen did not tread cautiously:

> "I hear Jesus speaking out of the experience of deep poverty and suffering to us, the rich, those of whom the world speaks well—not the Third World, which, like Jesus, does not speak well of us, but the world of corporate power. That world of wealth and power usually speaks well of Notre Dame graduates and Catholic archbishops."

Here was a key connection Hunthausen was making: weapons *and* wealth accumulation. "In considering a Christian response to nuclear arms, I think we have to begin by recognizing that our country's overwhelming array of nuclear arms has a very precise purpose: it is meant to protect our wealth. The United States is not illogical in amassing the most destructive weapons in history. We need them. We are the richest people in history."[55] Choosing the symbolic center of American Catholic intellectual life, Notre Dame, as the place to challenge the power elite, he reproached himself and the church hierarchy as a whole.

In doing so, he chronicled his own path back to what he called "that radical vision of Jesus from which the rich young man turned away. I think we need to find our way back, friends. We need to find our way back to the way of nonviolence, the way of love, which Jesus called us to in the gospel and on the cross." He spoke of the nonviolent campaign to resist Trident. "I have joined in that campaign because I cannot stand aside from it and claim to be proclaiming any good news. The good news of Jesus today is that through a way of nonviolence, nuclear war can be stopped." We could choose a world of peace and justice, he said, as he reflected back on the decision he had made to identify Trident as "the Auschwitz of Puget Sound." He told the Notre Dame crowd:

> "God calls us to name the evil our society has embraced so wholeheartedly in our nuclear arms, and to do so clearly. Trident is the Auschwitz of Puget Sound because of the massive cooperation required in our area—the enormous sinful complicity that is necessary—for the eventual incineration of millions of our brother and sister human beings. I say with deep sorrow that our nuclear war preparations are the global crucifixion of Jesus. What we do to the least of these; through our nuclear weapons planning, we do to Jesus. That is his teaching. We cannot avoid it and we should not try. Our nuclear weapons are the final crucifixion of Jesus, in the extermination of the human family with whom he is one."[56]

But many ask, why do war tax resistance? Hunthausen had come to his answer:

> "Now on a more blasphemous scale than any homage paid to a first-century Caesar, we engage in nuclear idolatry. It is not God in whom

> we place our trust, but nuclear weapons. Our tax dollars are our freely offered incense to a nuclear idol which scientists and physicians tell us may destroy life on earth. You and I, friends, are paying for that crucifixion, at least until we become tax resisters to our nuclear idol."

But then, many might still ask, why call for unilateral disarmament? "The way of nonviolence is the way of Christ. As Christians we are asked to embrace the cross and all its consequences.... As Christians it has taken us centuries to see thc nonviolent cross once again through the ruins of our war-making. May God give us the strength now to see and choose that nonviolent cross deeply enough to prevent nuclear war."

What would this mean for Catholic students and archbishops, he asked. "You who are students at Notre Dame, like me an archbishop of the church, need conversion to that divine way of unrestrained compassion which Jesus felt for the poor and the oppressed." Granted the enormous power and force of nuclear weapons, how could faith possibly be the answer in the face of such a threat?

> "I believe deeply that God's love is infinitely more powerful than any nuclear weapon, and that in seeking to rediscover the cross, we are on the edge of a discovery more momentous to the world than that of nuclear energy. Nonviolence, Jesus' divine way of the cross, is in its own way the most explosive force of history. Its kind of force, however, is a force of life—a divine force of compassion which can raise the people of this earth from death to life. I invite you to join me in finding our way back to that nonviolent force of life and love at the heart of the gospels, which offers a way out of our nuclear tomb."[57]

Once again, the soft spoken Hunthausen had delivered a speech that was powerful, prophetic, and provocative. In the question and answer session with the large assembly, he said that he did not like to be called disloyal and anti-patriotic. "We have to live with respect for law in society." But this was an extraordinary instance, he argued. "The very nature of nuclear weapons is such that as a Christian people, there is no way that we can support this.... We must take a radical stance. Our democratic system gives us the opportunity to speak."[58]

Back in Seattle after the Notre Dame speech, Hunthausen said that he did not know the extent of or type of reaction his tax resistance decision was engendering. He had been inspired by the personal witness of individuals and he wished in turn to inspire others to join him in changing the whole direction of the Reagan arms buildup. President Reagan's push for weapons development was the order of the day, and Hunthausen was having no part of it. "We are not going to turn this around until we say to do it differently."[59]

"Doing it differently" in his case, especially since he was a Catholic archbishop, was destined to bring Hunthausen a range of reactions. For example, a letter to the *Seattle Times* written by Enumclaw resident John McIntyre hit hard:

> "How and why, in so few short years, have the virile, stalwart, profoundly educated Catholic clergy, usually conversant in several languages, and certainly veracious to the body of Aristotelian-Thomistic principles, become double-talking, effete, moral tinkerers, elbowing their way into the already swollen ranks of the sociologists? What breakdown in Catholic structure, what failure in Catholic leadership, has allowed the Archbishop of the great city of Seattle to make such a fool of himself?"

In support of Hunthausen, on the other hand, Deborah Caplow of Seattle compared him with Reagan:

> "Unlike Rev. Hunthausen, who faces possible imprisonment for his acts of conscience, Reagan himself does not personally risk anything as he slashes social-welfare programs (cuts primarily affecting the poor, the elderly, women and children) in order to transfer the money into an ever-growing defense system.... It takes true courage to stand up against the war machine and to work for peace on earth. Archbishop Hunthausen is to be commended for his bravery."[60]

Gordon Zahn, a Catholic sociologist and conscientious objector, wrote an essay in the *National Catholic Reporter* after the Notre Dame speech. Many Catholics would find it shocking to have an archbishop actually doing civil disobedience, he observed. "The pattern of support for the government in all matters relating to what it chooses to define as national security and defense is so much a part of U.S. Catholic tradition that the very thought of such a protest will probably be difficult for most to grasp." The Catholic Church was not on the verge of becoming a "peace church," but was beginning to rediscover the gospel message. Zahn wrote that historically most U.S. Catholics "prided themselves upon their unquestioning obedience to the nation's call to arms." They might object to government policy in some matters, but not on war and defense. Something was changing. Hunthausen's lead could persuade others.

> "Let us hope his witness will be heard in Washington and counteract the immorality of the Reagan budget, which proposes to escalate the arms race and pay for it by depriving the poor and disadvantaged of necessary social programs. Hunthausen has challenged the immorality of those policies in this most dramatic act of conscience. By doing so, he has brought honor to the American Catholic community."[61]

Widely known religious historian Martin Marty was in Seattle in February 1982. He spoke about the Catholic bishops, and Hunthausen in particular:

> "If traditional pacifist churches of the sort I greatly admire were to do this (come out strongly against nuclear weapons) we would sort of yawn. But Catholic bishops are known for centuries of upfront realism. And communism has been their enemy. Their intelligence sources are not naïve. So this is done in the face of an awareness of the Soviet power."

Of Hunthausen's war tax resistance and redirection, Marty said:

> "I don't think it is going to become widespread. Too many people have too many fears of what would happen to civil order if we all did this.... There are times when certain people may make a gesture that doesn't look realistic in order to provoke the consciences of the realists. I guess that's what I see him doing at this time."[62]

What impact would Hunthausen's announcement to withhold (and redirecting it to the support of a Peace Tax fund, for instance) 50 percent of his federal taxes have on others? Richard Orosco, the acting district director of the IRS at the time, told a reporter that "he doubted that Hunthausen's announcement would fuel the protest movement, despite the archbishop's prominent position in the church's hierarchy."[63] Ironically it did help fuel a protest movement against him. One Catholic, riled up, wrote to the diocesan newspaper:

> "Unilaterally, he is taking a secular action because he has given up on the faith in the power of prayer that holocaust can be averted. He has despaired of his God's omnipotence when he hurls his frail body impotently against the elements.... To whom do we parishioners look for reassurance and a sense of comfort when we feel our archbishop has abdicated his pastoral duties and deserted his flock in an intellectual storm?"[64]

At that time John O'Connor, who would later become one of America's best known cardinals, was serving as auxiliary bishop of the Military Ordinariate. The *National Catholic Reporter* asked O'Connor to offer his perspective. *National Catholic Reporter* had just covered Hunthausen's Notre Dame address. O'Connor agreed with Hunthausen that the arms race and nuclear war were madness, but argued that "rational and legitimate defense of a nation is not madness." He countered the call for unilateral nuclear disarmament. "The nuclear age popes, Vatican II and the United States bishops as a body, while calling for multilateral and gradual disarmament, have specified that during the process, nations must be expected to maintain adequate security." What about the relationship between faith and reason? "What of faith? It is clear that Jesus Christ, prince of peace, was opposed to violence." At the same time, O'Connor wrote, "Catholics in general and their bishops have traditionally supported *reasonable* military security, given the tragic realities of human nature." Without careful reasoning, he argued, "we can compound the current dangers." Still, O'Connor felt it was important to be challenged by those who confront us with the call of Christ. "I am personally convinced that many soldiers of many nations are so very good and sincere that if Jesus made it clear to them that they should even unilaterally lay down their arms, whatever the cost, they would do so." Yet O'Connor's next line pointed a critique directly toward bishops such as Hunthausen: "But such an injunction coming from any *human source*, however sincere and convinced that this is what Jesus clearly wants, carries with it a staggering responsibility."[65]

THE FIRST TRIDENT FINDING ITS WAY FORWARD

At Oak Harbor on Whidbey Island in late February 1982, Hunthausen announced that he would be part of prayerful, peaceful protest at Bangor that coming summer for the arrival of the first Trident submarine. Active and retired Navy personnel were at the meeting, and some challenged him.[66] His critics were becoming more vocal, and so too were people who shared his outlook. Prayer vigils and marches alongside the Trident Naval Submarine Base Bangor became larger and more frequent. The Seattle Ecumenical Religious Peace Action Coalition and the Ground Zero Center for Nonviolent Action, with other groups such as Evangelicals for Social Action, made things happen. Mike Gogins, one participant at the "Vigil of Hope" scheduled every Sunday to continue that winter and spring until the arrival of the first Trident, said that Archbishop Hunthausen's announcement that he would do tax resistance was stimulating "a real groundswell of concern in the churches over the nuclear arms race...."[67]

The Catholic chaplain at Naval Submarine Base Bangor resigned his post in February. In an interview with Ground Zero Center for Nonviolent Action, he spoke about the influence Archbishop Hunthausen had on his decision. Like all the other priests in the archdiocese, Fr. David Becker had first received a "hot off the press" copy of Hunthausen's "Faith and Disarmament" speech back in June 1981. "I received it with a mixture of shock and exaltation, because as I read through it, it seemed to echo many of my feelings going back many years to Hiroshima and Nagasaki and feeling that this should never be allowed to happen again." Becker remembered the tension he felt inside. "I was immediately aware of a need to re-examine: What was I doing at Bangor?" By fall, he knew that he could not remain as Navy chaplain "because I felt that my presence was approving the Trident program and the arms race and the nuclear buildup and the amassing of more and more nuclear warheads."[68]

Becker's personal conversion of heart was just one of many buds of social change sprouting as spring 1982 approached. Judith Miller, writing for the *New York Times*, described the fresh momentum of the peace movement reacting to the threat of an atomic Damocles. "A growing number of political, religious and civic groups throughout the country are coalescing into a significant movement to try to halt the nuclear weapons race between the United States and the Soviet Union."[69] By this time, Archbishop Hunthausen was widely perceived as a hero in the peace movement, but of course in the eyes of others he was judged to be, if not a villain, certainly a dupe.

LEHMAN'S VERBAL ATTACK

On Sunday, March 7, 1982, at the Chapel of the Four Chaplains in Philadelphia, Navy Secretary John Lehman praised those he deemed to be authentic American heroes. At the same time he attacked Archbishop Raymond Hunthausen's "Faith and Disarmament" speech.

> "Today we do more than honor the memory of the great sacrifice made by these men of God, the heroic Four Chaplains. We also honor their spirit of patriotism, a spirit that sees no contradiction between serving God and serving in the defense of our nation, in time of peace or war. They knew that the great traditions of the faiths they represented have always viewed as honorable the defense of human values and freedoms—as the three altars bear silent but vigilant witness. This great spirit can be summed up in the traditional American phrase 'For God and Country.' It is a phrase that has always been closely tied to duty and honor.
>
> I believe that this spirit has been shared by the vast majority of men and women who—down through history to the current day—have dedicated their lives to God and their fellow men through religious vocation. We can be thankful that, in their time, they did not support the kind of pacifist ideology that has—most unfortunately—now captured a small and idealistic but vocal minority within the religious community. That wiser majority never called upon their countrymen to lay down their arms in the face of the totalitarian advance. Today, I am sorry to say, that call is being issued by a few of our countrymen.
>
> They did not urge others in the clergy and the souls in their care to stop building those weapons that alone stand between freedom and

slavery for our nation and its allies—weapons whose sole purpose is to defend our values and way of life. Such urging is now taking place.

Today we are told by a few religious spokesmen that even possession of nuclear arms by the United States is a grave evil. But all the evil seen in their lifetimes would pale beside the evil that our unilateral disarmament would inevitably produce in this country and throughout the world.

We are told that our effort to arm other nations so they might better resist Communist aggression is somehow immoral. I ask, where is the morality in Poland—in Afghanistan—in Ethiopia, Cambodia, Vietnam—in Hungary, Czechoslovakia, and inside the Soviet Union?

Can we expect morality—or justice—or restraint—from a Godless ideology? No, we cannot. History has proven that. What we can expect is oppression, power, and precious little mercy.

Those voices calling for unpreparedness and naked trust refer to themselves, naively I believe, as 'the church of peace.' What they are calling for would produce not only war—but the eventual loss of all freedoms for all mankind—religious freedom included.

Peace is not the result of unilateral disarmament. It never has been. And it never will be. Peace doesn't just happen; it must be forged. Peace must be made. That is why the Bible speaks of 'peace-makers.' Blessed are the peace-makers. This refers not merely to those who speak the words of peace but also—and with equal appropriateness—to those who take action to preserve peace. Even those of us who strongly agree that our Judeo-Christian tradition not only allows but, at times, demands, the ability and willingness to use force to protect our most precious human values, have not been energetic enough. We have taken too much for granted. We have stood by silently while vocal advocates of unilateral disarmament on the part of the United States have sought to capture public attention—and been lionized by the media.

In a particularly tasteless example of this unfortunate trend, the Catholic Bishop of Seattle publicly called our new naval submarine base at Bangor, Washington 'an American Auschwitz.' Such an ignorant and repugnant statement illustrates how far the abuse of clerical power has been taken by a few religious leaders. There is, I believe, something deeply immoral in the use—or misuse—of sacred religious office to promulgate extremist political views...."[70]

Lehman may have chosen a solemn and reserved setting for his speech, but he had not chosen to rein in his anger at the Seattle prelate. Archbishop Hunthausen did not seem to take the onslaught personally, but neither did he let Lehman's attack go unanswered.

> "I strongly reject the notion that because the episcopal office is a religious office a bishop may not speak out on issues that involve the political realm. Although it is true that the disarmament issue has a political side, it is also true that it has a moral side that religious leaders must address. To think that I and other religious leaders have no right to speak out on social and political issues that touch the welfare of persons is to reduce the role of the bishop and of Christianity to the realm of individual morality."[71]

He argued that "the bishop is supposed to speak out on the moral aspect of public questions. That is not only his right; more important, it is his duty. He has to make the effort to apply the values of the Gospel to the concrete social situation of his day."[72] The Second Vatican Council was really a commentary on the call to live a gospel way of life. "The Council found a way to open us to be a gospel people."[73] He turned to a scriptural foundation. "I have been touched by scripture and particularly the life of Jesus. How he himself responded to injustice."[74] Lehman had a right to speak his mind, Hunthausen added. "The secretary may disagree with my view, of course, and I respect that disagreement."[75]

I once asked Archbishop Hunthausen how his understanding of the life of Jesus informed his way of dealing with anger, such as one might feel after Lehman's *ad hominem*. "It's a loving response no matter how one might be dealt with that will eventually bring about conversion of hearts and transformation, if you will, of the human family." Could there be a place for anger? "There are moments when it seems to me that in order to be true to one's, if you will, response to situations, one has to be angry, but it's what one does with anger that makes the difference. Anger is a way of highlighting the deep conviction, the deep concern over a serious matter that an individual experiences."[76] To channel that anger we need contemplative awareness. "My openness to reflect, to allow God to touch me with that sense of love—that happens only by a willingness to step away from the noise of our busy lives and to find some time to do that, so that when we come back into the mainstream we come back with something that has been supplied by the Lord."[77]

Lehman may not have appreciated the practice of spiritual contemplation that informed Hunthausen's approach not only to Trident, but to all issues. Shortly before deciding to do conscientious war tax resistance, he had been on retreat with fellow bishops of the Pacific Northwest region. It was on the heels of this retreat that he announced his decision to resist. He had pondered the impact the decision could have. "I did it because I truly feel this issue is of that deep concern. I did it with honest and prayerful reflection about the many people who would be affected by my decision. I tried to examine the many publics, the different stances that Catholics and others in our area and beyond would have toward this."[78]

Richard Barnet, an influential author on international affairs, was in Seattle in March 1982 for a peacemaking conference at Pacific Lutheran University. Barnet's thinking sharply contrasted with the claims Lehman made on national security. Barnet had been conferring with peace movement leaders in Europe, and said that the peace demonstrations "there have spread to both sides of the Iron Curtain." He said that "the demonstrations in Europe, which are heavily based in the churches, speak not only to the people's fear of total annihilation in a nuclear attack but also to economic destruction by spending national resources on nonproductive weapons systems." Hunthausen, in Barnet's estimation, was stating "a truth ignored a long time" by calling into question the notion that security could be found in the threat to use nuclear weapons.[79] Speaking at the same conference, Hunthausen confirmed that he would participate in the planned boat blockade of the first Trident, the U.S.S. Ohio. "Americans apparently see their world neighbors as an expendable enemy population in a nuclear exchange, which goes against all of Christ's teachings," he declared.[80]

Given the announcement of plans for the boat blockade of the first Trident whenever it would eventually arrive, the media would now have a real clash to cover. And as spring began, the news that Hunthausen would be involved further aroused the fury of his detractors. The *Seattle Times* printed a full page of letters to the editor. William Kellman, of Auburn, accused Hunthausen of sedition. Why did Hunthausen not pay attention to Aleksandr Solzhenitsyn's description of the Soviet system, he asked. Kellman quoted Solzhenitsyn: "There has never been, on this entire planet and in all of history, a regime more cruel, more bloody and at the same time more diabolically clever. Only force can soften or make the Soviet system yield. The entire regime rests on brutal force and thus it recognizes only force." Hunthausen, some believed, failed to take seriously the crucial role that U.S. nuclear deterrence played in relation to such a brutal force. Bob McCauley, of Oak Harbor, wrote: "Article III. Section 3, of the Constitution of the United States of America fits Archbishop Hunthausen of Seattle to a 'T.' 'T' as in TREASON!" Keith Stonecypher, of Everett, wrote: "It is immoral to expect our military to defend our nation, including the Roman Catholic Archbishop and his ilk, by denying them nuclear retaliatory weapons. It is immoral for the Archbishop to let others pay their full share of taxes while he hides behind his clerical robes." Hunthausen was inciting "open rebellion," and therefore, honest taxpayers "have no choice but to demand his arrest and prosecution for his violations of laws enacted by his peers." Ralph Wright, Seattle resident, averred:

> "Navy Secretary John Lehman deserves a medal for his denunciation and criticism of the actions and attitudes of Archbishop Hunthausen. Mr. Hunthausen, who undoubtedly has a large following in this area, has publicly declared that he will withhold a portion of his income tax as a protest measure against the United States nuclear-arms program. He, along with pro-Communist radicals, feels that the United States should disarm unilaterally, which would leave this country open to invasion and subjugation by a foreign power, perhaps one which might even close his churches and prohibit free religious choice."[81]

As I was doing the research for this book, each time I found records of verbal attacks on Hunthausen an expression of support for him was also there in the same time frame. Writing an official letter from the Conscience & Military Tax Campaign (CMTC) to Hunthausen on March 14, 1982, CMTC leader Georgia Pearson emphasized the symbolic power of the archbishop's refusal to pay 50% of his federal income tax. "While you are not the first individual to take this step, you are one of the first national leaders to do so." Pearson thought Hunthausen was "courageous to stand somewhat alone in the public eye on such a controversial issue" and told him he was inspiring people all across the country. "From our mail we know that war tax resistance activity in the Washington area has increased tremendously since you first spoke out last June. Washington is now one of the top five states in Conscience & Military Tax Campaign–US activity." Much was happening, Pearson wrote, not only war tax resistance among the historic peace churches, but among Lutherans now circulating a nationwide call to war tax resistance. Other denominations were studying the question of resistance to the arms race, militarism, and the neglect of the poor. "We hope, as you do, that this is just the beginning of a large movement." Pearson asked Hunthausen to consider writing a cover letter that CMTC could then use with its letter—an appeal to consider joining with Archbishop Hunthausen in stepping forward on this issue—to send to "Catholic Bishops who would most likely be interested in the issues of conscientious objection to military taxes, passage of the World Peace Tax Fund Bill and military tax resistance." The original letter is pencil-marked, probably by Hunthausen himself or by his unflappable secretary, Marilyn Maddeford, with an arrow next to this request for him to write such a cover letter. "The image of fifty Catholic Bishops joining you followed by other religious leaders, followed by massive grass roots support is one that our 'leaders' in the government could not ignore." Pearson concluded, "During World War II, a delegation of the Historic Peace Churches met with President Roosevelt. This resulted in legislation which allowed conscientious objectors a program of alternative service to the military. We wonder if it is time for a delegation of religious leaders to meet with President Reagan to seek alternative service for military taxes."[82]

PRACTICING RESPECT

U.S. News & World Report in the spring of 1982 described the peace movement:

> "This time it's the middle class, not college radicals, leading an antiwar movement. Though quieter than European protesters, activists in rising numbers alarm officials worried about a Soviet edge in nuclear arms. Even as President Reagan presses the largest peacetime military buildup in the nation's history, a peace movement demanding a first-step global freeze on nuclear arms is quietly picking up support across the U.S."

The story described Hunthausen's announcement of tax resistance as a direct challenge to authorities. Many religious voices were being heard. Though he did not take a stand as radical as that of Hunthausen, even the world famous evangelist Billy Graham evinced these thoughts: "I am not a pacifist and I don't believe in unilateral disarmament, but I do believe in (eliminating) nuclear weapons. As long as any of these weapons exist, there is a danger." The story also cited conservative Catholic thinker Michael Novak expressing his criticism of the "peace bishops" in this way: "These clergymen appear unaware that Russia has been pushing a tremendous atomic-weapons buildup over recent years, while the U.S. was tapering off. To call a halt now would leave us at a serious disadvantage in numbers of military aircraft and with no antiballistic-missile system such as the Soviets possess." Certain factors, according to *U.S. News & World Report*, were prompting the new movement:

> "The major factor in triggering the country's new outburst of pacifism has been the breakdown of U.S.-Soviet efforts to control strategic weapons, starting in 1979 with the Senate's failure to ratify the Salt II treaty. Compounding this concern, peace campaigners say, are the stance and policies of the Reagan administration—the harsh anti-Soviet rhetoric, the coolness toward strategic-arms-control negotiations with Russia and the flurry of high-level talk last year of fighting a limited nuclear war in Europe."[83]

One might well wonder what Senator Henry Jackson, Democrat from Washington State, was thinking about Raymond Hunthausen. Jackson had long been a major "pork barrel" player, bringing robust military contracts thought to be so crucial to the economy of the state he represented. He lobbied effectively for Pentagon defense contracts which wound up with Boeing. United Press International reported that:

> "[Jackson] disagrees with Seattle's Archbishop Raymond Hunthausen, who is withholding half of his federal income tax to protest the proliferation of nuclear weapons. Jackson, a member of the Senate

> Armed Services Committee, said that he too would like to see the elimination of nuclear weapons, but that a freeze on construction of nuclear weapons would not solve the problem of proliferation. What Archbishop Hunthausen and others opposed to nuclear weapons should do, he said, is try to get the Soviet Union to bring about a reduction of such weapons."[84]

Hunthausen tried to deal respectfully with people no matter their views. Early on after "Faith and Disarmament," some of the most negative reaction came from Boeing. People working there had deep investment in the nuclear missiles, deterrence, and all of that military-related business. Justice and Peace Center director Don Hopps recounted what happened when one Boeing man came to the chancery.

> "There was one person in particular, from Federal Way. He was very adamant on the subject. So Archbishop Hunthausen said to him, 'well, come up and talk with me. I'd be happy to talk.' And so this fellow came up and as it turned out, the person was personally disturbed, but he said he found Hunthausen to be one of the most thoughtful people he had encountered on the subject. The Boeing man said of Hunthausen, 'He just wasn't knee jerk, attacking me or saying I was wrong. He wanted to know more, and the more we talked the more reflective the conversation became.' The upshot of this was that the guy went back, and there were other people in his group who were angry and shaking their fists and so on, and he said to them, 'you know, you have to go and meet Archbishop Hunthausen. This guy's the real deal.'"

In no time at all, a Boeing group developed and they often came to the chancery on Sunday evenings, for a long period of time. "It wasn't as if he was trying to convince them to quit their jobs at Boeing by any means. It was a dialogue that Archbishop Hunthausen really appreciated and he felt that he got a lot from them.... I thought, here is something that really says a lot about the person. He respected everybody."[85]

Just as Hunthausen welcomed the dialogue with the Boeing group, he gave his support to the Bangor to Bethlehem walk. A pilgrimage from the Trident Nuclear Submarine Base Bangor by the Hood Canal to Bethlehem in the Holy Land began with a group that ranged in age from 19 to 67, Protestant and Catholic, lay and clergy. Archbishop Hunthausen came to Bangor to join them as they began the long trek. The Bethlehem Peace Pilgrimage commenced on Good Friday, April 9, 1982. One newspaper announced it this way: "A commissioning prayer service at 1:30 p.m. Friday at the old main gates at Bangor on the Kitsap Peninsula will include blessings by the Most Rev. Raymond G. Hunthausen, Roman Catholic archbishop of Seattle, and chanting of an ancient peace mantra by a group of Japanese Buddhist monks."[86]

Nuclear disarmament actions were taking place simultaneously during Holy Week at different locations across the nation. Good Friday that year included the protest actions of Daniel Berrigan, joined by other demonstrators at the Riverside Research Center (with defense department contracts) in New York; the action of Daniel Ellsberg, arrested with other protesters at the Nevada Test Site; and the long walk that began at Bangor, all noted in an Associated Press report.

> "In Bangor, Wash., more than 400 anti-nuclear protesters turned out to march the first six miles with a dozen pilgrims on a 6,500-mile journey to Bethlehem in the Middle East. The trip started at the ammunition gate of the Navy's Trident submarine base. The pilgrims were blessed by Archbishop Raymond G. Hunthausen of Seattle. 'Nuclear weapons are in place around our earth, waiting like silent demons, to blow us back into the dark chaos unknown since the beginning of creation,' he said. Hunthausen asked that the pilgrims be blessed on their way across America, the Atlantic, through Europe and on to Bethlehem."[87]

Jesuit Jack Morris, the chief organizer of the walk, told me his recollections of the first part of the Bangor to Bethlehem journey. Hunthausen gave a brief talk and then walked with them for the first few miles of the pilgrimage, including the Stations of the Cross, from the Trident base to Poulsbo. "With us also was Fr. George Zabelka, who was the chaplain of the crew of the Enola Gay. Zabelka did the whole walk with us."[88] The Enola Gay had delivered the atomic bomb to its fateful destination, Hiroshima.

In a more secular context and on an international scale, concern over the threat of nuclear war was evident as the Second Congress of International Physicians for the Prevention of Nuclear War, which took place in Cambridge, England during the first week of April 1982. From Cambridge, Peter Rinearson reported for The *Seattle Times*: "Seattle is well known among the doctors and others who gathered here in the past week to plan a campaign against the threat of nuclear war. It is known, among other things, as the city of Hunthausen, Trident, Jackson and Boeing." Senator Henry "Scoop" Jackson was a household name, but with a very different symbolism than that which was associated with the name Hunthausen by that time. "The name of Washington's Sen. Henry M. Jackson arouses ire among many of the doctors gathered here to work against what some have come to refer to as 'the last epidemic'—the mass destruction that would come from nuclear war." One of the doctors labeled Jackson "an architect of the arms race."[89]

THE WORLD TAKES NOTE

By April 15, 1982, Hunthausen had decided he would place his war tax resistance revenue in an escrow account for the World Peace Tax Fund. He told a Seattle Press Club luncheon group that the amount of tax withheld was based on his estimated annual income of $9,000. He told them he hoped his action might spur others to take some action, whatever that might be. He was simply trying to live out his religious conviction, he said.[90] It spurred Bill Cate. The president-director of the Church Council of Greater Seattle announced on April 20 that he and his spouse would also begin withholding a symbolic portion of their income tax in protest against nuclear arms.[91]

On Tax Day 1982, widely read *Washington Post* columnist Mary McGrory focused national attention on Seattle: "Raymond Hunthausen has observed April 15 by withholding 50 percent of his income tax and publicly proclaiming it. He does not care for the way the Reagan administration would spend his money." Civil disobedience was undertaken "in the heart of the northwestern military-industrial complex" where "Washington state's economy is much tied to defense and nuclear enterprises." The archbishop represented a political threat to the Reagan administration.

> "He is one of many Catholic prelates who have taken a militant stand on the question. Remembering Vietnam, the White House had expected the hierarchy's solid support in the administration's anti-communist crusade. But on issues involving Central America and the 'peace through strength' nuclear buildup, the bishops have proved a disappointment.... His Eminence could go to jail if the IRS decides to make an example of him. It poses something of a dilemma. No administration would want to send an archbishop to the slammer. But about 75 percent of the American people share his views about the arms race, and they could, if frustrated, start following his lead. Prosecution would be as dicey as nabbing the thousands who have failed to register for the draft.... The archbishop is using his tax return as a weapon in the war against nuclear war. He is telling Ronald Reagan that until he listens to what the country is trying to tell him about nuclear morality he will get only half his allowance."[92]

Similarly, Columnist Colman McCarthy's April 18 opinion piece opened with a question:

> "Is the Internal Revenue Service preparing a jail cell for Archbishop Hunthausen of Seattle? If it jails him, the attending publicity would assure Hunthausen's style of protest would be pushed further to

> the front of the surging peace movement.... From behind bars, Hunthausen, a fatherly book-loving man, would lend immeasurable substance to conscientious tax resistance."

Yet supporters of Hunthausen needed to face a fact, McCarthy asserted. "The truth is that since Hunthausen announced his tax resistance last summer not one bomb has been dismantled and not one dollar diverted from the arms race. Hunthausen's protest needs to be seen as a mild startup of moral pressure on the government, not a grand finale."[93] As a matter of fact, Hunthausen would never be jailed by the IRS.

The *New York Times* also covered Hunthausen's act of resistance. "Last Thursday, Raymond G. Hunthausen, the Archbishop of Seattle, filed his Federal income tax return and deliberately held back $125. It was a milestone on a personal journey begun 37 years ago when the bombing of Hiroshima and Nagasaki left a young seminarian despondent and bewildered." He was asked what his peers would make of his action. "I am not in violation of anything the church would want me to say or not to say. If one were to look at the statements of the Popes in the last 10 years, Paul VI and so on up, or the statements of Vatican II about nuclear stockpiling, one would be expected to draw the conclusions I have drawn because the statements have been very powerful." Hunthausen cited a key passage from the Second Vatican Council: "The arms race is one of the greatest curses on the human race and the harm it inflicts on the poor is more than can be endured." He did not take this action lightly. "What I have done about taxes has left me with a whole spectrum of emotions. I have not found it easy to civilly disobey, whatever form that might take." As a church leader, in that role precisely, he felt he had to do something. "My message is that we can't leave it to others. I left it to others for a long time in my life and that's wrong."[94]

Catholic peace activist Kim Wahl appreciated Hunthausen's conscientious struggle to discern what action to take. She worked with him in a training as part of the white train tracks campaign.

> "Before a train arrived at the 'end of the line' or the train ammunition gate at Bangor, we would do a nonviolence training with anyone hoping to participate in the action. I was on the team of trainers who had the opportunity to 'train' Archbishop Hunthausen for this act of civil disobedience. He participated fully, engaging the process in ways helpful to the trainers. His role playing was really thoughtful and fun and I believe others were put at ease by his grace-filled participation. He decided not to do the action and I feel sure it represented that struggle he felt internally to act, not just 'leave it to others,' but pressure from many sources gave him pause."[95]

Hunthausen had become the subject of international attention. The well known German publication, *Der Spiegel,* described him as "the highest dignitary of the Catholic Church in America to join the peace movement with more than just words." Interviewing him, *Der Spiegel* asked, is it more Christian to be crucified than to threaten others with destruction? "Absolutely," replied Hunthausen:

> "The worst possible evil is not that we could be destroyed. The greatest evil is our willingness to destroy millions of others. Jesus teaches us the willingness to sacrifice our life for others. One thing he didn't teach us: protect yourself by killing as many as it seems necessary to you. But this is the worst imaginable scenario. It's my hope that the world would breathe a little easier if we began the nuclear disarmament and that the other side would follow suit."

The German magazine asked him about statements he had made that America's nuclear arsenal was there to protect wealth and property.

> "Yes, I believe that there is a connection between wealth and weaponry. If one were to examine all the forms of power one would probably arrive at the notion that force is almost always used when we want to hang on to something. Even in the personal sphere we become violent. We stand here today and say: if we don't continue to arm ourselves, if we're not the most powerful country, we'll be vulnerable. Jesus described this situation when he said: 'Oh you, who are rich!' He prophesied to the wealthy that they would one day grieve and weep. In reference to today, that means: if we choose the path of fantastic wealth and awesome might, we will get exactly the same nuclear war that we're threatening others with."

Hunthausen emphasized that in his view the arms race was "a terrible injustice to the poor of the world."[96]

It had not been that long, *Der Spiegel* reminded its interviewee, since the days when Cardinal Spellman, close friend of U.S. Secretary of State John Foster Dulles, "made more patriotic speeches before more soldiers than many generals." During the Vietnam War, there were few if any peace bishops. So, what had changed? Hunthausen:

> "During the Vietnam war I had uneasy feelings. I often wanted to express them but I didn't have the strength of my convictions. The crucial difference was that the danger of nuclear war was not discussed, although the danger was certainly present.... Technology has brought us to the point where we should have arrived a long time ago by faith, namely that wars are no means by which to settle problems."

What about the armament industry, Archbishop, what about Boeing and the large military bases? *Der Spiegel* added, "Senator Henry Jackson, whom the citizens of the state continually return to Congress, is one of the most famous hawks in Congress. Don't they accuse you of threatening their livelihood?" Hunthausen conceded that his statements and actions "have caused disquiet and pain for many. I have caused conflicts. But of the more than 500 letters that were written in response to my tax resistance, more than 85 percent agreed with my action." Calling the Trident nuclear submarine base at Bangor the "Auschwitz of Puget Sound," what did he mean by that?

> "Trident submarines are first strike weapon systems which I consider especially immoral and criminal. We have weapons therefore, that can extinguish the lives of hundreds of thousands of people—like the death camp Auschwitz. In addition to that, I believe that we are co-responsible for what goes on in our backyard. The more I've read, the clearer it has become to me that not many Germans knew what went on in Auschwitz, although a few were in the picture themselves. But whoever knew something and did nothing and said nothing was as much an accomplice in a certain sense. The same has to be said here and now: If we know about these weapons and that doesn't move us to action, if we don't say anything or do anything, then we're to a certain extent responsible for the consequences."[97]

Back home in the Pacific Northwest, the *Seattle Times* board editorialized on the war tax resistance actions of Archbishop Hunthausen and Rev. Bill Cate:

> "To their credit, neither Hunthausen nor Cate has publicly advocated that others withhold their taxes in protest. They both know their actions are against the law.... For either man to urge others to disobey the law would be irresponsible and illegal, as they must know.... We doubt that many people—even other members of the clergy—will follow Cate's and Hunthausen's example. Nor should they. Withholding taxes is a crude and ineffective way to change government policy, especially on such a complicated issue. Its final effect would be anarchy. The best function of such symbolic protests, as with much civil disobedience in the past, is to draw public attention to important issues and stimulate public debate.... We think that as many citizens as possible should do all they can to educate themselves on this vital issue. When they do, we think they'll agree with us that although the ultimate ends of Hunthausen, Cate and other nuclear-freeze activists are right, their preferred means of achieving them are wrong."[98]

The national magazine *Newsweek*'s April 26 story, "Who's Who in the Movement," captured the breadth of the peace movement in which Archbishop Hunthausen and Rev. Cate had a lot of company. The American Friends Service Committee, Business Executives Move, Clergy and Laity Concerned, Council for a Livable World, Federation of American Scientists, Fellowship of Reconciliation, Freeze Campaign Clearinghouse, Pax Christi, Ground Zero, Nuclear Network, Parenting in a Nuclear Age, Physicians for Social Responsibility, Union of Concerned Scientists, United Campuses to Prevent Nuclear War, and Women's International League for Peace and Freedom were just some of the groups noted. In addition to Hunthausen, the *Newsweek* story highlighted Thomas Gumbleton of Detroit, Leroy Matthiessen of Amarillo, and John Quinn of San Francisco. *Newsweek* recognized various secular leaders such as Randall Forsberg, so central to the whole nuclear-freeze proposal; Howard Hiatt of Harvard's School of Public Health; Jonathan Schell, whose book *The Fate of the Earth* was widely read; Ian Thiermann, who produced "The Last Epidemic," which imagined San Francisco after a nuclear strike; and Robert Jay Lifton, who investigated the psychological effects of the nuclear arms race. Harvard's Hiatt was, wrote *Newsweek*, part of:

> "[...] a group that met with President Reagan last December at the request of the Pope. Hiatt reminded the President of the blood he received for shock after he was shot and told him the hospital wouldn't have been able to handle five additional patients with the same needs. Hiatt says, 'I told him there would be 800,000 people in shock from burns and radiation if a 1-megaton bomb exploded over Washington.'"[99]

At a convocation in late April 1982 intended to rally the region's faith communities toward a vision of global peace, Hunthausen said:

> "I think we can read through the pages of the Gospel all our lives and never suspect that there's an infinite chasm there. Just turn your lives around and drop into that chasm. The kingdom of God is at hand when we are free-falling, when we've lost everything except a naked faith, a naked hope, a naked love, stripped of everything except a total reliance on the God who pushed us off the Gospel we thought we knew. Free-falling into the kingdom."

Was this a "high church" Roman Catholic archbishop in free-fall, we might ask. He continued, "The threat of nuclear holocaust has clarified the nature of faith: we cannot believe in both God and nuclear weapons. We cannot believe in the power of infinite love, yet choose to rely on world-destructive violence for our society. The two are incompatible." He foresaw the implications. "If we resist it strongly enough, our government like any other government will make us poor. You can count on it. Resist that nuclear crime with your life, and you may spend much of your life in jail."[100] He was keenly aware that people like Rev. Jon Nelson, Shelley and Jim Douglass, and a host of other people he knew well were risking incarceration.

As another contextual illustration painted on the global canvas of this time period, we note that a peace conference in Moscow took place in May 1982. Evangelist Rev. Billy Graham was among two dozen U.S. church leaders who participated in the pan-religious peace conference. The White House urged Graham not to attend but he went anyway. The Moscow event was dubbed the "World Conference of Religious Workers for Saving the Sacred Gift of Life from Nuclear Catastrophe" and involved representatives from Christian, Jewish, Muslim, Hindu, and Buddhist traditions across the planet. It was reported just ahead of the event: "It comes at a time both of nuclear fears and of reports of growing religious sentiment in the Soviet Union and efforts to stem it. A recent Pravda editorial calling for stronger atheistic indoctrination cited a growing presence of youth at religious services." Religious involvement in the peace movement, in the U.S., in Western Europe, and in the Soviet Union and its satellites was dynamic. The Associated Press described this as "a time when concern about the nuclear arms race has spiraled in the churches, when East-West tensions have heightened, when both sides are building more arms. But it also is a time when religious interest is reported growing among the Soviet people."[101]

FAITHFUL REALISM

On May 16, 1982, Archbishop Hunthausen made a speech in Brooklyn, New York. The question of whether the human family would destroy itself through nuclear war, he told the crowd, was "the greatest spiritual crisis in history." Faith and the cross could liberate us from our fear of losing our wealth, relinquishing our holocaust weapons. "I have been told often that it is politically realistic for us in the United States to keep on building nuclear weapons. That must mean also that it is politically realistic for us to prepare for their first use in a nuclear war, because that is where our counterforce policy and our new weapons systems, such as Trident II and the MX, are leading us—to a first-strike nuclear war." None of this could be truly realistic, he argued. "It strikes me that the realities on which such 'nuclear realism' is based are a terrible fear that we will lose what we have—our wealth—and a blind faith in our weapons to protect that wealth. A consuming fear of joining a world poorer than ourselves and a blind faith in our weapons are the overriding spiritual realities in our nuclear realism. They are demonic spiritual realities which determine our view of everything." Jesus faced this same false claim in his day, Hunthausen said. "In fact, Jesus shocked people by putting a different reality in place of a fearful power—the reality of an overpowering faith and love."[102]

Would we continue to rely on a "reality" predicated on fear and domination? "We shall either choose a new understanding of reality, centered on faith and the sharing of our lives, or we shall be destroyed by the ultimate fruits of our fear." Hunthausen recommended *The Call to Conversion*, a book by Jim Wallis of the Sojourners community. "The root cause of nuclear war is our lack of conversion, our utter lack of love," Hunthausen quoted Wallis.

> "Conversion, including the renewal of compassion for our neighbor, is the only enduring road to peace. Understanding and defending the humanity of enemy populations becomes increasingly important as pressures for war mount. Reviving our capacity to love has become an urgent political necessity as the superpowers come to regard millions of their neighbors as nothing more than expendable enemy populations in a nuclear exchange."

We must join with every potential victim, with every current victim of the arms race, he argued. That was a point Hunthausen felt was too often forgotten; U.S. military spending not only could lead to victims if the weapons were employed, but was already leading to victims simply because revenue for research and production of weapons could have been used to meet real human needs.[103]

> "This summer what may be the most destructive weapon in history, the Trident submarine, will come to its Bangor, Washington base, 14 miles across Puget Sound from Seattle. Each Trident submarine will have as many as 408 nuclear warheads, each with a destructive power five times that of Hiroshima, and capable of an accuracy of 100 feet after a 6,000 mile flight. I have said that I believe Trident is the Auschwitz of Puget Sound. In August of last year, I met with bishops and other church leaders of this area, where it was decided that we would take part in demonstrating our opposition to nuclear proliferation at the time of the arrival of the Trident submarine at Bangor. When this inconceivably destructive weapon travels down the Hood Canal, probably in July or August, it will be met by a nonviolent peace blockade to stop Trident.
>
> I intend to be present at that peaceful blockade, to support prayerfully those who will risk their boats and their lives to stop Trident.... In our nuclear age, I believe Jesus is calling us once again to conversion, to a way of nonviolence summed up in his cross, with the choices set before us: the kingdom or the holocaust. Each of us can and

> will make that choice between the kingdom and the holocaust in the most practical decisions we face—in our choices concerning the payment of war taxes, registration for the draft, involvement or not in nonviolent action; above all, in whether or not we choose to act on the most faith-filled vision each of us has in this desperate world of nuclear powers."[104]

At the cathedral there in Brooklyn a retired layperson held up a sign that read, "Archbishop Hunthausen: would you have us abandon the defense of our homeland and our loved ones?" Several others in the assembly expressed the same sentiment. Hunthausen responded to such concerns. "I love my country, and it is because I love my country that I say what I do. I would like for my country to put its confidence in the God we profess to believe in."[105]

In late May 1982, the *Seattle Times* addressed the simmering issue of Hunthausen and the Vatican. "Seattle's Roman Catholic Archbishop Raymond G. Hunthausen is not in the Vatican dog house for his strong stand against nuclear weapons, a spokesman for the local prelate said yesterday." Monsignor Ladislao Tulaba, rector of the Lithuanian Pontifical College in Rome, had said in "a news interview that Hunthausen should not withhold half of his income tax as a nuclear-arms protest as he has announced." Tulaba claimed that the Apostolic Delegate to the U.S., Pio Laghi, "had written to Hunthausen to tell him his arms protest was wrong." Rev. Michael Ryan, chancellor of the archdiocese, when asked about Tulaba's comments, said:

> "We have no knowledge of who this particular spokesman is other than he is rector of a small seminary in Rome. We presume he is speaking for himself. We have no reason to believe he enjoys any particular expertise in this matter. Further, we are sure he is not an official Vatican spokesman. In other words, we assume that he, like any priest interviewed by the news media, has the right to speak for himself and express his views on this controversial subject."

No letter asking Hunthausen to change his stand had been sent to Seattle.[106] The *Seattle Times* called it the "case of the Mysterious Monsignor." A spokesman for Archbishop Pio Laghi, the apostolic delegate, said he had never heard of Monsignor Tulaba. The spokesman did not say anything about Pio Laghi's views on Hunthausen's stand except "as a matter of policy we never, never comment on any communication between the delegation and the individual."[107] Pio Laghi's office did not explicitly refute the idea that perhaps the Vatican felt Hunthausen was wrong in advocating for unilateral disarmament and practicing civil disobedience. But we are getting ahead of ourselves; the Seattle-Rome conflict will come to the foreground later in the book.

At the very end of May, Hunthausen announced that a confidential registry of letters from conscientious objectors would be established and maintained by the Archdiocese of Seattle. As reported by the *Seattle Times*, the registry's purpose would be "to provide a means for sincere conscientious objectors to state their views about military service well in advance of receiving an induction notice." Archbishop Hunthausen indicated concrete concerns about U.S. policy and did so by putting emphasis on the role of conscience.[108]

Hunthausen also kept up his advocacy for gender equality in society as in the church. In early June 1982, Sister Maureen Fiedler, national coordinator of a group called Catholics Act for ERA, was one of several women participating in a hunger strike in Illinois in support of the Equal Rights Amendment. The ratification deadline loomed on June 30. Two weeks into the fast, Sister Maureen made public the names of 23 Roman Catholic bishops backing the ERA. One of them was Hunthausen.[109] Though the ratification effort ultimately failed, Catholics Act for ERA hailed the group of bishops, saying it was the first time church leaders had come together to urge states to adopt the amendment.[110]

On the peace issue, Hunthausen turned down an invitation to speak at a rally in Bonn, West Germany, in early June 1982. He did not want to give the impression that he was the official representative of American Catholics on the issue of nuclear disarmament. There was also some concern about the fact that the German Lutheran Church had withdrawn its support. Further, there was apparently no word from Germany's Catholic Church leadership that Hunthausen's presence at the rally would be okay with them.[111] Reading between the lines, one could infer that Hunthausen already felt pressure from Rome to tone down his profile and influence as an international symbol of Catholic leadership in nuclear disarmament.

It was Cardinal Krol of Philadelphia who, for Rome in those days, was a more appropriate voice for official Catholic views. "Carefully, with many pauses, he [Krol] enunciated his views on disarmament. And as they emerged, what was striking was that he could find himself involved in a movement that also engages such partisans as Raymond G. Hunthausen, Archbishop of Seattle, who has said he would withhold half of his income tax as a protest against production of nuclear arms." So wrote William Robbins in a *New York Times* profile story. At a June 1982 peace rally in Philadelphia with 15,000 in attendance, Krol declared, "We advocate disarmament—not unilateral but reciprocal or collective disarmament, proceeding at an equal pace, according to agreement and backed up by authentic and workable safeguards." Krol held to the right to legitimate self-defense of the nation. His approach to the role of the bishop—Krol had a reputation for being conservative and autocratic—was quite different than Hunthausen. Krol suited the Rome of Pope John Paul II and Cardinal Joseph Ratzinger.[112]

DIVISIONS IN THE CHURCH

In early June 1982, the *Wall Street Journal* highlighted the "divisive debate in the Catholic Church" and focused attention on the archbishop of the nation's capital. Archbishop James Hickey had just composed a pastoral letter calling for a nuclear-weapons freeze and asking whether it was moral to maintain a nuclear-weapons stockpile. "The archbishop is leading his flock into a thicket of moral, theological, political and military questions, questions that are being raised in rectories, chanceries and churches across the country. But the debate here in Washington could be especially sharp because some of the chief architects of President Reagan's arms-control policy don't agree with Archbishop Hickey. And they, too, are Catholics." As the *Wall Street Journal* pointed out, one of those Catholic chief architects was Edward Rowny, who would play a leading role in arms-control negotiations with the Soviets. Rowny had visited Hickey and his priests "in an attempt to head off any major differences between the church and the Reagan administration's policy of using a strong and credible nuclear deterrent as a lever to move the Russians into serious arms reductions." The *Wall Street Journal* reported on newly forming groups of politically conservative lay Catholics "who are preparing to do battle with what they see as a small but powerful elite within the U.S. church hierarchy that is turning toward pacifism as the one sure way to end the nuclear-arms race. There are 50 million Catholics in the U.S. and the political ramifications of a shift in that direction would be significant."[113]

Bishop Walter Sullivan of Richmond, Virginia, predicting that the "church is going to be on the cutting edge of the peace movement," had been too optimistic. Influential prelates like Cardinal Terence Cooke and Bishop John O'Connor were defending the just war tradition. The *Wall Street Journal* quoted O'Connor expressing his frustration with pacifists. "When you try to give a rational presentation and all you get back is the Gospels' manifestation of love," O'Connor said, "I think that's inadequate." A vigorous debate over the just war and pacifist perspectives would soon ensue among the bishops, a debate we will probe more deeply in chapter four. One of the most eloquent advocates for a move away from just war thinking was Bishop Thomas Gumbleton of Detroit. Back in 1972, as the war in Vietnam was starting to ebb, Gumbleton and friends formed a U.S. chapter of Pax Christi. Pax Christi began in Europe after World War II.[114]

A key moment for the American bishops to begin seriously grappling with their just war moral reasoning was the November 1980 meeting of the National Conference of Catholic Bishops. There was among some bishops "considerable gloom over the Reagan election and the plans for a nuclear-weapons buildup."[115] At the November 1980 meeting, Baltimore Auxiliary Bishop P. Francis (Frank) Murphy, a member of Pax Christi steeped in the study of peace, got the ball rolling. When all the bishops received a standard letter from the general secretary of the National Conference of Catholic Bishops asking if they wished to bring up anything during the *varia* (e.g. any new business?) at the November meeting, Murphy responded. Journalist Jim Castelli wrote in 1983 about this in the opening chapter of *The Bishops and The Bomb: Waging Peace in a Nuclear Age*. Murphy's *varium* called "for a concise summary of the church's teaching on war and peace and a strong educational effort on those issues within the church." Other bishops, including Bishop Edward O'Rourke of Peoria, Archbishop John Whealon of Hartford, and Cardinal Terence Cooke of New York, each with a different perspective, spoke. Though there was no unanimity of views, the bishops were ready to engage the issue of war and peace in light of Catholic moral teaching—and to evaluate that teaching in light of the realities of the nuclear age. When Gumbleton spoke, he echoed Murphy's call, saying there was an urgent need for a new examination of the morality of nuclear war. "If we need any convincing of it, a very quick review of what has happened in our country in the past thirty-five years since we entered the atomic era will help us realize that there is an urgency today that means, in fact, that time is very short before the nuclear holocaust could indeed happen.... We've just elected a President who has stated his conviction that we can have superiority in nuclear weapons; an utter impossibility. We have a Vice-President who has clearly stated that one side could win a nuclear war and that we must be prepared to fight one and to win it."[116]

Gumbleton also echoed Pope John Paul II's 1980 World Day of Peace statement, with its call for much greater attention to nonviolence and alternatives to war. This touched a chord with many of his colleagues, who affirmed what Gumbleton was articulating. Gumbleton described the moment: "It wasn't really loud, like somebody jumping up and down. It was just a quiet, sustained applause. It seemed to be an attempt by a number of bishops to say, 'Yes, this is what we have to do.'"[117] The peace pastoral letter, made possible by the initiative of Bishop Murphy, would be written. An ad hoc committee was soon announced and given the task of drafting a statement. In May 1982, the U.S. Catholic bishops' peace pastoral letter committee, which included Gumbleton and O'Connor, heard testimony in a closed session from Secretary Haig, Defense Secretary Caspar Weinberger, and the director of the Arms Control and Disarmament Agency, Eugene Rostow. Groups were actively preparing to challenge the bishops. Michael Novak was busy "organizing a group of 50 prominent Catholic laymen to be called the American Catholic Committee." In Chicago, Ed Marciniak formed the National Center for the Laity. Marciniak thought the bishops ought to lend their support to Catholic politicians and military leaders instead of condemning them. Paul Weyrick, another influential conservative, was forming the Catholic Center. "The center plans to send 'truth squads' to cities where bishops are supporting a nuclear-weapons freeze. At appearances by the bishops, the squads will raise questions from the audience, and they will hold news conferences of their own."[118] While the peace pastoral was in process, Hunthausen was busy not just thinking about what kind of letter he hoped the bishops would craft, he was gearing up for the possibility of nonviolent direct action.

WITNESS BOAT FOR PEACE BLOCKADE

In early July 1982, Hunthausen addressed Seattle's Downtown Kiwanis Club, telling his audience that he and other church leaders were not sure what they would do, given the fact that the federal government had just announced there would be security zones around the USS Ohio, the first of the Trident submarines, and around the submarine base Bangor. Mandating those security zones would make it a felony to be in the waters or air space of Hood Canal. Here was Archbishop Raymond G. Hunthausen, of the established, putatively conservative Roman Catholic Church, giving a speech about civil disobedience and a peace blockade to members of a mainstream American civic institution.[119] Hunthausen told the Kiwanis that the issue of whether the human family would destroy itself through nuclear war was the greatest spiritual crisis humanity had ever faced. This may have produced one of the most unique set of minutes of a Kiwanis meeting ever recorded.[120]

As could be expected, in the wider sphere, the attack campaign against Hunthausen persisted. One fledgling group named Catholics United Against Marxist Oriented Theology, urged Catholics to "send letters of criticism to the apostolic delegate to the United States, Archbishop Pio Laghi," *Seattle Times* writer Ray Ruppert reported. The group issued a statement on July 9, 1982: "Cut your (church) donations in half. If that does not work, cut them altogether. Then there will be no money for anti-American, anti-Catholic, anti-IRS propaganda.... We also ask our fellow archdiocesans to organize with us against Marxist-oriented theology in our churches and schools." The allegedly Marxist-oriented archbishop ought to "pay more intention to what he was installed to do, take care of the needs of this archdiocese and, in our opinion, keep his politically misinformed fingers more in the holy water and less in international politics."[121]

In mid-July, Ray Hunthausen joined Bill Cate and other local church leaders, as well as Jim Douglass, in plans to file a suit in federal court to overturn the federal government's regulations designed to keep demonstrators far afield from the USS Ohio. The Church Council of Greater Seattle issued a July 15 press release, announcing that several church leaders in the Puget Sound area were among the plaintiffs challenging the courts. Bishop Melvin Talbert, United Methodist Church, spoke for the religious leaders:

> "While we recognize the legitimate and responsible concern of the U.S. Navy for the safety of the Trident crew and also for the safety of those who have announced their intention to conduct peaceful demonstrations

in relation to the submarine's arrival, it is our contention that the establishment of the regulation has impact on people far beyond the bounds of national security. It is in our view an abridgement of the First Amendment rights of free speech and assembly."[122]

The American Civil Liberties Union and the National Lawyers Guild prepared the suit. According to Lynn Greiner, legal coordinator for the suit, the federal regulations would make "these religious leaders felons in that they intend to go out there and pray for peace."[123] *Seattle Times* journalist Carol Ostrom reported a day later that there were negotiations going on between officials of the Coast Guard and the local religious leaders, who would, despite the negotiations, still likely go ahead with the filing in federal court of the suit to overturn the "security zone" restrictions.[124]

The first Trident, built on the other side of the country, was soon to make its way from the Pacific Ocean, heading east through the Strait of Juan de Fuca, en route to the Hood Canal and south to the Bangor home port. On July 21, three representatives of the Peace Blockade organizing community, Jim Douglass, Jeanne Clark, and Ian Gaillard, sent a letter to Commodore Ted Lewin, commander of Naval Base Seattle. They spelled out the rationale for the planned blockade:

> "Dear Commodore Lewin:
>
> The Peace Blockade greets you in peace, love, and the unity of a human family threatened with nuclear extinction. We greet you in the faith that nonviolence can transform our family's conflicts from death to life. We greet you in the hope that you and we can be part of that nonviolent process.
>
> We ask you in the name of the God of Love, of all that lives, and of our precious Earth, to stop the imminent deployment of the first Trident submarine, the USS Ohio. Former Trident missile designer Robert Aldridge calls Trident 'the ultimate first-strike weapon.' The United States Navy describes Trident's destructive power in this way: 'Each Ohio class submarine represents by itself more explosive power than what was fired by all the world's navies in all the wars in history.' In view of these facts, we believe Archbishop Raymond Hunthausen's summation of Trident as 'the Auschwitz of Puget Sound' is accurate.
>
> A nuclear first-strike weapon of such inconceivable power is a violation of international law, as stated in the Geneva and Hague Conventions and in the Nuremberg Tribunal. Basing ourselves on principles of

> nonviolence and international law, people have been campaigning since 1975 to stop Trident's criminal threat to life on earth. We now appeal to your conscience, to the conscience of all our government leaders, and to the crew of the USS Ohio, to stop this criminal weapon. In this open letter we appeal for further support to the American public, who have been persistently deceived concerning the first-strike nature of Trident.
>
> As an expression of that appeal to conscience, our flotilla of small boats, the Peace Blockade, has been formed to intervene nonviolently between the USS Ohio and its Bangor base where it will be loaded with nuclear warheads. We in the Peace Blockade believe in the transforming power of nonviolence. We will use no force other than our bodies and lives in front of the submarine. We know that it is physically possible for the Ohio to stop before reaching our boats. We are asking that you and others make the decision in conscience to stop the Ohio, as an acknowledgment of our mutual humanity and as a sign that the Trident system can and will be stopped and dismantled. We are asking you not to participate in a crime against humanity, to choose life instead.
>
> We thank you, Commodore Lewin, for your reflection in conscience on this letter."[125]

On July 23, Carol Ostrom reported that a federal court judge had ordered the government and the would-be anti-nuclear demonstrators to try to work things out. Judge Barbara Rothstein "delayed until the first week in August a decision on a suit filed by religious leaders and others seeking to throw out government regulations restricting access to Hood Canal when the nuclear submarine Ohio comes to Bangor."[126] In late July, Ronald Auer, a Seattle resident, wrote to the *Seattle Times*:

> "This is not a new phenomenon, not something that is a consequence of nuclear weapons. The timid, the frightened, and the cowards have always been a vocal part of the American scene. We do well to remember that a minority of the American colonists fought in our Revolutionary War; and that then as now, there were those who sought peace at any price. Hunthausen and his kind should understand that for strong, free men and women there is a fate worse than death. It is the loss of liberty."[127]

On the first day of August, as a sense of imminence grew, Ostrom set the scene: The USS Ohio is "slipping silently through the ocean toward Washington state."

Once at its home port in Bangor, on the Hood Canal, it would be loaded with "24 nuclear missiles and become the most powerful war machine the United States has ever built." She retraced some of the history of protest at Bangor. There had been a "People's Blockade" back in 1972 to try to stop Vietnam-bound munitions ships. And in 1974, "protesters scrambled over barbed wire at the Trident base to plant a vegetable garden in symbolic protest." At "Bangor Summer" in 1977, there were some 2,000 people demonstrating against the Trident submarine, but meanwhile the submarine base was proceeding under construction. Unlike back in 1972, during the efforts to stop munitions shipments to the war in Vietnam, "the anti-Trident forces now have some formidable allies, such as Roman Catholic Archbishop Raymond Hunthausen, who has termed Trident 'the Auschwitz of Puget Sound' and intends to take part in a waterborne 'peace vigil' as the submarine churns through the Canal."[128]

Ostrom noted the Navy's concern. The submarine itself could be damaged, or "they worried that a hapless boater could be sucked into the vessel's powerful undertow." What about those who were planning to try to block the passage of the USS Ohio? She asked Jim Douglass. "What I learned from Dorothy Day—the woman who founded the Catholic Worker movement—is that we're on the edge of total destruction of the human family from total nuclear war, and that we're able to change that," said Douglass. "It's not as though we're expecting the peace blockade is going to end the Trident missile system," but the practice of "direct action" or civil disobedience remains vital to the anti-Trident campaign. If the broadening of the support for the peace movement "were to turn the Trident campaign in a direction that no longer included direct action, that would be a dilution and no longer what Gandhi called a 'truth force,'" Douglass believed.[129] Gandhi's *satyagraha* (truth force) entailed nonviolent direct action, and of course not everyone who wanted to be involved in the peace movement was ready to risk direct action.

Ostrom also interviewed Charles Meconis, the head of the Seattle Religious Peace Action Coalition of the Church Council of Greater Seattle. Meconis stressed the importance of mass participation, and yet he was growing impatient with some of the techniques. "You finally reach a point where you've given a million talks and you've written a million educational newsletters and you've sent a million letters to Congress…all the normal political channels, and you're looking for another channel of action," Meconis told Ostrom. "I cherish the normal political channels, democracy…. I am not an anarchist. In domestic affairs, democracy works very well. But by very tragic and bitter experience, I've learned that's not the case with military and foreign-policy issues." Meconis and many others, who would be risking a possible felony charge punishable by a $10,000 fine and 10 years in prison, were that weekend at an Olympic Peninsula campsite searching their consciences and preparing for nonviolent direct action.[130]

Sr. Mary Grondin had given a great deal of thought to the potential consequences of direct action. "It didn't change my decision at all. It just tightened the knot in my stomach. I think some people have to stand and say no.... Defense is one thing, but this is so grossly beyond defense that I see it as grossly immoral and evil. I feel it so strongly that I have to say it strongly. So I think the strongest way I can do that is to put my life on the line in the water. I think everybody has an obligation to stand against evil." Ostrom also included the vision shared by Shelley Douglass. She and Jim, at the Ground Zero Center for Nonviolent Action there at Bangor, had been providing retreat and nonviolence-training for a number of years. They were not trying to push people too fast. Shelley Douglass: "We're not primarily into getting the most number of people doing things, like blockading the submarine. We're into helping people think and grow."[131]

The *Bremerton Sun*'s "Thousands Protest Nuclear Threat" article described what happened August 8 on the shore of Hood Canal at Point Julia as "one moment to remember" for the anti-nuclear movement. Over 5,000 people came together on the Klallam Indian Reservation. Co-sponsored by Ground Zero Center for Nonviolent Action and the Seattle Religious Peace Action Coalition, the rally honored those who had died in the atomic blasts at Hiroshima and Nagasaki.[132] Archbishop Hunthausen led a prayer for the officers and crew of the Ohio, anticipating their arrival soon. "Do we pray for them because we believe they are bad-willed persons who want war and not peace?" By no means, he declared. They strongly desire peace, he felt. "Do we pray because we believe that we have a corner on the market of truth and we want to open the mind of our supposedly blind opponents?" Once again, Hunthausen insisted, "Not at all!" Truth is not something anyone could claim to know with such certainty.

> "As we struggle together over issues of foreign policy, we need to remember, then, that each of us possesses part of the truth, and so, be willing to work with compassion to understand the truth shown to us by the 'other side,' and to forgive mistakes and wrongs done us in a spirit of love. We are all—Navy and peace people—caught up in the same system; we all struggle to do the best we can to live according to our beliefs."

He continued to ask rhetorically, "Do we pray because we want God to persuade them to see things our way?" No, was his answer. "Prayer is not an attempt to persuade God to change things our way. It is much more an attempt to put ourselves in tune with the God who loves us all, a begging, really, that we find his will and follow it." Why do we pray, then, he asked. We pray for the crew of the USS Ohio, he said:

> "...because they are our brothers and we wish to express our solidarity with them. We pray because we are united in the goal of peace....

> We pray because we want these men to know that we respect their dedication, that we esteem them, and love them. We pray that they may better realize that we do not wish a barrier to grow between us.... The blockade is a kind of confrontation but it is not done with an attitude of antagonism, rather with respect and love for the people on board the Ohio."

He invited the large crowd to join him in asking God's blessing upon all the officers and crew of the submarine. "We pledge to continue to confront in love that which we feel is wrong, to listen attentively to one another's point of view, to respect the rights of others to believe as they do. We believe that if we enter this struggle seeking together for the truth, we will change together and the family which is now often obscured in our relationships will be revealed."[133]

The Trident submarine was seen, by many activists in the region trying to stop it, as a deep sea behemoth. Just one day before the behemoth arrived, Hunthausen and several other religious leaders, including good friend Bishop Bill Skylstad of Yakima, were out in a vigil boat. They had responded to what turned out to be a false report of the Trident's arrival. The Trident actually came down the Hood Canal quite early the next morning, August 12. Nonetheless, their intentions to be a prayerful presence giving support to those who would attempt the nonviolent blockade were fulfilled. Ecumenical leaders Bill Cate and Loren Arnett remember when all the bishops and church executives spent a fair amount of time in their Thursday morning breakfast meetings talking about how they were going to be supportive of their colleague, Ray Hunthausen. One thing they decided they could do was to participate with him in the blockade. Cate says Rev. Jon Nelson was intensely involved in the whole effort, as he was in so many aspects of the peace movement. And Fr. Harvey MacIntyre, the executive director of the Washington State Catholic Conference, "had a big boat he lived on, so we all got on that boat and we went out to be part of the witness vigil. Rabbi Norman Hirsch was with us," recalls Arnett.[134] The next day the blockaders—not the witness boats—faced the Coast Guard and Navy that employed water hoses, had guns drawn, and overturned some of the boats in the peace flotilla.[135]

Charlie Meconis recounts what happened. The effort to blockade the USS Ohio was fateful.

> "We were either going to end up dead, seriously hurt, or gone to prison for ten years. Several of us continued on with the planned blockade even after they raised the penalties. Fourteen of us were arrested. Seventeen more were detained. We had over one hundred support persons for the action. With regard to the Trident blockade effort, think about how bishops are always blessing fleets. So bishops were always blessing

> battleships etc. in that era, or especially before that time. And so here we had church bishops and other faith community leaders, twelve of them, in a witness boat. They all came out and blessed the blockade fleet. There were many witness boats kept outside the zone. This was a moment where the combined religious community was supporting a civil disobedience effort."

Meconis recalls how "they were out there with holy water to bless all the vessels there to be involved in trying to stop the submarine." And for the blockaders themselves, on the day when the submarine came in early in the morning, "there was a very dicey moment when a young coast guard member armed with a 50 caliber machine gun aimed at us, well, the kid was more scared than we were and that was a dangerous moment. After it was over, when eight days later they dropped the charges against us, they effectively had quashed the blockade and then eliminated our day in court. It was a great strategy on their part."[136]

On August 12 the Associated Press reported it this way: "The nation's first Trident submarine sailed into its home port in Washington today with Coast Guard boats spraying fire hoses to open a path through a rag-tag flotilla of protest boats. At least 14 people were arrested." The Ohio docked at Bangor home port mid-morning. "The protesters had been prepared to risk arrest to dramatize their non-violent opposition to the Ohio, which they view as a prime symbol of the nuclear arms race." Trident had indeed become a dramatic symbol. Hunthausen's stark words and actions helped make it so, and he had emerged as a prime emblem of religious opposition to Trident and the lethal first strike policy it represented.[137]

Sr. Mary Grondin was out there in one of the blockading boats, a fourteen foot long aluminum craft, operating the motor. Mary remembers how they would practice. The Pacific Peacemaker, a Greenpeace craft from Australia, was the flagship vessel for the blockade, with its hand painted sail done by Australian artists. "We would gather at the main flagship, and come into the shore every evening." Her colleague, Sr. Chauncey Boyle, and others brought food to support the people doing the blockade. The training process leading up to the blockade went on for about two weeks. There was wide press coverage. One Seattle paper had a cartoon with a small boat on the water just in front of the massive USS Ohio, with nun in the little vessel. All of this drama put even more attention on Hunthausen and the role of the Catholic Church in Western Washington. The Peace Blockade was, in the view of both Grondin and Boyle, a pivotal moment for so many people.[138] Afterward Hunthausen praised the actions of the protesters, saying that "...if one examines who they are and what they are about, you have to acknowledge they are not in it for themselves. How could they be? They're putting themselves out there at great risk to their lives."[139]

Jim Douglass later wrote: "The Peace Blockade was just confrontive enough to give one a sense of nonviolent revolution, really changing our lives and our structures as distinct from crying out in the night."[140] In the period after the Ohio's arrival, Ground Zero Center for Nonviolent Action prepared a welcome letter for the crew of the Ohio and their families:

> "Because you will be seeing us again and again, we would like to be clear that our disagreement is not with your presence but with the deployment of the Trident system. We welcome you to our community. You will be meeting people in the disarmament movement in many places. Like you, we have children in local schools, where we volunteer time to help out. Like you, we are involved in political parties, in sports, and in local churches. We shop in local stores as you do, visit local doctors, attend local cultural events and films. We look forward to meeting you and to being involved in dialogue with you."[141]

Archbishop Hunthausen's respect for direct actions of nonviolent prayerful resistance had grown deep like the waters. His critics deepened their attacks in tandem. *The Wanderer*, along with a Kelso, Washington-based group, Roman Catholic Laity for Truth, assailed Hunthausen's action in joining the witness boat vigil.[142] As mentioned earlier, Catholics Against Marxist-oriented Theology had recently sent a two-page letter to local newspapers and to the parishes of the archdiocese, urging Catholics to let the apostolic delegate to the U.S., Archbishop Pio Laghi, know that Hunthausen was politically misinformed.[143] Catholics should cut their donations in protest. Forces working to undermine Hunthausen were tenacious. Yet, rather than dropping off, the annual appeal for the archdiocese actually grew that year, and continued to grow in the following years. The jump between 1981 and 1982 alone was a 21 percent increase in total contributions and a 45 percent surge in the number of contributors. And letters to the archdiocese were overwhelmingly supportive of the archbishop.[144]

TARGET SEATTLE

Target Seattle was another way Hunthausen participated in social movements trying to stop the surge in arms. Target Seattle achieved an unprecedented coalescence of religious and secular organizations. In addition to the Church Council of Greater Seattle, Target Seattle included Americans for Democratic Action, American Jewish Committee, Arms Race Concern, Associated Students of the University of Washington, The Audubon Society, Boys and Girls Clubs of Seattle, Seattle City Club, Gray Panthers, and the Seattle Teachers Association, to name only a few.[145] It involved some 50 organizations, from September 20 through October 2, 1982. The Seattle and Puget Sound region would be a high prospect target in the event of nuclear war, given the extensive web of military and defense industries. Target Seattle's ambitious goal was to try to involve as many as 500 religious congregations. Although that goal was not reached, more than 200 faith communities were actively involved in Target Seattle, with sermons, adult forums, event ticket sales, and volunteer recruitment. Many conducted house-to-house visits to obtain signatures for the Tashkent (in the Soviet Union) Sister City letter. Backed up by 25,000 signatures, the letter read: "The people of Seattle and Tashkent are united through the Sister City Program, through our love of our cities, and through the hopes we share for our children's future. Yet if there is a nuclear war, all that we value would be destroyed. As people who live in the Puget Sound community, we pledge ourselves to work to prevent nuclear war."[146]

Archbishop Hunthausen was one of many Target Seattle speakers. On September 29 he spoke to a large audience: "I come to you tonight as a religious leader, if you will, but also as a fellow American whose love of country and concern for its survival give me no choice but to speak out."[147] His call for unilateral disarmament was a matter of taking initiative as a nation, dispelling the caricature that some critics had made. "I cannot believe that others would remain unchanged as we take these steps for peace. Divesting ourselves of holocaust weapons is not an overnight process." A year later he recalled the significance of Target Seattle and especially its atmosphere of dialogue and civility. "Target Seattle was truly the sound of a 'democracy at work.' It demonstrated that a community with both vested interests and firsthand involvement in the military and industrial complexities of defense, could at the same time mobilize its best human resources in a critical dialogue in the interest of the common good." He acknowledged there were many who did not share his convictions or his controversial notion of unilateral initiatives and unilateral disarmament. "We disagreed, but not as a community shattered by argument. We grew. We are no longer the same. We are still growing."[148]

ENDNOTES

1 Hunthausen, Raymond. "What It Means To Be A Peacemaker." Speech delivered at Interfaith Prayer Service, University of Washington, Seattle, 4 Oct. 1987. Archdiocese of Seattle Archives.

2 Ruppert, Ray. "Idolatry of weapons led archbishop to speak out." *Seattle Times* 28 June 1981. *Historic Seattle Times, 1900–1984*, 65.

3 "Cleric's stance draws criticism." *Seattle Times* 18 June 1981. *Historic Seattle Times, 1900–1984*, 65.

4 "Archbishop supported." *Seattle Times* 28 June 1981. *Historic Seattle Times, 1900–1984*, 65.

5 "Episcopalians back archbishop's stand." *Seattle Times* 2 July 1981. *Historic Seattle Times, 1900–1984*, 101.

6 Cate, William. "Clergy and Laity rally for peace." Source (*CCGS* newsletter) Oct. 1981, 1.

7 Ruppert, Ray. "Religious leaders to ponder plea for end to nuclear arms." *Seattle Times* 26 Aug. 1981. *Historic Seattle Times, 1900–1984*, 40.

8 Ruppert, Ray. "Catholic leaders back archbishop's protest." *Seattle Times* 28 Aug. 1981. *Historic Seattle Times, 1900–1984*, 18.

9 Ruppert, Ray. "Clerics seek support for weapons stance." *Seattle Times* 5 Sept. 1981. *Historic Seattle Times, 1900–1984*, 6.

10 "Archbishop Hunthausen's anti-nuclear speech is still creating ripples." *Seattle Times* 3 Oct. 1981. *Historic Seattle Times, 1900–1984*, 12.

11 Wooden, Cindy. "'Conservative' Catholic groups have diverse goals, procedures." *Progress* 29 Nov. 1984, 9.

12 Morriss, Frank. "The Bishop's Behavior is Inadmissible." *The Wanderer* (henceforth cited simply as *Wanderer*) 2 July 1981, 4.

13 Strand, Robert. "The teaching of the church is clear." United Press International 3 Oct. 1981. *Lexisnexis.com*. Web. 14 Aug. 2012.

14 McCarthy, Coleman. "Brave Bishops." *Washington Post* 3 Oct. 1981, A23. *Lexisnexis.com*. Web. 14 Aug. 2012.

15 Ruppert, Ray. "16 ministers urge end to arms buildup." *Seattle Times* 9 Oct. 1981. *Historic Seattle Times, 1900–1984*, 21.

16 Matt, A.J. "A Voice Worth Listening To." *Wanderer* 10 Sept. 1981, 4. Frank Morris. "Push for Women's Ordination Institutionalized in Seattle Archdiocese." *Wanderer* 17 Sept. 1981, 1,7.

17 Ruppert, Ray. "Churches taking the lead in the rebirth of U.S. peace movement." *Seattle Times* 17 Oct. 1981. *Historic Seattle Times, 1900–1984*, 12.

18 "Church groups announce peace-making event." *Seattle Times* 22 Oct. 1981. *Historic Seattle Times, 1900–1984*, 20.

19 Gelernter, Carey Quan. "Rally for nuclear-arms freeze has 'the time is now' mood." *Seattle Times* 25 Oct. 1981. *Historic Seattle Times, 1900–1984*, 32.

20 Hunthausen, Raymond. "The Calling to Lose Our Lives for Peace." 24 Oct. 1981. Archdiocese of Seattle Archives.

21 Moriwaki, Lee. "Push for peace: Growing movement cutting across class lines, generations." *Seattle Times* 1 Nov. 1981. *Historic Seattle Times, 1900–1984*, 3.

22 Associated Press 24 Oct. 1981. *Lexisnexis.com*. Web. 14 Aug. 2012.

23 Ruppert, Ray. "Episcopal bishop denounces buildup of nuclear weapons." *Seattle Times* 6 Nov. 1981. *Historic Seattle times, 1900–1984*, 18.

24 "Seattle archdiocese chagrined by stocks in arms-making firms." *Seattle Times* 16 Nov. 1981. *Historic Seattle Times, 1900–1984*, 6.

25 United Press International 18 Nov. 1981. *Lexisnexis.com*. Web. 14 Aug. 2012.

26 "Reader decries *Progress*' support for Archbishop's stand." *Progress* 12 Nov. 1981, 5.

27 Yzermans, Vincent. "A Catholic Revolution." *New York Times* 14 Nov. 1981, 23. *Lexisnexis.com*. Web. 7 Aug. 2012.

28 Ruppert, Ray. "Catholics tackling arms race, abortion, Central American issues." *Seattle Times* 5 Dec. 1981. *Historic Seattle Times, 1900–1984*, 14.

29 "A growing number of U.S. Catholic leaders are urging the 50-million member American church to join the movement against nuclear weapons." *Globe and Mail* 21 Nov. 1981. *Lexisnexis.com*. Web. 14 Aug. 2012.

30 McCarthy, Coleman. "The Flock of Peace; Catholic Bishops and The Call of Conscience; Flocking Toward Peace." *Washington Post* 21 Nov. 1981, C1. *Lexisnexis.com*. Web. 14 Aug. 2012.

31 "Bishop Resists Naming A-Sub Corpus Christi." *Washington Post* 26 Nov. 1981, E4. *Lexisnexis.com*. Web. 14 Aug. 2012.

32 Feinsilber, Mike. "A Grassroots U.S. Anti-Nuclear Movement." Associated Press 8 Dec. 1981. *Lexisnexis.com*. Web. 14 Aug. 2012.

33 Ruppert, Ray. "Editor sees nuclear arms, religious right as top moral issues." *Seattle Times* 19 Dec. 1981. *Historic Seattle Times, 1900–1984*, 8.

34 Strong, William. Letter to Raymond Hunthausen. 16 Dec. 1981. Archdiocese of Seattle Archives.

35 McCaulley, Neil. Letters to Raymond Hunthausen and Terence Cooke. 21 Dec. 1981. Archdiocese of Seattle Archives.

36 "The Church Divided." 24 Dec. 1981. *Wall Street Journal*. Archdiocese of Seattle Archives.

37 Buckley, William. "A sensible statement by the military vicar." *Seattle Times* 29 Dec. 1981, A8. Archdiocese of Seattle Archives.

38 Hyer, Marjorie. "Group Within Catholic Hierarchy Highly Critical of Nuclear Policy; Catholics Call Arms Race Immoral." *Washington Post* 25 Dec. 1981, A4. *Lexisnexis.com*. 14 Aug. 2012.

39 Huntley, James. "Best chance of avoiding N-war lies in credible deterrent." *Seattle Times* 23 Dec. 1981. *Historic Seattle Times, 1900–1984*, 7.

40 Weigel, George. Letter. *Progress* 20 May 1977, 7.

41 Weigel, George. "The 'Peace bishop' and the arms race: I." *Progress* 3 Dec. 1981, 4.

42 McCarthy, Coleman. "How the 'Peace Bishops' Got That Way." *Washington Post* 27 Dec. 1981, D5. *Lexisnexis.com*. Web. 14 Aug. 2012.

43 Ruppert, Ray. "Peace pastor preaches doctrine here." *Seattle Times* 10 Jan. 1982. *Historic Seattle Times, 1900–1984*, 20.

44 Ruppert, Ray. "Disarmament: Archbishop becoming major spokesperson." *Seattle Times* 17 Jan. 1982. *Historic Seattle Times, 1900–1984*, 22.

45 Walker, Richard. "US churches press for world peace, nuclear arms control." *Christian Science Monitor* 14 Jan. 1982, 7. *Lexisnexis.com*. Web. 6 Sept. 2012.

46 Weigel, George. *Tranquilitas Orndinis: The Present and Future Promise of American Catholic Thought on War and Peace*. New York: Oxford Univ. Press 1987, 170-171.

47 "Risking for Peace." *Ground Zero*. Spring 1986, 6.

48 Wahl, Kim. Personal interview. Seattle 11 Dec. 2012.

49 Ruppert, Ray. "Arms protest: Prelate to withhold tax." *Seattle Times* 28 Jan. 1982. *Historic Seattle Times, 1900–1984*, 1.

50 "Archbishop Says He Will Withhold Taxes to Protest Arms Race." Associated Press 28 Jan. 1982. *Lexisnexis.com*. Web. 6 Sept. 2012.

51 Hunthausen, Raymond. Pastoral Letter. 28 Jan. 1982. Archdiocese of Seattle Archives.

52 Ruppert, Ray. "N-arms: Archbishop's tax protest may unleash storm." *Seattle Times* 30 Jan. 1982. *Historic Seattle Times, 1900–1984*, 10.

53 "Nuclear arms: 'The very existence of humanity is at stake.'" *Seattle Times* 30 Jan. 1982. *Historic Seattle Times, 1900–1984*, 10.

54 Roemer, James. Letter to Archbishop Hunthausen. 29 Jan. 1982. Archdiocese of Seattle Archives.

55 Hunthausen, Raymond. Finding Our Way Back: A Christian Response to Nuclear Weapons. "'Our nuclear war preparations are the global crucifixion of Jesus'." *National Catholic Reporter* 12 Feb. 1982.

56 Hunthausen. Finding Our Way Back.

57 Hunthausen. Finding Our Way Back.

58 Hunthausen, Raymond. "Finding Our Way Back." 29 Jan. 1982. *National Catholic Reporter* audio cassette recording.

59 Ruppert, Ray. "Archbishop ready to go to jail over N-protest." *Seattle Times* 1 Feb. 1982. *Historic Seattle Times, 1900–1984*, 24.

60 "Archbishop Hunthausen: Foolish or courageous?" Letters. *Seattle Times* 3 Feb. 1982. *Historic Seattle Times, 1900–1984*, 15.

61 Zahn, Gordon. "'Sign of new Catholic American identity'." *National Catholic Reporter* 5 Feb. 1982.

62 Ruppert, Ray. "It's too soon to expect visible women leaders, says historian." *Seattle Times* 6 Feb. 1982. *Historic Seattle Times, 1900–1984*, 6.

63 Gough, William. "'Go to hell! Quintupling of protests in Washington." *Seattle Times* 14 Feb. 1982. *Historic Seattle Times, 1900–1984*, 3.

64 "There is safety in armament." Letter. *Progress* 18 Feb. 1982, 5.

65 O'Connor, John. "Facing Nuclear Buildup, Both Faith, Reason Must Converge." *National Catholic Reporter* 26 Feb. 1982.

66 "Hunthausen vows to protest Trident." *Seattle Times* 26 Feb. 1982. *Historic Seattle Times, 1900–1984*, 7.

67 Rader, P.J. "Prayer weapon of N-arms protest at Trident base." *Seattle Times* 1 Mar. 1982. *Historic Seattle Times, 1900–1984*, 26.

68 "A Chaplain's No to Trident." *Ground Zero*. July/Aug. 1982, 3,6.

69 Miller, Judith. "Effort to 'Freeze' Nuclear Arsenals Spreads in U.S." *New York Times* 15 March 1982, B12. *Lexisnexis.com*. Web. 7 Aug. 2012.

70 Lehman, John. "Nuclear Weapons Defend Judeo-Christian Civilization." See Bender, David. *The Arms Race: Opposing Viewpoints*. St. Paul, Minn: Greenhaven, 1982, 94-99.

71 Hunthausen, Raymond. Response to Lehman's statement. *Origins* 1 Apr. 1982, 673.

72 Hunthausen, Raymond.

73 Hunthausen, Raymond. Personal interview. Seattle, Washington 22 June 1989.

74 Hunthausen, Raymond. Personal interview. Seattle, Washington 16 Sept. 1988.

75 Hunthausen, Raymond. Response to Lehman's statement. *Origins* 1 Apr. 1982, 673.

76 Hunthausen, Raymond. Personal interview. Seattle, Washington 16 Sept. 1988.

77 Hunthausen, Raymond. *Ground Zero*. Summer 1987, 3.

78 Hunthausen, Raymond. "Coming to a Position on the Global Arms Race: A Personal Journey."

79 Ruppert, Ray. "Expert on defense urges freeze on nuclear arms." *Seattle Times* 12 Mar. 1982. *Historic Seattle Times, 1900–1984*, 7.

80 "Archbishop to join Trident-sub blockade." *Seattle Times* 14 Mar. 1982. *Historic Seattle Times, 1900–1984*, 1.

81 "Archbishop Hunthausen: Is he a traitor or a hero?" Letters. *Seattle Times* 21 Mar. 1982. *Historic Seattle Times, 1900–1984*, 21.

82 Pearson, Georgia. Letter to Archbishop Hunthausen. 14 Mar. 1982. Archdiocese of Seattle Archives.

83 Richardson, David. "On the March—U.S. Version of Peace Crusade." *U.S. News & World Report* 22 Mar. 1982, 24. *Lexis.nexis.com*. Web. 6 Sept. 2012.

84 United Press International 12 Apr. 1982. *Lexisnexis.com*. Web. 6 Sept. 2012.

85 Hopps, Don. Personal interview, Seattle, Washington 25 Mar. 2013.

86 "Good Friday trek to start at Bangor." *Seattle Times* 7 April 1982. *Historic Seattle Times, 1900–1984*, 57.

87 "Ellsberg, Berrigan Arrested In Separate Demonstrations." Associated Press 10 Apr. 1982. *Lexisnexis.com*. Web. 6 Sept. 2012.

88 Morris, Jack. Personal interview. Portland, Oregon 5 July 2011.

89 Rinearson, Peter. "Seattle is 'household name' to arms foes." *Seattle Times* 8 Apr. 1982. *Historic Seattle Times, 1900–1984*, 18.

90 Ruppert, Ray. "Archbishop begins withholding taxes." *Seattle Times* 14 Apr. 1982. *Historic Seattle Times, 1900–1984*, 33.

91 Ruppert, Ray. "Protest: President of Church Council to hold part of tax." *Seattle Times* 21 Apr. 1982. *Historic Seattle Times*, 1900–1984, 57.

92 McGrory, Mary. "Archbishop Makes a Simple Statement, in Dollars and Cents; REBEL." *Washington Post* 15 Apr. 1982, A3. *Lexisnexis.com*. Web. 6 Apr. 2012.

93 McCarthy, Coleman. "And the Meek Shall Pay All the Taxes." *Washington Post* 18 Apr. 1982, G7. *Lexisnexis.com*. Web. 6 Sept. 2012.

94 Turner, Wallace. "Tax Refusal Completes Prelate's Moral Journey." *New York Times* 19 Apr. 1982, A16. *Lexisnexis.com*. Web. 7 Aug. 2012.

95 Wahl, Kim. Correspondence with me as part of review of early draft of book manuscript. May 2014.

96 "Nuclear Armament–The Terrible Evil." *Der Spiegel* interview with Archbishop Hunthausen. 19 Apr. 1982. Archdiocese of Seattle Archives.

97 "Nuclear armament–The Terrible Evil."

98 "Cate and Hunthausen: Right end, wrong means." Editorial. *Seattle Times* 26 Apr. 1982. *Historic Seattle Times, 1900–1984*, 13.

99 "Who's Who in the Movement." *Newsweek* 26 Apr. 1982, 22. *Lexisnexis.com*. Web. 6 Sept. 2012.

100 Hunthausen, Raymond. "A Faith Response to the Nuclear Crisis." Speech, Seattle 30 Apr. 1982. Archdiocese of Seattle Archives.

101 "Graham, other religious leaders going to Moscow for conference." *Seattle Times* 1 May 1982. *Historic Seattle Times, 1900–1984*, 6.

102 Hunthausen, Raymond. "Faithful Realism." Speech at St. James, Cathedral, Brooklyn, New York 16 May 1982. Archdiocese of Seattle Archives.

103 Hunthausen, Raymond. "Faithful Realism."

104 Hunthausen, Raymond.

105 "Archbishop speaks in New York." *Progress* 20 May 1982, 5.

106 Ruppert, Ray. "Vatican, Hunthausen not at odds on arms." *Seattle Times* 27 May 1982. *Historic Seattle Times, 1900–1984*, 121.

107 "Catholic church officials puzzled over status of archbishop's critic." *Seattle Times* 29 May 1982. *Historic Seattle Times, 1900–1984*, 15.

108 "Archdiocese plans file for conscientious objectors." *Seattle Times* 29 May 1982. *Historic Seattle Times, 1900–1984*, 15.

109 "Further pressure on ERA hunger strikers." *Seattle Times* 3 June 1982. *Historic Seattle Times, 1900–1984*, 107.

110 United Press International 2 June 1982. *Lexisnexis.com*. Web. 6 Sept. 2012.

111 Ruppert, Ray. "Hunthausen declines European invitation." *Seattle Times* 5 June 1982. *Historic Seattle Times, 1900–1984*, 15.

112 Robbins, William. "Krol Assesses Position in Disarmament Movement." *New York Times* 9 June 1982, A24. *Lexisnexis.com*. Web. 7 Aug. 2012.

113 Fialka, John. "Nuclear Fission: Atom-Weapons Issue Stirs Divisive Debate In the Catholic Church." *Wall Street Journal* 9 June 1982. Archdiocese of Seattle Archives.

114 Fialka, John.

115 Fialka, John.

116 Castelli, Jim. *The Bishops and The Bomb: Waging Peace in a Nuclear Age*. Garden City, New York: Image Books 1983, 13-18.

117 Fialka, John.

118 Fialka, John.

119 "Trident security unsettle bishop." *Seattle Post-Intelligencer* 7 July 1982. Church Council of Greater Seattle collection at the University of Washington Archives.

120 Ruppert, Ray. "Federal curbs force clergy to reconsider N-sub protest." *Seattle Times* 7 July 1982. *Historic Seattle Times, 1900–1984*, 36.

121 Ruppert, Ray. "Lay group criticizes archbishop's actions." *Seattle Times* 10 July 1982. *Historic Seattle Times, 1900–1984*, 8.

122 News Release. Church Council of Greater Seattle 15 July 1982. Church Council of Greater Seattle collection, University of Washington Archives.

123 Ostrom, Carol. "Suit asks federal court to throw out N-sub security rules." *Seattle Times* 15 July 1982. Historic Seattle Times, 1900–1984, 39.

124 Ostrom, Carol. "No agreement yet in dispute over N-sub 'security zone'." *Seattle Times* 16 July 1982. Historic Seattle Times, 1900–1984, 39.

125 Clark, Jeanne, Jim Douglass, and Ian Gaillard. Letter to Commodore Ted Lewin 21 July 1982. Ground Zero collection, University of Washington Archives.

126 Ostrom, Carol. "Navy, Trident protesters told to negotiate." *Seattle Times* 23 July 1982. *Historic Seattle Times, 1900–1984*, 17.

127 Auer, Ronald. "Democracy reaps what it sows." Letter. *Seattle Times* 25 July 1982. *Historic Seattle Times, 1900–1984*, 15.

128 Ostrom, Carol. "Pesky protest fleet challenges a mighty war machine." *Seattle Times* 1 Aug. 1982. *Historic Seattle Times, 1900–1984*, 1.

129 Ostrom, Carol. "Friends, foes prepare to greet Trident submarine." *Seattle Times* 1 Aug. 1982. *Historic Seattle Times, 1900–1984*, 53.

130 Ostrom, Carol.

131 Ostrom, Carol.

132 Rothgeb, Jim. "Thousands Protest Nuclear Threat." *Bremerton Sun* 9 Aug. 1982. Ground Zero collection, University of Washington Archives.

133 Hunthausen, Raymond. "Blessing of the Crew of the 'Ohio'." 8 Aug. 1982. Archbishop Hunthausen Disarmament collection. Archdiocese of Seattle Archives.

134 Arnett, Loren. Personal interview. Bothell, Washington. 28 Mar. 2013. Cate, William. Personal interview. Bellevue, Washington. 28 Mar. 2013.

135 For a detailed version of what happened that day, see Paul Loeb's book, *Hope in Hard Times*.

136 Meconis, Charles. Personal interview. Seattle, Washington. 27 Mar. 2013.

137 Connolly, Patrick. Associated Press 12 Aug. 1982.

138 Boyle, Chauncey and Mary Grondin. Personal interview. West Seattle, Washington 11 Dec. 2012.

139 "Archbishop praises the protesters." *Seattle Post-Intelligencer* 13 Aug. 1982, A3.

140 Douglass, James. "Was the Peace Blockade Nonviolent?" *Ground Zero* Oct/Nov. 1982, 6-7.

141 Letter to the crew of the Ohio and their families. Ground Zero collection, University of Washington Archives.

142 Morriss, Frank. "Ad Apologizes For Archbishop Hunthausen." *Wanderer* 9 Sept. 1982, 1.

143 Oliver, Gordon. "Group forms to denounce Hunthausen." *National Catholic Reporter* 13 Aug. 1982, 9.

144 Burns, Jim. Personal interview. Edmonds, Washington 17 Sept. 2012. See also Gordon Oliver "Donations up in Seattle" *National Catholic Reporter* 17 Sept. 1982.

145 "50 Groups Join Target Seattle." *CCGS*. Sept. 1982.

146 "A Letter to the People of the Soviet Union." *CCGS*. Sept. 1982.

147 Hunthausen, Raymond. "The Case for Unilateral Disarmament." Speech at Target Seattle, 29 Sept. 1982.

148 Hunthausen, Raymond. "Target Seattle-Target Earth." Speech given in Seattle 7 June 1983. Archdiocese of Seattle Archives.

Part II

COURAGE

"I don't know any other way to live but to wake up everyday armed with my convictions, not yielding them to the threat of danger and to the power and force of people who might despise me."
—Wole Soyinka, Nobel Laureate

"The greatest challenge of the day is: how to bring about a revolution of the heart, a revolution which has to start with each one of us?"
—Dorothy Day, *Loaves and Fishes*, 1963

Chapter Four

IDOLS OF FALSE SECURITY

Advocates of the Reagan administration's nuclear arms buildup lambasted Archbishop Hunthausen and Target Seattle. Hunthausen called into question the dominant paradigm of national security—including nuclear deterrence—and the idolatry that he believed it represented. Many of his critics, however, simply thought Hunthausen's disarmament agenda would leave the nation defenseless. They rejected his assertion that the massive U.S. military imprint was making the world more insecure and, by diverting revenue from basic human needs, was also making the world more unjust. John Carlson, a former Reagan administration staff member, wrote in the *Seattle Times*:

> "The media and local intelligentsia have conferred a great deal of moral, intellectual and even political legitimacy on Target Seattle and on Archbishop Raymond Hunthausen, whose recent disarmament speech condensed most of what he's said in the past about American arms and nuclear war. That's too bad, because the clamor for Hunthausen's remarks revealed what conservatives have all along maintained; that in the propelling core of Target Seattle lies a political mindset determined to pursue virtually any course of action as an alternative to the Reagan administration's defense plan, even to the point of unilaterally disarming—a gesture which, assuming the Soviet Union's intentions are aggressive, is a call for surrender.... Everyone admits that it is desirable to limit, indeed to reduce the amount of nuclear weaponry in the world. But Hunthausen's remedy that the U.S. should disarm and continue to do so even if our adversary doesn't won't lead to less weapons and more peace. It will lead to more aggression, more killing, more destruction, and less freedom."[1]

Carlson's criticism was matched by that of famous conservative intellectual (and Catholic) William F. Buckley Jr., who derided Hunthausen in an October 1982 column printed in the same newspaper. Buckley reviewed three pathways of opposition to war. First, failure to register with the Selective Service; second, selective conscientious objection; and third:

> "...the pacifist, who, while recognizing that the U.S. government has for many years made provisions to spare conscientious objectors the

> obligation to do combat duty, nevertheless feels that a comprehensive negation of war requires also the negation of the administrative machinery of war, of which the draft is concededly a part. This thinking, by the way, is philosophically related to that of the post-draft-age citizen who decides to ventilate his defiance by refusing to pay his taxes. Or rather, by refusing to pay that much of his taxes used to create atom bombs. Archbishop Raymond G. Hunthausen of Seattle has, in his war against the atom, conveniently arrived at the figure of 50 percent. Well, the least of the bishop's sins is that he can't do arithmetic very well."[2]

If Buckley could be expected to criticize Archbishop Hunthausen, to no one's surprise the Jesuit peace activist Fr. Daniel Berrigan praised the Archbishop. Hunthausen was, Berrigan said:

> "...walking toward a new center, creating as he goes. It is a center of understanding. From it we may see ourselves anew—in church and in society. How strange it seems, and yet how fitting, that it should be a Catholic who is demonstrating that our true history is wrought anew by conscientious resistance against unjust laws! Hunthausen may perhaps take comfort. History will someday see him (as some of us see him now) hand in hand with all those who wrought our true vision; who stood somewhere, made their moral gesture, and paid up."[3]

Buckley's and Berrigan's views on Hunthausen in some ways exemplified the larger debate over the direction Catholic social thought ought to take in the pastoral letter on war and peace, very briefly noted in the last chapter, which was being developed by the U.S. bishops. It is time now to look more closely at the debate over that letter, and to explore in greater depth Raymond Hunthausen's reasoning on the core issues of war and peace. We will also observe how his critique of U.S. power applied not only to the issue of nuclear deterrence but also to the nation's lethal role in Central American wars. For Hunthausen the essential reality, common to both reliance on nuclear deterrence and to the general U.S. foreign policy propensity to rely on the threat of or use of military force, was this: the nation put its faith in idols of false security, and even though these idols could not bring true and lasting security, they were already bringing death and diminishment—both directly and indirectly—to our sisters and brothers in other lands, and to the poor everywhere. To be sure, Hunthausen's profoundly critical view of his nation's "security" doctrine was not shared by all of the American bishops, let alone by the Vatican at that time.

The American Catholic bishops adopted a consultative process as they worked through successive drafts of *The Challenge of Peace: God's Promise and Our*

Response. Their Ad Hoc Committee on War and Peace, chaired by then Cincinnati's Archbishop Joseph Bernardin, held its first meeting in July 1981. Detroit's auxiliary bishop, Thomas Gumbleton, served on the committee and brought a passionate commitment to the type of thinking that resonated with Raymond Hunthausen. John O'Connor, then an auxiliary bishop to Cardinal Cooke in the Military Ordinariate, brought an equally passionate commitment to the Catholic just war tradition, which remained the dominant ethic in official Catholic morality on war and peace. Two other committee members, Bishop Daniel Reilly of Norwich and Auxiliary Bishop George Fulcher of Columbus, were considered moderate. Bernardin, a master at consensus building, worked to find common ground among the disparate voices as the "letter"—in length, more like a book—moved through various drafts.[4] The final document was not completed until May 1983.

As the drafting process was underway, the nationally syndicated columnist Mary McGrory wrote that President Reagan and his administration were facing a challenge not only from recognized opponents, but from moderates such as Archbishop James Hickey of Washington, D.C. Hickey and another 152 American bishops had endorsed the nuclear freeze.

> "His careful, organized campaign to focus the thoughts of his flock on the nuclear question distresses the administration. Hickey is not a radical as some of his brothers, including Bishop Leroy T. Matthiessen of Amarillo and Archbishop Raymond G. Hunthausen of Seattle who advocate a much more frontal attack on the defense budget. But his stated determination 'not to permit the moral and human dimensions of the nuclear policy to be neglected or ignored in the deliberations of experts and politicians' is another reminder that the administration's campaign to make Americans more afraid of the Soviets than of nuclear weapons has not been a total success even in an institution with impeccable anti-communist credentials."

The hierarchy of the Roman Catholic Church was giving "the peace movement respectability for which people only prayed before."[5]

About a month before the November 1982 meeting at which the bishops were scheduled to debate the second draft, Archbishop Hunthausen was in Detroit to deliver one of the many addresses on war and peace he was being called on to make around the nation. As the most prominent "peace" prelate among the U.S. bishops, he was in high demand and had to turn down far more invitations than he could accept. At the National Conference of Catholic Charities in Detroit, Michigan, he emphasized the link between disarmament and economic justice. "In King County, Washington State, 422 companies alone do approximately $1.9 billion worth of Defense Department business." He bemoaned the fact that the huge arms budget devoured revenue needed for basic human needs. Public officials and citizens alike should "give serious and immediate consideration in all matters to the common good, to the welfare of society as a whole."[6] Days later in St. Paul/Minneapolis he said this: "During the past months, there has been heard across this nation and the world a swelling sound that echoes from the depths of our common experience: the universal longing for peace.... I do not believe that we are the only nation in the world to cherish our homes, to love our children, to yearn for peace and to feel compassion for human misery."[7] In Baltimore, the day before all the American bishops debated the draft pastoral, he reflected on his own way of going about the search for truth: "Again, I do not speak as an expert, but as one person deeply troubled by events." Gandhi counseled that noncooperation with evil is as much a duty as cooperation with good, Hunthausen reminded his audience. Each person should probe their own conscience and decide what to do, but we should seek the support of the community as we do so, he believed. Here he was giving a good sense of not only his approach to moral reasoning, but more importantly, his approach to moral practice. Noncooperation with evil should not be just a series of isolated acts. Clearly he wanted to see what might be named "the Catholic peace tradition" move from the margins to the mainstream of official Catholic thought and action. "We are not called to one action but to a life of searching, a risky journey. Each risk taken will deepen the joy, but no risk is ever the last one."[8]

But Hunthausen and the bishops who thought and acted like he did would have to work on developing a pastoral letter with other prelates who were sure that the just war tradition should remain the Catholic moral framework for evaluating U.S. nuclear arms policy. Some influential prelates were especially concerned to maintain a strong deterrent. When the bishops gathered on November 15, 1982, Archbishop Hannan of New Orleans argued for greater sensitivity to the dangers of totalitarianism. "The pastoral letter is minimally concerned with the horrible suffering, physical and spiritual, of those enslaved by communism and other dictatorships which disregard human rights." Archbishop Quinn of San Francisco, on the other hand, made the case that "the present moment is new because concern for peace and opposition to nuclear arms is not any longer sporadic and selective but widespread and sustained." Philadelphia's Cardinal Krol emphasized "the right and duty of governments to protect their citizens against unjust aggression." Yet, there was nuance in this just war argument. Krol argued that weapons of massive destruction exceeded the moral limits of the right of self-defense because such weapons would inevitably kill vast numbers of non-combatants. Cardinal Cooke of New York worried that the peace pastoral letter had the potential "for seriously dividing our church and our nation."[9]

While bishops raised numerous concerns and argued their various positions, what became most decisive was the debate on nuclear deterrence. There was nuance because many of the bishops wanted to find a way to bring together the two ethical frames—the Catholic pacifist view and the Catholic just war view. A reference in the arguments of several bishops was made to the June 1982 statement by Pope John Paul II to the United Nations, of which a key passage found its way into the final version of the pastoral: "In current conditions 'deterrence' based on balance, certainly not as an end in itself but as a step on the way toward progressive disarmament, may still be judged morally acceptable."[10] Archbishop Hannan, who two decades earlier had played a "just warrior" role during the Second Vatican Council by influencing the language on matters of war and peace in the *Pastoral Constitution on the Church in the Modern World*, argued that the whole pastoral letter idea should be dropped. This was his reaction to the second draft. Bernardin navigated the pastoral drafting process between the edges. "We are keenly aware of how important it is that the bishops present in this pastoral a moral theory which is in conformity with the totality of the church's moral teaching, but we believe our conclusion is fundamentally correct and in accord with the judgment on deterrence expressed by Pope John Paul II."[11]

During the debate on the second draft, when Hunthausen tried to make his case before his colleagues, he said: "My brother bishops, Christ calls us to proclaim his Gospel.... To many, my message seems like foolishness, but to many others and to me it is simply the Gospel of Jesus Christ." He supported several aspects of the second draft, such as the grounding of the letter in theological reflection, the willingness to give greater visibility to pacifism and conscientious objection in Catholic thought, the condemnation of specific first-strike nuclear weapons, the prohibition against first-use policies, the clear rejection of the concept of a limited nuclear war, the endorsement of an immediate bilateral nuclear freeze, the encouragement of unilateral initiatives toward disarmament, and the strong call to people to reject any efforts to legitimate the idea of nuclear war. But he also spelled out his differences. The bishops ought to define the whole strategy of nuclear deterrence as "a root cause of the continuing arms race." He named what deterrence actually meant in the concrete reality of U.S. policy: "If we are to proclaim the Gospel we need to state more clearly that nuclear deterrence is idolatry; and that, far from deterring the evil of nuclear war, living out the rationale of deterrence is engaging in that evil." He believed that "the evil of nuclear war is not simply the tremendous destruction that would come with a nuclear exchange, but it is the millions of acts of cooperation which you and I and our people do today, that will make the nuclear holocaust a reality tomorrow."[12]

Hunthausen had come to a full-fledged rejection of the sort of moral reasoning that would accommodate U.S. nuclear weapons: "In our pastoral letter we need to state simply but forcibly that we accept the reality of Jesus Christ and the power of His cross.... This, I believe, is the only way we as bishops can proclaim the

Gospel of Christ. We stand under the cross because it is the only power which can confound the power of the world. It is the one power that is free from corruption, equally accessible to all people however humble, the one power that endures and the one that you and I must preach when convenient and inconvenient."[13] After the bishops' meeting to debate the second draft, Hunthausen was back out on the speaker circuit. In Pittsburgh, he recalled again Hiroshima: "That awful event and its successor at Nagasaki sank into my soul, as they have in fact sunk into the souls of all of us, whether we recognize it or not." He evoked Pope John XXIII's prophetic encyclical, *Pacem in Terris*, "Peace on Earth," stating true peace consists not in a balance of military power, but in mutual trust. Hunthausen drew inspiration from the late Trappist poet monk of Gethsemane, Kentucky, Thomas Merton, who wrote that violence derives from illusions about ourselves and our world. Hunthausen found wisdom in *The Human Journey*, where author Anthony Padovano interpreted Merton's insight about the notion of the enemy: "The enemy is not the other but the tendency in all of us to make the other different and to declare ourselves the norm and the center of human behavior."[14] Nonviolence was not a struggle so much against the other but much more of a struggle to recognize our own true selves, Hunthausen believed—and he asked not only individuals but the nation as a whole to recognize what we were doing by threatening to use nuclear weapons against the people of the Soviet Union. This was the all too alluring idol of false security, Hunthausen believed: making "the other" different, and worshipping our own nation as the norm and the center of the world.

Archbishop Philip Hannan, on the other hand, forcefully challenged some of the same aspects of the second draft which Hunthausen lauded. Where Hunthausen put the emphasis on the moral questions around nuclear deterrence, Hannan worried that the draft pastoral showed little concern for the horrible injustices of the communist system. When I was examining the archival records of Archbishop Hunthausen's involvement in the pastoral letter process, I spotted what must have been his personal copy of a periodical. At some point he probably read the December 4, 1982 issue of *Human Events*, featuring "This Week's News From Inside Washington," which included remarks Hannan had given at the bishops' meeting in November. In the lead into Hannan's remarks, the editors wrote: "Many believe the letter is a virtual call for America to disarm itself unilaterally."[15] One week later, *Human Events* published "Bishops' Letter Ignores How Nuclear Deterrence Works," by Michael Novak, and Hunthausen had a copy of this as well. With an outlook not unlike Hannan's, the Catholic liberal-turned-conservative Novak wrote:

> "Why have the bishops not seen that their present position entails unilateral disarmament? One presumes that they have not forced themselves to face it. The more thoroughly pacifist among them do grasp the logic, however. They celebrate this draft as the indispensable

> pillar of their ultimate goal: pacifist surrender before aggression, which they hold is to follow the example of Christ. (It is one thing for individuals to hold this view; another to impose it on a pluralist state.) Nowhere in the bishops' draft do the bishops voice the by now classical Christian arguments against pacifism. They list none of the Christian reasons for rejecting pacifism—theological arguments, moral arguments, and political arguments. They give pacifism a free ride."[16]

The Reagan administration, with the help of Catholic intellectuals like Novak, worked hard to try to influence the direction of the pastoral letter. What was happening with these bishops? This was the question posed in London's *The Guardian* article published as 1983 began. Big changes had taken place in the Catholic Church in America. "As immigrants who believed in a faith whose head was in Europe, American Catholics felt they had to prove themselves to be super patriots. For many years the American hierarchy was exceptionally conservative and rarely critical of Government policies." Cardinal Spellman personified this approach, noted *The Guardian*. "But the civil rights movement, the Vietnam war, the influence of Latin American priests, but especially Pope John XXIII and the Second Vatican Council calling on Catholics to play a more active part in promoting social justice changed the thinking of many in the new generation of priests and bishops." There were prelates, such as Cardinal Terence Cooke, Spellman's successor in New York, representing the traditional strong support for the military. Yet Cooke, not merely a carbon copy of Spellman, was struggling to find his way into some type of critical stand. The bishops had to grapple with moral questions in the midst of a massive arms buildup during those early years of Reagan's presidency. *The Guardian* story continued:

> "During the past two years while the bishops were drawing up their letter, the Reagan Administration, worried that it would help the peace movement and supporters of unilateral disarmament, tried to influence the bishops through such Administration Catholics as National Security Adviser William Clark, who argued that the bishops should take into account the US's efforts at disarmament and the Soviet Union's threatening arms build-up."

The Reagan administration "has supported the formation of an American Catholic Committee by a group of influential Catholic laymen opposed to the hierarchy's support of 'leftwing causes' in Latin America." The American Catholic Committee was formed to challenge the bishops on the peace issue as well as on Central America. These pro-Reagan thinkers were facing a Catholic hierarchy that had changed. "The older generation of bishops were more autocratic and often seemed to separate theology and politics too rigidly and to be more interested in real estate than in social concerns. The younger generation sometimes reflects a guilt complex that the Church was late in turning away from the hawkish Spellman line in Vietnam." Now bishops on the dovish end of the spectrum, Hunthausen foremost among them, faced the charge from the Right of being soft on communism.[17]

This charge of being soft on communism was made adamantly in January 1983 by John Hugh McGee, a retired brigadier general in the U.S. Army. He wrote from San Antonio, Texas, enclosing with his letter to Archbishop Hunthausen what he described as "A Politico-Military Message to American Catholic Bishops From A Conquered Defender of American Territory." Hunthausen and the American bishops should think about this, he wrote: "I act as spokesman for the other American members of my two small groups of defeated defenders of territory of the United States during World War II. Defeated defenders who all lost their lives in a conquest of American territory that was provoked by failure of the United States to provide 'deterrence' for a 'strongman' defense of our nation's Philippine Commonwealth territory. Today, history is seemingly repeating itself for me and for them, with the politico-military difference that the American territory proscribed by an aggressor is our Homeland."[18] McGee expressed "great concern of either a destroyed world or a conquered United States, resulting from possible action of a majority of bishops at the 1983 National Conference of American Bishops." He worried "that my Church's bishops, like the militant American pacifists of pre World War II, are disregarding the biblical and historical lessons of relative armament weakness against an avowed conqueror." Bishops may be "eminently qualified, and most desperately needed today," as spiritual leaders, but unfortunately they have presumed "a dismally unqualified politico-military leadership." He chastised Hunthausen for claiming that America's deterrent nuclear strength, not the evil of Marxism-Leninism, was the chief obstacle to true world peace.[19]

Even after rebuke after rebuke from angry Americans, Hunthausen moved forward. He was fortunate to have a strong support circle of colleagues across various faith communities in the region. In late February 1983, religious leaders of the Church Council of Greater Seattle met with twelve visitors from the Soviet Union and a dozen U.S. leaders who were in town for the February 25-March 2 US-USSR 'Leaders in Dialogue' gathering. Lutheran bishop A.G. "Gib" Fjellman sketched the peace action history of the group of Seattle area religious leaders. Archbishop Hunthausen said to their Soviet guests:

> "We come on this occasion to express to you our good will and our love for our brothers and sisters in the Soviet Union and all the countries of the world...to acknowledge our realization that love of family and country, and the fear and anguish caused by the ravages of war are human experiences shared by your own people and the people of all nations, and not the exclusive prerogative of Americans...and to express to you our profound hope that these conversations, however

brief and unofficial, will advance the cause for universal peace as we share our individual concerns and fears as children of the same God."[20]

At Seattle University in March 1983, just two months before the final version of *The Challenge of Peace* would be rolled out, Hunthausen reflected on his own struggle of conscience. This personal journey, he told the audience, "has not been without its moments of pain and dark nights of the soul." Prayer was guiding him through the debate on the peace pastoral, he told them. He talked about his own effort to personally respond to peace as "a commitment to a life of nonviolence, a way of living that comes from the very heart of the Gospel and has Jesus as its model."[21]

His struggle of conscience was not made any easier when a hand-written letter with "confidential" underlined at the top and dated March 13, 1983, arrived from Helena, Montana. Bishop Elden Curtiss, who had been appointed to the office Hunthausen left when he went to Seattle, penned his concerns about the commotion being stirred up as Hunthausen traveled about the country making speeches in the spirit of "Faith and Disarmament." Among other places, Hunthausen had been speaking in his native Montana. Imagine how reading this letter could affect its recipient:

> Dear Dutch,
>
> This is a personal note about a delicate matter I need to share with you. You know you are always welcome here. I want you to be free to accept any invitation to celebrate or speak you want to accept here. Besides your strong roots here, and family, and many friends, I have grown to respect and love you as a personal friend and fellow bishop.
>
> My problem is your recent talk in Bozeman which resulted in a news release which hit the papers around the state—with the emphasis on unilateral disarmament whatever the cost. Because you are the former Ordinary here and in a continued leadership role, your public statements are not treated like those of another visiting bishop or celebrity—they carry much more weight.
>
> Bishop Murphy called me about the news release and its implications for us. He and I have worked out a position which we think will be reflected in our national pastoral on peace—multilateral disarmament which places as much pressure on the Soviet Union as on our own government. This is the expressed position we have assumed as the leaders of the Church in Montana.
>
> We feel considerable tension about your public statement regarding disarmament—how to respond to it without discrediting you but at

the same time maintaining the integrity of our own position. We have both been called by the press since your news release was published.

I guess what I am saying, because of your leadership role in Montana, which continues to be strong (and this is not a criticism, believe me) your public statements about unilateral disarmament are problematic for Bishop Murphy and myself in terms of our roles as the local Ordinaries.

I hope you do not misread what I am saying—I support your role in the disarmament debate, and have done so publicly—I just do not feel comfortable with you being the spokesman for the Church on this issue in the diocese (state)—and Tom Murphy and I feel that in some ways this is what is happening.

I share these perceptions and feelings with you rather than ignore them—it's not my nature, as you know, to suppress negative things. Your relationship to the diocese and state, and your relationship with me, is too important to let tensions build up when they should be analyzed and discussed and resolved.

I'll respond in any way you think appropriate—whether we should meet or exchange correspondence about this matter. I do not want you to have any negative feelings or to feel unwelcome in any way in the diocese.

You have my continued support and prayerful best wishes, in the Lord,

Elden[22]

We do not know how Hunthausen responded to this letter from Curtiss, except to say that it did not cause Hunthausen to pull back from making his case for disarmament. On Tax Day, April 15, 1983, David Anderson, religion writer for United Press International, wrote "Conscience, defense and the income tax" with reference to Hunthausen's prior year announcement that he would do war tax resistance. Anderson described the tensions that could face participants in this type of civil disobedience: "Although tiny, the tax resistance movement underscores a growing awareness of the connection—or tension—between religious ethics and government policies.... Although for the individual, the dictates of conscience may be an absolute, maintenance of the social fabric has also posited the idea of 'compelling state interest' against untrammeled exercise of that conscience."[23] Standing at the three-way fork in the road of individual conscience, Catholic faith, and the national interest, Hunthausen believed that his conscientious war tax resistance and redirection action was in the true public interest—and was also true to the original Christian faith—but this did not therefore make things easy for "big tent" Catholic bishops such as Curtiss and Murphy. And when it came to the direction of the pastoral letter on war and peace by the collective body of U.S. bishops, Hunthausen and prelates of his outlook could expect push-back from some bishops in other corners of the country, not just Montana. The most consequential push-back, at least in terms of *The Challenge of Peace*, came in the thrust of the moral argument in the third draft.

When that draft was debated in the spring of 1983, Hunthausen commented on the positive spirit of the dialogue which marked the widely consultative process for which the peace pastoral letter was already gaining fame. The church, in this participatory dialogue, was becoming what the Second Vatican Council had envisioned, he remarked. But anticipating the May 1983 meeting in Chicago where the bishops would finalize the letter, he voiced his misgivings: "The root problem with our discussion of nuclear war and deterrence is that the distinction between the moral and political dimensions of these issues has become hopelessly muddled." In his estimation, the third draft obscured the Gospel basis for a clear stand. "We must return to the roots of our moral tradition and speak clearly, forcefully, without equivocation, to the moral dimension of these issues."[24]

Just prior to the meeting in early May, when the pastoral letter would be completed, the *Seattle Times* raised the question of whether the U.S. bishops, when they issued the third draft in March, had succumbed "to pressure from the White House, as many news reports suggested, by retreating from some of the stronger stands in the second draft?" The newspaper reminded its readers that President Lyndon Johnson once said, "As long as I've got the cardinals on my side, I don't care about the kids." The *Seattle Times*:

> "Now President Reagan is fighting for a trillion-dollar defense buildup that can only be achieved in the Cold War atmosphere of a new national consensus. In a speech to the National Association of Evangelicals earlier this year, he warned religious leaders against 'the temptation of pride—the temptation of blithely declaring yourselves above it all and label(ing) both sides equally at fault, to ignore the facts of history and the aggressive impulses of an evil empire, to simply call the arms race a giant misunderstanding and thereby remove yourself from the struggle between right and wrong and good and evil.'"

The bishops as a body had not only questioned nuclear policies but also Reagan's policy in Central America, making it clear that "they no longer can be counted on to back all things labeled anti-communist." They were no longer predictably in line with American government policy, but they were also not adopting the kinds of policies Hunthausen advocated on nuclear deterrence, although many bishops did agree with the stand he took on U.S. policy in Central America.[25] That stand will be reviewed shortly.

Seattle Times reporter Carol Ostrom, writing about Archbishop Hunthausen's role in the peace pastoral letter process, quoted Hunthausen's justice and peace director, Don Hopps: "In a very real sense, the archbishop here is something of the spiritual leader of the peace group within the circle of bishops.... I think he has the opportunity to assert a strong leadership role." And Ostrom described Hunthausen as "in many ways the antithesis of a political animal, appearing uncomfortable with the trappings and assumption of power." She also asked theologian-activist Jim Douglass what he thought might happen as the bishops gathered to decide on the pastoral letter. "The question is," said Douglass, "when they get to Chicago, which will they feel more strongly: the Holy Spirit or politics?"[26]

NOT CHAPLAINS TO THE REAGAN COURT

Amendments Hunthausen made during the period just before the final version was adopted, opposing nuclear deterrence, failed. Yet when asked about the pastoral letter at the end of the two-day meeting in Chicago, Hunthausen did not appear unhappy. The *Seattle Times* reported: "Although several proposals supported by Hunthausen failed—including one yesterday backing unilateral nuclear disarmament—he was pleased because dozens of amendments toughened language in the document." Hunthausen could imagine a direct confrontation between the bishops and the Reagan administration ahead. This was because the peace pastoral, in its final form, provided a *strictly conditioned* acceptance of deterrence policy. A defense based on the threat of using nuclear weapons was conditioned on efforts to reduce, and in time, eliminate nuclear arms—with urgency. "If we are going to be honest with the document, there are going to be some pretty gutsy confrontations in the next few years," Hunthausen said, noting how the Reagan administration at that time kept pushing for buildup rather than cutbacks.[27]

The pastoral letter did not call for unilateral nuclear disarmament, even though Hunthausen's prominence had brought that notion a great deal of publicity. Kenneth Briggs of the *New York Times* wrote that "some Catholics mistakenly believe that the pastoral letter calls for unilateral disarmament by the United States. For that reason, some material intended to help priests preach on the subject stresses the need to emphasize that the pastoral letter explicitly rejects that idea, and calls for a negotiated disarmament by both the United States and the Soviet Union." Don Hopps, who would help Hunthausen move *The Challenge of Peace* into dialogue processes in the parishes of Western Washington, described for Briggs the region's situation: "The nuclear issue hits people in the pocketbook here. The issues have been debated here for some time, so the positions of lay people on the pastoral letter tend to be more polarized in Seattle than in many places."[28]

Indeed, however polarized the nuclear issue may have been, Hunthausen made the most of the new peace pastoral. At a press conference on May 5, 1983, he introduced plans for a two-year pastoral letter study process in parishes all over the region. Bill Cate announced that the ecumenical community would participate in grassroots programs in the congregations as a broad endeavor to study and debate the Catholic letter. During the press conference, Hunthausen dodged a question that had also been posed to his colleague Joseph Bernardin, by then named Chicago's cardinal—whether President Truman would have ordered the atomic bombing of Hiroshima and Nagasaki if he had relied on the pastoral letter. Bernardin would not speculate, and nor would Hunthausen. "I can understand why Cardinal Bernardin didn't answer the question. I think you are going to have to meet President Truman in heaven to find out the answer." He added, "I'm definitely in support of what the pastoral is saying, but the pastoral clearly gives us the right to speak out in a direction that may be interpreted as going beyond it."[29] Hunthausen himself clearly was going beyond the letter, but in launching the two-year pastoral letter study process he was simply trying to encourage more dialogue. He was never comfortable being the center of attention, so the point was not to dwell on his own stand. He made it clear he wanted the dialogue and debate prompted by the pastoral letter to be a widely participatory process.[30]

Bishop Thomas Gumbleton was a major force in the peace pastoral, although, like Hunthausen and other nuclear disarmament-minded bishops, he did not prevail in the letter's chief argument. Cardinal John Dearden was responsible for Gumbleton's appointment as an auxiliary bishop in Detroit in 1968. At that time Gumbleton told Dearden, "Your eminence, this is a great honor, but I'm not sure I can be a bishop in the way I understand bishops are supposed to be." Dearden's response was, "Tom, you have to assume they knew what they were doing when they made you a bishop, and just be yourself." Hunthausen and Gumbleton hardly fit the conventional expectations for Catholic hierarchs, although that convention itself was "shape-shifting" since many bishops wrestled not only with how best to govern the life of the local church but also how best to clarify the differences, as well as the continuities, between the just war and nonviolence ethics of their complex Catholic heritage. Archbishop Maurice Dingman of Des Moines, just a few days after the passage of the pastoral letter, spoke about U.S. policy and the bishops' call for a reversal in the arms buildup. "If they haven't done it in three years, we'll go the Hunthausen route," he said. "We'll tell our people to quit paying their taxes and to quit their jobs in the defense industry." Archbishop Francis Hurley of Anchorage acknowledged Hunthausen's impact. "I don't agree with Dutch on all the issues," he said. "But he made me think about them. He is our teacher." Hunthausen,

Gumbleton, and other Pax Christi bishops may not have won the central argument in the letter's debate, but they certainly helped Cardinal Bernardin steer the letter away from moral approbation of the prevailing national policies. George Kennan, recognized as the dean of U.S. foreign policy throughout much of the Cold War era, commenting in the *New York Times*, called *The Challenge of Peace* "the most profound and searching inquiry yet conducted by any responsible collective body into the relations of nuclear weaponry, and indeed modern war in general, to moral philosophy, to politics and to the conscience of the national state."[31]

If Bernardin could look to colleagues such as Hunthausen to help keep the letter from edging toward any tacit approval of the Reagan administration's nuclear arms buildup or its de facto first-strike policy, he had to keep his eye on Rome all the while. This is not to suggest that the Vatican outlook was consonant with the Reagan administration. After the peace pastoral was accomplished, the *Seattle Times* reported that Pope John Paul II had told Cardinal Bernardin and three other U.S. church officials in a meeting in Rome back in January that he had concerns about the letter when it was still in its second draft stage, the version Hunthausen and other Pax Christi bishops had found more agreeable. John Paul wanted hierarchies around the world to be on the same page. He had in mind the American, West German, and French bishops. While U.S. bishops were edging toward a "no first-strike" doctrine and, in fact, achieved it in the pastoral letter, the West German bishops were concerned about NATO's need to retain the threat of nuclear retaliation to ward off the potential of an invasion by Warsaw Pact conventional forces. Though the distinction between principles and their application had been noted from the beginning of the drafting process, the pope wanted to strongly emphasize this distinction. The bishops must not give the impression that the church supports nuclear pacifism—and unilateral nuclear disarmament—as public policy. The superpowers needed to negotiate. The pope's expressed concerns were addressed in changes in the draft of the letter.[32] Yet in its final form, *The Challenge of Peace* certainly did not give *carte blanche* to the Reagan administration.

To the *Washington Post*'s Colman McCarthy, examining the third draft, it looked as though the bishops were going to "behave as proper chaplains to the Reagan court," but instead, the final version, *The Challenge of Peace: God's Promise and Our Response*, questioned the Reagan administration at a time when the administration was "turning up the heat for still greater military excesses." Nevertheless, McCarthy thought *The Challenge of Peace* would now face its own big challenges:

> "For the bishops, the hard part of their peacemaking now begins. The media, having reported the stunning conversion of a hierarchy that was pro-war in the '60s under Cardinal Spellman to being anti-nukes in the '80s under Cardinal Bernardin, aren't likely to be fascinated by the slow progress, if any, the bishops make in getting their pastoral letter into the

> heads of their flocks. Misunderstandings already have occurred in places like Seattle, where the tax-resisting archbishop, Raymond Hunthausen, is depicted falsely by some as a traitor to the flag. The bishops' bind is that they can't force their letter on the faithful as if it were official church teaching, nor can they walk away quietly and let the government conclude that the pastoral was all talk. How, then, to build a genuine peace church?"

He sounded like Hunthausen when the columnist wrote: "The origins of their religion are in nonviolence and peaceful resistance." McCarthy may have been more enthusiastic about the future than Hunthausen when in the next line he added: "The pastoral letter is the beginning of a return to the original creed."[33]

CALLED AS A CHARACTER WITNESS IN THE CASE OF WORLD CITIZENSHIP

A pastoral letter could never be a substitute for prophetic action. That same May 1983, Hunthausen served as a character witness at the trials of several people arrested for nonviolent actions at the Trident base Bangor. They had opposed the deployment of the Trident submarine and its first-strike missile system. Hunthausen drew on the Nuremberg principles, positing the responsibility of individuals to dissent from laws when these are superseded by international law, specifically when a government engages in crimes against humanity: "It is my understanding that, in their defense, the protesters not only cite the principle that the claims of conscience are superior to the claims of civil law; but also the principle that we owe allegiance to all the human family which goes beyond loyalty to the nation state." He placed his thoughts on civil law in the context of personal conscience and the common good. "Catholic social teaching holds that the authority in which law is founded emanates from God and has as its object the common good." Legitimately established civil laws cannot be treated lightly, he argued, but both divine law and international law must be recognized. "I see the Trident protesters as acting on their world citizenship."[34] They helped inspire his shift of consciousness. "I know for myself—and I believe for a great many others besides—this transformation owes a great deal to the revelations that have been given to us through the courage and conviction of those who have chosen to brave the strictures of lesser law to witness nonviolently to the truth." When Hunthausen gave this testimony in a secular courtroom it happened to be the liturgical week of Pentecost. "Together, we pray that the transforming power of the Spirit again comes to us, and that we will be open, and God will renew the face of the Earth."[35]

Another trial was underway at Kitsap County Superior Court. In Port Orchard, Washington, five people were facing possible prosecution for their attempt to block a train that carried nuclear warheads to the base at Bangor. According to United Press International's Joni Balter, the jury was deliberating after hearing testimony, including that of Archbishop Hunthausen. Balter quoted Hunthausen: "I have to say I'm saddened at the whole notion of breaking the law.... I would not advocate it as a normal procedure but I personally feel there is a higher law. One must be responsible to his or her own conscience." One defendant in the case, Jeanne Clark, a Dominican nun, had called Hunthausen as a witness. "Part of my defense is why I was there," she said. "My deepest commitment is as a Christian." Sr. Clark asked Hunthausen to explain the moral foundation in support of conscientious civil disobedience. He responded that non-violent civil disobedience may be valid when, based on prayerful examination of one's conscience, a person feels that they must be responsible to God.[36]

Reporter Carol Ostrom covered the trial of the three defendants, Shelley Douglass, co-founder of Ground Zero Center for Nonviolent Action, Sr. Mary Grondin, teacher and member of the Sisters of Providence, and Karol Schulkin, also of Ground Zero, who had walked into Bangor Trident Submarine Base on Ash Wednesday, February 16, 1983. The defendants were found guilty; Schulkin and Grondin charged with trespassing, and Douglass charged with re-entering government property. Hunthausen testified that civil disobedience such as these people had enacted was part of what had pushed him to make public his views about the nuclear arms race. "I truly believe society owes them a debt of gratitude.... I can't help but believe that these actions have helped bring people to greater awareness."[37] At about the same time the five men and women were found guilty in Kitsap County Superior Court for trying to stop that Bangor-bound train thought to be loaded with nuclear warheads.

After testifying at both trials, Hunthausen came to a forum in support of all of the defendants, and said this: "The virtue of patriotism means that as citizens we respect and honor our country.... But our very love and loyalty makes us examine carefully and regularly its role in world affairs, asking that it live up to its full potential as an agent of peace with justice for all people." It had not been easy for him to accept the validity of civil disobedience, given that Catholics have a long tradition of obeying the law, but, he said, "We must accept responsibility for the rights and obligations that the new reality of nuclear arms and the threat of worldwide annihilation imposes." He cited from paragraph #231 of the new peace pastoral letter: "The relationship of the authority of the state and the conscience of the individual on matters of war and peace takes a new urgency in the face of the destructive nature of modern war."[38]

In early June 1983, the two-year study and discussion of the peace pastoral letter commenced. At the kickoff held at Camp Cabrini near Issaquah, Hunthausen told the assembly: "We must put aside that combination of naiveté and complacency that allows Congress to think that they can pass the freeze resolution one month and fund the MX missile the next, and that somehow we will not notice." He called on the group of some 80 people at this initial session to make citizen mobilization a priority.[39] The Dialogue for Peace with Justice Program, initiated through the Catholic justice and peace center, became a broad ecumenical enterprise.[40]

Within a year, over 40,000 people across several Christian denominations had participated in the process—35,000 in the Dialogue survey, and 5000 in the series of five discussions that went into the issues in greater depth. Don Hopps summarized the results of the May 1984 interim report on the peace pastoral Dialogue Project:

> "It is clear from this material that the great majority of the people involved in the dialogue process do not see our world as a bi-polar world. The dialogue explicitly rejects the notion our world can be defined in terms of the conflict between the Soviet Union and the United States. Instead, the participants express a wide-spread and profound concern for the third world. Second, the dialogue sees the roots of conflict in the present inequities which press down on the third world; it sees our policy toward the third world as determining whether that conflict will grow.... There is overwhelming support for a bi-lateral nuclear freeze.... There is a very strong sense that we must end our military involvement in the third world.... There was a strong feeling that we cannot discount the Soviet threat. There was agreement that the militarization of the third world and the prevalence of injustice there ultimately serve the cause of the Soviets. The dialogue thus rejected disarmament as a solution, as an end in itself. The dialogue saw the pursuit of peace as much more complex; it saw disarmament as being more a result than a cause of peace. In the end, there was a strong feeling, expressed by most, that peace begins with the creation of a spiritual force."[41]

The Dialogue discussions on disarmament—that disarmament ought not to be viewed as an end in itself—need to be stressed. Indeed, it would be a mistake to reduce Raymond Hunthausen's full view of peace simply to disarmament. As in the "Faith and Disarmament" address, he continually linked his personal path of religious conscience and his call for disarmament to a constructive public vision of social justice as democratic participation involving the redistribution of power and wealth. In short, his call to conscience was simultaneously a call to the common good.

In the spirit of the common good, he met with Seattle's Rotary Club in July 1983. Someone described it as an appearance akin to Ralph Nader before the board of General Motors. "More than 400 men in suits sat quietly at lunch yesterday, amid remnants of sirloins and seafood salads," wrote Carol Ostrom, reporting on the talk and the question and answer session. A veteran of World Wars I and II asked, "Do you think we should approach Russia from a standpoint of weakness?" Hunthausen responded that "it depends on what you mean by weakness. I think we're living in an age where if we don't take cognizance of the nature of the weapon there will be no winners. And I sometimes wonder whether that which we identify as weakness isn't really strength." He truly hoped that the leaders of the two nations would meet, even to share lunch together once a week. "I am convinced that until and unless we get to know and respect one another as people, there will not be an opportunity to get away from this sense of hostility." But if a mutual verification of disarmament could not be reached, "someone has to take a radical step," he said, and the United States should take that step.[42] After the meeting was reported in the *Seattle Times*, one letter writer to the editor evaluated the archbishop this way:

> "I can't thank you enough for writing the article on Archbishop Raymond Hunthausen as seen through Rotarian eyes! How could that man urge people to adopt his dangerous views? To practically overthrow our government, and have a flowered pathway made for Russia's grand entry into our world. I think the pope should have ordered him into exile for creating such a disruptive element in Seattle's life, as well as outside towns."[43]

Missing from this harsh rhetoric was any acknowledgement of Hunthausen's argument that unilateral initiatives might well stimulate constructive dialogue between the two superpowers in search of the international common good.

In September that same year Henry "Scoop" Jackson, a member of the U.S. Senate since 1953, passed away. "He gained a national and international reputation for his stinging criticisms of the Soviet Union. He continually warned that the Soviets were aggressively seeking to expand their sphere of influence and domination," wrote Dean Katz for the *Seattle Times*. Because of his linchpin support for defense contracts in the region, Jackson was known as "the Senator from Boeing."[44] Jackson took the same stand during the Vietnam War that Hunthausen's predecessor, Archbishop Connolly, had taken, advocating the bombing of North Vietnam. Jackson was a chief architect of the Pacific Northwest military-industrial powerhouse that Hunthausen and the region's peace movement sought to dismantle.

In late autumn 1983, Hunthausen was on the University of Washington campus, having just watched *The Day After*, a film starkly imagining the consequences of nuclear war. With this heightened sense of immediacy, this horrific picture of the planet or of a city in the aftermath of a nuclear conflagration, he asked the Kane Hall audience, "Are we willing—individually and collectively—to forego the use of violence as an answer to human problems...any violence, violence of any kind?" The peace pastoral letter, he said, moved away from a numbed collective acceptance of violence. Yet the letter, alas, reinforced the notion of nonviolence only as a personal stance. It was as if the ethic of nonviolence had heroic merit for individuals seeking the counsels of perfection. What was missing from *The Challenge of Peace* was a serious argument showing how the just war principle of defense of the common good could be reframed and transformed into a practical and efficacious policy of collective training in nonviolence as a force for the common good and as a means of collective security. The pastoral letter ought to have given greater consideration to the role active nonviolence could play as central to public policy—to the collective life of a society, not just the conscience of the individual.[45]

What was so clear in his thinking, yet could be missed when all the media attention focused on his provocative talk of unilateral disarmament, was the idea that disarmament steps must go hand in hand with an active endeavor to shape the good in common. This would in turn make genuine security more likely. Just as war-preparations and war-making stole from the poor and secured a system of gross inequality, disarmament steps and active peacemaking could win what had been ironically dubbed in the 1960s, "the war on poverty". Hunthausen joined with other Church Council of Greater Seattle leaders in late December 1983, announcing their plans to create a 10-part statement on foreign policy. A principal purpose was to link the arms race and the challenge of hunger and poverty. The plan was to move the issue out into local congregations and community groups for discussion to stimulate grassroots reflection and action. "It's a question of the rich nations being more willing to respond to the needs of the poorer nations," Hunthausen said. "Maybe we are in the arms race to protect that which we treasure so much—our lifestyle."[46]

CONSCIENCE IN THE MARKETPLACE—AND ON THE TRAIN TRACKS

At First Congregational Church in Vancouver, Washington, in the first month of 1984, Hunthausen spoke to an issue of poignancy not only in the context of the peace pastoral letter, but also in relation to Rome's investigation of his leadership. That investigation, the subject of the next chapters in this book, was well underway. He addressed the symptoms of divisiveness and raised the issue of whether the peace pastoral had become a factor. A greater value than unity is the search for clear and truthful stands on issues affecting humanity, he argued. As to the role of the ecumenical religious community in the relatively "unchurched" Northwest region, the religious community "has redefined the proper role of the churches and religious leaders as the voices of conscience in the marketplace." We are called "to fully accept the role of moral leadership into which we have been cast—or, perhaps, more accurately, have cast ourselves—for <u>more</u> than just a <u>moment</u>, on <u>more</u> than just a <u>solitary</u> issue."[47] (Emphasis in the original text)

The great challenge, felt Hunthausen, was to honor the central message of the Gospel. In February 1984, he spoke directly to its relationship to the peace pastoral.

"The pastoral letter has added nothing to the Gospel but it has put the challenge of the Gospel where it belongs—at the center of our lives in an age of holocaust."[48] There was a song then that remains a staple of hope even today, and it arose from the brilliantly talented Cat Stevens, who later converted to Islam and took the name Yusuf Islam. He called it "Peace Train." It was a song contagious with spirit and goodwill. Many, figuratively speaking, jumped aboard the peace train in that era and it is true that the peace movement was sounding louder; but meanwhile, the United States was literally loading nuclear warheads onto trains and shipping these instruments of mass destruction across the nation.

In late February 1984, a dozen Catholic bishops called on the people in their churches to join in a "prayer vigil" along the route where these trains were carrying nuclear warheads on their way to submarine bases. The story made the *New York Times*. The bishops encouraged nonviolent protest against these shipments along the routes from Amarillo, Texas. After trigger installation at the Pantex plant in Amarillo, nuclear weapons were being delivered to Charleston Naval Weapons Station in South Carolina, later to Kings Bay Submarine Base near St. Mary's, Georgia, and to Bangor, Washington, where the weapons would be placed on submarines. The bishops announced: "Our stand in the pastoral letter is that no further deployment of nuclear weapons can possibly be justified. Every missile and nuclear weapons shipment is both a significant step toward a first-strike holocaust and a violation of the moral stand we have taken, with the support of many other U.S. citizens, especially people of faith. What we can do along the tracks when these shipments come through is stand in prayerful witness to the alternative power of divine love and nonviolent action." There were other bishops whose dioceses included portions of the train routes and who were asked to sign the statement but declined. The Ground Zero Center for Nonviolent Action, based at Bangor, took the lead in organizing the trackside vigils just as it had helped to "spearhead" the attempted peaceful blockade of the first Trident submarine.[49]

The bishops' collective statement announcing the "prayer vigil" along the path of the white-painted freight train included these words: "We are Catholic bishops whose dioceses are along the route taken by missile parts and nuclear warheads shipped by rail.... We believe that a further escalation of the arms race by the shipment and deployment of such weapons is in violation of international law, the Gospel of Jesus Christ, and the teaching of our pastoral letter, *The Challenge of Peace*." They supported the Agape Community, a nonviolent community living along the tracks. "Since 1981 the Agape Community has sought the transforming power of love through a nonviolent campaign of education, prayer vigils, and civil disobedience in response to these missiles and warhead shipments. Our teaching responsibility and the location of our dioceses along these tracks make it imperative for us to join with this community in its campaign."[50] Hunthausen called upon the people of his archdiocese to weigh prayerfully the moral significance of the white train reality and the vigils. He said, "We will join in the Agape Community's prayer vigils when missile and nuclear warhead shipments pass our locations. We will also sponsor or join in a prayer vigil to be held at many sites along the tracks on Peace Pentecost, Sunday, June 10, 1984."[51]

In June 1984, at about the mid-point in the two year dialogue process on *The Challenge of Peace*, Hunthausen participated in a symposium on "Shaping a Peaceful World: Practical Ways of Implementing the Peace Pastoral," at St. Martin's College in Lacey, Washington. He made explicit his criticism of the dominant moral theory in official Catholic thought on war and peace. "The Just War theory provides good answers to what we can or cannot do in difficult situations. As a minimum standard to guide moral decision-making, it is more than adequate. But Christianity is not, ultimately, about moral standards. As the poet Blake once pointed out—'If morality was Christianty, Socrates was the Savior.' Christianity is about a transforming liberation, the building of peace with justice." The just war theory provided good answers to the wrong questions. He continued:

> "*The Challenge of Peace* effectively cut away any moral defense for the use of nuclear weapons. It clearly and forcefully exposed the moral bankruptcy of violence. But, it failed to come to grips with the moral bankruptcy of the policy of deterrence and the prevailing theory of peace, the balance of power. Our ethical theory worked to show that we have gone far beyond the limits of morality in contemplating nuclear war; but it could not provide us direction in criticizing our current approach to guaranteeing peace."[52]

The bishops in *The Challenge of Peace* spelled out the just war theory's central premise, which St. Augustine put forth some seventeen hundred years earlier. The quotation from the pastoral itself: "In his view war was both the result of sin and a tragic remedy for sin in the life of political societies. War arose from disordered ambitions, but it could also be used, in some cases at least, to restrain evil and protect the innocent. The classic case, which illustrated his view, was the use of lethal force to prevent aggression against innocent victims. Faced with the fact of attack on the innocent, the presumption that we do no harm, even to our enemy, yielded to the command of love understood as the need to restrain an enemy who would injure the innocent."[53] The presumption would always be for peace but in some situations war would be necessary. If so, criteria for determining whether or not war could be morally justified would include just cause, competent authority, comparative justice, right intention, last resort, probability of success, and proportionality. The bishops grappled with the crucial question of whether just war criteria could really have application in the context of nuclear war. Foremost among their concerns would have to be proportionality—could the damage inflicted and the costs incurred by war be proportionate to the good that would come from going to war?

Hunthausen called for a return to a Christian vision before the time of the emperor Constantine. "In the first three centuries of our Christian history, Christianity spread because the Christian community—though powerless—exemplified the Gospel message of peace with justice. Christian communities were models of nonviolent resistance. Through them Christianity penetrated the consciousness of their age, and worked history's greatest and most lasting change." What could the original Christian witness mean for us today?

> "This will require us, first, to become what we want the world to be. The Christian revolution—unlike any other—works it change from the heart outward. The revolution is a movement of communion—incorporating many diverse and unique parts into community. But before we can attain this communion, we must practice reconciliation. We must become a reconciling Church. As our first centuries demonstrated, it is the very process of being Christian which will create the change we seek."

Peace in the world would require real change in the life of the church itself. "As a Church, we must dismantle those structures which do violence and replace them with processes which affirm us in our differences as they bring us together in our common bonds.... As a Church, we must give power to the powerless and voice to the voiceless, so that all the parts of the body, equally honored, can fulfill their mission with confidence."[54] He voiced these ideas during the very time when Pope John Paul II and Cardinal Joseph Ratzinger were questioning his way of being a bishop. As a Vatican II bishop, Hunthausen took seriously Pope Paul VI's dictum, "If you want peace, work for justice." In his spirit, thought, and practice, Hunthausen emphasized the inextricable relationship between justice and peace—in society, to be sure, but also in the church.[55] John Paul II made many eloquent arguments in support of justice in society, but his model of church governance was another story. Hunthausen may have gotten into trouble with Rome partly because in many ways he put into practice this notion: if you want peace, work for justice in society and in the church.

In late September 1984, Archbishop Hunthausen, Bishop William Skylstad of Yakima, and Bishop Lawrence Welsh of Spokane were at a public forum just a few miles away from the Hanford nuclear reservation. Hanford began as a vital link in the Manhattan Project, processing the plutonium used in the bomb dropped on Nagasaki. "We each are faced with these moral decisions and we cannot escape the fact that many of the people here are involved in the nuclear-defense industry," Hunthausen said. "My deepest pastoral concern goes out for people and communities who must grapple with these moral concerns." The arms race was the most serious spiritual crisis facing the world. "We must reject any preparation on the part of any nation for the ultimate holocaust. The very existence of the human spirit is at stake. The decisions we are faced with are very urgent." He and his two bishop colleagues were challenged by some audience members as naïve about the motivations of the Soviet Union. Hunthausen responded. "The greatest evil is not that we may be destroyed, but our willingness to destroy. I'm not ready to say what the bishops would do if disarmament does not materialize, but we have an awesome responsibility to take some radical steps. We must make ourselves vulnerable in hopes other countries will follow. Those kinds of radical steps must be taken."[56]

Hanford, on the Columbia River near a relatively modest-sized population, was a powerful symbol of the U.S. nuclear-industrial complex, yet much of the peace movement energy in the region continued to focus on Bangor—located much closer to a large metropolitan area. According to Wallace Turner, writing for the *New York Times* in February 1985, if the base at Bangor was a central symbol in the antiwar efforts, it also was a symbol of the power of U.S. policy despite the protests. "It symbolized the fact that, despite all the protests, lawsuits, fence-climbing into forbidden areas, attempts to stop trains and jail demonstrators, the Navy had built, equipped and was bringing to full operation its base on Puget Sound for submarines armed with Trident missiles."[57] This all happened despite what Hunthausen and so many other people had done to stop what Trident represented.

Hunthausen faced pressures from many quarters. He tried to balance the call of personal conscience with his responsibilities as the symbol of unity. As an official religious leader, the stand he took could potentially be more influential than if he were not in such a role. But the call of personal conscience, even though it was intended to further the common good, could often collide with the desire for unity. Hunthausen knew this. This was made clear by how Hunthausen handled the matter of his war tax resistance, as reported in a United Press International story in early January 1985: "Hunthausen said he told the church to cooperate with the IRS's demand for wage garnishing because if it did not the federal agency could take action against the church as his employer. He said that as a person to whom the material goods of the archdiocese had been entrusted, he felt he had an obligation to 'always seek to represent the overall interest and concerns of the people of the archdiocese.'"[58]

On October 25, 1986, the Associated Press reported on a Friday night ecumenical service in Seattle billed as "Deadly Cost and Lively Resistance," with speakers including Hunthausen and Bishop Michael Kenny of Juneau, Alaska. Kenny said he had come to Seattle to join Hunthausen and other peace activists "in demonstration against the arrival earlier this month of the USS Alaska, the latest Trident submarine to join the fleet at Bangor." Hunthausen told the crowd,

"Isn't it so, so hard to think of the arms race and the USS Alaska and all that it means? We don't want to think about it. It's too horrible. It's too beyond us. Yet we have to think about it, because we have a responsibility to each other and to our world." According to the AP report, "many people at the packed service sported buttons that read 'I love Hunthausen.'" By that time, autumn of 1986, it was widely known that Hunthausen had been "stripped of some of his authority over church matters by the Vatican," and in an act of collective solidarity the crowd gave him a standing ovation. Cardinal Joseph Bernardin of Chicago had said just one week earlier that this action against Hunthausen by the Vatican was causing an "extreme negative reaction" affecting morale among Catholics. One could surmise from what happened at the Central Lutheran Church that evening that in fact, Catholics and other people who supported Hunthausen were more energized than ever, rather than having their morale dampened.[59]

Hunthausen often said that his own nonviolent actions came out of tough grappling with questions of conscience. Others might have been inspired by his actions, but, he said, "It makes me feel a little uncomfortable because I certainly haven't provided them with answers. But what they're saying is that it got them wondering and thinking and moving. Not that they are totally in command of all the answers either. But it seems to me that they are struggling with what life is all about."[60] What was the struggle like for him? "There isn't any question about my commitment to the concept of nonviolence. Do I live it out? There are so many moments in my life when I stop and question and wonder, when I am forced to discern."[61] In this vein, he struggled with discernment on the issue of abortion. "Abortion is a product of the tensions and injustices of a patriarchal society. It is often reduced to a 'woman's' problem by men who will not take responsibility for their sexual activity nor for the ongoing nurturing and development of their children, as well as for their financial support."[62] Hunthausen linked the sanctity of human life to concern for economic justice. At a "Mass for Life" liturgy at St. James Cathedral in 1988 he avoided a narrow agenda. "A respect for life demands that we do everything to preserve life from the moment of conception to the moment of natural death. But if we are to take our relationship to others seriously, as the Word of God asks us to do, then our respect for life must include a commitment to eradicate all the contradictions of life present in our society today."[63]

It cannot be overstated how deeply Hunthausen rejected any moral support for nuclear deterrence. When he made an April 1986 speech on "Peace and Pastoral Ministry" at St. Meinrad's Seminary in Indiana, he drew a relationship between nuclear deterrence and the disregard for the spirit of law among nations. Deterrence is based on "the assumption of an international order without rules, a stage on which a depraved human nature is free to pursue self-interest without care or scruple." Deterrence reinforces a culture of violence. "We soon become the very kind of people—self-centered, manipulative, fickle and violent—which we assumed the world was peopled with when we began to build the nuclear tower of Babel." Nonviolence could play an active role in "helping to reverse the policies and cultural attitudes which lock us into the use of violence as an acceptable solution to human problems." He saw a collective dimension to conscience. "Having examined our individual consciences on the place of violence in our lives, we must examine our collective conscience and the place violence inhabits in the policies and activities of our nation, and the daily lives of our people."[64] One thing Hunthausen had made clear in his own mind was that the continued reliance on a deterrence ethic and strategy would simply justify more investment in nuclear weapons, and this would mean less investment in economic justice.

I once asked Archbishop Hunthausen about the peace pastoral letter, which, by the late 1980s, no longer seemed to be what many originally hoped it would be. "Today, one of the most discouraging things is that we do not ever talk about discontinuing the manufacture and research of deadly weapons. We make agreements but we keep researching and manufacturing them. We as bishops could have put a condition. The manufacture of these weapons must cease."[65] At the Pax Christi national assembly in Chicago on July 31, 1987, Hunthausen worried about this lack of a definitive stand in the peace pastoral and the continuing pattern of military research and manufacturing of weaponry. "In my view, we are rapidly approaching the point where our courageous pastoral letter will no longer be seen as the challenge it was meant to be; it will become, instead, the nuclear equivalent of a blank check. Should this happen, I would regard it as a deeply tragic conclusion to the peace pastoral."[66] He asked, "How can we as Christians become a prophetic, reconciling community in response to our world-destructive violence? How can we at this critical moment in history be converted more deeply to that transforming, nonviolent vision of our Lord?"

He was at the point in his annual schedule, August, "where I always take a month away from my office in order to go fishing in the mountains and just be at peace in God's creation." A week later he would be, he told them, where he would like to be at that moment, "wading in a stream in what feels like the heart of creation, rather than grappling again with our inconceivable evil of preparing to destroy creation." But if we are going to retreat to God's creation for sustenance, he said, we must also defend creation "in God's name and grace, in that world where our own greed, irresponsibility, and violence have brought on this ultimate crisis." The long years of work by Pax Christi, the Catholic Worker, and other peace activists paved the way, he said, for the Catholic Bishops' peace pastoral letter issued four years earlier. That pastoral letter was prophetic in some ways, though its conditioned acceptance of nuclear deterrence was not something he could accept. Back in the 1976 U.S. Bishops' prior pastoral letter, *To Live in Christ*

Jesus, the moral unacceptability of deterrence was stated clearly, he noted. It stated, "As possessors of a vast nuclear arsenal, we must also be aware that not only is it wrong to attack civilian populations, but it is also wrong to threaten to attack them as part of a strategy of deterrence." This quotation from the 1976 pastoral was in the first two drafts of *The Challenge of Peace*, but was deleted from the final version for obvious reasons, he said. "How could we call something 'wrong' and 'morally acceptable' at the same time?" Even though he had voted for the 1983 pastoral letter, which included the strictly conditioned moral acceptability of deterrence, he felt "compelled at this moment to wonder out loud whether perhaps we weren't right the first time."[67] Bishop Thomas Gumbleton, reflecting back on that era, thinks Archbishop Hunthausen saw the situation correctly. The condition for a transitional acceptance of deterrence as a means to disarmament was never applied by the bishops to hold the U.S. government accountable.[68] Collectively the bishops hesitated to put real leverage into their conditional acceptance of nuclear deterrence.

CENTRAL AMERICAN CONCERNS

Archbishop Hunthausen, however, did not hesitate to speak unequivocally on the immorality of deterrence or on the immorality of U.S. conduct in Central America. What was going on with U.S. policy in Central America, of course, was closely associated with the Cold War issues shaping the nuclear debate. The Reagan administration's aggressive action in the region went hand in glove with its first-strike nuclear weapons buildup. Involvement in the regional proxy wars was part of an integrated national and international security strategy.

It was nearly the second anniversary of the death of El Salvador's Archbishop Oscar Romero on March 24, 1980, and the new Archdiocesan Justice and Peace Center was considering what approach to take. Don Hopps, the director, had been encouraged by some leaders within the local church, including his own supervisor in Catholic Charities, to help Hunthausen become a little more "politically savvy"—that is to say, to perhaps walk a more diplomatic or establishment-friendly path. According to these "shrewd" advisers, Hunthausen had gotten too close to "peace radicals" like Jim Douglass, and consequently took stands that were not always politically astute. So at a meeting with Hunthausen, Hopps was beginning to lay out a detailed description of Central American issues. The plan was to give the archbishop a 'policy backgrounder' about El Salvador and what the church should do about the situation there, especially given the Reagan administration's role supporting the oppressive regime. "When I started to give my speech, he let me go for about three or four sentences and then looked at me and said, 'Don, what do you think is the right thing to do?' And I just thought, whoa, because he was putting me on the line. So I said, 'I think the right thing, Archbishop, is we need to take a stand on this.' He said, 'fine, that's what we're going to do, go for it, do it.'" Hopps had decided not to buy into the advice he had been given to help Hunthausen become more politically savvy. He and Hunthausen shared a call to conscience. Hunthausen trusted Hopps to make the right decision, and this gave Hopps courage. This archbishop did not pay attention to what would or would not wash politically.[69]

In the early 1980s, Hopps also chaired the newly formed Seattle Commission on Central America. In 1983 they drafted a city initiative—like Madison, Wisconsin and Cambridge, Massachusetts had done—critical of U.S. Central America policy. They wanted to do something different rather than just a quick initiative statement. Seattle could be the first big city with a public vote on the issue. This took place a couple of years after there had already been large annual Romero processions. "We wanted a public vote on the initiative before it went to the city council. We asked for funding for a Seattle Commission on Central America. The city of Seattle was the only city that ever had a vote on U.S. foreign policy in Central America and we established the Commission on Central America." Patsy Collins, who had many connections with King TV and the Bullitt-funded media conglomerate, had lots of awareness regarding U.S. covert actions. Patsy Collins told Hopps, when he was chairing the commission, that there was a Central Intelligence Agency guy who wanted to meet with them off the record, to give them the lowdown on the situation in Central America. She arranged for the meeting. Hopps remembers the CIA guy "told us that the Roman Catholic Church in El Salvador and Guatemala was linked to the armed rebellion, that these groups were getting funds from the Soviets, that there are a lot of these people we consider dangerous and we are going to eliminate them. He told us that we were being used, that we needed to realize that the Soviets were serious about all this. The Sandinistas, the CIA person told us, are not supported by the people." The CIA person was surprisingly frank and honest about U.S. involvement with torture, assassinations, and attacks on ordinary people in the wrong places, although he did not use the term "collateral damage." He told Hopps that the Jesuits and other clergy were at least collaborators and, thus, legitimate targets. They were communists in clerics. "This was odd," because "he and another person with him were giving us information that, paradoxically, only made us more convicted in our critical stand against U.S. Central America policy."[70]

According to Washington Association of Churches leader Rev. Loren Arnett, Central American issues were a big matter for the religious leaders in the region. "The Washington Association of Churches organized the Central American refugee program, and Catholics were very involved in this effort. We raised money for bail for the refugees when they were arrested by the U.S. government. The FBI got hold of all of the files of that program later on to see what was going on."[71] Already by early in 1982, a broad base of religious leaders called for an end to American military aid to El Salvador. The Catholic bishops on a national scale were engaged. This thrust of faith-based criticism troubled the Reagan administration. The effort involved many religious voices, not only the Catholic community. This was the beginning of a major challenge by churches to United States policies in Central America.[72]

Joel Connelly, writing for the *Seattle Post-Intelligencer* in 1990, cited the ecumenical practice that for many years was so significant. Each Thursday morning, "Hunthausen drives out to St. John Lutheran Church near Woodland Park and sits down for breakfast with friends who call him Ray. Hunthausen is one of a group of Catholic and Protestant church leaders who break bread weekly, and have broken a lot of ground during their years together." Though the Seattle area has a small percentage of churchgoers compared to other parts of the country, "denominational barriers to those who preach and practice religion may be less of an obstacle than in most places." Those breakfasts each week had been instrumental to help these folks move forward with their words and actions on an array of justice and peace issues. "We probably would never have done anything had we not done these breakfasts," said Hunthausen. One key area of their work together had to do with Central America.

> "They've been spurred on by the presence of Northwest church workers in El Salvador and Nicaragua. Such prominent congregations as Plymouth Congregational Church and St. Mark's Cathedral have sister churches in Nicaragua. Church leaders have been particularly vocal in opposing the U.S.-sponsored Contra war in Nicaragua and military aid to the government of El Salvador.... After six Jesuit priests were killed by Salvadoran soldiers, Hunthausen told a protest rally that America's 'involvement in El Salvador and other Central American nations spins from an idolatry of power. This false sense of power, this illusion that with sufficient might our will will be done, allows us to cynically wash our hands of the torture and death of thousands of people in order to support those few we call our friends.'"[73]

The weekly breakfast meetings were crucial. The breakfast group, Hunthausen said, had become his "sounding board" and many of his actions came from these conversations and the ideas that were presented there.

A good deal of Hunthausen's attention to Central American concerns was channeled through the Justice and Peace Center (JPC). When Hunthausen returned from the November 1982 meeting of the U.S. bishops, he told Don Hopps that he had met with Archbishop Rembert Weakland of Milwaukee, who had talked about his own growing interest in sanctuary for Central American refugees. Weakland gave his support to any parish that wanted to provide sanctuary for Guatemalan and Salvadoran refugees.[74] Inspired by the example in Milwaukee where the effort was an interfaith sanctuary program, Hunthausen asked the JPC to provide him with background on the larger issues of U.S. policy and Central America and to help him consider the sanctuary idea.

In late January 1983, Hunthausen sent a letter on the issue to the people of the archdiocese. "Many refugees from civil strife in Central America are finding their way into the United States. Some have come to our own state. These refugees need our help and protection." The Immigration and Naturalization Service was denying refuge to these people. "It is my judgment that one of their reasons for doing so is that they find it politically embarrassing to admit that the governments which the United States supports cannot protect their citizens from violence. In fact, these governments are often the perpetrators of that violence." As on nuclear arms, Hunthausen directly challenged U.S. policy on this issue. "The effect of these policies is to subject these refugees to deportation and to further exposure to the vindictive actions of authorities in their countries." And, he wrote, it is "our obligation as Christians to offer these innocent people sanctuary." Individuals and parish communities could help these refugees by giving them food, shelter, and clothing, by providing them opportunities to support themselves, and by forming support groups for those working directly with the refugees. A few individuals and parishes, he said, "will be able to go the last step and offer refugees from Central America sanctuary from the law, which in this case, is being applied unjustly. I want you to know that the Archdiocese will support any and all of these efforts on behalf of Central American refugees."[75] These decisions were up to the conscientious choice of individuals and parish communities. They were not mandates. He asked people to ground their choices in prayer and reflection. The Archdiocesan JPC would provide coordination, technical assistance, and legal support for the activities chosen by individuals and parish communities.

Hopps has emphasized that the focus was not simply on sanctuary. "The last thing most refugees wanted was to be 'in sanctuary.' Rather, the vast majority craved complete anonymity for fear of compromising people back home in their country. We worked hard to give as many refugees as we could the support they needed and wanted."[76] Participants in the Sanctuary Movement were risking the legal consequences of civil disobedience, just as Hunthausen was doing by his practice of war tax resistance. Sanctuary for Central American refugees had been pioneered in the region especially through the efforts of people at University Baptist Church in Seattle and kindred spirits in the region's ecumenical community. The Church Council of Greater Seattle, so active in social issues, was gearing up for widespread discussion and action on sanctuary and other Central American-related concerns. The Rev. Donovan Cook of University Baptist Church coordinated educational efforts and actual sanctuary with other leaders in a nation-wide movement that began in Arizona through the actions of Quaker Jim Corbett and others. Cook and others in the Puget Sound area were actively responding to the plight of refugees who would face the immediate expectation of death if deported back to their countries.[77] Sanctuary was important, to be sure, but the core attention of the Archdiocesan Justice and Peace Center was on addressing Central American concerns as a whole and critically examining U.S. policy there. The real focus, says Hopps, was on generating mindful dialogue on the issues, fostering support for our fellow sisters and brothers, and working with the refugees on a host of needs.[78]

The Sanctuary Movement had a broad base of activity ranging from meeting basic needs to working for political change. Delegations went to refugee camps in El Salvador and Guatemala as part of the integrated effort that involved people from all over Central and North America. Sanctuary had inspiration from America's past. When the Fugitive Slave Act of 1850 made it illegal to provide refuge and assist a slave in gaining freedom, many churches participated in the Underground Railroad to provide a path to freedom. In the early 1980s, the Sanctuary Movement for Central Americans became known as "the new underground railroad."[79] Hunthausen felt moral urgency over the plight of the refugees. Solidarity with the people of Central America was at the heart of the message he shared in late March 1983. He saw injustice being perpetuated by his own government. He commemorated the death of Oscar Romero, the archbishop of San Salvador who was slain on March 24, 1980. "Most especially today, Oscar Romero must now be a teacher to us. To all the actions—covert operations, fraud, manipulation, and surrogate violence—we as a nation have employed to influence the outcome in Central America—Oscar Romero holds up the truth."[80] Hunthausen put matters in stark terms. "Either we will, as a people, choose to abjure the temptation to impose our will by force, because we believe we are right, or see the blood in the streets of San Salvador on our hands."[81]

A letter to the editor of the *Seattle Times* in mid-May 1983, by Nancy Krieger, a Seattle resident, applauded Hunthausen: "In light of the criticism Archbishop Hunthausen is receiving from certain conservative quarters for his public progressive stands, I am writing this letter to commend the archbishop. Like his brethren in countries where repression is rampant—such as in El Salvador and in the Philippines, Archbishop Hunthausen is using his post to speak out against the abuse of human rights in light of the moral teachings of the church." Hunthausen also denounced the repression of the Marcos regime in the Philippines, standing in solidarity with the labor movement there.[82]

The Church Council of Greater Seattle, the University Baptist Church, and the archdiocese's JPC were all active in Central American concerns. By late spring of 1983, the JPC had held forums at more than two dozen parishes. For the Center the primary partners were parishes, Catholic Community Services, the other dioceses (Spokane and Yakama) in the state, the Washington Association of Churches, and the Seattle City Commission, along with many secular groups. The Washington Association of Churches raised financial—and other—support for refugees. And since February a group of Roman Catholic nuns were hiding Salvadoran refugees in their basement, responding to the challenge of conscience presented by Hunthausen and others to support the refugees in any way people could do so.[83]

Parishioners of St. Leo's Catholic Church in Tacoma voted in June 1983 to offer sanctuary to El Salvadoran refugees. Fr. Charles Schmitz had proposed the question to the parish after he got the letter from Archbishop Hunthausen back in February. Schmitz said he felt obligated to the archbishop and to this issue to bring it to the parish. The vote was overwhelmingly in support of providing sanctuary, which parish members knew meant breaking the law as a matter of conscience.[84] In this case, the civil disobedience was the act of an entire parish, not a sole individual. It was an act of collective conscience.

An Associated Press story in early July 1983 reported that "conservative Catholics are dismayed by what they perceive as their bishops' leftward trend." Exhibit A in the story was Hunthausen and his anti-nuclear weapons stand. But the story also cited conservative Catholic concerns over the bishops' pastoral letter on war and peace and the emerging pastoral letter on the U.S. economy. That pastoral letter's drafting committee chairman, Milwaukee Archbishop Rembert Weakland, was reported to be one of several bishops who "have supported parishioners who have defied U.S. immigration authorities—and risked a $2,000 fine and five years in prison—by harboring illegal Latin American immigrants who might be endangered if returned home." Critics such as James McFadden and Michael Novak charged "that the bishops, many of them liberals who rose to power after the Second Vatican Council, are ignoring Vatican II's ideal of lay participation by trying to instruct lay people on matters about which the laity are equally well, or better, informed." Novak was quoted saying, "The old authoritarian style...has not changed. Only this time, the progressives are running things."[85] Novak need not have been so discouraged. Progressives were not running things in Rome.

A July 4, 1984 interdependence (on American Independence Day) event in Seattle, at Plymouth Congregational Church, emphasized this message: Central American refugees are in danger from violence and repression in their homelands, and deserve refuge here. The *Seattle Times* reported that a caravan of "up to 40 cars had made it in eight days from Tucson, Arizona through California and Oregon to Seattle with five illegal Guatemalan refugees." The caravan made its plans known to immigration authorities. The strategy of the movement had changed from one of secrecy to a public action.

> "Yesterday's ecumenical service to welcome campesinos Alfredo, 23; Maria, 22; their children Isabel, 3, and Anita, 3 months, and medical student

> Mario, 25, drew some 350 people downtown, among them a number of prominent religious leaders, including Archbishop Hunthausen. Cleo Gold, program coordinator of the Catholic Church's Justice and Peace Center, set the tone when she welcomed the refugees, declaring, 'Here we are not illegal people.... Here we are not people without papers. Here we are all brothers and sisters of God here in his house."

Mayor of Seattle Charles Royer was there in a show of solidarity. The refugees described the abuse they had suffered at the hands of the army and the police in their native country, Guatemala.[86]

Hunthausen analyzed connections between many social justice issues and there was a particular way that he reflected on these ties. This can be seen clearly in a speech he gave even after the whole Vatican investigation was completed and after the Reagan presidency. The speech underscores how the real concern about Central America was, for Hunthausen, much broader and deeper than the act of sanctuary alone.[87] In March 1989, Hunthausen received a peace award in Denver, Colorado, and took the opportunity to speak about the struggle for justice and peace in Central America. He had just recently been reading about the lives of five catechists in the village of Santa Cruz El Quiche, in Guatemala. Hunthausen had a particular connection to Guatemala, because when he was the bishop of Helena the diocese established a mission there. In the early-to-mid 1980s, the Guatemalan army, under the dictator General Rios Mont, was brutally repressive. Hunthausen told his audience in Denver the story of what happened to the five catechists. "As you know, at that time any position of leadership in the Indian community was tantamount to a death warrant. Leaders in the church were a special target. And so it was inevitable that when the army finally came to Santa Cruz El Quiche, they came to kill the catechists who lived and worked there." The soldiers also sought to intimidate and humiliate the people.

> "They had to find some way to kill the spirit. They chose a particularly cruel method. They told the inhabitants of the village that if they did not themselves search out and kill these much-loved and respected ones that they would return and slaughter all of the inhabitants of the town. The condemned persons urged their fellow villagers to act, offering themselves up for sacrifice. They knew any other option they chose would inevitably lead to the death of many of the people of Santa Cruz El Quiche. So it was. They were martyred by their own friends and relatives."[88]

SPEAKING TRUTH TO THE AMERICAN EMPIRE

Hunthausen told his Denver audience that as citizens of the United States they, like he, shared in some responsibility for what the soldiers did. "Just as with the citizens of ancient Rome, we are the power upon which the violence of the Guatemalan military rests and which that military serves. Years ago, we made the armed revolution that overthrew the only democratic government Guatemala has ever known. Now we train and arm the military in which the ruling oligarchy is institutionalized. During this decade, as a matter of deliberate policy, our government has promoted low intensity conflict throughout Central America." He asked his audience there in the mile-high city to recognize another level of responsibility.

> "Just as you and I share a responsibility for the events in Santa Cruz El Quiche by virtue of our citizenship, we share a second and higher responsibility to them through the bond of our common creation and the divine image we bear. The events at Santa Cruz El Quiche violated human community certainly; they also point up how far we have to go to build in actual fact the community to which we were formed, and to which we are called. The martyrdom of the catechists, indeed the collective martyrdom of the poor of Latin America, is the end result of the basic denial of community that is so deeply rooted in our culture."

We must examine the individualism and alienation of U.S. society, he said. "In so far as you and I contribute to the isolation and separation manifest in our restless search for immediate gratification, our identification of a self-centered independence with freedom, and the growing passivity and negativism toward social action for the common good, we contribute to the process which ends in the dusty streets of a hundred Latin American towns." To overcome this pattern and its destructive consequences we would need to cultivate empathy. We would also need to squarely examine our understanding of security.

> "Security: this word haunts us. Security is the word that justifies our presence in Central America; security is the word that justifies each and every new warhead that we add to our nuclear arsenal. Security is the salvation promised to us by the idols of our age. But the idols we create in turn create the fears which drive us, drive us down to the depth of the unspeakable terror that the nuclear holocaust will come. All around us the pervasiveness of this fear is revealed: uniformed Central American children toting automatic rifles, our own children shot down in a schoolyard. All around us the very nature of idolatry is revealed; idolatry is fear. The idols of old did not fall until confronted with a faith that drove out fear.... I firmly believe that there will be no end to the nuclear arms race, there will be no end to poverty, there will

be no end to violence of any and all kinds until we step up and accept the risk of believing, truly believing in a God who took the ultimate risk: to accept death out of love."[89]

Hunthausen could see his nation worshipping Mammon, the god of wealth, and constructing warrior gods to defend avarice, conspicuous consumption, and gross inequality. In its hubris, the American Empire was contributing to injustices in hinterlands such as Central America, justifying its brutal conduct in the name of national security. Unless it underwent a conversion of heart, an empire habitually bowing to idols made in its own image would never know freedom from fear.

ENDNOTES

1 Carlson, John. "Moral Disarmament: Is Hunthausen really so naïve?" *Seattle Times* 11 Oct. 1982. *Historic Seattle Times, 1900–1984*, 14.

2 Buckley Jr., William. "Draft Dodgers: The Motivation is irrelevant to legal issues." *Seattle Times* 21 Oct. 1982. *Historic Seattle Times, 1900–1984,* 17.

3 Berrigan, Daniel. "Hunthausen's moral gesture." *National Catholic Reporter* 19 Feb. 1982.

4 Castelli, Jim. *The Bishops and the Bomb: Waging Peace in a Nuclear Age*. Garden City, New York: Image Books 1983.

5 McGrory, Mary. "Catholic Bishops Take On the Bomb—and Maybe Reagan, Too." *Washington Post* 21 Sept. 1982, A3. *Lexisnexis.com*. Web. 6 Aug. 2012.

6 Hunthausen, Raymond. Speech delivered at the National Conference of Catholic Charities in Detroit, Michigan. 7 Oct. 1982. Archdiocese of Seattle Archives.

7 Hunthausen, Raymond. Speech delivered at Faith Gathering event of the Archdiocese of St. Paul/Minneapolis. 6 Nov. 1982. Archdiocese of Seattle Archives.

8 Hunthausen, Raymond. "Arms Against the Poor." Speech delivered at Baltimore, Maryland. 14 Nov. 1982. Archdiocese of Seattle Archives.

9 See "Presentation of Five Bishops on Proposed War and Peace Pastoral." *Origins* 2 Dec. 1982, 402.

10 John Paul II. "Message to the Second Special Session of the United Nations General Assembly Devoted to Disarmament." Cited in *The Challenge of Peace*, paragraph 173.

11 Briggs, Kenneth. "Catholic Bishops Begin Arms Debate." *New York Times* 16 Nov. 1982, D26. *Lexisnexis.com*. Web. 6 Aug. 2012.

12 Hunthausen, Raymond. *Origins* 2 Dec. 1982, 403-406.

13 Hunthausen, Raymond. *Origins* 2 Dec. 1982, 406.

14 Padovano, Anthony. *The Human Journey—Thomas Merton: Symbol of a Century*. Garden City, NY: Doubleday, 1984, 67.

15 "A Bishop's Response to the Bishops." *Human Events*. 4 Dec. 1982. Catholic Archdiocese of Seattle Archives.

16 Novak, Michael. "Bishops' Letter Ignores How Nuclear Deterrence Works." *Human Events* 11 Dec. 1982. Catholic Archdiocese of Seattle Archives.

17 Weatherby, W.J. "How America's bishops learned to loathe the bomb." *The Guardian* 2 Jan. 1983, 6. *Lexisnexis.com*. Web. 6 Aug. 2012.

18 McGee, John Hugh. Letter to Archbishop Hunthausen. 11 Jan. 1983. Catholic Archdiocese of Seattle Archives.

19 McGee, John Hugh. A Politico-Military Message to American Catholic Bishops from a Conquered Defender of American Territory. 26 Dec. 1982. Catholic Archdiocese of Seattle Archives.

20 Hunthausen, Raymond. Address to Young Leaders from the Soviet Union. 28 Feb. 1983. Catholic Archdiocese of Seattle Archives.

21 Hunthausen, Raymond. "The Challenge of Peace: A Personal Response." Speech delivered at Seattle University. 16 Mar. 1983. Archdiocese of Seattle Archives.

22 Curtiss, Elden. Personal correspondence with Archbishop Hunthausen. Archdiocese of Seattle Archives.

23 Anderson, David. "Conscience, defense and the income tax." United Press International. 15 Apr. 1983. Lexisnexis.com. Web. 6 Aug. 2012.

24 Hunthausen, Raymond. "Statement on the Third Draft of the Pastoral." Statement prepared in anticipation of the 3 May 1983 NCCB meeting in Chicago. Archdiocese of Seattle Archives.

25 Casey, Rick. "Bishops' letter : How the Catholic leaders decide what to say about nuclear arms." *Seattle Times* 1 May 1983. *Historic Seattle Times, 1900–1984*, 3.

26 Ostrom, Carol. "Seattle archbishop is 'spiritual leader in peace group'." *Seattle Times* 1 May 1983. *Historic Seattle Times, 1900–1984*, 3.

27 Casey, Rick. "Catholic bishops adopt letter against nuclear weapons." *Seattle Times* 4 May 1983. *Historic Seattle Times, 1900–1984*, 7.

28 Briggs, Kenneth. "Roman Catholic Consciousness-Raising Against Nuclear Arms." *New York Times* 16 Dec. 1983, B1. *Lexisnexis.com*. Web. 9 Aug. 2012.

29 Casey, Rick. "Nuclear-arms pastoral letter 'only beginning,' says Hunthausen." *Seattle Times* 6 May 1983. *Historic Seattle times, 1900–1984*, 14.

30 Hopps, Don. Comments on first draft of manuscript helped bring out this point about dialogue process. May 2014.

31 Casey, Rick. "Pathfinders: Catholic bishops tackle tough issues." *Seattle Times* 7 May 1983. *Historic Seattle Times, 1900–1984*, 56.

32 Casey, Rick. "Secret role: Pope warned bishops on N-freeze." *Seattle Times* 7 May 1983. *Historic Seattle Times, 1900–1984*, 1.

33 McCarthy, Colman. "Hard task ahead for the bishops." *Seattle Times* 10 May 1983. *Historic Seattle Times, 1900–1984*, 10.

34 Hunthausen, Raymond. "In Support of Protesters." Testimony delivered on 18 May 1983. Archdiocese of Seattle Archives.

35 Hunthausen, Raymond.

36 Balter, Joni. "Archbishop defends anti-nuclear civil disobedience." United Press International 20 May 1983. *Lexisnexis.com*. Web. 6 Aug. 2012.

37 Ostrom, Carol. "3 N-arms protesters guilty of trespassing at Trident base." *Seattle Times* 24 May 1983. *Historic Seattle Times, 1900-1984*, 35.

38 Ostrom, Carol. "Trident protesters lose trials, but make point." *Seattle Times* 28 May 1983. *Historic Seattle Times, 1900–1984*, 11.

39 Ostrom, Carol. "Time to halt arms race, archbishop tells panel." *Seattle Times* 9 June 1983. *Historic Seattle Times, 1900–1984*, 12.

40 Historical Background of the Dialogue Project. No date. Catholic Archdiocese of Seattle Archives.

41 Hopps, Don. Summary of Interim Report. May 1984. Catholic Archdiocese of Seattle Archives.

42 Ostrom, Carol. "Hunthausen sincere, but to some Rotarians he's wrong." *Seattle Times* 14 July 1983. *Historic Seattle Times, 1900–1984*, 40.

43 Root, Caroline. Letter. *Seattle Times* 24 July 1983. *Historic Seattle Times, 1900–1984*, 19.

44 Katz, Dean. "Dedication was hallmark of Senate career." *Seattle Times* 2 Sept. 1983. *Historic Seattle Times, 1900 -1984*, 4.

45 Hunthausen, Raymond. "The Peace Pastoral." Speech given at Kane Hall, University of Washington, Seattle. 21 Nov. 1983. Archdiocese of Seattle Archives.

46 Ostrom, Carol. "Local churches to draft 10-part statement on foreign policy." *Seattle Times* 23 Dec. 1983. *Historic Seattle Times, 1900–1984*, 12.

47 Hunthausen, Raymond. "Beyond The Pastoral on Peace." Speech delivered at the First Congregational Church, Vancouver, Washington 20 Jan. 1984. Archdiocese of Seattle Archives.

48 Hunthausen, Raymond. "The Pastoral and the Gospel." Feb. 1984. Archdiocese of Seattle Archives.

49 Lindsey, Robert. "Bishops Protest Train Carrying Atom Weapons." *New York Times* 24 Feb. 1984, A10. *Lexisnexis.com*. Web. 6 Aug. 2012.

50 Hunthausen, Raymond. "The Pastoral and the Gospel." Feb. 1984. Archdiocese of Seattle Archives. This statement was signed by Hunthausen and also by Bishop Eusebius of Tulsa, Bishop Leroy Matthiessen of Amarillo, Bishop Arthur Tafoya of Pueblo, Bishop Charles Buswell of Pueblo, Archbishop James Casey of Denver, Bishop George Evans of Denver, Bishop William Skylstad of Yakima, Bishop Francis Quinn of Sacramento, and Bishop Joseph Madera of Fresno.

51 Hunthausen, Raymond. "The Pastoral and the Gospel."

52 Hunthausen, Raymond. "Shaping a Peaceful World: Practical Ways of Implementing the Peace Pastoral." Speech delivered at St. Martin's College in Lacey, Washington 8 June 1984. Archdiocese of Seattle Archives.

53 National Conference of Catholic Bishops. *The Challenge of Peace: God's Promise and Our Response*. 3 May 1983, paragraph 80.

54 Hunthausen, Raymond. "Shaping a Peaceful World."

55 Hopps, Don. Comments on draft of manuscript. May 2014.

56 "Nuclear-arms race is moral issue, say bishops." *Seattle Times* 25 Sept. 1984. *Historic Seattle Times, 1900–1984*, 17.

57 Turner, Wallace. "Despite Protests, Missile Fleet Patrols." *New York Times* 5 Feb. 1985, B5. *Lexisnexis.com*. Web. 6 Aug. 2012.

58 "Feds garnishes archbishop's pay." United Press International 10 Jan. 1985. *Lexisnexis.com*. Web. 6 Aug. 2012.

59 "Bishops Call For Activism Against Arms Race." Associated Press 25 Oct. 1986. *Lexisnexis.com*. Web. 6 Aug. 2012.

60 Hunthausen, Raymond. Interview by Michael Gallagher (unpublished).

61 Hunthausen, Raymond. Personal interview. Seattle, Washington 16 Dec. 1988.

62 Hunthausen, Raymond. "Protecting and enhancing life." *Progress* 23 Jan. 1986, 5.

63 Hunthausen, Raymond. "Mass For Life Homily." Delivered at St. James Cathedral 2 Oct. 1988. Archdiocese of Seattle Archives.

64 Hunthausen, Raymond. "Peace and Pastoral Ministry." Address delivered at St. Meinrad's Seminary, St. Meinrad, Indiana 28 Apr. 1986. Archdiocese of Seattle Archives.

65 Hunthausen, Raymond. Personal interview. Seattle, Washington 22 June 1989

66 Hunthausen, Raymond. "The Christian Community: Prophetic and Reconciling." Speech delivered to the Annual National Assembly of Pax Christi USA, Loyola University, Chicago 31 July 1987. Archdiocese of Seattle Archives.

67 Hunthausen, Raymond.

68 Gumbleton, Thomas. Correspondence in review of draft manuscript, May 2014.

69 Hopps, Don. Personal interview. Seattle, Washington 20 Sept. 2012.

70 Hopps, Don. Personal interview. Seattle, Washington 10 Dec. 2012.

71 Arnett, Loren. Personal interview. Bothell, Washington 28 Mar. 2013.

72 "Clergymen united against U.S. aid to El Salvador." *Pacific Stars and Stripes* 19 Feb. 1982. Church Council of Greater Seattle collection. University of Washington Archives.

73 Connelly, Joel. "Preaching Peace And The Social Gospel; Activism Unites Many Of Seattle's Church Leaders." *Seattle Post-Intelligencer* 11 April 1990, A1.

74 Golden, Renny and Michael McConnel. *Sanctuary: The New Underground Railroad.* Maryknoll: Orbis, 1986, 6.

75 Hunthausen, Raymond. Letter to the people of the Archdiocese of Seattle. 24 Jan. 1983. Archdiocese of Seattle Archives.

76 Hopps, Don. In correspondence in review of draft. May 2014.

77 Golden, Renny and Michael McConnel, 37.

78 Hopps, Don. Correspondence in review of draft. May 2014.

79 Golden, Renny and Michael McConnel, 15.

80 Hunthausen, Raymond. "Commemorating Oscar Romero." Mar. 1983. Archdiocese of Seattle Archives.

81 Hunthausen, Raymond. "Commemorating Central American Martyrs." Address at Blessed Sacrament Parish. 27 Mar. 1983. Archdiocese of Seattle Archives.

82 Krieger, Nancy. Letter. *Seattle Times* 19 May 1983. *Historic Seattle Times, 1900–1984*, 14.

83 Gelernter, Carey Quan. "Community responds to Salvadorans' plight." *Seattle Times* 12 June 1983. *Historic Seattle Times*, 1900–1984, 1.

84 Smith, Carlton. "Church offers have for Salvadorans." *Seattle Times* 13 June 1983. *Historic Seattle Times, 1900–1984*, 26.

85 "Some Conservatives Disturbed by Bishops' Attitudes." Associated Press 6 July 1983. *Lexisnexis.com*. Web. 6 Aug. 2012.

86 Gelernter, Carey Quan. "Five refugees arrive safely in Seattle." *Seattle Times* 5 July 1984. *Historic Seattle Times, 1900–1984*, 16.

87 Hopps, Don. Correspondence in review of draft. May 2014.

88 Hunthausen, Raymond. Denver Peace Award Speech. 27 Mar. 1989. Catholic Archdiocese of Seattle Archives.

89 Hunthausen, Raymond.

Chapter Five

NOT JUST A FRATERNAL VISIT

As far back as 1978 the Holy See had asked for information about pastoral practices in Seattle, but such inquiries with various dioceses were more or less normal.[1] Since Archbishop Hunthausen was given no indication of any special Vatican concern, correspondence with Rome seemed fairly routine to him. However, he came to realize that relations were no longer routine when, in the spring of 1983, he was informed that a formal Apostolic Visitation to the Archdiocese of Seattle would take place.[2] He learned of this in Chicago from the Vatican's Washington, D.C.-based apostolic delegate to the United States, Archbishop Pio Laghi, who was attending the May 1983 meeting of the National Conference of Catholic Bishops (NCCB), at which *The Challenge of Peace* was approved. "When Pio Laghi told Hunthausen it was just a friendly thing, a visit, Hunthausen said to himself, this does not sound so good, but then he thought, this could be good, we are implementing Vatican II in many imaginative and creative ways. The agenda was foggy and murky from the start," commented Seattle's chancellor and vicar general Fr. Michael Ryan, who was in Chicago accompanying Hunthausen. Timothy Schilling, whose well-researched dissertation on the Seattle-Rome conflict is a key source for the present chapter and the next, learned from Ryan that Laghi's hurried revelation about plans for an apostolic visitation took place during a coffee break in the NCCB proceedings.[3]

Just what would the "apostolic visit" be about? Hunthausen wanted to try to clarify the intent of Rome's plans, but Laghi had already left Chicago, so Hunthausen sought counsel from the president of the NCCB, Archbishop John Roach. Roach recommended that he demand a 'bill of particulars' specifying the reasons for the visitation. When Hunthausen was later able to reach Laghi, he was told that the visitation was a family matter. No bill of particulars would be necessary. Things should be kept in the family and, Laghi told him, "You must never let this go public. Keep it quiet." By midsummer Laghi had told Hunthausen that the visitation would be conducted by Washington, DC's Archbishop James Hickey. Hickey then wrote to Hunthausen to indicate it would be arranged for the coming fall.[4] Hunthausen in turn asked Hickey for a bill of particulars, but in step with Laghi, he replied that such a legalistic approach would be unnecessary, for this was going to be just a fraternal visit.[5]

So the formal visitation was set for November 1983. Hunthausen was in Rome two months earlier and had the opportunity to meet face to face with Cardinal Joseph Ratzinger, the prefect in charge of safeguarding church doctrine. He told the prefect that if a visitation were to take place he hoped it would happen in an open and constructive spirit. He invited Cardinal Ratzinger to come out to Seattle to see the church there for himself, but the Cardinal did not take him up on the invite. As autumn drew near, Hunthausen urged Laghi and Ratzinger to let the process be transparent. They in turn kept insisting on secrecy. Somehow news of the impending visitation was leaked to the press. Hunthausen claimed that the leak came from the East Coast and not from Seattle.[6]

Habitual Vatican opaqueness persisted, however, for when Archbishop Hickey prepared to conduct the visitation, he required interviewees to be sworn to secrecy.[7] Even so, news was out and, therefore, the Vatican and its apostolic visitation team had to deal with the media in some fashion. In a public announcement made jointly with Hunthausen on October 26, Hickey stated: "I go as a brother bishop to observe the situation first hand and to offer appropriate fraternal assistance and support. I look forward to my days in the Northwest and a visit with my colleague, Archbishop Hunthausen." Hunthausen for his part reiterated his aspiration that the visitation process be informed by an open spirit. In fact, he wrote to the people of the archdiocese optimistically: "Because my faith tells me that this renewal in the church is the work of the Holy Spirit, and because I am convinced that our efforts here in this archdiocese are in keeping with the spirit and intent of the Council, I do welcome Archbishop Hickey's visit here."[8]

The press understandably wanted to know if Hunthausen's highly publicized nuclear disarmament stand and war-tax resistance had been factors. Such was not a factor, Hickey asserted.[9] Archbishop Hunthausen had been criticized, as *Seattle Times*' Carol Ostrom reported, "for statements and activity concerning homosexuals, women, contraception, abortion, peace and sanctuary for illegal aliens, among other issues." Catholic sources told her that "several disgruntled groups, some of which include priests, have gained the attention of influential people close to the pope." What were detractors saying? "It's about time to straighten him out, to bring him back to a level course," said Danny Barrett with Catholics Against Marxist Theology, who claimed his group represented about 30,000 people in the region. Yet Fr. Kurt Wuelner, the associate pastor of St. Philomena's in Des Moines, where Barrett was a member, countered that critics like Barrett, though vocal, were few in number.[10]

In late October, a Vatican spokesman explained the purpose of an apostolic visitation. The visit would involve trying to clarify whether the complaints about Hunthausen's ministry were of a religious or political nature. "If it is a political question, we're most concerned that the Ordinary (the Archbishop) not come across as identifying with any one partisan group but that he relate to all as pastor and father. He should be receptive to those in his diocese who are not of his political persuasion." The visitation would be done in a spirit of "brotherly correction."[11]

Regional and national attention just ahead of the November visit heightened. "Hunthausen stirs the Vatican," the *Seattle Post-Intelligencer* editorialized, continuing:

> "As a result of dissent and opposition among more conservative members of the Catholic community to Hunthausen's potent and highly visible views and positions on various contemporary issues and his fervent social activism, the archbishop this coming week is to be the subject of a church inquiry commissioned by no less than Pope John Paul. Whether the substance and style of Hunthausen's leadership faithfully and effectively serves his church is a matter solely for the church hierarchy itself to decide."

Yet in the view of many people in the region skeptical about what they saw as Rome's authoritarian propensities, this was itself the problem: the paternalistic assumption that only the hierarchy should make decisions. The *Seattle Post-Intelligencer* editorial continued:

> "More than any other Catholic leader in the history of the Pacific Northwest, Hunthausen has opened the doors of his church to religious ecumenism in the spirit of the Second Vatican Council. He has been an active supporter of the Protestant-dominated Church Council of Greater Seattle and its efforts to end discrimination against homosexuals in housing and employment, as well on behalf of food and shelter for the poor, programs for the handicapped, and church sanctuary for political refugees from Latin America and Asia."[12]

Kenneth Briggs of the *New York Times* wondered about the close ties between church control of authority and church doctrinal decrees on sexuality. "John Paul, like some popes before him, has worried about the impact of a democratic society on a church that claims hierarchical authority." Strong papal insistence on Catholic allegiance to church teachings on sexuality was one way to try to reassert central authority, Briggs observed. Bishops should be forthright in fighting any dissent on sexuality, came Rome's unequivocal message. There was also the question about how Rome wished to see American bishops relate to U.S. superpower. "Many bishops believe that the Pope especially wants the American church to become a model of fidelity to authority because of its strategic position within an international superpower and its financial strength." Much of the Seattle-Rome case, not to mention the larger tension between Rome and many liberal dioceses in America, turned on the meaning of church power. "The present stress between the Pope and the Americans stems in part from new definitions of church power introduced by the Second Vatican Council."[13]

Bishop Walter Sullivan wondered just why both his Richmond, Virginia diocese and Seattle were being investigated, even though the broad campaign to discredit progressive and even moderate bishops was not limited to one or two dioceses. "The letters are being sent to Rome. It's an organized effort to discredit the direction of the church in the United States." Who was behind it all? "Well, I don't have any names. I would say it's coming from groups that are opposed to renewal." Sullivan felt "there is certainly a relationship between Seattle and Richmond in the sense that both bishops are certainly very strong in the peace movement. That has caused opposition to that position." His own diocese had been visited secretly in June 1983 by Archbishop John May of St. Louis, dispatched by Pio Laghi.[14]

SEATTLE PRIESTS STAND WITH THEIR BISHOP

The president of the Archdiocese of Seattle's Senate of Priests, Rev. Theodore Marmo, announced that a statement pledging support for Hunthausen was being circulated among priests in response to word of Hickey's imminent visit. Marmo proclaimed, "If anybody knows the man himself, he's just a great and courageous churchman." Two hundred seventy-one parishioners of St. Patrick's on Capitol Hill signed a petition which read:

> "[Archbishop Hunthausen] has taken seriously the principles of Vatican II and has encouraged their implementation throughout the archdiocese. In his role as teacher and unifier, he has not once negated Catholic tradition. In his role as prophet, he has been a leader in proclaiming the Gospel, which is not always popular with the crowds. Even so, he has never attempted to impose his positions on the faithful; he simply challenged us to hear the Gospel and to respond as the spirit directs each of us in our own consciences."

Fr. James Moran, the pastor of St. Patrick's, said many parishioners and priests were pleased with Hunthausen's leadership. "But for many of us, this is the first time we've heard someone in the hierarchy taking issue with the government position. This is a real change in the U.S. Catholic Church.... You're asking people to separate loyalty to God on the one hand and loyalty to country on the other hand." Not only has Hunthausen taken a strong stand on the nuclear-arms race and other issues, he has also been open and "responsive to people in need."[15]

The Senate of Priests statement pledging "respect, loyalty and love" for Hunthausen had received signatures of 252 of the 280 archdiocesan and religious order priests. The Archdiocesan Pastoral Council, designed during Hunthausen's first years in Seattle and made up of elected priests, nuns, and lay men and women from across the archdiocese, stood up for Hunthausen in a statement to Hickey: "The church of Christ is truly present and active in Western Washington because of the inspired, courageous and prayerful leadership of our Archbishop Hunthausen."[16] Sister Lucille Dean, provincial superior of the Sisters of Providence and the head of a leadership conference representing six religious orders of women, likewise publicly affirmed Hunthausen. Detractors made their views public as well. Pat Matsun, a Catholic woman, told the *Seattle Times*:

> "There are a lot of us who do not support him and are afraid of him. Nobody wants a nuclear war, but this country needs a defense. If we do not defend our own country, there will not be a cathedral for this guy to preach in. I think people would be amazed at the people who are against him, but just don't take the time to call or write."[17]

Hunthausen's protests of nuclear weapons would not be an issue—or so claimed Hickey publicly. The focus would be on issues of doctrine, liturgy, and morality. This would include, Carol Ostrom reported, Hunthausen's stance on the role of women in the church, divorce, remarriage, homosexuality, abortion, and theological issues such as the infallibility of the Bible and the divinity of Christ. "The Seattle situation, Hickey said, appears to reflect church wide conflicts between the old traditions and a church wide renewal set in motion by the Second Vatican Council after 1962." Debate was healthy, Hickey felt, but he said that in a church rooted in strong doctrine not everything is "up for grabs, up for debate." Fr. Michael Ryan told Ostrom that Hunthausen was especially vulnerable to attacks by the "very traditional and ultraconservative" critics because he was on the cutting edge of change in the church.[18] Yet Ryan was optimistic. "I feel there will be a clear finding that Archbishop Hunthausen is doing what he was sent here to do. He's carrying out his ministry."[19]

Rome's wish to keep the visitation low profile was not working.[20] In early November 1983, the *New York Times* reported: "One by one, men and women are being ushered this week into a small conference room here to speak about Raymond G. Hunthausen, the Roman Catholic Archbishop of Seattle. Although they are participating in a theological process that is centuries old, they are discussing 20th century issues: thermonuclear weapons and modern attitudes toward sex and society." The Vatican's investigation of Hunthausen had to do with larger Vatican concerns about the Catholic hierarchy in the United States, or so speculated the *New York Times* writer:

> "American Catholic bishops have not only become more active in speaking out about the nuclear arms race, the American military presence in Central America and other temporal matters; many have also made the Vatican uncomfortable by veering from its hard line in

opposition to artificial birth control, homosexuality and the ordination of women as priests while tolerating greater dissent from within the laity than is customary in other countries."[21]

Fr. Harvey McIntyre, executive director of the Washington State Catholic Conference, thought Hickey's "energy would be more effectively utilized in an investigation of the resistance to the spirit of Vatican II by archconservative organizations."[22] McIntyre may have had a good argument, but the "visit" spurred by some of those archconservative groups was on. Asked what he felt would be its impact, Hunthausen alluded to Vatican II and the struggle for the soul of the Catholic Church: "I would be the last to deny that our efforts at renewal have met with criticism both legitimate and questionable. Any serious attempt at renewal can hardly be expected to avoid this sort of thing."[23]

Hickey and his entourage interviewed Hunthausen for more than four hours and held some seventy interviews with various supporters and detractors. They also reviewed documents the archbishop had issued as part of programs implementing the Vatican II ecclesiological paradigm shift to shared responsibility.[24] Hickey met with people such as Danny Barrett of Catholics United Against Marxist Theology, Erven Park of *Catholic Truth*, and members of the staunchly conservative Catholics United for the Faith, including former president Dave Mitchell. Mitchell told *Seattle Times* reporter Ostrom that Hunthausen was always gracious, nice, and available, but "His job is to teach the true faith." He was not doing his job, in Mitchell's judgment. "Let's put it this way: I don't think the Catholics of this archdiocese truly know their faith. And just like the captain of a ship, if somebody opens a valve and sinks the ship, it's the captain's fault." Hickey received letters or telegrams directly from many people, and critics also contacted Pio Laghi. Hickey's secretary, Rev. Godfrey Mosley, used the family metaphor to explain why the whole matter should have been kept in-house: "For some reason, everyone feels it should be an open kind of thing, but it's like in your own family—if something should go wrong, some disagreements, you sit down and talk about it. It's an in-house kind of thing." The Seattle-Rome affair, so concentrating the mind on broader tensions which characterized Catholicism in that era, could never remain in-house.[25]

Mary Royer, Portland-area president of the National Parent's League, told *Seattle Times*' Ostrom that homosexuality was the chief concern motivating her to meet with Hickey. Erven Park, a former Grand Knight of the Knights of Columbus, wanted Hickey and anyone else who would listen to him to know that Hunthausen was naïve, anti-American, and dangerous, a bishop straying from obedience to Rome. Hunthausen's stand on the role of women could be troublesome, reported Ostrom. His approach was always to be sensitive to the struggles a given person was going through instead of immediately "asserting the doctrine," a priest close to Hunthausen told her. "Archbishop Hunthausen is a very pastoral man. He's a very compassionate man for the situations that people find themselves in, and on account of that, people might say he's not holding a firm line on doctrine. But I don't think that's the case." There was controversy over Hunthausen's stand on abortion. In June the archdiocesan Respect Life advisery committee resigned *en masse*. Don Hopps, who staffed the committee for Hunthausen, said the archdiocese was taking a multi-issue approach to life, not single-issue, and that this may have frustrated the committee. Ostrom tried to convey what some Catholic conservatives felt: "Hunthausen has often linked the abortion issue with the nuclear-arms race in his own talks. But in many ways, Hunthausen's bold activities on behalf of peace brought him trouble on the abortion issue. If he could put himself in a boat in Hood Canal in protest of the Trident, why not put himself onto the sidewalk in protest of an abortion clinic, some reasoned."[26]

Erven Park apparently told Archbishop Hickey what he also told the secular media: "The Mass is central to the faith, and any abuses are an offense to the Holy Father and to God." Park claimed such abuses included allowing liturgical dancers to perform during Mass, extending communion to Catholics and non-Catholics alike, priests neglecting to genuflect before communion, letting girls and women be altar servers, and lay persons distributing communion while priests remain seated. Betty Sifferman, vice-president of Catholics United for the Faith, reportedly presented to Hickey her accusations of abuses regarding the role of women in the church: "They're pushing this feminist business on us. They get into women in the priesthood, they get into women at the altar, which is forbidden by canon law." Youth in the Catholic Youth Organization (CYO) program were discussing disarmament. Peace and justice programs were infiltrating Catholic schools, she told Hickey.[27] Hunthausen's vocal opposition had to wonder, would their voices be heard by the Vatican and would Rome intervene to make much needed corrections in a region gone astray.

"I found so many good things here," an upbeat Hickey announced as he prepared to leave. He would get his report to Pio Laghi, who would make emendations and then send it on to the Vatican. Rev. Peter Chirico, Hunthausen's theologian, told a *Seattle Times* reporter that he thought most criticisms generally had to do with "liturgical discipline" and were not about "the essence of Christianity."[28] Hickey thanked Hunthausen and the people of the archdiocese for their cooperation. "I have observed the progress made in the Archdiocese of Seattle, and have gained, I believe, an insight into the range of viewpoints."[29] Rome's reading of the situation in Seattle was not going to be so sanguine. Fr. Ryan took Archbishop Hickey to the airport and on the way there Hickey encouraged him to consider how he could draw upon his training, since Ryan had studied in Rome, and could play a pivotal part in helping Hunthausen meet Rome's expectations. But as the Seattle-Rome conflict developed, Ryan remained steadfast in supporting Hunthausen and his Vatican II-inspired vision of church.[30]

IN NEED OF SOME PERSPECTIVE

Hunthausen was aboard a ferry crossing Puget Sound on his way to a conference sponsored by Catholic Community Services one day in mid-November 1983. Carol Ostrom captured Hunthausen's feelings as he expressed them to the audience the next day at the conference:

> "It was on the ferry to Friday Harbor that Archbishop Raymond Hunthausen, staring at the water and struggling for perspective, received a gift and a message from a very small and special friend. Hunthausen, on the boat a week ago, was visiting a parish in the San Juan Island town while in Seattle Archbishop James Hickey, sent by Pope John Paul II, was investigating complaints and interviewing Hunthausen critics. Hunthausen, despondent, had sought out an isolated corner of the ferry to stare at the water and the islands. But…he wasn't to be alone for long. Searching through the ferry, a four-year-old girl he had meet briefly earlier with her parents found the archbishop in his corner. She had a present for him, she said. Hunthausen showed it to the audience. It was a page taken from a Christian coloring book captioned with the words: 'I'm special. God makes things right.' Above the words was a place for a self-portrait, which the little girl had filled in, surrounding her face with squirrels and bunnies and frogs, Hunthausen told the audience. On the bottom of the gift page were instructions: Put your picture in the middle and hang the page on the doorknob of your room. His little friend, Hunthausen told his audience, will never know how he appreciated her gesture. While he wasn't feeling 'totally sorry for myself,' he admitted, 'I was in need of some perspective.'"

The conference was at St. Francis of Assisi, a parish where, during the previous summer, members came out of the church to find fliers on their cars criticizing Archbishop Hunthausen and urging them to send letters to Pio Laghi. Hunthausen told the audience that he had received an outpouring of support with calls, letters, telegrams, and flowers ever since the Vatican visitation was announced. "I have been ministered to in recent days," he said, "and I can't tell you how deeply that touches me."[31]

Hunthausen had feelings, of course, but apparently vindictiveness was not one of them. Fr. Jack Walmsley, director of priest personnel, could not recall Hunthausen ever saying anything negative about those who were going after him.

"Hunthausen was genuinely surprised by the visitation and all that followed it. He just thought he was doing the Vatican II work of the church. He felt surprised and disappointed. He was motivated by his heart and spirit." I told Walmsley that in one of my interviews with Hunthausen in the late 1980s he said the whole Vatican investigation felt a little like a visit from the "thought police". Hunthausen's sincere motivations were so much deeper than the cognitive or doctrinal level, Walmsley told me, so that even if he had to deal with officers of doctrine they really could not police the spirit that moved within him. "He really prayed about things. He could bring compassion and strength in the same moment. He could speak truth and yet be profoundly compassionate at the same time." They might attempt to control his thoughts (or their public expression) but they could not do surveillance on his inner spirituality. He had a spiritual center that manifested itself in good-natured unpretentiousness. Walmsley recounted an episode when he saw a parishioner trying to remove a picture of Archbishop Hunthausen from the vestibule of the church. He asked the parishioner to put the picture back. Later, when Hunthausen came to the parish to meet with the people, they could not believe this earthy and humble fellow was the person they had vilified.[32]

Before Christmas 1983, Hunthausen received a cordial letter from Cardinal Ratzinger saying the visitation process was in good order and thanking him for his loyalty to the church and his devotion to the Holy See.[33] "It was precisely because we did not want to give uncritical acceptance to extremist viewpoints that this demanding work was undertaken," he wrote.[34] He did not, however, share with Hunthausen the contents of Hickey's report.[35] Archbishop Laghi suggested to Hunthausen that he might want to seek out the confidential advice of a brother bishop. He provided Hunthausen with the names of possible advisers, one of whom was Anchorage Archbishop Francis Hurley. Hunthausen and Hurley already knew each other well since both were part of the regional group of bishops of the Northwest and Alaska. Hurley became a key Hunthausen adviser and close confidant as the Seattle-Rome affair developed.[36]

In spite of the conciliatory tone of Cardinal Ratzinger's letter, by 1984 Rome proposed the idea of sending a coadjutor archbishop to Seattle. Hunthausen was not happy, since he had expressed his desire for an *auxiliary* bishop, someone within the region who he knew and could help him with the creative yet demanding challenges of Vatican II-style leadership.[37] His former auxiliary bishop, Nicolas Walsh, had retired due to poor health. An auxiliary would be the normal request. The idea of a coadjutor would only be considered necessary, normally, if an archbishop was in some way incapacitated. Whatever Rome was up to, it did not keep Hunthausen from persisting with his call for church renewal. "We have to set our own house in order. The peace and justice which we would bring to other societies must first take hold, and flourish, within our own Catholic communities. We have not yet evaluated for reform, in the light of the Gospel, some of our more public institutional values and ecclesial structures."[38] This was in a message he made affirming the Sisters of St. Joseph of Peace, one of the various orders of women religious in the vanguard of church reform. After Hunthausen stated his displeasure with Rome's coadjutor archbishop idea, the Vatican decided to appoint an auxiliary bishop—but one from outside the region. Hunthausen, trying to find some common ground, said he could accept the idea of Rome appointing an auxiliary from outside the archdiocese if he could also have one from within. Rome dismissed this request.[39]

Friction mounted. Just before Christmas 1984, Hunthausen suffered a mild heart attack. He had complained about symptoms, but thought it was just a cold or perhaps a bronchial condition. His workload—without an auxiliary bishop—and the pressures from the Vatican had probably been factors. After the heart attack, it was several months before Hunthausen could resume his full duties. In April 1985, he wrote to the people of the archdiocese:

> "God, who is never short on surprises, nor on surprising ways to speak to us, has used the experience of this illness to reawaken in me a deep sense of how truly blessed I am both in my vocation as priest and bishop and in you, the people who are the Church here in Western Washington, the people whom it is my privilege to serve.... My experience of illness has helped me come to terms with my own limits and vulnerability...."[40]

On September 30, 1985, Cardinal Ratzinger sent Archbishop Hunthausen a long letter that would remain private until May 1987. Hunthausen was required to keep it secret by order of the Vatican. Fr. Ryan many years later speculated in an interview with the doctoral researcher Schilling as to why Hunthausen was not allowed to release the letter:

> "My feeling about it all along is that they wanted things quiet. It's just their preferred way of doing things. And that was true from the beginning with regard to the visitation itself, it was true with regard to the letter, and it was true, later, of the special faculties. The whole notion of disclosing these kinds of things...that people have a right to know these things, is not in their vocabulary."[41]

Some issues raised in the letter and, more to the point, the conservative mindset of its author, figured into subsequent "acts" of what might be viewed as a sort of reality play. Ratzinger's "script" deserves a full recitation because it lays out a veritable litany of concerns that motivated the efforts to discipline Seattle. Imagine being in Hunthausen's shoes—playing the lead in this Catholic reality theatre—as he laid eyes on the "Inquisitor" cardinal's confidential letter. He had waited almost two long years to learn what the Vatican's chief doctrinal officer had concluded after the fraternal visit by Hickey. He never saw Hickey's report.

CARDINAL RATZINGER'S SEPTEMBER 30, 1985 CONFIDENTIAL LETTER TO ARCHBISHOP HUNTHAUSEN

Your Excellency,

I am writing to bring to a close the Apostolic Visitation process, which was assisted by the visit of Archbishop James Hickey of Washington, DC, to the Archdiocese of Seattle from November 2-8, 1983.

Prior to that visit, both significant criticism and considerable praise had been directed toward your own pastoral ministry and that of your collaborators in Seattle. To quote from this Congregation's own October 4, 1983, letter to you, "It was precisely because it did not want to give uncritical acceptance to the published and private criticisms made about the Archdiocese of Seattle, that the Holy See... has undertaken this project." Toward that end, the Visitor conferred with at least sixty-seven members of the clergy, religious and laity. In addition, he examined many pertinent documents, statements issued by the Archdiocese, and letters. Principally, though, Archbishop Hickey spent some four to five hours of intense discussion with you. That interview, taped and transcribed, was later reviewed by you and approved. Archbishop Hickey, with a model sense of co-operation and collegial concern, filed a lengthy and exhaustively documented report with this Congregation, and with that, his involvement with the Apostolic Visitation process ended.

After a careful review of the entire body of testimony, and of other materials as well, this Congregation is now in a position to make the following observations which, we hope, will be received by you in the spirit in which they are offered, and will be of assistance to you as Archbishop of Seattle.

1. There are many indications that you have striven with heart and mind to be a good bishop of the Church, eager to implement the renewal called for in the decrees of the Vatican Council II. You have worked zealously to bring into existence the various consultative bodies promoted by the Council and mandated by the recently revised Code of Canon Law. Numerous people spoke of your laudable and conscientious efforts to involve the laity in the work of the Church

and you have sought diligently to be open and accessible to your people. You have been repeatedly described as a man of Gospel values, sensitive to the needs of the sufferings and the aggrieved. Your concern for justice and peace is well known. Time and again you have given clear evidence of your loyalty to the Church and your devotion and obedience to the Holy Father.

2. It is also true that you and those who assist you have suffered from exaggerated criticism and routine misunderstanding. Our observations are based neither on the complaints of your more strident critics, nor on publications that are obviously biased. Nor do we wish to encourage extremist groups who are wholly lacking in a spirit of co-operation and seek to destroy or suppress whatever is not to their liking. It is our attention, rather, to support what you have done to promote the renewal of the Church in Seattle and to point out, at the same time, areas which we consider are in need of correction and improvement.

3. It is with this background of your own commitment to the real service of the Lord and the authentic renewal of His people, that this Congregation wishes to outline these problems and to enlist your cooperation in resolving them.

4. It appears that there has been a rather widespread practice of admitting divorced persons to subsequent Church marriage without prior review by your Tribunal, or even after they have received a negative sentence. Catholics have been advised that after divorce and civil remarriage, they may in conscience return to the Sacraments. Such a practice lacks foundation in the Church's clear teaching about the indissolubility of a sacramental marriage after consummation, and in sound jurisprudence. A clear presentation, then, of the sacramentality and indissolubility of Christian marriage should be made to all your people. Every effort must be made to avoid written materials which equivocate regarding the essential properties of marriage and which may encourage the divorced to attempt a second marriage without the Tribunal's declaration of nullity. At the same time, steps need to be taken to ensure that your Metropolitan Tribunal, both in its constitution and practice, conforms with all the prescriptions of the revised Code of the Church's public law.

5. A number of other basic doctrinal problems can be identified. While it is impossible to judge how widespread they are, and although they

may seem to be abstract, they too often have had real implications and concrete effects in the day-to-day life of the Church in Seattle.

a. It is important that clear and firm guidance be offered to those in the Archdiocese who seem reluctant to accept the Magisterium as capable of giving definitive direction in matters of faith and morals.

b. It is important that the nature and mission of the Church be taught in their entirety. The Church should be understood as more than a merely social entity, governed chiefly by psychological, sociological and political processes. When it is viewed in this way, its institutional or visible dimension is placed in opposition to its divine origin, mission and authority. Such a view misunderstands the meaning of the Church and destroys all prospects of the authentic renewal for which the Vatican Council II so clearly called.

c. Incorrect notions of the Church's mission and nature, as well as flawed understandings of the dignity of the human person, can frequently be traced to faulty Christologies. It is imperative that every effort be made to ensure that the Church's integral faith concerning Christ be handed on: his divinity, his humanity, his salvific mission, his inseparable union with and Lordship over the Church.

d. Vigorous efforts must be made to engender in priests, religious and laity, a correct appreciation of the sacramental structure of the Church, especially as it provides for sacred ministry in the Sacrament of Holy Orders. An effective seminary program needs to be established which inculcates in candidates for the priesthood an understanding of the sacraments as the Lord's gifts to His Church. While efforts to encourage the laity to fulfill their apostolate and assume their proper roles in the Church should continue, the unique ministry and office of the Bishop, as well as that of the priests who assist him, must never be obscured.

e. A critical reexamination of policies and programs of the Archdiocese should be conducted to ensure that they are based on the clear vision of the human person which is at the heart of the Gospel message. An anthropology which is dominated by the tentative conclusions of the human sciences could well undermine many pastoral initiatives, however well intentioned.

f. There is a need to correct misunderstandings concerning the role which conscience plays in making moral decisions. In particular it is necessary to highlight the valid claim on the Catholic conscience which is made by the authoritative teaching of the Church.

In all these areas it is vitally important to consult with competent, faithful theologians, clergy and religious to determine how best to proclaim the Church's entire deposit of faith in our changing times.

When guided by an authentic theological method such efforts are not only not in conflict with the teaching of the Church, they are a faithful response of her constant call to vindicate the rights of the poor.

It is also important that the faith be imparted in a way which is sensitive to the suffering and the powerless.

No bishop should hesitate to overrule advisers who propose opinions at variance with the authentic teaching of the Holy See. At the same time, he must seek ways to hand on that teaching convincingly.

6. As per your letter of March 14, 1984, we realize that you have taken steps to correct the practice of contraceptive sterilization which had been followed in local Catholic hospitals. Such procedures are clearly and explicitly forbidden in all Catholic institutions. The clear moral teaching contained in this Congregation's 1976 Declaration on Sexual Ethics, as well as the teaching found in the documents of the U.S. Bishops' Conference must be maintained and explained in an effective manner.

7. In matters of pastoral practice, first Confession should precede first Communion. This decision, which terminates any authorized experimentation, was incorporated in c. 914 of the revised Code. Accordingly, the sequence of first Confession prior to first Communion is not optional, nor can a custom to the contrary be established.

8. Similarly, the use of general Absolution must be strictly limited to the conditions listed in the relevant documents of the Holy See and in particular in c. 961 par. 1. The fact that many penitents would naturally congregate at the times of great feasts, Christmas and Easter for example, would not of itself constitute the necessary condition that they would be deprived of the grace of the sacrament for a long time if general absolution were not given. Responsible supervision on the part of the office for Liturgy is indicated.

9. Likewise, the attention of the clergy and the faithful should be drawn to the fact that non-Catholic Christians may be admitted

occasionally to communion in the Catholic Church under specific conditions as listed in c. 844 par. 4, and in the related documents of the Holy See on this question. Catholics, however, are permitted in some cases to receive the Eucharist in non-Catholic churches, but only in those whose sacraments are recognized by the Catholic Church, as is clear from c. 844, par. 2.

The Catholic Church believes the Eucharist to be a sign of unity already achieved. Routine intercommunion on the occasion of weddings or funerals, wherever it is the practice, should be recognized as clearly abusive and an impediment to genuine ecumenism.

10. Efforts to encourage full and lively participation in the sacred liturgy should be fostered. However, practices which are not in accord with the Roman Sacramentary and the related directives of the Holy See should be eliminated. The appointment of a carefully trained priest to aid in the supervision of sacramental and liturgical discipline is indicated here as well.

11. Concern for priests who have left the ministry is obviously a duty of a bishop, but he must always be aware of the Church's discipline. Laicized priests are excluded from performing certain roles, as amply described in their rescripts of laicization. The status of priests who have left the ministry but who have **not** been laicized must be recognized as much more irregular, and they can hardly be employed formally or informally by the Church in any way. The same applies for their civilly married wives.

12. It has been noted that in 1976 and in 1979, the Archdiocese of Seattle devised questionnaires to obtain information useful for the formation and conduct of Archdiocesan programs. Some, unfortunately, understood these questionnaires to be a kind of voting process on doctrinal or moral teachings. The questionnaire did reveal certain deficient doctrinal understandings and the results point to the need for a more careful and extensive catechesis for both children and adults.

13. With regard to the role of women in the Church, the teaching of the Church regarding their God-given dignity and importance should be given full weight. The current fierce politicization of this issue must not impede the Church's efforts to vindicate the rights of all. The exclusion of women from Sacred Orders was dealt with at length in this Congregation's 1975 Instruction, Inter Insigniores and should be explained unambiguously.

14. A final question of pastoral practice pertains to ministry to homosexual men and women. The Archdiocese should withdraw all support from any group which does not unequivocally accept the teaching of the Magisterium concerning the intrinsic evil of homosexual activity. This teaching has been set forth in this Congregation's Declaration on Sexual Ethics and more recently in the document, Educational Guidance in Human Love, issued by the Congregation for Catholic Education in 1983. The ill-advised welcome of a pro-homosexual group to your cathedral, as well as events subsequent to the Apostolic Visitation, have served to make the Church's position appear to be ambiguous on this delicate but important issue. A compassionate ministry to homosexual persons must be developed that has as its clear goal the promotion of a chaste life-style. Particular care is to be exercized by any who represent the Archdiocese, to explain clearly the position of the Church on this question.

In bringing all the above points to your attention, it has been our purpose to assist you as effectively as possible in your office as Archbishop of Seattle. We commend you for your kindness and patience during the Apostolic Visit and during the many months needed by the Holy See for careful review and appropriate action.

May the Holy Spirit of Christ be with you and with His people whom you serve.

With my own best wishes, I am

Sincerely yours in the Lord,

Joseph Cardinal Ratzinger, Prefect[42]

Hunthausen and Laghi soon thereafter met at the apostolic nunciature in Washington, D.C. Hunthausen once again was denied the right to see the full Hickey report. He insisted on sharing publicly the Ratzinger letter, but Laghi had orders not to allow it.[43] The Holy See formally concluded the visitation by way of a mid-November 1985 letter from Laghi, which Hunthausen published later that month. While naming general areas of concern it lacked the specific detail of Cardinal Ratzinger's letter.[44] When Hunthausen shared Laghi's letter with the people of the archdiocese, he wrote his own letter to them, acknowledging his limitations: "Because of this, I am particularly dependent on your prayers, your support, your advice, and your constructive criticisms. At the same time, for the sake of the unity and well-being of the Church, I call those of you who have supported me and those who have stridently criticized me to join together to build up this Church. To the extent we fail to do this we wound and, in many cases do serious harm to our unity in Christ."[45] One could sense Hunthausen's anguish.

THE WUERL WIND BLOWS IN

Rome proceeded to impose an "auxiliary" bishop from the outside. Laghi made the announcement on December 3, 1985. Donald Wuerl was to be that person. Fr. Donald Wuerl, a priest of the Diocese of Pittsburgh, had worked as executive secretary to the papal representative for the study of U.S. seminaries.[46] Even though Rome was making decisions without dialogue, Hunthausen welcomed the word that Wuerl would be coming. He tried to put the best face on things. Still, in an interview he spoke anew about the problem of secrecy: "I have always maintained that it would be terribly important for me to be able to share with all of our people as fully as possible the results of Archbishop Hickey's evaluation. I felt that I owed this to our people, since I knew that the results of the visitation, whatever they were, would involve all of us because it is together that we are church." The Vatican remained adamant that Hickey's report would remain undisclosed. But Hunthausen, while speaking his mind, would never rebel against his superiors.

> "I have always, to the very best of my ability, striven to carry out my ministry as archbishop in faithfulness to the Gospel and according to the rightful demands and expectations of the Church. This, of course, is what I will continue to do in the days ahead. The direction I have received as a result of the visitation should assist me positively in this regard. As archbishop it is, of course, my task and my duty to do all I can to see to it that our people have no question as to what is the authentic doctrine of the Roman Catholic Church. This is a solemn duty that I accept with utmost seriousness."[47]

Hunthausen attended Pope John Paul II's ordination of Donald Wuerl as a bishop on January 6, 1986. The next day, January 7, John Paul II met with both of them. Like so much in the nebulous Vatican stratosphere, what took place in that brief meeting has not been disclosed. Even though he could not print it, on January 23, 1986, Hunthausen read aloud to the priests Ratzinger's September 30, 1985 letter. According to one priest whom Schilling cites, the reason for the gathering was "to hear the letter and get out their anger and frustration" prior to Bishop Wuerl's arrival. Many at the meeting, said the priest, vented "great anger at the process." On January 30, 1986, Auxiliary Bishop Donald Wuerl celebrated his first liturgy in Seattle. Fr. Michael Ryan read aloud the letter from Pope John Paul II appointing Wuerl, which included this line: "We have willingly heard the request of our venerable brother, Raymond Hunthausen, Archbishop of Seattle, and grant him an auxiliary bishop." In fact, Rome was not granting Hunthausen his request, for Wuerl was not really meant to be an auxiliary. He was Rome's whirl wind of discipline blowing in to subdue the alleged excesses of liberal Catholicism near Puget Sound.[48]

REMAINING FAITHFUL TO THE CHURCH IN A TIME OF TENSION

When members of the National Federation of Priests Council met in Salt Lake City in April 1986, they gave Archbishop Hunthausen an award recognizing his commitment to gospel values. Accepting it, he spoke on something he was in the throes of trying to live out and he knew that they too were grappling with: "Remaining Faithful to the Church in a Time of Tension." He asked them, what is a Catholic priest to do? "In order to remain faithful as a priest, one must get back to, and renew, the deepest font of his personal life as a follower of Jesus Christ." He wondered how one's commitment to follow Jesus could be lived out in the face of policies and practices at odds with the gospel and the good of the church itself. One should be "publicly committed to love and to serve the Church, and to faithfully persevere in this commitment despite the cost." The audience of priests knew that his own existential situation in that tense time lent credibility to what he was saying to them. "As the Church has resolutely moved from the sanctuary into the world's market place, with an agenda that is not always clear or agreed upon by all, increasingly priests have become public men. They live with tensions from liberals and conservatives, popes and laity, bishops and fellow priests, councils and media."[49]

In June 1986, Hunthausen was on the Maryknoll grounds by the Hudson River in New York State. He gave the "Departure Day" talk for a Maryknoll group getting ready to depart for foreign mission work: "I have come to believe that the crucible for conversion for the American Catholic people is today the issue of power and our attitudes toward it." American society and culture encourage a fascination with power and a love of domination, he observed. Jesus calls us to leave this behind, he told them. "We who find it so difficult to view life from any perspective other than dominance and self-preservation and the use of power in the name of progress and peace, need to hear your story of going forth as powerless disciples to touch and be touched by the hands and hearts of people of other lands."[50] He did not mention that he himself was facing the marginalization brought on by power and domination.

By the end of that summer of 1986, Hunthausen announced that he had been forced to yield several areas of authority to Donald Wuerl. This was a bombshell. We have to go back to earlier that year to understand what had happened. Apparently, in a meeting a few months earlier, Wuerl and Hunthausen were with other members of the archdiocesan staff. An issue came up involving a King County decision that included homosexuals under protection of equal employment laws. Differences between Archbishop Hunthausen and Bishop Wuerl on this matter brought to the fore the question of authority.[51]

Don Hopps, Hunthausen's justice and peace director, was there for the meeting when the authority issue came to a head. Even then, Hopps believes, Ryan and others in the meeting figured that Bishop Wuerl was there to control things. When the gay rights issue came up, Hopps and his colleague Tony Lee provided the political lay of the land. They explained public policy issues involving the King County ordinance changes which were being proposed. Those changes would have implications for the gay and lesbian community. Other voices were present, including Seattle University's president, Fr. William Sullivan, and Fr. Peter Chirico, Hunthausen's theological adviser. At some point, the meeting got into Thomistic theology, and the Jesuit Sullivan challenged Wuerl's doctrinal claims about the concept of objective disorder and the evil of homosexuality. Tony Lee, a lawyer adept at cross-examination watching Sullivan maneuver Wuerl into a box, became incredulous as he considered where Wuerl's line of thought was leading. So Lee asked Wuerl, "Do you think that someone who is gay is worse than a murderer?" Wuerl, trapped in his own logic and probably frustrated by being ganged up on by a room full of thinkers hardly aligned with a rigid side of Catholic moral theology, apparently answered "yes." The temperature in the room shot up.

One person kept his cool. Hunthausen calmly said to everyone, "stop." As he settled them all down, he shared a personal experience he'd had of being visited by a school teacher who came to him to confide that he was worried. Because he was gay, he was anxious about what would happen if he were to be found out. The prejudice against gay people might cost him everything, he'd told the archbishop. By sharing that parable, Hunthausen said to the group in the meeting that day that surely they must ensure that the schoolteacher's human rights would be protected. Right then the *deus ex machina* of one type of authority dropped down onto the stage. Wuerl, taking umbrage with Hunthausen's conclusion, said, "I am going to decide on this area," and he asked to have a word with Hunthausen in private. So Wuerl and Hunthausen and Ryan went off into another room. Wuerl told Hunthausen that he had final authority in this area.[52]

By mid-summer 1986, Rome had communicated with Hunthausen in no uncertain terms. Cardinal Gantin, prefect of the Vatican's Congregation of Bishops, wrote to Hunthausen confirming that Wuerl was to have final say in five key areas, and asked Hunthausen to put in writing to Wuerl that he was granting these special faculties. Of course this was not the case, since Hunthausen was forced to "grant" them. He did as Gantin requested, in a letter to Wuerl on July 28, 1986.[53] After the Vatican had clarified what powers Wuerl was to possess, and Hunthausen at the beginning of September had made this public, Seattle's archbishop was asked how he could have been mistaken for several months on such a significant matter of governance:

> "My conversation with Archbishop Laghi about the visitation and how it might be concluded and what some of the consequences of that would be engaged us in the possibility of an auxiliary bishop with special faculties. That was always presented as one of the possibilities that we might try to work with. I resisted that, quite frankly, because I felt it was fraught with real difficulties. It would create, as it has created in the minds of many people, a sense of division in the authority of the church and I wondered whether it was workable; I seriously wondered whether it was workable and I felt that it would be better if we avoided it.... (So) when Wuerl's appointment was determined, I had come to believe from my conversations with Archbishop Laghi, that his appointment would be as auxiliary bishop. Of course I was aware of the concerns in these special areas and I indicated that I was open to, clearly, not only his involvement in these special areas, but in the whole governance of the archdiocese. But I was absolutely convinced that I was to retain final authority in all aspects of the governance of the archdiocese. I felt that was our understanding. I honestly and truly felt that was our understanding."[54]

Things were not easy then, and they were going to get even harder. On more than one occasion during the whole Seattle-Rome affair, Hunthausen considered resigning. There were many times during his various exchanges with the Holy See that this thought entered the archbishop's mind. However, Pio Laghi again and again let Hunthausen know that the Holy Father did not want him to step down.[55]

Hang in there, he was told, even as he was *forced* to relinquish some of his responsibilities. The irony must have been glaring. It seemed he was told to "share" power with Bishop Wuerl in part because Rome felt he had been sharing too much power with the people. He had taken too seriously the Second Vatican Council's call to broadly share responsibility. A conflict over divergent conceptions of power and authority was bound to receive media hype. The *New York Times*, in early September 1986, announced: "Vatican Moves To Curb Power Of A Liberal Prelate In Seattle."[56] Jim Burns, Hunthausen's development director, remembers that when he saw the *Seattle Times* headline announcing that the archbishop had been stripped of major powers, he called his boss on the phone. Characteristically shifting the conversation away from his own plight, Hunthausen told him, "Jim, isn't it amazing that the church still has something to say to the wider society?" Jim, almost in tears, replied, "Archbishop, I just want you to know, I love you."[57]

Early that September, Hunthausen wrote to his brother priests. Much had taken place over the summer months, developments that would "have a notable impact on our shared ministry here in the Archdiocese," he began. He noted the "special and unique relationship" they shared because of the sacramental bond uniting the priests and bishop and "the fraternal and personal relationship that we have come to enjoy over the years." He wanted to be clear about what was happening and why. He was aware that "speculation has taken place, both in printed form and in less formal ways, regarding the roles and responsibilities of Bishop Donald Wuerl." The fact that Wuerl was appointed to Seattle shortly after the apostolic visitation had formally concluded, "made it inevitable that people would wonder whether, in appointing him as my Auxiliary, the Holy See had not also intended for him to have some specific additional responsibilities with reference to the findings and conclusions of the Visitation." Indeed, this was the case, "but at the time of his appointment, both Bishop Wuerl and I, along with the Apostolic Pro-Nuncio, judged it best to make no public announcement to that effect." Hunthausen told the priests that the reason for not giving full public acknowledgment of all the specifications of Wuerl's appointment had to do with ensuring "the best possible climate for beginning his ministry among us."

"Subsequent events, however, which I will almost certainly have an opportunity in the near future to relate to you in detail greater than allowed by a letter such as this, have led me to the conclusion that it is now vitally important—even absolutely necessary—that I make the matter public." He recounted how the Holy See had decided to give him an auxiliary bishop who would help him in the areas which the Vatican deemed to need greater clarification and vigilance. Wuerl was judged by the Holy See as up to the task.

> "Anyone familiar with his many gifts and impressive background can well understand why. However, at the time of his appointment, I did not understand the nature and extent of Bishop Wuerl's role. After considerable discussion with the Holy See, it was confirmed that it was the understanding of the Holy See in December 1985 when appointing Bishop Wuerl that he not only assist me by assuming a general oversight and responsibility for these five areas, but that he actually be delegated by me to have complete and final decision-making power over them. The clarification of this decision took place in June at the Collegeville meeting of the bishops where I met with the Apostolic Pro-Nuncio."

Hunthausen said he took steps to carry out the Holy See's wishes. He had shared the matter with his close collaborators in the ministry and administration of the archdiocese. They needed this information, he said, because without it "a dangerous vacuum…would have deprived all the key people within our organization of the most vital sort of information imaginable; namely, that having to do with lines of accountability as well as with ultimate responsibility." Bishop Wuerl "now enjoys complete and final authority within this Archdiocese for each of the five areas." He and Wuerl would strive to work together, supporting each other in their respective areas. It would take some time to work things, he said, as to how to implement their common and distinct responsibilities, but both of them were firmly committed to a fraternal and collegial spirit.

"Our relationship, which has come to mean so very much to me personally, will, I know, continue to grow stronger and closer as the days unfold." He could not predict how those ensuing days and weeks would unfold.

> "Among the duties that are mine as your Archbishop, none are more important or more sacred than the preaching and teaching of the saving Gospel of Jesus Christ and of witnessing to that Gospel, to the very best of my ability, by all I say and do. I am firmly committed to doing this, but I cannot do it alone. None of us can. We can only do it with the strength that comes from God's grace. We can only do it in union with each other and with the Church Universal. Thus united, we have a power that we can never have merely of ourselves."

Our ministry is one, he reminded them. "It is always shared, and it can even be delegated. But it must never be divided." The Spirit of the Lord "has formed us into one Body, one holy and gifted people." Hunthausen called on the priests to join him and Bishop Wuerl in "this unified and shared ministry we have been given." He did not try to conceal his anguish, writing that "the long days and the complex events which have brought us to this particular moment as a Church have been extremely trying and agonizing ones for me." And he imagined things could not be easy for them either. "Understanding has not come easily. Decisions have come only after a good deal of painful and prayerful struggling and searching." But through it all, the grace of God had been present and "God has allowed me to grasp better than ever before just what it means to live by faith."[58]

ETERNAL CITY CRACKDOWN

In mid-September 1986, Marjorie Hyer's front page *Washington Post* story chronicled the evolution of a Vatican crackdown across America consistent with the pressure on Raymond Hunthausen. "After Pope John Paul II became pope eight years ago, moves to restore orthodoxy to the multi-hued church in this country began so quietly that at first they caused little notice. But lately they have been coming so thick and fast that there can be no question, as University of Chicago church historian Martin E. Marty puts it, that 'an efficient process is at work to force a kind of conformity' on the American church." Examples she cited:

bishops ordered to remove their imprimaturs from books; a popular catechism ordered withdrawn; continuing investigations of seminaries and religious orders; heightening church control over Catholic colleges; a Jesuit sociologist "who polled the nation's bishops on the sensitive topics of clerical celibacy and the ordination" told to either "destroy his research or leave the order." Especially noteworthy were the Curran and Hunthausen cases, Hyer wrote.

> "When the Vatican notified the Rev. Charles E. Curran in mid-August that it considered him neither 'suitable nor eligible' to continue his career as a Catholic theologian, it signaled for many a new stage in efforts by John Paul II to force American Catholics back into line. That conviction was strengthened when Washington Archbishop James A. Hickey, in explaining the church's stance, declared that 'there is no right to public dissent' within the church.... The shock over disciplining Curran, whose views place him squarely in the mainstream of contemporary Catholic theology, had not subsided when Archbishop Raymond G. Hunthausen of Seattle disclosed that he had been stripped by the Vatican of some key powers, which had been given to an auxiliary bishop picked by Rome."

University of Notre Dame theologian Rev. Richard McBrien felt the forces on the right were now fully in charge. Daniel Maguire, a theologian at Marquette University, saw evidence of a classic power struggle. Since the Second Vatican Council, Maguire said, "laymen and women entered into the study of theology on university campuses where academic freedom is sacred. The laity became theologically literate and ecumenical. The Vatican has taken poorly to this loss of power and is struggling to regain it."[59]

Hunthausen, in some ways, was an icon of the liberal side in this struggle, and at the same time was caught in the middle. He never fancied himself a rebel engaged in a direct power struggle with the Vatican. If he was ever angry about the actions of the Holy See, he did not express it. Others did. Around 140 local Catholic leaders gave vent to their anger. They presented a letter of protest entitled "What Kind of Church are We Becoming?" and launched a petition to challenge the Vatican decision. Sister Chauncey Boyle, who worked on the letter, expressed their thinking and sentiments: "We are angry because this happened to us without any input from the Archbishop. Since Vatican II, we were attempting to become more collegial. This decision is not very collegial." On the other side, of course, Catholic conservatives were encouraged by the Vatican's move to curb Hunthausen's authority. William Gaffney, chairman of Catholics United by the Faith, called the Vatican action "reasonable and necessary."[60]

Divesting Hunthausen of his faculties, however, was far more explosive than Rome must have anticipated it would be. It brought people out—in the local church, in the regional ecumenical community, across the nation, and beyond. In Seattle, a mid-September 1986 prayer service called "The Church in Conflict" took place at St. Mary's Parish in the southeast part of the city. Over 300 personal reflections on Rome's action were gathered to be given to Archbishop Hunthausen and Bishop Wuerl. "I fail to see the ministry of Jesus at work in the way the Church has been dealing with our Archbishop over these past two years," said one participant. In a hopeful spirit someone else wrote: "I am overjoyed that there is such solidarity in support of Archbishop Hunthausen. I truly believe that he represents our future—one of integrity and hope and promise." Another person said: "Anger, frustration, confusion and depression rise up in me when I hear the Roman Church speak one way and then act in a totally other way. The church calls for collegiality, gospel values, Christian behavior and yet treats one of its most outstanding examples of Christian leadership in the shamefully, medieval, unethical manner." Still another participant in the prayer service put it this way: "I do not believe the Vatican fully understands what has happened here. For Archbishop Hunthausen has always proclaimed the Gospel of Jesus, and he has lived it. The reason I am so committed to Christ is largely due to his living example of his love for Christ. We are the church." A Protestant church member who participated in the prayer service at St. Mary's wrote that "it doesn't make any sense to me that the hierarchy at the Roman Catholic Church will in many ways silence the prophetic voice of one of its well-loved leaders."[61]

As reported in a *Seattle Post-Intelligencer* story, Fr. Michael Ryan, vicar general and chancellor, stated respectfully, hoping Rome might hear his plea: "Our archbishop has not been understood. We understand him. We love him." The case should not be misinterpreted as a war between Hunthausen's supporters and Rome, he argued. The media would be wrong to interpret this as a 'win-against-Rome' struggle. "We are nothing if we are not the Roman Catholic church," Ryan said.[62] On Friday, September 12, most of the priests of the Seattle Archdiocese met with Hunthausen and Wuerl for over six hours. Two days later, one of the priests spoke with his parish community in his Sunday homily about that meeting: "The priests were quite honest throughout the meeting with both bishops. It was the consensus of the majority of priests that these special faculties must be reversed. It was also the consensus of the priests that the investigation of our Archdiocese was flawed and unjust." He worried aloud with his congregation. "It seems that the primary focus of ministry in our Archdiocese will become church discipline and doctrine." That would be acceptable, he told the parishioners, "only if they are held in tension with the Church's sense of mission—a mission of ministry; a ministry of love that welcomes, receives and extends compassion. Jesus does not do less than this. Dare we?"[63]

For the September 12 gathering, one priest, Fr. Pat Carroll, described the situation:

> "The issue is much larger than what is happening now. It has to do with our ability to focus on the essential mission of the Church. Some might get the idea that the really important issues in the Church are not whether we have a nuclear war but in what order we have to have first communion/first confession. Everything that we are about—in my very socially active parish—is undermined by the Vatican's action."

Fr. James Mallahan, sharing responses of people from the Central Seattle area, asked why Archbishop Hunthausen was "picked out for the visitation when what is happening here seems to be happening all over the United States?" Fr. Joe Kramis, sharing responses from South King County parishes, offered this perspective: "The Archbishop has brought unity to the majority of priests and people and if his external powers are taken from him, nevertheless his internal authority remains, whereas Bishop Wuerl has not been able to establish his internal authority and therefore has no power even though that power has been granted." He added, "The National Federation of Priests Council has given the Archbishop their highest award. When the Vatican slaps this penalty on the Archbishop what does this say about the priests of our country and our own presbyterate?" Fr. Michael J. Ryan (not to be confused with Fr. Michael G. Ryan, the chancellor and vicar general), representing the South Sound deanery, said:

> "We ask the Vatican to tell us specifically what the Archbishop did that was wrong and why he was stripped of his rights?…We heard Bishop Wuerl express again and again that he does not feel he has any credibility here in the Archdiocese. We know what that is like because our Archbishop and we priests have experienced that during and since the investigation. If Bishop Wuerl could honestly make a public statement supporting the style of leadership the Archbishop is known for throughout the world, and if Bishop Wuerl would publicly affirm our Archbishop, our priests and religious as well as the laity of our Archdiocese—our credibility would be restored. If Bishop Wuerl could make that statement—then he would have our credibility."[64]

Joseph Berger, writing for the *New York Times*, analyzed authority in the church. The American Catholic bishops lived in a hierarchical church and were still subject to the authority of Pope John Paul II, and yet "they were staking out a clear identity as an American Catholic group steeped in the country's democratic style." They "have largely been silent about the dramatic decision by the Vatican disciplining one of their colleagues, Archbishop Raymond G. Hunthausen of Seattle, because they are caught in a dilemma involving their own authority." Only a few bishops were frank about what they saw the Vatican doing. One was Bishop Thomas Gumbleton, the auxiliary bishop in Detroit, who described the Vatican's treatment of Archbishop Hunthausen as "cruel" and "demeaning." Gumbleton predicted that the Vatican action against Hunthausen would intimidate the American bishops. "They'll always be looking over their shoulder to see who's watching and afraid to speak or act," Gumbleton said. "It's a serious loss if every bishop is afraid to act out of his own faith commitment, but only act on the basis of what he thinks somebody else wants him to do." Bishop Leroy Matthiessen of Amarillo, Texas, said it "certainly strikes me from a distance as being part of the effort to centralize, to control." Representing the more moderate and cautious view among bishops at that time, Bishop Thomas Kelly of Louisville told Berger that, though he had great respect for Hunthausen, "any one of us can fall afoul." Berger observed: "What Bishop Kelly alludes to is the fine diplomatic line bishops must walk between respecting the official teachings of their church and being sensitive to the constituents who feel they need to ignore those teachings on birth control and divorce." Theologian Rev. Richard McBrien worried that many Catholics who had been inspired by the bold initiatives of bishops would be discouraged by the unwillingness of most bishops to speak up firmly in support of Hunthausen. Other Catholics not so inspired by all the reforms of the Second Vatican Council, however, agreed with one bishop, Patrick Ahern of New York, that the church was "in a crisis of diversity right now" and was seeking "a presence of uniform teaching on major issues of dogma or morals."[65]

In mid-September the Archdiocesan Pastoral Council (some thirty members signed their statement) wrote to Archbishop Hunthausen:

> "We wish to express our support for you. We have experienced you as a gifted teacher, leader, pastor. We have seen you as someone who loves God and who serves the people God loves. Vatican II states as a bishop's ultimate goal to enable all people to walk 'in all goodness and justice and truth.' We have seen you constantly and clearly demonstrate this to be your ultimate goal, personally and professionally. By your person you stand as testimony of unity between theology and ordinary life, between the work of holiness and the work of church policy, between the life of faith and the life of the 20th century world. We have known you to listen to the concerns of all the people of God. We have experienced you as one who with great ease shares his vision of church. You have, as a good shepherd to your flock, taught us the meaning of the leadership to which our faith calls us. You have consistently inspired us by the way you have modeled Gospel values. As we shared with you and Bishop Wuerl at our recent meeting, we have experienced in our parishes, from Vancouver to Bellingham, from Aberdeen to Olympia,

> great confusion, pain, disillusionment, and sadness. Many people in our parishes are confused as to why this division of power was necessary, and how such a split authority can ever be effective. We feel a special sensitivity for the pain many are experiencing because of what this action implies about the Vatican's confidence in your leadership of the Church in Western Washington. Certainly the private and public outcry which followed the announcement of the Vatican's action is testimony to the tremendous pastoral influence you have been on our church. We have heard parishioners who are disillusioned because so little has been made known about the accusations which led to the visitation, and because many see the very nature of the process as unfair and unjust. We are a concerned Church."[66]

Making this a public statement, they called for the petitioning of the Holy See to restore Archbishop Hunthausen's full faculties and authority.

The St. Mary's Parish Hispanic Community, represented by Gudelia Alejo, also a member of the Archdiocesan Pastoral Council, made a statement in late September. "The Archbishop is a man who loves everybody, especially the poor. As Hispanic people we are really sad about what is happening to him. He is a humble man who lives the true Gospel."[67] Fr. Phillip Bloom was in charge of Seattle Hispanic Ministry. He called the investigation "foolhardy and unjust." It was foolhardy because Rome could have simply inquired about life in the archdiocese in an open and transparent way. "The secrecy has however served to create a mystique which immobilizes response." The archbishop was being unfairly tried.

> "Inasmuch as our pastoral ministry as priests has legitimacy only in union with the Archbishop, we also have been unfairly tried. That unfairness can be seen clearly in one of the areas where the Archbishop was stripped of his authority—the marriage tribunal. All of us in pastoral ministry have seen the tribunal serve as an instrument of healing and reconciliation, but now those people whose consciences were once eased are again made uncertain. Yet…no one had explained to the Judicial Vicar of the tribunal what the problem was. I consider that not only incompetent, but unjust—to him, to us, to all the people served by the tribunal, as well as to the Archbishop."[68]

Fr. Phillip Bloom had written candidly to Archbishop Pio Laghi expressing his concern—a concern shared by many people—that perhaps there was something going on between Rome and the U.S. government to suppress Hunthausen for mutually beneficial reasons. Laghi replied saying he appreciated the frank expression of concerns Bloom provided regarding the split-power arrangement in Seattle. "With equal candor, I can assure you that the rumor concerning the cooperation of the Holy See with the Administration of President Ronald Reagan in censoring those critical to the advocated positions of this government is totally baseless. There is no truth to that rumor at all."[69]

Bishop Wuerl wrote to the priests of the archdiocese on September 19. He noted something that had come up at the September 12 meeting: "You may recall that I was asked repeatedly at the Friday meeting to denounce the visitation process as 'unjust.' This, as I said, I cannot do. The fact that the process indicated in the September 30, 1985 letter of Cardinal Ratzinger is a process with which we Americans may be unfamiliar or uncomfortable does not of itself make the process 'unjust.'" His presence in Seattle as an auxiliary bishop was precisely to help Archbishop Hunthausen work with the issues highlighted in Ratzinger's letter, he said. "To continue to debate the visitation, its process and outcome here in Seattle seems futile and ultimately divisive."[70]

Archbishop Hunthausen wrote again to the priests. When they met at St. Thomas Center the prior week, they agreed on the need for a second meeting. It would take place on Friday, September 26. To that meeting he was inviting all the priests, the members of the archdiocesan pastoral council, the finance council, and the central agency department directors. He and Bishop Wuerl had met with members of the presbyteral council for what was, he wrote, "the very frank and fruitful discussion we had around the suggestions" put forth. Knowing that "not everyone got to speak or share fully what was in his heart," he wanted to give all the priests the opportunity to share their views. So he invited them to prepare statements that would be shared at the meeting on the 26th.[71]

Here is a sample of the many statements submitted. Rev. G. Barry Ashwell asked, "Where do they begin? How can they succeed in disturbing a whole people? On the surface anyway, they began their diatribe twenty some years ago at the sign of peace during Mass. They couldn't give it instinctively." He alluded to those who, in his estimation, had been against the whole spirit and direction of Vatican II from the outset. Of Archbishop Hunthausen, Ashwell wrote, "He has embraced the Magdalenes among us and has eaten with them. He has, yes, engaged the tax collectors. He has tried to raise the lowly to high places and from the dung he has lifted up the poor."[72] Fr. Patrick Carroll, the Jesuit pastor at St. Leo's in Tacoma wrote:

> "Our very faith is at stake, our understanding of the Church, our belief in Jesus. This is not big, it is everything. Our Archbishop who has helped shape this vision has effectively been called inadequate to help us be more faithfully Church. I assert simply, out of the only Faith I have: Nuclear war is a much more gospel value than general absolution, or the order of confession and communion. Compassion

to gay people is far more a gospel value than clarity about our church teaching on homosexuality. Shared responsibility, trust, empowerment are far more gospel values than secret investigations, vague charges or relatively trivial matters of Church discipline. Until Bishop Wuerl is able to admit, face, feel the pastoral pain in our entire vision of Church, ecclesiology, ministry, and most importantly, Jesus, we have no future to move into, together."[73]

On the other hand, a limited number of priests criticized Hunthausen's leadership. Fr. W.R. Harris, from St. Francis of Assisi Parish, hoped that Archbishop Hunthausen would "call upon all of his priests and lay leaders without exception to cooperate fully" with the decision to comply with the remedial measures outlined by the Holy See. Hunthausen should discourage all activities that would "only continue to divide our archdiocese and thwart our efforts to address the concerns which were delineated in the letter from Cardinal Ratzinger."[74] Jesuit Fr. Harry Kohls was troubled by the liberal propensity for dissent from the position of the Holy See: "I can only conclude that both bishops and priests in this country seem to take dissent from the Holy See as a matter of course involving no danger to the faithful." Bishop Wuerl was playing an indispensable role, thought Kohls. He asked, "Do we have the honesty, the humility and the courage to accept his help in bringing our archdiocese back into conformity with the norms of renewal of Vatican II, e.g. paragraph 25 of *Lumen Gentium*, as interpreted by the Holy See and not by the dissenters?"[75]

As Schilling documented in his dissertation, at the big gathering held at St. Thomas Center on September 26, words between Wuerl and some of the more outspoken priests got heated. Some accused Wuerl of trying to strong-arm Seattle. Wuerl in turn accused some priests of fomenting division. Hunthausen and Wuerl spelled out their plan to go to Rome to resolve things, an idea that had surfaced when the priests had gathered on September 12. The Rome trip, however, would never materialize. The Vatican, for its part, did not want to provide a forum suggesting that its authority was up for a vote.[76] Meanwhile, like streams feeding rivers during a Pacific Northwest rainstorm, statements of support for Archbishop Hunthausen came in from all over the region and beyond. For instance, the Renton Ecumenical Association of Churches, Pax Christi USA, and the National Conference of Diocesan Vocation Directors all sent messages.[77]

On September 29, Archbishop Hunthausen sent a memorandum to "Designated Leaders in the Archdiocese of Seattle," in which he included the April 29th report on the apostolic visitation, which he had mentioned to most of them who were present for the September 26th meeting at St. Thomas Center. Archbishop Hunthausen had appointed Bishop Wuerl, Chancellor Ryan, and Director of Administration Michael McDermott to carefully review the September 30, 1985 letter from Cardinal Ratzinger, and based on that, to develop the outline of a plan to address the issues therein noted.[78] The committee (Wuerl, Ryan, McDermott) had outlined a plan for addressing all the concerns identified in Cardinal Ratzinger's letter. They met with parties responsible in the areas of concern and engaged them in discussions of how to approach specific problems. Hunthausen was trying to respond to Rome's concerns in the best way he could, and he was attempting to work with Wuerl and with his own core staff.[79]

Coincidentally, also on September 29, Fr. Phillip Bloom wrote back to Archbishop Pio Laghi. He appreciated Laghi's prompt reply to his earlier letter but still had questions:

> "The unanswered questions have to do with the reasons for the investigation and the failure to deal with the injustice that followed it.... Being a priest who serves the Hispanic community those questions have an intensified urgency. In our community there are many Latin American refugees from both communist and right wing regimes. Some bring powerful stories of a church that risked itself to defend human rights. Others have sad, even bitter memories of a church that was silent, and sometimes cooperative with repressive governments. For example Argentine refugees, some of whom were imprisoned and tortured during the 'dirty wars,' tell about a church that largely ignored their plight—a church that seemed deaf to the mothers of the *desaparecidos* [disappeared]. We have so much more to lose by silence and stonewalling than by trying to identify injustice and deal with them. Of course, the case of Archbishop Hunthausen does not equal the human rights violations in Argentina and other countries. Still, if we cannot deal with a clear injustice done to a bishop, how can we hope to apply our teachings effectively in other areas?"[80]

Laghi had served as Rome's representative in Argentina, so these questions being posed by Bloom must have made the D.C. apostolic delegate ponder his own history. The theory about ties between the Vatican and U.S.—let alone U.S. allies in Latin America or elsewhere—will be looked at more closely later in this book. If Laghi had answers for Bloom, there is no record that he provided them.

The pastor of St. Paul's Parish in Seattle, Fr. Jerry McCloskey, wrote to Bishop Wuerl on September 30. He was deeply disappointed with the priests' meeting that took place the previous Friday:

> "As I reflected on why the meeting went the way it did, it became apparent to me that you were not really hearing us at all. We were talking about two different things. Your opening statement, for example, as well as your letter of September 19, seemed to imply

that we should forget the past and deal only with the issues raised by the investigation. You do not seem to appreciate the fact that, for most of us, the investigation itself is the issue. The concerns expressed by the Vatican are their concerns, not ours. This is not to say that we dismiss these concerns lightly or that we are unwilling to address them.... Please try to understand where we are coming from. We have lived and worked under the leadership of Archbishop Hunthausen for over ten years. We greeted his arrival in the diocese as a welcome change from the rather despotic rule of his predecessor. We saw his appointment as the beginning of a new era for the Church in Seattle.... We agonized with him as he (and many of us with him) bore the vicious, slanderous, and to us totally unjustified attacks of the radical right, both religious and political. We were fully aware of the so-called abuses which they were alleging. We were also aware that most of these 'abuses' were pure fabrications of twisted and theologically illiterate minds. We had no reason to believe that anyone would take these ridiculous charges seriously."

Bishop Wuerl ought to seriously consider a creative way to surmount the impasse, wrote McCloskey. He could let the Vatican know that Archbishop Hunthausen and the diocesan leadership could manage the issues raised by the investigation. "A vote of confidence by you in Archbishop Hunthausen and in us could redeem your credibility in the diocese and enable us to work together with you in addressing the concerns of the Vatican in a responsible manner." McCloskey urged Wuerl not to "underestimate the depth of feeling that exists among both clergy and lay people in this diocese. Your refusal to recognize and deal with that feeling can only result in greater harm to the Church than anything Archbishop Hunthausen ever did or ever would do." McCloskey felt that Wuerl was a victim in the situation as well, but Wuerl could change course. "The difference is that you are in a position to do something about it immediately and with a minimum of pain and embarrassment to all concerned."[81]

Mary Buckley, an associate professor of theology at St. John's University, Jamaica, New York, wrote a letter the *New York Times* published in late September. It is just one example of how the rumble over the Hunthausen case, along with other cases, was reverberating across the country:

> "As a Roman Catholic woman theologian, I dissent in anger and sorrow from three recent actions of the Catholic hierarchy: *The firing of the Rev. Charles E. Curran as theology professor at Catholic University for his more thoughtful stance on contraception, divorce and homosexuality. *The proclaimed policy of the New York Roman Catholic Archdiocese barring all who publicly disagree with 'church

> teaching' from speaking in parishes of the archdiocese. *The almost unheard-of curb by the Vatican on the authority of Archbishop Raymond Hunthausen of Seattle, who was directed to give over control to his auxiliary bishop in five major areas."

The rumble had a lot to do with the fact that women were not honored as equal with men. These actions Buckley wrote about were repressive and part of a patriarchal pattern of control, she argued. Issues dealing with Catholic doctrine on matters related to sexuality were of foremost concern. "Women are the ones who bear, nurse and in great measure socialize children. They are most immediately affected by all pronouncements on sexuality, yet they have nothing to say about decisions in this immense field, have no sacramental jurisdiction and no contribution to doctrinal development."[82]

Representatives of the new group in the archdiocese, Concerned Catholics, met with Hunthausen and Wuerl on October 1st. The group organized and represented lay people, women religious, priests, and others challenging the Vatican's decision. They put together petitions and circulated these among an estimated 14,000 Catholics, asking that Hunthausen's powers be restored and that the results of the investigation be fully disclosed. They presented the signatures to Wuerl at that October 1 meeting. According to Timothy Schilling, "Participants in this meeting said that, while the meeting itself was cordial, Wuerl shared his view that press coverage had been detrimental in the Seattle situation thus far and that, unless the 'decibel level is lowered' in Seattle, the Vatican might yet take sterner action against Hunthausen."[83] Sr. Kathleen Pruitt, representing Concerned Catholics, wrote to all the bishops of the Northwest region (several states including Alaska) that same day:

> "This letter is a follow-up to the one we sent to you shortly before the installation of Archbishop Levada in Portland. In that communication we expressed our grave concern for our Archbishop and for the Church here in the Archdiocese of Seattle. We asked that you, as a collegial and concerned brother of Archbishop Hunthausen, use your influence as forcefully as possible to seek a meeting with Archbishop Pio Laghi to present our petition that the full pastoral powers of the Archbishop be restored, that the specifics of the investigation be made known to the Archbishop so that he, and the members of the Church here, might address them in an open and collegial manner.... We had hoped that you, as a group of Bishops of the Northwest, would have spoken more strongly to the issues at hand. The statement which you issued fell far short of our hopes and our expectations. Many of us read it with dismay and disappointment.... We know that we are faced here in the Archdiocese and elsewhere in the country, with differing ecclesiologies. That fact should not make it impossible to speak to issues of injustice,

nor should it make impossible the raising of legitimate questions.... Question, dissent, and dialogue: these are not the marks of radical, undisciplined members of the church. They are marks of faithful and loyal sons and daughters of the Church who ask to be heard and taken seriously. We ask it for ourselves—we ask it for you as our leaders.... You hold our hope for bringing our concerns more directly before the Conference of Bishops and requesting solidarity in seeking restoration of the pastoral powers and authority of our Archbishop. We need this kind of courage and support and action from you so that the healing that needs to take place in this Archdiocese will happen."[84]

In his 1992 book *Holy Siege: The Year that Shook Catholic America*, Kenneth Briggs documented the broad mobilization in support of Hunthausen: "News of the archbishop's dressing down by Rome unleashed a torrent of protest by the most active elements in the Seattle church, who were solidly behind their archbishop."[85] When the drama was unfolding, *The Wanderer*, the archconservative newspaper, depicted the energies of all of these Hunthausen advocates as "a campaign of resistance to the Vatican's action."[86] Hunthausen avoided any tone of contention. Individual bishops close to him in the region, such as Bishop Sylvester Treinen of Boise and Bishop Skylstad of Yakima, made public statements supporting their brother bishop. His fellow bishops of the Northwest made a collective statement, the one Sr. Kathleen Pruitt referred to in the above letter. In it, the regional group of bishops said that Hunthausen stood "as a testimony of unity between theology and ordinary life, between the work of holiness and the work of church policy, between the life of faith and the life of the 20th century world."[87]

Their message was fine with Apostolic Pro-Nuncio Pio Laghi, who quoted them when he sent a letter to Rev. Richard Hynes, then serving as the president of the National Federation of Priests Council. Hynes had written to Laghi asking for an explanation of what was going on in Seattle. Laghi replied: "In the best interests of the Archdiocese, it would be helpful if endorsement were to be given to the objectives as expressed by the Bishops of Region XII who stated: 'The seventeen bishops unanimously support the efforts of Archbishop Hunthausen and Bishop Wuerl in their process to deal with the situation in Seattle to move beyond this moment and to continue to build up the unity of that local Church among its own members and its unity with the Universal Church.'"[88]

When William Levada was installed as the new archbishop in Portland, Oregon on September 22, 1986, retiring Archbishop Cornelius Power said when asked about the Seattle affair, "I think what you want to ask me about, I don't want to talk about."[89] Most bishops of the region, as of the nation, were cautious and circumspect. Not so, other people who cared deeply about the fundamental questions of authority raised by Seattle's predicament. The Vatican's action was causing a groundswell of nationwide solidarity with Hunthausen. Of course, the mild-mannered character at the center of all this did not in the least bit wish to be an emblem of American Catholic anger toward the Vatican. The early October issue of the *National Catholic Reporter* featured letters from across the country. Wrote one person: "The recent Vatican intervention in the Seattle archdiocese is one more clear example of the violence that occurs when maintenance of a power structure, in this case the institutional church, takes precedence over such values as hearing and living the Gospel of Jesus Christ." Anticipating the November 1986 meeting of the U.S. bishops in Washington D.C., another person wrote: "The credibility of the leadership of the American church rests upon our bishops' making it known that they will challenge injustice even when it comes from within." Power entered the observations of another contributor: "The time has come for us as church to reclaim the kind of power that is the heritage given us by Jesus: power to heal, teach, preach, power to love, to serve, to extend compassion to all; power to nurture that which brings life and to say no to violence and that which destroys…."[90]

The Rev. Charles Curran had been stripped of his right to teach theology at Catholic University. Ari Goldman, writing for the *New York Times* in early October, put this issue in context: "Both conservatives and liberals agree that the Vatican's steps concerning educational institutions are part of an effort by Pope John Paul II and some United States bishops to quell dissent in the American church. Among the other actions mentioned were the curtailing of the power of Archbishop Raymond Hunthausen of Seattle, the threat to discipline 24 nuns who signed an advertisement in 1984 on abortion, and criticism of Governor Cuomo by the Archdiocese of New York."[91]

At about the same time, the Jesuit and Anaconda native, Jack Morris, situated the Seattle story in a global struggle for the soul of Catholicism. What was happening to Hunthausen and bishops like him was happening as well to theologians and others who listened to grassroots liberation movements.

> "Boff, Schillebeeckx, Curran, Hunthausen, Sullivan—and the way they (Rome) are appointing bishops world-wide without listening, without consultation with the indigenous church—Boff and Schillebeeckx are both dangerous because they portray a church that is based on love, on servanthood, and the Spirit. Somewhere a beginning has to be made to develop tactics, and strategies to show others as well as to solve our own problems. I feel very strongly that we needn't allow it to happen—I mean the undoing of Vatican II and the movement of the church into the modern world."[92]

By mid-October, as various commentators in the *National Catholic Reporter* and other media were anticipating the Seattle controversy becoming a major focus of the November meeting of the National Conference of Catholic Bishops, Hunthausen wrote to the people of the Archdiocese of Seattle.[93] The last few weeks had been extremely demanding:

> "The range of reaction from you and from people throughout the country has been overwhelming. I refer not only to the variety and depth of feelings expressed, but also to the myriad explanations offered for the Visitation and subsequent events. I am sure I will never know exactly how many factors have brought our Archdiocesan Church to this present situation. What I do understand is the pain and confusion so many of you have shared with me. You speak with tears of your distress and you speak out of a lifelong fidelity to Catholic belief and practice. I apologize to you for whatever I may have unwittingly done or not done to contribute to the pain you feel."

He would not deny the "hurt and uncertainty that now exists in our hearts and minds." It would be so important to "move past this painful moment" and to do so by reflecting "on how we can best help one another renew our faith, our hope and our love." We need above all to ask the Lord for healing and guidance, he wrote. "It is vital to the life of the Church that you as individuals and as parishes, other faith communities, organizations, institutions and Chancery departments continue to work and interact as you have been doing to develop our Church. This is my first concern as your Archbishop."

He went on to describe how he hoped they would all approach the future:

> "We must choose to walk every moment of this journey as genuine disciples of Jesus. In His ministry, Jesus always placed His own pain and confusion into that larger mystery of God's loving fidelity to this world. By our willingness to move into the future we will witness to the power of God's redemptive love ever active in our midst. In a word we are called to be Catholic—encompassing all, wide-ranging, universal in extent.... We must try to understand the other side, not simply take stands.... Our Catholic spirit will urge us to embrace our sharpest critics with love and an effort to understand. Our Catholic spirit will continue reaching out to those excluded everywhere else. Our Catholic spirit will call us beyond our shallow securities to the deeper mystery of total trust in God who calls us to be one in Christ."[94]

Here he was officially a sign of unity as a bishop, and yet he had become an emblem of division, a role he never wanted to play. He gave a kind of *cri de coeur*:

> "My earnest plea to all our people and, indeed, to all who find themselves in any way affected by these matters, is this: let us help

> break the cycle of tension that now exists by making every sincere effort in word and action to rise above any contentious spirit, and let us do all we can to preserve the bond of unity that is ours as faithful members of the Church, committed always to witnessing to the truth of love."[95]

Esther Lucero Miner, Hunthausen's first multicultural ministries director, remembers once, during a cabinet meeting, when all the cabinet members were in the room. It was at the peak of all the hurt over the Vatican investigation, she says, and people were crying, tears coming down their cheeks, and Archbishop Hunthausen said to them all: "I want your forgiveness. This would not be happening to you if it were not for what is going on with me," he said.[96] She was moved in a way she would never forget. Hunthausen was asking them to forgive him as if he was causing the whole problem when, like so many others, she felt that the source of the trouble was in Rome and in the designs of a small but vocal group close to home. And here was Hunthausen, asking his cabinet members to forgive *him*.

TRYING TO CONTROL THE NARRATIVE

Could things get worse? On October 27, 1986, Archbishop Hunthausen wrote to the priests and other co-workers once again, enclosing for them a copy of "Chronology of Recent Events in the Archdiocese of Seattle," which had been sent over the weekend to all the American bishops. It had also been released to the news media, along with a detailed statement he was issuing in response. In the cover letter he said:

> "As I told the Bishops of the country when I circulated my response, I debated long and hard before deciding to make even this brief statement at this time. In the end, I became convinced that I had no real choice because to have remained silent would have seemed to signal a level of agreement with Archbishop Laghi's Chronology that quite simply is not there. I further indicated to the Bishops that my statement is not in any sense made in an accusatory spirit but only with the deepest sentiments of respect for Archbishop Laghi himself and for the position he holds. Lastly, I shared with the Bishops the same prayerful and heartfelt hope that I will share with you, my closest collaborators in the ministry; namely, that in the next few weeks these matters will have calmed to the point that we Bishops, who have a collegial concern for the good of the entire Church, will be able to discuss them openly and constructively in that spirit of love, trust and mutual respect they most assuredly deserve."[97]

"Vatican, Replying To Critics, Explains Curb of U.S. Bishop" was the title of the *New York Times* story on October 28. "The Archbishop first came to national attention several years ago when he said he would not pay a large share of his income taxes, to protest Federal spending on nuclear arms. The chronology specifically denied that that protest formed any part of the Vatican's investigation."[98] Pio Laghi had been under growing pressure to make the Vatican's version of events public. Laghi and National Conference of Catholic Bishops (NCCB) President, James Malone, apparently had planned for a Laghi-crafted chronology to be released together with a cover letter from Malone. Malone was going to endorse the Vatican version of events, but after conversations with other key bishops he decided to remain neutral. The NCCB executive committee at the time included Malone, NCCB Vice President John May of St. Louis, Boston Cardinal Bernard Law, Washington Auxiliary Eugene Marino and Rockville Center Bishop John McGann. Though that group would not be like-minded on the direction the American Catholic Church ought to head, they came to an agreement that the Vatican version of the Seattle-Rome matter would only be released if a version by Hunthausen were to accompany it. The *National Catholic Reporter* (*NCR*) investigated the details of what happened.[99] (Schilling traced all of this and more for the historical record in his excellent dissertation in 2002, providing a great source to guide many detailed turns in the story recounted in this chapter and chapter six.)

Laghi called Cardinal Joseph Bernardin of Chicago and told him that the Vatican was upset that his chronology would not be released as planned. Bernardin in turn, told Malone that Laghi had spoken with Cardinal Ratzinger and Cardinal Gantin, who was prefect for the Congregation of Bishops. The "triumvirate" of Ratzinger, Gantin, and Laghi wanted Laghi's chronology distributed. Bernardin talked with Malone about how things could be handled in a way that would meet both the expectations of Rome and the desires of the NCCB. Bernardin encouraged Malone to convene the NCCB executive committee again. Bernardin was in the middle on this matter, as so often he was on many issues between the Vatican and the Americans. His moderating role was influential here as it had been in the peace pastoral. The *NCR* story continued: "Malone then called Laghi, who related the Vatican 'request.' A second hastily called conference took place and the decision to distribute the Laghi chronology was made." Hunthausen's earlier request to both Malone and Laghi to not distribute the pro-nuncio's version was, in the end, disregarded. Hunthausen had told them that the Vatican chronology's release would only further the polarization in the church. The NCCB walked a fine line attempting to align itself ultimately with the wishes of the Holy See and yet showing some independence. The *NCR* account concluded:

> "Several sources said the Vatican and Laghi's office have been 'deluged' in recent weeks with Hunthausen support letters. One source said this

had 'irritated' at least some Vatican officials; another, however, said it was pushing them to answer critics' complaints that it had failed to explain adequately what exactly led to the Vatican move to give Seattle Auxiliary Donald Wuerl final authority in several ecclesial areas in the archdiocese. A spokesperson for the Seattle archdiocese said Hunthausen was 'discouraged' by the developments and had not yet decided how he would respond."[100]

At one point or another during the conflict, Pio Laghi told Seattle's archbishop that his own role was simply to be an official intermediary. He told Hunthausen, "I am only a conduit."[101] The "conduit" had been assigned the task of taking control of the narrative. Let's look closely at what he came up with as the Vatican's way to tell the history of the Seattle-Rome conflict. Imagine a theatrical recitation, with Laghi dressed as one might imagine an actor would dress if playing the part of "a conduit" on stage. Conduit Pio Laghi, dutiful and solemn, recites the Roman Chronology:

1. Decision for an Apostolic Visitation of Seattle

a. For the past several years, at least since 1978, the Holy See, through the then Apostolic Delegation, has corresponded with Archbishop Hunthausen on matters related to pastoral practices and the presentation of the Church's teachings. Through this exchange the Holy See sought the assistance of the Archbishop of Seattle in responding to the high volume of complaints that were sent to Rome by priests, religious and faithful in the Archdiocese. The Holy See's interest in this matter reflected its responsibility for the well-being of the Universal Church, as outlined in the Constitution on the Church of the Second Vatican Council. It should be stressed that at no time did the Holy See pursue with Archbishop Hunthausen the criticisms it received on controversial issues, e.g., nuclear weapons and the payment of taxes. The concerns were strictly and solely of a doctrinal and pastoral nature.

b. The Archbishop agreed that there were abuses in a number of cases and that corrective action was needed. In fairness to Archbishop Hunthausen, he did address some of the problems brought to his attention by the Holy See.

c. Substantiated complaints nevertheless continued. But, the decision to inquire further was primarily provoked by the documented responses of the Archbishop himself. Moreover, in expressing their fraternal concern for Archbishop Hunthausen and the Church in Seattle, certain Bishops suggested that there was a need 'to clear the air.' Prominent among their recommendations was the appointment of a brother Bishop to visit Archbishop Hunthausen and the Church in Seattle in order to gather factual information on behalf of the Holy See. Accordingly, on July 6, 1983, the Most Reverend James A. Hickey, Archbishop of Washington, was named Apostolic Visitator.

2. Preparation of the Apostolic Visitation

a. From the beginning, the priorities of the Holy See were two-fold: 1) to promote the building up of the Church in Seattle in harmony with the Universal Church and 2) to protect the good name of Archbishop Hunthausen. Consequently, it was determined that publicity would be kept to a minimum, so as to avoid fostering criticism of the Archbishop. Furthermore, it was the firm intention of the Holy See that any action required would come only after fully informing Archbishop Hunthausen and making every effort to secure his agreement and support.

b. Before Archbishop Hickey began the Apostolic Visitation, he consulted with Archbishop Hunthausen both in a long telephone conversation and in a day and a half meeting in Chicago. Both the procedure and the various doctrinal and pastoral aspects were reviewed in detail. Many of those who had lodged complaints against Archbishop Hunthausen had sent him copies of their letters to the Holy See and/or spoke to him personally. Archbishop Hickey discussed these persons with Archbishop Hunthausen and asked for an evaluation of the authenticity of their remarks and their reliability. The Visitator also asked Archbishop Hunthausen's help in drawing up a list of persons to be questioned. Archbishop Hickey stressed his desire to gain a balanced view of the Archdiocesan situation, the positive as well as the negative.

c. Archbishop Hunthausen insisted that a public announcement be made about the Visitation. Once this was done, the statements of Archbishop Hickey were designed to offer support and advice to Archbishop Hunthausen in accord with the initial and constant wish of the Holy See.

3. The Visitation

a. Information was gathered from the following sources: 1) Public documents such as Archdiocesan policy statements on matters dealing with Church teaching and discipline. 2) The testimony given by those on the list prepared in advance. This was done through consultation with Archbishop Hunthausen and the Reverend Michael Ryan, Vicar General of the Archdiocese of Seattle, so that a cross section of the priests, religious and laity in the Archdiocese would be represented. In all, this included seventy individuals, nearly one half of whom were priests of the Archdiocese. 3) The testimony of the Archbishop himself, a written copy of which he reviewed and signed. It should be noted that the Visitator spent 13 hours in conversation with Archbishop Hunthausen. Every effort was made to assess the credibility of the persons who had complained to the Holy See.

b. Throughout the investigation a number of allegations were judged as insufficiently based in fact or as corrected by an adequate response of Archbishop Hunthausen. However, after careful attention was given to the facts verified by the three sources of information noted above, five areas of concern remained: the tribunal, liturgy, clergy formation, priests leaving the ministry or who are laicized, moral issues in health care institutions and ministry to homosexuals. The testimony of "unfriendly" witnesses added little to the data on which the criticism of the Holy See was based.

In more specific terms the problems included the following:

The Tribunal – the misunderstanding and systematic misapplication of the so-called internal forum solution, and the lack of a plan to employ degreed personnel in the Tribunal.

The Liturgy – the widespread use of general absolution on a regular basis and the practice of First Communion before First Confession; repeated instances of intercommunion, e.g. permitting non-Catholics to receive communion at Catholic masses and Catholics in Protestant services.

Health Care – the continued inadequate response in both teaching and practice to the directives of the Holy See and the National Conference of Catholic Bishops regarding contraceptive sterilizations in Catholic Hospitals.

Homosexuals – the need to develop a ministry to homosexuals that is at once unequivocally based on the teachings of the Magisterium, rather than on erroneous doctrines, and which avoids affiliations with groups promoting doctrines contrary to the Church's teachings.

Inactive Priests – the employment of those who have left the active ministry and/or who have been laicized, in teaching positions and for service in the liturgy contrary to the directives of the Holy See and the terms of their rescripts of laicization.

Clergy Formation – because of concern regarding the admissions practices of candidates for the priesthood and because of concern and questions surrounding the continuing formation of the clergy, efforts must be taken to ensure that the continuing education of priests be done in ways that emphasize the bond of the local Church and the Universal Church, and which are firmly rooted in sound theology, especially in these areas: Christology, Anthropology, the Role of the Magisterium, the Nature of the Church and Priesthood and Moral Theology.

c. After hearing a preliminary report on the Visitation, Archbishop Hunthausen concluded that the Holy See judged him to be an effective bishop in many respects. At the same time, Archbishop Hunthausen understood that the Holy See considered him lacking the firmness necessary to govern the Archdiocese. The Archbishop would dissent from such judgment, but stated in a letter to the Pro-Nuncio (September 11, 1985) that "if it (the judgment) has been made, then I can perhaps begin to understand why the Holy See might reason that the only workable solution to this matter is the appointment of a man to assist me whose principal responsibilities will be to supply or 'fill in' in those areas where it is thought that I am lacking."

4. The Decisions after the Visitation

a. On October 8 and 10, 1985, the results of the Visitation were again shared with Archbishop Hunthausen in extensive consultation at the Apostolic Nunciature. It should be noted that the actual raw data from the interviews were not released to him given the confidentiality assured to those who provided the information. However, the specific areas of concern to the Holy See were reviewed in detail and the Archbishop was given the possibility to offer a response and seek clarification. In large measure he did not dispute the facts. Rather, it was his interpretation of the importance of these matters and the inadequacy of his response that were the principal concerns.

b. Before his request for an Auxiliary was granted, consideration was given to a number of ways that another Bishop could be of assistance in addressing the five problem areas, e.g., the appointment of a Co-Adjutor with full power, the temporary appointment of an

Administrator, the appointment of an Auxiliary with special faculties from the Holy See. In considering the alternatives, the Holy See gave careful attention to the effects that any decision would have on the Church and the Archbishop of Seattle.

c. The Code of Canon Law (canon 403 #2) does contemplate cases when the Holy See grants special faculties. However, upon the recommendation of members of the hierarchy in the United States, it was agreed that Archbishop Hunthausen, after accepting the Auxiliary, would himself give Bishop Wuerl responsibility over the areas of particular concern to the Holy See. This compromise, which the Archbishop formally accepted in a letter dated December 2, 1985, was not to lessen the significance of those special faculties. Rather, it allowed the Archbishop to follow a procedure analogous or similar to that used by other Diocesan Bishops, who share authority with Auxiliaries in areas or over a territory. Simultaneously, the Archbishop of Seattle did acknowledge that the Holy See could reserve to itself, in an uncontested way, the right to adopt such measures as may subsequently become necessary. At no time did the Holy See require Archbishop Hunthausen to make a public announcement that he had agreed to surrender any episcopal duties. This was never contemplated.

d. For more than six months after the arrival of Bishop Wuerl, the agreed-to faculties were not given. When this was brought to the attention of Archbishop Hunthausen, he stated that, in his original understanding, he agreed that the Auxiliary would supervise or manage these areas of concern as he, the Archbishop, determined. This could be attributed to a misunderstanding or misinterpretation on his part. The Pro-Nuncio, therefore, reminded him of the sequence of events that led to the compromise. The faculties, which were originally to be given by Rome, would be given instead by him as Archbishop, but with the same effect. The Archbishop of Seattle then petitioned the Holy See for an authoritative clarification.

e. When this was given, the Archbishop of Seattle granted the faculties and made the announcement that they were mandated by Rome. In fact, a more precise description would have been that this was the agreement reached between Archbishop Hunthausen and the Holy See after much discussion and effort to support him. Regretfully, the surprise announcement made by Archbishop Hunthausen after granting the faculties was interpreted as portraying this whole process as a one-sided affair.

> f. The efforts made by the Holy See after the Visitation were designed to address and strengthen those areas that were found wanting, and at the same time, to respect and recognize the position of the Archbishop. Meeting these goals required the corresponding cooperation of the Holy See, of the man who was selected and accepted as Auxiliary, and of the Archbishop of Seattle.[102]

If Rome was trying to control the narrative, this did not hamper the phenomenal outpouring of support showered on Seattle's Archbishop Hunthausen. Rev. Joseph McMahon, chair of the board of the Federation of Diocesan Liturgical Commissions, sent Hunthausen a letter and a resolution of support endorsed at the mid-October national meeting of the Federation held in Portland, Maine. Diocesan liturgical commissions and offices of worship all over the nation were backing Hunthausen. The delegation of complete and final authority to Auxiliary Bishop Donald Wuerl in the area of liturgy in the Archdiocese of Seattle was a "most unusual action of the Holy See and [we] find both the process and conclusions confusing and divisive, and declare that this is an issue of significant and immediate concern to them."[103]

On October 30, 1986, the *New York Times* reported:

> "Archbishop Raymond G. Hunthausen, called anything from saint to heretic in more than four years of dispute with the Vatican, shows no sign of letting up in the public activism that has thrust him into the limelight. As the Vatican was preparing to issue a detailed documentation of church complaints that led to his disciplining, the Archbishop of Seattle was busy protesting the arms race and urging all Christian denominations to fight nuclear weapons."

He was out at the Trident nuclear submarine base at Bangor on the day before the Vatican issued the chronology. "When Archbishop Hunthausen left to attend a funeral Tuesday for his mentor, Bishop Bernard Topel of Spokane, on the other side of the state, other church officials rushed to his defense." Ryan, the chancellor, rejected the Vatican claim that the power-sharing arrangement was voluntary. "There were no alternatives. It was made clear by certain highly placed church authorities that he had to accept these conditions." One of Hunthausen's good friends, Archbishop Francis Hurley of Alaska, described Hunthausen as "the most unlikely hero" for liberal church activists. "When it comes right down to the ultimate question, he is obedient, he respects the church authority," Hurley said. Hurley also said that the real question was no longer Hunthausen. "It's a question of the state of the church."[104]

Nationally syndicated columnist Mary McGrory suggested in an allusion to a poem by Dylan Thomas that Hunthausen, known as a gentle pastor, would not "go gentle into that good night," which the Vatican "seems to have in mind for him." Something was happening, she wrote:

> "...an occurrence unthinkable a generation ago: a wave of protest by Roman Catholics, including clergy members from Seattle and across the United States, over the treatment accorded Hunthausen. The Hunthausen story begins with Pope John XXIII, who appointed him. The beaming peasant believed that all God's children belonged to the 'people of God' and convened the Vatican II Council in 1962 with the idea of 'throwing open the windows of the church.' The current pope, John Paul II, is much more concerned with the people inside and protecting them from the contamination of heretical thought."

The Catholic bishops were quite different from those a generation earlier. Now they were "in the vanguard of resistance to President Reagan's anticommunist crusade in Nicaragua." Was John Paul II going after Hunthausen as an attack on collegiality?

> "Anyone seeking the difference between the old and the new need look no farther than Cardinal Francis Spellman, who blessed the Vietnam war, and Archbishop Hunthausen, who not only withheld 50 percent of the income tax on his annual $9,000 salary to dramatize his objections to the arms race and advocates unilateral disarmament but who, on the day the bill of particulars against him came out, was on a picket line protesting the Trident submarine, harbored at a base he calls the 'Auschwitz of Puget Sound.'"[105]

The *New York Times* portrayed Rome and Seattle in "a war of words." "The Vatican's quarrel with Archbishop Raymond G. Hunthausen of Seattle was taking on the look of a press release war last week."[106]

"Many practices for which Archbishop Raymond G. Hunthausen of Seattle was reprimanded by the Vatican are common across the United States, Roman Catholic officials say." So began *New York Times* writer Joseph Berger in his November 10 story. For example, Dignity (the gay Catholic group) had Mass in churches in several other dioceses across the country, he noted. "These churches are in dioceses led by some of the church's foremost figures, including John Cardinal O'Connor of New York, regarded as a leading exponent of greater church orthodoxy...." Other concerns raised by the Vatican in the case of the Seattle archdiocese "are prevalent in dioceses around the country." So why Hunthausen? Berger noted that in the view of Rev. Joseph O'Hare, the president of Fordham University, Hunthausen's activism on the issue of nuclear arms may have been the catalyst that sparked so many complaints about other practices in Seattle. "As a result, people gave his actions closer scrutiny than they might have the less conspicuous ordinaries," O'Hare said. Berger continued: "Other church leaders said they believed that the action against

Archbishop Hunthausen was part of a firmer stance by Pope John Paul II against the liberties taken with orthodox Catholic doctrine by a democratic and diverse American church."[107]

Bishop Emeritus Nicolas E. Walsh, then living in Boise, said in early November that he had made a trip to Rome the previous month "to show my personal solidarity with Pope John Paul II and the archbishop, and to visit the cardinal-prefects of the Vatican offices handling the case." Walsh had been auxiliary bishop with Hunthausen for several years. "Walsh said everyone he met with at the Vatican expressed surprise at the publicity Hunthausen's case has received."[108]

There should not have been so much surprise on their part. After all, the Vatican by this time was well into its sometimes heavy-handed effort to dismantle the reform patterns and moderate-to-liberal thinking that had come out of the refreshing *aggiornamento* spirit of the Second Vatican Council. John Paul II and Cardinal Ratzinger, among others working to restore central command and control, were giving considerable hope to the very people who had long been critical of "quintessential Vatican II bishop" Raymond Hunthausen. Ken Vanderhoef, an active lay Catholic in the region, a lawyer and an early leader in the national Right to Life movement, felt Hunthausen had for many years been very visible in the peace movement but could rarely be seen in the pro-life movement. Hunthausen had shown a longstanding unwillingness to interact with people who held a conservative political perspective. He speculated that perhaps one reason for what he perceived to be Hunthausen's reticence to take a more outspoken stand on the abortion issue could be the unchurched character of the region. That demographic fact made more precious the need to sustain bonds of unity in the ecumenical community, so that the churches could have a unified voice in a largely secular atmosphere. Hence, Vanderhoef suggested, Hunthausen avoided topics which would tear away at the ecumenical bonds.[109]

The Wanderer, the newspaper out of the Twin Cities, had been going after Hunthausen, especially since the June 1981 Tacoma speech. Hunthausen was muddled, irresponsible, and unpatriotic. In 1983, the paper made the claim that this archbishop was part of fundamental problems plaguing much of the Catholic Church in the United States. After the pastoral letter on peace was completed, *The Wanderer* described Hunthausen as one of the key leaders among those turning the U.S. Catholic Church into a vehicle of partisan politics.[110] Now it seemed Rome was responding to critical voices such as *The Wanderer.*

Homosexuality came under the newspaper's watch. Hunthausen was said to be pampering homosexuals. The decision to open St. James Cathedral to Dignity showed that Hunthausen was one of many U.S. bishops trying to establish a new nationalist church that would reject Rome's authority. "Catholics in the Seattle Archdiocese are finding out just how far practitioners of the New American Catholic

Church are willing to subject them to in the way of insult ranging from indignity to immorality."[111] When the decision to have the visitation became public knowledge, the conservative newspaper reported that during the previous years the Vatican had received large quantities of mail from U.S. Catholics expressing criticism of Hunthausen. *The Wanderer* unabashedly stated that much of this mail had to do with Hunthausen's stand on war and peace issues.[112]

Running through the paper for many years was the basic conviction that something very serious had gone awry in the Catholic Church in America. *The Wanderer*'s Frank Morriss wrote in December 1983 that those who ridiculed this paper and called it a fringe archconservative work of zealotry were missing a crucial truth. All the negative focus on Hunthausen and other religious leaders came from "a genuine and well-based anxiety for the integrity of the Catholic Faith."[113] Curiously, the criticisms of Hunthausen in this newspaper were comparatively limited during the 1984 and 1985 period, up to the time when Pio Laghi announced that the visitation was formally closed. Denunciations had been feverish and pronounced in the period before the visitation and during its early period.

The Wanderer received a letter from Ronald Reagan on the eve of the 1984 presidential election. Reagan wrote: "By encouraging the examination of public policy from the perspective of Catholic teaching and values, you are fostering the spirit of reasoned debate and inquiry which assures that the beliefs and views of all citizens will be considered with respect in the marketplace of ideas."[114] Reagan liked the paper's strong American patriotic martial pitch. The paper drew a parallel between pacifism and what one of its writers described as "spiritual pacifism." If a church leader is pacifist on the issue of war, so went the argument, he was frequently found to be "weak" and "passive" with regard to the church and doctrine. A country must be militarily strong to defend itself against the menace of communism, argued one writer, and a bishop must be a strong authority figure fully in command of his local church. Hunthausen, like some other bishops who had gotten so engaged in the peace pastoral letter, was a pacifist on both fronts, and therefore a danger to both society and church.[115] Frank Morriss, commenting on Rome's decision to investigate Hunthausen and the specific move of assigning Wuerl to Seattle, claimed all of this sent a signal to the American church as a whole.[116] Another writer put it this way: "There are undoubtedly other bishops in America who have sinned against Catholic teaching in the same manner as had Archbishop Hunthausen, and it is essential that they also should be persuaded to mend their ways."[117]

Robert Auer, a lay Catholic from Bellevue, felt that Hunthausen was undermining both U.S. democracy and the Catholic Church. Auer, writing in the Bellevue newspaper *Journal-American*, claimed Hunthausen's major mistake was that of becoming a politician priest who neglected his duties as chief shepherd of the archdiocese.[118] Auer saw things much as Eleanor Schoen did. As a lay person long active in church life in the archdiocese, Schoen felt that Hunthausen had neglected his official duties when he became so involved in the peace movement. She insisted that letters of complaint sent to Rome were not the product of any heavily organized effort. They arose spontaneously. She rejected the argument that there had been some sort of plot against the archbishop's peace stand. People were upset for a host of reasons, not only because of his peace stand. "He is the archbishop; he should be dealing with church issues per se."[119]

Margaret Hoffman, a member of a group calling itself the Sons of St. Peter Coalition, felt that ecclesiology and authority were the crucial matters. All too often people, especially people in positions of religious leadership in Seattle, ignored the legitimate authority of Pope John Paul II. Many people in the archdiocese were understandably angry and strident in their criticisms of Hunthausen. Many felt betrayed, she said, by what they perceived to be Hunthausen's tendency to view himself as an autonomous bishop unbeholding to Rome.[120] William May, a professor of moral theology at Catholic University, argued that the Vatican's action in disciplining Hunthausen was a serious and necessary effort to safeguard Catholic teaching. The Hickey visitation, he maintained, involved a careful examination of the Seattle situation. The Vatican correctly concluded from the evidence that something needed to be done to remedy the state of affairs in Seattle. The Vatican action was vital to ensure that the local bishop fulfilled his responsibility to express the "mind" of the Catholic Church.[121]

I asked one person who worked with him how Hunthausen was coping with all the criticism. John Reid came in 1979 to direct the Channel Program, working in young adult ministry. When all the conflict between Seattle and Rome heated up, there were prayer services in the churches. They were giving out "I love Hunthausen" buttons (with the heart symbol located between "I" and "Hunthausen"). On one occasion Reid went with Hunthausen to an event at a high school:

> "I [Reid] asked him how the investigation was treating him. We got close to Kennedy High School and we saw people wearing those buttons. And he said, really clearly, 'You know, I'm really uncomfortable about that. I didn't become a priest to be loved myself. I don't like that, the I love Hunthausen focus, that shouldn't be.' So I said to him something like, 'well, you know, Archbishop, it's still, it's a good thing, if people like you, if they respect you, they're going to listen to you.' He kind of thought about it, and I remember as the car stopped he said, 'I guess it's okay if people love me as long as they love the church even more and the gospel even more and Jesus, and the God Jesus reveals even more.' I thought to myself, you know, Hunthausen was being attacked by the church, and yet he does not focus on himself but instead says this."

Once, when he was visiting Hunthausen in his office and was really angry about the investigation, Reid was bold enough to think that he had an insight about what the archbishop could do, namely tell them to shove it. "Archbishop, how come you're not angry? I'd be really angry that I was being maligned, being attacked. I don't understand. Teach me about how to deal with being attacked." Hunthausen replied, "Well, you know, first of all, I took a vow of obedience that I take seriously. I took a vow first to the bishop when I was ordained a priest, I took a vow of obedience to the pope when I agreed to be a bishop back in Helena, and so I take that vow very seriously and I think I need to find appropriate ways to live with this challenging situation without impugning any one in any way." And Reid asked him, "Well, your vow of obedience, doesn't it leave room for, you know, faithful dissent, or respectful disagreement?" Hunthausen said, "I don't see how that would do anything to build up the church. I think it would divide the church into camps and that's not what I am about."[122]

Once the public knew by the fall of 1986 that Hunthausen's authority had been attenuated, news skyrocketed to heights exceeding even the media coverage enveloping Hunthausen's "Faith and Disarmament" words and actions in 1981-1982. At one point in 1986, he called Don Hopps on the phone and asked him to come over to his apartment at St. James Cathedral. Hopps got over there and when he came into the archbishop's residence, there was Aldolfo Perez Esquivel, the Argentinean justice and peace activist who had just received the Nobel Peace Prize. The Nobel laureate said people around the world were worried about Hunthausen. "We know that the attack on Hunthausen is bigger than is being said, that the big forces are manipulating things behind the scene." Perez Esquivel told Hopps, "Look, take care of Hunthausen; he can't take care of himself alone." He surmised that the forces going after Hunthausen were the same repressive forces at work in Central America, Argentina, and elsewhere around the world. He had flown out to Seattle from New York, taking a detour on his way home from the Oslo Nobel ceremony, to let Hunthausen know that people in other countries were concerned about the injustice they felt was happening to him and to the church in Seattle.[123]

Hunthausen had been speaking his truth to power—specifically, to American wealth and power. In that secular realm he spoke his conscience and put his words into the practice of civil disobedience. In the religious drama, on the other hand, he was not going to practice ecclesial disobedience. Yet he did speak truth to ecclesiastical power—to Roman Catholic 'command and control' power. As we shall see momentarily, he called into question the official Vatican-approved chronology of what had happened to date in the Seattle-Rome conflict. What happened when he made his case before his brother bishops at their November 1986 NCCB meeting? Those brother American bishops had all taken a vow of church obedience just as Hunthausen had. How would they respond when he asked for their help?

ENDNOTES

1 Reese, Thomas. *Archbishop: Inside the Power Structure of the American Catholic Church.* San Francisco: Harper and Row, 1989, 337.

2 Hunthausen, Raymond. "Archbishop Hunthausen's Response to Vatican Chronology." *Origins* 20 Nov. 1986, 406-408.

3 Schilling, Timothy. *Conflict in the Catholic Hierarchy: A Study of Coping Strategies in the Hunthausen Affair, with Preferential Attention to Discursive Strategies.* Utrecht, The Netherlands 2002, 316.

4 Ryan, Michael. Personal interview. Seattle, Washington 13 Dec 2012.

5 Schilling, 316.

6 Schilling, 148.

7 Schilling, 150.

8 "A Letter from Archbishop Hunthausen." *Progress* 27 Oct. 1983, 5.

9 Schilling, 149.

10 Ostrom, Carol. "Vatican to investigate Archbishop Hunthausen." *Seattle Times* 27 Oct. 1983. *Historic Seattle Times, 1900–1984*, 1.

11 Ostrom, Carol. "Vatican official: Visit aimed at fact-finding." *Seattle Times* 29 Oct. 1983. *Historic Seattle Times, 1900–1984*, 8.

12 "Hunthausen stirs the Vatican." 20 Oct. 1983. This editorial from *Seattle Post-Intelligencer* was located via *Historic Seattle Times, 1900–1984,* 30.

13 Briggs, Kenneth. "Pope Tells U.S. Bishops: Fight Dissent On Sexuality." *New York Times* 31 Oct. 1983, A1. *Lexisnexis.com*. Web. 9 Aug. 2012.

14 "Virginia bishop blames conservatives for Vatican probe." *Seattle Times* 31 Oct. 1983. *Historic Seattle Times, 1900–1984,* 9.

15 Ostrom, Carol. "Support for Hunthausen grows as probe nears." *Seattle Times* 1 Nov. 1983. *Historic Seattle Times, 1900–1984*, 13.

16 Michels, Erich. "Archdiocesan leaders react to investigation." *Progress* 3 Nov. 1983, 10.

17 Ostrom, Carol. "Local groups affirm support for Hunthausen's social views." *Seattle Times* 2 Nov. 1983. *Historic Seattle Times, 1900–1984*, 77.

18 Ostrom, Carol. "Doctrine, not disarmament, point of Hunthausen probe." *Seattle Times* 3 Nov. 1983. *Historic Seattle Times, 1900–1984*, 1.

19 Ostrom, Carol. "Vindication predicted for Hunthausen." *Seattle Times* 4 Nov. 1983. *Historic Seattle Times, 1900–1984*, 1.

20 Schilling, 151.

21 Lindsey, Robert. "Witnesses Discuss Views Of Prelate." *New York Times* 6 Nov. 1983, 37. *Lexisnexis.com.* Web. 9 Aug. 2012.

22 Michels, Erich. "Archdiocesan leaders react to investigation." *Progress* 3 Nov. 1983, 10.

23 "Vatican Investigation begins this week." *Progress* 3 Nov. 1983, 9.

24 Schilling, interview with Fr. Michael G. Ryan, 316.

25 Ostrom, Carol. "Vatican representative holds court with friends, foes of Hunthausen." *Seattle Times* 5 Nov. 1983. *Historic Seattle Times, 1900–1984*, 9.

26 Ostrom, Carol. "Is probe a blessing in disguise?" *Seattle Times* 5 Nov. 1983. *Historic Seattle Times, 1900–1984*, 13.

27 Ostrom, Carol. "Hunthausen critics list 'abuses'." *Seattle Times* 8 Nov. 1983. *Historic Seattle Times, 1900–1984*, 14.

28 Ostrom, Carol. "Vatican's envoy says he found good things." *Seattle Times* 9 Nov. 1983. *Historic Seattle Times, 1900–1984*, 86.

29 Reese, Thomas. *Archbishop: Inside the Power Structure of the American Catholic Church*. San Francisco: Harper and Row, 1989, 338.

30 Schilling, 316.

31 Ostrom, Carol. "4-year old's message sustained archbishop." *Seattle Times* 12 Nov. 1983. *Historic Seattle Times, 1900–1984*, 8.

32 Walmsley, Jack. Personal interview. West Seattle, Washington 8 Dec 2012.

33 Ratzinger, Josef. Letter published in *Progress* 26 Jan. 1984, 5.

34 Ostrom, Carol. Vatican letter thanks Hunthausen, boosts 'moderation'." *Seattle Times* 28 Jan. 1984. *Historic Seattle Times, 1900–1984*, 31.

35 Schilling, 149.

36 Schilling, 316.

37 Schilling, 317.

38 Hunthausen, Raymond. Transcript of videotaped address to the Sisters of St. Joseph of Peace, July 1984. Archdiocese of Seattle Archives.

39 Schilling, 317.

40 Hunthausen, Raymond. Letter to the people of the archdiocese. 25 Apr. 1985. Archdiocese of Seattle Archives.

41 Schilling, 320.

42 Ratzinger, Joseph. Letter to Archbishop Hunthausen. 30 Sept. 1985. See *Progress* 28 May 1987, 5; also available as "Cardinal Ratzinger's Letter" *Origins* 4 June 1987, 41-43.

43 Schilling, 156.

44 Wooden, Cindy. "Holy See concludes investigation." *Progress* 28 Nov. 1985, 13.

45 Hunthausen, Raymond. Letter to the people of the archdiocese. *Progress* 28 Nov. 1985, 1.

46 Schilling, 160.

47 "Interview with Archbishop Hunthausen." *Progress* 5 Dec. 1985, 4-5.

48 Schilling, 162.

49 Hunthausen, Raymond. "Remaining Faithful to the Church in a Time of Tension." Speech delivered at the National Federation of Priests Council Convention in Salt Lake City. 21 Apr. 1986. Archdiocese of Seattle Archives.

50 Hunthausen, Raymond. "Departure Day Talk." Speech delivered at Maryknoll, New York. 7 June 1986. Archdiocese of Seattle Archives.

51 Schilling, 317.

52 Hopps, Don. Personal interview. Seattle, Washington 20 Sept. 2012.

53 Schilling, 317.

54 Schilling, 163. He cites Hunthausen's interview from *Progress* 11 Sept. 1986, 3.

55 Schilling, 317.

56 "Vatican Moves To Curb Power Of A Liberal Prelate In Seattle (National Desk)." *New York Times* 5 Sept. 1986. *Global Issues In Context*. Web. 7 Aug. 2012.

57 Burns, Jim. Conversation and comments on draft manuscript. Lafayette, Oregon 20 May 2014.

58 Hunthausen, Raymond. Letter to the Priests of the Archdiocese. 3 Sept. 1986. Concerned Catholics File. The Concerned Catholics File is a rich trove of historical materials (minutes of CC meetings and much more) and I have found it of great help as will be noted throughout this chapter and chapter six. Sr. Louise Dumont, Sisters of St. Joseph of Peace, loaned the CCF to me.

59 Hyer, Marjorie. "The Vatican and Dissent; Crackdown in America Increasingly Evident." *Washington Post* 15 Sept. 1986, A1. *Global Issues in Context*. Web. 7 Aug. 2012.

60 "Vatican Change In Seattle Protested (National Desk)." *New York Times* 6 Sept. 1986. *Global Issues In Context*. Web. 7 Aug. 2012

61 "The Church in Conflict." Prayer Service held at St. Mary's Church, Seattle 14 Sept. 1986. Archdiocese of Seattle Archives. (Note: Some sources I have relied upon came from the late Kay Lagreid of the Public Affairs Office of the Archdiocese when I was doing my doctoral dissertation research in the late 1980s. I refer to the Archdiocese of Seattle Archives as the present source for these documents on the assumption that these documents are probably there at present.)

62 Young, Caroline and S.L. Sanger. "Priests want Hunthausen's powers restored." *Seattle Post-Intelligencer* 13 Sept. 1986, A6.

63 Homily (priest not identified in the records). 14 Sept. 1986. Concerned Catholics File.

64 Responses from Individuals and Regions, Meeting of the Presbyterate, 12 Sept. 1986. Concerned Catholics File.

65 Berger, Joseph. "Bishops and Vatican: U.S. Prelates Tread a Fine Line. (National Desk)." *New York Times* 18 Sept. 1986. *Global Issues in Context*. Web. 7 Aug. 2012.

66 Letter from Archdiocesan Pastoral Council to Archbishop Hunthausen. 17 Sept. 1986. Concerned Catholics File.

67 Statement of Support. St. Mary's Hispanic Community. 26 Sept. 1986. Concerned Catholics File.

68 Bloom, Phillip. The Investigation: Foolhardy and Unjust. 24 Sept. 1986. Concerned Catholics File.

69 Laghi, Pio. Letter to Rev. Phillip Bloom. 16 Sept. 1986. Concerned Catholics File.

70 Wuerl, Donald. Letter to the Priests of the Archdiocese of Seattle. 19 Sept. 1986. Concerned Catholics File.

71 Hunthausen, Raymond. Letter to the Priests of the Archdiocese. 19 Sept. 1986. Concerned Catholics File.

72 Ashwell, G. Barry. Statement. 23 Sept. 1986. Concerned Catholics File.

73 Carroll, Patrick. Response to Archbishop in preparation for Friday's meeting. No date specified. Concerned Catholics File.

74 Harris, W.R. Statement. No date specified (but likely part of the series of statements made in late Sept. 1986). Concerned Catholics File.

75 Kohls, Harry. Letter to Archbishop Hunthausen. 25 Sept. 1986. Concerned Catholics File.

76 Schilling, 174.

77 Letter to the Editor, from the Renton Ecumenical Association of Church, no date specified; Pax Christi USA News Release 24 Sept. 1986; Letter to Archbishop Hunthausen from the executive director of the National Conference of Diocesan Vocation Directors 11 Sept. 1986. Concerned Catholics File.

78 Memo from Archbishop Hunthausen to Designated Leaders in the Archdiocese of Seattle. 29 Sept. 1986. Concerned Catholics File.

79 Schilling, 174-175.

80 Bloom, Phillip. Letter to Archbishop Laghi. 29 Sept. 1986. Concerned Catholics File.

81 McCloskey, L. J. Letter to Bishop Wuerl. 30 Sept. 1986. Concerned Catholics File.

82 Buckley, Mary. "Repression Is Undoing Work of Vatican II." *New York Times* 22 Sept. 1986. *Global Issues In Context*. Web. 7 Aug. 2012.

83 Schilling, 175.

84 Pruitt, Kathleen. Letter to Bishops of Region XII, on behalf of the group Concerned Catholics. 1 Oct. 1986. Concerned Catholics File.

85 Briggs, Kenneth. *Holy Siege: The Year that Shook Catholic America*. HarperCollins, San Francisco 1992, 17.

86 Schilling, 172.

87 Wooden, Cindy. "Northwest bishops support efforts of Archbishop Hunthausen, Bishop Wuerl." *Progress* 25 Sept. 1986, 3.

88 Laghi, Pio. Letter to Rev. Hynes. 3 Oct. 1986. Concerned Catholics File.

89 Schilling, 173.

90 "Cloud over Seattle." *National Catholic Reporter* 3 Oct. 1986, 1.

91 Goldman, Ari. "Catholic Colleges In U.S. Debate Academic Freedom Amid Disputes." *New York Times* 8 Oct. 1986. *Global Issues in Context*. Web. 7 Aug. 2012.

92 Morris, Jack. Letter to Concerned Catholics. 3 Oct. 1986. Concerned Catholics File.

93 Schilling, 175.

94 Hunthausen, Raymond. Letter to the People of the Archdiocese of Seattle. 14 Oct. 1986. Concerned Catholics File.

95 "Archbishop writes concerning recent events in Seattle Archdiocese." *Progress* 16 Oct. 1986, 3.

96 Lucero Miner, Esther. Personal interview (with small group). Edmonds, Washington 8 Dec 2012.

97 Hunthausen, Raymond. Letter to Priests of the Archdiocese (and letter to colleagues and co-workers in the ministry). 27 Oc. 1986. Concerned Catholics File.

98 Berger, Joseph. "Vatican, Replying To Critics, Explains Curb Of U.S. Bishop." *New York Times* 28 Oct. 1986. *Global Issues in Context*. Web. 7 Aug. 2012.

99 Schilling, 175. See *National Catholic Reporter* 31 Oct. 1986.

100 Schilling, 176. See *National Catholic Reporter* 31 Oct. 1986.

101 Schilling, 317.

102 Laghi, Pio. "A Chronology of Recent Events in the Archdiocese of Seattle." *Origins* 6 Nov. 1986, 361-364.

103 Letter and Resolution sent to Archbishop Hunthausen. Rev. Joseph McMahon, Federation of Diocesan Liturgical Commissions. 29 Oct. 1986. Concerned Catholics File.

104 "Archbishop At Odds With The Vatican: A 'Most Unlikely Hero'." *New York Times* 30 Oct. 1986. *Global Issues In Context*. Web. 7 Aug. 2012.

105 McGrory, Mary. "Guilty of Compassion?" *Washington Post* 30 Oct. 1986, A2. *Global Issues in Context*. Web. 7 Aug. 2012.

106 Mansnerus, Laura, and Katherine Roberts. "Ideas & Trends; A War of Words Between Seattle and the Vatican." *New York Times* 2 Nov. 1986. *Global Issues In Context*. Web. 7 Aug. 2012.

107 Berger, Joseph. "Practices Cited In Seattle Rebuke Are Common In U.S. Catholicism." *New York Times* 10 Nov. 1986. *Global Issues In Context*. Web. 7 Aug. 2012.

108 "Bishop From Boise Met With Pope To Discuss Hunthausen." Associated Press 4 Nov. 1986. *Global Issues in Context*. Web. 7 Aug. 2012.

109 Vanderhoef, Ken. Personal interview. Seattle, Washington 9 Sept. 1988.

110 Morriss, Frank. "Archbishop Hunthausen Moving Deeper Into Politics." *Wanderer* 30 June 1983, 1,7.

111 Morris, Frank. "Pampering Homosexuals No Substitute For Truth." *Wanderer* 21 July 1983, 1,6.

112 "Holy See To Investigate Complaints Against Archbishop Hunthausen." *Wanderer* 3 Nov. 1983, 1,5.

113 Morriss, Frank. "Where There's Smoke, There's Usually Fire." *Wanderer* 8 Dec. 1983, 4.

114 "Greetings From The President." *Wanderer* 1 Nov. 1984, 4.

115 Connell, Anne Stewart. "The Spiritual Pacifism of the leadership of the NCCB." *Wanderer* 7 Feb. 1985, 4.

116 Morriss, Frank. "A Change In The Direction of Orthodox Catholicism." *Wanderer* 19 Dec. 1985, 4.

117 Mulloy, John. "Can There Be Any Public Criticism of Bishops?" *Wanderer* 23 Jan. 1986.
118 Auer, Robert. "Hunthausen neglected duties." *Journal-American* 5 Oct. 1986, D8.
119 Schoen, Eleanor. Personal interview. Seattle, Washington 14 Sept. 1988.
120 Hoffman, Margaret. Personal interview. Seattle, Washington 13 July 1989.
121 May, William. Letter "Catholic Faith." *Washington Post* 16 Nov. 1986, K6.
122 Reid, John. Personal (small group) interview. Seattle, Washington 25 Mar. 2013.
123 Hopps, Don. Personal interview. Seattle, Washington 20 Sept. 2012.

Chapter Six

WHAT KIND OF CHURCH?

Archbishop Hunthausen's case was about to be taken up by his fellow American bishops. While everyone wondered what the bishops would do, a lot of folks did much more than speculate. They organized to support him. For instance, most of the priests of the Seattle archdiocese put their sentiments together in a shared communication to the U.S. bishops. Another example involves the organizing work of Concerned Catholics (CC). The scrappy group brought together the energies of lay people, women religious, and priests in the vanguard of voices advocating for Hunthausen. Sr. Louise Dumont shared with me the CC's trove of documents and recounted how the CC seed was planted. "We were in the car, Fr. Dave Jaeger, Fr. Mike Raschko, and myself, and we discussed the idea of forming a group to talk about what was going on." Sr. Dumont was the first woman to be appointed to head the Seattle chancery's office representing women religious. I asked her about Hunthausen's character as a religious leader:

> "Hunthausen was not a person who pushed himself forward. He was very accepting of people. He responded, he listened to people to hear what they had to say. He never wanted to be a bishop, much less an archbishop. He was very much a man of the church. He never criticized the investigation, he never labeled them. He did not accuse Wuerl. He just did not think negatively about others. Eventually he came to realize this but he did not think it initially. He endured great suffering. What troubles me is the lack of respect. To do what they did sending Wuerl here without telling Hunthausen the true mission they had given to Wuerl, this was wrong. It was not just. So often the church is not concerned about justice."[1]

Dumont's Sisters of St. Joseph of Peace colleague, Sr. Kathleen Pruitt, helped lead CC's organizing efforts on his behalf, though of course Hunthausen himself did not try to instigate any of this. "We were active and vocal. I remember saying to him, 'Dutch, you don't need to speak out on this, the rest of us will do this.'" He could have been more vocal himself, she thought. "Part of me wishes he would have taken a more critical position. In some ways Hunthausen was a very private person, he was reluctant to be in the public eye. But remember, he was a leader who opened space for others to be leaders, to share their voices, to be empowered."[2] When the

U.S. bishops were gathering in November 1986, Pruitt, Dumont, and the growing CC membership, sent the bishops an open letter:

> "As you meet in Washington, D.C. we ask you to look west to the other Washington and see our confusion, pain and distress over what has happened to your brother and our Archbishop, Raymond G. Hunthausen. We ask you to do this out of love for and loyalty to our Holy Father, Pope John Paul II, and out of concern that he exercise his universal ministry in a way that safeguards the truth and builds up the Church for its mission. We are not certain that the Pope really knows and understands the facts and the meaning of what has happened here.
>
> We ask you to support us in our efforts to unmask the secrecy and expose the basic unfairness and injustice of the Apostolic Visitation of 1983. We ask you to join us in calling for the restoration to Archbishop Hunthausen of full, ordinary, proper and immediate power required for the exercise of the pastoral office of Bishop in a diocese.
>
> We ask you to do this because our reaction to what has happened here is spreading across the country and is now shared by thousands of people. We are concerned because an orthodox, competent, compassionate and prophetic leader has been publicly humiliated; because the Church's credibility has been damaged by this scandal; and because the kind of Church we have worked hard to become since Vatican II is now threatened.
>
> The Apostolic Visitation was unfair and even unjust because Archbishop Hunthausen's basic rights as a person and Bishop in the Church were violated. He was not told who asked for this investigation, nor the reasons for the investigation, nor what the specific findings of the investigation were. When the Visitation was concluded by a letter from the Apostolic Pro-Nuncio praising the Archbishop for his many gifts and asking him to exercise special care and vigilance in certain areas of Church life, he set up a process to do just that. As the work was beginning, he was asked to delegate complete authority in these areas to his auxiliary. We see this as an arbitrary and capricious act of authority in the Church.
>
> We ask for full disclosure first to the Archbishop and then to the public of the reasons for the investigation, the contents of the final report to the Holy See, and disclosure of the special and serious circumstances that warrant the removal of his faculties. We know the Archbishop wants to deal in an open and collegial manner with whatever serious issues may be behind this Visitation and its unfolding aftermath. We do too.

> We ask that you and the Holy See develop an open, just and collegial process for any future Apostolic Visitations or investigations. We do not want to see what has happened here repeated elsewhere.
>
> The issue of Seattle has now become a national and even international issue. It goes to the heart of who we are as Church. If we are to preach justice in the world with credibility, we must be seen as practicing justice in our own community of faith.
>
> We support your gathering with our prayer that the Spirit grant you depth of compassion and breadth of vision and wisdom."[3]

The D.C. meeting of the American bishops began. Bishop James Malone, completing his term as president of the National Conference of Catholic Bishops (NCCB), expressed concern to his colleagues about the rising distrust between some American Roman Catholics and the Vatican. "What makes the question of dissent all the more complicated in our local church is the passion we have in this country to let all persons have the freedom to give their point of view," Malone said. "As citizens we will die to protect this freedom of speech. As Catholics we must further defend the revelation given us in Christ and the church's responsibility to continue that revelation in its care for authentic teaching." A central question pressed on the bishops: "Wherever you stand, this division presents the church in the United States with a very serious question: How will we move to address this developing estrangement, to strengthen the cognitive and affective bonds between the Church here and the Holy See?" The *New York Times* described the laden-with-anticipation atmosphere at the Capitol Hilton, telling readers that "Archbishop Hunthausen sat quietly in the rear of the meeting room for most of today's business session." As a prelude to the closed executive session where they would focus on the Hunthausen case, Malone made an attempt to produce as much harmony as possible. He insisted that the NCCB would not "inject itself into the special relationship between the Holy Father and a local bishop."[4] Malone wanted the body of bishops to steer clear of second-guessing Rome.

> "Nor have we any intention of engaging in a retrospective review of events which have already occurred and which have been placed in the public record. The purpose therefore of addressing this matter in our executive session is simply this: to offer fraternal support to Archbishop Hunthausen and Bishop Wuerl in their future efforts to minister to the church in Seattle. We look to this as a constructive expression of the collegial spirit which unites us with one another and with the Holy Father."[5]

Following Malone's remarks, the apostolic pro-nuncio (prior to 1984 he was the apostolic delegate, since then, full diplomatic relations between the Vatican and the U.S. government had not been formalized), Archbishop Pio Laghi took to the podium and sounded rather pleased when he said: "As I look out over this assembly permit me to express my satisfaction at the presence of so many who have been appointed to the hierarchy during my tenure as papal representative. We have not yet reached the 'magic number' of 100, but we are not yet far from it." Laghi conveyed a message from the Holy Father about "the mystery of the church…and our own relationship of ecclesial communion," which is "discovered in the same mystery of the church."[6] In keeping with all this talk of mystery, the executive session to debate the Hunthausen case would take place behind closed doors. Not even Hunthausen's Fr. Mike Ryan was allowed in the conference room.[7]

Despite, or because of, the Vatican-tailored cloak of secrecy over the bishops' deliberations, Hunthausen backers demonstrated and marched outside the Capitol Hilton. Inside, the bishops faced a dilemma. "One church official said the difficulty was finding how to support the Archbishop without offending the Vatican," reported the *New York Times*. How much influence could a national conference wield? Bishop Malone had been, added the *New York Times*, "a forceful advocate of the national bishops' groups in face of criticism by some Vatican officials that the groups have no real teaching authority. In church law, individual bishops, and not their national conferences, are given that authority." A national conference could become a threat to Rome's control, and on this issue Cardinal Law, Archbishop of Boston and Archbishop Weakland of Milwaukee, exemplified polar views. "Cardinal Law has been a strong supporter of recent Vatican moves to impose orthodoxy on the United States church; Archbishop Weakland has publicly questioned the wisdom of the Vatican crackdown."[8] The people outside the Hilton were not going to leave the debate to the hierarchy. *New York Times* reporter Lydia Chavez wrote "A Red Letter for a 'Martyr'," describing a group from New Jersey "that made its stance known by wearing large patches of the letter 'H' cut from red cloth." Red denotes martyrdom. The group had petitions in support of Hunthausen signed by hundreds of New Jersey Catholics.[9]

CHALLENGING THE LAGHI CHRONOLOGY

At the center of the drama, Raymond Hunthausen was preparing to address his colleagues. Before they met face to face, he had sent them a detailed rebuttal challenging the Laghi chronology. Just as Laghi's chronology was cited in full in the last chapter, Hunthausen's is presented here:

> Because of necessary time restrictions limiting my presentation about the Apostolic Visitation of the Archdiocese of Seattle and related

matters, I have decided it will be best for me to convey to you in printed form my response to the "Chronology of Recent Events in the Archdiocese of Seattle," released on October 24, 1986, by the Apostolic Nunciature.

As you know, I chose to make a generic response at the time the Chronology was released. My respect for Archbishop Laghi and for the position that is his made it difficult for me to do otherwise. I was convinced that a point-by-point response at that time would only have escalated an already tense situation and that it would cause further confusion for our people. Also, I had been offered by Bishop Malone, our President, the opportunity to present a further response at this meeting.

I hesitate to burden you with reading material at this time. I do so only because I think the record demands it and because, from my perspective at least, what follows will shed light on an extremely complex situation.

I want to say, too, that it frankly embarrasses me to be engaging in this form of exchange of information. I have the greatest respect and admiration for Archbishop Laghi and appreciate his time and efforts to resolve this matter. I trust you will understand, then, that the matters which I will set forth herein are in no sense an attack upon his person or his integrity. That our recollections and interpretations differ in some important respects should not be so surprising when one considers that we are both attempting to present in capsule form a very long and complicated series of events.

In the first place, it is probably important for you to know that, after I first read the Chronology, I asked Archbishop Laghi not to publish it because I felt it would raise more questions than it could possibly hope to answer. I feared it would generate a whole new round of publicity in a setting in which accusations and counter-accusations rather than the voices of reason would dominate and that, in the minds of many, it would ultimately reflect unfavorably on the Holy See, the very thing both Archbishop Laghi and I had striven to avoid all during this time.

From the very outset of these events, which now go back some three-and-one-half years, I have been concerned about adverse publicity for the Holy See. I expressed this concern in my earliest correspondence and in all my conversations with the Holy See, with Cardinal Ratzinger, Archbishop Laghi, Archbishop Hickey, and even with the Holy Father himself. It was always my deepest desire and my strongly expressed wish that, whatever steps might be taken to address certain concerns in Seattle, that they be taken in a way that would strengthen and cement our relationship with the Holy See, and not in any sense detract from it.

As far as the Chronology itself is concerned, let me say that I believe it either attempts to do too much (i.e., to tell the whole story in too brief a space), or to do too little (by that I mean that it doesn't really get to some of the deep, underlying problems which are at stake here).

As to particulars which are set forth in the Chronology, I must say that I find that the Chronology contains some misleading things, some things that were quite new to me, some rather disappointing things and some very real inaccuracies. I will address each of these four headings in sequence:

(1) The Chronology contains some misleading things:

For example: reference is made early on to "substantial complaints" against my teaching or with regard to certain pastoral practices in the Archdiocese of Seattle. My observation is that if there were substantial complaints I was never told who made them or who substantiated them and on what basis. Nor was I told till considerably after the Visitation was decided upon and announced to me, (and then only in the most generic manner) what *some* of those complaints were.

The Chronology goes on to indicate that certain responses I myself gave to inquiries were primary among the causes that led to the decision to mount a Visitation. That may be so. But I would have to state clearly (and our files certainly bear this out) that if certain responses I provided to inquiries by the Holy See—some of them as far back as 1978—were viewed as unsatisfactory, then I must ask why I was never informed of this fact at the time I made those responses. Why, instead, was I politely and routinely thanked for the information I provided only to hear nothing further at all until the major decision was made to undertake the extraordinary step of the Apostolic Visitation. If my responses were inadequate, surely some dialogue on the matters in question should have taken place before a decision was made that only an Apostolic Visitation could set matters straight in Seattle. So, for anyone to review that correspondence now and to suggest that it was the cause of the Visitation troubles me greatly.

Another misleading point: the Chronology states that at the time I announced the granting of special faculties to Bishop Wuerl I indicated that they were "mandated" by Rome" when, in fact, a more precise description would have been that this was the "agreement" reached between the Holy See and myself. As a matter of fact, in my letter to our priests and people, I made no reference to a "mandate from Rome." I spoke only of carrying out "the wishes of the Holy See," which was manifestly what was at stake here. That I "agreed" to go along with those wishes is clear, too, although I did not do so with any sense of freedom since the consequences of my not agreeing to do so had been made clear to me on more than one occasion.

(2) The Chronology contains some new learnings:

From the Chronology, I learned for the first time that the problem with our formation program for seminarians (we have no seminary in Seattle) had to do with the admissions practices followed by the Archdiocese. That was news to me. I had never before been told that. I also learned that the rather all-encompassing theological concerns (embracing such things as the relationship of the local Church to the Universal Church, the teaching of Christology and of a sound anthropology, the role of the Magisterium, the nature of the Church, of priesthood and moral theology) were apparently all concerns that related to the programs followed in the Archdiocese for the Continuing Education of priests. I do not find this particularly enlightening since our priests are certainly orthodox on these matters and our education programs employ the same personnel and deal with the same themes as those of dozens of other dioceses in the country, but I do find it revealing to discover that this was the context for all those serious theological concerns which I first learned of last year at this time in a letter from Cardinal Ratzinger.

Whatever the case, it would have been helpful to have had this information during this past year when painstaking efforts were being made to understand the precise nature of Cardinal Ratzinger's concerns so that we could address them in a conscientious and responsible manner.

I would also have to say that it came as a surprise to me that I had been judged by the Holy See to lack the necessary firmness to govern the Archdiocese of Seattle. I had, of course, wondered out loud whether this might indeed have been the case. I had even speculated about it openly in a letter to Archbishop Laghi, but while I had learned from him that I enjoyed no credibility whatever in Rome, I had never been told until the publication of the Chronology that the judgment had been made that I lacked the necessary firmness to govern my Archdiocese.

(3) The Chronology contains some disappointing things:

I found very disappointing the intimation that in dealing with Bishop Wuerl and, specifically with regard to his special faculties, I did not carry out my promises, that I exhibited a certain intransigence, or even that I acted in bad faith. This is simply not true. The misunderstanding that came to light regarding the nature and extent of Bishop Wuerl's faculties was a genuine one. Indeed—and I don't say this in any sense to be self-serving or contentious—it is difficult for me to believe how anyone who was present to the conversations and who saw the correspondence could interpret it in any way other than the way I did. From the start of the Visitation and all during the long process that took place with regard to the appointment of an Auxiliary Bishop, I had made certain things abundantly clear. Among them was the fact that I would gladly resign the Archdiocese should that be the wish of the Holy See or, of course, of the Holy Father himself.

Secondly, I made it clear that I would never carry out a public charade by pretending to be something I was not. I am just not constitutionally capable of that. In other words, if significant or substantial powers were to be taken away from me (and here it goes without saying that if final decision-making authority for critically important areas of Archdiocesan life and governance were to be taken from me), I would choose to resign rather than to stay on and pose as the Archbishop of Seattle when, in fact, I would scarcely be that except, perhaps, in some vague, legalistic, and rather meaningless sense. My thinking in this regard, incidentally, had nothing to do with any need I had to hold on to power. It had to do with my need for personal authenticity and my willingness to get out of the way entirely if it was perceived that I was the source of some grave problems in my Archdiocese. I always presented these convictions to Archbishop Laghi as matters of conscience for that is what they were. With him I tried to discern as best I could what was for the good of the Church.

In a crucial letter dated December 2, 1985 which I wrote to Archbishop Laghi, I agreed to give substantive authority without, however, relinquishing my ultimate authority. These are the words I used: "this arrangement will not impinge upon my ultimate authority as Ordinary of the archdiocese." I went on to quote the Code of Canon Law to make the matter unmistakably clear. Archbishop Laghi's response stated: "While this does not lessen your authority as the local Bishop, it is understood that this action is being taken at the specific instruction of the Holy See." For this reason, it troubles me greatly not only that a great misunderstanding could have later ensued, one that in the end I was informed was mine, but also that it would later be suggested publicly that I might have acted in bad faith. I did not.

Perhaps it is at this point that I need to say a word about why, in the end—this past July, to be exact—after the Holy See had given its decisive interpretation of the precise nature and extent of Bishop Wuerl's special faculties, I agreed to accept the arrangement. Above, I indicated that, as a matter of conscience, I had always resisted such an arrangement, preferring the course of resignation to what would amount to pretending to be what, in fact, I was not. In the end, my very reluctant decision to remain as the Archbishop of Seattle was made on the basis of what several trusted brother bishops and close advisers convinced me would be for the ultimate good of the Church in the Archdiocese of Seattle.

(4) The Chronology also contains some very real inaccuracies:

The Chronology speaks of my "insistence" that a public announcement be made at the time the Apostolic Visitation was undertaken. A more accurate statement would have referred to my earnest desire, expressed to Cardinal Ratzinger, Archbishop Laghi, and Archbishop Hickey that, if the Visitation did indeed have to take place, I would like it to do so in as open and positive and constructive a spirit as possible. I took this position because I honestly recognize the value in my own life of careful, objective evaluation, and because I felt that our priests and people were mature enough to deal with such a process, particularly if they understood that I supported it—even welcomed it—as a step toward answering some of my more vocal critics and toward improving certain aspects of a Church which is *semper reformanda*. In addition, I repeatedly expressed my fear that to undertake the Visitation under the cloak of secrecy would be a mistake for at least two reasons: first, it would smack of a method of operating that was more characteristic of the pre-Vatican II Church than of the post-, and, second, it was clear to me that no amount of effort to maintain the curtain of secrecy would ever succeed, and that the embarrassment which would follow any disclosure by "leak" would be far greater than that which might accompany an open and honest disclosure from the start.

I made these points clear from the beginning, and I brought them personally to Cardinal Ratzinger during my 1983 *ad limina* visit. I even offered to personally and publicly invite him or his designees to come to the Archdiocese so that the onus for the Visitation would be on my shoulders. But my invitation and my point of view were not accepted. Secrecy was to be the rule, and I adhered to it.

As matters turned out, when the inevitable leak did come, it came not from Seattle but from the East Coast. Archbishop Hickey called to tell me about it and to say that, after consultation with Archbishop Laghi, he had decided that we needed to issue a news release that would be given out simultaneously in Washington, D.C. and Seattle. That is what, in fact, took place.

A second inaccuracy: the Chronology makes reference to my "surprise announcement" at the time I granted the Special Faculties to Bishop Wuerl, the implication being that I did something that was outside of or contrary to prior agreement or understandings between myself and the Pro-Nuncio. The record will show, however, that I repeatedly made the point in my conversations and exchanges with Archbishop Laghi at Collegeville this past summer, that, in the then unlikely event that I would agree to accept the special faculties arrangement according to the manner in which they were being understood by the Holy See, I would have no choice but to make this matter known to all my priests and close collaborators since it would be absolutely essential for them to know to whom they were accountable and from whom they would receive orders and directives. I never left the slightest doubt about this matter since I knew that to have acted in any other way would have resulted in a chaotic situation with regard to the governance of the Archdiocese.

For this reason I am simply unable to understand how my subsequent announcement about the Special Faculties could have been the source of surprise for anyone who had been party to our conversations, or how it could be stated in the Chronology that my actions had never "been contemplated." I also find it difficult to understand how anyone could ever have believed that keeping the Special Faculties a secret

> could possibly have worked in the first place. If nothing else, the early history of the Visitation to which I have just referred should have clearly indicated otherwise.
>
> To the best of my ability, I have reflected on the contents of the Chronology and presented my understanding of events. Since there seems to be such a divergence of opinion between my understanding and interpretation and that set forth in the Chronology, I would certainly welcome some sort of review of all these matters should that be the wish of the members of the Conference.
>
> In my oral presentation during the Executive Session, I will attempt to address these and other matters from a different perspective than that demanded by a response of this sort.[10]

Hunthausen had made a strong rebuttal. This did not mean he wanted to disparage or disrespect Rome's authority. In the executive session on November 11, face to face with his colleagues, he asked them to view the whole matter not as a personal struggle or as a "battle of wits between a maverick Archbishop and the Holy See." But he did think that the shroud of secrecy the Vatican kept over the process was causing confusion and anger across the country. It contradicted the open spirit of the Second Vatican Council, he said. As to apparent doubts about his own pastoral judgment, he said that he always tried to discern the guidance of the Holy Spirit faithfully and in fidelity to church teaching. Recalling his 1983 decision to allow Dignity to celebrate Mass at St. James, he reminded his brothers that this act of hospitality was common in several of their dioceses. He had never deliberately defied church regulations. As to the priesthood candidate process and the formation program, Seattle had become something of a model. "I hold with the Magisterium conscientiously and I make every effort—personal and professional—to deepen my understanding of the Church so that I will be able to present it to my people as the vital and living tradition it is—the very Gospel of Jesus...." The attitude of Jesus, he believed, must always be "the most identifying mark of our own lives." A public religious leader must be committed to dialogue. The whole issue of the shared responsibility of national episcopal conferences was at stake in the Seattle case, he argued, and the visitation ought to have involved close collaboration between the Vatican and the NCCB. At the same time, the case pointed to the need to value the legitimate diversity and particularity of each local church. The church must commit itself to honest and just relationships. This was not a match between adversaries. "I do not feel the need to win so that others will have to lose. Winning or losing is not what this is at all. The good of the Church is what is at stake." Concern for the good of the church as a whole led him "to say more than I normally would in a situation like this."[11] The virtue of obedience could never allow him "simply to acquiesce." Genuine obedience has "prompted me to engage in a process of dialogue, one which, to the best of my ability, I have always carried out in a respectful, docile and faith-filled manner." A more open and forthright approach to the visitation process would have conveyed the respect for the people who have "come of age," and "deserve to be treated as adults."[12]

Though he never would have described what he was doing in such terms, Hunthausen was speaking prophetic truth to an overly-centralizing power. "What kind of church," he asked, "are we trying to be and to become?" He objected to the methods of the investigation and the process Rome used to arrive at its conclusions. The issue was not whether there should be accountability, but what form and approach should be involved in this relationship. "I have to take to heart the need I have to be evaluated, and I accept the fact that I must work very hard with my priests and people, and as conscientiously as possible, in order to address and correct any areas in which I have been found wanting." But Rome's arrangement granting special faculties to Wuerl was simply unworkable. "For the good of the Church in Seattle and beyond, I am absolutely convinced that the matter of the governance of the Church of Seattle needs to be returned to normal as soon as humanly possible. I would even say <u>at once</u>. [Emphasis Hunthausen's]"[13]

What happened after the bishops had heard Hunthausen? Did they grapple with his core question: what kind of church? Many bishops, thinking about what Hunthausen had said and about what he was going through, must have been seriously pondering that question, but it did not drive their collective statement toward anything even remotely prophetic. Bishop Malone, speaking for the NCCB, said "bishops are conscious that in such matters…the Holy See proceeds carefully and charitably, employing procedures developed over many years to protect the rights of individuals and promote the common good of the Church."[14] Still, they did not simply cave to the Vatican. The American bishops did not say that the Vatican had been just or reasonable, only that its action had been carried out in accordance with general procedures. In fact, the administrative committee of the NCCB had recommended that the bishops should indicate their support for Rome's action in Seattle as "fair and just." Instead, the Malone statement representing the majority of U.S. bishops reflected only the Vatican's prerogative. This was hardly an enthusiastic endorsement of Rome's action in the Seattle situation. And the American bishops sent a critical message to Rome in another way—with a majority vote to defeat conservative bishops seeking key NCCB leadership posts.[15]

The *New York Times* summarized what the bishops had tried to balance with two words: sympathy and loyalty; sympathy for Hunthausen, but loyalty to John Paul II. Bishop Malone stated: "On this occasion the Bishops of the United States wish to affirm unreservedly their loyalty to and unity with the Holy Father." John

Cardinal O'Connor, spinning the proceedings in favor of Rome, said at the time: "I think it's a very well balanced statement.... It shows the unity of the bishops, it shows the loyalty to the Holy See and it demonstrates our explicit recognition that the Holy See has acted very charitably and very justly." Not all agreed. Bishop Michael Kenny of Juneau, Alaska, who on several occasions joined his Seattle colleague in anti-nuclear protests, called it otherwise: "The statement does not adequately address the widespread perception that both the process and the decision were unfair. The Holy See must not only be just, but appear just."[16] When Bishop Malone made the statement affirming unreserved loyalty to and unity with Pope John Paul II, Bishop Thomas Gumbleton told me recently, "he was not speaking for a significant number of us."[17]

THE QUESTION OF AUTHORITY

The Pope's authority was being questioned by many people in the United States, not to mention elsewhere in Europe and Latin America. The *New York Times* quoted a senior aide to John Paul II: "In the past the difficulties have been posed in terms of disagreements on several different moral issues like abortion and contraception. Now everyone seems to realize that something much more fundamental is involved: the structure of the church and in particular the bishops' allegiance to the Pope." Another papal aide reportedly said: "This could be a turning point. Even though the divisions will not go away overnight, the bishops are now focusing their relationship with Rome and perhaps realizing that disagreements can only go so far." John Paul II had made his outlook clear in that message read by Laghi at the opening session of the NCCB: "You are, and must always be, in full communion with the Successor of Peter." As a matter of global context, it should be noted that John Paul had tried to rein in two other national conferences, the bishops of the Netherlands in 1980 and the bishops of Brazil in 1985.[18]

While Hunthausen himself was not attempting to question papal authority, he was asking key questions. Timothy Schilling, in his dissertation's analysis of the Seattle-Rome conflict, identified three major themes Hunthausen had touched on when he spoke to his brother bishops. Hunthausen asked first about the mutual involvement of leaders. Schilling spelled it out this way: "How does a diocesan bishop who is himself the Vicar of Christ in his particular church, carry out his role with the degree of independence which this role implies at the same time doing so in full union with and under the rightful authority of the Supreme Pontiff?" Secondly, Hunthausen asked the bishops to think about legitimate diversity in the Church. Third, Hunthausen placed "a challenge before the bishops. Church leaders, Hunthausen asserts, need to be as eager to establish just structures inside the Church as they are to promote them outside the Church."[19]

On the other hand, the NCCB statement relied much more on the type of "family matter" language we saw used by the Vatican in its description of the apostolic visitation in 1983—a way to gloss over the crucial structural questions Hunthausen had raised. Bishop Malone's statement included this rhetorical question aimed at transcending the nitty gritty conflict over ecclesiologies: "Is it paradoxically possible that what has happened in the Archdiocese of Seattle has given, and continues to provide, a vivid demonstration of the unity of the Church, perhaps the best demonstration we have seen in many years?" The family analogy was employed by Malone to help resolve a problem, but without getting to the roots: "I am deeply convinced that the degree of pain which has been felt and enunciated in Seattle, but far beyond Seattle, really is the kind of pain that can only be felt by members of a family.... If my analogy is correct, it suggests some of the directions in which we must go. There are certain things that a family must do when it wants to resolve a problem." The bishops as a body had already followed the code of canon law and the norms of a national conference of bishops. They met the Holy Father's wishes, and in so doing, they failed to advance a collective self-critical examination of the patriarchal authority structure of their family. "A family comes together. Each member expresses the pain, the anxiety, the doubts they feel. These things are listened to with respect and sympathized with, deeply, and in the heart. Then support is expressed, for the persons as persons and for the responsibilities they must bear. This we bishops have done together in these days." Seemingly oblivious to the irony, the Malone statement's analogy ignored an entire gender. Where were the voices of the women in the Catholic Church *family*? The male half of the family that was in the room might have been more introspective if it had speculated on the ways family secrets and shame can keep members from being honest with one another. Granted, Malone was trying. He suggested that a family "takes steps to see that, in so far as possible, a painful situation does not happen again." But the bishops never examined the male-only character of their power structure. They showed fraternal sympathy for Hunthausen instead of honestly examining the unfair structure. In keeping with John Paul II's paternalistic call to communion with Rome without critique, "the mystery of the church" became the opportunity for prayer minus real debate. Malone: "There is at least one more thing a family of faith does when it is in difficulty, and that is pray."[20] He might have said, if he had been more cognizant of the patriarchal culture shaping things, that there is one thing a patriarch does when he senses a possible rebellion against abuse of authority: get everyone down on their knees to pray to the Father.

Schilling critiqued Malone's family analogy:

> "Neglected in the analogy...is the fact that the whole family is not at the table. While the brother bishops commiserate and share their pain and anxiety, the patriarch—the Holy Father—is present to the

discussion only in the form of an abstract statement. Also missing is a candid assessment of accountability. Who caused the pain that everyone is feeling so deeply? Though according to this image a highly meaningful conversation, marked by mutual vulnerability, has taken place, no change is the result. 'Archbishop Hunthausen and Bishop Wuerl have been given a job to do by the Holy See.' The bishops offer their assistance, but essentially Hunthausen and Wuerl are invited to make peace with the very arrangement that Hunthausen has come to the meeting to protest and has just called 'unworkable.' The family problem-solving covers up the genuine disharmony that exists and pretends that a solution has been reached."[21]

In his analysis Schilling captured both the candor and the frustration Hunthausen must have felt.

> "It is almost as though, on the Hunthausen side, no plausible argument is left untried in this forum with the bishops. The text creates an impression of Hunthausen venting accumulated frustration (near the end, Hunthausen says explicitly, 'I guess a lot has built up within me during the past three and a half years')—and of his doing so on the occasion of his last stand, his last best chance in a conflict where the odds are against him."[22]

The bishops did not truly stand up to Rome; to do so would have required them to question the structure and culture of its authority. Others, unconstrained by a Roman tether, did. Peace marchers walking across the nation to call for nuclear disarmament gave petitions bearing 1,000 names to Archbishop Pio Laghi. "As the Great Peace March completes its transcontinental pilgrimage in Washington, we would like to express our appreciation and solidarity to Archbishop Raymond Hunthausen of Seattle," said their statement.[23] Another unambiguous stand arrived in a letter Hunthausen received from a group of inactive priests and nuns (including the spouses of those who were married): "We write you because we are shocked and saddened by the recent announcement of the radical reduction of your full authority as Archbishop. This has confused the faithful and brought insult to your dignity, to your ministry and to our Church in this Archdiocese. We are with you in this difficult time. We are inspired by your openness, compassion, and fidelity to the Gospel." They deplored "the actions of those who deliberately forced this confrontation." In their estimation, "the mean spirited criticism from a small, but vocal minority has spread to the highest level of the Church to re-appear as a disciplinary action."[24]

Hunthausen had learned some time before he addressed his colleagues in D.C. that he would have only a limited amount of time to speak, a fact Schilling documented:

> "In the week before the conference, a discussion ensued between Hunthausen and two friend-advisers, Fr. Michael G. Ryan and Archbishop Hurley (Anchorage, Alaska), about how best to use the time Hunthausen had available for oral remarks. Drawing on this input, Hunthausen decided upon a set of select remarks to share with the bishops at the beginning of the closed session on November 11. This was a valuable opportunity for Hunthausen, since public speaking was one of his strengths. As an orator, Hunthausen possessed a low-key eloquence: he was persuasive in an understated way. In general, Hunthausen came across as a person internally at peace, as one who was nonthreatening and who had integrated his own values."

The *National Catholic Reporter* covered what happened when Hunthausen faced his brother bishops. Hunthausen appeared to be "visibly tense" as he stood up to speak. "He talked of his pain and of the hurt the episode was causing the church; he said he was personally embarrassed by the affair. Never did he have any intention of challenging papal authority, he said, adding he implied no ill will on anyone's part and saying it was understandable that differences in perception could occur regarding events which took place over several years." When Hunthausen sat down, "applause broke out throughout the chamber, a 'sustained applause,' according to one bishop."[25] They may have come close to giving him a standing ovation, but at the end of the day, they did not stand up for him.

Nevertheless, they had been willing to hear his side of the story. "Archbishop Hunthausen just wanted to be heard," said fellow peace bishop Michael Kenny of Juneau. Hunthausen had released more than 30 pages of documents and statements in the course of the four-day NCCB meeting. So all he wanted was to be heard? Kenny tried to put the best face on what had happened, as did Hunthausen. Graciously, if less than convincingly, Hunthausen called the NCCB statement a good one "that has emerged from a very honest exchange of many different points of view."[26]

The *National Catholic Reporter* wrote more candidly about the NCCB meeting and noted the differences among bishops that could be missed if one simply looked at the final Malone statement:

> "Among the principal themes to emerge in the bishops' addresses were their desires to avoid being or appearing to be critical of the Vatican action, to be viewed in full accord with Rome, to address honestly any injustice that may have occurred, to pass to Rome the ever deepening

> distress of growing numbers of mainstream Catholics, including many priests, across the nation, and to be credible in the eyes of the public, especially the press."

Archbishop Rembert Weakland was apparently:

> "[...] among the first to call for a change in the Malone letter. He said it lacked credibility in light of the Hunthausen documents. Seattle Auxiliary Donald Wuerl spoke early, calling for the bishops' support in making the situation work according to the Vatican's wishes. Cardinal Joseph Bernardin, speaking on behalf of 'four cardinal ordinaries,' offered his support for the Malone letter. He said it was essential that the conference offer Rome its support and also said unity was necessary so a climate of reconciliation could occur and the situation could move toward normalization."

The *National Catholic Reporter* story continued:

> "Washington Archbishop James Hickey, who conducted the Vatican apostolic visitation in Seattle, spoke about his personal involvement in the case, saying he did what was asked of him and carried out the visitation in accordance with church procedures. Hickey said he had prepared the documents and knew them well, implying, in the eyes of several bishops, that there was definitely more to the story than was coming across in the Hunthausen documents. His remarks later moved Anchorage Archbishop Francis Hurley—a close personal friend of Hunthausen's and the man who served as his informal legal counsel—to speak as well. Hurley reminded the bishops that they were not gathered to discuss the specifics of the Vatican visitation. Then he said that, because Hickey had raised the subject, he felt free to reassure the body of bishops he, too, had seen many of the documents in the case and could attest to the correctness of Hunthausen's version."[27]

As Schilling noted, the bishops faced a dilemma:

> "All of the American bishops have an incentive to preserve their own autonomy of action—individually and as an episcopal conference—which is symbolized in Hunthausen's predicament. But protecting their own freedom to move (including vertically within the hierarchy) requires not offending the Holy See, which has the power to grant and limit freedoms. It is a delicate balancing act, taking shape in words in Malone's statement on behalf of the conference."[28]

Rome, under John Paul II, would not let "the balancing act" get close to a balance. As Schilling pointed out, when Cardinal Ratzinger referred to the Pope in his

December 12, 1983 letter to Hunthausen announcing his receipt of the Hickey report, Ratzinger described the pontiff in a fashion that the Pope himself later used in his message to the U.S. bishops conveyed by Archbishop Laghi. That description —"the successor of Peter has been constituted for the whole church as pastor"— was, according to Peter Hebblethwaite, a long time student of the Vatican, quite recent in origin and has come to be used "to mean that the pope can intervene anywhere, at any time, without consultation, thus usurping the pastoral function of the local bishops."[29] Concerned for "the unity of the Church" and "communion with the Pope" the bishops conceded to a centralizing papacy. Hunthausen's hopes for a truly just process were dashed. Theologian Richard McBrien wondered at the time whether historians would laugh or cry when they looked back at the mixed signals coming from the bishops and their response to the Hunthausen case.[30]

BACK IN SEATTLE, STILL HANDCUFFED

At a news conference in Seattle, Hunthausen said that the archdiocese "should return to normalcy as soon as possible. Normalcy means the authority is in the hands of the Archbishop. I don't see how we can function any other way without creating serious confusion." He described the split-authority problem in a metaphor: "I've mentioned to Bishop Wuerl that the only way he and I could carry this off would be to be handcuffed together for 24 hours a day." Of the charge that his approach was in violation of church teaching, he said, "In no way are we deliberately trying to fly in the face of church practice or authority." The whole episode was unprecedented, this he acknowledged. "It's been one of the most moving and profound experiences of my life." In fact, when he had stepped off the plane at Sea-Tac International, returning from D.C., hundreds greeted him with flowers.[31]

Reporters asked him about the abrasiveness supporters and detractors seemed to be aiming at each other. "I really believe that our people, I know they are concerned that in the last week and beyond and continuing, there's an element of prayer, there's an element of concern, there's a coming together. I've had more people speak to me about the fact that they are fasting in the hope that we might find a resolution to this." The situation could be a unique opportunity for growth. "I think if you look at the documentation coming out of this experience you will see that it's a unique moment in the life of the National Conference of Catholic Bishops. Nothing like this has ever happened before."[32] Someone at the press conference asked him how the whole ordeal had affected him. "I've struggled every day with what I ought to do, what is the best approach for me to take, how can I deal with this and affect what is truly my deepest concern." How could he live out his vision of the Second Vatican Council? "How does one try to identify what he feels really needs some fixing, if you will? In the nature of the Church this becomes sensitive because in so doing one almost immediately gives the impression that he's setting himself up against the Holy See or against the Holy Father." He did not want to rebel. He just wanted to do the right thing. "I really feel it has forced me to recognize that the answers are in the Lord, that I can only do my best, but this is so complex that it's going to take...all of us in the Church to seek the wisdom and the response of the Spirit."[33]

Hunthausen had talked with close colleagues about resigning, he said. "They felt it would be far, far worse for the Church and for all concerned if I were to resign." He pondered aloud the meaning of the conflict: "I think that if the story can be told, and be told, if you will, as I truly believe it is in reality, then I think it's a marvelous moment for all of us to become more aware of what is Church and how we need to address the concerns in Church and grow out of adversity, to recognize that we're not a perfect Church, but that unless we identify what we need to do to be better and acknowledge that honestly, we...will not be building the Kingdom." In that press conference he said "this is a moment when we, I think, can recognize the need to find the means to grow together, to come together, to be, if you will, as we say in the Roman Catholic Church, the Body of Christ. But beyond that, to somehow be a human family that recognizes the need to work out stress and strain so that we don't have wars." His vision of peace and justice for the world had to relate to the situation at hand as well. "This is a conflict. This is, it's the irony of it, that I am in the midst of the kind of conflict that has the potential of causing serious rift in the Church. And I'm constantly talking about the need to avoid that very thing in the human family and on the world scene." More than anything he sought a way to resolve the conflict between Rome and Seattle. "We've got to recognize that there are ways of working it out, and let's continue to pray and make that happen."[34]

Joseph Berger of the *New York Times* shed some light on what the bishops had done—and not done. For many people who understood the politics and authority structure of the Catholic Church, he concluded, there never was any choice. "As bishops in a church where Pope John Paul II is not simply an institutional leader but one with a theologically endowed status whose power determines their own, the bishops had to support the Pope publicly. The only questions were how they would do so while expressing some affection for their colleague, and what hints they might include of the displeasure many felt with the way the case was handled." When Berger wrote of a "theologically" endowed status, it would have been more accurate to describe it as canonical, not theological. In any event, status is socially constructed—not God-given. Dr. Germain Grisez, a professor of Christian ethics at Mount St. Mary's College in Emmitsburg, Maryland, looked at the matter this way: "It's the nature of the church. If the bishops didn't support the Vatican, they wouldn't have any status themselves. It's like pulling the plug on your own rowboat."

Catholic liberal writer and psychologist Eugene Kennedy saw something quite telling, something not addressed above, regarding the family metaphor used by Malone. Kennedy referred to this line in the Malone statement: "A family also takes steps to see that, in so far as possible, a painful situation does not happen again." This sentence in particular indicated to Kennedy that many of the bishops were not pleased with what had happened and that they wanted to pursue "some effort to moderate this crisis and to bring about some as yet not clear positive resolution to it." Based on official church law, the NCCB had no authority to intervene in the case, yet if they intervened they could experience authority of another sort—legitimacy among many liberal and progressive Catholics. Conservative intellectual Michael Novak thought the meeting represented a "watershed" or "turning point" in the American church. "In a dramatic way," Novak said, "the bishops gave evidence of the central role that communion with Rome plays in the life of the Catholic community." Orthodoxy and loyalty would grow, Novak hoped. "The bishops had to make a choice in this experience, and they had to think through their relationship to Rome very clearly in the light of intense public opinion and pressure building in the media for them to distance themselves from Rome," Novak remarked. "They recognized the pitfalls."[35]

With standing room only and standing ovations wherever he spoke, support overwhelmed Hunthausen. He did not want the attention or adulation. "It hasn't been easy," he said. "I've struggled every day with what I ought to do. I have found myself a stronger person spiritually because of all of this."[36] He had come of age with Vatican II in the early 1960s. Now, in the mid-1980s, he was under fire in part because he had taken so seriously the Second Vatican Council's call to share leadership with the people. Fr. Michael McDermott, who worked closely with him, has tried to explain Hunthausen's basic attitude. Hunthausen did not want to rally all the social energies that were targeting the Vatican:

> "In all of the issues with Rome, he did not go overboard in trying to defend himself. His talk with the bishops was his clearest statement about the good of the church and the importance of a fair process. He was forceful in his presentation with his brother bishops. At the same time, when Dave Jaeger and others were developing Concerned Catholics, this was not something Hunthausen would have supported. Anything that would get close to the protest model vis á vis the church, he would not have wanted. He loved the church, and his sense of unity was so deep. He felt the way was to sit down and dialogue, not protest."[37]

When it came to Trident or U.S. policy in Central America or the massive concentration of wealth and power among some while others went hungry on the margins, Hunthausen was willing to engage in significant protest—even to act conscientiously in civil disobedience. He had not taken a sacred vow of obedience to the secular government. Nor was he an officer in that government. The church was a different matter.

We have learned a lot about what Hunthausen was thinking, but what was Pope John Paul II thinking about the Seattle-Rome case and particularly what did he make of the American bishops? According to Schilling's review, one Vatican official, speaking on condition of anonymity, said that "the U.S. bishops came out surprisingly strong on the side of the Holy See in the Hunthausen affair. They were on the right track." Another Vatican official felt there was a "general sense of relief and satisfaction" at the Vatican.

> "The Pope's only public comment on the affair came on November 19 aboard the papal plane, en route to Bangladesh.... Asked about a possible rift between U.S. Catholics and the Vatican, the Pope replied, 'Sometimes one creates divisions that do not exist' by 'talking and writing.' 'Our task—that of myself and the bishops of the United States—is the same, the good of the church. It is our common ministry.... The American Church is part of the universal church and still wants to be a part of the universal church.' When asked specifically about the Hunthausen case, the Pope said, 'I know only the statement by the (bishops' conference) president, and it was correct.'"[38]

The American bishops, hardly all on the same page, were not yet through with the whole matter. Malone suggested that the bishops ought to have a meeting with Pope John Paul II to discuss the "growing and dangerous disaffection" in the American church that was evident. Nevertheless, in the weeks following the NCCB meeting, other influential prelates suggested that tensions would blow over. Archbishop Roger Mahony of Los Angeles believed the Hunthausen affair, along with the Charles Curran case, were not that important. "You hardly ever hear these kinds of concerns," Mahony said. "I really feel people who have voiced concern may represent a fraction of our church and in our diocese a very, very small fraction of our people." Newark's Archbishop Theodore McCarrick expressed similar sentiments. Archbishop William Levada, in Portland, Oregon, asserted that orthodoxy "is the natural condition of a pope or bishop." Bishop Thomas Welsh of Allentown, Pennsylvania, added that religion "is not a democratic process."[39]

Of course the "demos"—the people—as members of a religion may not all agree. On December 1, Seattle-based Concerned Catholics wrote the NCCB members asking the prelates to "take practical action...to bring to concrete and practical reality your offer of assistance to Archbishop Hunthausen in bringing resolution to the unworkable situation resulting from the separation of episcopal authority and power in the Archdiocese of Seattle." They should also "seek constructive ways to address the deep and serious issues that need to be addressed around the relationship of the local church (i.e. the Church in the U.S.) to the universal Church (i.e. the Holy See and the Holy Father)." What were these issues?

> "The issues are many and reach far beyond the person of Raymond Hunthausen and the Archdiocese of Seattle. In our understanding, as we grapple with the issues, they have to do with the nature, role and responsibilities of the office of bishop; the relationship of the local church to the universal church; the process and practice for the appointment of bishops; the theological questions surrounding this new practice of separation of episcopal power and authority through 'special faculties'; the shroud of secrecy in the conduct of internal church affairs resulting in perceived injustices and lack of respect in dealing with persons in the church."[40]

In early December, the Association of Pittsburgh Priests, a voluntary organization of some fifty priests serving in the Diocese of Pittsburgh (Wuerl's home diocese), called on Bishop Wuerl to resign and said:

> "We feel that in serving the Church in Seattle Archbishop Hunthausen has offered exemplary prophetic and pastoral leadership. He has been an advocate of the poor and powerless and has shown remarkable sensitivity to people who are frequently put on the fringe of life. The bishops of Vatican II once said, 'The joys and hopes, the griefs and anxieties of the people of this age, especially those who are poor or in any way afflicted, these too are the joys and hopes, the griefs and anxieties of the followers of Christ.' Bishop Hunthausen's ministry in Seattle is a sign to us that he has tried to make these joys and hopes, griefs and anxieties his own."

The process employed to limit Hunthausen's authority, they said, was "secretive, arbitrary, and unjust." As to why Hunthausen was subjected to Vatican scrutiny, they stated: "It is painful for us to conclude that Archbishop Hunthausen was singled out for censure because of his strong public witness to the Catholic Church's call for an immediate end to the arms race and a halt on the construction of more nuclear weapons, and because he sought a pastoral approach to problems instead of rigid enforcement of the norms of Canon Law."[41]

Bishop Thomas Gumbleton recently talked with me about the role of the American bishops at that D.C. meeting in November when Hunthausen had asked them to come to his aid:

> "Hunthausen had a remarkable honesty and spirit of shared responsibility with the people of the archdiocese. When Rome gave

> the areas of authority to Wuerl, or when this became somewhat clear and Wuerl had a letter from Rome showing his official authority, in such a situation most bishops would keep the matter secret and just accept what Rome had done. Hunthausen said that the people in the archdiocese have a right to know about this. He called Rome's bluff, if you will, and said, 'if you are going to kick me out or take some of my areas of authority away, be open about it.' The way he tolerated the horrendous treatment by the rest of the NCCB, the majority view, that we just must not embarrass the Holy Father, this is remarkable. It was the idolatry of the papacy. The bishops, again the majority approach, wanted to keep a good image of full unity with the Holy Father and did not want to embarrass him and the Vatican. And Ray in effect went along with all this."

Some bishops wanted to stand up to Rome, Gumbleton said:

> "Look at what Paul writes in his letter to the Galatians. He says he stood up to Peter and told him he was wrong. Paul stood up, and this is what the bishops of the NCCB ought to have done, stand up to John Paul II and Cardinal Ratzinger in defending their brother bishop, Hunthausen, at the NCCB meeting when he shared his perspective on the Seattle situation. We had a perfect opportunity to bring life into that part of Paul's letter. But the bishops as a whole, as the NCCB, would not do this."

This troubled Gumbleton, who likened Hunthausen to Archbishop John Dearden. The latter was so instrumental in the period right after Vatican II, as the national conference began to develop a strong voice. He was the archbishop of Detroit when Gumbleton first became auxiliary bishop in 1968. "Dearden, like Hunthausen, did his work without any desire to have the spotlight. Similar types of persons, the two of them."[42]

A battle for the soul of the American church was being waged. The Catholic conservative mindset was a formidable opponent that knew it had a receptive ear in the Vatican and among the growing number of prelates who had been appointed by Pio Laghi. In the Seattle region, Nicholas Holzschuh, with the Foundation for the Promotion of Orthodoxy, on November 26, 1986, wrote a "Dear Brothers and Sisters in Christ" letter seeking signatures. He wrote as one of "all of us Catholics in Western Washington" who, during the past few weeks, "have been inundated by a staggering amount of crossfire between the Archbishop, the Auxiliary Bishop, The National Conference of Catholic Bishops, The Vatican, and The Holy Father himself." In Holzschuh's view, Hunthausen was resisting "acceptance of an investigation which according to his peer bishops conforms to standards set forth in canon law." Instead, "he is inciting rebellion against" the whole process. Holzschuh:

> "Is then the Archbishop responding to The Holy Father with obedience, or is he employing political maneuvers designed to achieve his own ends? Is he asking us to be united with Rome, or rather to raise our voices in support of his own interests and ambitions? Will similar actions to these here, and in other archdioceses, if allowed to continue in the future, express the reverence and obedience that is due to Peter's Successor, or will Peter's Successor become merely another political force to do battle with? Will our Holy Father continue to be our temporal link to Jesus Christ Himself, or will he at some point in time, be known simply as the Bishop of Rome and nothing more?... The Archbishop and Fr. Ryan, the chancellor, have publicly stated that the aberrations that were of concern to Rome either never existed, have been taken care of, or are being attended to. If you feel otherwise, from your observation of the facts, write to the Archbishop listing and documenting, if possible, liturgical and dogmatic aberrations that are still occurring. Help the Archbishop bring the Archdiocese into line by contacting your pastor, pointing out those areas in which he is not following the Universal Church. If your efforts have no results, follow the chain of command and send copies of your experience to the Archbishop, papal legate, and appropriate curial offices in Rome. Talk to fellow Catholics. Explain this is not a battle for or against the Archbishop. This is a battle to save the Church in the United States from those who want to split us off from the Holy Father, the Vicar of Christ."[43]

Hunthausen now had his own physical battle to deal with; a life threatening illness. On December 10, 1986, he had major prostate cancer surgery. Surgeons removed a malignant tumor from the prostate gland and lymph node tissues.[44] Jim Burns, Hunthausen's development director and tireless advocate, was among those who gathered and sang Christmas carols outside the window at the hospital where Archbishop Hunthausen was recuperating. "A group of us from the chancery and the Burns family and others all stood outside and sang. He came to the window."[45] Hunthausen was released from Seattle's Providence Medical Center on Christmas Eve, sooner than anticipated. While still in the hospital he received a telegram from Pope John Paul II: "I have been informed of your recent operation and I wish to assure you of my fraternal solicitude for your speedy recovery." He told him that he would include him in his prayers during the celebration of the "mystery of the incarnate word of God."[46]

Along with pop icon Bette Midler, Iran-Contra figure Lt. Colonel Oliver North, Nicaraguan President Daniel Ortega, and Dr. Seuss, Archbishop Raymond Hunthausen was one of People Magazine's "25 Most Intriguing People of 1986."[47] Celebrity had zero attraction for a man hoping the controversy would end. As a matter of fact, shortly after 1987 began, Archbishop Hunthausen asked a group of nuns and lay members to refrain from holding a fast and vigil on his behalf. They'd been planning to hold these to push for the full restoration of his authority. He felt it could only lead to more polarization.[48] Hunthausen held out hope for constructive action by the NCCB.

Archbishop John May, the new NCCB president, said the bishops would offer to help devise a process "of restoring peace and unity to the pastoral administration of the Seattle Archdiocese."[49] The NCCB would have to work with Rome, of course, so therefore what Pro-Nuncio Archbishop Pio Laghi was thinking would matter. *New York Times* writer Joseph Berger interviewed Pio Laghi at the Vatican Embassy in D.C. in late January 1987. Laghi explained his view of what had happened with the Hunthausen affair. The Vatican was trying to be discreet. Hence much of what happened was not done in the open. Americans want candor, Laghi said. Americans have a Watergate-complex, he said, referring to the Nixon debacle and cover-up from the mid-1970s. "When something is behind the door there is the impression that something is wrong." The Vatican put more stock in charity and sensitivity, Laghi explained, than merely confidentiality. Too often criticism of Vatican action was aimed at the process, when in fact Rome was concerned about doctrinal deviation. Berger wrote that Laghi:

> "contended that the Vatican had a good sense of the American mood and style because more than 30 Americans were in high positions there. He said the Vatican was very well aware that many of the attacks on Archbishop Hunthausen came from conservative groups, such as Catholics United for the Faith, and 'absolutely' did not give those voices improper weight in their final decision. Moreover, the Vatican diplomat said Archbishop Hunthausen had not been singled out, as some critics have charged, because of his well-publicized opposition to nuclear weapons. Archbishop Laghi said that issue played no part in the Hunthausen case."[50]

Rome certainly wanted to find a solution.

Most of the major parties in the Seattle-Rome conflict, as Schilling documented, wanted a way forward. Plans were being made to employ three American prelates to help resolve the situation. Cardinal Joseph Bernardin of Chicago was instrumental.[51] The Seattle archdiocesan newspaper printed a Vatican announcement on February 12, 1987: "The Holy See has appointed an ad hoc commission of Cardinals Joseph

Bernardin and John O'Connor and Archbishop John Quinn to assess the current situation in the Archdiocese of Seattle. Archbishop Raymond Hunthausen has expressed his concurrence."[52]

Quinn was considered somewhat progressive, Bernardin moderate, and O'Connor firmly in the conservative camp.[53] Schilling documented the origins of the commission:

> "On February 10, Bernardin, O'Connor and Quinn issued a joint statement, saying that they had been notified of their appointment in a January 26 letter from Archbishop Laghi. The commission members noted that the formation of the commission was in keeping with a longstanding plan of the Vatican. The assessment 'was envisioned by the Holy See and agreed to by Archbishop Hunthausen when the auxiliary, Bishop Wuerl, was appointed more than a year ago.' The work of assessment was already underway. 'We initiated our task in Dallas and will make our report to the Holy See when it has been completed.'"[54]

As calendars would have it, most of the U.S. bishops were in Dallas, Texas for a workshop on medical ethics, and Hunthausen and Wuerl met with the commission, together with Laghi, on the morning of February 10. Later that same day, they had meetings with Hunthausen and Wuerl without Laghi present.

In mid-February 1987, the *National Catholic Reporter* broke the story that the Federal Bureau of Investigation had kept files on Hunthausen and Bishop Thomas Gumbleton of Detroit.[55] The *National Catholic Reporter* fueled even greater speculation about the nature of the relationship between the Reagan administration and the Vatican. Columnist Colman McCarthy had raised the theory in November of 1986. Other stories speculating on the connection had come out, including one in *Seattle Weekly*, on January 13, 1987:

> "Conspiracy theorists note that the same Archbishop Laghi who implemented the pope's discipline is the Vatican's first-ever delegate in the U.S. (sic: actually, Laghi was the first to have the status of an ambassador; apostolic delegates had previously represented the Vatican in the U.S.), sent when the Reagan administration and the Vatican established formal diplomatic relations in 1984. They figure that reining in the tax-resisting archbishop was part of a quid pro quo for those formal ties. Laghi's statement that 'at no time did the Holy See pursue with Archbishop Hunthausen the criticisms it received on controversial issues, e.g. nuclear weapons and the payment of taxes.' is accordingly taken as evidence that the opposite must be true."[56]

In his research Schilling asked, was it possible that churchmen were "protesting too much" when they kept denying that Hunthausen's stand on nuclear arms had no part in the Vatican's motivations? Schilling saw no evidence to prove the theory, although the *National Catholic Reporter* investigation showed FBI and Naval files indicating that the U.S. government was at least paying some attention to Hunthausen. This was not enough evidence, in Schilling's view, to prove the allegation that a deal had been cut between Rome and Reagan. Schilling considered another strand of the conspiracy theory:

> "...persons in the Seattle archdiocese who were unhappy with Hunthausen for political reasons sought to attack him on other grounds that were more telling for the Vatican: i.e., doctrinal and pastoral issues. Though its population was politically liberal in many respects, the Puget Sound area was also home to a number of key military bases...and was a good example of the military-industrial economy at work, with military contractor Boeing being the most prominent local employer. Thus, any number of persons would have reason to be unhappy with Hunthausen's challenge to stop building and deploying weapons that were not only part and parcel of the nation's security strategy but also the source of paychecks to tens of thousands of local citizens. This theory may have been more plausible, and certainly was being discussed as the controversy continued, but again it seemed to result more from speculation than from hard evidence that emerged at the time."[57]

Meanwhile, as Schilling has documented in his chronicle of the Seattle-Rome conflict, Bishop Wuerl went to Rome a few days following the meetings in Dallas. He met privately with Pope John Paul II. According to the Vatican spokesman Joaquin Navarro-Vals, this meeting, brief as it was, focused only on Wuerl's work heading up the study of U.S. Catholic seminaries, and thus had nothing to do with the Seattle situation. Wuerl did not comment when asked by media about whether the meeting with the Pope related to the Seattle situation.[58] "No comment" was not the method of those who kept up their activism on behalf of Hunthausen. A national group, Catholics Speak Out, advocated for the full restoration of Hunthausen's authority, running a full-page ad in the January 9, 1987 issue of the *National Catholic Reporter*.[59]

The Bernardin-O'Connor-Quinn commission trio held a round of interviews in March 1987 in Menlo Park, California on a Friday and Saturday. They met with bishops, priests and archdiocesan lay officials, including Archbishop William Levada and retired Archbishop Cornelius Power, both of Portland, Bishops William Skylstad of Yakima, Sylvester Treinen of Boise, Thomas Connolly of Baker, Elden Curtiss of Helena, Thomas Murphy of Great Falls, and Eldon Schuster, retired, also of Great Falls. Archdiocese of Seattle Board of Consultors members who advised Hunthausen were interviewed, including Revs. Anthony Domandich, Richard Hayatsu, Joseph Kramis, James Mallahan, Theodore Marmo, Gerald Stanley, and William Treacy. The commission also interviewed Rev. Michael McDermott, archdiocesan director of administration; Rev. Michael Ryan, chancellor and vicar general; Rev. David Jaeger, director of seminarians; Mr. Patrick Sursely, associate director of administration; and Ned Dolejsi, director of faith and community development. The three-member commission then went to Seattle shortly after Menlo Park and met with both Hunthausen and Wuerl.[60] On March 12, Wuerl and Hunthausen met individually with the commission and Laghi in Chicago. On March 19, Archbishop Quinn interviewed Fr. William Lane, a member of the Archdiocese of Seattle board of consultors, who was not able to attend the Menlo Park meetings. Quinn and Bernardin met with Archbishop Hickey on March 25 in Washington, D.C. Quinn met with Archbishop Hurley of Anchorage on March 29 and with both Hurley and Juneau's Bishop Kenny on March 31.[61] All these sessions were intended to help Bernardin, Quinn, and O'Connor in their effort to find a resolution that would satisfy the Vatican, while showing that they had listened and had tried to understand the Seattle situation objectively.

Hunthausen met with the trio again in Chicago on April 8. News was about to break that would lead to speculation about what had transpired between the commission members and Hunthausen. It so happens that Hunthausen was out at the Ground Zero Center for Nonviolent Action, adjacent to the Trident submarine base on the Hood Canal, on the night of April 15, 1987. The *National Catholic Register*, not to be confused with the more liberal *National Catholic Reporter*, announced that Hunthausen had agreed to resign if the Vatican would restore his full powers. The *Register* declared that, "according to highly placed sources," Wuerl was going to be sent to another diocese. Hunthausen would be retired from office, but he would have a face-saving period when all of his powers would be restored. The public affairs director for Seattle, Russ Scearce, called it "a speculative story and we do not have a comment. This is not the kind of news we were hoping to receive during Holy Week." Fr. Ryan wrote a letter to the priests of the archdiocese urging them to "disregard the *National Catholic Register* article, because not only is it speculative; it is incorrect.... The information that formed the basis of the article was apparently leaked to the reporter by an uninformed and irresponsible party in Rome or Washington, D.C....."[62] Ryan wondered out loud if the *Register* story may have been put out there as a "trial balloon" to see how U.S. bishops would react if Hunthausen were forced into early retirement, or the leak could have been intended to thwart a possible proposal coming from the commission that would fully restore Hunthausen's authority.[63]

PASSION NARRATIVE

On Good Friday, April 17, 1987, Fr. Paul Magnano wrote to Hunthausen encouraging him to seek help from a canon lawyer. "Over the months I have remained in contact with a friend and Canon Law Society official whom you have met, Father Jim Cuneo from Bridgeport, Connecticut.... He feels...it would be very useful to conduct a thorough canonical review with one or another of the most competent and respected canon lawyers in the church."[64] Magnano and Hunthausen talked. The next day, Holy Saturday, Magnano wrote a follow-up:

> "He [Cuneo] suggests that you note carefully if the appointment of a coadjutor affects your authority in any way and that the coadjutor not be able to act independently from you.... He feels you have been a 'defendant' who is perhaps far too obliging to the 'prosecutor.' He notes that the presumption of the law is that you are still archbishop, until removed by the pope himself. Thus he continues to strongly affirm the important role of Canon Law, with awareness, however, as you indicated yesterday, that it could make the whole matter worse. He feels, at least, that you should continue to negotiate with the three members of the commission to the pastoral and practical sense of the pope against the perceived idealism of Ratzinger. He also feels as archbishop you still have an avenue of appeal personally and directly to the pope. And if you choose to go to Rome you should go with the assistance of a canon lawyer."[65]

Given the time of year, Hunthausen's ordeal evoked the story at the heart of the Christian faith. Fr. Jerry McCloskey, in his Easter Sunday Homily, April 19, 1987, interpreted the Passion Narrative thus:

> "I want to tell you a story. It is a story that all of us have heard this past week, and one which took on special meaning for some of us.
>
> It is the story of a very special man. He was born in a small town in a remote part of the country of simple, hard-working parents. He spent most of his life in that remote town unknown by anyone outside his own circle of family and friends. He never wanted more than that. He did not care about money, power, or the trappings of power. He just wanted to live his life as God wanted him to and to do the best job he could.
>
> But then one day, a call came to him. He did not seek this call and would have avoided it if he could. But he came to believe that it was the will of God for him. And so he accepted. And his whole life was changed.
>
> Before long this man was doing things and saying things that got people excited. He was unlike anyone who had come before him, at least in

recent memory, a breath of fresh air in a world that had become rather stale. His popularity with the common people increased daily. Many began to place great hope in him. Some even called him a prophet.

His overriding concern in everything he did or said was *people*—especially those who were hurting, the outcasts, those who had been excluded from power, those who were discriminated against. In his concern for these people—the little people—he didn't hesitate to bend some of the rules if he felt they were too restrictive or too burdensome. Yet he always remained steadfastly loyal to the laws of God and to the traditions of his people.

His concern for people also led him to challenge the civil and religious leaders of his day. He called them to account publicly for laying heavy burdens on others and for being concerned about the externals of religion while forgetting its spirit.

Naturally, those in power didn't like what he was saying and they decided that he had to be gotten rid of. But they had to be very careful. They could not attack him outright because of his popularity. They had to find some more subtle means. They tried to set traps for him, but they were never able to pin anything on him that would justify their taking public action against him.

Finally, they found someone who agreed to lead him into a trap where his popularity could not save him. This man claimed to be a friend and supporter. But behind his back he was laying the groundwork by which the authorities could get rid of this man who was becoming such an embarrassment and a threat to them.

Eventually he was arrested and a secret trial was held which was illegal by all standards of justice, even by their own law. Charges were brought against him which were manifestly ludicrous. People were brought forward who made the most outrageous claims without a shred of proof. Conflicting testimony was ignored. He was not given an opportunity to face his accusers, nor to answer the charges brought against him.

But the authorities were not about to let a little thing like legality stand in their way now that they had this man where they wanted him. With persistence and threats, they eventually got him condemned and sentenced to death.

> During his trial, most of his supporters abandoned him—some because they didn't realize what was going on, some because they didn't want to challenge the authorities, some because they felt it was hopeless to come to his defense, some because they were afraid for themselves. And so this good man, who had never done harm to anyone, was put to death. And for most of the people life went on as it had before.
>
> But that was not the end of this man. They had taken his life, but they could not destroy his spirit. That spirit lived on in a few of his followers who continued to believe in him and in what he stood for. They abandoned everything—jobs, family, security—to keep that spirit alive. And slowly, but inevitably, they prevailed.
>
> And because of those few who never lost faith, that man's spirit is alive today. And *he* is alive—in each of us who share his spirit and are willing to give up everything to keep that spirit alive.
>
> That is our Easter hope—that those who sincerely try to do God's will and who are not afraid to put their lives on the line for what they believe in, even if they are put to death, can never be destroyed, and in the end will triumph. That was true for Jesus Christ; it will be true for Archbishop Hunthausen; and it can be true for you and me."[66]

As I was going through the extensive records Sr. Louise Dumont had held onto from the days of Concerned Catholics, I happened onto one perceptive analysis from the pen of an anonymous author. It was written when the apostolic commission was into its decisive period and all the media were speculating as to what it would be recommending. The writer hoped to see a constructive outcome. As a "real time" (spring 1987) contextual study shedding light on many aspects of the complex case and directed to Bernardin, O'Connor, and Quinn as its primary audience, it is well worth quoting at length.

> "It has been brought to my attention that tensions are rising in the Archdiocese of Seattle as the Hunthausen affair again is making headlines. The return of the special commission from Rome and the visit of Archbishop Hunthausen to Chicago to see the commission members a few weeks ago, the strain of the long, silent period of waiting for some resolution of the matter, the speculative articles in the *National Catholic Register*, the *National Catholic Reporter* and the *New York Times*, and the rumors that are proliferating have the Archdiocese on edge. This is not doing the Catholic Church in Seattle or elsewhere any good. The damage could get worse. It is my opinion that any resolution which is viewed as punitive toward Archbishop

Hunthausen or which results in what appears to be a forced resignation or retirement or a loss of his position will hurt both the Archdiocese of Seattle and the Holy See. It would do inestimable damage to the Archdiocese of Seattle, robbing a vibrant diocese of much of its vitality and causing harm it would take at least a generation to repair. The Holy See would suffer too in the inevitable alienation, sense of betrayal and loss of loyalty and good will of countless otherwise loyal priests, religious, and lay persons in the United States and beyond.

It would be tragic for the case to end this way, tragic not only for Seattle and the Holy See, but also for the larger Church. For what is happening in Seattle is but a microcosm of tensions in the universal Church. In many ways Seattle could become the victim of complexities which confront the Universal Church without our ever facing those complexities nor using this particular case to move toward a solution.

What is essential at this time is for the Commission and the Holy See to view the 'Seattle situation' as an opportunity for the development of greater unity and understanding in the Church rather than as a problem that could ultimately lead to greater scandal and deeper division. The following thoughts are shared with the hope that they can help you view the matter from this perspective.

1. The Second Vatican Council has been a great gift to the Church, but the renewed life and growth it has brought has not been achieved without difficulties. It has brought confusion, and mistakes have been made in the attempts to implement it not just in Seattle or the United States but throughout the world. This was and will continue to be unavoidable because whenever old ways give way to new and the Church is called to move into the future through the guidance of the Holy Spirit and under leadership of the hierarchy, there will be frustrations, fears, negative reactions and at times mistakes. In the midst of it all, however, the inspiration of the Holy Spirit and the wisdom of the hierarchy keeps us faithful to the Gospel and to our Tradition. It has not been nor will it become easy, but it is lifegiving. Thus in the work of implementing the decrees the ambiguities and tensions present in the documents themselves have moved from the text into the very life of the Church. Many of the issues which seem to be at the heart of the Seattle question are issues which arise from this struggle to understand and carry out what was begun at the Council. Thus they are issues for the whole Church, not simply issues for the Archdiocese of Seattle or the United States. To take punitive action

there and think the problems are then solved is to deceive ourselves and others, to fail to face the issues and to leave ourselves open to similar situations in the future.

2. Another factor at play in the Seattle situation is the relationship of the dioceses in the United States to the Holy See. The unique civic tradition with its relationship of Church and state, the American sense of justice, democracy and the pioneering spirit, and the way of life of the American people are not always completely understood by the Holy See. This does not make the dioceses in the United States a separate church or a church that must go its own separatist way. But it does mean that the Church in America must take its unique cultural circumstances into account in the renewal of its life. The signs of the times to which the Church is called to respond are different in the United States than they are in other places in the world. The many problems of the Catholic Church in the United States are a sign of the need for the Holy See to be more directly involved with the Church in this country in responding to these needs in a positive fashion. To do so, however, stronger forms of communication and collaboration between the bishops of the United States and the Holy See need to be developed so that misunderstandings might be avoided and more importantly true unity and growth might be fostered in the Church. The Seattle situation should be seen in the light of this approach. For much of what is at issue in Seattle is at issue throughout the whole country. Rather than taking punitive measures in Seattle, this is an opportunity to expand the conversation and help the Holy See understand the American situation more clearly and to bring the broader view of the Universal Church to play in the American situation. Dialogue rather than disciplinary measures will ultimately bring greater life to the Church.

3. A third complexity manifest in the Seattle situation is unique to that Archdiocese. It is the person of Archbishop Hunthausen himself. His style of leadership and its roots in his personality and spirituality may not be understood by those who do not know him well. He operates out of a great trust in people, a trust they themselves may not wholly understand. He gives people a task or responsibility and trusts that they will carry it out within the broad parameters which he has set. Like a good parent of teenagers he allows them to make their mistakes but expects them to reflect on these mistakes and grow from what they have learned. He expects the same integrity and level of commitment in others that he himself practices. He draws the best out of people

by his leadership style. He leads in a collegial manner, involving in decisions all those who will be affected by his decisions. This may not be a traditional style of leadership and may be misinterpreted as not being firm enough. But it is effective and calls his people to a deeper commitment and responsibility for the work of the Church. It is important that the Commission help the Holy See better understand the Archbishop as a person and as a leader. Then what are seen as weaknesses may be seen in the larger context of the Archbishop's overall style as the inevitable price of a style which has many strengths. Ultimately the Archbishop should be judged on the basis of the deeper faith and commitment on the part of his people and not on mistakes that have been made along the way to this goal. Rather than simply punishing mistakes the visitation and its aftermath could strengthen his style, help him overcome his weaknesses, and affirm and build on the many positive aspects of his leadership.

The Holy See must be helped to see the real person of Archbishop Hunthausen. A judgment on him and his work as Archbishop should not be made on misinformation. He is utterly loyal to the Holy See, and he is a man of irreproachable integrity. He is as confused by this whole situation as anyone else, because he has always acted as he felt the Church had called him to act as a bishop. It would be tragic if a judgment were made about him without an adequate knowledge of the man.

4. Another element of the problem is the clear perception of many Catholics in the United States that the Holy See is trying to deal with the ambiguities and concerns that have emerged with implementation of the Second Vatican Council by replacing bishops who have taken a pastoral approach to the implementation with bishops, brought in from regions geographically distant from their new dioceses, who are seen to take a hard line conformist approach to Church discipline. This appears to be an indirect method of dealing with the problematic issues the pastoral implementation of the Council has raised. This is a method often used by corporations to change the direction they are taking, but it cannot work within the Roman Catholic Church without undermining the role and the theological understanding of the office of bishop. The Holy See needs to be convinced to deal with these issues directly by engaging bishops who are clearly loyal in processes that may lead to needed reforms without cutting off great numbers of the priests, religious, and lay people who need to support the direction of the Church. Clearly Archbishop Hunthausen, in spite

of the faults the Holy See has found in him, is the type of bishop who can be engaged in this process and can bring with him the support of many of the priests, religious and lay people not only of his own diocese, but of the wider Catholic Church in the United States. If the Catholic Church is to be truly universal, he and bishops like him are essential to this process.

5. The fifth complexity emerging from the Seattle situation lies in the method of the investigation itself. Whether it was canonically proper or not, it was doomed to failure by the different cultural contexts of those involved. It was Roman in style and relied heavily on secrecy. Those kept in the dark by the secrecy were not just members of the wider public, but principal parties involved including the Archbishop. In other contexts this may be proper, but it would never be seen as such by the American public. Our cultural traditions call for an openness which includes at least those who are involved in an investigation, clear procedures which are understood beforehand, a clear statement of the issues involved, and some sense that both the procedures and their results will be carried out with a dispatch that is appropriate to the issues at hand. The process of the investigation was incomplete because it looked only at what were viewed as problems and not the whole life of the Church in the Archdiocese of Seattle. There may be problems in the Archdiocese of Seattle, as there are in any diocese, but these must be viewed in the light of the life of the diocese as a whole. Any judgment of the ministry of Archbishop Hunthausen should be made in the light of its entirety.

In conclusion, then, the Seattle situation involves complexities and issues which are found throughout the Church. It could end in tragedy for Seattle and a great deal of embarrassment and loss of public stature on the part of the Holy See, as the Holy Father himself would be seen as making an unwarranted attack on a loyal and holy brother bishop and a local church, which by theological definition subsists in the person of its bishop. Or on the other hand, it could be taken as an opportunity to widen the constructive involvement between the Church in America and the Holy See. I encourage the commission to take the latter path…."[67]

It was a strong analysis. The question remained, would the next move—with the Vatican hoping to ensure its objectives would be met through the commission trio's assessment—be perceived as just in the eyes of American Catholics?

REACTION TO THE COMMISSION'S ASSESSMENT

By late April 1987, the commission's assessment and recommendation, which was not what many American Catholics would have hoped for from three American bishops, had been shared with Archbishop Hunthausen. He in turn shared it with his board of consultors and close staff, the very people who had visited with the commission in Menlo Park. That group wrote of their disappointment, to Bernardin, O'Connor, and Quinn:

> "We are very sorry that the Holy See and now you, as reflected in your document, seem to have the impression of our Archbishop and our Archdiocese that you do.
>
> We are grateful to you for more clearly stating what seems to be the core issue, namely, that the ultimate flaw in the Archdiocese is twofold:
>
> a) The one flaw consists in an attitudinal climate which allows continual aberrations to occur with regard to magisterial teaching and Church discipline. These aberrations consist mainly in arbitrary modifications of church teaching or discipline by some pastors or other persons charged with archdiocesan activities. This attitudinal climate persists, you say, because the Archbishop's communications to those in responsible positions are inadequate in the sense of being ambiguous… or because he is too tolerant in his allowance of time for them to form mature and responsible consciences in carrying out Church teaching and discipline.
>
> That Church discipline has not always been properly observed can be demonstrated. That some may not have presented Church teaching as clearly as possible could also, we have no doubt, be demonstrated. But we have to disagree with the idea that all of these cases are serious in nature or that they are due to a permissive attitudinal climate or one that persists because of the Archbishop.
>
> b) The other flaw, you state, consists in the Archbishop's practice of shared responsibility, which can lead people to think and act as if the Church is not hierarchical but rather 'congregational', that is, a church in which the voice of others competes equally with the Archbishop's.
>
> We state categorically and without reservation that this is not the understanding of the pastors, chancery staff, religious and lay leaders of the Archdiocese. We acknowledge that there may be some who hold these views, but they are not in significant leadership positions.

If your analysis were correct we would understand the concern, because these two forces would work hand in hand and soon create a church totally foreign to the one, holy, catholic and apostolic Church we know as the Roman Catholic Church.

Your assessment makes clear what we have suggested from the Fall of 1985, when Cardinal Ratzinger finally communicated the results of the Visitation, namely that the real issue was not the concerns themselves but rather the Archbishop's style of leadership. Naturally our suspicions were strengthened by subsequent events, namely the appointment of Bishop Wuerl, the granting of Special Faculties, and Archbishop Laghi's chronology in which he states that 'the Holy See considered him (Archbishop Hunthausen) lacking the firmness necessary to govern the Archdiocese'. But you are the first to say so clearly. We appreciate this fact even though we disagree with your assessment.

You mention that the 'climate' has remained substantially unchanged since the Apostolic Visitation. What else could be expected, since the Archbishop did not have a clear idea what the Holy See's concerns were and there was no public report until Cardinal Ratzinger's letter almost 3 years later. And immediately after the letters closing the Visitation, Bishop Wuerl was appointed precisely to correct the aberrations and change the 'climate'. Thus we ask, why, in your assessment of the Seattle Situation, is there no mention of Bishop Wuerl and his activities or lack thereof in addressing the concerns of the Holy See? After all he has had for some time now the formal responsibility and authority to act in five major areas and yet you say that it is Archbishop Hunthausen's fault that the 'climate' remains unchanged....

The appointment of an Auxiliary Bishop with Special Faculties has not improved the Seattle Situation. It is not clear why you think that the appointment of a Coadjutor Bishop will be any more successful. If the Coadjutor Bishop is selected from a *terna* submitted by the Archbishop won't this person be one similar to him in leadership style? Since the Holy See is already criticizing the Archbishop's leadership style it seems highly unlikely that such a candidate would be selected. And so isn't the only other option the Archbishop's forced resignation? In addition whether or not the Holy See approves one of the candidates named by Archbishop Hunthausen the underlying issue will be far from settled. We see this issue as the right of an Archdiocesan Church to an appropriate opportunity for clearly demonstrating its unity with the Holy See in Church teaching and discipline.

> And so we fear this 'final solution' will only continue to damage the Holy See's reputation. The Holy See will be seen as trying to save face rather than dealing with the fundamental issues at stake. This will further demoralize pastors, religious and lay leaders, and it will unleash new attacks from the far right. Pastorally speaking, we feel all of this will be very traumatic for this church and, we suspect, the larger church.... We would like the chance to address the Holy See's concerns as indicated in Cardinal Ratzinger's letter and demonstrate that the 'climate' of this Archdiocese and the approach of Archbishop Hunthausen to sharing responsibility are not what they seem to you or others. The major stumbling block has been that we have never been given a chance to do so. It was just days after the public letter closing the Visitation, that Bishop Wuerl was appointed. Progress was definitely being made in addressing the issues and in establishing a new 'climate' when Special Faculties were mandated. While adjusting to this reality, the Presbyteral Council and the Chancery staff made still new efforts to assist Bishop Wuerl in addressing the concerns.
>
> We ask for a suitable period of time to address the Holy See's concerns on our own, without an auxiliary bishop with special faculties or a Coadjutor. Should the Holy See agree to this approach, we would gratefully accept your continued assistance as well as the assistance of the NCCB during this time. If after this period of time your assessment remained the same as it is now it would be appropriate for the Holy See to ask for Archbishop Hunthausen's resignation.
>
> We believe the best interests of the Church will be served by this approach which has our full commitment and we judge the full commitment of our priests, religious and lay leaders.
>
> In closing we repeat our disappointment with your current assessment and recommendation. We are disillusioned, for it doesn't at all reflect our conversations with you in San Francisco and we would gladly state this in a face to face meeting. In fact we would welcome a follow up meeting to clarify our position."[68]

I asked Fr. Michael McDermott, one of this letter's authors, about his recollections of the Menlo Park meetings:

> "Bernardin, Quinn, and O'Connor wanted to talk with several of us.... They were first asking us questions concerning the archbishop. We were pretty consistent in our responses to them. They were very polite and all. You couldn't tell whether you were having any impact on

> them. It was very cordial. We were able to say what we wanted to say. We wanted to try to get across to them that Archbishop Hunthausen was faithful to the church and was in both words and actions neither against the church nor trying to undermine the church nor trying to do something that was against church teaching. We were trying to confirm that he was, from our perspective, totally in line with the church. Because we never knew the reasons for the official investigation, it was a little hard to respond to general kinds of questions. So I think we each spoke from our different perspectives given where we were, what our responsibilities were at that particular time."

McDermott was responsible for the archdiocesan financial office and also coordinated Hunthausen's cabinet meetings. I asked him about the commission's depiction of a "general climate of permissiveness" in Seattle. The only thing ever even alluded to in this regard, as far as he could remember, was the issue of the Dignity Mass. Whether it had come up at the Menlo Park meeting he could not remember, but he figured that it was probably related to their concern.

> "If there was a question of permissiveness I think it was probably something along that line, the gay and lesbian issue. The only other thing, and again I don't remember if this came up at Menlo Park, was that it was a pastoral judgment that Archbishop Hunthausen had made. He had carefully consulted with Fr. Peter Chirico, the theologian at the time. Subsequent to that event Dignity came to call for change in church teaching."

McDermott went on to say that when Archbishop Hickey came out for the visitation in early November 1983, he asked McDermott about the bicentennial process, which used in part Fr. Andrew Greeley's sociological study about American Catholics. "We found out, through our bicentennial process, that our Catholics here in the archdiocese were very similar to Catholics elsewhere in terms of their religious understanding. One of the questions I was asked at the time was, 'What have you done about this?' I said, 'Well we haven't had a chance to figure out exactly how to respond to the data.'" McDermott continued:

> "I think it's partly because there were some questions that showed us some people were beginning to question the real presence and other questions like that. But this is a statistical response. So the fact that we asked people a variety of questions about their religious understanding and practices, is this permissiveness? Was the whole bicentennial process and survey interpreted by some critics as allowing the church to try to become a democracy? Did the bicentennial create the worry that Seattle was becoming, through Hunthausen, a church based on

popular opinion? That could be. The whole bicentennial process was part of a national effort. We had the survey and then we had deanery listening sessions. We listened to what people were saying and we took the results of our process and the data to Chicago for the national meeting. Fr. Jim Dunning was in charge of all of this.

You see, with Hunthausen you have a person fully committed to shared responsibility and collegiality with all. He is the paradigm of a good coach. And so when you bring people together and you start talking with them instead of telling them what to do, you say, this is where we need to go, and you listen to them, to the people and their responsibility, well, that can be interpreted as a climate of permissiveness. I guess it could be. You see Hunthausen's whole model of shared responsibility could have been interpreted this way. He was formed as a bishop at the Vatican Council those four years. When he came to Seattle he was able to build a team, treat people as adults, and work with people. He was very clear about what the church taught. There was no permissiveness in terms of dogma, morals, or what the church taught. It was a question of how best to make it a reality in the lives of the people. Now did he challenge the government on nuclear disarmament? Absolutely. Did he, when the peace pastoral was being written, speak in terms of saying that nuclear arms were immoral? Yes. But does that go against church doctrine or church teaching? At the time the Bishops as a whole were trying to sort that out."[69]

A GOOD COACH, HE'S OUR ARCHBISHOP

A sense of personal connection to Hunthausen was felt by many people in the region, Catholic or not. One *Seattle Post-Intelligencer* headline announced: "He's Our Archbishop." Bill Cate of the Church Council of Greater Seattle described Ray Hunthausen this way and said such sentiments were shared in diverse faith communities. Charlie Meconis, forever up to his neck in the peace and justice movement, remembered that many folks rallied for Hunthausen at Rev. Jon Nelson's Lutheran congregation up on Capitol Hill. "The news media covered it widely. Margaret Casey, Kathleen Pruitt, and others were leading the whole effort in that period to support him. By all the organizing we did," Meconis told me, "we succeeded in getting the powers to pull back, to retreat some from what they were doing to Hunthausen."[70]

Fr. David Jaeger spoke out forcefully. "This is a call for help. Do not let the Holy See do something that is going to do damage to the Catholic Church here and beyond. Stop them." Jaeger argued that "loyalty means more than consenting to something that is wrong." Most of the priests of the archdiocese came together at St. Paul Parish in Seattle on April 20. They made a statement. Hunthausen was a "faithful and orthodox teacher of the Catholic faith" and the Vatican action against Hunthausen was unjust. The Archdiocesan Sisters' Council made their own statement, saying that "witnessing such scandalous actions against a highly respected prelate causes doubts and questions about the Catholic Church's commitment to living out its principles and pronouncements about justice." The April 24 edition of the *National Catholic Reporter* announced that the commission had come up with a proposed solution, which it presented to Rome and which was accepted after John Paul II amended it. A point of contention was the issue of a coadjutor. Hunthausen would be required to accept the appointment. A coadjutor would normally only be appointed in the circumstance when a bishop is incapacitated, so the symbolism had significance. According to the *National Catholic Reporter*,

> "Hunthausen was taken aback and would not agree to the proposed compromise during his meeting with Bernardin in Chicago. The commission members are irritated, even angered, by what they perceive to be Hunthausen's recalcitrance.... Though neither side is altogether happy with the compromise plan...it is the only way Hunthausen will be able to stay on as archbishop of Seattle. If he rejects the compromise, Rome will appoint an administrator and ask Hunthausen to step down, the sources said."[71]

On April 29, 1987, intrepid Hunthausen advocate Fr. Jerry McCloskey wrote to Cardinal Bernardin and the commission. He included with his cover letter a statement of support for Archbishop Hunthausen that had been signed by most of the diocesan and many of the religious priests. In his letter he wrote with a tone suggesting a revolt was very close to erupting:

> "It is no exaggeration to say that the diocese is a powder keg at the moment. The only thing that has kept many people from taking more drastic action has been their love for and trust of Archbishop Hunthausen and their respect for his desire to give the process every opportunity to succeed. Once that restraint is removed and there is no longer any hope for justice through the process, an explosion could be set off that will rock the whole Church. And the only thing that can prevent that explosion from happening would be the full and unconditional restoration of Archbishop Hunthausen's authority. Nothing less than that will be acceptable to the majority of the people of the Archdiocese."

Bernardin, Quinn, and O'Connor would grasp the situation, he hoped, but if they should choose to ignore its gravity, "you do so only at great peril to yourselves and to the entire Church. When you agreed to serve on the Commission you accepted a grave responsibility, not only to those who appointed you, but to the entire Church which you represent as bishops. We trust that you will discharge that responsibility as befits those at the highest levels of authority in the Church."[72]

Hunthausen had come to McCloskey's parish, St. Paul's, for the Confirmation ritual. It was just one week later following his last correspondence with the trio that the pastor of St. Paul's wrote again to the commission, describing Hunthausen's visit:

> "As is our custom, I invited him to dinner and, as is his custom, he accepted. Our housekeeper, a wonderful and gracious woman, spent literally days planning the menu, preparing the food, and setting the table. She loves to entertain and had outdone herself for 'the Archbishop'—chicken a l'orange, sliced tomato salad, strawberries and pineapple served in a dish carved out of a melon in the shape of a swan, and 'Bishop's bread' (which she had 'elevated' to Archbishop's bread).
>
> Everything was ready when we received a phone call to say that the Archbishop would not be able to make it to dinner because 'something had come up.' The 'something,' of course, was his conference call with you. When I got home in the afternoon, the housekeeper was sitting at the kitchen table with her head in her hands, looking somewhat dazed. She was heartbroken, though she is much too gracious to have admitted it. Archbishop Hunthausen made it to the Confirmation (barely), looking somewhat frazzled and having eaten only a peanut butter sandwich. He finally got to sample some of the dinner about 9:00 p.m., re-heated in the microwave.
>
> The Gospel reading for the Mass was Matthew 5:1-12 (the Beatitudes.) It was hard for me to read those words in the presence of a man many of us consider the living example of what they mean. But when I got to the last sentence, I choked on the words and had to hold back the tears. 'Blest are you when they insult you and persecute you and utter every kind of slander against you because of me. Be glad and rejoice, for your reward is great in heaven; they persecuted the prophets before you in the very same way.' It is one thing to read mere words; it is quite another to see those words in action before your very eyes.
>
> I tell you this just to let you know how your actions have affected a whole lot of little people. Not that it really matters to you. If you can keep us in the dark and negotiate the future of an entire diocese

> behind closed doors, I would hardly expect you to care about a mere housekeeper. But I'm sure that you have all lived in rectories enough to know that you can mess with the bishop and you can mess with a pastor, but you don't mess with a housekeeper.
>
> It is callousness such as this (which we clergy have been experiencing for four years) which will doom to failure any attempt you may make to impose a 'solution' on Seattle. If you try to force us to accept anything less than the full and unconditional restoration of Archbishop Hunthausen's authority without fully and clearly justifying such an extraordinary action, all hell will break loose. And I, for one, will personally see that it does."[73]

Pro-Nuncio Laghi, in an interview held at his D.C. office on May 8, said he was hopeful that the Seattle controversy would soon end. "I am the first one to hope there will be some reconciliation, but reconciliation without compromising" on principles. Anticipation of some sort of closure, some sort of negotiated settlement, was in the air—or so the Vatican prayed.[74] From the excellent investigative work of Kenneth Briggs, in his early 1990s book *Holy Siege: The Year that Shook Catholic America*, it is known that negotiations between Hunthausen and the three-member commission did not go well in late April and early May. The trio was willing to recommend that Hunthausen's full powers be restored, but he would have to accept a coadjutor who would have the right of succession. But, from his point of view, if he agreed to a coadjutor, he would be giving tacit support for the notion that Seattle required Rome's help to address problems in the local church. Hunthausen had not found the early draft of the commission report, with its sharply critical tone, palatable. So the commission tried to work things out so that the archbishop would have some influence over the selection of the coadjutor. The three names to be forwarded to Rome by Pio Laghi would be names Hunthausen could approve. Still, he would not be given the freedom to pick these people. Hunthausen went ahead with his desire to provide the names of three of his own preferences, Bishop Michael Kenny of Juneau, Archbishop Francis Hurley of Anchorage, and Bishop William Skylstad of Yakima.[75] Briggs chronicled what happened:

> "Archbishop Hunthausen and his aides had resisted the coadjutor concept before, viewing it as a tacit admission that things were indeed so amiss in the archdiocese that special Vatican assistance was needed to clean it up. They had never fully acknowledged the existence of the laid-back climate described by Cardinal Ratzinger in his 1985 indictment of the archbishop's leadership, and they were no more inclined to give ground now. In addition, the archbishop and his advisers were shocked by the commission's preliminary evaluation

> of the archdiocese. Not only did its dour tone surprise them, but its criticisms seemed to some even harsher than Cardinal Ratzinger's censure. From previous dealings, they had read the commission's attitude as highly positive. But the evaluation shattered that optimism.
>
> The archbishop had long felt misunderstood by Rome but had reason to expect better treatment from his fellow American bishops. His hope suddenly crumbled when the cardinal, the supposed mediating influence on the commission, had handed him the proposed settlement, including the evaluation. As April wore on, he and his advisers were running low on the most indispensable ingredient, trust. At one low point, he even denounced the process as 'evil.'"[76]

The main issue at core, as Briggs correctly analyzed the significance of his conscientious character, was "Archbishop Hunthausen's integrity as a church leader. Rome's severest blow was to judge him unfit. In its 'chronology' of events released the previous November on the eve of the showdown over the Hunthausen case at the annual meeting of the bishops, the Vatican had asserted that although the archbishop had been 'an effective leader in many respects,' he nonetheless lacked 'firmness necessary to govern the archdiocese.'" Briggs continued, "By the first days of May, the tension between the archbishop and the commission was at the breaking point. The archbishop remained adamant that his acceptance of a coadjutor was contingent on his choice of both nominees. The commission refused to back down from its offer. At this point, the four of them were wearing down each others' nerves daily during long, grueling conference calls." The commission had agreed to submit two names, Bishop Skylstad, who was Hunthausen's preferred choice, and Bishop Thomas Murphy of Great Falls-Billings, Montana, "a man the archbishop liked and respected but had some immediate qualms about placing in that role. The question was still whether acceptance of any coadjutor constituted, in principle, an admission of guilt that he could not make in good conscience."[77]

Although, Briggs wrote, "the settlement seemed rational, even generous," to the members of the commission, Hunthausen saw it differently. "As the commission tried to seal the deal, an exasperated archbishop threatened to go over their heads by flying straight to Rome, only to have the Vatican put the kibosh on his plans. There would be no meeting with the pope or top Vatican officials, they informed him, without what amounted to a signed confession and a pledge to mend his ways." Would Hunthausen now take his story directly to the people through the press? He was a hugely popular figure. The commission was worried he might do so. Briggs:

> "As the pressures to accept the commission's settlement increased, Archbishop Hunthausen became more solitary and downcast. He did

> not welcome the commission's argument that if he loved the church he would submit. He believed that through sleight of hand by the commission or the Vatican he might end up with a coadjutor who would be no more satisfactory in the long run than Wuerl had been. He could not be sure about Murphy as coadjutor. He could not be sure about anything. If a successor were to be appointed, what would be the sense of carrying on anyway? He couldn't see how it could possibly work."[78]

Briggs continued: "Alarm was growing on both sides. But from the commission's perspective, the jittery impasse could not go on much longer. What resulted amounted to an ultimatum: accept the assignment of a coadjutor, agree to submit the names of Skylstad and Murphy, and go along with a final, revised assessment. He held out for the choice of both names." Hunthausen had wanted Bishop Michael Kenny of Juneau among his choices. "Without agreement, the settlement talks would break off. The consequences appeared dire. Archbishop Hunthausen would be forced by the Vatican to leave the archdiocese." Even on May 4, it appeared that Hunthausen would reject the package and quit. "To do otherwise, some of his associates believed, would be to accept defeat and egregious compromise." Things did not look good from any point of view. But all changed in three days.

> "On May 7, the Archbishop had accepted that which he had nearly spurned. The deal was struck. The two names would go forward, one chosen by the archbishop, the other by the commission. What happened to bring about the change? Witnesses described the reversal in transcendent terms, as the product of a spiritual transformation that swept over the Archbishop. Both the archbishop's partisans and those involved with the commission spoke of the intervention of the Holy Spirit in bringing about what the human principals could not. Archbishop Hunthausen's supporters attributed the change to his ability to place the dictates of the gospel above his own wishes. In the end, they said, he also believed he owed it to the church in Seattle and most especially to his loyal backers to stay. It was God's will as he understood it. To those who saw the situation more from the commission's vantage point, the success had been largely due to the commission's heroic forbearance."[79]

Reconciliation involved, in no small measure, Briggs noted, "the ministrations of a skilled lay intermediary who helped the archbishop sort through the tangle of factors involved in the dilemma. On the purely human side, that assistance was credited more than any other single element with saving the settlement. The archbishop was counseled on his way to a new vision."[80] The two names that would go forward were William Skylstad and Thomas Murphy, Skylstad chosen by the archbishop and Murphy by the commission.

The intermediary who helped him through the tangle of factors was Tom Fox, editor of the *National Catholic Reporter*. When I spoke with Fox, he shared the inside story, which had never been told before. Fr. Michael Ryan and Tom Fox got to be pretty close, since Ryan was serving on the *National Catholic Reporter* board. So with Ryan as the conduit to a relationship, Fox got to know the archbishop. As time went on, Hunthausen and Fox, regularly on the phone together, had some very personal conversations. According to Fox, at some point in the spring, Hunthausen lost trust in the three bishops of the commission, and Bernardin, the lead member of the trio, lost trust in Hunthausen. Fox found himself in a 'go-between' role. Well-published Catholic thinker and psychologist Eugene Kennedy was close to Cardinal Bernardin and knew Tom Fox well, therefore he also played a role. Since they were no longer talking directly, Hunthausen and Bernardin had Fox and Kennedy as their proxies.

So Hunthausen had to decide whether to take the commission's offer or resign. It was at that decision-making moment that Fox had an intimate conversation with Hunthausen. Hunthausen wanted to understand just what the commission's offer was really all about, since he was trying to decide whether to accept it. Fox: "We prayed together, the 'Our Father'. Hunthausen said, 'I just want to make this decision based on my understanding of the Gospel, what the Gospel would require.'" Fox was in a critical moment in American-Roman Catholic history there on the phone—in a shared prayer experience. Fox then listened as Hunthausen came to the conclusion that he would accept Bernardin's offer. Hunthausen asked Fox to convey the news. Fox called Kennedy, who in turn called Bernardin. Fox wondered many years later, in retrospect, if that was the right decision, hoping and praying that he was not an accomplice to a slow death. For in the years that followed, in the view of Tom Fox, Rome effectively cut Hunthausen out of office.[81]

After speaking with Fox, I contacted Eugene Kennedy. He described the drama as he remembered it:

> "If Tom Fox had not been working with Mike Ryan, things would not have gone so well. Bernardin was trying to find a solution that would preserve Hunthausen's position but also deliver something to Rome. Cardinal Bernardin told me that Hunthausen did not get the nickname "Dutch" for nothing. Hunthausen was at times intransigent and stubborn. Just when Bernardin thought he could close the deal, Hunthausen would get stubborn. There was a great deal of conversation between myself and Tom Fox in this time. Hunthausen was unwilling to give the commission his full cooperation. Mike Ryan was key in

all of this. The Hunthausen case was resolved at the personal level. Tom Fox had gotten Hunthausen to agree to the final settlement. The conversation between Fox and Hunthausen was poignant, deeply spiritual. Hunthausen was planning to resign, seriously considering it. He did not like what Bernardin and the commission was saying. Hunthausen overcame his reluctance to accept the resolution. Ryan and Fox played key roles in this. I called Bernardin to tell him that Dutch had accepted the resolution."[82]

On May 19 and 20, 1987, the three-member commission met with top officials and Pope John Paul II in Rome. Cardinal Ratzinger signed off on the settlement, but reluctantly. John Paul II was, relatively speaking, more enthusiastic. He must have thought that this settlement could finally put an end to all the negative press the Seattle-Rome conflict produced. The end result: Hunthausen would be restored to full authority; Bishop Murphy would become coadjutor archbishop to help Hunthausen in overcoming the problems the Vatican identified. The commission would stay on for another year to monitor the efforts, and Wuerl would be re-assigned.[83]

When the unanimous judgment of the Holy See's appointed commission came out in late May 1987, it summarized the Seattle church situation, saying that "no matter how personally firm in his teachings and practices the Archbishop himself may be, without intending it, he is perceived as generating, or at least accepting, a climate of permissiveness within which some feel themselves free to design their own policies and practices." Hunthausen's compassion was leading many in Seattle to take advantage of the permissiveness. Here was, according to the American hierarchy trio cum-Vatican endorsement, the essence of the problem:

> "the overall attitudinal 'climate' or psychological and ecclesiological orientation of the Archdiocese…is the ultimate key to the situation. No substantive changes will perdure until this climate or orientation changes. And this climate or orientation seems to have remained substantially unchanged since the time of the Apostolic Visitation and the letter of the Congregation for the Doctrine of the Faith."[84]

Commission head Cardinal Bernardin, in a *New York Times* interview, commented: "I think that what we try to do in this proposal is attend to the concerns of both the Holy See and the Archbishop and I think it's a good solution. I'm confident that all the parties will do everything they can to make it work and I'm very pleased with the way it turned out." Was "a good solution" a just solution? One thing could be said: Hunthausen would not have to deal with the "unworkable" arrangement he had been saddled with beforehand, but now he would have to deal with a coadjutor—and remember the role which coadjutors had played as precedent was to step into a situation when a bishop has been incapacitated. While officials insisted the settlement was a win-win, *New York Times* writer Berger noted the subtle nuance in the language of some church officials who were saying the Vatican's appointment of a coadjutor meant that Hunthausen "will probably consider it 'prudential' to consult with his new assistant on important matters."[85]

Donald Wuerl was sent to back to Pittsburgh. Bishop Thomas Murphy of Great Falls-Billings, Montana was appointed Coadjutor Archbishop of Seattle. Hunthausen had taken steps to carry out certain provisions which had been specified in Ratzinger's confidential September 1985 letter (cited in chapter five), which by the spring of 1987 was in the public record. Hunthausen's compassionate spirit and his pastoral approach were publicly lauded by the commission. In fact his abundant compassion was judged to be part of the problem of permissiveness. The commission recommended that Rome establish target dates for the completion of objectives specified in Ratzinger's letter. The commission would be mandated to assist in the accomplishment of these tasks.[86]

On May 27, 1987, the members of the Seattle Archdiocesan Board of Consultors and leadership group of the central agencies of the archdiocese commented critically on the commission's final document:

> "The document purportedly bases its assessment on learnings gained largely from interviews which the members of the Commission conducted with each one of us and with the Bishops of the Northwest on March 6 and 7 at St. Patrick's Seminary in Menlo Park, California. While we cannot presume to speak for the Bishops of the Northwest, we do strongly assert that the negative judgments contained in the document in question do not begin to fairly or accurately reflect either the content or the spirit of the testimony which we presented to the Commission with regard to the current state of the Church in our archdiocese. In fact, we state without hesitation that the document, in its judgment that the overall attitudinal climate or psychological and ecclesiological orientation of the archdiocese needs to be substantially changed, simply does not describe the Church we know and serve...."

This statement by these people, key clergy and lay leaders with Hunthausen, must have been viewed by the Vatican as post-facto evidence of the problem they had to solve. These Seattle folks just didn't get it—Rome's need to control Seattle's climate and clip Hunthausen's wings. "We further state that the solution proposed by the Commission, i.e., the naming of a coadjutor archbishop who will share leadership with and eventually succeed Archbishop Raymond Hunthausen, is completely out of keeping with the ideas and proposals which we were asked to respond to in our personal interviews with the Commission members." They nevertheless supported Archbishop Hunthausen in his acceptance of the decision of the Holy See to appoint Bishop Thomas Murphy as coadjutor archbishop.[87]

The new Coadjutor Archbishop Thomas Murphy was side-by-side with Hunthausen at a Seattle press conference in late May. Asked what he thought about Hunthausen's prominent anti-nuclear stand, Murphy replied simply: "I respect Archbishop Hunthausen's stand on peace and justice." Hunthausen, asked if he thought that his politics had angered the Vatican, replied: "I have never understood why we have been singled out. I can't answer that."[88] Joseph Berger for the *New York Times* interpreted what had just happened in the Catholic world: "When a panel of three American bishops announced an arrangement last week allowing Archbishop Raymond G. Hunthausen to resume control of the Archdiocese of Seattle, the commission appeared to be affirming the right of Catholic institutions in the United States to go about their business in the open, democratic manner to which they have grown accustomed." The Vatican had to accept that their earlier solution, the appointment of Wuerl, was not working. Berger continued:

> "But the Vatican prevailed on the principle it held most fundamental: the integrity of Roman Catholic doctrine. The commission, in so many words, affirmed most of the Vatican's findings of doctrinal abuses in Seattle. Sterilizations had been performed at Catholic hospitals, though the Archbishop allowed the procedure only for non-Catholics. Archbishop Hunthausen had permitted Dignity, a group of Catholic homosexuals, to use the cathedral for a mass. Catholics were advised by some priests that after divorce and civil remarriage, they could return to the sacraments, a policy that contradicted the Vatican view. Although the commission found that the Archbishop may not have been personally to blame for all these problems, it agreed that a 'permissive' atmosphere had developed."

The commission made sure that Hunthausen knew of every person they had interviewed and he was shown all documents, unlike what happened with the Vatican visitation by Hickey. The three-member commission was relatively transparent. But what really had just happened? Berger wrote that the commission was "affirming the right of Catholic institutions in the United States to go about their business in the open, democratic matter to which they have grown accustomed." That conclusion was too sanguine.[89] The truth, easier to see from hindsight perhaps, is that Hunthausen lacked "the necessary firmness" required of an American bishop serving during the reign of Pope John Paul II and Cardinal Joseph Ratzinger and therefore needed a coadjutor archbishop to ensure a tighter ship—one that would get on course with Rome's central (and centralizing) flagship.

So how did Hunthausen handle the news conference on May 27, where the proposed resolution to a difficult situation was made public? "The result is a good one," he told reporters packed into the room at the chancery. Asked about the assessment, he disagreed with some important aspects of the commission's report and then went on to say rather candidly that he could not support it. The prior day he had written to the priests of the archdiocese: "I want you to know that while I am not in agreement with a number of important aspects of the assessment and am therefore not prepared to endorse it, I have nonetheless come to the point of accepting the commission's proposed resolution to our situation." Hunthausen made it clear that Bishop Murphy would not have any special authorities. As Kenneth Briggs put it in *Holy Siege*, it "was the archbishop's forced surrender of five areas of the archdiocesan operation to Bishop Wuerl that had touched off the rebellion the previous fall, and the Vatican apparently did not intend to rub that raw wound again. Coadjutors normally were given special faculties, but Archbishop Hunthausen said he was sure an exception had been made in this case." From the perspective of many of his supporters, his full authority had been restored because enough people vocalized their resistance. "Perhaps the most crucial aspect of the agreement, many supporters said, was that in their view the Vatican had backed down. It had forced Wuerl on them, and that had sparked a rebellion that had caused Rome to retreat."[90] Many supporters understandably wanted to put as positive a face on the outcome of their long struggle as possible.

Conservative elements in the American Catholic world were not happy in the least. *The Wanderer*'s June 4, 1987 edition judged the settlement

> "a clear victory for the 'Americanist' wing of the U.S. Episcopacy which has long campaigned for more input into the resolution of tensions between the Holy See and the local Church.... While many observers view this latest settlement as a compromise, others see it as a retreat by the Holy See in the face of determined and organized opposition from Seattle dissidents supported by a network of Americanist allies throughout the country."

Briggs observed that perhaps it was "natural that the far right, which had rallied its forces nationwide to urge the Vatican to discipline Archbishop Hunthausen, should see the outcome as a triumph by a far-flung network of 'Americanist' conspirators."[91]

One troubling irony, having to do with Bishop Wuerl, made itself apparent in his interview with the *Pittsburgh Post-Gazette* (his hometown newspaper) in late June 1987. He reflected back on the experience in Seattle. "I had to remind myself, 'They are not angry at me personally. I am a symbol of the malfunctioning.' The solution they tried was not working." Wuerl was a symbol of Rome's intervention and therefore became a target of the anger many felt over what the Vatican had done to Hunthausen. But Wuerl did not go deeper in the interview. He did not say that Hunthausen was the real symbol at the center of the drama. He did not say candidly that the Vatican had targeted Hunthausen, and that Hunthausen was being attacked by the Vatican in part because of some flaws in the structure and culture of the Vatican authority system. In the eyes of Wuerl, the Vatican's crackdown on Hunthausen had been vindicated. "There was a great deal of feeling that the action against Hunthausen was unjust, but that is not heard now," Wuerl said. "Now an American commission has said there is a problem—they are saying the same things the Holy See saw have to be corrected. It had to do with issues of church doctrine and practice."[92] No critical examination of Vatican power entered into Wuerl's perspective. When he was later installed as the new bishop of the Diocese of Pittsburgh, in February 1988, he was asked again to comment on what he had gone through in Seattle. "That chapter is closed. It's finished."[93]

He might have added that Archbishop Hunthausen's whole endeavor to move the church in the spirit of the Second Vatican Council was pretty much "finished" as well. The commission completed its work in spring 1989. Hunthausen, always trying to see things with as much of an irenic attitude as he could muster, was relieved to know the matter seemed to be reaching closure. In April he said:

> "Both Archbishop Murphy and I acknowledge the trial the Church here has faced over the past several years, yet we are also able to view the whole experience as a time of grace, a grace which, with the Lord's help, will enable us to offer our leadership to the Church in Western Washington in the years ahead with renewed dedication and commitment to the Gospel and the Universal Church under our Holy Father, Pope John Paul II. We ask for your prayers as we continue to meet the challenges of being a Roman Catholic community of faith here in Western Washington."[94]

In its report to the Holy See on the situation in Seattle, the Bernardin-Quinn-O'Connor commission had written that they tried to keep in mind charity and compassion, fairness, and openness, but "we also kept in mind the nature of a bishop's role in the Church." Referring, without any hint of irony, to the Second Vatican Council, they underscored the power bishops exercise in their own right, but wrote:

> "...the Council also teaches that every bishop, by reason of his episcopal ordination, is a member of the College of Bishops. He is not an independent agent, standing in isolation. As a member of the College of Bishops, he exercises his office only in communion and obedience to the Head of the College of Bishops, the Pope, the Successor of Peter and Bishop of Rome. Indeed, every bishop in his ordination publicly

> declares his promise to fulfill his ministry in obedience to Peter and his successors."

Why would the commission dedicate the closing page of its report to this topic of obedience, not exactly the theme most widely associated with Vatican II? The commission's closing message was not about collegiality but about centrality:

> "From the first century to this, it has been the role of the Bishop of Rome to intervene in local, regional or national situations when required by the greater good of the Church, as attested by the earliest documents of Christian history. If the Church, spread through many cultures and existing on all continents is to remain one and maintain its identity, the Pope must make decisions which must be binding on the whole body of the Church."

Also, with no apparent sense of irony, they quoted the great theologian Karl Rahner, as if to suggest that he would endorse the action taken by Rome in Seattle. For "the Church cannot be a debating society: it must be able to make decisions binding on all within it."[95] Both Rahner and Vatican II were employed here, out of context, to make a case for a tide that was turning away from the Council in an effort to restore a centralizing papacy. Actually, as Bishop Thomas Gumbleton pointed out in a retrospective conversation, it was not until the fourth century that the Pope was recognized as having special powers, but even then he could not be viewed as a lone ranger, but always as a member of the college, *primus inter pares*, first among equals.[96]

J.L. Drouhard worked with Hunthausen and has continued to work in justice and peace ministry ever since, including the Catholic Campaign for Human Development, in the Archdiocese of Seattle. Since Drouhard has long served as a lay professional in a role not unlike the one I had for several years in the Archdiocese of Portland, I wanted to know his thoughts about Hunthausen:

> "I remember the investigation. I saw there so much conflict going on. I watched him. He seemed to be not wanting to bring conflict into the archdiocese. Or if it was there, not to fan the flames. By not hearing much about it I thought that must be his approach. The investigation was a travesty. But there was for Hunthausen this whole spirit of collegiality. I remember reading his statement from when he met with all the bishops at the NCCB and I remember thinking, what a terrible position to be in. I could see that he was very adhering to the way the church had a hierarchy and there was a sense of apostolic succession and there was collegiality but you also had the bishop of Rome leading. Just all the struggle Hunthausen must have felt with this. Looking back now, I would say he was not

a person who relished the idea of engaging in conflict. I am not sure if that ever got really worked out in his mind. How could anybody in that position as a bishop deal with the situation that presented itself to him?"

Hunthausen just did not want to confront Rome. "He modeled a way of ministry that I try to emulate," J.L. said. But Drouhard expressed some ambivalence, something I could identify with as well:

> "As a lay person, most of my life working in the church, I have this ambivalence about how Hunthausen dealt with the crucial issue of the church injustice he faced. Why did he not confront Rome more directly? When he spoke to the general assembly of the NCCB about the situation, he was not quiet. With his brother bishops he was saying, 'we're kind of all in this together, if it happens to me, who am I, I'm just a guy from Anaconda, and this is my local church. I happen to be the person there, it could happen to any of us.' I guess that he did this out of a brotherly thing. This is part of the struggle I have with who he was as a hierarch. It was thrust upon him, it wasn't what he chose. He just lived through it. I'm not a hierarch but my check comes from them and, as they say, I am an extension of the archbishop's ministry in my work. That grates against me at times but all I have to do is think of Dutch and say, okay, he is a model. It's not like he's superman. It just comes out of that humility. He's just a regular guy who had his values that I really admire, but he embraced those in a way that was fed by something that I think we could all draw on."[97]

The system both supported and constrained Hunthausen. He internalized some of the oppression. This can partly be explained by the grip of family secrets in a patriarchal family to which he was a loyal—as well as prophetic—son, and by the formal duties of the hierarchy of which he was a member. He challenged Rome publicly. He countered Laghi's chronology, and he never accepted Rome's fundamental shift away from Vatican II. That shift away would continue through the rest of John Paul II's long papacy and that of his successor, Benedict XVI—Cardinal Ratzinger. Hunthausen tried to practice peace in the church controversy. Could he have practiced more directly the struggle for justice in the church?

It seems that in almost everything he did as a religious leader, Raymond Hunthausen turned first and foremost to prayer; to the example of the life of Jesus as best he could interpret it from Scripture with the help of good exegesis; to reflections on his many interpersonal encounters that were so influential in his discernment, such as that personal testimony of the gay school teacher who told him about his anxiety over the official Catholic stand; and to his best general reading of the signs of the times. He did this with respect to his call for unilateral nuclear disarmament, to be sure, but also in how he handled the conflict over the split-authority imposed by Rome. Yet he chose to endure the authority structure of the church when it was being taken in a direction contrary to the Vatican II call for greater collegiality and lay empowerment. He walked on a path of conscience, courage, and communal loyalty. It took remarkable loyalty to Rome to stay in Seattle even after the heavy beating Hunthausen had endured. Yet at the same time, it took courage to boldly ask—and answer, through his example, during the era of John Paul II and Joseph Ratzinger—the question Raymond Hunthausen had made so defining for his life work ever since the Second Vatican Council: what kind of church are we trying to become?

ENDNOTES

1 Dumont, Louise. Personal interview. Seattle, Washington 10 Dec. 2012.

2 Pruitt, Kathleen. Personal interview. Seattle, Washington 3 Dec. 2011.

3 Open Letter to the Bishops of the United States from Concerned Catholics of Western Washington. November 1986. Concerned Catholics File.

4 Goldman, Ari. "U.S. Bishop Urges A Papal Audience On 'Disaffection'." *New York Times* 11 Nov. 1986. *Global Issues In Context.* Web. 7 Aug. 2012.

5 Malone, James, Nov. 10, 1986 statement at NCCB meeting, as cited by Schilling, 185.

6 Cited in Schilling, 185.

7 Schilling, 318.

8 Goldman, Ari. "2 Centrists Win In Vote To Head Bishops In U.S." *New York Times* 12 Nov. 1986. *Global Issues In Context.* Web. 9 Aug. 2012.

9 Chavez, Lydia. "Reporter's Notebook: A Red Letter For A 'Martyr'." *New York Times* 13 Nov. 1986. *Global Issues In Context.* Web. 9 Aug. 2012.

10 Hunthausen, Raymond. Letter to fellow bishops. 11 Nov. 1986. See *Origins*

11 Hunthausen, Raymond. Address to Members of the NCCB, delivered in Washington, DC 11 Nov. 1986. See "Archbishop Hunthausen to the U.S. Bishops." *Origins* 20 Nov. 1986, 404-405.

12 Schilling offers thoughtful analysis of Hunthausen's whole address, 194.

13 Hunthausen, Address to Members of the NCCB (emphasis in original).

14 "The Situation in Seattle." *Origins* 20 Nov. 1986, 400-401.

15 See Reese 342 and Lernoux, 225.

16 Goldman, Ari. "Prelates Endorse Steps By Vatican On Seattle Bishop." *New York Times* 13 Nov. 1986. *Global Issues In Context.* Web. 9 Aug. 2012.

17 Gumbleton, Thomas. Correspondence in review of manuscript, May 2014.

18 Suro, Robert. "Vatican Aides Say Bishops' Talks In U.S. May Mark Turning Point." *New York Times* 13 Nov. 1986. *Global Issues In Context.* Web. 9 Aug. 2012.

19 Schilling, 194.

20 "Malone Statement And Excerpts From Hunthausen Statement." *New York Times,* 13 Nov. 1986. *Global Issues In Context.* Web. 9 Aug. 2012.

21 Schilling, 208.

22 Schilling, 198.

23 "Peace Marchers Back Embattled Archbishop." Associated Press 19 Nov. 1986. *Global Issues In Context*. Web. 9 Aug. 2012.

24 Letter to Archbishop Hunthausen. Group of 35 inactive priests and nuns (including the spouses of those who are married). 15 Nov. 1986. Concerned Catholics File.

25 Schilling, 201, and citing from *National Catholic Reporter* 21 Nov. 1986.

26 Goldman, Ari. "Censured Archbishop Quietly Departs For Seattle." *New York Times* 14 Nov. 1986. *Global Issues In Context*. Web. 9 Aug. 2012.

27 Schilling, 202, citing *National Catholic Reporter* story of 21 Nov. 1986.

28 Schilling, 204.

29 Schilling, 207, citing from Hebblethwaite's story in the 7 Nov. 1986 issue of the *National Catholic Reporter*.

30 McBrien, Richard. "The bishops and Archbishop Hunthausen." *Progress* 11 Dec. 1986, 6-7.

31 "Hunthausen To Press For Return Of Full Powers In Archdiocese." *New York Times* 15 Nov. 1986. *Global Issues In Context*. Web. 9 Aug. 2012.

32 See "Transcript of Hunthausen's Press Conference." Held at Chancery Place, Archdiocese of Seattle, Seattle 14 Nov. 1986. Archdiocese of Seattle Archives.

33 "Transcript of Hunthausen's Press Conference."

34 "Transcript of Hunthausen's Press Conference."

35 Berger, Joseph. "Bishops' Parley: A Bow To The Pope, But Dissatisfaction Is Expressed, Too." *New York Times*, 15 Nov. 1986. *Global Issues In Context*. Web. 9 Aug. 2012.

36 "500 Pack A Rural Gym For Hunthausen's Mass." *New York Times*, 17 Nov. 1986. *Global Issues In Context*. Web. 9 Aug. 2012.

37 McDermott, Michael. Personal interview. Tacoma, Washington 14 Dec. 2012.

38 Schilling, 212. Schilling cites from a *Seattle Post-Intelligencer* story of 11 Nov. 1986 and from *Progress* story of 27 Nov. 1986.

39 Berger, Joseph. "Rift Exaggerated, U.S. Prelates Say." *New York Times* 1 Dec. 1986. *Global Issues In Context*. Web. 9 Aug. 2012.

40 To Cardinals, Archbishops, Bishops of the NCCB, from Concerned Catholics of Seattle. 1 Dec. 1986. Concerned Catholics File.

41 Press Statement by the Association of Pittsburgh Priests. 2 Dec. 1986. Concerned Catholic File.

42 Gumbleton, Thomas. Telephone interview. Detroit, Michigan 10 June 2013.

43 Holzschuh, Nicholas. Letter. BIOP Foundation for the Promotion of Orthodoxy. 26 Nov. 1986. Concerned Catholics File.

44 "Archbishop Undergoes Operation for Cancer." *New York Times* 17 Dec. 1986. *Global Issues in Context*. Web. 9 Aug. 2012.

45 Burns, Jim. Personal interview (with small group). Edmonds, Washington 8 Dec 2012.

46 Schilling, 213. citing from a *Seattle Post-Intelligencer* story of 25 Dec. 1986.

47 Schilling, 212.

48 "2D Seattle Bishop Taking A More Visible Role." *New York Times*, 19 Jan. 1987. *Global Issues In Context*. Web. 9 Aug. 2012.

49 Schilling, 212, citing *Progress* 8 Dec. 1986.

50 Berger, Joseph. "Vatican Envoy Defends His Handling Of Case Against Archbishop Of Seattle." *New York Times* 30 Jan. 1987. *Global Issues In Context*. Web. 9 Aug. 2012.

51 Schilling, 325.

52 See Schilling, 216, citing from *Progress* 12 Feb. 1987.

53 Schilling, 216.

54 Schilling, 216.

55 Schilling, 217.

56 From story in *Seattle Weekly* 13 Jan. 1987, as quoted by Schilling, 217.

57 Schilling, 218.

58 Schilling, 218.

59 Schilling, 218.

60 "Vatican Panel In Seattle." *New York Times* 16 Mar. 1987. *Global Issues In Context.* Web. 9 Aug. 2012.

61 Schilling, 219.

62 As recounted by Schilling, 220.

63 As documented by Schilling, 220.

64 Magnano, Paul. Letter to Archbishop Hunthausen. Good Friday, 17 Apr. 1987. Concerned Catholics File.

65 Magnano, Paul. Second letter to Archbishop Hunthausen. Holy Saturday, 18 Apr. 1987. Concerned Catholics File.

66 McCloskey, Jerry. Easter Homily. 18-19 Apr. 1987. Concerned Catholics File.

67 Author unknown. Date not indicated, but was written before the commission report came out in April 1987. Concerned Catholics File.

68 Letter to Archbishop John Quinn and also sent to Bernardin and O'Connor, from Michael G. Ryan et. al. 20 Apr. 1987. Concerned Catholics File.

69 McDermott, Michael. Personal interview. Tacoma, Washington 25 Mar. 2013.

70 Meconis, Charles. Personal interview. Seattle, Washington 27 Mar. 2013.

71 Schilling, 321, citing the *National Catholic Reporter* story of 24 Apr. 1987.

72 McCloskey, Jerry. Letter to Cardinal Bernardin. 29 Apr. 1987. Concerned Catholics File.

73 McCloskey, Jerry. Letter to Cardinal John O'Connor (and to the other two members of the commission as well). 5 May 1987. Concerned Catholics File.

74 Schilling, 222.

75 Briggs, Kenneth. *Holy Siege: The Year That Shook Catholic America.* HarperSanFrancisco: 1992, 338.

76 Briggs, 338.

77 Briggs, 338-339.

78 Briggs, 340.

79 Briggs, 340.

80 Briggs, 340-341.

81 Fox, Tom. Personal (telephone) interview. 12 Sept. 2013.

82 Kennedy, Eugene. Personal (telephone) interview. 12 Sept. 2013.

83 Briggs, 341.

84 See "Excerpts From Recommendations On Bishops." *New York Times* 27 May 1987. *Global Issues In Context.* Web. 9 Aug. 2012.

85 Berger, Joseph. "Catholics Work Out Compromise In Dispute On Seattle Archbishop." *New York Times* 27 May 1987. *Global Issues In Context.* Web. 9 Aug. 2012.

86 "Commission report explains process, conclusion of assessment." *Progress* 28 May 1987, 3. "A Restoration of the Situation in Seattle." *Origins* 4 June 1987, 37-41.

87 Statement by the Archdiocesan Board of Consultors and the leadership group of the Archdiocesan Central Agencies. 27 May 1987. Concerned Catholics File.

88 Tuner, Wallace. "Seattle's Bishop Resumes Control." *New York Times* 28 May 1987. *Global Issues In Context.* Web. 9 Aug. 2012.

89 Berger, Joseph. "Catholics Reach Accord In Seattle Case." *New York Times* 31 May 1987. *Global Issues In Context.* Web. 9 Aug. 2012.

90 Briggs, 342.

91 Briggs, 342-342, and citing *Wanderer*, 4 June 1987.

92 "Bishop Calls For Sharing Of Authority An Unworkable Venture In Seattle." *New York Times* 24 June 1987. *Global Issues In Context.* Web. 9 Aug. 2012.

93 "Prelate in Seattle Dispute Named Pittsburgh Bishop." *New York Times* 13 Feb. 1988. *Global Issues In Context.* Web. 9 Aug. 2012.

94 Hunthausen, Raymond. News Release. 11 Apr. 1989. Archdiocese of Seattle Archives.

95 Report of the Holy See Presented by the Commission Appointed by the Holy See to Assess the Current Situation in Seattle. Published in *Progress* 28 May 1987, in *Origins* 4 June 1987 and included in Schilling's dissertation, 369-372.

96 Gumbleton, Thomas. Correspondence in review of manuscript, May 2014.

97 Drouhard, J.L. Personal interview (small group). Seattle, Washington 25 Mar. 2013.

Chapter Seven

PARACLETE IN THE LABYRINTH

The Eternal City's equivalent of surveillance cameras, figuratively speaking, had been fixed on Hunthausen and the Catholic community of Western Washington for several years by the time (April 1989) the three-member commission finally wrapped up its work. In *Prophets in Their Own Country: Women Religious Bearing Witness to the Gospel in a Troubled Church*, Sandra Schneiders critically analyzes the Vatican's much more recent investigation of women religious in the United States. When Schneiders published her perceptive book in 2011, Benedict (formerly Cardinal Ratzinger) was still in the papal office. Few students of Catholicism could have predicted that Benedict would resign, let alone be replaced by an Argentinean Jesuit who would take the name Francis and begin moving away from the centralizing ethos championed by his two immediate predecessors. John Paul II and Benedict XVI, writes Schneiders, "resolutely pursued a restorationist agenda that has polarized the Church between those who long ardently for a return to the Tridentine era and those who have passionately espoused a conciliar renewal." Speaking from personal experience as well as scholarship, she claims women religious know that "their fidelity to their own living of the conciliar renewal and their promotion of it in the Church and the world will not endear them to the Curia or to the ultraconservative episcopacies that were created by John Paul II, much less to the magisterial fundamentalists among the laity."[1] The Leadership Conference of Women Religious (LCWR) was being subjected to something evocative of Raymond Hunthausen ordeal. The Vatican's heavy-handed treatment of the LCWR could not help but bring to mind, from a long list of cases too numerous to cite, the silencing of the Latin American theologians Ivone Gebarra and Leonardo Boff, not to mention the suppression of Charles Curran and Elizabeth Johnson. Whether as the prefect in charge of doctrine or later as the pope, Joseph Ratzinger was instrumental in all of these disciplinary actions. It was as if Ratzinger had found his true character playing a certain unforgettable role, the grand inquisitor, in Dostoyevsky's *Brothers Karamazov*.[2]

RATZINGER'S WORLDVIEW

What was Rome's agenda? The archivist at the Archdiocese of Seattle let me study files on disarmament and related social concerns. Only two people had access to the records dealing directly with the Seattle-Rome conflict—the current archbishop and the archivist. Those files would remain off limits to researchers indefinitely, I was told. Archbishop Peter Sartain judged that too much divisiveness continued to surround the topic. By extending the Vatican's cloak of secrecy, Sartain may have also been trying to respect Raymond Hunthausen's desire to remain out of the public eye for the remainder of his life.[3] When, in the autumn of 2012, I made that inquiry about pertinent archives, Archbishop Sartain was taking charge of the Vatican's investigation of the Leadership Conference of Women Religious. As Seattle's archbishop, Sartain held the very post that Hunthausen once held, an office now ironically assigned the task of implementing a Vatican investigation instead of being the object of one. Sartain claimed old wounds would fester if the Seattle-Rome case files were opened. Yet he must have known that all this Vatican-guided oversight of the LCWR, even if he tried to be personable and cordial about it, could not help but inflict new wounds. Though William Faulkner's tale was set in a different context, a well known passage from his (applicably entitled) novel, *Requiem for a Nun,* came to my mind: "The past is never dead, it's not even past."[4]

Key documents—in Seattle, Rome, and elsewhere—remained sealed. Nevertheless, the official church statements presented earlier in this book give us some indication of Rome's agenda. We remember that a Vatican spokesman explained in advance of Archbishop Hickey's visit that usually a combination of different concerns, not just one specific issue, could bring on a visitation. The objective was to determine whether the complaints Rome received about Archbishop Hunthausen's ministry were of a religious or political nature. His political activity would be a concern only if he appeared to be engaged in partisan efforts that could divide the local church. Archbishop Hickey insisted that Hunthausen's activities against nuclear weapons and other political matters were not objects of scrutiny. Doctrine, liturgy, and morality were. This notion that Hunthausen's stand on issues of war and peace was not a key concern begs the question. A fair review of the historical record could reasonably postulate that the apostolic visitation happened in part because so many complaints about Hunthausen had been lodged, and more to the point, the record shows that Hunthausen's controversial criticism of certain U.S. government policies sparked many of those complaints.

When Cardinal Ratzinger communicated with Archbishop Hunthausen before Christmas in 1983, he said that among Hunthausen's critics the voices of moderation would be given priority. Did that mean his office was ignoring extreme criticisms? In the September 30, 1985 letter, Ratzinger told Hunthausen that "significant criticism" had been brought to Rome's attention prior to Hickey's visit. Ratzinger claimed that Rome did not wish to give uncritical acceptance to strident voices, and yet the record suggests such voices probably reached the Vatican ear. And another point should not be forgotten. As the official Vatican explanation of its action toward Seattle evolved over time, Hunthausen's alleged "non-cooperative" response to Vatican concerns became the "blame the victim" evidence for further suppression. It may seem astounding to some that Hunthausen would be told by Laghi that he had lost all credibility in Rome but was never told that the well-organized letter campaigns against him lacked credibiliy.

Recall that one of the areas of concern Ratzinger pointed to in the September 1985 letter was liturgy. The report of one alleged liturgical abuse may have made it to the top of the prefect's desk. It apparently happened in January 1983. According to one account of what transpired at St. Michael's Parish in Olympia, conduct at a funeral troubled the mother of the deceased. A dancing clown tied balloons to the casket. In reaction to this and other aspects of the ritual, the distraught mother wrote to Rome.[5] Some of the liturgical creativity may have come across as lacking empathy for a mother in grief. Beyond this single case the focus on alleged liturgical abuse was fed by "Truth squads" who practiced creative liturgical-policing by such means as lining up in the queues of certain parishes, looking for communion hosts made of ingredients not meeting strict Eucharistic requirements.[6]

As seen in the full letter to Archbishop Hunthausen, Cardinal Ratzinger had a merciful litany of problems he wanted to see corrected. When Hunthausen was told to yield authority to Wuerl, the areas corresponded to several items on that list. More significant than all the concerns Rome laid out, however, was the *sea change* that commenced when John Paul II took office. Hunthausen faced the impact of that sea change most consequentially through the office of Cardinal Ratzinger. For that reason we must try to appreciate more carefully the worldview guiding this bishop from Bavaria.

When named archbishop of Munich in 1977, as John Thavis points out in *Vatican Diaries*, Joseph Ratzinger had almost no pastoral experience. When John Paul II appointed him as prefect of the Congregation for the Doctrine of the Faith in late 1981, Thavis writes, this "took him even further away from the day-to-day reality of most Catholics. This was a man who had found a refuge in the church from social conflict, criticism and doubt."[7] He was just twelve when he was enrolled in a minor seminary in 1939, the same year Hitler drove into Poland, and "except for a brief stint in the army, from that moment the church was his entire life." He was more at home in some ways with books than with people. His thinking had not always been focused on restoring a pre-Vatican II model of church or promoting what he would later call a "hermeneutic of continuity." Early on, he brought some innovative analysis to Vatican II. However, it was when he was on the theology faculty at the University of Tübingen that he witnessed, Thavis says, an "increasing Marxist influence and radicalization, culminating in the protests and riots of spring 1968. By all accounts that experience gave his worldview a permanent shift to the right."[8] His great cause, which would make him the darling of many conservative Catholics, became the defense of the faith from ideological distortion and from modernity's pervasive relativism. What he saw in Seattle was the quintessential liberal experiment coming out of Vatican II.

In *Cardinal Ratzinger: The Vatican's Enforcer of the Faith*, John Allen, Jr. also describes the shift in Ratzinger's thinking. Ratzinger was present at all four sessions of the Council and was one of the young theologians who challenged the old guard led by archconservative Cardinal Ottaviani.[9] Ratzinger helped shape passages of *Lumen Gentium* ("Light of All Nations") dealing with collegiality and the collaborative role of the bishops. On a number of issues, including ecclesiology, he was not far apart from progressive theologians such as Yves Congar, Johannes Metz, Karl Rahner, Edward Schillebeeckx, and Hans Kung.[10] "The drift of Ratzinger's thinking at the council is clear. The church was too centralized, too controlled from Rome, and there was a need, both practical and theological, to shift power back to the bishops."[11] But later, Allen writes, when he became the Vatican's "enforcer," he went after some of the same thinkers with whom he had collaborated at the council, including most famously Hans Kung, his old Tübingen colleague. Ratzinger traveled quite a distance. Though while at Vatican II he had sounded a positive note regarding ecumenism and decentralism, two of the areas Hunthausen would encourage in his ministry, what he experienced at Tübingen in 1968 shocked him. Even in theological faculties, he detected the influence of Marxist ideology. "That experience made it clear to me," said Ratzinger later, "that the abuse of the faith had to be resisted precisely if one wanted to uphold the will of the council."[12] So, going forward after the campus turbulence, he would challenge the liberalizing force he had supported earlier. By the 1970s, he was arguing that "council enthusiasts had lost their perception of the 'whole church' in their passion for reforms…."[13] Hans Kung, never hesitant to speak his mind, described what it felt like for him as a theologian facing Cardinal Ratzinger as the guardian of orthodoxy. "He is the chief authority of the Inquisitorial office. It's like having a general conversation about human rights with the head of the KGB," he told Allen.[14] Given that Cardinal Ratzinger probably, and Pope John Paul II certainly, understood the repressive reach of the Soviet Union, Kung's use of the KGB metaphor might have been a stretch—or at least painfully ironic.

A Latin American dimension to the story is especially pertinent here, not only because it helps further elucidate Ratzinger's worldview, but also because it relates to Rome's concern over Raymond Hunthausen's liberation model of church. In *Church: Charism and Power*, the Brazilian theologian Leonardo Boff criticized the pattern of authority so often adopted by Church powers. In the early to mid-1980s, Boff laid out a strongly liberationist vision of Catholicism. He asked: "What is the truly Catholic attitude?" And he confidently answered: "It is to be fundamentally open to everything without exception, something that the New Testament encourages. To be authentically Catholic is to be free and open to the totality of the

Gospel. Pathological Catholicism is to follow exclusively certain paths or to hold to only certain currents that express faith."[15] For his candor, Boff was soon hit by a Right-powered tide from across the Atlantic that struck hard on the shores of Latin America's liberation theology. That assault on liberation theology was part of an even larger agenda.

In *The Silencing of Leonardo Boff*, Harvey Cox placed the Boff case in context. Cox observed in Joseph Ratzinger three major preoccupations. First, Ratzinger saw too much openness to the outside world. Concepts such as Karl Rahner's "anonymous Christian" and notions of the equality of religions were dangerous to the true Catholic faith. A second worrying trend was the decline Ratzinger perceived in the courage of individual bishops, something he blamed in part on the post-Vatican II rise of national and regional conferences of bishops as collective bodies. In the Latin American context, CELAM (Conferencia Episcopal Latinoamerica, Latin American Bishops Conference) had hosted liberation theology at Medellín, Colombia in 1968. There was a tragic irony in Ratzinger's anxiety about cowardice among individual bishops. Drawing on deep spirituality, on the example of church workers all around him and on a popular religiosity that challenged the status quo Church hierarchy then in bed with the El Salvadoran power elite, Archbishop Oscar Romero showed unflinching courage, which cost him his life. He did not get much support from Rome or from some of his fellow Salvadoran bishops when he confronted the oligarchy, asked soldiers not to kill their fellow citizens, and challenged the United States to end its policy of military aid to the corrupt regime. Apparently Romero did not show the kind of individual courage Ratzinger was looking for. What he wanted were bishops with the courage to uphold orthodoxy. His third preoccupation was the decline he observed in strict Catholic moral teaching. Here he also decried "radical feminism" (anticipating the investigation, when he was pope, of the LCWR), not to mention calls for the ordination of women.[16] Contrast this fortress church attitude of Ratzinger with the thinking of Boff, who simply asked which comes first, the community or the hierarchy? Hunthausen answered, as did Romero. Earlier in this book it was noted that a number of Hunthausen's critics wrote to Rome alleging he was promoting a Pacific Northwest version of liberation theology.[17] To the degree that he did so, he could expect to get in trouble.

So Ratzinger perceived a basic crisis of ecclesiology. In one of the interviews that shaped *The Ratzinger Report*, he said of ecclesiology: "Herein lies the cause of a good part of the misunderstandings or real errors which endanger theology and common Catholic opinion alike."[18] When it came out in 1985, *The Ratzinger Report* was promoted assiduously by Al Matt and his *Wanderer* newspaper. To paraphrase Ratzinger, when, in the name of democracy and inclusiveness, people reject the authority inherent in the hierarchical structure of the Catholic Church, they reject an authority willed by God. On what did he predicate the legitimacy of this bold claim? "Her deep and permanent structure is not *democratic* but *sacramental*, consequently *hierarchical*. For the hierarchy based on the apostolic succession is the indispensable condition to arrive at the strength, the reality of sacrament."[19] (Italicized emphasis in the original) This assertion had serious implications for how a theologian could think or how a bishop could govern. He was trying to reassert a pre-Vatican II paradigm that had long predominated. Judged to be a laboratory in liberal sociology if not liberation theology, Seattle became a beachhead in a war to purify Catholicism. Hunthausen's style of leadership became a target.

HUNTHAUSEN'S LEADERSHIP STYLE

Ray Hunthausen would tell his good friend and ecumenical colleague, Bill Cate, that his model for pastoral ministry was Pope John XXIII.[20] John XXIII inspired people with his gentleness, integrity, personal warmth, and humor. This is how Hunthausen felt about him and, Cate says, this is also how so many people felt about Hunthausen. And the Second Vatican Council, commenced by beloved Pope John, gave Hunthausen an unforgettable experience of collegiality with bishops from all over the world. It also set the stage for significant structural reforms. A shift was happening in the meaning of authority and leadership. The central document of the Council, *Lumen Gentium* ("Light of All Nations"), turned the spotlight away from a clerical culture so that it could shine on the whole people of God.

> "This was to be the new people of God. For, those who believe in Christ, who are reborn not from a perishable but from an imperishable seed through the Word of the living God (cf. 1 Pet. 1:23), not from the flesh but from water and the Holy Spirit (cf. Jn. 3:5-6), are finally established as 'a chosen race, a royal priesthood, a holy nation, a purchased people.... You who in times past were not a people, but are now the people of God.' (1 Pet. 2:9-10)."[21]

The first session happened at the same time as the Cuban Missile Crisis. JFK was killed the next fall. The civil rights movement pushed forward with the Voting Rights Act by the time the Council met in 1964. By 1965, LBJ was ramping up military involvement in Vietnam, a place Pete Seeger would soon prophetically sing about, "knee deep in the big muddy." The Council experience of sharing prayer and debate with colleagues from all over the planet resonated with Hunthausen. Shared responsibility, a key notion in Vatican II, became his watchword. Many years hence, on Pentecost Sunday, May 1978, he expressed this sentiment: "The real meaning of shared responsibility is to be found in an attitude of mutual cooperation and mutual accountability...." For indeed, "shared responsibility is as old as the Church itself; we see it operative in the community of believers in the Acts of the Apostles...."[22]

The Council spirit of shared responsibility and collegiality resonated with Hunthausen's colleague, John Dearden of Detroit, who became instrumental in organizing the National Conference of Catholic Bishops to bring moral vision to major social issues including peace and economic justice. The American bishops developed a bold agenda. In time, their collective efforts led to the watershed pastoral letters on peace and on economic justice. But at the same time as the American bishops completed the incisive letter on economic justice in 1986, they were faced with the tension between Seattle and Rome. And as we saw, they were not of one mind. What they really faced were the same forces of Vatican recentralization that went after the Brazilian and Dutch bishops. A chief weapon in the Vatican's arsenal was episcopal appointments, something like what can happen when a U.S. president changes the complexion of the courts with judicial appointments. As time went on, bishops who thought like Hunthausen were being replaced by ones who helped Rome achieve a roll-back of Vatican II.

Though the tide had turned, Hunthausen never stopped moving forward with a model of shared leadership inspired by the Council experience. On the Washington coast in June 1988, Hunthausen met with the priests for their annual retreat. He remembered their first meeting years earlier. "My first talk with all of you when I came to the archdiocese as your bishop thirteen years ago was about shared responsibility because I knew clearly that I could never do the job alone."[23] Working with Management Design Incorporated (MDI) of Cincinnati, Ohio, with Rev. George Wilson, S.J. as key consultant, Hunthausen had set in motion a process to make shared responsibility come alive all across the archdiocese.[24] With the help of MDI, Hunthausen tried to shift the authority structure. Seattle became a pioneer attempting to change the basic decision-making paradigm. Back when his work in Seattle began he said, "We do not know precisely what this sharing of responsibility will ask of each of us, what form it will take, what challenges and stresses it will bring." Reaction and resistance were not so apparent in the early days. "Step by step we will have to build a common outlook, looking at each piece of the mosaic of shared responsibility, trying out our new learnings together.... When we learn to see ourselves as Church differently, we will behave differently."[25] One can imagine Pope Francis beckoning the Church today in much the same spirit.

Alas, Hunthausen's style of shared responsibility clashed with the "restorationist" model of ecclesiology. His vision, attitude, and practice of broadly shared leadership factored into Rome's intervention. Consider, as documented in previous chapters, Archbishop Hunthausen's way of responding to Rome. He tried to invite the Vatican's people into relationships of collegiality and openness. This only bolstered the Holy See headquarter perception that the real error to be corrected in Seattle was "permissive" governance. In truth, the "error" was to suppose that Vatican II still guided the Vatican.

In 2012, Raymond Hunthausen wrote a reflection on Vatican II as part of "A Church Reborn," a special 50th anniversary issue of the *National Catholic Reporter*:

> "If Pope John XXIII surprised the world when he called the council, he surprised me when he called me to be a bishop. Absolutely nothing could have been further from my thoughts. I was living out my priestly call very contentedly in the world of Catholic higher education: teaching chemistry, coaching a variety of sports, and serving as president of Carroll College, a small but wonderful, diocesan-operated liberal arts college in Helena, Montana. Then out of the blue came the call to be bishop. I answered it with more than a little hesitation and was ordained in late August 1962. I was 41 years old. Six weeks later, I was in Rome, beginning my on-the-job training. For me, the council was liberating, challenging and exciting. I have often reflected that if the timing had been different—if I had become a bishop years earlier or even years later—things might have turned out quite differently."

He spent those four years learning about laypeople and their baptismal call, about bishops and their servant role and collegial relationship with one another and with the bishop of Rome, about the centrality of Sacred Scripture, about the importance of ecumenical and interfaith relations, and about "the ways our church was called to come out of its fortress and, through honest dialogue and prophetic witness, to become engaged with the modern world."[26]

Jesse Dye, who helped Hunthausen on mediation issues including the difficult matter of the sex abuse crisis, a topic to be considered in chapter ten, shared a hunch about what worried Pope John Paul II and Cardinal Ratzinger when they tried to figure out what to do with Seattle:

> "We were inspired by a more powerful message, responding from our sense of the Gospel teachings, not a disloyalty to the Church, but a more powerful message. It was our message, we owned it. That's what Hunthausen had, he owned it inside. It didn't belong to the Vatican hierarchy. I think maybe the deepest message from the Hunthausen story is that people's spirituality belongs to them. It doesn't belong to the Magisterium."[27]

So perhaps Dye's observation about spirituality belonging to the people—and Hunthausen honoring this—indeed gets to the heart of the leadership matter. Is this what Timothy Schilling concluded? In his dissertation, which has been a valuable reference at different points in this book, Schilling analyzed the causes of conflict between a center (Rome) and a periphery (Seattle). He worked from the theoretical assumption that conflict happens when one party's pursuit of its interest is viewed as incompatible with another party's pursuit of its interest. "In the Rome-Hunthausen case, we can express the apparent interests at stake most simply as follows: Rome's interest (the center's interest) lies in seeing Hunthausen govern Seattle Rome's way; Hunthausen's interest (the periphery's interest) lies in governing Seattle his way without alienating Rome." Hunthausen appeared:

> "...to be trapped between a number of personal principles that are difficult to reconcile in the context of the affair: he wants to be true to his own experience of the local Church and his own belief about what is best for it, but he also wants to be loyal to Rome. As the conflict progresses, his loyalty to Rome undergoes serious tests when power is taken from him. Hunthausen's ideal solution would be to honor his own experience and beliefs while pleasing Rome: but how to do this?"[28]

In Schilling's analysis the intra-hierarchical conflict was the central drama. Notice how he framed the conflict:

> "What Rome saw as Hunthausen's main weakness, his flexible and tolerant leadership style (his lack of 'firmness'), was in Hunthausen's view a necessary and valuable component of Church leadership. Hunthausen presented himself as treating Church members as adults, making room for participation and tolerating the unavoidable failures that accompany participation as an acceptable cost. Hunthausen also showed a higher comfort level with intraecclesial diversity. The Vatican position (expressed most concisely by Ratzinger), however, saw in this approach of toleration a threat to the full realization of the Church's own ideals. Toleration might make Hunthausen popular in his own archdiocese, but it could also interfere with those same people's ability to face up to the difficult challenges that God has placed before them. In simple terms, Hunthausen's ecclesiology of forgiveness and charity clashed with the Roman emphasis on the demands of the cross. Both are central and fully orthodox perspectives within Christian theology; they are theologically inseparable but not always easily reconciled."[29]

Yet one might ask, thinking about "Faith and Disarmament" for instance, just who was emphasizing the demands of the cross? From another point of view, Hunthausen's prophetic witness was actually calling the people—and Rome—to face the difficult challenges that God was placing before them. One could argue that it was Hunthausen's "full realization of the Church's own ideals" that got him in trouble, just as it got Archbishop Romero killed. The difficult challenges placed before Hunthausen, from where did they originate? The Vatican line about

Hunthausen's alleged "climate of permissiveness" may have kept some analysts from giving sufficient attention to Cardinal Ratzinger's tacit concern, perhaps even an unconscious anxiety, that Hunthausen was fostering a climate of civil—and therefore potentially ecclesiastical—disobedience. He did this not by any rebellious intention, but simply by taking the demands of the Gospel seriously and by empowering the people to take the lead themselves—to examine their own consciences and, as Jesse Dye perceptively put it, to own their own spirituality.

Schilling evaluated Hunthausen as a leader adept at asserting his personal identity:

> "The key to Hunthausen's success with the strategy lay in highlighting his charismatic personality and reputation for integrity, and establishing a link between his conflict positions and these qualities. Also critical was the fact that he personalized his position (humanized it) without giving the appearance of grandstanding or willful disloyalty. His individualized stance came to be associated with integrity and a commitment to principle and not with putting himself above the best interest of the Church."

This is a curious way of assessing Hunthausen. Those who knew him well say Hunthausen never tried to "assert his personality" as part of a planned strategy. His stance never "came to be associated with integrity" by design to achieve or maintain power. Instead, Dutch Hunthausen developed habits of heart and mind over the years, and the linchpin for understanding how he dealt with Rome was to be found in his basic character. Schilling's rather abstract approach juxtaposes Hunthausen and his personal identity, imagined as a strategy in contrast to the strategy the Vatican adopted. "The Vatican's disinclination to highlight individual personalities appeared to be related to overriding commitment to managing the conflict out of public view (and perhaps to limit the opponent's access to the conflictual partner)." So much reliance on his center-periphery theory, quite helpful in some aspects of an ecclesiastical power analysis, kept Schilling from paying adequate attention to Hunthausen's essential character. Of course that character could only be appreciated either by knowing him well or by learning his life story from those who knew him well. The same point, to be fair, would have to apply to the other persons who played key roles in the drama. Some of the personality traits of certain leaders in the Vatican and like-minded prelates in North America seemed to be more authoritarian. Research into those characters could shed light as well. Earlier in this chapter we focused some on the formative character of Cardinal Ratzinger precisely for this reason, but a much fuller study would be preferable. It seems reasonable to think that authoritarian structures and authoritarian personalities have what Max Weber described as "elective affinity" or a deep rapport. Affinity draws them together (rather than suggesting that one dimension, say, an authoritarian culture and institution, simply produces the other, the authoritarian character).

In Hunthausen's case, there was an elective affinity between the collegial culture engendered at the Second Vatican Council and the collaborative traits so evident in his character. Archbishop Hunthausen was not simply a member of the hierarchy who behaved according to some sophisticated theory about what such officers tend to do. Based on my own experience getting to know Raymond Hunthausen and from the measure of his character by those much closer to him, one would have to conclude that he could not be understood accurately through such a theoretical lens. The Hunthausen story at its heart has to do with the ways in which he did not do "what intra-church hierarchical officers" tend to do. Part of the present book's task is to illustrate why he did not. Part III, illustrating Dutch Hunthausen's formative character, will attend directly to this task.

Still, Schilling made a major contribution by weighing the influence of the hierarchical structure and culture on Hunthausen. Schilling tried to draw a multi-dimensional picture, "supplying enough data so that multiple potential influences on the case handling (personal factors, organizational factors, societal factors) could be identified and considered."[30] These dimensions, however, need to be examined along with other factors across a longer time than the period he so carefully covered, 1983-1989. To place the Seattle-Rome conflict in proper context, one must come to know Hunthausen's character in relation to the larger public history that unfolded alongside his personal biography. That is the structure and intent of the present book. To understand Hunthausen's leadership in Seattle and what Rome did to him and also to contemplate why all this matters for the future, we have to focus on much more than "the case handling" dynamics.

Schilling has written, "The Church is an organization that seeks to forge unity from diversity. The tension between central control and local (peripheral) autonomy is a reflection of the effort to cull oneness from plurality." True enough, center-periphery conflicts and tensions seem to be inherent in large-scale centralized and bureaucratized multinational organizations. Yet there were specific people involved and specific reasons why Hunthausen was taken to the Vatican woodshed. Schilling has persuasively evaluated the Vatican culture and system of secrecy. He has also reflected on the limits of his own analysis.

> "This type of analysis makes no room, really, for consideration of altruistic impulses and for the participants' own professions that God is somehow present to the conflict handling. Nor does it account for more tortured kinds of wrestling with questions of power and ideals (of the sort that the novelist Graham Greene described so well) that bishops may experience internally. The result of this approach is a two-dimensional depiction of the participants' exchange: we see a shadow drama about power and not much else."

Schilling has rightly argued that his attention to how "power is manipulated in intra-hierarchical conflict is a topic worthy of consideration that has been neglected… the way power is employed is crucial and is, without question, a legitimate focal point."[31] Think, for instance, about how Hunthausen related to power—especially the social power of the people. Hunthausen encouraged every person to make their decisions as adults through prayer and conscientious reflection. He did not insist that others take the same personal positions as he took on nuclear arms, Central America, or on any other subject. To be sure, he could make church decisions that impacted parishioners directly. In the civic sphere, he could only encourage, challenge, and model a different way.

He did try to interpret church teaching in light of the Gospel. As one colleague of his has said, he was not inclined to be unorthodox. That was never his objective. He was inclined to follow a prayerful reading of the Gospel, and this could get one into trouble. At various points, Cardinal Ratzinger (and later as Benedict XVI) argued that the view of Jesus as a revolutionary was a misreading. He made that case vehemently in his 1984 evaluation of Latin American liberation theology. Hunthausen's mode of leadership, authority, shared responsibility, and conscience encouraged personal and social transformation, and in that sense, he too was promoting liberation. He may not have been a revolutionary, but he was not the type of prelate desired in that era. Rome made him an object lesson as a warning to other bishops.

In *The Limits of the Papacy*, Patrick Granfield observed the range of views that influenced what happened between Seattle and Rome. At one end of the spectrum were Catholics, who viewed the Roman interventions in the Hunthausen and Charles Curran cases, among others, as "long overdue and absolutely necessary if the purity of the faith and the uniqueness of Catholicism is to be preserved." Loyalty to the papacy was what mattered. At the other end of the spectrum were those who viewed "Roman action as unjustified, ill-timed, and detrimental to the vitality of Catholic life; they insist that such events weaken the high hopes generated by Vatican II and point to excessive centralization in the Church."[32] Many bishops were caught between pressure from the grassroots Vatican II expectations on the one hand and directives from Rome under John Paul II on the other. Hunthausen, to a significant degree but not entirely and never intentionally, broke out of the Vatican sphere, not as a rebel, to be sure, but just by trying to be the bishop he thought he was supposed to be.

In the twenty years or so after Vatican II, many bishops had become more engaged in social concerns. Writing in the late 1980s, historian Gerald Fogarty noted this, as well as the fact that there was anything but a monolithic view among Catholics in America.

> "For many American Catholics this new episcopal activism was a deviation from the legitimate spiritual sphere of the Church. For others it represented the bishops recognizing their role in not becoming identified with the national culture. For some Roman officials the activism of the NCCB and other national conferences has raised the question of the canonical status and teaching authority of episcopal conferences."[33]

To the degree that Rome eventually backed down under public pressure and restored Hunthausen's authority, it could be argued that the Hunthausen affair gave the NCCB the opportunity to try to assert some collective independence. Yet as we have seen since then, the days of such independence were numbered.

In her dissertation, Carol Arlene Aseltine cited Archbishop Hunthausen from an occasion when he addressed Cardinals Joseph Ratzinger and Bernardin Gantin, head of the Congregation of Bishops. Hunthausen was in Rome for his *ad limina* visit, and he met with Pope John Paul. The two of them sat down together privately on December 1, 1988, for the first time since Hunthausen had his full authority restored. Although Aseltine was not able to determine what was shared between Pope John Paul and Archbishop Hunthausen, she noted what Hunthausen said to Ratzinger and Gantin:

> "I believe that the apostolic visitation and its long aftermath, the appointment of Bishop Wuerl as auxiliary bishop with special faculties, the unfortunate misunderstanding about the precise nature of those special faculties and the appointment of Cardinal Bernardin, Cardinal O'Connor and Archbishop Quinn to serve as special apostolic commission, have all combined to create a time of pain and severe tension for ourselves and the Archdiocese of Seattle."[34]

As we saw previously, the Vatican treatment of Hunthausen had stirred intense reaction. Lawrence Lader, in his 1987 book, *Politics, Power, and the Church*, described the scene this way:

> "[Hunthausen] would become the highest American prelate in recent times to be the subject of Vatican punishment. Whichever of a long list of his supposed transgressions angered the Vatican the most, whether opening his cathedral to a homosexual mass, the use of young women to serve at the altar, or his generous approval of marriage annulments, nothing he did seemed to merit the scope of Vatican wrath. The real issue is why the pope singled him out for extraordinary punishment. After Hunthausen was investigated for years and his case seemingly closed with appropriate warnings, a large part of his responsibilities—morality in health care, liturgical and parish programs, among

> others—was transferred in 1986 to his auxiliary bishop. Father Richard P. McBrien, head of the University of Notre Dame's theology department, said that, 'As a theologian, I don't know of any instance like this before.' Rick Anderson, a *Seattle Times* columnist, thought it left Hunthausen 'with nothing more to minister than the check-in-counter at the Catholic Seamen's Club'."[35]

In Lader's church power analysis:

> "By virtually stripping the archbishop of his authority, the pope was undoubtedly putting all U.S. bishops on notice that no deviance from his policy would be tolerated. Other bishops protested, including Matthew Clark, John Fitzpatrick, Leroy Mattheisen, and Francis P. Murphy, but there was no way of gauging the size of the rebel bloc. Bishop Thomas J. Gumbleton called the punishment 'clearly unjust and demeaning.' Pax Christi USA warned that it would 'increase the polarization with the Catholic church in the U.S.'"[36]

One of the most hard-hitting assessments of church power issues in the 1980s was *People of God: The Struggle for World Catholicism* by Penny Lernoux. Lernoux put the Seattle situation in context:

> "Under the influence of Vatican II and sister churches in the Third World, particularly in Latin America, the U.S. bishops had begun to take a more prophetic stance, challenging the Reagan administration on such issues as its Central American policy, nuclear warfare, and economic policy, and encouraging greater pluralism in the church. But just when these initiatives were beginning to bear fruit, Pope John Paul II intervened in an attempt to force the U.S. church back into the pre-Vatican II mold of an authoritarian institution that demanded unquestioning obedience to Rome's commands."[37]

Doing so "strengthened President Reagan's hand by undercutting the most outspoken American bishops, particularly in regard to the arms buildup, and by providing support for his policies in Central America and elsewhere." William Wilson, Reagan's first ambassador to the Vatican, felt "a parallelism of viewpoints" existed between Washington and Rome. Washington could benefit from Rome's capacity to "damage, even destroy, the religious leaders who have given the people a new faith in themselves."[38]

If Hunthausen was giving most of the people a new faith in themselves, he was giving some a feeling of deep disruption. Catholics in the United States who wanted to turn back the tide of Vatican II "made common cause with Reagan's evangelical supporters and the Roman Curia in the attack on liberal Catholic leaders." The critical issue was, Lernoux wrote, "the unfinished business of Vatican II." On this the right, left, and middle could agree. Vatican II had particular implications for the question of power and authority. "Vatican II did not resolve basic questions about power-sharing among the bishops, pluralism among churches of diverse cultures, or the role of the laity or women."[39] It did, however, point the way and bishops such as Raymond Hunthausen had their roadmap.

Consider this thought experiment. Try placing two characters, Archbishop Hunthausen and Pope John Paul II, side by side. They were both athletic, loved the outdoors, skied, had infectious smiles, enjoyed people, and drew from deep wells of prayer. They were both sons of the church through and through. They were ordained in the same year, 1946. John Paul II was a much more extroverted personality, or at least he seemed to wear public life and celebrity in a way that Dutch Hunthausen could not. Archbishop Hunthausen, in Lernoux's view, listened to people whereas John Paul II, the former Archbishop of Krakow, did not. "The tragedy of John Paul is that, with all his many gifts, he has lacked the one most needed at a time when the church is changing from a European to a world institution—the ability to listen."[40] George Weigel, John Paul II's official biographer and hagiographer, would vigorously disagree. Even though Weigel thought Hunthausen to be a likable person, he thought prelates like Hunthausen were too stuck in Scriptural literalism to listen, for instance, to the nuance of just war theory that Weigel believed John Paul II and Joseph Ratzinger keenly understood.[41] It could certainly be argued that John Paul II played a huge role listening to the hearts of the Solidarity movement in the shipyards of his native Poland.

Yet Lernoux understood that as far as the church itself was concerned, notwithstanding his support for such efforts as Solidarity, Pope John Paul II wanted to reinforce, not dilute, distinctions between the laity and a clerical class. This made Hunthausen's agenda of shared responsibility a target. There was also the tight link between Rome and Washington when Reagan realized he had a fellow conservative in the papacy. John Paul II's hostility toward the Sandinistas in Nicaragua was one example of where the two could work together. The Sandinistas rejected control both by Washington and Rome. "The specter of religion-fueled rebellion worried both power centers, which saw liberation theology as the wedge for Marxist revolution."[42]

Lernoux also saw clearly that Hunthausen's peace stand "provoked the animosity of Seattle's powerful defense industry and of right-wing Catholics, who launched a campaign against him in Rome." How did Rome respond? In Lernoux's reading, "the Roman Curia was prepared to believe the worst of Seattle's archbishop, perhaps because he is so thoroughly American in his tolerance of religious and social diversity." Hunthausen went through a grueling period.

> "It cost him 'incalculable pain,' said a fellow bishop. Hunthausen later acknowledged that 'the long days' had been 'extremely trying and agonizing ones for me.' At one point, when asked if he had considered resigning, Hunthausen hesitated, then said he preferred not to answer the question. 'I'm just as human as anyone else,' he admitted, adding that he had gone through 'the whole gamut of emotions' during the investigation."[43]

Why was Hunthausen singled out? Lernoux spent time in Seattle in the late 1980s trying to answer this question, meeting with locals around the large dining room table at the home of Don Hopps and Pam Piering on Queen Anne Hill just north of downtown. Lernoux wrote:

> "The pope himself had spoken out against the nuclear threat, so there had to be more reason for the attack on Hunthausen than his aggressive peace stand. It was also possible that by singling out the archbishop, rightist Catholics had provided the Vatican with a convenient whipping boy for all the perceived ills in the American church."

Bishop Walter Sullivan, of Richmond, Virginia, had told *Sojourners* magazine that Hunthausen's punishment on "ecclesiastical issues" made no sense unless it was related to the peace questions because so many other dioceses followed the same religious practices. Sullivan himself was investigated by Rome. Like the Seattle region, the Richmond area had formidable ties to the military-industrial complex, as documented by Phyllis Theroux in her recent biography, *The Good Bishop*.[44] Lernoux made the educated conjecture that going after Hunthausen or Sullivan would not be as costly as it would be to go after a prelate in one of the places, say Chicago or New York or Los Angeles, upon which Vatican finances relied more heavily. "His ecclesiastical positions made him vulnerable to Vatican discipline, and his stand on the nuclear issue assured that any moves the Roman Curia made against him would be endorsed in the United States by right-wing Catholics and powerful business interests. He was, as they say in Rome, dispensable."[45]

Lernoux described a revealing moment in San Antonio, Texas, when 200 priests serving as vocation directors were gathered to hear the keynote speaker, Spokane's Bishop Lawrence Welsh, chairman of the U.S. bishops' committee on vocations. During the question and answer period, a Seattle priest asked Welsh why Hunthausen had been punished. The Vatican had never explained the true reasons. "Clearly upset, Welsh gripped the lectern, his head down, remaining silent for so long that people began to worry. Eventually he looked up: 'The archbishop is a friend of mine. I want you to know I am struggling along with you.'" Later, well after Lernoux wrote about this emotional moment, it would be revealed that Welsh was having his own personal struggles with alcohol and abuse. In any event, the situation with Hunthausen at the time of the intense Seattle-Rome conflict was beyond comprehension. This was itself part of the pain felt by so many people. "Would an itemization of specifics reveal some fundamental flaws in Archbishop Hunthausen," Archbishop Francis Hurley, of Anchorage, close friend and adviser to Hunthausen, asked. "Or would they appear trivial and, therefore, provide feeble basis for the extreme action taken?" Lernoux thought she had a pretty good idea what was really going on.

> "In fact, the stated charges against Hunthausen were not the real issue. Vatican II had firmly restated the right of bishops to share in the government of the church in unity with Rome, but the Vatican wanted to end such collegiality, making the pope a supreme monarch and his curial court a new class of Catholic nobles. Forcing the bishop to bow to Rome's wishes—as the pope had done with the Dutch hierarchy—was one way to reassert that power. If the apparent causes were trivial, that only added to the intended humiliation."[46]

SUPPORT FOR WOMEN AND GENDER EQUALITY

Hunthausen's style of leadership had to be curbed. Among other reasons, he dared share leadership with women. In September 1984, when Pope John Paul II was in Vancouver, British Columbia, *Seattle Post-Intelligencer* reporter John McCoy wrote about the Polish pope. McCoy, who a few years later became the communications chief for the Archdiocese of Seattle, also wrote about Cardinal Joseph Ratzinger.

> "It was Ratzinger who was behind last year's investigation of the ministry of Seattle Archbishop Raymond Hunthausen. The Vatican's problem, some insiders say, was not Hunthausen's opposition to nuclear weapons nor his offer of sanctuary to illegal Central American refugees...but the fear that the Seattle archbishop would do something doctrinally objectionable such as ordain a woman."

McCoy reported that Seattle University President William Sullivan felt the issue of the role of women in the church was the most explosive issue facing the church in North America. And, McCoy noted, a few months earlier, Hunthausen was ordered by Ratzinger, as was another U.S. archbishop, to remove his stamp of approval from two popular books that supported the reform movement in the church.[47]

It will be recalled that Ratzinger, in the September 30, 1985 letter to Hunthausen, expressed concern about the role of women in Seattle church. "With regard to the role of women in the Church, the teaching of the Church regarding their God-given dignity and importance should be given full weight." He continued. "The current fierce politicization of this issue must not impede the Church's efforts to vindicate the rights of all." Seattle was not being sufficiently clear about stating the official stand opposing the ordination of women. "The exclusion of women from Sacred Orders was dealt with at length in this Congregation's 1975 Instruction... and should be explained unambiguously."[48]

Other U.S. bishops also supported gender equality. So on this issue, as on others, why was Hunthausen in special trouble with Rome? Hunthausen's 1980 pastoral statement regarding women and the church was among the first such letters by a Catholic bishop in the U.S. Just as with nuclear disarmament and other issues, he did not limit his rhetoric to a sort of safe harbor of general principles. He took specific actions intended to prepare the ground for a change in the patriarchal structure, establishing a women's commission to make real the recommendations spelled out in the pastoral letter. As noted early in the book, some people felt strongly that if anything was going to happen anywhere in the country to really change the sexist patterns in Catholicism, it would happen in Seattle.

I asked Sr. Kathleen Pruitt, a working associate with Hunthausen in areas including ecumenical relations, what she thought was behind Rome's investigation. She named several issues. One of them was his receptiveness for gender equality. Her understanding of what various sociological analysts call the "intersectionality of issues" could be seen in how she answered my question:

> "A variety of things got people of tender conscience riled up. Dignity's use of the Cathedral was the straw that broke the camel's back. He angered the secretary of the U.S. Navy, Lehman. Lehman may have gone to the U.S. ambassador to Rome or to Rome itself. Pio Laghi may have brought pressure. Rome is an eminently political institution. An archbishop of the church was taking a very public position. This was embarrassing for the U.S. elite and for Rome. Therefore they put pressure on Hunthausen. His opening of the door to the role of women in the church was for some more than they could handle. Many factors were involved in what led to the investigation. You keep throwing stuff into the mix, it's big, and you don't know which really carries the greatest weight."

His strengths were in pastoral presence. "Dignity, the organization, was a big thing." When Pruitt went to Rome much more recently (but before the papacy of Francis), representing the Leadership Conference of Women Religious, homosexuality was a huge issue. The LCWR itself was being investigated on some of the same issues: homosexuality, the role of women in the church, and not being crystal clear about the divinity of Christ. "Homophobic fear permeates the place," and, she said:

> "Hunthausen was a lightning rod on many issues. It would not have taken a rocket scientist to figure out that Hunthausen could have

> lifted a finger and raised an army. Think about this, he chose not to do so. He was a quiet charismatic authority, but he could have raised a huge ruckus on the church investigation if he had wished to do so. He supported equality between women and men in various ways. Hunthausen opened the doors for women in the church. He opened doors for pastoral leadership by women. The closing down of the permanent diaconate (only available to men) in the diocese was partially to say women can do this, therefore we do not need a permanent diaconate. He was always trying to find ways to open space for women to assume leadership. There was a way in which the role of women in leadership in the church was lifted up when he was here."[49]

The closing down of the all-male permanent diaconate took place in the late 1980s, so this action as such, happening after the height of the Seattle-Rome drama, could not be claimed to have provoked Rome's investigation. The larger point, however, was Hunthausen's approach to leadership as expressed in his commitment to share it equally with women. Victoria Ries, among the first lay women to lead a parish, saw Hunthausen unavoidably having to operate from within a male-dominated hierarchical approach. "And yet he was a person led by listening to the Holy Spirit, it was about God and not about himself. He was prayerful and disarming, this is core to his bold stands. He would wait for the Holy Spirit to give him the long perspective." Like Pruitt, Ries also felt that Hunthausen's welcome of Dignity was one of the catalysts for the investigation.[50] These women could see the "intersectionality" of various issues involving religious tradition, patriarchal power, sexuality, and gender.

By the late 1980s, people like Patty Repikoff, Victoria Ries, Dominican sister Kay Lewis, and a couple of the Providence sisters were serving as *de facto* pastors. Patty Repikoff took over at St. Therese Parish, above Lake Washington. Since she had been at St. Leo's in Tacoma for years, when I sat down with her she remembered when the great spirituality writer Henri Nouwen came to St. Leo's one eve in the early 1980s. It turns out I was in the audience that evening as well, having traveled north from Mt. Angel Abbey, where many of us were engaged in issues involving Christianity and the crisis in Central America. Nouwen conveyed an image (picturing the geographical map of Central America) of Christ being crucified. It was a time of great bloodshed, and we, the U.S., had blood on our hands. St. Leo's provided sanctuary for Central American refugees. As noted in chapter four, Hunthausen supported this effort. But even more than his prophetic stands, she remembered how Hunthausen "was so filled with the presence of the holy, and he could see the enemy as holy, as teacher, and he could be kind to those who would profane him. I was trying to be a woman leader. I got many nasty notes, attacks. Hunthausen inspired me to see all these people as teachers." He would reflect with her, not out of bitterness but with sadness, about what was going on with the church in the investigation and all.

> "There is a strong sense of loyalty in Hunthausen. He pushed things as far as he could. He could put women in roles as pastoral leaders through the Viable Faith Communities project, finding leadership to match the need. He pushed the envelope through the spirit of Vatican II. 'Let's make a church that works.' But he understood that if you go too far off the rails you lose your credibility and your authority. He simply loved being a Catholic priest. Hunthausen taught us how to try to listen to one another, to look each other in the eye and try to have respectful conversations. He convened people in groups. He got us all doing this convening."

She remembered a moment that exemplified Hunthausen's commitment to engage and respect people regardless of where they stood on a given issue, such as Trident, for instance. "There was a person in the role of Hunthausen's liturgy director. The liturgy office taped Hunthausen for a video-liturgy for sailors aboard a Trident submarine. Somehow they had not prepared a video-Mass for Christmas. Hunthausen in his most unobnoxious way preached on peace."[51]

In 1982, Hunthausen was one of five U.S. Catholic bishops awarded "for furthering the cause of women in the church." This award, made by the magazine *U.S. Catholic*, included Weakland, Buswell, McAuliffe, and McManus.[52] Just shy of two dozen Roman Catholic bishops were listed as Equal Rights Amendment supporters in a United Press International report on June 2, 1982. "The group which announced the bishops' support—the Catholics Act for ERA—said it is the first time a group of church leaders has banded together to urge adoption of the amendment."[53] These bishops, one of whom was Raymond Hunthausen, formed a very small percentage of bishops. Others could have supported the ERA but did not do so. Sister Maureen Fiedler, national coordinator of Catholics Act for ERA, was one of several women participating in a hunger strike in Illinois in support of the ERA, with the ratification deadline looming. Two weeks into the fast, Sr. Maureen made public the names of the bishops who were backing the ERA.[54] Stories like this one about Sr. Maureen Fiedler, published in papers around Puget Sound, irritated traditional Catholics. When the June 30 deadline for ratification passed, the necessary level of support had not been garnered, so the ERA failed to become part of the U.S. Constitution.

In the spring of 1983, *Seattle Times* reporter Lisa Konick focused on women's listening sessions. Happening throughout the Seattle archdiocese, these sessions grew out of the work of the archdiocesan women's commission. Hunthausen had asked this commission to help enlighten him about concerns important to Catholic women. He promised that such concerns would be a top priority when he visited Pope John Paul in the late summer of 1983. Hunthausen made his promise before Pio Laghi told him that Rome was planning to pay Seattle a visit. The Vatican had its own concerns, from a very different vantage point, about women's issues. Konick reported on the gap between what Hunthausen supported and what often happened in the local parish. Many women wanted to see a change in the structure of the church hierarchy. "Archbishop Hunthausen is really concerned about women's issues but that concern doesn't always get down to the parish level," said Sister Catherine Patch, O.P. "The pastor really has the power to organize the parish any way he wants to."[55] In some parishes there were people, probably including some pastors, letting Rome know they did not like the direction Hunthausen was moving on this issue.

Carol Ostrom wrote "Women in the Catholic Church" for the November 19, 1983 issue of the *Seattle Times*. Sister Ann Wetherilt, of the Sisters of St. Joseph of Peace, told Ostrom she saw some parallels between the Catholic Church and a repressive political regime, both characterized by secrecy, a top-heavy patriarchal hierarchy, and one-way communication. She was just back in Seattle from a conference of Catholic women held in Chicago. Hunthausen had been among dozens of bishops attending the conference, after which the bishops headed to Washington D.C., where they voted to write a major pastoral letter on the role of women in church and society. The bishops would try to affirm the rights of women while making sure there was no crack in the door to let them think they might be ordained. That pastoral letter would eventually be shelved, another indication of the rightward turn of the papacy. Ostrom zeroed in on the tension. "The pope has told bishops to oppose discrimination against women but at the same time, he opposes ordination of women because he says that issue is linked to Christ's own design for his priesthood and is extraneous to the issue of discrimination."

According to Wetherilt and Katherine Dyckman, the latter a Holy Names sister and member of the Archdiocesan Women's Commission, in Chicago women were calling for much deeper changes than just access to ordination. Networking, bonding, and sharing feelings went hand in hand with analyzing power, patriarchy, and dominance. "It's like the whole mindset has to change. There has to be a shift in how we relate to each other on a personal level." What they want, Ostrom wrote, "seems revolutionary, tantamount to rebuilding the very structure of the church itself." Wetherilt agreed. What the institution had become, she wanted to dismantle. The question was this: "Does the Catholic Church exist to perpetuate itself as institution, or does it exist to bring about the reign of God?...Is obedience listening to the hierarchy and doing what you're told? Or is obedience a much higher listening, listening to the movement of God in your own life, and listening to the culture you're in, and relating that to the wider reality, and to the church?" Catholic women in Seattle were getting more support from the bishop than elsewhere. "I think Hunthausen is a marvelous pastoral archbishop, and that although he keeps within the—I'll say 'regulations' from Rome, he is able to employ a good pastoral sense which tends to mitigate some of the frustration," said Dyckman.[56]

In May 1987, *The Guardian* published a story about women religious confronting the male power structure. Sister Connie Driscoll, a member of the Mission Sisters of the Poor, worked with the homeless in a slum in Chicago. Her view on the religious vow of obedience refuted Vatican male control: "We take vows of poverty, chastity and obedience—but it's obedience to the Holy Spirit, not to Rome." Sister Margaret Traxler, who helped women prisoners in the U.S. fight for their rights, told *The Guardian* that she saw "women as victims of male exploitation that pervades their church as insidiously as their society." Three years earlier, Traxler, together "with 23 other American nuns, two brothers and two priests, signed a full-page advertisement in the *New York Times* challenging the Church's dogmatic teaching on abortion." The women religious refused to recant publicly when they were told to do so by the Vatican's prefect for religious orders, although the priests and the brothers retracted their support. Traxler clarified the matter. "We don't favor abortion, but women must have free will and real life must be taken into account. We have pregnant girls of nine and ten. Anti-abortion laws are made by men to enhance their own power and domination." *The Guardian* reported that Bishop Walter Sullivan of Richmond, Virginia, had been "sternly disciplined because he allowed a Catholic homosexual group to celebrate mass in one of his churches." A Jesuit scholar, Fr. Terrance Sweeney, was "expelled from his order for publishing the results of a research project (which had been approved by the order) on the attitude of bishops toward the idea of women priests and married priests." Issues of gender, sex, and power were linked:

> "Yet the tussle over sex must also be seen as a disguised power struggle. Authority is male, as the embattled sisters of Chicago insist. Power can never be really devolved until women get their share—and the nuns think this has to begin with power over their own bodies and end with married priests and women priests. There is much sympathy with these women. Archbishop Hunthausen's vicar-general, Father Michael Ryan, said 'These nuns are deeply faithful people. Naturally, if you continue to marginalize people they will only get more and more radical.'"[57]

Hunthausen's resistance to U.S. Cold War policy was more deeply related to his approach to other issues than some might have thought. He confronted the military and geopolitical domination made possible through the concentration of power and wealth. That domination, in the form of the threat of nuclear annihilation with advanced first-strike technology, was an expression of a hegemonic attitude.

He did not condone domination—whether expressed through nuclear arms and a first strike threat, big corporation-based structural violence (as in the poverty he saw when he visited Peru), or top-down male control of the church. They all had to change. In the mid-1980s, Betty Reardon wrote *Sexism and the War System*. While Reardon and Hunthausen would have disagreed on some issues, if they had ever met he would probably have agreed with her thesis: "The crux of the argument set forth in this book, that neither sexism nor the war system can be overcome independently from the other, lies in the assumption that structural, even revolutionary, changes in the public order without significant inner psychic changes in human beings will be ineffective, old wine in new bottles…."[58] Reardon's passage, applied to Hunthausen's religion, would mean that Catholicism could not effectively call for peace and disarmament if its leaders failed to make significant inner psychic changes along with a shift in the structure.

Rev. Bill Cate of the Church Council says they debated for years what was behind the investigation. He remembers those Thursday morning breakfast meetings and the private discussions among the bishops and executives of various denominations:

> "Hunthausen would talk about things, just like others would. He would say priests should be married, women should be priests, and that sort of thing. He would talk among us and say these things. The matter of women clergy was pretty active among the Protestant denominations then. We talked, we were all good friends. Hunthausen was a liberalizing force in the Catholic church and in the whole area."

Ecumenism did not sit well with some Catholics. One time Cate was asked to give a speech on Christian Unity during the Week of Christian Unity at a Catholic parish in Auburn, and "lo and behold there was a big demonstration of Catholics out around the church and the priest apologized for it." Bill's wife, Jan Cate, a leader of Church Women United, says "Hunthausen operated on what he thought was the Christian position, he acted on being a Christian, not many people do that. Hunthausen was fully supportive of women taking leadership." Bill Cate speculates that Hunthausen's peace action precipitated the negative reaction from right wing Catholics, but there were many issues at work. Hunthausen had liberal views on matters such as the ordination of women but publicly he could not take that stand. Jan Cate says, "think about when the women's movement hit the Catholic Church. Keep this in mind. In 1970 the Church Council of Greater Seattle had only 2 out of 50 people, as women, on the board. Everything changed in the next two decades, and Hunthausen was right in the middle of all this period." They had big discussions on the role of women in the church. Jan Cate says "we all knew that Hunthausen would support us as women, Catholic and Protestant." When we sat down together in their Bellevue home during Holy Week 2013, Bill Cate recalled feeling very angry about what the Vatican was doing to Hunthausen. "I remember there was a big hall. I got up and gave a speech." Cate spoke up to defend his good friend. The self-effacing head of the Church Council never thought of himself as a gifted orator. Jan and Bill sprang into laughter after he gave me a wry smile and said, "I'd never gotten that positive a response before to any speech."[59]

Abortion and reproductive rights, an intensely controversial "culture war" at the time, remains divisive today. Hunthausen, like Cardinal Bernardin, argued for a consistent ethic of life. On various occasions he stated his opposition to abortion on demand. This opposition was part of official Catholic teaching. But there was nuance. On various issues Hunthausen paid attention to the real world challenges facing women. Don Hopps remembers this:

> "Kenneth Vanderhoff and Kathy McEntee, of the Right to Life effort here in the Archdiocese of Seattle, had direct connections to Cardinal O'Connor and the Vatican. They were very outspoken in their criticism of Hunthausen. They wanted him to lead the battle against abortion rights, and they felt he wasn't 'true blue'. They felt Hunthausen was not forcefully fighting on the issue. Hunthausen once said, 'I just don't think that God is going to condemn all those unbaptized babies to hell or limbo. I fully believe God loves those babies and will save them.' This is not to say that he didn't think abortion was a problem. He just did not make it the only issue. Hunthausen once told me, 'you know, Don, we every day deal with women who every day face great difficulties.' The archbishop was very supportive of the Providence Sisters and their theologian, Larry Riley, who was unorthodox on abortion in those days. Riley said once that for the Right to Life folks, if we accepted their position we would have to hold that God is the greatest abortionist of all because the vast majority of conceptions are aborted naturally."

Hunthausen once told Hopps, "you know, when we took that vote at the bishops' conference to oppose the Roe v. Wade decision, when I came back my Catholic Community Services director in Helena said to me, 'you know, bishop, that was the biggest mistake you have made. It's a very complicated issue and the position that the church took on the matter was very simplistic.'" Hunthausen added, "you know, in retrospect I think he was right." Hopps staffed the Archdiocesan Right to Life Committee for a couple of years. "What we did was focus on positive efforts, how we could support people so that it's possible to make positive choices. Hunthausen approached this issue in the way he approached all the issues. He looked to the 'victim' first. To him, most of the times, the women were the 'victim' first and last." The standard church approach to attempting to prevent an abortion was still a process of victimizing women. What was needed was to find different ways to promote the right to life so as to be true to the consistent ethic of life. In time, Kathy McEntee stopped coming to the meetings. So this would have been one of the areas of concern brought to the Vatican as well.[60]

In his 1980 pastoral statement Hunthausen wrote:

> "All of us have become increasingly aware of the struggle of women to attain equality, freedom, dignity and identity as full human persons. As they have gained a new sense of personhood, women have experienced new life and hope. However, progress toward full human status in society has been accompanied by anxiety, stress, confusion and alienation from family, friends and community. Significantly, there has been a growing acknowledgement by women and men of the social and cultural oppression of women that has marked our history."

He could have stopped there, commenting solely on society, but he added:

> "I am indeed aware that many, possibly a majority, of women in the archdiocese do not view themselves as oppressed. This fact removes nothing of the pain of those whose study of social and religious history, and whose personal experience reveal inconsistencies in the religious doctrine of universal salvation when set against the realities of exclusion and discrimination. It is helpful to remember that one does not identify a present condition as painful or oppressive as long as there is no hope for improvement; we all protect ourselves psychologically from despair. It is thus imperative we continue to proclaim the message of hope, of the possibility for all peoples to advance as ever-new persons toward the fullness of the Kingdom promised to all."[61]

This kind of language troubled Cardinal Ratzinger. Like John Paul II, he did not identify church patriarchy as painful or oppressive. Because Hunthausen had been listening to critically-minded Catholic women, he was learning otherwise. One of the best analyses of the larger context of the times and the many efforts toward gender equality made over the course of many years before the 1980s is Mary Henold's *Catholic and Feminist: The Surprising History of the American Catholic Feminist Movement.* She argues that Catholic feminism was not an import from secular feminism, but rather grew organically from within Catholicism itself.[62]

In the specific case of Raymond Hunthausen, his own awakening to the issue took place in the same way that he was drawn into nearly every issue, through personal encounters and an ethics grounded in empathy. Jim Burns, Hunthausen's development director, shared a pithy anecdote emblematic of the attitude Hunthausen brought to gender equality. One time Burns and Hunthausen were in a car together, returning from a visit with a female pastoral minister, a dynamic and empowering leader in one of the parishes. The archbishop looked at Jim, put his fist gently but firmly down on the dashboard, and said, "I could ordain her tomorrow and the parish problem would be solved."[63]

RESPECTING THE HOMOSEXUAL COMMUNITY

The guardians of orthodoxy were fighting what they perceived as a corrosive culture of moral relativism. Armed with the moral tradition of natural law as they chose to interpret it, their battle had to be waged especially on fronts having to do with gender and sexual ethics. As will be recalled from chapter five, Cardinal Ratzinger's September 30, 1985 letter informed Archbishop Hunthausen that his support of the gay and lesbian community was not winning him any graces. Whether that was true or not would have to be left to divinity, but one thing was certain: it did not win Hunthausen any Vatican curial office graces. His decision to open the door of St. James Cathedral to Dignity only heightened Ratzinger's vigilance. "The Archdiocese should withdraw all support from any group which does not unequivocally accept the teaching of the Magisterium concerning the intrinsic evil of homosexual activity." Hunthausen was making "the Church's position appear to be ambiguous on this delicate but important issue."[64]

A recent book, *Gay Seattle: Stories of Exile and Belonging*, provides rich social and historical context. Author Gary Atkins writes a particularly pertinent chapter, "On Catholic Hill: The Clash of Dogma and Ministry," which includes the story of Norm DeNeal and Bert Bokern. "In 1978, both were members of a group in Seattle then six years old, Catholics who had affiliated with a national organization called Dignity whose purpose was both social and religious. Dignity provided a way for gay men and lesbians to meet one another and to share experiences of faith, as well as to seek a more visible role within the religious conversation." DeNeal and Bokern, encouraged by Vatican II, immersed themselves in social justice struggles in the 1960s and 70s. In March 1978, they were interviewed by the archdiocesan newspaper as part of a series of articles regarding the church and homosexuality.[65]

The prior year, Archbishop Hunthausen had affirmed Seattle Mayor Wes Uhlman's proclamation of a Gay Pride Week, saying it was a "special week to call our attention to the injustices suffered by many homosexuals in our community." For this, Atkins writes, he faced "a torrent of dissent from more conservative and anti-gay Catholics, criticism that seemed to throw the archdiocesan newspaper into the fight to explain precisely what the Catholic Church's post-Vatican II stance was." Both Bokern and DeNeal challenged natural law dogma that involved a theological distinction between homosexual orientation itself and the sex act—the latter being denounced as a sin. "My orientation is gay," said DeNeal, "and I engage in activity. I don't think it's valid for the Catholic Church to deny the actualization of a person's feelings, of a person's gift."[66]

Fr. Kirby Brown, then serving as Dignity's chaplain, expressed his view that Rome was being unrealistic in demanding celibacy for all gays and lesbians. The campaign in 1978 to repeal gay and lesbian rights in Seattle, Initiative Thirteen, had been challenged by the Catholic archdiocese and other mainstream church bodies. The follow-up Atkins brings to light: "But four days after the initiative was defeated, the *Northwest Progress* [the official newspaper of the archdiocese]...finally took a stance against what DeNeal, Bokern, and Brown had said. Dignity, the newspaper editorialized, was refusing to adhere to Catholic doctrine." Archbishop Hunthausen was trying to promote civil rights for homosexuals, yet he could not alter official church teaching.[67]

Fr. Kirby Brown and others pushed for a change in church dogma. The obvious tension between compassion and doctrine troubled Archbishop Hunthausen. After he had endorsed Uhlman's first declaration of Gay Pride Week, some angry letter-writers to the editor of the archdiocesan paper excoriated him. More to the point, some fiercely attacked the community Hunthausen was trying to support. One condemnatory sentence from one of these letters, if unsurprising in the context of its time, remains sobering: "Homosexuals should be legislated out of a civilized society to remove their vile influence."[68] Hunthausen wanted no part of this mean-spirited attitude. Nevertheless, his own religion officially deemed homosexual activity to be intrinsically evil. He tried to downplay the doctrinal emphasis of Rome's 1975 declaration on homosexuality while highlighting the much more pastoral statement made by the U.S. bishops in 1976. Meanwhile, as Hunthausen navigated through doctrinal and pastoral crosscurrents, Seattle Dignity moved forward to see if they could gather on church grounds. St. Joseph's, a Jesuit parish up on Capitol Hill, became the site for a Dignity Mass on Sunday evenings.[69]

The issue stayed somewhat calm for a period after the aforementioned 1978 episode, writes Atkins. "Then in the summer of 1983, when a strange new virus began to make its way into Seattle's gay community and raise the visibility of homosexual sex and relationships toward a new peak, the underlying conflict over dogma began fatefully rumbling toward an explosion." Activists called on the Washington state legislature to change state civil rights law to stop employers from discriminating on the basis of sexual orientation. Hunthausen and the other Catholic bishops in the state endorsed this amendment. It was defeated, but the Catholic bishops issued a teaching document, "The Prejudice against Homosexuals and the Ministry of the Church." Hunthausen and his colleagues in Spokane and Yakima reiterated church doctrine about the immorality of the homosexual sex act. Yet, Atkins notes, they made "remarkable pastoral statements of appreciation for homosexuals." For example, they wrote: "A homosexual person may manifest virtues and qualities that are admirable by any standard. In fact, there is some evidence that many homosexuals possess important attributes that are often, unfortunately, lacking in their straight counterparts. Thus, it appears that sensitivity to the needs of persons and the ability to express warm feelings toward both men and women are frequently present in gays." That same month, June 1983, while he was speaking on the issue of peace and disarmament at the Mayflower Park Hotel in downtown Seattle at a gathering of the major gay activist Dorian Group, Hunthausen voiced his support and respect. Writes Atkins: "It was the first time in Seattle that someone with such rank in the Catholic Church had met officially and publicly with a gay activist group." We know that by that time Raymond Hunthausen knew Rome was preparing to conduct an apostolic visitation, for Pio Laghi had told him so at the May 1983 NCCB meeting in Chicago. When he met with the Dorian Group, whether he had a foreboding about the upcoming visitation he said something most prescient: "I hope it's not the last."[70]

Members of the local Dignity chapter asked Archbishop Hunthausen if St. James Cathedral could host a special Mass for a national Dignity conference. He considered it, made his decision, and expressed his thoughts in a long interview published at the beginning of September, just as the Dignity Mass was about to take place. "They must be recognized as full members of the church, integrated into the parish community." Hunthausen acknowledged that this would be "painfully hard for many of our people to accept."[71] Hunthausen's welcome, according to Atkins, led directly to "a titanic clash over dogma and ministry between Rome and Seattle." For the Saturday, Labor Day weekend Dignity Mass, Archbishop Hunthausen—in Rome making his case that the upcoming apostolic visitation ought to be conducted in the open, and hearing from Ratzinger and others including the head of the Congregation of Bishops, Sebastian Baggio, about some of their concerns—had prepared a videotaped message to the Dignity members assembled in St. James Cathedral. The Vatican moved swiftly, according to Atkins: "Fewer than eight weeks passed before the Vatican ordered a special investigation.... The catalyst, it would become clear, was the Dignity Mass at St. James."[72] Yet as we know, Rome's decision to conduct the visitation had been made as early as May of 1983. Nonetheless, Atkins' broader point was true. Hunthausen's support for the homosexual community was raising eyebrows.

Interviewed for the September 1, 1983 issue of the Seattle archdiocesan paper, the archbishop said he would "stand clearly with the church on this matter," but he thought the official position could change in time. Various theologians saw the possibility. He awaited "with great interest the findings of our theologians and the ensuing dialogue between them and the church's Magisterium." Alas, such hopes would have to wait a long time in "limbo." In fact, moral theologians whom he felt could bring insight into a dialogue were being systematically put through purgatory. In the following years the guardians of orthodoxy only tightened doctrine. Characteristically, Hunthausen felt ministry to the homosexual community ought to be modeled after Jesus. "It must recognize that the homosexual person has a need for self-worth, for love and a sense of community, for prayer and worship...." He was asked about Dignity and its national convention coming to the cathedral that very weekend. "It can hardly be denied that the homosexual in the Catholic community has been the recipient of misunderstanding and prejudice. Because of this, most of these people have felt unwelcome in our parish communities and many have drifted away." People in such circumstances would naturally seek a support group or organization and would seek dialogue with the church, he said.

"It was an awareness of these kinds of needs that prompted me to tell the leadership of Dignity that they were welcome to hold their convention in this Archdiocese. Over the past few years, the official church has begun to dialogue with members of the homosexual community and to minister in new and more open ways to persons with homosexual orientation." He was then posed with this question: What about people in the Catholic community disturbed that St. James Cathedral would be opened? "I am certainly aware that some of our people are concerned—perhaps that's too mild a word—about this. One thing about being a bishop, you are continually faced with issues that bring pain to some...that cannot prevent a bishop from acting or from addressing controversial issues." He would not shut the cathedral door. "To do so would be to judge their standing before God."[73]

Kirby Brown graciously shared with me firsthand knowledge that illuminates the history with key details. He began with what happened at St. Mary's Parish. Brown's account illustrates how one community tried to include gays and lesbians and how Archbishop Hunthausen approached the case. Brown was St. Mary's pastor at the beginning of the 1980s, and had been serving as the chaplain to the local Dignity group for five years. Dignity was in search of another place to meet since St. Joseph's was such a busy parish. The St. Mary's Parish Council considered whether or not to rent the church and school hall to Dignity on Sunday afternoons. "It soon became clear that feelings on this proposal ran high on both sides. Since a majority of the Parish Council favored the proposal, those with concerns about it wrote a letter to the entire parish and appealed to Archbishop Hunthausen." Consistent with his style of leadership in most matters, Hunthausen listened and then encouraged the parish to reach its own decision. The atmosphere grew tense. Strong arguments were made by opponents at a well-attended meeting held in the school hall.

> "The final vote was very close, but in favor of the proposal. Noting the split vote and the extremely strong feelings of the opposition, including the threat to involve the press, the Dignity President then stood and declined the offer to come to the parish. He decided that it would be best to stay at St. Joseph's where they could carry on their mission to

> their own members without having to deal with how to help a parish (namely St. Mary's) unify around the gay Catholic issue."[74]

Brown wrote about his experience in the Catholic world in a 2012 autobiographical reflection. He was in Rome studying for the priesthood during the last two sessions of Vatican II.

> "Over time that Council profoundly impacted the life of every Catholic throughout the world.... Returning home in 1968, I focused my ministry as a priest on helping Catholic Church change come about. I kept hoping for even more developments such as allowing married priests and women priests, greater acceptance of divorced Catholics, more openness toward gays and lesbians, approval of birth control, and more democratic ways of decision making."

He got involved in the peace movement, nuclear disarmament, civil rights, and the global women's movement. He served at St. James Cathedral and at St. Edward's Parish in Seattle before he became the pastor at St. Mary's. After six years at St. Mary's and serving as Dignity chaplain, he joined Maryknoll's program that sent priests to poor countries. He worked with the Aymara people in the high Peruvian Andes.

> "By this time, a new Pope, John Paul II, was effectively stifling many of the advances of the Second Vatican Council. He emphasized his own authority over other bishops. He cracked down on innovative theologians and bishops' groups all over the world.... Back in Seattle, Archbishop Hunthausen and his many supporters were fighting against Rome's moves to limit his authority. I began to see that my future in the priesthood would no longer be one of helping the Church change. I would have to live with and defend many teachings and practices that I felt were out of date. I saw little hope for more change in my lifetime. This wasn't the priesthood I had signed up for."

Brown realized that he needed to stop trying to change the Church and focus instead on personal change. Celibacy had always been a burden for him. "But now I felt the type of priesthood I was facing wasn't worth paying that price anymore."[75]

Brown's experience with Dignity can help us better understand Archbishop Hunthausen. Brown remembered hearing confessions at St. James Cathedral in the late 1960s and early 70s. Among the penitents, some were gay. "They had grown up Catholic and wanted to be faithful to the teachings of the church. But they had also come to realize they were gay.... These men came to confession hoping for some way out of their dilemma. How to live with a sexual orientation they didn't choose and still be a good Catholic?" As a young priest he did not feel prepared to provide them much insight. "They didn't know that the 30-year old priest hearing their confessions was terribly ignorant of things sexual." After five years at St. James Cathedral he enrolled in pastoral counseling programs on the other side of the nation, in New York City. "My academic programs began in September 1973. Three months later in December, the American Psychiatric Association removed homosexuality from its official list of illnesses." During those years, Brown "came to understand that the major sin connected with homosexuality was not the sexual activity of gay persons but the bigotry and hypocrisy of those who condemned them. The church and the rest of society had a lot of work to do to root out homophobia along with racism and sexism."[76]

When he returned to Seattle, openly gay men met with him at St. Edward's and asked him to accompany them as they developed Seattle Dignity. The Seattle chapter had formed in 1973. "I remain proud to say that I was the group's chaplain from 1975 to 1982." Brown's role was not official. One major focus during his time with Dignity was their effort to achieve official acceptance. "My superior then was Archbishop Raymond G. Hunthausen. In 1975 he had just come to Seattle. He was above all a very prayerful, holy man. He also espoused many progressive views, including respect and love for all people including gays and lesbians." Dignity members had been meeting in gay friendly non-church settings such as the Gay Counseling Center on Capitol Hill, but "the members wanted to be in a truly Catholic setting, an established church." Being in a parish church would symbolize that both their faith and their sexuality were central to who they were.[77]

In about 1980, they developed a presentation called "Growing Up Gay and Catholic" through which several members explained what it had been like to grow up surrounded by an anti-gay culture and then discover their own true orientation. They offered "Growing Up Gay and Catholic" as a panel and a presentation was sponsored by the Archdiocese of Seattle at the meeting of the Religious Education Congress held at the Seattle Center. Brown believes that the national convention of Dignity celebrating Mass at St. James Cathedral precipitated the Vatican effort to remove Hunthausen from Seattle. "The Vatican in these years steadily pursued ways to force the U.S. bishops to promote compassion to gays and lesbians as persons while declaring immoral all of their sexual behavior." While Dignity still exists in the U.S. today, Brown says that "due to its affirmation of gay sexuality it has been systematically excluded from holding meetings, Masses or any other functions on Catholic property." As the Vatican came down on Hunthausen, he was eventually forced to close the church doors. The final Mass at St. Joseph's Parish took place in July 1988. "I participated in the pews, praying, singing, and sharing Holy Communion with a group of Catholics whose joys and struggles I had come to know. My face streamed with tears as the whole group formed a procession and marched off of Catholic property together in a symbolic exodus.

A portion of God's people were now going into a type of exile singing hymns with their heads held high."[78]

Dignity was welcomed into churches in many parts of the nation. Even Cardinal O'Connor in New York, a leading exponent of orthodoxy on many fronts, allowed Dignity Masses. Yet O'Connor was no Hunthausen. The tide was turning to the right. Hunthausen was already a target of right-wing Catholic groups and ultra-conservative media. He became the object of concentrated letter writing on this issue, on women, on liturgical abuse—whatever the campaigners thought might stick. *The Wanderer* felt Hunthausen—in his welcoming people regardless of their sexual orientation—was leading "the New American Catholic Church" in a range of insults, indignities, and immoralities that would offend upstanding and morally sound Catholics.

I met with Dave Jaeger, who was Fr. David Jaeger when he worked closely with Hunthausen. On a late Sunday morning in Advent, mid-December of 2012, over breakfast at the International House of Pancakes across the street from Seattle University, Jaeger self-consciously struggled with the onset of dementia. He asked me to forgive him, for he did not think he could remember everything. Yet Jaeger grew animated and lucid as he described his good friend, Raymond Hunthausen:

> "He made the church much better here. He went all over the area. He went all over the archdiocese in a simple car. When he was paid, he would give it to people who needed it. He did not use the money himself. Hunthausen was a Vatican II bishop. John Paul II and Cardinal Ratzinger wanted to move the church away from Vatican II, and this was the key to what happened. Look at the bishops who were appointed. The peace stand taken by Hunthausen came right out of his Vatican II way of being a bishop. At one point Ratzinger called him in, and said to him, 'you should not be welcoming those gay people into your church.' Hunthausen told Ratzinger, 'I talk with those people, they are very nice people, they have families.' Hunthausen told Ratzinger, 'they are good people.' Hunthausen never said anything about sex. Hunthausen is a holy man. He made a big change in Seattle. When he left Helena in 1975 the apostolic representative, Archbishop Jean Jadot, had to ask him three times. At last he gave in. 'I'm a bishop in Montana and what do I know about Seattle.'
>
> When I first saw him I knew he was a very special human being. He beamed in joy, and the people, thousands of them on the day of his arrival, cheered and cheered for him. The next morning he was at his desk and he went to work to know all the priests, sisters, parishioners. He immediately became close every week with bishops and executives

in other faiths. He met with the priests, sisters, and members of parishes, all over the archdiocese. He wanted to know what they were thinking. The Vatican was upset with him because he stood up for his beliefs. They just couldn't figure him out.

Hunthausen asked me to spend time with AIDS victims. My partner, Steve, has HIV now. Steve early on was afraid he was going to die. Steven and I have been together now for about 24 years. It was the Dignity Mass that prompted Ratzinger to call Hunthausen to Rome. The lecture in Rome did no good. Hunthausen just smiled. Hunthausen did not agree with Ratzinger. He just smiled and did not look upset. Ratzinger did not know what to do with him. Hunthausen would never yell at those with whom he disagreed. We all learned a lot from Hunthausen. Even those who did not agree with him liked him if they got to meet him. But some of the older priests and older folks, some did not like him. They were from Archbishop Connolly's world. Connolly also was at Vatican II, but soon realized that Vatican II was giving too much power to the people. Connolly was not happy when Jadot sent Hunthausen to Seattle."[79]

Dave Jaeger died of Alzheimer's in late July 2014. Shortly after my meeting with him, a newspaper ad from three decades earlier seemed to leap out of my research files. At the outset of September 1983, timed to coincide with the Dignity Mass, the *Seattle Times* printed a paid advertisement that began with bold face upper case letters, "**DON'T BE MISLED**," and followed with this statement: "WE, ROMAN CATHOLIC LAITY OF THE ARCHDIOCESE OF SEATTLE, ARE SADDENED BY THE WELCOME EXTENDED BY ARCHBISHOP RAYMOND HUNTHAUSEN TO THE HOMOSEXUAL ORGANIZATION KNOWN AS 'DIGNITY' FOR ITS BIENNIAL INTERNATIONAL CONVENTION. WE ARE MORE SADDENED THAT 'DIGNITY' WILL BE ALLOWED TO USE OUR ST. JAMES CATHEDRAL FOR ITS 'MAJOR LITURGY'." The ad included quotes from Dignity alongside quotes from "The Holy Scripture Speaks" and "The Church Speaks" and ended: "BECAUSE WE BELIEVE THIS CONVENTION TO BE NOT ONLY AN OCCASION OF CONFUSION, BUT ALSO OF SCANDAL, WE ARE PAYING FOR THE PUBLICATION OF THIS ADVERTISEMENT. THOSE WHO WISH TO SUPPORT THIS APOSTOLATE MAY SEND CONTRIBUTIONS TO: National Parents League Inc., P.O. Box 30789, Seattle, WA 98103. Mary Royer, Chairman."[80]

The same day, the *Seattle Times* began a two-part series entitled "Gays: Receiving pastoral help from churches" with a woman by the name of Margaret Regan recounting what she experienced when, after a long time away, she returned to the church as an avowed lesbian. Regan kneeled at the confessional at Blessed Sacrament, where she had attended long before, and said, "I'm a homosexual, father, and I'm leading a homosexual life." The priest replied through the screened partition, and said, "All right, so you're a homosexual. You're a child of God. Now what are your sins?" She experienced genuine reconciliation in that confessional. Regan had been the director of nursing at one of Seattle's largest Catholic hospitals. Now she was co-chairing the Dignity convention. More than 1000 delegates and participants from as far away as Australia and the West Indies were with her. Wrote Lisa Konick, *Seattle Times* reporter: "For Regan, who can remember when Dignity conventions 'held all their Masses in hotel rooms because they weren't welcome in any of the churches,' a special welcome from Archbishop Hunthausen and an invitation to celebrate Mass in St. James Cathedral seem almost miraculous, an encouraging sign of the careful negotiations now going on between gay Catholics and their church." It was a time when many denominations were grappling with their own ambiguities. Rev. Bill Cate, speaking for the Church Council of Greater Seattle, described the difficult process that took place over a year long debate until finally the Seattle Metropolitan Church was welcomed as a member of the Council. "I must confess for my own part I really had to struggle with the issue," Cate said. "I had all kinds of homophobic problems, but I did eventually come to grips with it, as did most of our members."[81]

"Catholic gays pray in cathedral while protesters chant outside" was the headline of a *Seattle Times* story reporting that, on the sidewalks outside of St. James, some 100 people were chanting the rosary and protesting. They called the Dignity Mass a "sacrilege." But if there were protests outside, inside there was welcome. The Mass took place after a full week of seminars. Kenneth Van Dyke, one of the planners of the Dignity convention, said he "personally knew of a great number of people who were disenchanted or felt disenfranchised from the church. I heard people say, 'I was away from the church for 20 years,' and now they have found a place to find home in the church again."[82]

Bill Gaffney, member of St. Joseph's Parish and local leader of Catholics United for the Faith, led the movement against Hunthausen on this issue. Welcoming Masses had been going on in several parishes for years before the September 1983 Mass at St. James. The Catholic gay and lesbian community was already well developed. The Dignity Mass idea itself probably reached a point of becoming a concern to Rome when, instead of gays and lesbians just showing up for a Mass, it was specifically oriented to them. Because of Gaffney and others, this would have been on the radar of the Vatican well before Dignity's day at St. James.[83]

I asked Fr. Mike McDermott, since he served for many years as a central administrative member of Hunthausen's cabinet, for his perspective:

"If you go back to the issue of the Dignity Mass, he consulted with people before he made the decision to go ahead and allow it. He asked, 'Is this going to be a violation of church teaching?' And at the time, his theologian Fr. Peter Chirico and others let him know this would not be a violation. Pastorally speaking he felt it was the reasonable and right thing to do. Archbishop Hunthausen asked questions, sought advice, then acted for the good of those involved."[84]

In June of 1983, Hunthausen wrote to the priests of the archdiocese. He noted how the bishops, in their 1976 pastoral letter *To Live in Jesus Christ*, had denounced prejudice against homosexuals. Why was he going to open the cathedral door? "In the final analysis, the measure of our pastoral care can, of course, only be the example of Jesus who time and again chose to minister directly to those whom society found most difficult to accept."[85] As the Dignity participants gathered in St. James, and several dozen angry people stood outside to protest the archbishop's decision by carrying signs, candles, and praying the rosary,[86] Hunthausen through his videotaped message told the Dignity participants, "I am surely with you in spirit." He prayed that their efforts would be guided by Jesus and the Gospel of love:

"You know as well as I do, that for some, your presence here is a source of wonderment and confusion, even anger and resentment. They find it difficult, if not impossible, to understand why the church should engage in a special ministry to persons of homosexual orientation. They are confused and perplexed by the statements of church leaders such as the one made several years ago by the American Bishops when they called for understanding and compassion on the part of the Christian community, and encouraged homosexual persons to play an active role in that community. Perhaps your first duty in love during your days here will be toward those very people who find it so difficult to understand you and why you have come here."[87]

Fr. John Heagle and Sr. Fran Ferder worked with Hunthausen for many years, providing professional training and guidance for pastoral ministers, priests, women religious, and lay ministers. I sat down with John Heagle for an interview at their Therapy and Renewal Associates center now located on the Oregon coast:

"On the issue of the gay and lesbian community, Hunthausen saw how the community was being attacked. Dignity was trying to be recognized as part of the Roman Catholic community. Hunthausen was trying to walk a creative role regarding doctrine and yet being compassionate. In all five areas that Cardinal Ratzinger noted, they all had something to do with sexuality in one way or another. Gender roles, identity roles. Hunthausen was open to change on the question

> of celibacy. He wanted to be present to people. Each year, for example, he sent into Rome the names of married people who he thought would be good candidates for the priesthood. He was so open to the idea of ordaining women or men, married. He envisioned them all being ordained.
>
> Dignity was trying to make some demands. Dignity was, like other organizations, pushing hard to advocate. To the majority of the population they looked rebellious as they pushed. Hunthausen was trying to walk a creative role there. He did not want to go against church doctrine and yet he wanted to be compassionate. At the time this got a little blurred.
>
> When it came to the basic things like the Apostles Creed and the Nicene Creed, at core he was an obedient participant in the church. The whole visitation was so confusing to him because he could not understand why they were getting so upset. In retrospect he began to see later on that his convictions about applying the gospel were in conflict with the institutional vision of the church. How could the institutional church have gotten it so wrong? How could they misread Seattle so badly? How could their reaction to the church in Seattle be so off? What were the behind-the-scenes factors that led to such?"

Heagle believes the political right wing, including many Roman Catholics, used the Ratzinger list to cover their chief concern. "The American Catholic Right leaned on the Republican machine that then went to the Vatican. They used other things as excuses. This is the untold story. Knowing what the CIA was doing all over, it is not hard to imagine that there were folks going after Hunthausen. There was a strong reaction against communism. Reagan and John Paul II were tight on this." So many Catholics, when Heagle was young, would pray to Our Lady of Fatima for the conversion of Russia. "Think about it, with the Roman Catholic institution that he challenged with his vision and practice, the system reacted. It is a patronage system. Who you know, who you owe, and who owes you, a patronage system, not just a patriarchy. He did not ever play the patronage game." Heagle thought about the global scene. "How did all of this relate to what was going on between JPII and Reagan? You will hear this from so many quarters, people convinced that this is the untold story, the connection between the government at the time, right wing Catholics (in government as well) and the Vatican." Going back to the Gospel and moving forward with Vatican II was bound to put Archbishop Hunthausen in conflict with Rome in those days.[88]

Regarding Hunthausen and the issue of homosexuality, Cardinal Ratzinger's outlook was no small factor. In the aforementioned book, *Cardinal Ratzinger: The*

Vatican's Enforcer of the Faith, John Allen examined "Ratzinger's campaign to hold the line on homosexuality."[89] The year 1983 was pivotal. The Congregation for the Doctrine of the Faith attempted to prevent the publication of *A Challenge to Love: Gay and Lesbian Catholics in the Church*, an anthology edited by Robert Nugent. Fr. Nugent and Sr. Jeannine Gramick were actively ministering to the gay and lesbian community across the country. While many assumed that Hunthausen's problems with Rome stemmed from his reputation as a peace activist, "the origin of Ratzinger's interest in Hunthausen had to do with homosexuality." This was the conclusion Allen came to in his book. The Dignity Cathedral liturgy was celebrated by Jesuit John McNeill, "who would later be forced out of the order for his advocacy of changes in church teaching on homosexuality." The message sent from the whole disciplinary action toward Hunthausen, including his loss of authority over ministry to the gay and lesbian community, put bishops "on notice that pastoral ministry to homosexuals, unless it is based on clear condemnation of homosexual conduct, invites serious trouble with Rome."[90] Yet, as the evidence suggests, Raymond Hunthausen was inviting serious trouble with the Vatican on several fronts.

RESISTING U.S. NUCLEAR WEAPONS AND CENTRAL AMERICAN WAR

Let's return for a moment to "Faith and Disarmament," June 1981. The full speech was presented in this book's opening chapter. Hunthausen said that he felt the call to the cross "was a call to love God and one's neighbor in so direct a way that the authorities in power could only regard it as subversive and revolutionary." He called the Trident Bangor base the Auschwitz of Puget Sound, appealed for unilateral disarmament, and envisioned a social movement for conscientious war tax resistance. U.S. political leaders should pursue peace, not war and increased armaments. He then began to practice civil disobedience himself. Did the authorities, including some in the church, see his words and deeds as subversive and revolutionary?

The real reason behind the U.S. arms buildup, argued Hunthausen, was to retain power and privilege. Weapons protected and produced wealth. He confronted the defense industry. The region epitomized the military-industrial complex President Eisenhower had famously warned about. "This conjunction of an immense military establishment and a large arms industry is new in the American experience," Eisenhower said. "We must not fail to comprehend its grave implications.... The potential for the disastrous rise of misplaced power exists and will persist."[91] Twenty years later, Archbishop Hunthausen saw Ike's admonition going unheeded. Hunthausen focused on Trident as early as 1976, and some people in the region began to criticize him years before the June 1981 speech in Tacoma. Just as Trident became an object of social forces trying to resist the Reagan buildup, so Hunthausen became an object of countervailing social forces. If some saw Trident as a sea monster, others saw Hunthausen as a traitor.

Hunthausen denounced the Reagan arms escalation. At Notre Dame early in 1982, he explained that the Auschwitz metaphor for the Trident submarine base at Bangor was apt because our society was embracing an evil system. The train-delivered weapons placed on Tridents could lead to a nuclear holocaust. Massive military expenditures were already inflicting pain on people who lacked life's basic necessities. As some argued at the time, Hunthausen represented a political threat to the Reagan administration on the nuclear weapons issue. He also challenged the Reagan administration's Central American policy.

Fr. Phillip Bloom, active in Seattle's Hispanic Ministry, wrote in the tense climate of September 1986, "Some people might say the deeper motive behind the investigation was episcopal jealousy. We are all familiar with clerical jealousy and its effects, but could it be that some bishops were simply jealous of another bishop who was liked by his priests, effective in running his diocese and, without seeking it, gaining an international reputation for his gospel witness?" But if it were just this, the whole story would be easy to grasp. It looked like something more than envy. "Archbishop Hunthausen, perhaps more than any U.S. bishop, has distinguished between the gospel and nationalism. He has shown by example that to follow Jesus Christ puts one at odds with certain directions of our government." Letter writing campaigns had taken place. "Did the energy for all those letters come simply from people upset about general absolution? Or are they enraged because Archbishop Hunthausen is a 'subversive' U.S. citizen?" Bloom, speculating that links between the Reagan administration and the Vatican could have been a nudge, noted a book by Anna Maria Ezcura, entitled *Administración Reagan y el Vaticano*. Ezcura argued that the Reagan administration tried to employ the Vatican to further its Central American policy. Bloom: "Could some of Reagan's people not also have used their Vatican connections to discredit a bishop who is seriously challenging them?" Bloom had asked Archbishop Hickey and Archbishop Laghi if the Reagan administration was involved. Though they told him "no," he was not sure whether they would necessarily know the answer, and even if they did, they might not tell him. "We have been shown a lot of duplicity in all of this."[92]

Jesuit Fr. Richard McSorley, who authored the 1976 article "It's a Sin to Build a Nuclear Weapon" that so affected Hunthausen, argued his theory on the heels of the 1986 NCCB meeting in D.C. where Hunthausen appealed in vain for robust support from his brother bishops. McSorley believed what was really behind the investigation was Hunthausen's prophetic peace posture.

> "His accusers knew that there was no use complaining to Rome about his condemnation of the arms race and about his refusal to pay some

of his taxes that are used for nuclear weapons, so they attacked him on other points on which they thought Rome might listen. But their real objection was his peace stand. Since Vatican II this same group has opposed everything the Church teaches about justice and peace. In this case they have been listened to and rewarded for their criticism and disobedience."[93]

Fr. Jack Morris, another Jesuit, told me in 2011 what he thought. "The military powers got to him. When he called the Trident base at Bangor the Auschwitz of Puget Sound, they took note."[94]

Morris convinced me to start working on this book. There could have been any number of concerns prompting a visitation to Seattle, but the question always remained, was it Trident, Central America, and civil disobedience? I asked Archbishop Hunthausen directly face to face about this when I met with him in Yakima, Washington on Memorial Day of 2011. He clearly did not wish to talk about the Vatican investigation. "If we were to get started on this we would be here for days," he sighed. I pressed him. "Frank," he said, "this is freaking me out." However, before we left the topic he mentioned a name, Cardinal Sebastian Baggio, who was the prefect of the Vatican Congregation of Bishops when Hunthausen went to Rome that late summer of 1983. "We had a conversation when I was back there for an *ad limina* visit in Rome. Baggio said to me something like, 'you know, we have some concerns about some of your activities regarding nuclear arms and your civil disobedience.'"[95]

A few months later, I phoned retired Archbishop Weakland of Milwaukee, who knew Baggio well. I learned that the head of the Vatican Congregation of Bishops was candid. "If he said that to Hunthausen, he must have meant it." Baggio would not make that up, felt Weakland.[96]

> "Baggio was very supportive of the Jadot-appointed bishops and he was his own man.... Rome's problem with Dutch was this: the public case would not be built around his stand on the military issue and peace. They would not want a public show on such matters. Both John Paul and Vatican Secretary of State Cardinal Casaroli were great admirers of Reagan. Rome was concerned about Hunthausen's military stand, but would not want to appear to take sides with the Reagan administration. They would never want to appear to take such a stand."

Weakland remembered another *ad limina* visit, probably in 1988, when he and Hunthausen were together in Rome. The famous writer James Michener happened to be there. Pope John Paul II gave communion to Michener, who would have been turned away if strict guidelines had been enforced. With a grin, Hunthausen quipped to Weakland afterward that, given all he and Seattle had been through, "perhaps there ought to be an apostolic visitation of the papal household." It all came down to a control issue, in Weakland's estimation. The peace stand was a factor, but the bottom line was, in the days of John Paul II and Cardinal Ratzinger, the Vatican wanted central control, and Hunthausen personified the model of church they wanted to rein in.[97]

For McSorley and Morris, Hunthausen's peace stand was *the* factor. For Weakland, that stand was *a* factor. Throughout this examination of various perspectives, keep in mind the diversity of interpretations among people close to the scene. When meeting with Fr. Ryan, I wanted to know if he thought there was any merit to all the speculation about the White House-Vatican collusion theory. "Let me say that I have always thought that there was a connection…at DC or at the Vatican, top level people, such as William Casey, Alexander Haig, others, and someone saying to a Vatican diplomat, 'can't something be done about that,' if I may use the phrase, 'that loose cannon out there in Seattle?'" Ryan used "loose cannon" with deliberate irony.

> "I told him that his talk at the Lutheran Synod in Tacoma was the shot heard 'round the world, very ironic too. I've always imagined that that conversation happened, whether it was at a cocktail party or some other way. A lot of things in this world happen that are sort of off the record conversations that are far more significant than one might think. The timing is such that you could make a pretty good case for it. There were letter-writing campaigns about a lot of bishops. I don't know if he was perceived to be more 'out there' than others, but I think that in Rome they were probably happy to have those other concerns to hang out on the clothes line rather than the real one, if my theory is right that the real one was his position on tax resistance. When I was preparing the talk that Hunthausen would give to the bishops at the November 1986 meeting, I noted that the things Hunthausen was being called on were realities in many dioceses. This is something we are all involved in. It is possible that the real kicker was that this upstart bishop was so engaged in the war issue. The Vatican would have responded to a Reagan challenge; realpolitik as the way to handle it. 'We can hang other things on Hunthausen, get this and this and this from so and so, and we (the Vatican) will tell the public that all this has nothing to do with the government and the peace issue.'"

Wasn't Hunthausen's call for unilateral nuclear disarmament a position that the peace pastoral pulled away from, with pressure from the Vatican and some American bishops pushing the just war doctrine?

"I think it is instructive that he was not given a role in the peace pastoral. He did have an interview with the committee. It is significant that he was not given a role. It was also during one of the meetings on the peace pastoral letter that he was pulled aside by Pio Laghi to be told about the visitation. He was there for a meeting having to do with the peace pastoral, he was pulled aside during a coffee break, I mean in the most informal of circumstances, talk about cocktail party, and he was told, 'by the way, the Holy Father....' He heard this, it was disconcerting, but then he thought, 'we are doing such wonderful things in Seattle,' which indeed we were, so he chose in one sense to think, 'maybe they want to learn from us.' He was not naïve, but he was not church smart. The whole church power structure, how it works, this was really not his *forte*. He was never on the trajectory to be a bishop. That was totally outside of his mind. He was the president of Carroll College. No one was more surprised than Dutch Hunthausen the day that he got the call. The inner workings are not something that he understood.

There is a man, a Montanan, by the name of John Driscoll, researching what I will call the conspiracy theory, and John has been like a heat-seeking missile in terms of getting Freedom of Information Act high level information. He has not gotten information from the Vatican, that's a hard place to get information from, isn't it?... I don't know what he intends to do with what he has done but he has uncovered a lot that I think is going to substantiate that this was part of the issue, even though Laghi always insisted that the visitation had nothing to do with Hunthausen's peace stance. He said it so many times that he 'protesteth too much, me thinks.'"[98]

I followed up on Ryan's tip, making contact with retired U.S. Army Colonel John Driscoll. He proved valuable and his discoveries will be cited shortly. In an interview for Timothy Schilling's dissertation, Ryan spelled out his understanding of the persons and groups that launched complaints about Hunthausen: (1) Erven Park, the publisher of *Catholic Truth*; (2) readers and affiliates of *The Wanderer*; (3) people who had greater status when Archbishop Thomas Connolly was in charge and felt pushed aside as Hunthausen developed his different model of leadership; (4) folks who passionately disagreed with Hunthausen on the issue of nuclear arms and related policies; (5) those who had wished Hunthausen would have been more outspoken and prominent against abortion; (6) people critical of laicized priests being allowed ministerial and teaching roles; (7) people concerned about liturgical experimentation; and (8) last but certainly not least, in ego, Gary Bullert, author of *The Hunthausen File*. Bullert not only opposed

Hunthausen's nuclear arms stance, but felt that he, Bullert, had been unjustly relieved of teaching posts within the archdiocese.[99] Bullert's book revealed more about the right-leaning ideology of its author than about Hunthausen. Chapter titles such as "The Parallel Church," "Empowering Radical Feminism," "The Pansexual Subversion of Catholicism," an "American Liberation Theology," suggest his agenda.[100] George Weigel was another critic of Seattle's archbishop. Weigel, elegant and hagiographic about John Paul II, was dismissive of any "Holy Alliance" theory about a White House-Vatican effort to bring about the fall of communism, let alone the fall of Hunthausen.[101]

Ryan gave Schilling three reasons why he believed there was something to the collusion theory: (1) the visitation came very close in time to the American government's granting of diplomatic status to the Holy See (Hickey came to Seattle in November 1983 and formal diplomatic ties were secured in January 1984); (2) a visitation of another religious leader, Bishop Walter Sullivan of Richmond, Virginia, happened at about the same time as the Seattle visitation (although the Sullivan case did not get the same level of publicity) and Sullivan too was outspoken against nuclear arms; and (3) the Holy See's representatives in the Hunthausen case, Pio Laghi especially, but also Archbishop Hickey and Cardinal Ratzinger, seemed to "protest too much" as they claimed that Hunthausen's nuclear arms stance had nothing to do with the investigation. Schilling commented:

> "If Ryan is correct in his view, then my own findings here suffer from some serious deficiencies, because then the conflict would have been about something very different than what I have believed it to be about. Moreover, there would have been a crucial participant involved (one or more representatives of the U.S. government) that I have failed to identify.... Regarding Ryan's theory, I can only say that I have not found enough evidence in my own investigation to establish its credibility. The only additional piece of information that I have come across that might fit in with this theory concerns the revelation of the FBI and U.S. Naval Intelligence files on Hunthausen's anti-nuclear activity. But this surveillance activity does not surprise me and seems not, in and of itself, to increase the likelihood of there having been some sort of cooperation/conspiracy between Rome and Washington. Perhaps someday further evidence will give us an entirely new picture of the Hunthausen case. But in my view the evidence presently available suggests that Rome was indeed concerned with pastoral issues and maintaining its control over local churches. Involvement by the U.S. government in the affair is only speculative at this point."[102]

Still, there were quite likely some "off the record" conversations. The brief admonition Sebastian Baggio conveyed to Hunthausen is at least suggestive.

At the Archdiocese of Seattle's Justice and Peace Center, Don Hopps got a phone call from a person who identified himself as a lieutenant in the U.S. Navy. "I am Roman Catholic, and I am kind of bothered by this, and I want you to know your phones are being tapped." This call came in at some point after March 1982, says Hopps, because he remembers that Navy secretary Lehman had already publicly denounced Hunthausen (see the Lehman speech cited in chapter three). The call lasted only about 30 seconds.

> "We knew there was this group of conservative Catholics led by John Lehman. We knew about groups like the Knights of Malta, the international group of conservative Catholics, with Haig and others involved. While Lehman was obsessed with Trident, Haig was much more broadly pushing a vision of a grand alliance of the Vatican and the U.S. in a crusade against communism. In this context, we know Haig saw himself as the puppet master. As with other things Haig did, he probably attempted to build his vision outside of the administration process."

In Hopps' thinking, Haig was probably the only Reagan administration person pushing this alliance. It was not long before Haig was out of favor and power. By the time the Vatican was considering Archbishop Hickey's report on the situation in Seattle, Haig was no longer a player. The important point, however, would be to think about the connections between the Vatican's concerns about Latin American liberation theology and how those concerns might relate to Hunthausen. "Later on, Penny Lernoux was out here visiting some of us and she was focused on what was going on in the U.S. People out here, we were all asking, and Lernoux was asking us, about Ratzinger and Laghi and the Latin American connection and liberation theology concerns." Alfonso Trujillo, the Colombian archbishop, was "Ratzinger's agent against liberation theology," Lernoux thought. Some of Ratzinger's funds, when he was the archbishop of Munich (bishops received public funds from the German tax for churches), went to support Trujillo and other "missionary work" in South America and to prevent the spread of liberation theology in Central America and Mexico.[103]

Another pertinent background note: In 1980, the Council for Inter-American Security produced a report, *A New Inter-American Policy for the Eighties*, which became known as the *Santa Fe Document* after Santa Fe, New Mexico, where it was conceived. As Lernoux wrote in *People of God*, the *Santa Fe Document* showed there was a clear effort by the Reagan team to go after liberation theology. Reagan's early advisers on Latin America shaped *Santa Fe*.

> "The Reagan administration supported the papacy's get-tough policy with local churches, not because Washington cared in the least who

> was appointed a bishop or how religious rites were conducted but because the American bishops comprised an influential opposition group in the United States, and a strongly anticapitalist liberation theology challenged U.S. hegemony in Latin America."[104]

In the Archdiocese of Seattle, says Hopps, "El Salvador, Nicaragua, and Guatemala were huge concerns of ours." Secretary of State Alexander Haig and his dealings with the Vatican were important. At the very outset of the first Reagan term, Haig was working to get his boss a personal envoy to Rome, which the Vatican desired. Haig, a conservative Catholic, wanted the liberal apostolic delegate to Washington D.C., Jean Jadot, out. Whether or not he had a hand in it, Jadot was soon out, and Laghi, with a Latin American track record favorable to the Reagan people, was soon in. Hopps:

> "Hunthausen once told me, right after the Hickey visitation was announced publicly, that he believed JPII had changed significantly after the papal assassination attempt. He seemed to loosen his grip on the day to day running of the Vatican. This is when Ratzinger really began to have major power in the Vatican power structure. Before the assassination attempt JPII was much more the person the theologian Gregory Baum was excited about due to the strong social justice encyclical *Laborem Excercens*. After the assassination attempt, Ratzinger's power surged. Hunthausen, at the 1983 *ad limina*, asked JPII, 'why am I being investigated?' JPII acted as if this was nothing. 'Do not worry about this, employing the bureaucracy this is just one of those things Cardinal Ratzinger does.' Hunthausen was surprised that JPII was not more aware of the visitation. The pope's response seemed unusually cavalier. By the time of the Vatican evaluation of Seattle, Ratzinger had major power. There were key actions against other prelates such as the archbishop of Milan in that same period. Ratzinger was willing to use the power of inquisition to undermine any number of people. The investigation of Hunthausen was not an isolated action. The Latin American church was hit especially hard.
>
> However, Hunthausen, unlike some of the other cases, had become an international figure by that time. He was moving onto the international stage and this troubled the Roman hierarchy. He was a charismatic figure in a global people power movement. He was a threat as a globally recognized person. He had international awareness among people engaged in the anti-nuclear weapons movement. And Hunthausen's involvement in Central American concerns was a second wave of controversy that caught the attention

of the U.S. government and the Vatican. In this context, the Romero Day commemorations and marches, Hunthausen's speeches, and civil disobedience actions would have been especially troublesome, not so much sanctuary by itself. The U.S. government, especially people like Haig who was directly in contact with the Vatican, and Lehman, wanted Hunthausen suppressed. Another key player in all this was Richard Viguerie. He was a very conservative Catholic who had a secret meeting in the early 1980s in Portland with about 80 or 90 people from the Archdiocese of Seattle. The focus of the meeting was how to get rid of Hunthausen. Viguerie's direct mail strategy would be used to send massive mail to generate letters to Rome to attack Hunthausen. Paul Weyrich and Richard Viguerie, both masters of direct mail campaigns, were closely linked to Grover Norquist. Weyrich and Viguerie came out and met with Catholics on a pretty regular basis. They were key in helping people organize the letter writing campaigns against Hunthausen."[105]

Around the same time period, when Hopps got the very brief phone call from the Navy lieutenant, another man came in to talk. He claimed to be a trained assassin with the Australian Special Forces. He told Don Hopps that he and a group had been contracted to do a killing in Nicaragua. They had been sent there to assassinate a Contra leader who lost the trust of those in charge. The CIA was obviously involved. To this day Hopps is not clear why the Australian chose to visit him, but it reminded Hopps of the cloak-and-dagger practices affecting Central America. Hunthausen was taking a strong stand against U.S. policy in that region. As to the Navy connection, of one thing Hopps was sure, Secretary John Lehman took a special interest in Hunthausen. Trident was Lehman's "flagship" for a huge Navy expansion during the military spending surge. "Lehman is a good example of a conservative Catholic who finds a highly authoritarian church structure to suit him well. Lehman linked this kind of church power structure to the military command structure. Lehman had direct personal ties with people in the Vatican. And he had close ties with Alexander Haig."[106] The army generals at Fort Lewis, the admiral at Bangor, the admiral at Sandpoint Naval Base (who was also in charge of Whidbey Island and Bremerton—all the bases except Bangor, which had its own separate command) and the air force leadership at McChord—these people would have been working mostly behind the scenes, Hopps thinks. Lehman was recognizable. Navy personnel would have done his bidding. Gregory Barlow, who had served in Vietnam, was the adjutant general for the Washington State National Guard. Apparently Barlow did not like Hunthausen's stand at all. Another Hunthausen close associate, Jim Burns, remembers once getting a phone call from him. "Jim," Barlow said, "we are going to cut him off at the pockets." A Catholic,

Barlow was connected to power and wealth in Seattle and obviously had strong ties in the military of the region.[107]

As to what brought on Rome's action, it was a combination of factors, thinks Hopps:

> "You have the militant 'nuke'em' Catholics in the U.S. These folks had a great deal of influence at least at the beginning of the Reagan administration. You have militant anti-communist Europeans who are in charge at the Vatican (Ratzinger and John Paul II). They were totally focused on what's going on in Eastern Europe in that era. Then you have the locals here who were a combination of the conservative proponents of a strong military and anti-gay and anti-any Vatican II changes."

A coalition came together to go after Hunthausen. Where the nuclear issue played big was in the context of the regional military-industrial complex. Also, intense reaction against communism was heightened due to the fact that communism was historically vigorous in the region. Hopps thinks the Dignity issue was covered with the other issues that Ratzinger and Laghi noted in their letters and statements. "To the Vatican Hunthausen was viewed as a liberation movement bishop, the North American version of Latin American liberation theology."[108]

I also wanted to know what Fr. Paul Magnano thought, since he too worked closely with Hunthausen. He also did advanced study in the field of psychology, and served as a pastor. We met at his parish, Christ Our Hope, in downtown Seattle in December of 2012.

> "There was a combination of factors that led to the Vatican scrutiny. Certainly the 'Faith and Disarmament' speech, and steps Hunthausen took following it, and Lehman's anger, all this was a factor. Hunthausen also was so pastoral in how he approached church issues, such as allowing Dignity to have the Mass in the Cathedral. The fact that Hunthausen was such a real person, fully present to the people, troubled Rome. Some people would have said of Hunthausen, 'we wanted a pastor, after Connolly, but we ended up with a prophet.' Hunthausen was a bishop who stepped out of line. This troubled John Paul II and his people as well as the U.S. government. Hickey, at the time the archbishop of DC, was doing the bidding of both Rome and the Reagan administration. Hunthausen was always honest to himself and honest in every way. He never wanted to draw attention to himself and he always loved the church. He loved Jesus. Jesus and his followers are the church. He was rooted in prayer. He was never out to get the church. It hurt him that he could not keep people together, united. He was

> surprised by the divisions. He was a human being. He would go out of the front door of the Cathedral residence to get the newspaper, and if he saw a person out on the street or sleeping by the rectory he would invite that person inside for coffee. He knew he was a bishop, but the key is, what kind of bishop. 'Golly by Gee' is what he would say if surprised by a person or if he did not understand something, such as the whole investigation. He seemed baffled by it."[109]

Patty Repikoff, another trailblazer for gender equality, feels the real reason may well have been that Hunthausen's stand on Trident angered the Reagan administration. "And there were people especially in the Vancouver, Washington area who organized to put money into getting Hunthausen." The peace stand was key, but other issues could be used as a "two prong approach" to undermine him. "Well-heeled business people, Roman Catholics, in Vancouver, Washington, some of them, were quite conservative and big *Wanderer* fans. They formed organized groups throughout the archdiocese. Not just the Ervin Parks. There were politically astute, quiet and wealthy people involved."[110]

Charlie Meconis had moved Hunthausen by his own personal example of conscientious war tax resistance. So I asked Charlie what he thought was behind Rome's investigation. Lehman was vociferous in his blowback after Hunthausen branded Trident as immoral. "Lehman had tight connections with the Vatican. Lehman's attack on Hunthausen was a clarion call for the conservative attack. Lehman was tight with the archconservative group *Opus Dei* and had connections with Pio Laghi and others." Charlie remembers there was a significant bump up in right-wing Catholic criticism almost immediately after the "Faith and Disarmament" speech.

> "The Catholic Right has been aroused. Hunthausen's position on the nuclear arms race and his statement calling for civil disobedience really convinced powerful people in the Reagan administration and in the Vatican that this needed to be watched. This was serious. Of course it wasn't just Hunthausen. Tom Gumbleton, Michael Kenny, Walter Sullivan, Leroy Matthiessen, and other bishops were also there."

But the Navy would have tried to get some dirt on Hunthausen.

> "It's one thing when you have the Berrigans out there, but it's another when you have bishops, it's another ball game. With *The Challenge of Peace* coming along, the truth is, they could not find anything on Hunthausen on the peace issue. Absent any dirt, they could not get at him directly. And the pope was largely on Hunthausen's side on the nuclear issue. The Vatican had made strong statements for disarmament."

Meconis adds:

> "The Navy and the Reagan administration realized they needed to have a much broader attack against Hunthausen. George Weigel began his ascent as a neo-conservative Catholic when he took on the peace bishops. Hunthausen embodied the genuine spirit of Vatican II in all of its ramifications. He was certainly a faithful man of the church but he absolutely took to heart the central message of the *Pastoral Constitution on the Church in the Modern World*. The central message is that because the Holy Spirit works in the world the church must be open to the Holy Spirit wherever the spirit moves and bring that wisdom into the church and into its internal structures. So then the world will pay attention to the church because the church has paid attention to the world and is fully engaged."

Meconis thinks it is crucial to note Hunthausen's openness to many issues:

> "...his openness to women's issues in the church, this was a matter of core human rights. Allowing the Holy Spirit to work, this same outlook shaped how he approached the matter of sexual orientation. Hunthausen had this essential openness to the work of the Holy Spirit in the world. Having failed to dig up dirt on the peace and justice front, the neo-conservatives highlighted the gender issues and sex issues. Any flexibility he showed at all on issues of birth control, abortion, celibacy, women in the church, homosexuality...if they could catch him in any way that's where they would go after him, and they did.... The whole counter-reform (counter Vatican II) has been going on now for more than 30 years, and has had a tremendously negative impact on the role of the church in the world and on the attention that the world pays to the church, and this is a time when we so need leadership like Hunthausen's."[111]

During Holy Week of 2013, I met not only with Meconis, but with other folks who had worked with Archbishop Hunthausen in an ecumenical context. In Bothell, near the north end of Lake Washington, where he and his spouse retired, Washington Association of Churches executive Rev. Loren Arnett told me he thought Hunthausen's push for U.S. nuclear disarmament was part of the motivation for the crackdown. "There was a great deal of resistance to Hunthausen by lay people over his peace stand. A lot of those people were using whatever channels were available to them to complain about this 'radical archbishop' who was not in line with their views. He was taking a stand that was pretty risky. Nobody else in our group was taking that stand."[112]

Jesse Dye, who worked with Hunthausen and the Archdiocese of Seattle for several years in the capacity of professional mediation, and now works on environmental concerns in the Pacific Northwest region, shared with me her angle on Rome's motives:

> "John Paul II was a pope of the Cold War. Reagan also hated communism. Don't you think that at some point Reagan turned to JPII and said 'will no one rid me of this meddlesome priest?' I think this is almost certain to have happened. See T.S. Eliot's *Murder in the Cathedral.* This is at the heart of the story. Hunthausen's story is a modern reenactment, or a variation on a theme, of this situation with Thomas Becket. The Vatican tried to undercut him by sending out Wuerl, and basically failed to do so. This is the story. Hunthausen did not let them take him down. As a result it's a better story than the classic one T.S. Eliot tells. Here there's a new narrative. Hunthausen is not a tragic figure. He is a person full of joy and life, a happy person. But the investigation weighed on him heavily, but it did not break him. Hunthausen does not need to tell his story. He did his work. He was a model of collaborative and loving conflict resolution. He had huge grief about it, but he was also at peace about it all. To be sure, he is holding within himself a story that we all could so benefit from his perspective on it all, for religion and society. I wish he would share what he is holding within.
>
> But he was not trapped into the bindings of the hierarchy. He lived through the story impeccably, better than the rest of us. Many of us were much more manipulated by the machinations of the Vatican. Hunthausen just followed his own conscience. He was not manipulated by their machinations. Maybe he has done the better thing, which is to live the story impeccably. To talk about their bad behavior would not further anything, he must feel. The real point is that he lived through it with grace and dignity. For him the key was to live in the present, not to revisit it later. This is key to his spiritual journey.
>
> There is enormous corruption in the church, let me tell you, I'd rather deal with trying to stop the extinction of all life on the planet than with the Catholic Church. This is a fair comparison because that is what I do, work on environmental concerns.
>
> The nuclear stand he took was on the global stage. It took place during the height of the Cold War. Reagan and John Paul II were friends. They shared a hatred for the Soviet Union. Reagan says to the Pope,

'hey, I got this problem in Seattle, can you help me?' In the mean time there were the attacks. The Mass of Dignity might have been a bit of a problem, but it and other issues, such as approving too many annulments etc., these were pretty petty matters. They were all not a huge deal. Hunthausen would discuss this all at times, say, on the elevator at the chancery he would say, 'I don't understand what they are objecting to?' The matter of sterilization was a false issue, etc. with other matters Ratzinger listed in the letter. Nuclear weapons, Hunthausen's stand on this, was the key, because none of the other matters really added up from a factual standpoint."[113]

Like others involved with the Ground Zero Center for Nonviolent Action, Jim Douglass knew the consequences one could face taking on U.S. war policy. Douglass, we know, had a personal impact on Hunthausen, who found him prayerful and conscientious. He spent many periods as a prisoner of conscience. When I reached Jim by phone at the Catholic Worker community in Birmingham, Alabama, I asked him what he thought:

"The official church reasons for the investigation were linked to the political issues. Bishops Matthiessen and Hunthausen led a retreat at Ground Zero. They sent an appeal to the other Catholic bishops along the tracks. This made the *New York Times* front page story. The people picketing Ground Zero were the same people appealing to the Vatican. Pope John Paul was being briefed every morning by the CIA.[114] Hunthausen was in many ways the catalyst for the peace pastoral letter. The June 12, 1981 speech was the first statement. Other bishops followed from this speech. There was push back from the U.S. government and the Vatican to ensure that the pastoral letter would not be a Hunthausen approach. There is no way that the Vatican would ever come out at that time, or now, and say that the reason they were suppressing, visiting, investigating Hunthausen was because the Reagan administration did not want him voicing his stand on the disarmament issue, but it was certainly key."[115]

When reports came out in 1987 that the FBI and Navy had been keeping files on Hunthausen, the Archbishop reacted to the first disclosures. "I must say I am surprised and concerned that the FBI would monitor and keep records on occasions or events when I simply exercised my right as a citizen to speak out on public issues."[116] The Navy began keeping a file on Hunthausen back in 1982. The *National Catholic Reporter* obtained the Navy records through the Freedom of Information Act, just as it had done to obtain the FBI files on both Hunthausen and Detroit Auxiliary Bishop Thomas Gumbleton. One report from Navy intelligence noted that Hunthausen spoke of "Auschwitz of Puget Sound," and another had a newspaper story about a week-long "peace dialogue" ahead of the planned blockade of the Trident submarine, the U.S.S. Ohio. Parts of the report were blanked out.[117] If there were some FBI and Navy files on Hunthausen, the files dealing with Douglass were far more extensive and covered many years.

Fortunately, another Ground Zero Center for Nonviolent Action participant, Glen Milner, had been making Freedom of Information Act requests for files related to the peace movement in the region. Many of the FBI and Navy records on Douglass were among his collection. Milner guided me through his basement, stacked wall to wall with filing cabinets. He pulled out the most pertinent records and loaned them to me. So I had more homework to do. After I drove south from Seattle to Tacoma, then west to the Bangor Navy base, Ground Zero Center host Constance Mears provided me hospitality and a quiet space to myself. The following morning, I began going through the trove of once classified materials. Good Friday and Holy Saturday were dedicated to studying government files on anti-war activists. I sat in a retreat center near Trident subs with unimaginably destructive payloads. The setting and timing were the epitome of paradox. As I worked my way through Milner's FOIA research, I thought about how Rev. Dr. Martin Luther King Jr. had once said, "Good Friday must give way to Easter." I thought about those times when Archbishop Hunthausen had been here next to the base, acting on his beliefs with others just down the road at the gates to one of the nation's largest concentrations of nuclear firepower.

In one news-clipping I found in the government files, the Associated Press described a Sunday in early June 1987. Hunthausen, with dozens of other peaceful demonstrators, was standing outside the gates. "Sunday's appearance at the Trident missile base was the 65-year-old Hunthausen's first anti-nuclear speech since his powers were restored on May 27." Asked to comment on the Vatican's action, the archbishop instead focused on the stunning beauty of the Olympic Mountains to the west, and on Trident: "I'm going to reflect on the wonders of creation and I'm going to, I hope, reflect that this is God's creation and that we are being unmindful of what we are about in this arms race and especially seemingly unmindful of the awesome nature of the weapons," he said.[118]

I began to read an April 1982 report (marked "Confidential") by the Naval Investigative Service (NIS) of the U.S. Department of the Navy, sent with a cover memorandum from the NIS director to the director of the Federal Bureau of Investigation. The topic had to do with demonstrations surrounding the anticipated arrival of the first Trident submarine, and included significant references to Hunthausen as well as Douglass:

> "Anti-Trident dissident groups have been protesting the existence of Naval Submarine Base Bangor, since about 1975. These groups

feel that the Trident system is a 'first strike' weapon and is therefore morally and legally wrong.... The whole thrust of the movement has been to stop the Trident submarine from becoming operational. With the arrival of the USS Ohio in the summer of 1982, they have their first opportunity to stage a protest action that could accomplish this goal. These organizations have threatened to blockade the Hood Canal preventing the Ohio from reaching Navsubase Bangor.... Ground Zero is the primary anti-Trident group that poses the greatest threat to the uneventful arrival of the USS Ohio.... In June 1981 Douglass purchased a one acre plot of land near the southern rail entrance to Navsubase Bangor. These rail lines are critical to the function of the base.... In late 1981, protest activity directed against the Trident project increased dramatically. Hunthausen, Catholic Archbishop of Seattle, called Navsubase Bangor the 'Auschwitz of Puget Sound' and he threatened to withhold fifty percent of his taxes to protest nuclear arms. The media devoted and continues to devote an inordinate amount of coverage to the archbishop. The archbishop's speech touched off a debate within the religious community and most leaders side with him against nuclear weapons. The Seattle Ecumenical Religious Peace Action Coalition organized church groups to hold 'prayer vigils' at the gates of Navsubase Bangor every Sunday afternoon. The archbishop is a leader with stature and easy access to the media. His position made participation in anti-Trident demonstrations legitimate.... Ground Zero announced plans to blockade the Hood Canal upon its (USS Ohio) arrival and Archbishop Hunthausen stated he would join in this blockade.... The largest demonstration this base has faced was approximately 5000 people in 1978.... Indications are that the Aug. '82 protest will be much larger.... Violence is not anticipated as long as Ground Zero's non-violent philosophy is followed.... The threat to Navsubase Bangor has never been greater. Dissidents such as Douglass have spent years trying to stop the Trident triad (submarine-base-missile) from coming together. In the case of Douglass, the anti-Trident movement is his occupation and preoccupation. He and his closest followers are totally dedicated to stopping it.... He states that his followers must be prepared to risk their lives and suffer to the end to stop Trident. Although Douglass has been non-violent in the past, this is no guarantee he will remain so. He is totally committed to stopping the USS Ohio. What risks will he take? How aggressive will he be? Only more in depth intelligence or time will tell."[119]

Three observations struck me on that Good Friday, pondering this report thirty years after it was made: 1) Douglass never broke his commitment to the philosophy and practice of nonviolence; he and others with him never let up in their effort to nonviolently resist what they saw as a massive war machine; 2) the head of the NIS wanted the FBI director to understand that Archbishop Hunthausen's involvement was making participation in the anti-Trident demonstrations legitimate; and 3) the federal government, certainly Secretary John Lehman's Navy, expressed serious concern about the anti-Trident campaign—especially the anticipated attempt to blockade the USS Ohio.

On June 1, 1982, FBI chief William Webster wrote to Captain Joseph Soriano, NIS head, indicating the FBI could not "conduct an investigation of the group(s) reportedly planning the demonstrations." It seemed clear that the group (Ground Zero) "has a history of nonviolent activity, and has publicly stated it has nonviolent intentions; that being so, the group does not come within the AG (Attorney General) Guidelines which govern the conditions under which we can conduct an investigation."[120] Webster assured Soriano that the FBI's Seattle office would be "closely monitoring this situation" and would take whatever action was deemed appropriate depending on events. But the files also showed that Soriano persisted in making the case to Webster. The FBI should coordinate with the Department of Justice "to determine courses of action open to the Bureau to develop substantive information regarding the identity, strength, plans and intentions of those who currently contemplate the conduct of civil disobedience and blockade against the OHIO. This determination may also serve as guidance for response to subsequent threats to military functions by anti-nuclear groups." Webster needed to understand that time was growing short, so Soriano wrote again in mid-June 1982, reminding Webster that the anticipated arrival of the Ohio was less than two months out.[121]

Archbishop Hunthausen was one of the most prominent mainstream religious figures anywhere contemplating civil disobedience as part of a peaceful blockade. A more frequent focus of government attention was Jim Douglass, but the records show that the government perceived the influence between Douglass, the Ground Zero Center for Nonviolent Action, and Hunthausen as significant. The U.S. Coast Guard, in coordination with the Navy and the FBI, closely tracked Ground Zero's activities. In mid-July 1982, one Coast Guard report, "Law Enforcement Special Inquiry," included this note: "The Catholic Archbishop of Seattle will bless the crews and boats taking part in the boat blockade." In a later section of this same report, minus words that could not be seen because they had been redacted with a heavy black marker, I noticed the following: "On 18 June 1982, [a word or two, presumably the name of an 'intelligence operative' marked out] provided the following information: A speaker from the Seattle Peace Coalition, [marked out] urged the congregation to become active in anti-nuclear activities. [Marked out] spoke to [marked out] about the dangers involved in blockade activities. [Marked out] informed [marked out] the Archbishop's vessel would be piloted by a LCDR (NFI) in the Coast Guard."[122]

When writing in chapter three about the attempted blockade of the USS Ohio, I failed to emphasize that the pilot of the witness boat was the boat's owner, Fr. Harvey MacIntyre, Hunthausen's director of the Washington Catholic Conference at the time. Remember that Hunthausen, to a crowd of over six thousand activists at Point Julia on August 8, 1982, said everyone, including the Navy and the peace people, were "caught in the same system. We all struggle to live according to our beliefs." Then and later, when he and the other religious leaders went out on the water in the witness boat, the government watched them closely. In subsequent years, as Hunthausen supported the broad-based peace campaign to block the white train and its delivery of nuclear missile warheads to Bangor, he remained under federal scrutiny.

There are some suggestions of how government surveillance may have related to what happened when Hunthausen came under Vatican scrutiny. Latin America-based Penny Lernoux, the intrepid journalist, tried to document the ways she suspected the Reagan administration's links with the Holy See were "aided by quasi-government organizations which had their own lines to the Vatican."[123] The Institute on Religion and Democracy's prominent Catholic member, Michael Novak, had access. The Institute, highly critical of the Sandinistas, was supportive of Nicaraguan Archbishop Obando y Bravo, who was fiercely opposed to the Sandinistas. Lernoux had no doubt that the CIA cooperated with the papacy. But such Cold War ties and the special affinity between Reagan and John Paul II did not prove that there was some deal focused on suppressing Hunthausen.

> "The FBI's spying on Archbishop Raymond Hunthausen at least suggested links to subsequent Vatican disciplining of the Seattle prelate.... Since the FBI sometimes shares information with the CIA, it is not impossible that the data on Hunthausen was passed on to the Vatican. Hunthausen had been particularly outspoken in his opposition to the arms race, and he and Gumbleton had played key roles in persuading the U.S. bishops to write the letter on nuclear warfare. A stream of important U.S. officials had visited the Vatican in the same period, including President Reagan, Vice President Bush, Secretary of State Shultz, Defense Secretary Weinberger, and General Walters, all of whom may have complained about the bishops' peace stance, although William A. Wilson, Reagan's first ambassador to the Vatican, insisted that they did not mention the letter."[124]

As already noted, Republican activist Paul Weyrich and New Right Catholic fundamentalists, including *The Wanderer*, flooded the Vatican with criticisms of the Seattle archbishop.

> "As in Brazil, where tensions between the local church and the papacy were basically about politics, the attack on Hunthausen was not direct, allegations about religious sins serving as a smokescreen for the real attack. Hunthausen needed to be disciplined, it was said, because there was too much democracy in his archdiocese and he had sanctioned all manner of liturgical innovations. But since many other dioceses in the United States were guilty of the same practices, there was no convincing reason for Hunthausen to be singled out except for his antiwar activism."

Archbishop Pio Laghi "confirmed that Hunthausen's refusal to pay taxes for defense and his protests against nuclear weapons had been the subject of many of the complaints." But Laghi continued to insist that the Holy See never went after Hunthausen on his peace stand, regardless of the criticisms. Lernoux concluded that by "punishing Hunthausen, Rome sent a warning to the U.S. bishops to pay more attention to spiritual matters and less to political ones, and at the same time gave some of its most important allies, especially Germany and the United States, symbolic support in the controversy over the arms race."[125]

Archbishop Pio Laghi pivoted between Pope John Paul, President Reagan, the Roman Curia, and a select number of the American bishops. "Laghi, who was called upon to apply the punishment, was furious when Hunthausen went public with the matter." Laghi supported the repressive regime in Argentina during the late 1970s. As a journalist working in Latin America, Lernoux knew a lot about this. "In 1976, in the early months of the military regime, he gave a speech to the army in which he cited the church's just-war theory to sanction the military's campaign against dissent. He then blessed the troops." He ignored those who wanted him to speak out against mass torture and murder. If Laghi was the point person for Rome, William "Bill" Wilson played that role for Washington. Wilson, a member of the Knights of Malta, was appointed to serve as the U.S. ambassador to the Vatican in 1984.[126] Lernoux's account led me to another investigative work.

Gregory Vistica, in *Fall From Glory: The Men Who Sank the U.S. Navy*, tells of a three-star Lieutenant General Le Bailly, who wrote a note to Navy Secretary John Lehman in March 1982 from the state of Washington. "The Archbishop said that he plans to be in the group who, in their small boats will try to prevent the first Trident sub to sail up the Hood Canal to Bangor next summer." He added, "A couple of thoughts for the Archbishop to ponder, The Berlin Wall,

Poland—Where would he choose to live other than the U.S.—In Russia he could not speak like this. He criticized the U.S. continually—never the other side." Le Bailly had worked for Lehman at Abington, a defense consulting and contracting firm. Le Bailly "was one of the spies quietly reporting to" Lehman about Hunthausen.[127]

Also tracking Hunthausen was the Knights of Malta, a Catholic organization with ties to the CIA and the Vatican. Membership included the Reagan administration's ambassador to the Vatican, William Wilson, and Secretary of State Al Haig. Reagan's Richard Allen and Bill Casey were Knights. Vistica noted that many of Lehman's friends belonged, as did Jim Watkins, his new chief of naval operations. The Knights "disagreed not only with Hunthausen's antidefense positions, but also with his stance on homosexuals and his liberal interpretations of church doctrine. They wanted him fired, and they were a formidable alliance." Michael Schwartz, a conservative Catholic close to many prominent Republicans, "helped coordinate the effort in the United States and noted with some pride that much of the Reagan administration's national security apparatus was composed of conservative Catholics."[128]

We know that Hunthausen had infuriated Lehman. "A comment made by the Navy secretary to a friendly bishop then located in Montana—that he was out to get Hunthausen and that he would do it before a certain date—had circulated widely within church circles. It would be a calculated risk on Lehman's part, but the odds were not all that bad when the conservatives weighed in on the side of the Navy." There were conservative bishops who "feared that Hunthausen was becoming the symbolic head of a peace movement within the church that actively opposed not only the Navy's Trident sub program, but Reagan's plan to modernize the nation's nuclear arsenal. A similar alarm struck Lehman and other conservative Republicans, who were concerned that under Hunthausen's leadership the church's rank and file could become a formidable foe of the administration."[129] Vistica continues:

> "Lehman's spies, the Knights of Malta, and conservative Republicans continued to shadow Hunthausen until the controversy reached a climax. This coalition funneled information to Wilson at the Vatican, and Wilson in turn rang the administration's bells that something had to be done about the American bishops—and Hunthausen. Finally the Vatican moved to silence Hunthausen. The Holy See ordered an investigation that focused on Hunthausen's liberal interpretations of the scriptures, primarily his push for more freedoms for women and homosexuals in the church. Although the Vatican did not acknowledge Hunthausen's antiwar protests, privately Pope John Paul, who had a reputation as a staunch anticommunist, was trying to establish strong

> ties with the Reagan administration. The Vatican felt it had no choice but to strip Hunthausen of his powers."[130]

That's how Vistica saw the matter. When I spoke with Jim Douglass, he urged a close look at the investigative work of Gordon Thomas and Max Morgan-Witts, who in 1984 published *Averting Armageddon: The Pope, Diplomacy, and the Pursuit of Peace*, a U.S. censored edition, that in its uncensored version was entitled *The Year of Armageddon: The Pope and the Bomb*. Douglass wrote to the authors in early 1986. He had just finished re-reading *Averting Armageddon*.

> "A particular reason why I found your book both illuminating and alarming comes from my being a good friend of Archbishop Raymond Hunthausen of Seattle.... It is not what you say specifically about the Vatican's attitude toward Archbishop Hunthausen which alarms me—that I already knew—but rather the ramifications of other information, such as the remark on page 277 that William J. Casey and the CIA have explained to John Paul how they are 'updating the strategy formulated by a predecessor, Richard Helms, to combat clerical dissidents.'"

Douglass wanted to know more about the updated strategy.[131]

Thomas and Morgan-Witts, like Carl Bernstein and Marco Politi (*His Holiness: John Paul II and the Hidden History of Our Time*), were criticized for alleged embellishments of "journalistic fantasy" in their work. George Weigel claimed that all the theories about a supposed "Holy Alliance" between John Paul II and Ronald Reagan were left-wing fairy-tales. Douglass did not agree. His own life under government surveillance gave him good reason to believe their claims probably had substance. When studying the files Milner had loaned to me, I found documents showing that U.S. authorities had been tracking Douglass as far back as the late 1960s. One FBI file dated October 1969 reported on Douglass teaching at the University of Notre Dame. He was taking a year's leave from his post as assistant professor of religion at the University of Hawaii, where he had already been involved in civil disobedience against the war in Vietnam. The FBI described him as "a leading figure in The Resistance here" and said his work, such as *The Non-Violent Cross,* "constructs a proposal for revolutionary action through non-violence based on the traditions of the Judeo-Christian faith and the experiments in truth of Gandhi." An October 15, 1969 "Resistance" Mass was held, according to the FBI file, "at the reflecting pool in front of the Memorial Library on the campus of the University of Notre Dame." Though heavily redacted, the documents show that the FBI kept a close eye on the relationship between religion and resistance. In that case Douglass and others were explicitly linking their nonviolent civil disobedience to a liturgy in the faith tradition of Notre Dame. The FBI wrote in its report on Douglass that the Mass at Notre Dame "was held in conjunction with the October Moratorium which called for an end to the war in Vietnam." As part of the liturgy, "six men from UND…tore up their draft cards."[132] With a long history of watching Douglass, the FBI began to track the developing relationship between him and Hunthausen.

On the other hand, Douglass was trying to trace the relationship between the White House and the Vatican. And he saw evidence in *Averting Armageddon* pointing toward ties between Washington and Rome. One of those links involved the Sovereign Military Order of Malta. Consider this passage from *Averting Armageddon*:

> "Both the CIA and the Vatican know that now, more than ever before, it is essential for the Holy See never openly to be seen to ally itself with the political aims of the CIA and the Reagan administration. Working through the order—an honorific society, in the case of the United States, of the country's leading Catholics—the CIA can more safely engage in wider and longer-term contacts with the papacy than its Rome station could ever achieve. Using the order, Casey has opened a sophisticated conduit which allows the CIA, on an indirect and informal basis, to exchange ideas and opinions with the Pope.… There are powerful emissaries in the order who can convey the CIA's views to John Paul, in that essential 'informal' way which distances the agency from the papacy."

Knights of Malta members reinforced to the Pope the CIA view that Latin American liberation theology was a great danger to the church.[133] Some of them may have reinforced to the Vatican a view that there was a troublesome archbishop in Seattle, a North American manifestation of liberation theology.

Could there be firmer evidence allowing us to move beyond suggestions and speculations? Fr. Mike Ryan encouraged me to contact John Driscoll. I reached him by phone at his home in Hamilton, Montana. He was tenaciously trying to uncover evidence that might confirm suspected ties—specifically regarding Hunthausen—between the White House and Rome. Driscoll's own experience drove his search. In September 1983, about the same time that Archbishop Hunthausen was in Rome pleading that the apostolic visitation ought to be conducted in the open, Captain John Driscoll was on active duty with fellow army personnel in a forest near Frankfurt, West Germany. A U.S. army general asked if anyone was from Montana. Driscoll replied that he was and asked the general where he was from. When he replied, "Anaconda," Driscoll said, "Oh, then you must know Dutch Hunthausen!" The general then said, "Oh, yeah. My brother's working with a group out in Seattle that's about to take care of him."[134]

Driscoll, now a retired colonel, grew up in Butte, Miles City, and the Bitterroot Valley, and spent thirty years serving as an army officer. He was on the Joint Staff, working in the new section of the Pentagon, on September 11, 2001. He has written that several years of reflection about "what could have been lost to the world that day, had the attack been nuclear, have caused Driscoll to read the thoughts of Catholic thinkers, regarding the morality of nuclear war." Remembering what the general had said in the forest outside Frankfurt, he decided to dive into research in the Reagan Presidential Library and archives at other locations around the nation. The full record of his investigative research can be found in a series of articles in his web-based *Steward Magazine*. I draw from his work here, including "The Storm of a Lifetime."[135]

According to Driscoll's interpretation of the record, the Vatican helped the Reagan White House by trying to quiet Hunthausen on the issue of nuclear weapons. This may have been done with a wink and a nod, but it definitely happened. Controlling Hunthausen served the conservative Vatican's purpose of wanting to cow the rest of America's liberal hierarchy until many were replaced or discredited. Hunthausen was the target of religious and secular powers working together. He was subjected to an assault—without tying the assault to its true source—in order to hamper his credible effective moral and nonviolent leadership to end nuclear weapons. Let us now see how Driscoll arrived at this conclusion.

Close ties between the White House and the Vatican, both intent on pressuring the Soviet Union, began early in the Reagan administration. Some national security policy-makers, who happened to be Catholic, such as Reagan's National Security Adviser William Clark, spent time with John Paul II. Clark, together with William Casey, CIA Director, often met with Archbishop Pio Laghi on Embassy Row. Laghi, in turn, had easy access to the White House. Clark, with Dr. Chris Lehman, National Security Council Legislative Liaison and brother of Navy Secretary John Lehman, tried to convince the U.S. bishops to support the Reagan administration's approach as they were developing their pastoral letter, *The Challenge of Peace*. Secretary of the Navy Lehman had leverage to try to get the Vatican to go after Hunthausen. His brother was working for Clark, who had strong conservative Catholic ties with Wilson and the Vatican.

According to Driscoll, Clark kept in close contact with Reagan's envoy in Rome, William Wilson. There was one time when Cardinal Ratzinger met with Wilson. Although there is no explicit evidence, Driscoll believes that this meeting had to include a discussion about Hunthausen. Studying Wilson's papers, he found a message from State Department Foreign Service Officer Michael Hornblower, then working at the U.S. Embassy's Vatican desk in Rome. Hornblower informed Wilson by telex that he had an appointment on Monday, March 28, 1983 with Cardinal Ratzinger. Driscoll writes about what was implicit:

> "This message is the only document, among all of Wilson's papers, which indicates anyone from the Reagan Administration ever met with Ratzinger.... The only subject the two men had in common to discuss would have been Archbishop Hunthausen. Wilson, a convert to Catholicism, had the title "Ambassador Faux Pas," because he was so candid, enough to convince the Vatican that something dramatic needed doing about a likeable guy like Hunthausen. Being a U.S. ambassador to the Holy See was Wilson's highest personal goal, and the Vatican diplomatic corps, oldest in the world, wanted formal diplomatic recognition from the U.S. From Ratzinger, Wilson would have learned about the pending Apostolic Visitation before it became a papal secret. Though not the sort of person to go blabbing around about something that important, he would have passed the word of the reassuring disciplinary action back to Clark."[136]

The two Catholic Lehman brothers, one working with Clark and the other running the Navy, were tight. "The Navy Secretary would have got the news from his highly placed brother, who got it from Clark, who got it from Wilson's report of meeting Ratzinger."[137]

Drawing on Gregory Vistica's research, Driscoll learned that John Lehman had talked with Elden Curtiss, who at the time was the Catholic Bishop of Helena. He recently arranged to meet with Archbishop Emeritus Curtiss, in Omaha, Nebraska. Curtiss remembered one of the first things that happened when he became the bishop of Helena in 1976. "The very first letter I opened was from Cardinal John Wright's office in the Vatican, telling me, 'You've got a laicized priest saying Mass out there. What are you going to do about it?" The priest was Fr. Mike Miles, who ten years later wrote *Love Is Always*.[138] Curtiss disagreed with Miles' interpretation of what happened. No surprise, since Miles painted Hunthausen as the pastoral bishop and Curtiss as the Vatican enforcer. When the Miles book was published in 1986, Archbishop Hunthausen, by then under intense Vatican scrutiny, said he did not agree with the claim Miles made that he had been given permission by Hunthausen to exercise a married priesthood for five years.

"Whatever a reader might construe from the book, at no time did I ever agree to, much less foster, any kind of experiment in married priesthood."[139] By referring to the Miles case, Curtiss was telling Driscoll he believed that the apostolic visitation was purely an internal church matter, even though Hunthausen's stand on nuclear weapons made some of the bishops nervous. We can remember that confidential letter, cited in an earlier chapter, from Curtiss to Hunthausen. Helena's Curtiss and Great Falls Bishop Murphy had to deal with all the "fallout" from Seattle Archbishop Hunthausen's Montana talks. The letter is evidence that Curtiss had been made nervous—and not by "purely internal church matters."

The letter from Curtiss to his colleague in Seattle was written in the midst of the peace pastoral drafting process, just as the White House was working to try to sway the tenor of the pastoral away from the views advocated by bishops such as Raymond Hunthausen.

Hickey, then the Archbishop of Washington, D.C., had convenient lines of communication not only with Pio Laghi, but with the White House as well. Hickey's views on the peace issue were not consonant with the Reagan folks, but he did not agree with Hunthausen's unambiguous moral refutation of deterrence. It was probably not by pure coincidence that it was Archbishop Hickey, after all, who was sent to Seattle to "visit" Hunthausen. Driscoll provides a colorful canvas for Hickey:

> "Beneath a sleeping volcano, inside an airport between the seaports of Tacoma and Seattle, a man dressed in black stepped from a jet-way into a concourse, filled with lights, cameras, microphones and reporters. Archbishop James Hickey might have slipped unannounced into the Pacific Northwest on November 2, 1983, except that he had been forced to ask Seattle's Archbishop Raymond Hunthausen, to release a joint statement downplaying the visit. Hickey wanted to pre-empt misunderstanding caused by a mysterious leak emanating from the U.S. East Coast. So, on October 27th the two archbishops made Seattle front-page news, pushing back reports of 400 Koreans protesting the September 1 Soviet shoot-down of Korea Airlines Flight 007 and funeral plans for Washington State Democrat U.S. Senator Henry 'Scoop' Jackson. Jackson was the man responsible for making the Puget Sound home to hundreds of Trident nuclear missiles, deployed in huge submarines or stored at their base, the naval ammunition supply point at Bangor, Washington, on the nearby Hood Canal. 'The Senator from Boeing' also helped advance Boeing Corporation's nuclear capable B-52 bombers and Minuteman and Cruise missiles. Unknown to anyone in the U.S., when Hickey arrived in Seattle, the Soviets perceived signs of a nuclear attack on their country by the U.S. and its NATO allies.
>
> In light of real world events, it seemed to the Soviets that our military exercises were hiding a surprise nuclear attack in peacetime. After unusually aggressive fleet exercises by the U.S. and the Soviet downing of KAL 007 as a spy plane, NATO military activity increased. The first week in September 170 aircraft, flying on radio silence, transported 16,044 U.S. troops, with their personal equipment and arms, to West Germany. Drawing pre-positioned armored and wheeled vehicles, they

> and many other troops moved close to the border with East Germany and Czechoslovakia. Then the world's airwaves filled with an October burst of secret communications fitting doctrinal templates for 'Nuclear consultation in NATO.' In reality that encrypted U.S. and U.K. traffic concerned the October 25 U.S. invasion of the Queen of England's tiny island of Grenada. Now more activity had started around NATO's command centers. In Seattle's layer of reality everyone questioned if Hickey's Apostolic Visitation was for Hunthausen's protests against nuclear weapons."[140]

Hickey, as previously noted, waylaid such speculation by saying the visit was purely about internal church matters. He and his two assistants spent the next several days deposing clergy, religious and laity, reviewing documents, and engaging in several hours of intense discussion with Hunthausen. "On November 8 they departed at the height of the worst nuclear war scare since the Cuban Missile Crisis. As Hickey stepped back into the jet-way for Washington, D.C. the Soviets expected a secret U.S. nuclear attack within 36 hours, and began their doctrinal response, which is to strike sooner with their nuclear weapons." Driscoll writes that nuclear war seemed almost inevitable. When the crisis ended on November 11, Hickey was writing his secret report. Ten days later, Vatican Secretary of State Cardinal Agostino Casaroli arrived in D.C. On November 22, Casaroli and Laghi met informally with President Reagan, and again the next day in a more official meeting to finalize details of U.S. formal recognition of the Holy See.[141]

Driscoll was fastidiously detailed in his research. Reagan's close friend, Judge William Clark, did not attend the November 23 meeting because by that time he was no longer serving as Reagan's National Security Adviser. Nancy Reagan thought Clark had been pulling her husband too far to the right. Clark had asked Dr. Chris Lehman to serve as Legislative Liaison for the National Security Council, and in that capacity Lehman interacted with Milwaukee Democratic Congressman Clement Zablocki. Zablocki, who backed the Nuclear Freeze effort, was also the author of a house resolution that would enable funding of a U.S. diplomatic mission to the Holy See. On December 31, 1983, the State Department announced that formal diplomatic relations with the Vatican would begin the next day. Just a few days later, the White House put out the word that President Reagan would be nominating William Wilson as the first U.S. ambassador to the Holy See.[142]

Congressman Zablocki was based in Milwaukee, Wisconsin, as was the Catholic League for Religious and Civil Liberties. Jesuit Fr. Virgil Blum founded the Catholic League in 1973. Theologically and politically conservative, the Catholic League avidly advocated for formal diplomatic relations between the U.S. and the Vatican. Blum saw blatant anti-Catholicism in the 1867 law that had for over one hundred years prohibited the use of federal funds to support formal diplomatic ties. When formal ties were finally made, Blum described it as "a great triumph that routine diplomatic business in the national interest can at last be openly conducted with the Vatican." Blum and the Catholic League worked with Zablocki and Senator Richard Lugar to overcome what Blum called a "petty and childish symbol of religious bigotry."[143] Driscoll found many "Virg" and "Clem" letters in Zablocki's files indicating that Blum and Zablocki were close. Going through Blum's files, Driscoll made an interesting discovery: a contract historian for the CIA was also working for the Catholic League.

Driscoll points out that when Dr. Anthony Czajkowski, the CIA historian, was at the Catholic League, his immediate supervisor was a young priest named Fr. Peter Stravinskas. Stravinskas gave testimony in support of Wilson's confirmation at a Senate Foreign Relations Committee meeting in early February 1984. Despite the fact that here was opposition to Vatican recognition, by February 21, Wilson was confirmed as the first U.S. ambassador. Wilson had full diplomatic credentials at the Vatican and Laghi in turn had the same at the White House. Driscoll interviewed Stravinskas in May 2013. Stravinskas had already been with the Catholic League more than a year before Reagan was first elected and Laghi was posted to D.C. When he spoke with Driscoll, Stravinskas made clear what he thought of Hunthausen. "The man is a heretic. He was running a Protestant archdiocese out there. Jadot should never have appointed him. It was incredible what was going on out there in both the Diocese of Helena and the Archdiocese of Seattle. I worked in Idaho 5 years, I know. There was already a body of complaints from priests and religious in Laghi's office. John Paul knew this." Stravinskas could still picture the "tense-muscled look of anger that swept his friend Laghi's face, as Chicago's Cardinal Joseph Bernardin unexpectedly opened a discussion about the Vatican's treatment of Hunthausen."[144]

Stravinskas coordinated the May 1983 tenth anniversary celebration of the founding of the Catholic League. Pio Laghi went to New York's St. Patrick's Cathedral for the Solemn Papal High Mass and for a dinner afterward at the Waldorf-Astoria. President Reagan was to be the recipient of the Catholic League's "Pope John Paul II Religious Freedom Award" but could not attend the fête in the Big Apple, so Stravinskas, Blum, Czjakowski, and Catholic League Secretary Ann Brosnan met at the White House to give Reagan the award. As Driscoll writes, Reagan asked Stravinskas and Blum "to stay behind for a chat, during which Blum complained about the failure of public funding for Catholic schools. Reagan calmed him saying, 'I'm not your enemy Father. Your enemy is the National Conference of Catholic Bishops."[145]

It turns out that the Catholic League's Director of Public Affairs was Michael Schwartz, who came up in Gregory Vistica's *Fall From Glory*. Vistica claimed

Schwartz, a conservative Catholic who was tight with prominent Republicans, coordinated the effort—strongly pushed by Navy Secretary John Lehman—to go after Hunthausen. So Driscoll interviewed Schwartz in 2012. Schwartz could not recall the 1990s interview with Vistica, but he did not deny that there had been a concerted effort to target Seattle's archbishop. He told Driscoll that he thought perhaps the Vatican's investigation of Hunthausen came about "because of his high profile."[146]

Driscoll, anxious to learn more about Navy Secretary John Lehman's role, followed up on other leads from Vistica's research. In Lehman's archived files, Vistica had found hand-written notes by U.S. Air Force General Le Bailly, in which Le Bailly let Lehman know Archbishop Hunthausen said he planned to be in the group that would try to stop the first Trident sub from sailing to Bangor. Driscoll looked up Le Bailly's son, Stephen, a combat helicopter pilot. His father had worked for Lehman's Abington Corporation and also consulted for Boeing. Stephen Le Bailly remembered hearing from his dad that Lehman was determined to do something about Hunthausen. He told Driscoll about Melvyn Paisley, who worked as Lehman's Assistant Secretary for Research, Engineering and Systems. In the years prior to Reagan's election to the White House, Paisley handled international sales for Boeing Aerospace in Seattle and managed Boeing's relationship with Lehman's Abington Corporation. By December 1981, then working for the Navy Secretary, Paisley was in charge of the Trident II D5 missile development program, which the Reagan administration was accelerating. Trident was getting a lot of media attention in part because Archbishop Hunthausen had called its Bangor base "the Auschwitz of Puget Sound." Lehman assigned his monitoring of Hunthausen to Paisley out in Seattle.[147]

Remembering his personal experience in the West German forest back in 1983, Driscoll started looking for connections between Paisley and the person he figured must have been working with a group in Seattle to "take care of Hunthausen." Charles "Chuck" McLean was a graduate of Anaconda Public High. McLean worked for Paisley on the Minuteman missile in Boeing's Applied Physics Laboratory, back in the 1960s. Driscoll tracked down his son, Mark McLean. Mark's dad worked at various points with Fluke Engineering, Trident manufacturer Lockheed, and Boeing. Fluke had an arrangement with Lockheed on the Trident missile. All this Cold War military-industrial linkage was TOP SECRET thirty years ago, writes Driscoll. By the late 1970s, Chuck McLean was popular, respected, and active in the Catholic Church around Seattle, especially the Knights of Columbus. Chuck McLean was really no enemy of Archbishop Hunthausen. In fact, McLean had sponsored his fellow Anacondan to be a Fourth Degree Knight. One member of the local Knights Council (at Saint Brendan's Parish in Bothell) remembered Hunthausen missing Vocation Night and sending a representative because he had to be at an anti-nuclear weapons demonstration. What did Driscoll learn from the local council? "They were adamant that, regardless of the problems Hunthausen might have encountered from 'letting homosexuals get close to the liturgy' or protesting nuclear weapons, no one in the Washington State Knights of Columbus would ever 'back door' him with the Vatican. He was too widely loved and respected."[148]

The Knights put Driscoll in touch with Mike Hanrahan, an old fishing buddy of Chuck McLean. He and McLean had started the Bothell Council of the Knights. Hanrahan told Driscoll that McLean and Hunthausen had a positive relationship. As any researcher into complex interpersonal and social history might expect, Driscoll was getting different interpretations. McLean's son, Mark, told Driscoll that his dad was "not happy about Hunthausen protesting against Trident nuclear weapons 'with his collar on.'" His dad frequently said, "It's as though Hunthausen's speaking for the Catholic Church, when he's just speaking for himself." Driscoll also spoke with another of Chuck McLean's sons, Mike. He felt that the relationship between his dad and Hunthausen was "not all it should be at times." Driscoll writes, "I decided to visit a second time with Hanrahan about the impression I'd gotten from McLean's two sons that their father disagreed with Hunthausen taking such public positions while wearing the collar." Did Hanrahan think McLean was torn by conflicting feelings he had about Hunthausen? "No way. You've got to understand these were grown men. They're supposed to disagree and they told each other as much."[149]

This image of two friends disagreeing led Driscoll to at last try to make direct contact with the army general whose brother out in Seattle was working "to take care of Hunthausen." General William "Tim" McLean, a graduate of Anaconda Central High School, which happened to be the school also attended by Raymond Hunthausen, was the person Driscoll had talked with there in the forest outside Frankfurt. Driscoll reached Tim McLean by phone, 28 years after their encounter.

> "This time the General was more reflective, and he told me that at times 'Charles' could be a little hot-headed. He remembered his brother telling him that, during Mass, he asked the rest of the Congregation to pray for members of the Clergy who wanted to withhold taxes that bought protective equipment for people like his brother Tim who risked his life in Vietnam. McLean told the General that Hunthausen, having just given a homily to the same Congregation on the subject of withholding taxes, was furious. This still made the General laugh."[150]

In Driscoll's view, Raymond Hunthausen was targeted by the Reagan administration—including some of the inner circle who were politically and theologically conservative Catholics and some of whom were Knights of Malta—because, as an influential archbishop, he had become such a prominent voice in the peace movement very early in the Reagan era. Pio Laghi, in particular, used the attitude and network relations of the Catholic League to help achieve two objectives, including the relationship the Vatican wanted with the U.S. government and the critical energy the Vatican wanted to direct toward certain liberal bishops. Paul Weyrich and the numerous "truth squad" attacks on Hunthausen meshed with the outlook and activity of the Catholic League. The connections between Navy Secretary Lehman, his brother, and the Catholic Right, were part of the multi-faceted attacks. It did not matter that Hunthausen was seen by almost all who came to know him as a likable guy. To the array of forces aligned against him, as a representative symbol he was not likable.[151] The 1984 establishment of formal diplomatic relations between the Holy See and the U.S. government aided the Vatican of John Paul II and Cardinal Ratzinger in their effort to control American Catholicism, especially the liberal bishops and the NCCB. It helped, more specifically, with the effort to control a high profile Hunthausen, who was taking the church in a direction unattractive to the Vatican and calling his country in a direction inimical to the White House.

In the late 1980s, I had a conversation with a key member of the Seattle business community who wished to remain anonymous. He told me that within the Puget Sound area there were people in the business community who viewed the Trident submarine and missile system as a vital peacekeeper. Some members of the business community respected Archbishop Hunthausen's sincere convictions while believing him to be misinformed. Some thought he relied too heavily on the counsel of pacifists like Jim Douglass. A top executive at Boeing told me that several business leaders in the region were incensed by Hunthausen's anti-Trident stand and his war tax resistance. The nation needed a strong military. This Boeing executive voiced the popular "peace through strength" argument. Archbishop Hunthausen's tax resistance had the potential to incite anarchy and disrespect for the rule of law. The religious leader's rhetoric was at times inflammatory, claimed this critic. At the same time, he thought Hunthausen was courageous and holy, a person who often played a creative role in public dialogue on many issues.[152]

Don Hopps believes that many of the local power players in the area liked Hunthausen. "He had the same kind of aura Pope Francis has. He was especially well liked by the media, not only the working stiffs but also the owners. The major media power player in Seattle at the time was the Bullitt Family led by Patsy Collins. Also, he fit this area's interest profile to a tee—from his progressive politics (during this era, Washington was still the last bastion of progressive Republicanism) to his interest in the outdoors." There was no monolithic local power elite, no single power structure. Rather, there were several overlapping structures such as media, political, corporate, labor, and "old" money, and the "operative" power structure would vary depending on the issue.[153]

Whether trying to fathom the power complexities regionally or nationally, as Hopps argues, one would have to look at the details closely. At the national level, some of the overlapping structures, cultural values, and power players come more clearly into focus if we zero in, briefly, on Ronald Reagan's top hand, Judge William Clark. A devout Catholic, in his younger years he had been influenced by St. Augustine, St. Francis of Assisi, G.K. Chesterton, Thomas Merton (early writings), and Fulton Sheen. Famous Catholic convert Clare Boothe Luce, who promoted Merton's own conversion story, *Seven Storey Mountain*, knew Clark. In the 1950s, Bishop Fulton Sheen had an influential television program, and his *Communism and the Conscience of the West* affected Clark.[154] When Clark was serving as National Security Adviser for President Reagan, he brought with him a Catholicism wary of the Soviet Union and any groups involved in communist thought.

Eugene Kennedy, who was close to Chicago's Bernardin, told me that Clark was angry over the direction the U.S. bishops were taking in the early stages of the peace pastoral. Clark was the lead agent from the Reagan administration trying to move the bishops away from ideas—especially the challenge to the core notion of deterrence—promoted by Hunthausen and other Pax Christi bishops.[155] Clark, who passed away in August 2013, was perhaps Reagan's most trusted friend and ally in D.C. It was during his tenure as Reagan's national security adviser that he had great influence, especially reinforcing Reagan's pressure on the Soviet Union. Clark arranged a key meeting between Reagan and John Paul II, at which the two leaders shared their common concern to support the struggle for freedom in Poland and Eastern Europe. In an interview a few years ago, Clark was asked about this relationship between the two leaders. "I firmly believe that President Reagan and Pope John Paul II are most responsible for the fall of the Soviet empire, which had enslaved 300 million people prior to its surrender and dissolution. The two men shared the belief that atheistic Communism lived a lie that, when fully understood, must ultimately fall."[156]

This Clark trail leads from the White House to the Vatican. While there may not have been a full blown "holy alliance," there was a special affinity between the Reagan presidency and the John Paul II papacy. Clark was at its center. For the official biography about Clark, *The Judge*, Paul Kengor and Patricia Clark Doerner sat down with Clark to learn about the links. Poland was seen by both Clark and Reagan as "the hub of the Soviet empire—of the seven adjoining countries, second only in priority to Russia itself," Clark told them. Crack open the Iron Curtain in Poland, and much more might happen. A most significant meeting between Reagan and John Paul took place on June 7, 1982. By then Clark had been with the National Security Council just half a year. Clark went to Rome early to help prepare for the historic rendezvous. He met with Vatican officials, "and before the President arrived, Clark conferred with the Pontiff for a couple of hours, the first of several discussions they would have in the years ahead."[157] Pope John Paul II and President Reagan, face to face in a room at the Vatican Library, talked about the attempted assassinations both had survived the prior year. They had another thing in common, a desire to help bring about the collapse of communism in the Soviet bloc.[158]

Clark was struck by how both men described their survival as "miraculous" and how they saw their work as part of a Divine Plan to help rid the world of atheistic communism. Clark's role then was to concentrate energy on developing a strategy dedicated to that end. The White House and Vatican relationship developed in ways that may have impacted Hunthausen. In Washington, D.C., William Clark and another Catholic on the Reagan team, CIA director William Casey, met frequently with Archbishop Pio Laghi. On occasion, they had coffee or breakfast together and discussed whatever might have been of common concern, especially Poland. Reagan's attorney general, Edwin Meese, told the authors of *The Judge* that Clark and Casey "would brief Laghi on items the Reagan team thought the Pope should know…Laghi, in turn, would do the same from his end."[159] Clark and Laghi developed close professional and personal ties. At some point they probably discussed a high profile archbishop out in the Pacific Northwest who, as reported in papers including *Washington Post*, called a nuclear submarine base "the Auschwitz of Puget Sound."

By 1982, as the Reagan administration moved full speed ahead with record level military spending on many fronts, the anti-nuclear movement, especially the nuclear freeze movement, was building some momentum to challenge the escalation. With MX missile deployment plans, the plan for Pershing II missiles, the B-I bomber, the Trident fleet, and on and on, the Reagan administration was all hands on deck. In such a context, the National Conference of Catholic Bishops took on the development of the peace pastoral, and Clark, in response, took on a special role with the bishops. He was in contact with Bernardin, the head of the pastoral letter committee, and with others, such as Hickey, right there in D.C.[160] One of the prelates more likely to share some of the sentiments of the Reagan administration was New York's Cardinal Terence Cooke, who affirmed Reagan's belief that he had a divine mission. On Good Friday, April 17, 1981, just a couple of weeks after the assassination attempt, Cooke told President Reagan that the hand of God was upon him.[161] Cooke and Hunthausen were not on the same page regarding nuclear deterrence. Even so, Cooke was not as conservative as his predecessor Cardinal Spellman and folks like Bishop Fulton Sheen from the era when American Catholicism and anti-communism often went hand in hand.

Clark needed allies to try to influence the drift of the pastoral letter, since such a document could influence the largest religious demographic in the nation. Clark had ties with another famous Catholic anti-communist, Clare Boothe Luce. Clark and Reagan looked to her. "Clare was there at the core of the team," Clark told the authors of *The Judge*. "She was enormously helpful." Other Catholic heavyweights trying to draw the bishops away from the kind of outlook espoused by Hunthausen included Michael Novak. In that time period, and especially into 1983, when the National Conference of Catholic Bishops raised serious concerns about the administration's policies in Central America, the bishops and Reagan did not see eye to eye. As Hopps had cautioned, to understand the power dynamics at work, one needed to look at each issue and each relationship. In 1984, Clark and Reagan had another occasion to meet briefly with the Pope from Poland. By then, Clark was serving as Secretary of the Interior. It turned out that Pope John Paul II was stopping over in Fairbanks, Alaska to refuel en route to South Korea. Reagan was coming home from an historic visit to China. This was the first meeting between the pontiff and the president since formal diplomatic relations between them had been established.[162] The two were close on their Cold War outlook, including on Central America, especially their common vexation over the Nicaraguan Sandinistas. From the very beginning of the Reagan first term, Secretary of State Al Haig had firmly linked the Reagan approach to the Soviet Union directly to the proxy battles in Central America. This linkage had not been entirely absent from the Carter administration before, especially when the Sandinistas came to power in 1979 and the Soviets invaded Afghanistan. The kind of thinking coming out of the White House once Haig and Clark were handling Reagan's "State and Security" operations resonated with the Vatican's deep distrust of liberation theology and its use of Marxist social analysis. This is why we must not take lightly the implications of the claims of some of Hunthausen's critics that he was fostering a North American version of liberation theology. His critique of U.S. nuclear policy went hand in hand with his critique of U.S. policy in Central America.

What held the Reagan team and the Polish pope's team together, even though they did not concur on any number of other issues, was their common antipathy toward all things tinged with communism. The Chinese communists would not let John Paul visit their country. The Soviets were oppressing his own homeland. Liberation theology in Latin America was giving support to Marxist critiques. And in the United States, even if they were not communist sympathizers, there were some bishops who seemed to be willing to leave the country defenseless before the Soviet Union. Moreover, a significant number of West German and French bishops were concerned about the possibility that their U.S. counterparts might undercut the moral backing for nuclear deterrence. People living in countries near the Iron Curtain depended on nuclear deterrence for their defense against an otherwise overwhelming Soviet army.

As a matter of fact, back in 1979, when Pope John Paul II first flew to his native land, he was accompanied by the cardinal of Munich, Joseph Ratzinger, along with Cardinal Krol, who had his own deep roots in Poland.[163] Krol, like Cardinal Cooke, did not concur with the unilateral nuclear disarmament arguments of Hunthausen. Wary of the Soviet threat, Cooke firmly, and Krol perhaps ambivalently, held to a nuanced argument, as did John Paul II. They supported conditional acceptance of nuclear deterrence if efforts were being made toward eventual nuclear disarmament. During that first trip to Poland as pontiff, John Paul II visited Auschwitz. After walking through the camp entrance with its infamous "*Arbeit Macht Frei*" hanging above the gate, he delivered an emotional speech comparing the camp to the place where Jesus Christ had been crucified. "This is the Golgotha of the modern world." John Paul II met with survivors of the death camp, including priests whose forearms displayed identification numbers the Nazis had tattooed on them. John Koehler writes in *Spies in the Vatican: The Soviet Union's Cold War Against The Catholic Church*: "For the rest of his time as pope, it seems that John Paul II paid special attention to memorializing the Holocaust. Perhaps this visit to Auschwitz was a watershed for that as well."[164] Karol Wojtyla, after studying in secret during the Nazi occupation, had been ordained in 1946, the same year as Raymond Hunthausen. Just as Pope Paul VI would appoint Hunthausen to Seattle, he appointed Wojtyla to Krakow. Each time John Paul II returned to his homeland, he called on the people to resist the forces of tyranny. When he and Cardinal Krol heard the news that Seattle's archbishop was comparing a U.S. nuclear submarine base to Auschwitz, they probably did not feel the metaphor was appropriate.

On the other hand, during the process of the pastoral letter on peace, Krol voiced the notion that if it is wrong to use a weapon, it is also wrong to threaten to use it. So Krol was questioning the central notion of nuclear deterrence, since Defense Secretary Caspar Weinberger made it clear that nuclear deterrence depended for its viability on the belief that the threat was real. Bishop Gumbleton at one point specifically asked Weinberger if deterrence was only a threat. Weinberger explicitly said that it was not merely a threat. So it would be a mistake to imply that Krol was in full agreement with the Reagan administration's nuclear policy. Perhaps for Krol the greater concern about Hunthausen had to do with the issue of control of the church itself. In Philadelphia, Cardinal Krol ran a tight ship, and from his vantage point, Hunthausen had simply lost control of Seattle.[165]

Another figure in Reagan-JPII relations was Vatican Secretary of State Cardinal Agostino Casaroli, who visited the White House in mid-December 1981, discussing, among other things, the planning for Reagan's June 1982 trip to meet with the pope. At that time, martial law had been imposed in Poland. Stirrings of freedom and the organizing of Solidarity at the Gdansk shipyards and elsewhere were being crushed. Lech Walesa, elected to chair the labor movement's Solidarity that would ultimately play a pivotal role in the downfall of the puppet regime, was under arrest. On the eve of that meeting with Casaroli, Reagan telephoned John Paul II to express his shock and that of the American people over the crackdown in Poland. "Your Holiness, I want you to know how deeply we feel about the situation in your homeland.... Our country was inspired when you visited Poland, and to see the people's commitment to religion and belief in God. It was an inspiration for the whole world to watch on television.... I look forward to the time when we can meet in person."[166]

By June 1983, John Paul II was back in Poland, while at the same time, Ronald Reagan was in Chicago to address the Polish National Alliance and the Polish American Congress. Reagan told his audience that, despite the brutality of martial law, the people of Poland held their spirits high. "And the papal visit to Poland, which ends today, is truly a ray of hope for the Polish and an event of historic importance. During these short eight days, the pope's message of hope and faith has helped to inspire millions of Poles to continue their struggle to regain human rights taken from them by the Polish authorities 18 months ago."[167] Reagan and John Paul II built close White House-Vatican ties. Reagan believed, and said so, that all across the world freedom-loving people were being inspired by this pontiff. That same year, in the fall of 1983, Lech Walesa was awarded the Nobel Peace Prize. Throughout those early years of the Reagan administration, it was Cardinal John Krol of Philadelphia who kept the White House informed about Solidarity's situation.[168] It was in fact that same fall of 1983 that Archbishop Hickey was conducting his evaluation of the Seattle church.

There was a "holy alliance," at least to some noteworthy degree. The White House team included Reagan's first national security man, Richard Allen; his successor, William Clark; Secretary of State Al Haig; Reagan's Vatican liaison and eventual ambassador, William Wilson; CIA director William Casey; retired General Vernon Walters who served as Reagan's ambassador-at-large; John Lehman; and Lehman's brother, who worked for Clark. This suggests the breadth of informal and formal ties between the White House and the Vatican. The relationships did not mean there was a monolithic alliance, but they did indicate significant inter-communication. Leading Rome's team was a person with a strong thespian background, a charismatic communicator like Reagan. John Paul II had on his team Secretary of State Cardinal Casaroli and Congregation of the Doctrine of the Faith prefect Cardinal Ratzinger, as well as the prefect of the Congregation of Bishops, Cardinal Sebastian Baggio, and later Cardinal Bernard Gantin; John Paul II's D.C. liaisons, Archbishop Pio Laghi and Archbishop James Hickey; and, among other American prelates (who would have included Cardinal Terence Cooke and his successor in New York, John O'Connor), Philadelphia's Cardinal John Krol.

The "holy alliance" was a set of close personal relations and a strong worldview of "elective affinity" between a more theologically (including model of church governance) conservative brand of Catholicism and a deep Cold War political conservatism. CIA Director William Casey was a fervent Catholic who went to Mass almost daily and adorned his home with statues of the Virgin Mary. Casey played a central role in ties between the Reagan administration and the Holy See.[169] Much of that was done through covert channels. The links between Rome and Washington, with the CIA in a covert but crucial role, would have involved common concerns about the situation in Poland and the rest of Eastern Europe, as well as the situation unfolding in Central America. William Clark worked closely with Casey. Those concerns would have been part of their regular round of discussions with Pio Laghi. Archbishop Hickey, based in D.C., was in the mix. And of course it was Hickey who conducted Rome's apostolic visitation in Seattle. Cardinal Krolm figured prominently given his ancestral bonds to Poland and close connection both to Pope John Paul II and Ronald Reagan.[170]

One ego seemed to leave almost everyone else in his wake. As we saw in his March 1982 speech, John Lehman was most outspoken in his attack on Archbishop Hunthausen. Hunthausen had the audacity to "demonize" Lehman's pride and joy, the Trident submarine and the Bangor base. But Trident was the spearhead of Lehman's larger agenda that persisted for decades. Lehman seemed to embody America's military-industrial and personal superiority complexes. John Lehman long pursued massive American military might and large profits through defense contracts. He pushed for a 600-ship navy when he was with Reagan and made a similar push much more recently as adviser to Republican Presidential candidate Mitt Romney in 2012. Lehman was deep into the defense "pork barrel" before he became Reagan's navy secretary. People like Senator Henry "Scoop" Jackson's staff member, Richard Perle, who would loom large in the Project for a New American Century and a more recent period of American war-making, were linked with Lehman when he ran a defense firm early on. In the early 1970s, Lehman served under Henry Kissinger at the National Security Council, when Kissinger and the CIA were involved in the Nixon administration's covert effort to help General Augusto Pinochet oust President Salvador Allende in Chile. Raised and educated

Catholic, he saw himself a strong adherent to the true expression of the faith. He breathed dragon fire on a religious leader out in Seattle who had the audacity to call his Navy base "the Auschwitz of Puget Sound." Lehman was one of the less subtle members of the Reagan team. One twist on Lord Acton's famous phrase ("Power corrupts. Absolute power corrupts absolutely."), which Lehman apparently made into a personal motto of sorts, fit his inflated ego to a tee: "Power corrupts. Absolute power is kind of neat."[171]

OTHER FACTORS AND PERSPECTIVES

It may seem a stretch to suggest that Hunthausen's ecumenical and interfaith outreach might have been a concern to the Vatican. After all, Pope John Paul II, manifested a strong interfaith spirit of dialogue with his hosting of an historic meeting in Assisi of religious leaders from across many traditions. On the other hand, there were pockets of insular Catholics trying to protect "the true faith" in a relatively unaffiliated region of the country. Some of them saw religious indifferentism and moral relativism being smuggled in through the ecumenical movement as well as through the wider secular culture all around them. Hunthausen attended the Thursday breakfast meetings regularly and found there an ecumenical group of religious leaders with whom he could share some of his thoughts and develop some of his stands. For Catholics inclined to see the ecumenical movement and interfaith dialogue as threats to Catholicism, Hunthausen's approach to both church governance and social issues may have looked Protestant to them. Ray Hunthausen often confided in Bill Cate, Loren Arnett, and other ecumenical leaders, discussing controversies and listening to their views. His ecumenical and interfaith activity probably ended up on the radar screen of some Catholics in the region. Cardinal Ratzinger's 1985 letter did reference concerns about intercommunion. Perhaps the concern of orthodoxy watchdogs was not only the improper sharing of the communion host during the liturgy but also the ecumenical communion of minds—especially when that communion of minds and hearts helped a religious leader find the courage to move into a conscientious *protestant* ethic of civil disobedience.

His ethic of *pro test* (to witness for) was both deeply individual and communal. We know that a very important aspect of Hunthausen was the emphasis he placed on the role of individual conscience in moral decisions and actions. Some people thought Hunthausen did not adequately distinguish his personal positions from what they felt were his official duties, particularly his unifying role as bishop. This tension between being a witness for peace on the one hand and a sign of Catholic unity on the other was a factor. Hunthausen vexed Rome, because his personal conscience led him to take courageous stands on certain issues (such as war and peace, women's issues, gay and lesbian issues). If a bishop took a bold and even divisive stand that aligned with the Vatican, of course, that bishop would be rewarded for the courage of his conscience. If one looks again at Cardinal Ratzinger's 1985 letter (see chapter five), it will be noted that he raised concerns about "the role which conscience plays in making moral decisions." By his example and rhetoric, Hunthausen took bold stands in personal conscience and became prominent. The Vatican (or one should say, more precisely, those with the most clout in the Vatican) was concerned about the empowerment of individual conscience as modeled by Dutch Hunthausen.

Hunthausen became a representative character, in the sense defined by Robert Bellah and colleagues in *Habits of the Heart*. He became a personification of what many felt were the best traits of a religious leader in American public life. He was, to many people in various faith traditions and in the secular world, an exemplary individual who had the courage of his personal convictions and at the same time practiced inclusiveness and an egalitarian ethos with soft spoken tones of hospitality. He had the guts to speak truth to power. And he respected each person to honor their own conscience. To others, who thought he was leading the "one, holy, Catholic, and apostolic Church" off the cliff into liberalism and democracy, he undermined what they felt a member of the Catholic hierarchy ought to uphold.

The interpretive battle over the meaning of Vatican II itself became divisive, and Hunthausen became a symbol of one side of that battle. People who backed him often projected onto him whatever was their primary issue. He did not always meet the expectations of Catholics and others who wanted him to be their prophetic archbishop on their issues. Those who worked against him did likewise, projecting onto him whatever was ruining their traditional Catholic faith. The divisiveness he represented was probably as much a reflection of the social forces aligned against each other as a reflection of Hunthausen himself.

Fractiousness troubled him. Remember he once said: "I am in the midst of the kind of conflict that has the potential of causing serious rift in the Church. And I'm constantly talking about the need to avoid that very thing in the human family and on our world scene." Think of the irony. The Vatican investigation of Raymond Hunthausen was largely a response to his having become a representative character of the Catholic peace tradition and of Vatican II church renewal. He carried the torch passed forward to him from the long legacy that Ronald Musto chronicled in *The Catholic Peace Tradition*, a classic study of peacemaking dating back to the early church.[172] The Vatican's heavy-handed action provoked social resistance. The Vatican then blamed Hunthausen and his supporters for this tension. When he spoke up at the NCCB meeting in November 1986, and on other occasions to defend himself, he infuriated Laghi. But he did not do this to be a dissident. Rome failed to appreciate the depth of his commitment to the vision of church gained from his experience of Vatican II. Or perhaps people such as Cardinal Ratzinger actually grasped this very point and decided that Hunthausen would be a lesson for other bishops to ponder.

It seems that many factors were at work in the Vatican's effort to suppress Seattle's prophetic archbishop. Bishop Thomas Gumbleton, involved deeply in justice and peace action for half a century, recalled how Hunthausen caused quite a commotion with his war tax resistance talk in 1981. Gumbleton had already taken the same position *de facto*. He did so for years by keeping his income low enough to avoid being taxed on it, thus not feeding the coffers of the defense industry. He may well have been the person Hunthausen had in mind when, before the "Faith and Disarmament" speech, he spoke about "another bishop" having brought up the notion of war tax resistance. Gumbleton told me he was not yet convinced that the Reagan administration was the primary agent behind the Vatican investigation. "After all, Walter Sullivan and others were also being harassed by Rome. Think about Kenneth Untener of Saginaw, who was harassed by Rome, and he was not a peace activist. And Wuerl never was given authority over issues related to peace and so on." Gumbleton had much experience with the pastoral letter *The Challenge of Peace*, since he served on the drafting committee. Reagan's defense secretary, Caspar Weinberger, according to Gumbleton, "was very open about talking with the peace pastoral letter core committee about the U.S. position and expressing the Reagan view. None of the committee members ever felt harassed in any way for the positions they held."

Many years later, Rome went after Gumbleton. By this time, Cardinal Ratzinger was Pope Benedict XVI. The Vatican removed Gumbleton from his role as Auxiliary Bishop in Detroit. This was because he was so critical of the way the church failed to confront its pattern of covering up sexual abuse by priests and also because of his progressive views on homosexuality and on gender equality. In Gumbleton's view, the Hunthausen case became a way for Rome to send a message to the National Conference of Bishops.

> "Keep in mind that Cardinal Ratzinger never liked the whole structure and authority of national bishops' conferences. Over a period of time he took away the teaching authority of these national conferences of bishops. Ratzinger did not want the NCCB, or any other national conference of bishops in other places in the world (e.g. Brazil) to provide what people would see as authoritative statements. Ratzinger worked to undercut the pastoral letters of the NCCB unless they were totally in line with the Congregation for the Doctrine of the Faith."[173]

Gumbleton does think that Rome was concerned that Hunthausen, through his peace stand and in other ways, was dividing the community. "A pastor can be removed if he is seen as splitting the people up into divisions. Rome might have gone after Hunthausen because he could have been viewed as sparking division in the church in Western Washington, this is a plausible thesis," Gumbleton told me.

> "But not specifically because he was so outspoken in his opposition to U.S. military policy. Think about the case of Leroy Matthiessen. Rome may have been prompted to go after him because his stand (re: challenging Catholics to drop their work at Pantex, the nuclear arms producing plant there in his diocese in Texas) divided the people so much. In the Hunthausen case, the very areas where Wuerl was given authority were indeed likely areas of genuine concern to the Vatican—gay issues, liturgical area (women preaching, leading) where Wuerl was given authority."

The likelihood of the military stand being central as a motivating factor for the Vatican's action would be more persuasive if Hunthausen had garnered a broad following in his call for war tax resistance. He inspired many to take up this type of civil disobedience, but a broad-based war tax resistance and redirection movement never materialized.[174]

Bishop William "Bill" Skylstad, who was with Hunthausen and others in that witness boat during the Trident peace blockade in August 1982, shared with me his thoughts about his colleague. "Those were days of creative tension," he said. "Nuclear disarmament, in those days, was challenging a massive buildup, enough to blow the world up a dozen times or more. So often what happens is people's hearts change. Consider the huge price we are paying for the whole Iraq War." Think about how Hunthausen approached it all.

> "He saw the craziness of the arms race, and how any kind of flashpoint could be terribly destructive. To threaten someone is just not the way the gospel is lived.... You have to remember the context, two World Wars, the Korean War, Vietnam War, and the Cold War. Hunthausen had a deep sense of the global community, that we need to respect one another and be people of peace. The whole spirit of intimidation and nuclear deterrence was abhorrent to him. And it was a terrible waste of resources on war. Remember that Hunthausen was always very respectful of the Holy Father and his role."[175]

Skylstad never detected any bitterness toward the Vatican in his good friend Dutch.

Holy Week 2013 had just passed, it was Easter Monday morning and I had just returned from a round of interviews with folks in Seattle. Bishop Skylstad and I were sitting in a hotel café in downtown Portland. All around us were other bishops in town for the installation of a new archbishop in Portland. I asked him about the tensions involved in being a bishop, for Hunthausen or for himself, when it came to taking personal stands. Skylstad said:

> "Well a bishop has an unusual role of fostering a sense of unity and community. Hunthausen was very pastoral. In those days that was the dramatic shift from the model of bishop that was predominant before Vatican II. Hunthausen saw the role of the bishop as being deeply pastoral. He also was one who saw his role trying to bring people together from divergent viewpoints in pastoral respect. Even with regard to the Bangor situation, for example, he did a videotape to be used on board the submarines for a Eucharistic service. Regarding the church investigation, he would see that, well, as past history, not something you necessarily forget, but you move on beyond that. And with all that has happened, I can honestly say this, I've never detected a sense of bitterness on his part. There are a lot of things in life we cannot control. A deep part of our spirituality as Catholics is letting go. You know, it's like Jesus in the Garden, 'Father, not my will but yours be done.' And there's a mystery about this. We need to let go. We are tempted to grasp and hang onto the hurts, injustices. We lose all sense of perspective when this happens."[176]

PARACLETE IN THE LABYRINTH

Some people wish Hunthausen would have more assertively confronted John Paul II and Cardinal Joseph Ratzinger. He could have taken up the practice of ecclesiastical as well as civil disobedience. With courage he challenged the Vatican's narrative at the meeting of bishops in D.C. in November 1986. He could have done more, some of his supporters believed. They were ready to raise a larger ruckus. Many hoped he would resign as a matter of principle in that tense "standoff" in the spring of 1987. Hunthausen let go, forgave, and moved on, but not without going through a lot of pain. The last thing he wanted was a house divided. He wanted the church to be a more perfect union. He was not a religious rebel. Yet he was prophetic in some profound ways.

The stifling grip on Hunthausen and Vatican II left little air for him to breathe. The big sky and the fresh air in Montana, where he had retreated every August during the sixteen years he was Seattle's archbishop, must have looked better than ever when August 1991 rolled around and, at age seventy, he headed home. At the same time, he would keep ties with many people he worked with and would visit Seattle often after he retired. There was a complexity of emotions. Not one single representative from the papacy of John Paul II or from Benedict XVI's era ever made a phone call, wrote a letter, or sat down with Raymond Hunthausen to level with him candidly about just why he and the people of the Seattle archdiocese had been subjected to an "apostolic" trial, verdict, and sentencing without due process. Plenty of other victims of Rome's suppression, in plenty of other places, probably faced this same cold fact. Seattle's Archbishop Hunthausen could wait in vain for a Vatican act of contrition. But as we shall see in Part III, Hunthausen just let it all go through forgiveness.

The official line from Rome persisted: Archbishop Hunthausen's civil disobedience, his war tax resistance, his stand on nuclear disarmament, his strong stand on Central American issues, and in general his high profile influence as a voice of resistance to U.S. superpower had no part in a "purely internal and purely doctrinal" probe. A prophetic prelate from another faith tradition, Archbishop Desmond Tutu of Capetown, published a poignant account of the work of the Truth and Reconciliation Commission in South Africa near the end of the twentieth century. *No Future Without Forgiveness* almost jumped, of its own accord, off my bookshelf when I got home after the Easter Monday time with Bishop Skylstad's soft spoken reflection on forgiveness. Tutu writes that perpetrators of injustice—in some cases horrific acts—were given amnesty after the collapse of the apartheid regime if they were willing to come forward and tell the whole truth. The situation in South Africa was awful. What happened in Seattle cannot begin to compare. Yet the whole truth about what really motivated the Vatican has never been brought forward.[177]

What can be concluded about the Vatican's action and Hunthausen's response? Two words point to the heart of the Hunthausen story: faith and disarmament, his profound faith and his multi-faceted call for disarmament. Hunthausen's faith—how he envisioned it, how he practiced it, and how he encouraged others—made Rome uneasy. His call for nuclear disarmament and how he put this call into practice made the Reagan administration uneasy. The faith that guided his vision of U.S. nuclear disarmament and his denunciation of the empire's Central America policy was the same faith that guided him to take courageous stands on each of the other major issues reviewed in this book—how he challenged Rome's chronology and its restorationist ecclesiology; how he approached leadership, authority, shared responsibility, and personal conscience; how he supported women and gender equality; how he respected gays and lesbians and welcomed Dignity; basically how he handled almost every sphere where the approach he took was destined to get him into trouble. He challenged, with a disarming spirit, a fortress church and a militarized nation. His vision of peace was grounded in an ethic of social justice—understood in the biblical sense of a call to right relationships.

When Hunthausen spoke "Faith and Disarmament" in 1981, he focused on his nation. Archbishop Raymond Hunthausen told the Pacific Lutheran University audience that he believed Jesus' first call to us is to love God and our neighbor. "But when He gives flesh to that commandment by the more specific call to the cross, I am afraid that like most of you I prefer to think in abstract terms, not in the specific context in which Our Lord lived and died. Jesus' call to the cross was a call to love God and one's neighbor in so direct a way that the authorities in power could only regard it as subversive and revolutionary." Hunthausen laid out in two sentences the contours of what was to become his own fate. As this seventh chapter has illustrated, his fate was tied not only to the stands he took in the secular realm but also to the stands he took in the church.

Almost as if the Paraclete, the Holy Spirit, were being imprisoned in a labyrinth, he had to be suppressed not only because he was challenging American hegemony. His prophetic vision of faith called the church itself to disarmament and social justice. What he challenged by his way of being a bishop were the resurgent patterns of Roman Catholic authoritarianism. Hunthausen espoused shared responsibility and shared authority. His working concept of social justice was close to the notion developed by the U.S. bishops in their 1986 economic pastoral letter. They asked, what does the economy do for people, to people, and how do people participate in shaping the economy? Hunthausen asked, what do all these nuclear arms and this destructive policy in places like Central America do for the people, to them, and how do they participate in shaping this? He asked his church, what does the church do for the Catholic people, to them, and how do they participate in shaping this church?

The claim has been made by many people that the official Vatican reasons were mostly smokescreen for "the real deal," which was to put the hammer down on Hunthausen because that is what the Reagan people wanted. Pro-God, Pro-America folks—and their like-minded Reagan Catholics in the pews—got their message across to Rome. Plenty of indicators traced in this book suggest that some people high up in the Reagan administration or people closely linked to it, made deliberate efforts to encourage Vatican suppression of Hunthausen. By 1982, he was the most high profile of peace and disarmament bishops. A coalition of forces, some within the halls of secular power, others in the halls of religious power, and some folks in the pews, and in the jobs tied to the defense industry, wanted Hunthausen quieted.

John Paul II and his administration, or at least key members including Cardinal Ratzinger, did not subscribe to the unequivocal and unconditional rejection of deterrence. They did not share Hunthausen's proposition, and they were not inclined to set aside the just war tradition. By the time of the U.S. 2003 invasion of Iraq, John Paul II would develop what became a full-throated call for nonviolence as public policy. But that is not what he expressed in the context of the Cold War. He, and especially his prefect for doctrine, did not agree with Hunthausen's position on Central American issues either. Hunthausen was not the only bishop to take such a stand. But to suppress Hunthausen, both on the political matters important to the Reagan folks and on ecclesiastical matters important to Rome, was to make him an object lesson for other bishops—and for that troublesome "people of God" Vatican II movement. In some ways, Hunthausen was the liberation theology bishop of the Pacific Northwest, for liberation has that overlap of meanings that Leonardo Boff articulated in the line of reasoning that got him into Ratzinger's dog house. Justice in society and justice in religion must go hand in hand.

So there was a coalition of shared thought that included John Paul II, some of his curia and especially those who were in charge of doctrine and of D.C. relations, some U.S. prelates with considerable influence, and other prelates including West German bishops (this was the base for Ratzinger before he went to Rome in 1981) who did not want to see the U.S. bishops go down a path that could leave Western Europe open to Soviet conventional aggression. There were affinities between the White House, players in the military-industrial complex, and right-leaning Catholics in high and low places, proxy organizations, certainly in some sectors of the U.S. hierarchy itself, and in Rome. Distinct affinities did not neatly cover all the concerns. What mattered, however, was something Sr. Kathleen Pruitt pointed out earlier. Hunthausen became a lightning rod on many issues.

> "It would not have taken a rocket scientist to figure out that Hunthausen could have lifted a finger and raised an army. Think about this, he chose not to do so. He was a quiet charismatic authority, but he could have raised a huge ruckus on the church investigation if he had wished to do so. He supported equality between women and men.... He angered the secretary of the U.S. Navy, Lehman. Lehman may have gone to the U.S. ambassador to Rome or to Rome itself. Pio Laghi may have brought pressure. Rome is an eminently political institution. An archbishop of the Church was taking a very public position. This was embarrassing to the U.S. elite and for Rome. Therefore they put pressure on Hunthausen. His opening of the door to the role of women in the church was for some more than they could handle.... Dignity's use of the Cathedral was the straw that broke the camel's back.... Many factors were involved in what led to the investigation. You keep throwing stuff in the mix, it's big, and you don't know which really carries the greatest weight."

The official Vatican reasons for the apostolic visitation in Seattle, the long investigation itself, the disciplinary action including the split-authority with Wuerl, and the steps taken by the apostolic commission to find a "solution," all made for a labyrinth that could perhaps discourage even the Holy Spirit—for a while.

Archbishop Weakland knew of what he spoke when he told me there was no way the Vatican would come out and say publicly what Cardinal Sebastian Baggio told Hunthausen privately in late summer 1983, that his stand on the nuclear issue and related war tax resistance and all that civil disobedience stuff was something he had better do something about. The Vatican, especially the Congregation for the Doctrine of the Faith, had enough to go on with its intra-church agenda. Hunthausen and his Vatican II Seattle became a beachfront in the great battle for the soul of the church. The Vatican investigation was indeed prompted in part by concerns that actually were, as Rome claimed, matters of doctrine and morality. Some concerns, such as lax annulments or dubious altar bread or pesky altar girls, would not alone have prompted an investigation. And as many have argued, Hunthausen, permitting an array of practices also happening in many dioceses around the country at the time, would probably not have been targeted as an object lesson had he not become such a high profile leader. His tax-resistance and his opposition to Trident thrust him into that prominent controversial place. The fact that Hunthausen became so prominent on the disarmament issue and social justice, and that this bothered many who wrote their letters of complaint to Rome and loaded up their letters with other intra-church concerns as well, fed the Vatican's appetite for a crackdown.

In Vatican II's *Pastoral Constitution on the Church in the Modern World*, Hunthausen had found the seeds of his call to disarmament and economic justice—since massive weaponry was stealing from the poor—just as that same document, and the substance and process of the Council, provided him with inspiration and guidance to encourage reform in the church. Some powerful forces wanted to brake (and break) this whole thrust. It did not matter that he was so likable. Perhaps that fact about his character only added subconsciously to the sense that this popular personality needed to be stifled. Small wonder he kept asking himself what the true agenda really was. He did not have the type of character that would easily think ill of others.

When Archbishop Raymond Hunthausen, soft spoken and sad, stood before his brother bishops in the nation's capital in November 1986, he asked them, what kind of church "are we trying to be and to become?" Imagine how in the years since that time he may have asked in some bewilderment, what kind of church are we trying to be and to become? Rome left him and his vision of Vatican II out in the wilderness. When he stood before the gates of "the Auschwitz of Puget Sound" with the people of the Ground Zero Center for Nonviolent Action, when he stood there in Tacoma in June 1981, when he got in the boat to join in a blockade to protest the first Trident submarine, he was asking, what kind of a nation are we trying to be and to become? When he opened the doors of the church to Dignity, when he invited women to take leadership, when he asked parishes to be sanctuaries for refugees who would otherwise be deported to face grave harm, when he practiced a style of leadership that encouraged each person to find their own voice and listen to their conscience, and when he simply tried to be the bishop he thought he was supposed to be as inspired by John XXIII, he was asking, what kind of church are we trying to be and to become?

When I reached him by telephone at his home in East Helena about a year before the meeting we had in the Yakima Red Lion Inn on Memorial Day 2011, I was getting back in touch after many years had gone by since I met with him for spiritual direction in 1991. I said I hoped we could meet because I had been thinking a lot about his witness for peace and justice. I asked him how he was doing. He replied, "well you know, Frank, pretty well, except the structure is collapsing." Such words could refer to the church or society, I thought in that moment. But I did not comment, since I knew he was not talking about the Catholic Church or the United States. He was simply saying that his legs were giving out. That reality must have been hard to accept for an athletic soul who loved to hike, ski, and use those sturdy legs to keep balance while fly-fishing in many a Montana stream.

In the journey to understand what happened to Dutch Hunthausen and why it happened and what it all means, each person to whom I have listened has conveyed memories, aspirations, and frustrations. These perspectives obviously do not provide all the answers. Certain people who could say more have remained silent. Some have taken that silence to their graves. Records are still under seal. To know the fuller truth could help us better grasp the suffering inflicted and endured in a case that has reverberated far and wide. Berkeley's Robert Bellah wrote in *Habits of the Heart: Individualism and Commitment in American Life* of how communities of honest memory can become communities of hope, effecting real social change.[178] Both a country and a church could benefit from knowing why Archbishop Hunthausen was put through a crucible. He loved his country, though some Americans accused him of treason. He loved his church, though some Catholics accused him of heresy. Yet in the end, neither religion nor nation held his ultimate allegiance. At their best, religions, and perhaps societies, point beyond themselves to the ineffable. They resist the idolatrous inclination to treat doctrine as deity. Hunthausen tried to discern God's will, acting from conscience fed by stillness and conversation. He never claimed a monopoly on truth.

Paradox accompanied him. He operated in a vertically structured institution. His deepest vow, no doubt, was to try to follow in the footsteps of Jesus. That required a life of prayer. He once sent to every priest in the Seattle Archdiocese a wood-mounted bronze plaque on which was inscribed one of his favorite prayers, from Thomas Merton's *Thoughts in Solitude*:

> "My Lord God, I have no idea where I am going. I do not see the road ahead of me. I cannot know for certain where it will end. Nor do I really know myself, and the fact that I think that I am following your will does not mean that I am actually doing so. But I believe that the desire to please you does in fact please you. And I hope I have that desire in all that I am doing. I hope that I will never do anything apart from that desire. And I know that if I do this you will lead me by the right road though I may know nothing about it. Therefore I will trust you always though I may seem to be lost and in the shadow of death. I will not fear, for you are ever with me, and you will never leave me to face my perils alone."[179]

When Raymond Hunthausen was ordained a priest he made a vow to obey the bishop, and as a bishop and archbishop he made vows of obedience to the Holy Father. Imagine for a moment a quiet retreat setting where we might come upon a labyrinth designed for a walking meditation. Yet in Greek mythology a labyrinth was not so irenic. In one version of the ancient myth, the Minotaur had a man's body and the head of a bull, and was held captive in a maze-like prison.[180] Hunthausen practiced contemplation, but had to contend with a hierarchical culture marked by strange labyrinthine passageways. From ancient Crete to modern Seattle, one application seems apropos. Dutch Hunthausen was partly imprisoned in a labyrinth of hierarchical obedience fortified by a centralizing papacy. Yet his hierarchical status as a Catholic archbishop helped lend him a public voice in the first place. There are layers of paradox. Just by his down to earth nature, he embodied effortless protest against the vertical framework itself.

Trying to follow the guidance of the Holy Spirit, Archbishop Hunthausen remained a loyal son of the church and became a prophetic witness. He internalized some of the system's oppression, not always confronting the arbiters of injustice as candidly as some people wish he had. Yet he disarmed some of the very forces that went after him by taking a page from *satyagraha* (truth force) and *ahimsa* (nonviolence), ideas expressed as "soul force" in the American Civil Rights movement. Dr. King, Septima Clark, Fannie Lou Hamer, and hundreds of thousands of movement participants drew inspiration from Gandhi's truth force and nonviolence, and from great wellsprings of endurance-resistance spirituality, to challenge racism, militarism, and classism. By intentionally absorbing the violence inherent in an unjust system, people can dramatize the situation and try to effect positive change. Suffering can be redemptive, calling out to the conscience of the oppressor.

With gentle charisma and the radical peace and justice challenge, Hunthausen practiced active and contemplative nonviolence. He did not blithely ignore what Ronald Reagan described as "the evil empire," but focused primarily on his own nation's moral responsibility. The United States had to move away from the kind of mindset that produced Trident. It had to end its militarism in Central America and elsewhere. In response to these and other cries for change, Hunthausen was hindered. And he faced suppression due to his way of being a bishop. Theologian Gregory Baum wrote that the logic of maintenance could overwhelm the logic of mission. Any organization needs an authority structure, for without some sort of structure the whole thing easily falls apart. But if maintenance—including doctrinal vigilance—is exaggerated, the logic can "refuse the integration of dialogue, consultation, conciliarity and synodal responsibility in the exercise of ecclesiastical government."[181]

Hunthausen's willingness to speak truth to power had its limits. During and after what some dubbed "the Seattle Inquisition," he knew *pathos*. I saw it briefly on his face when we met in Yakima in 2011. When I asked what lay behind Rome's treatment of the church in Western Washington, he sighed. He was not going to say much. "Frank, if I get started on this we'll be here for days." Yet I would have been wrong to detect only grief. The silence from within the walls of the Red Lion may have had another meaning, compassion. Those who know him well say he held no bitterness or anger toward Cardinal Ratzinger or anyone else.

Each of us has experiences in life that seem to evoke reflection on comparisons and contrasts. Paul Simon and Art Garfunkel once sang "The Sound of Silence"; in Beijing a few years back, their voices and their magnificent harmony and lyrical prophecy wafted out from amplifiers next to a trinket vendor's table. I heard the song almost every morning as I walked down the steps into a throng that then bottle-necked through narrow gates at the *Xibei* (northwest) subway station. China is governed by an authoritarian system running at breakneck speed amassing wealth and power, but to what end? As I thought about "the sound of silence, written on the subway walls," something deep inside my own life made me reflect on the religion and society of my upbringing. I asked myself, what really happened to Raymond Hunthausen and to so many people inspired by Vatican II? The Chinese Communist party and the Roman Catholic curia were certainly not the same systems, far from it. Still, the Catholic system can be stifling even while it has so much depth to offer. Silence imposed from "on high" can be so oppressive, and yet there remains a rich Catholic contemplative wellspring of silent prayer and communal liturgy from which Hunthausen drew strength. Raymond Hunthausen had a quiet but charismatic authority that inspired so many and yet proved troublesome to others. Though reluctant, he could be prophetic. He relied on the guidance of the Paraclete, the Holy Spirit, a spirit at work in the Second Vatican Council and a spirit alive in the natural wonder of his beloved Montana.

The Paraclete even if sentenced to languish in a labyrinth for a long winter, could never be trapped there in perpetuity. It would blow free again in the wind. Raymond Hunthausen had first discovered the divine spirit alive in his family, in the stunning geography, and in the social resilience of his native Montana, and the town of Anaconda, where he grew up.

ENDNOTES

1 Schneiders, Sandra. *Prophets In Their Own Country: Women Religious Bearing Witness to the Gospel in a Troubled Church.* Orbis 2012, 25-26.

2 See, for a record of this sad saga about many victims as told by one of its victims, Matthew Fox's, *The Pope's War: Why Ratzinger's Secret Crusade Has Imperiled the Church and How It Can Be Saved.* Sterling Ethos 2011.

3 Dalby, Seth. Archdiocese of Seattle archivist; conversations (in person and by telephone) with the author. Fall 2012.

4 Faulkner, William. *Requiem for a Nun.* Act One, Scene III.

5 "Checking up on Dutch," *Time Magazine* 28 Nov. 1983. As referenced by John Driscoll in "The Storm of a Lifetime" Jan. 2014. See www.stewardmagazine.com.

6 Recall from chapter two the discussion of altar breads, and Hunthausen's greater concern about how massive spending on weapons was stealing bread from the hungry.

7 Thavis, John. *The Vatican Diaries.* Viking, Penguin Group 2013, 262.

8 Thavis, 281.

9 Allen, Jr., John. *Cardinal Ratzinger: The Vatican's Enforcer of the Faith.* Continuum 2000, 44-47.

10 Allen, 56.

11 Allen, 59.

12 Ratzinger, Joseph. In *Salt of the Earth* (1997) as quoted by Allen, 82-83.

13 Allen, 83.

14 Allen, 126.

15 Boff, Leonardo. *Church: Charism and Power: Liberation Theology and the Institutional Church.* Wipf and Stock 1985, 77.

16 Cox, Harvey. *The Silencing of Leonardo Boff: The Vatican and the Future of World Christianity.* Meyer Stone 1988, 80-81.

17 See chapters two and three and the references to groups attacking what they called "Marxist-oriented" activities in the church of Western Washington.

18 Ratzinger, Joseph with Vittorio Messori. *The Ratzinger Report: An Exclusive Interview on the State of the Church.* Trans. Salvator Attanasio and Graham Harrison. Ignatius 1985, 45.

19 *The Ratzinger Report,* 49 (emphasis in the original).

20 Cate, William. Personal interview. Seattle, Washington 2 Sept. 1988.

21 Abbot, Walter, ed. *The Documents of Vatican II.* New Century 1966, 25.

22 Hunthausen, Raymond. "Shared Gifts, Shared Responsibility, Shared Spirit." May 1978. Archdiocese of Seattle Archives.

23 "Newsletter, Ministry to Priests." August 1989. Archdiocese of Seattle Archives.

24 Bautsch, John Eugene. "Analysis of Change Within a Normative Bureaucratic Organization: A Case Study of The Catholic Archdiocese of Seattle." Ph.D. dissertation, Seattle University, 1987.

25 Bautsch, 285.

26 Hunthausen, Raymond. "A bishop receives 'on-the-job training" *National Catholic Reporter* Vatican II 50th Anniversary 11 Oct. 2012, 35-36.

27 Dye, Jesse. Personal interview. Seattle, Washington 28 Mar. 2013.

28 Schilling, 298-299.

29 Schilling, 338.

30 Schilling, 339.

31 Schilling, 341.

32 Granfield, Patrick. *The Limits of the Papacy*. New York: Crossroad, 1987, 31.

33 Fogarty, Gerald. The Vatican and the American church since World War II. In *The Papacy and the Church in the United States*, ed. Bernard Cooke. Paulist Press, 1989, 136-137.

34 Hunthausen, Raymond. Report during quinquennial visit to Rome, 1988. As quoted by Aseltime, Carol Arlene. Impact upon Catholic higher education in the United States of the communicator style and message of Pope John Paul II in the cases of two significant Catholic educators. Ann Arbor: UMI, 1992, 83.

35 Lader, Lawrence. *Politics, Power and the Church*. Macmillan, 1987, 230-231. As quoted by Aseltime, 84.

36 Lader, 231. Quoted by Aseltime, 86-87.

37 Lernoux, Penny. *People of God: The Struggle for World Catholicism*. Viking Penguin, 1989, 10.

38 Lernoux, 10.

39 Lernoux, 12.

40 Lernoux, 13.

41 See his *Tranquilitas Ordinis: The Present Failure and Future Promised of American Catholic Thought on War and Peace* and his biography of Pope John Paul II, *Witness To Hope*.

42 Lernoux, 66.

43 Lernoux, 207-208.

44 Theroux, Phyllis. *The Good Bishop: The Life of Walter F. Sullivan*. Orbis Books 2013.

45 Lernoux, 208-209.

46 Lernoux, 291-220.

47 McCoy, John. "The paradoxes of John Paul II." *Seattle Post-Intelligencer* 16 Sept. 1984. Found via *Historic Seattle Times, 1900–1984*, 94. John McCoy is the author of *A Still and Quiet Conscience: The Archbishop Who Challenged a Pope, a President, and a Church*. Orbis Books 2015.

48 See the full text of Ratzinger's letter, cited in chapter five.

49 Pruitt, Kathleen. Personal interview. Seattle, Washington, 3 Dec. 2011.

50 Ries, Victoria. Personal interview. Seattle, Washington 10 Dec. 2012.

51 Repikoff, Patty. Personal interview. Seattle, Washington 14 Dec. 2012.

52 Associated Press story 22 May 1981. *Lexisnexus.com*. Web. 6 Aug. 2012.

53 United Press International story 2 June 1982. *Lexisnexus.com*. Web. 6 Aug. 2012.

54 "Further pressure on ERA hunger strikers." *Seattle Times* 3 June 1982. *Historic Seattle Times, 1900–1984*, 107.

55 Konick, Lisa. "Listening: Catholic women discuss church problems." *Seattle Times* 23 Apr. 1983. *Historic Seattle Times, 1900–1984*, 11. Web. 28 Sept. 2012.

56 Ostrom, Carol. "Women in the Catholic Church." *Seattle Times* 19 Nov. 1983. *Historic Seattle Times, 1900–1984*, 57.

57 Schwarz, Walter. "The US Catholics: A Church in Crisis—Rebels against the 'dead hand of Rome'." *The Guardian* 5 May 1987. *Lexisnexis.com*. Web. 6 Aug. 2012.

58 Reardon, Betty. *Sexism and the War System*. Syracuse Univ, Press 1985. As cited in Barash, David. Ed. *Approaches to Peace: A Reader in Peace Studies*. Third Edition. Oxford Univ. Press 2014, 298.

59 Cate, William and Jan. Personal interview. Bellevue, Washington 28 Mar. 2013.

60 Hopps, Don and Pam Piering. Personal interview. Seattle, Washington 25 Mar. 2013.

61 Hunthausen, Raymond. "Pastoral Statement On Women." Archdiocese of Seattle Archives. 1980.

62 Henold, Mary. *Catholic and Feminist: The Surprising History of the American Catholic Feminist Movement*. University of North Carolina Press. 2008.

63 Burns, Jim. In one of many conversations I enjoyed with Jim Burns throughout the process of working on this book.

64 See the full text of Ratzinger's letter, cited in chapter five.

65 Atkins, Gary. *Gay Seattle: Stories of Exile and Belonging*. Univ. of Washington Press, 2013, 272.

66 Atkins, 273.

67 Atkins, 274.

68 Atkins, 282.

69 Atkins, 283.

70 Atkins, 284.

71 Atkins, 285.

72 Atkins, 286.

73 Hunthausen, Raymond. "Archbishop Addresses Issue of Homosexuality." Excerpts from *Progress*, 1 Sept. 1983. Archdiocese of Seattle Archives.

74 Brown, Kirby. Record of "St Mary's Struggle With Gay/Lesbian Issues," St. Mary's Parish, Seattle, 2000, provided to author by Kirby Brown as part of email exchange, 22 June 2013.

75 Brown, Kirby. "The Major Branching Points in My Life." 9 Oct. 2012, personal document shared by Brown with me as email exchange, June 2013.

76 Brown, Kirby. "Growing Up with Dignity." July 2011. Personal document, shared with me via email exchanges in June 2013.

77 Brown, Kirby.

78 Brown, Kirby.

79 Jaeger, David. Personal interview. Seattle, Washington 9 Dec 2012.

80 "Don't Be Misled." Paid Advertisement. *Seattle Times* 3 Sept. 1983. *Historic Seattle Times, 1900–1984*, 51.

81 Konick, Lisa. "Gays: Receiving pastoral help from churches." *Seattle Times* 3 Sept. 1983. *Historic Seattle Times, 1900–1984*, 52.

82 "Catholic gays pray in cathedral while protesters chant outside." *Seattle Times* 6 Sept. 1983. *Historic Seattle Times, 1900–1984*, 42.

83 Hopps, Don and Pam Piering. Personal interview. Seattle, Washington. 25 Mar. 2013.

84 McDermott, Michael. Personal interview. Tacoma, Washington 25 Mar. 2013.

85 Hunthausen, Raymond. Letter to priests of the archdiocese. 8 June 1983. Archdiocese of Seattle Archives.

86 Dodds, Bill. "Dignity convenes amid protest, welcome." *Progress* 8 Sept. 1983, 6.

87 Hunthausen, Raymond. Transcript of video-tape message of "Archbishop Hunthausen's welcome" for Dignity Convention, Aug. 1983. Archdiocese of Seattle Archives.

88 Heagle, John. Personal interview. Gleneden Beach, Oregon 16 Mar. 2013.

89 Allen, John. *Cardinal Ratzinger: The Vatican's Enforcer of the Faith. Continuum*, 2000, 200.

90 Allen, John. 201.

91 Thomas, Evan. *Ike's Bluff: President Eisenhower's Secret Battle to Save the World.* Back Bay Books/ Little Brown and Company. 2012, 3-4.

92 Bloom, Phillip. "The Investigation: Foolhardy and Unjust." 24 Sept. 1986. Concerned Catholics File.

93 McSorley, Richard. "Real Objection to Hunthausen Was His Stance on Peace." *National Jesuit News* Dec. 1986.

94 Morris, Jack. Personal interview. Portland, Oregon 5 July 2011.

95 Hunthausen, Raymond. Personal interview. Yakima, Washington Memorial Day, 2011.

96 I also received corroborative word while working on this chapter, from Jim Burns, close friend of Hunthausen and Seattle Archdiocese development director for many years, who says that once he was told by the archbishop about the one time that the Vatican had brought to the archbishop's direct attention a concern; something like, he better do something to clear up the situation regarding his nuclear stand. Burns remembered Hunthausen telling him that this brief conversation was with the Prefect for the Congregation of Bishops, and that Hunthausen was asking for an auxiliary bishop at the time, and in that context he was told to take care of his nuclear "to far out there" stand (ergo, this conversation must have been with Sebastian Baggio).

97 Weakland, Rembert. Telephone interview. Milwaukie, Wisconsin 11 Nov. 2011.

98 Ryan, Michael. Personal interview. Seattle, Washington 2 Dec. 2011. Also Personal interview. Seattle 12 Dec. 2012.

99 Schilling, 316.

100 Bullert, Gary. *The Hunthausen File*. (No publisher indicated, March 1992).

101 See for example, his huge hagiographic book *Witness To Hope: The Biography of Pope John Paul II*, (HarperCollins, 1999) in which Weigel writes briefly about the general claim that John Paul II and Ronald Reagan entered into a conspiracy to bring about the downfall of the Soviet Union (and, one might infer, though Weigel does not say this, by implication may have colluded through some of their respective people in the attempted downfall of people such as Hunthausen), calling this "journalistic fantasy" (see p. 441).

102 Schilling, 331.

103 Hopps, Don. Personal interview. Seattle, Washington 20 Sept. 2012, and correspondence in review of draft, May 2014.

104 Lenoux, Penny. *People of God: The Struggle for World Catholicism*. 89-90.

105 Hopps, Don. Personal interview. Seattle, Washington 20 Sept. 2012.

106 Hopps, Don.

107 Burns, Jim. Conversation in review of manuscript draft. Lafayette, Oregon 20 May 2014.

108 Hopps, Don. Personal interview. Seattle, Washington 20 Sept. 2012.

109 Magnano, Paul. Personal interview. Seattle, Washington 10 Dec. 2012.

110 Repikoff, Patty. Personal interview. Seattle, Washington 14 Dec. 2012.

111 Meconis, Charles. Personal interview. Seattle, Washington 27 Mar. 2013.

112 Arnett, Loren. Personal interview. Bothell, Washington 28 Mar. 2013.

113 Dye, Jesse. Personal interview. Seattle, Washington 28 Mar. 2013.

114 See Gordon Thomas and Max Morgan-Witts, *Averting Armageddon: The Pope, Diplomacy, and the Pursuit of Peace*. Doubleday 1984.

115 Douglass, Jim. Telephone interview. Birmingham, Alabama 26 Apr. 2013.

116 "FBI releases 4 pages of clippings on Hunthausen." *Seattle Post-Intelligencer* 24 Feb. 1987, referring to a quotation from *National Catholic Reporter* story. See *National Catholic Reporter* 20 Feb. 1987, "FBI admits it has files on U.S. 'peace bishops'.

117 Associated Press. "Naval Intelligence Kept File on Archbishop" 8 April 1987. *Leixsnexis.com*. Web. 6 Aug. 2012.

118 Associated Press. "Catholic Archbishop Raymond Hunthausen Appears At Trident Rally" 8 June 1987. *Lexisnexis.com*. Web. 6 Aug. 2012.

119 "Physical Threat to the USS Ohio" Confidential report, Department of the Navy, Naval Investigative Service, 9 Apr. 1982. In personal collection of various government FOIA records, held by Glen Milner, Seattle.

120 From personal collection of government FOIA records, held by Glen Milner, Seattle.

121 "Security Threat to the USS OHIO and Naval Submarine Base Bangor" Dept. of the Navy, NIS, memo from NIS director to FBI director. From personal collection of gov. FOIA records, Glen Milner, Seattle.

122 "Law Enforcement Special Inquiry," U.S. Coast Guard. 12 July 1982. See Glen Milner collection.

123 Lernoux, 68.

124 Lernoux, 69-70.

125 Lernoux, 70-71.

126 Lernoux, 71-72.

127 Vistica, Gregory. *Fall From Glory: The Men Who Sank The U.S. Navy*. Touchstone 1997, 148-149.

128 Vistica, 150.

129 Vistica, 150.

130 Vistica, 151-152.

131 Douglass, Jim. Letter to Gordon Thomas and Max Morgan-Witts, 14 Jan. 1986. Copy of letter was shared with me by Jim Douglass.

132 See Glen Milner's files. From FOIA request; FBI file, IP 25-20753, 15 Oct. 1969.

133 Thomas, Gordon and Max Morgan-Witts. *Averting Armageddon: The Pope, Diplomacy, and the Pursuit of Peace*. Doubleday 1984, 275-277.

134 Go to www.stewardmagazine.com. See the various issues beginning in 2011. In 2016, John Driscoll published a book that gathers together his analysis, *The Storm of a Lifetime: A Report to U.S. Catholic Bishops and Pope Francis*. Old Glory Books. Helena, Montana 2016.

135 Driscoll, John.

136 Driscoll, John. "The Storm of a Lifetime" *Steward Magazine*. Jan. 2014, 20. See Driscoll's website, www.stewardmagazine.com/Current_Issue/Spring_2014.

137 Driscoll, 22.

138 Miles, Michael. *Love Is Always: A True Story of a Man and Woman's Challenge to Catholicism's Forbidden World of the Married Priesthood*. William Morrow and Company 1986.

139 See "Book's portrayal of archbishop denied" *National Catholic Register*, Vol. 62, 10 Aug. 1986, 2.

140 Driscoll, 1-2.

141 Driscoll, 3-4.

142 Driscoll, 8-9.

143 Driscoll, 10.

144 Driscoll, 12.

145 Driscoll, 13.

146 Driscoll, 14.

147 Driscoll, 25-30.

148 Driscoll, Summer 2011 edition of *Steward Magazine*, Section VI.

149 Driscoll, Summer 2011, Section VI.

150 Driscoll, Summer 2011, Section VI.

151 Driscoll, "The Storm of a Lifetime" 34.

152 Based on a conversation I had in the late 1980s with a key member of Boeing who wished to remain anonymous.

153 Hopps, Don. Correspondence with me, January 2014.

154 Kengor, Paul and Patricia Clark Doerner. *The Judge: William P. Clark, Ronald Reagan's Top Hand.* Ignatius 2007, 44-46.

155 Kennedy, Eugene. Telephone interview. 12 Sept. 2013.

156 Lawler, Phil. "Judge William Clark, RIP—a Reagan confidant, an unsung hero of the Cold War." 12 Aug. 2013. Blog post, *CatholicCulture.org.*

157 Kengor, Paul and Patricia Clark Doerner. *The Judge: William P. Clark, Ronald Reagan's Top Hand.* Ignatius 2007, 171.

158 Kengor and Doerner, 172.

159 Kengor and Doerner, 173, interview with Edwin Meese 7 June 2005.

160 Kengor and Doerner, 190.

161 Kengor and Doerner, 127.

162 Kengor and Doerner, 282-283

163 Allen, 123.

164 Koehler, John. *Spies In the Vatican: The Soviet Union's Cold War Against The Catholic Church.* Pegasus 2009, 78-79.

165 Gumbleton, Thomas. Telephone interview. Detroit, Michigan 16 May 2014.

166 Koehler, 195-196.

167 Koehler, 223.

168 Bernstein, Carl and Marco Politi. *His Holiness: John Paul II and the Hidden History of Our Time.* Doubleday 1996, 267.

169 Bernstein, Carl and Marco Politi, 11.

170 Bernstein and Politi, 268-269.

171 See www.nndb.com/people/230/000043. Re: John Lehman.

172 Musto, Ronald. *The Catholic Peace Tradition.* Peace Books 2002.

173 Gumbleton, Thomas. Telephone interview. Detroit, Michigan 10 June 2013.

174 Gumbleton, Thomas.

175 Skylstad, William. Personal interview. Portland, Oregon 2 Apr. 2013.

176 Skylstad, William.

177 Tutu, Desmond. *No Future Without Forgiveness.* Doubleday 1999.

178 Bellah, Robert, et. al. *Habits of the Heart: Individualism and Commitment in American Life.* University of California Press 1996, 152-155.

179 Merton, Thomas. *Thoughts In Solitude*. Farrar, Straus and Giroux, originally published in 1958; 1999, 79. Raymond Hunthausen sent me a card in 2012 which included a prayer card with this Merton passage on one side and on the other side: "Please pray for Archbishop Hunthausen."

180 Morford, Mark and Robert Lenardon. *Classical Mythology*. Seventh Edition. Oxford University Press 2003, 567.

181 Baum, Gregory. *Theology and Society*. Paulist Press 1987, Chapter 13, "Contradictions in the Catholic Church."

Dutch with his sister Marie, probably taken in late 1923 or early 1924, at their home in Anaconda. (Photo and context provided by Dick Walsh)

Dutch, first communion day, wearing first suit, circa 1927, standing in front of the Hunthausen family home at 701 West Third St., Anaconda. (Photo and context provided by Dick Walsh)

Taken in front of the family home in Anaconda, circa 1936, with all seven siblings, from oldest to youngest: Dutch, Marie, Tony, Jack, Edna, Art, Jean. (Photo and context provided by Dick Walsh)

Dutch, standing on the running board of the Hunthausen family car, friend (taller) to his left, with other kids (could be siblings, or neighborhood kids) playing in the vehicle. Photo was taken with the Hunthausen family home in background, day of his first communion. (Photo and context provided by Dick Walsh)

St. Peter's Grade School and High School, across Fourth St. from St. Peter's Catholic Church in Goosetown. Built about 1907, the school was administered by Dominican Sisters. When Dutch attended St. Peter's High, he had to travel east down Third St. on the trolley to get to school. (Photographer unidentified; photo provided by Patrick Morris. Source: Marcus Daly Historical Society, Anaconda)

St. Peter's High School, Anaconda, basketball team, 1939, the year Dutch graduated. Both Dutch and his brother Jack were all around good athletes. Dutch is number 10 (the number is not fully visible), standing behind the teammate wearing number 11. Pat Walsh, who later would marry Dutch's sister Marie, is wearing number 6. (Photo and context provided by Dick Walsh)

Fr. Hunthausen's ordination to the priesthood, at his home parish of St. Paul's Catholic Church, Anaconda, 1946. Back row, left to right: Pat Walsh, Marie Hunthausen Walsh, Grandparents Mary and Gerhardt Hunthausen, and Jack Hunthausen (later, Fr. Jack). Front row, left to right: Jean Hunthausen (later, Mrs. Stergar), Art Hunthausen, Edna Marie Hunthausen (Dutch's mother), Dutch as Fr. Hunthausen, Anthony Hunthausen (Dutch's father), and Edna Ruth Hunthausen (later, Sr. Edna). (Photo and context provided by Dick Walsh)

First trip (and liturgy) in the Bob Marshall Wilderness Area, early in Helena Bishop Hunthausen's tenure. Left to Right: Mike Miles (seminarian at the time), Nick Walsh (priest of Boise, later would become auxiliary bishop of Seattle), George Speltz (auxiliary bishop of St. Cloud, MN), Bishop Hunthausen, Fr. Jim Hogan, and Pat Estenson (seminarian). (Photo provided by Dick Walsh; context by Fr. Jim Hogan).

Archbishop Hunthausen together with others gathered at an anti-Trident rally at the gates of the Bangor base, late 1980s. (Photographer: Elizabeth M. Harburg for the Northwest Progress, Archdiocese of Seattle newspaper; photo provided by the Archdiocese of Seattle Archives, Cat. No. VR610.909)

Archbishop Hunthausen speaking, Shelley Douglass adjusting the microphone, probably at Peace Pentecost 1987, near the "Railroad Track Gate" entrance to the Trident sub base Bangor. (Photo taken by Molly Rush; photo and context provided by Shelley Douglass)

On the Witness Boat, Oak Harbor Bay, August 1982, looking in anticipation of the first Trident submarine. From left to right: Rev. James Halfaker (Washington North Idaho Conference, UCC); Sr. Margaret Casey, SCJP; Rev. Robert Brock (NW Regional Christian Church); Archbishop Hunthausen; Bishop William Skylstad (behind Hunthausen); Rev. Loren Arnett (Washington Association of Churches); Rabbi Norman Hirsch (Temple Beth Am, Seattle); Sr. Sharon Park, OP. (Photographer unidentified; photo and context provided by Seth Dalby, Archdiocese of Seattle Archives, Cat. No. VR610.910)

Archbishop Hunthausen preparing for a press conference when he would announce the results and conclusions of the Vatican's investigation. Taken in a conference room at the Chancery of the Seattle Archdiocese, in 1985. (Photo and context provided by Brad Reynolds, SJ)

Two horseback riders, off their horses and hamming it up, at trailhead of the Bob Marshall Wilderness Area. Bishop George Speltz (St. Cloud, MN) and Bishop Hunthausen. (Photo provided by Dick Walsh; context by Fr. Jim Hogan)

Jim Douglass and Archbishop Hunthausen at the Ground Zero Center for Nonviolent Action, mid to late 1980s. Shelley and Jim Douglass keep this photo, mounted and framed, at their Birmingham, Alabama home, part of the Catholic Worker community there. (Picture of the mounted photo, provided by Shelley Douglass; photographer and newspaper source unidentified)

Rev. Michael G. Ryan with Archbishop Hunthausen, Holy Thursday, spring of 1986, at Holy Rosary Parish in West Seattle. (Photographer unidentified; photo and context provided by Maria Laughlin)

Gathering at St. Joseph's Catholic Church, Seattle, set to march with crosses to the Federal Building in downtown Seattle, late November 1989, marking the death of Jesuit priests and their housekeepers in San Salvador. (Photograph by Jeffrey Wahl, context provided by Kim and Bill Wahl)

The "Elders" gathered on "Pat's Deck" at Moose Lake, July 25, 1992 (Jack's 65th birthday). In the foreground, Dutch and Tony Hunthausen, and in back, from left to right, Donna Hunthausen (Art's spouse), Jean Stergar, Art Hunthausen, Sr. Edna Hunthausen, Harriet Hunthausen (Tony's spouse), Marie Walsh (Marie's husband, Pat, died in 1991, and he had built the deck with others), John Stergar (Jean's spouse) and Fr. John "Jack" Hunthausen. (Photo shared by Tony Hunthausen; context provided by Dick Walsh)

Taken in 2012, when Carroll College named a street on campus as Hunthausen Avenue. Dutch is surrounded by family. (Photo and context provided by Dick Walsh)

Family reunion at Legendary Lodge, summer of 2012. This is the last reunion attended by Dutch and his siblings together. Dutch and his sister, Marie (Walsh), are front and center and behind them, from left to right, are Harriet (Tony's spouse), Tony, Jack, Edna, and Jean (brother Art had passed away in 2010). Four generations are gathered for this picture. (Photo and context provided by Dick Walsh)

Part III

CHARACTER

"The character of a man is his guardian spirit."—Heraclitus, circa 500 BCE

Chapter Eight

FROM ANACONDA CHILDHOOD TO WARTIME TRAINING FOR PRIESTHOOD

Anaconda came into being four decades before the person at the heart of this book began his life. In southwestern Montana's Deer Lodge Valley, the town of Anaconda is surrounded by mountain ranges, streams, and lakes. With abundant trout, elk, black bear, deer, big horn sheep, mountain lions, moose, and golden eagles, a nature-loving eye might have seen it as "God's country." Other eyes focused on what lay under the ground, especially in nearby Butte. They turned things—literally the earth—upside down. Anaconda owes its origins to "copper king" Marcus Daly and the Anaconda Copper Mining Company (ACM). Daly wanted to call the place *Copperopolis*, but in those mine-frenzied times in Montana there was already a town with that name. The spot for what became Anaconda, some twenty-five miles west of Butte, was chosen by Daly partly because of the readily available water from upper Warm Springs Creek. Butte, with three thirsty smelters of its own, did not have enough water to handle yet another one. Daly linked Butte and the smelter operation in Anaconda with the indispensable structure for industrial transport: a rail line.[1]

Patrick Morris, in his two-volume history of the town, points out that by the time Anaconda had been established to support Daly's smelter, various Indian tribes who in times past had roamed the Deer Lodge Valley—bands of Blackfeet, Crows, Pawnee, Shoshone, Snakes, Flathead, Pend d'Oreilles, and Nez Perces—were mostly a memory. Those who had survived the genocidal onslaught were on reservations. One can ponder Anaconda today and recollect its past of suffering endured and suffering inflicted. It is a town within a watershed, ecological as well as historical. Warm Springs Creek in upper Deer Lodge Valley, as well as other creeks, eventually flow into the Clark Fork River and in turn into the Columbia River. Anaconda is located west, by only just a few miles west, of the Continental Divide.[2]

The city plot was filed in 1883, Morris notes, a year after Daly made a major discovery of copper in Butte. Butte was short not only on water but other crucial resources, including wood, needed to support the massive smelter operation. Many of the trees around Anaconda were devoured to fuel the smelter.[3] As to the origins of the town's name, an actual mine in Butte had been given the name "Anaconda". An Irish immigrant, Thomas Hickey, owned that mining claim. The story goes that Hickey, who had been a Union soldier in the Civil War, remembered reading lines from Horace Greeley writing that the Union would "encircle Lee's forces and crush them like a giant anaconda."[4] In time, the ACM would put more pressure on nature than a thousand anacondas ever could. Among the victims were water, trees, air, and as well the area around the lime quarry operations that provided a key chemical source for the blast furnace. This degradation reached into many spheres. For example, arsenic emanating from the smelter stack would eventually destroy the mortar holding the stain glass windows in place in Anaconda's St. Peter's Catholic Church.[5]

ACM was the town's principal economic lifeblood. In its early days, Anaconda could afford elegant electric streetlights, some of which continue to light up the evening in places such as the corner of Third and Walnut where the Hunthausens lived beginning in the 1920s. A trolley line ran along West Third and extended to East Third, where workers would board it to ride up to the smelter. East of Main, in the area known as "Goosetown," saloons could be found on almost any corner.[6] The name "Goosetown" is reputed to have originated from the practice these saloons had of raffling live geese.[7] While noticeable, wealth-poverty contrasts between the west side, where the Hunthausens would reside, and Goosetown, to the east, were not sharp. Anaconda was a small community with ties that reached across most neighborhoods.[8] By 1900, many homes in Anaconda had running water and indoor plumbing. Yet its people often lived under a haze of smoke from the smelter stacks and suffered from arsenic-laden dust.[9]

George Everett's "When Toil Meant Trouble" offers a vivid description of the health hazards facing the workers in the Butte mines and smelters, including Anaconda's. Everett notes that soldiers who went off to the war in 1917 were thought—in some cases—to have had "a safer workplace ahead of them in France. Odds for survival may have actually *improved* by going to war." Yet, "if the mines and smelters brought death, they also gave life and a decent standard of living to thousands who gambled with their lives and health. The role of the union was to increase the odds of maintaining that health and the decent standard of living despite a trend of falling wages and more dangerous working conditions."[10] Daly could be generous, but the fact remained that Anaconda was *his* town, and dominance by the Company he created was to mark the town's character persisting well beyond the death of this "copper king" in 1900.[11] By the time the Hunthausens were settled in Anaconda, Daly had been dead for several years. Standard Oil owned the Company since 1899, and it was henceforth officially called the Amalgamated Copper Company.[12] Working conditions were dangerous for the smelter workers spanning the Daly and Standard Oil eras. Smeltermen had to contend with mineral dust, toxic fumes, and other maladies. Alcoholism was a major problem. The town had more than its share of bars and brothels. Racism was a fact of life. "One of the most dangerous places on the smelter was the tram railway that carried the red-hot calcine from the roaster to the reverb. This was one of the departments where the few blacks who worked at the smelter were assigned. They had to be on constant guard against being burned by molten calcine when explosions occurred as a result of blasts of cold air getting into the roasting furnaces."[13]

Anaconda had a mix of immigrants, including Irish, Welsh, English, Scottish, Swedish, Norwegian, Croatian, Serbian, Slovenian, French-Canadian, Chinese, German, and Italian, among others.[14] Both of Raymond Hunthausen's parents were German immigrants, his mother's family having moved to Anaconda from Wisconsin in 1901. Hunthausen's mother, Edna Marie Tuchscherer, was the daughter of Adam Jacob Tuchscherer and Matilda Frances Trilling. Anthony Gerhardt *Hunthausen*, Dutch's father, was the son of Gerhardt *Hundhausen* and Mary Ann Lutz. Raymond Hunthausen's grandfather, Hundhausen, had immigrated to the U.S. from Windeck, Germany and Mary Ann Lutz was from Tipton, Missouri, where they were married.[15] In their early twenties, Anthony Gerhardt Hunthausen and a friend were traveling west from Missouri heading for Seattle when they found work in the Butte/Anaconda area. Anthony decided to stay while his friend ended up making it to Seattle. His sister Mary moved to Anaconda some years after he had settled there and worked as a telephone operator. The rest of the Hunthausen family stayed in Tipton, Missouri. Archbishop Hunthausen's brother Tony remembers visiting Tipton where their dad was born. "We saw on some of the grave stones there it was written Hundhausen. In Germany, even my dad's grandparents spelled it that way. We used to say, our name is Dog House."[16] That was family humor decades before his brother ended up in the Vatican's "dog house."

Anthony Gerhardt Hunthausen and Edna Marie Tuchscherer were married in Anaconda in October 1920. At the end of August 1921, the *Anaconda Standard*'s Sunday edition included a short announcement tucked back on page ten. "Mr. and Mrs. Anthony Hunthausen are the parents of a little son, born to them last Sunday. Mother and son are doing nicely."[17] Born on August 21, 1921, Raymond Gerhardt Hunthausen was the first of seven children born to Edna and Anthony. Ray was only sixteen months old when his sister, Marie, was born, and he was four years old when Tony arrived. He was not quite six when Jack—who, like Ray, would become a priest—took his first breath. Ray was almost eight when Edna, who would become a nun, was born; ten when his youngest brother Art joined the fold; and thirteen when the birth of his youngest sister, Jean, made them the "lucky seven." Soon after they were married, Anthony and Edna Hunthausen opened a grocery store. They lived simply, but avoided the abject poverty and insecurity of blue collar Anaconda, especially when the Depression years came. They were Catholic to the core. Dutch attended parochial school. Ursuline sisters were his teachers, and outside of school hours his family often visited their convent, which was close by. The Hunthausen children sang in the Sunday choir at St. Paul's Parish. Explaining his continued habit many years later of visiting the Ursuline teachers, Dutch quipped, "I'm their boy."[18] The sisters made a lasting impression. When he was old enough, he was coached into giving a welcoming speech for the bishop of the diocese. "It was good for people to push me. They saw things that I should do even if I didn't want to do them."[19]

In an Archdiocese of Seattle newspaper story for Archbishop Hunthausen's celebration in 1987 of 25 years as a bishop, reporter Cindy Wooden wrote that his mother liked to tell the story of what happened on the day Raymond was born. "She was ready to go to the hospital, but had to wait for Anthony to change into his good suit." Edna remembered he wanted to dress up for that special occasion of meeting his first son. One central aspect of Raymond's early life and that of his siblings seems evident. The seven kids grew up knowing they were loved and secure. "Their memories of growing up are seldom duets or trios, they're whole bands: the clan driving in a 1930 Nash to visit relatives in Missouri; hiking in the mountains with Teddy, the dog, tagging behind; large holiday gatherings at Grandmother's house. As much joy as noise."[20] "It was a sharing community," Fr. Jack Hunthausen told Wooden. "The Depression years gave people in Anaconda a sense of needing each other. We grew up with a good set of values." From talking with Jack and others, Wooden was able to capture that sense of Anaconda as a close knit community that helped shape the character not only of Dutch, but of all seven siblings. "Neighborhoods, with houses snuggled close together, were cohesive—kids running in and out of each other's homes, parents keeping an eye on the whole gang. It didn't matter whose kids they were. Grandparents, aunts, uncles and cousins often lived just a few houses away."[21]

On the edge of town, up on Smelter Hill, there was a giant smoke stack. Just a couple of years before little Ray was born, a huge cylindrical tower replaced a smaller stack that was "only" three hundred feet high. Before she married, and because her family name was prominent in town, Edna Tuchscherer was one of the Anacondan residents invited to ride the elevator up through the center to the top of the new stack to lay one of the final ceremonial bricks.[22] One local historian described the stack, still standing today (the smelter has been closed for several decades) at just over five hundred eighty five feet, taller than the Washington Monument, a memorial to Anaconda's social and economic history, if not its basic faith: "Everybody would get up in the morning and look to see if there was smoke coming out of the stack, and if there was, God was in His heaven and all was right with the world and we knew we were going to have a paycheck."[23] That was the deity of industry, not the one associated with, "God's country." There were, however, times when there was no smoke and no work. The same year Raymond Hunthausen was born, the Amalgamated Copper Company shut down the mines in Butte along with the smelter in Anaconda, citing depressed copper prices.[24] In that decision, as in numerous other decisions over the decades, the deity of capitalist calculation was in charge.

By the 1920s, Anaconda was a town of about 13,000. The atmosphere could be rough. Archbishop Hunthausen recalled, "I can still see images of back-alley fights that just turned me sick because I saw people really get hurt. I saw people who got knocked to the ground and were treated very cruelly; and one side would be shouting and raging and celebrating, and the other side would be vowing revenge."[25] As a lad, he witnessed broken bones, blood, swollen eyes, and missing teeth. Still, he said that the more typical experience of his childhood was the security and love of his family and a wider community that shared burdens and together celebrated joys. Dick Walsh, a nephew, says that even at age 92 or 93, "Uncle Dutch" could remember being five-years-old and playing with friends in the neighborhood. "He recalled his grade school teachers by name."[26]

I once asked Tony how his brother got his nickname. "There were kids from all over the place. The town was full of immigrants from all over. He was from a German family, so other kids started to call him Dutch. 'You're an old 'Dutch man'. It stuck. It's always been Dutch. We called him Dutch too, always."[27] His childhood friend Eddie Dolan, with a knack for giving out nicknames, was probably the first person to call him Dutch.[28]

Archbishop Hunthausen once said, "I don't have any hesitation in saying that I had a very loving family and extended family: grandparents, uncles, aunts, cousins. I think it's fair to say, a loving neighborhood. Church was influential. It was part of who I was to be close to church and all it represented."[29] His parents were gentle, good humored, down to earth, exhibiting practical compassion for those less well-off. What truly shaped Dutch and the rest of his siblings were the love and support they got from the family of Hunthausens and Tuchscherers. Adam Tuchscherer, Raymond Hunthausen's maternal grandfather, was a pioneer businessman. The Tuchscherers got into the beer brewing business, and had considerable success over the years—with the noteworthy exception of the Prohibition era. Adam Tuchscherer became president of the Anaconda Brewing Company in 1908. When Prohibition went into effect in Montana and all the breweries and liquor stores closed, the Anaconda Brewing Company became the Anaconda Products Company for a stretch.[30]

Andy Hunthausen, one of Tony and his wife Harriet's children, heard what it was like back when they were kids:

> "Dutch was always out in the streets of Anaconda organizing games and engaging with his peers. I often hear stories of him leading neighborhood kids up Warm Springs Creek to a number of local

> swimming holes. They had swimming holes marked by the numbers on telephone poles along the road. They might say, 'let's go swimming at 99 today.' Grandpa Hunthausen would run pretty good credit at times for folks who did not have a way to pay for their groceries. My dad and Dutch often joked about not knowing or ever seeing a yellow banana. Grandpa would bring home brown bananas and brown lettuce. They often ate all of the stuff that couldn't be sold at the store anymore. The best food and produce from the store was to be sold, but during the Great Depression or when there was a labor strike at the smelter Grandpa always tried to do his part to share food with people in need. They just did not waste food through those tough years. They grew up right in the middle of all this economic chaos and turmoil. Dutch's father struggled with the Anaconda store during the Depression. They were the working poor during that period. It was tough times but the community helped each other out."

Dutch and Andy's dad Tony would tell stories about the brewery business and how it was really hard going through the Prohibition years. The business faltered, of course, when they could not sell beer, but Adam Tuchscherer figured out how to hold on for better times. "Great-Grandpa Tuchscherer tried to make investments in some of the bars in town hoping that eventually, if they could hang on, Prohibition would end. When it did end he had a large investment in the community," says Andy.[31]

The Hunthausens lived "uptown," as their area west of Main Street was called. Jack Morris, younger brother of the historian Patrick Morris whose work has helped give us a picture of the town, was the Jesuit who figured into the story in chapter one, right after Archbishop Hunthausen made his "Faith and Disarmament" speech. Jack Morris grew up as a good friend of Jack Hunthausen and lived in the Goosetown area, which he described as "rough and tumble and economically challenging." Jack told me that he could always recall the warm and personable spirit of welcome he felt when hanging out with the Hunthausens at their place. It was, after all, a small town and the two neighborhoods were just blocks apart. "Hunthausen's dad was a great golfer, a well known, outgoing, and affable sort much at ease with the locals, helpful and generous, no matter their circumstances, with anyone. This people-centered spirit was passed onto his oldest son and the whole family."[32]

Morris shared with me his insights about how those early years in Anaconda helped to form Hunthausen's kindred spirit with the "open-to-the-world-and-concern-for-social-justice" outlook of the Second Vatican Council decades later. "Some mixture of the American spirit was alive in that town, in many ways. Anaconda itself had a powerful influence. It was a very diverse ethnic town. People all worked for the Anaconda Mining Company. Butte and Anaconda were both quite Catholic. Immigrants were all brought over to work for the mining company." At that time, he said, the largest copper refining center in the world with the world's largest smoke stack shaped everything that went on in every part of town.[33]

Early on Dutch seemed to be accident-prone, frequently getting a bruise or cut, something his mother shared about her oldest son when she was interviewed in 1975 after the news broke that Hunthausen would be sent to Seattle.[34] In 1987, for his silver anniversary as a bishop, Cindy Wooden wrote, "The family made a real effort to go to Missouri for part of the summer every other year to visit Anthony's family." It was apparently with reference to something that happened on that trip that Marie, Dutch's sister, told Cindy Wooden: "Mother used to tell a little story about Dutch, when he was maybe 4 or 5. He used to play with our grandfather's tools. One day he missed the nail and hit his thumb with the hammer. He told everyone, 'I fooled the nail.'"[35] One time when Dutch was in high school he was learning to pole vault. He knocked himself out when his bamboo pole broke and he hit the ground. "He's dead!" shouted his brother Jack.[36] This mishap evidently happened in the back of the old Tuchscherer brewery, where they had a big pile of sawdust just a block or so away from the house on Third Street. The kids ran into the house and shouted, and Ray's mother heard them, "Dutch is dead!" He was just knocked out for a brief spell, but it gave everyone quite a scare.[37] Ever since then it has given the family quite a laugh.

While he may have suffered little aches and pains from time to time as a kid, these pale when compared to the pain that he observed around him in Anaconda. His father had the habit of extending credit to those in need. His sister Edna, a member the Sisters of Charity of Leavenworth, Kansas, told me that her oldest brother helped his dad at the grocery store and delivered groceries around town.[38] His youngest sister, Jean Stergar, welcomed my wife and me into the very home, located at 701 West Third, where the seven siblings grew up together, and where she still lives today. As she showed us the house and took us upstairs to the room that had been her brother's so many years ago, she remembered how he used to ride "a big red bike" to deliver those groceries to people who often had to "charge" rather than pay cash. Her father always wanted to be in solidarity with the unions when they were on strike, and this was one way to support the people.[39] Carolyn Miller, one of Jean's daughters, told me that she heard "Grandpa Hunt" would take in people and give them odd jobs. Everything was a handshake, times were simple. When someone wanted to call the grocery store, the phone number was simply 7, just that sole number. And it was a party line.[40] In some ways, the party line symbolized the community bonds of those times—although it probably also fed small town gossip.

Marie's son Dick Walsh helped me appreciate something about the character of Dutch's parents.

> "I loved my Grandma very much but when I was young I do not recall her as soft and sweet. She was strong willed and when she visited us at our homes she would appear to take control and let you know if you were out of line. She had a wonderful faith and along with my grandfather did an incredible job in raising seven amazing children. I would say that Dutch's mother influenced him more in faith and his father in business and adventure. They were both wonderful examples of how to live a Christian life. I am sure that is where the foundation comes from. To think of others and not yourself."

The family took in two housemaids. "They helped with cooking and such. I have always understood from Dutch this was an act of compassion as much as the family's need for help. This was their way of helping these two young women. The second girl hired was Rita Dunn (O'Rourke) and her brother was also given employment at the Hunthausen grocery store."[41] Dutch not only worked with his dad in the grocery store in Anaconda and delivered groceries by bicycle and later by automobile, but also worked in his maternal grandfather's Anaconda Brewery in high school and during the summer when he was in college. By then Dutch's uncles, Walter and Arthur Tuchscherer, ran the brewery. And he traveled with his dad to golf tournaments and golf outings. "Their dad was an excellent golfer and Anaconda Club champion. Dutch was already a great golfer back then."[42]

The golfing background did not mean economic aloofness. The family was of the small business class in town, to be sure, but consistent with Catholic social teaching they supported the rights of workers to organize. Jack Hunthausen's friend Jack Morris knew well the harsh conditions facing so many in the labor class. Jack's dad was a member of the Mine, Mill, and Smeltermen's Union, Lodge No. 1. His dad worked in the smelter all of his life. Jack had keen memories of what it was like to see his dad affected by alcohol and to live so close to the smoke stack. His dad never went to church and had no use for the Catholic churches or any others there in town—or anywhere. It was Jack's mother who encouraged the kids to go to church. What was true of both of his parents, and was a characteristic of Anaconda's culture, was a no nonsense struggle for the rights of the workers whether the official church stood up for them or not.[43] Dick Walsh had another illustration of this culture of labor unions. "Uncle Dutch told me a story once describing the union hold on Butte and Anaconda area when he was growing up. He had come home from college or seminary and was painting his parents' home. He noticed people driving by and looking at what he was doing. Finally someone approached him to ask him what union he belonged to. The union climate was such that even when you painted your own home there was suspicion."[44] Dutch was not suggesting anything negative about unions by telling this story, but rather was letting his nephew know that the whole community defended the union tradition and wanted to be sure that his taking on the painting of the house was not seen as a scab operation.

Fr. Dan Shea grew up in Anaconda in the 1940s and 50s, a decade or two after the Hunthausen clan, but he had a sense of what the town was like for the generation that preceded him. He, like Jack Morris, grew up in Goosetown.

> "The Hunthausens lived on the 700 block on West Third, while our family lived on the 700 block of East Third. We would joke about Goosetown being the real town, the ethnic part, the parish of St. Peter's founded by Slovenians and Croatians. Most folks born in the Goosetown area would, if and when their situation improved, migrate to the west side. Recently I joked with Dutch when I visited him, and said to him, 'you guys think you're classy up there in the West side. Come on, I'm gonna prove that you guys are really Goosetowners at heart no matter where you lived.' So Dutch says to me, 'how are you gonna do that?' I says, 'now you tell me, you get up in the morning, and you wash your face. What do you wash your face with?' He says, 'well, you wash with a wash rag.' And I says, 'that's incontrovertible truth that you are a Goosetowner at heart. If you took on airs as the *nouveaux riche* of St. Paul's you would have called it a wash cloth.'"

They had a lot of fun with that kind of joking.[45]

Throughout his life, Hunthausen's social concerns had reference to personal experiences. I learned of this in a very special way when his brother Tony, together with wife Harriet, welcomed me into their home in East Helena. Tony could still recall something that happened when he was in the fifth grade at St. Paul's. His big brother was a freshman in high school at St. Peter's. "One day I came to school with a brand new pencil sharpener. During recess that morning, this guy who was from a rough family having a lot of difficulty—well, most of the kids in school were kind of afraid of him—that day he wanted that sharpener that I had. I didn't want to give it to him. We got into a fight. Well, he really beat me up. I wasn't a very good fighter. I didn't see very well then. I had bad eyesight." Tony headed home, only a few blocks from the school. His big brother also came home from high school not too far away over in Goosetown.

> "I was so mad. I was even crying. I told my folks that he had taken my pencil sharpener away from me. Dutch said, 'well, tell me where he lives and I'm going to go right down there and talk to him.' I knew where he lived. I can't remember exactly, but we tried to talk with this kid. Evidently his parents were there too and they tried to talk with him as well. Anyway, he opened a window up on the second floor; I

suppose it was his bedroom. I don't remember what Dutch said to him, but the kid finally threw the sharpener down and Dutch caught it and gave it to me and off we went. The thing I remember is that this kid who was a 'toughie' in school became, in time, my very good friend. He changed. I remember later we learned to drive a car together in the eighth grade. We were very good friends by then. I don't know how he changed, but somehow he did change and it may have had something to do with what Dutch said to him that day. His name was Ray too."[46]

Tony remembered also how there was a little grocery store every few blocks in those days. When he was in high school, Dutch learned how to drive.

"He would drive the little red truck we had. In those days you delivered groceries to people's homes. I remember during the summer we did this all day long. The rest of the year we did it after school. But during the summer, Dutch would drive that truck and deliver groceries. I would deliver them on bicycle. One day I was at the store helping my dad. We all kind of worked there. Dutch was so capable and interested in sports. He'd be out delivering groceries and time would go by and I remember my dad in the store saying, 'Where did that kid go? I've got more stuff to be delivered. Tony, get out there and find that guy and get him home.' So I'd take my bike, ride about a block away from our house where a kid had a basketball hoop set up and where they would play basketball like crazy. Sure enough, there was the truck parked in the alley and Dutch would be playing basketball. Other times, football or baseball was going on at the Commons right in the middle of town. It's where we had ice skating in the winter. Often times too he'd just forget all about his work when he got to playing. He was so good at those games. I so often had to chase him down for dad."[47]

Tony noted the feel of Smelter Town. To work up on "the hill" meant to work up where the smelter was. During the Great Depression, the smelter was often shut down. "During the 1930s you wanted to work for whatever pay. You were glad to get any job." The family often had trouble getting money out of people but his dad would give them the food anyway. "My dad always went to work at the store. People who did not have money, he would carry on credit for a long time. If they got a job he would start getting paid by them. I'm not sure if he could himself buy his groceries (for the grocery store) on credit. My dad was under a lot of financial pressures, but never talked about it."[48]

Tony recounted what it was like to work at the brewery. "In those days they bottled all the beer, that was before cans. You had to carefully be sure they could wash all the bottles. The way Dutch started, and later me too, was we got the job to take care of sorting the bottles, all by hand, which bottles for beer, which for sodas. Right next to the brewery was the bottle shop." In those days the bottle shop could not be in the brewery itself. "They had to pipe the beer over to the bottling building. They would brew the beer very early in the morning. Then late morning they would scrub the brewing tanks. I remember scrubbing those tanks. We had a large tank where the bottles were washed. You had to work fast as the tray went by on the conveyor belt. I remember how proud we were if we could learn to do all this without help."[49]

The Hunthausens handled groceries, but they were not alone. Patrick Morris writes that, by 1925, Anaconda had as many as forty grocery stores. "It was a time when a little bit of capital and a lot of hard work could create and sustain a small enterprise and provide a modest income for its owners."[50] Yet, by 1933 and deep into the Great Depression, when Dutch Hunthausen was twelve, unemployment in Anaconda was over 50%. The National Recovery Act of 1933, with President Roosevelt's leadership, gave labor the right to organize and bargain collectively. Anaconda had a strong Democratic Party loyalty. The Social Security Act of 1935 was just around the corner.[51]

Dave Stergar, a son of Dutch's youngest sister, a coach and avid athlete, shared with me his experience of Uncle Dutch. "He tells stories about the football teams he played on. He talks about all the players he played with. He talks about how they worked together well as a team." Dave keeps a picture of the spot in Anaconda where Dutch skied as a kid. Back then, Nordic ski-jumping was a big thing. People of Dutch's generation would probably have done Nordic jumping before Alpine skiing became popular.[52] Only about ten miles to the west, Wraith Hill was the place where Dutch took his younger brothers skiing back when there was no modern equipment.[53]

More ought to be noted about the religious context of Anaconda and the state as a whole, since Dutch's Catholic background proved so influential. The authors of *Montana: A History of Two Centuries* point out this interesting demographic feature: "Roman Catholicism has always been Montana's dominant religion. In 1906, a major census of religions by the federal government found that about 74 percent of all regular communicants in the state were Catholics, exactly twice the national percentage. The heavy concentration of Irish in western Montana explains the high number."[54] The relatively small Catholic German population had their Irish Catholic fellow believers to thank for the pronounced Catholic atmosphere. This was especially true in Butte. Anaconda must have felt a strong Catholic influence as well, as it was fifty percent Catholic for a long time. The presence of Catholics from elsewhere besides Ireland was evident, for instance, in Anaconda's St. Peter's Austrian Roman Catholic Church, which had Masses in Serbo-Croatian.[55] Irish Catholicism dominated in nearby Butte, a fact documented by David Emmons in *The Butte*

Irish: Class and Ethnicity in an American Mining Town. Emmons claims that the Catholic Church in Butte was—or seemed to be—almost "the unchallenged moral and social arbiter it had always been in Ireland."[56] Emmons notes a close alliance between the Church and the Democratic Party, and points out that neither of them supported working-class radicalism or socialism.[57]

The Hunthausen family attended Mass at St. Paul's Catholic Church located on the corner of Park and Cherry Streets on the west side of town. St. Paul's was the first Catholic church in Anaconda. According to Cornelia Flaherty's history of the Diocese of Helena, *Go Haste Into The Mountains*, Butte is the place in western Montana where the Catholic Church "saw its greatest development."[58] The growth in Butte in the first part of the twentieth century was reflected in Anaconda as well. Catholic education thrived. In addition to the Ursulines who taught in the grade school of St. Paul's, where Hunthausen went to elementary school, Dominican Sisters taught in the grade school and high school of St. Peter's.[59]

Flaherty opens the chapter about Bishop Hunthausen by emphasizing the formative Catholic influences. "Raymond was the oldest of seven children, three of whom entered the religious life. He was baptized by Father Amatus Coopman of St. Paul's Church. He received his early education at St. Paul's grade school and graduated from St. Peter's Central Catholic High School in 1939."[60] It seems he was a born athlete. In 1934, Dutch played football with the lightweights of St. Paul's school in Anaconda.[61] The August 1962 edition of the Catholic newspaper, a souvenir edition produced when he became the bishop of Helena, has pictures of him as a very young athlete and of his First Communion. He played both football and basketball at St. Peter's, known later as Anaconda Central Catholic High, and excelled in scholarship as well. Andy Hunthausen says of his Uncle Dutch, "the simplicity of it is the depth, the essence, of who he is. There is nothing complex or secret about it. All those experiences as a kid shaped him. From what I hear, he was always a peacemaker. If there were conflicts in the games, on the field, he just wanted to keep playing rather than have arguments about who was in or out."[62] Not everything was angelic in the world of young Dutch Hunthausen. He and his buddies on occasion threw apples at passing cars. And apparently at some point in his high school years he wrecked the family car, though luckily no one was hurt.[63]

Dutch told another story, relayed by nephew Dick Walsh, of what he and two friends, Greeno and Kelley, did when he was a sophomore in high school. They teamed up and purchased a Studebaker for $19.00. The plan was to share the vehicle with a daily rotation among the three of them. "Dutch says the floor boards had holes in them and exhaust would come into the car. When Dutch's dad learned of the purchase he asked about insurance and other expenses. That pretty much ended the ownership of the car and they sold it back to the person from whom they had bought it, for $10.00. They owned it for just a week or two."[64]

CARROLL COLLEGIAN AND PRIESTLY VOCATION

When Dutch was 18, he and some buddies, including his cousin Jack Sugrue, took a trip to Catalina Island (off the coast south of Los Angeles) to celebrate graduating from high school. The island was known for casinos, ballrooms, and big bands. Dutch and a buddy were walking through the casino and noticed Jack Sugrue and a friend on the monitor being interviewed. They told Dutch that some fella came up to them and asked if they wanted to be televised. They said "sure, as long as it does not hurt." They had never heard the word 'television' until that moment.[65]

Guido Bugni, one of the first people Hunthausen recruited for football, has described Hunthausen's college achievements. "During his undergraduate days at Carroll he distinguished himself as an outstanding student and athlete. He captained the first Carroll football team to win the Montana Collegiate Conference championship and he lead the 1941 team through an unbeaten and unscored upon season. He also has the distinction of serving as captain of the first team to win a championship in that other sport—basketball."[66]

John Semmens did extensive research for a senior thesis on Hunthausen's impact on Carroll College. When Hunthausen received his high school diploma in late May 1939, Semmens writes, "he did so with only a vague notion of what his life journey might entail. He had spoken with his father about the possibility of studying chemistry at Montana State University in Bozeman, as that could allow him to take over his grandfather's Rocky Mountain Brewery." Or he could go to Carroll College, where a number of his friends were headed. He just could not make up his mind. "There was one certainty, however, floating amidst the sea of confusion on that May afternoon: Raymond would be starting his freshman year of college in roughly three months.... Raymond traveled to San Francisco in the summer of 1939 to experience the World's Fair, visit local universities, and chart a course for the future. When the trip came to a close, however, Raymond still had not made up his mind." When he got home he learned that he had a scholarship offer from Carroll College. Carroll's Coach Ed Simonich, "a legend among the Anaconda boys because of his football career under Knute Rockne at Notre Dame, drove to Anaconda and asked Raymond to play on the gridiron of the Fighting Saints."[67]

Semmens describes the situation at Carroll College after the U.S. entered the Second World War. The college experienced a rapid drop in enrollment and there was concern the place might close. Monsignor Emmet Riley, the college president in those years, "solicited the help of Mike Mansfield, then a member of the United States Congress, to secure a much needed V-12 program." That program was awarded to Carroll College in the spring of 1943. It brought in some 700 trainees just in those next two years, keeping the college alive.[68] Hunthausen told

Semmens that Carroll College "proved to be a real fit for me and I was happy from the outset." One of Hunthausen's close college buddies, Dr. Jack Lowney, told Semmens, "He was into sports, but he was superior in all aspects of academics.... He was a guy we all really admired as a leader."[69] Fr. Bernard Topel (who later became Spokane's Bishop Topel), Hunthausen's math and chemistry professor, really began to influence Hunthausen and asked him to consider whether he might have a vocation in the priesthood. Hunthausen had been putting most of his energy into chemistry but in his junior year, with Topel's influence, he began to take classes in Latin and Philosophy. And because he was in the Borromeo program as a pre-seminary ministry student, he had a deferment from military service.[70]

Hunthausen once described his college life:

> "While a student at Carroll College I participated in almost every sport that was available on campus and enjoyed them all, with one exception. I was never interested in boxing so I never really took time to go out for the spring smoker. The irony of it is that now they have a new athletic center at Carroll College, and when it was erected they revived the old smoker concept of a number of boxing bouts, and without asking me they decided that the major award would be the 'Bishop Hunthausen Boxing Trophies.' I am confident that had they asked me I would have said no; any other sport but not boxing."[71]

While he was at Carroll, Pearl Harbor was attacked.

> "Prior to that I remember with my friends going down to the local civic center to register for the draft. Recalling as best I can the sentiments that were present in my life and in my mind at that time, I dare say that they weren't a whole lot different than those that were in the minds of my friends. I saw war, and the Second World War in particular, with a great deal of dread. I saw it as a horrible and vicious evil, but at the same time I had it surrounded with a great deal of glamour, particularly because I was training at that time to fly an airplane. I was looking with great interest to becoming a pilot in the secondary program. I was in the primary program and nearing its end when the federal government indicated that in the case of our involvement in the war, one in either of these programs was automatically in the Army Air Force. And so I didn't get to do the aerobatics that attracted me so much because my counselor at that time, Fr. Topel, now Bishop Topel, encouraged me to continue to think seriously about priesthood. I had far from convinced myself that this was what I ought to do, but he made it clear that it would be foolhardy for me to cut off my options.... When Pearl Harbor occurred, many of my friends in a

matter of 24 or 48 hours were off in the service. Almost all the rest of my classmates continued on through college as long as they were able before being drafted in one direction or another, and almost all of them ended up in the officer training program. I remember one day playing golf with my father. He had come over to visit me. He was a quiet man; he never really talked to me much about what I ought to do. He gave me good counsel and tremendous example, and I always felt the closest kindred to him. I can still remember the exact spot when he had to bring up an issue that was very important to him. He wanted to know what I was going to do about military service. And that was the first time that I shared with him the fact that I had made up my mind to at least pursue for the moment the priesthood. Finish college in the next year or so and then go on to the seminary. He said, 'Tremendous, I think that's just the greatest thing you could tell me. The reason I brought the issue up is because I was in the First World War and I remember how much better life the officers had, and I was going to encourage you to go into officer training.' I still remember that, just as vividly as though it happened yesterday. I remember when he wrote to me on the occasion of my ordination to the sub-diaconate. He recalled that moment in our lives and that really touched me deeply that he remembered it so keenly."[72]

His dad wrote, "My Adam's apple has jumped with delight as I reflected on the direction you were moving."[73]

Fr. Joseph Oblinger was a classmate of Hunthausen's at Carroll College. Both Oblinger and Hunthausen were in the Borromeo program for those preparing for seminary. So, Oblinger says, they were studying side by side with their military buddies and finding themselves in a commando training program of extensive physical fitness effort. When they graduated in 1943, there were only eighteen members. Some went off to seminary and others to the war in the Pacific or Europe.[74]

At St. Edward's Seminary in Seattle, Hunthausen was in an accelerated program, three years instead of the traditional four years of theology. This involved summer classes. Joseph Oblinger was in the same seminary training program and has described it as tightly regimented. "We were plunged immediately into the routine of the Seminary. That meant finding our rooms, getting unpacked, then dressing in our black cassock or soutane, and finding our way to the lecture hall where we were instructed about seminary life. Among the most difficult aspects of this new life was the silence. Silence above the first floor; silence in and between classes, silence during meals (special occasions excepted)." Oblinger writes that seminary life did seem to have some aspects of three worlds: Boot Camp, Boarding School, and Penitentiary.[75]

A typical day began with morning prayer and meditation in community at 6 a.m. By 10 p.m., lights were out. Oblinger has recalled other aspects of their life in seminary at St. Edward's. Fr. John Galvin was one of the Sulpician priests who taught dogmatic theology at St. Edward's. Both Oblinger and Hunthausen were under Galvin's tutelage. He helped them develop, Oblinger says, "an attitude of criticism, i.e. not to swallow everything you hear or read on sight. There are more ways than one to express a given truth. He was a student of John Henry Cardinal Newman, who developed the idea that doctrine or truth is a seed that develops over the years as man applies his intellectual gifts to its study."[76]

August 1945 brought the nuclear age into Hunthausen's consciousness:

> "I was well along in my seminary training. I recall the announcement of Hiroshima and Nagasaki.... My life was dramatically changed at that time. I can recall exactly where I was, maybe all of us can, when that announcement was made. And while many around me were ecstatic with their happiness that now the war was probably over, I have to tell you I walked off in another direction and I was sad to the depths of my being. In one sense I was rejoicing, yes, that this might mean the end of the war, but I somehow felt that as a world we had taken a dramatic step, that we were no longer the same and we never would be the same again. I could not comprehend an instrument of destruction that was capable of annihilating so many people in such a short period of time. I just did not want to accept that. I guess what I did not want to do was in any way have a part with it, and yet I felt as if I were implicated. There was no way I could not be part of it. I was depressed for days and I'm sure many others were. But as time went on my life came back into focus and I along with the rest of the world pretty much took our new weapons in stride and went on with my life."[77]

The next year Hunthausen became a priest. Bishop Gilmore ordained him on June 1, 1946, at St. Paul's Church in Anaconda. St. Paul's was the home parish of not only Hunthausen, but also Bishop Gilmore and William Morley, who was ordained with Hunthausen that day.[78]

> "It was a happy occasion. I was ordained in my home parish church... which was a break from tradition. Prior to that time, ordinations were always held in the cathedral. But this was at the tail end of the war. Gas rationing was still on, and the bishop, sensitive to that, decided to ordain us in our own parish. I remember the gathering of the clan. My grandparents came from Missouri, along with some aunts and uncles and cousins. It doesn't seem 50 years ago."

In 1996 he was asked about his first Mass:

> "It's etched in my memory. It was on a Sunday—that would be June 2—in the convent chapel at St. Paul School. It was just my immediate family, and the Sisters, and Father Topel, who later became bishop of Spokane. I can still remember that, probably more clearly than Mass celebrated just a few days ago. Those are events that touch one very deeply."[79]

On his 50th anniversary of priestly ministry he was also asked about the process he went through in deciding to become a priest:

> "Throughout the seminary, I wasn't always certain that this was where I belonged and what I ought to be doing. But I couldn't honestly say that I knew what I *was* supposed to do. In those days, six months to a year before being ordained a priest, one was ordained sub-deacon. That's when I really had to decide. And, quite frankly, from that time on, any doubts disappeared. I've never had any question that this is very truly where I was meant to be. And I consider that a great grace."

How had his call to the priesthood come about?

> "More than my own intuiting that this is where I was supposed to go, I was responding to people whose opinion I really respected. Father Topel was one of my teachers in college, and he became my spiritual guide and a wonderful influence in my life. He simply asked the question, 'Are you sure that this is *not* what you're supposed to do?' And I said, 'Well, no, I'm not sure.' And he said, 'Why don't you think about it, and why don't you pray about it.' And that's how it all began. I was convinced, of course, that the priesthood was wonderful and we needed priests. Somebody ought to be a priest, I thought. But I'm not sure I ought to be one. I prepared myself for the seminary and wasn't sure how long I might stay. There was a great tug at the time. The war was on, and all my friends were in the military. I had taken a civilian pilot training course that the government was offering. There was a fascination, a romantic sense about wanting to fly these planes. And, of course, I love children. I was attracted to married life and family. Those were all part of my reflection and entered into my prayer and discernment."[80]

Dutch's brother Tony tried to make it home in time for his older brother's ordination. Just after Tony finished high school, the summer of 1944, he joined the U.S. Army. Tony tells me that he and Dutch never spoke much about this, but Dutch knew the story:

> "I remember I spent my birthday, January 25, 1945, in Belgium on the frontline. I was in the 102nd Infantry Division. What I saw from January to May was enough for anybody my age to bear. I remember thinking, this couldn't be true, mom's going to wake me up any minute and say, 'Get up and get to school.' I remember thinking that way. But it was a reality alright. Luckily for me I only had a few months in the service. They were getting a lot of people shot up. I was hit in the leg. A guy with a machine gun was shooting at us."

It was April 12, 1945, when Tony was wounded. His wound seemed to heal up rather fast. But they sent him to a doctor back from the frontline.

> "He said to me, 'you know what, I'm going to have to do something even though I'd rather not because we don't have the equipment for it. But I've got to, because if I don't that's bound to be infected and you are going to lose your leg.' So he put me on the table. That hurt so bad. He said, 'I have to do this and I can't give you anything to numb the pain.' So he went in there and dug the lead out. Luckily he saved my leg. I was there on that table a couple of hours. They did not have anesthetic up there near the front and there was no antibiotic then."

Tony would never forget how it felt on that table. In time he healed but he had to stay in the service to wait his turn while other soldiers who had served longer were able to head home sooner. At some point, when he was informed of the plans for his brother's ordination scheduled for June 1, 1946, he made every effort to get home in time to be there. But since he was the youngest in his whole division he had to wait much longer than he would have wanted to. He did leave Europe in the middle of May, but then the weather turned foul and this delayed things. "All kinds of things happened. We hit storms in the North Atlantic. The ship was a little tiny thing, why you could have fit it so easily into the Queen Mary that I had come over to Europe in." He got on the train in New York City and made a connection in Wisconsin, but could not get back to Anaconda until over a week after Dutch had been ordained.[81]

In a way, even Dutch was not able to be fully present for his own ordination; that is to say, with his powers of concentration focused entirely on the solemnity. This is because a charley horse struck him at one point during the ritual. Dick Walsh recalls the laugh he and his uncle enjoyed when they were together recently. "We were looking at pictures and came across the one where he was lying prostrate on the altar at his ordination. He said he had the worst muscle cramp in his leg and was not able to concentrate much at all on the service as he was just trying to make it through the moment of pain with the charley horse."[82] Now it need not be interpreted as some sort of omen presaging the constraints Rome would "hobble" him with decades later in Seattle.

ENDNOTES

1 Morris, Patrick. *Anaconda Montana: Copper Smelting Boom Town on the Western Frontier* and the sequel, *Anaconda Mountain: In Changing Times*. Swan Publishing 1997 and 2010.

2 Morris, Patrick. *Anaconda Montana: Copper Smelting Boom Town on the Western Frontier*. Swan Publishing 1997, 22.

3 Morris, Patrick, 27.

4 Morris, Patrick, 2.

5 My spouse and I learned of this when we visited the town in the summer of 2011.

6 Morris, Patrick, 190

7 Finnegan, Alice. *Goosetown in Their Own Words*. Sweetgrass Books 2012, 15.

8 Morris, Patrick, 286.

9 Morris, Patrick, 184.

10 Everett, George. "When Toil Meant Trouble" Outback Ventures 1999.

11 Morris, Patrick, 149.

12 Morris, Patrick, 260.

13 Morris, Patrick, 184, 187.

14 Morris, Patrick, 132.

15 Shipman, Raymond. "The Descendants of Henry Adam Trilling: A Book of Family History" Self-Published, Dillon, Montana 2014, 11, 18, 19.

16 Hunthausen, Tony. Personal interview. Helena, Montana. 4 Aug. 2014.

17 "The Week in Anaconda Society" "Hunthausens Have Son" *The Anaconda Standard* 28 Aug. 1921, 10. Found at Butte Historical Society in Butte, Montana.

18 Wilson, Cynthia and Rebecca Boren. "The Peace Bishop." See in David Brewster and David Buerge, eds. *Washingtonians: A Biographical Portrait of the State*. Sasquatch Books, 1989, 470.

19 Atkins, Gary. "Archbishop Hunthausen." *Seattle Times* 20 June 1982, 9-10.

20 Wooden, Cindy. "Faith, family and friends continue to guide Archbishop Hunthausen" *Progress* 1 Oct. 1987, 9.

21 Wooden, Cindy, 9.

22 Walsh, Dick. Telephone interview. Polson, Montana. 23 Aug. 2014.

23 "Stack stands as remembrance" (the local historian was Bob Vine) *Anaconda Visitors Guide*, 2011, 16.

24 Everett, George. "When Toil Meant Trouble" *Outback Ventures* 1999.

25 "It Comes From Faith: An Interview with Archbishop Raymond Hunthausen." *Ground Zero*. Summer 1987, 2.

26 Walsh, Dick. Telephone interview. Polson, Montana. 23 Aug. 2014.

27 Hunthausen, Tony. Personal interview. Helena, Montana. 4 Aug. 2014.

28 Walsh, Dick. Telephone interview and email correspondence. Polson, Montana. 23 Aug. 2014.

29 "It Comes From Faith." 2.

30 Shipman, Raymond. "The Descendants of Henry Adam Trilling: A Book of Family History" Self-Published, Dillon, Montana 2014, 8.

31 Hunthausen, Andy. Personal interview. Helena, Montana. 3 Aug. 2014.

32 Morris, Jack. Personal interview. Portland, Oregon 5 July 2011.

33 Morris, Jack.

34 Clark, Paul. "New Seattle Archbishop is a 'people's prelate'" *Progress*, Special Souvenir Edition 23 May 1975, 5.

35 Wooden, Cindy. "Faith, family and friends continue to guide Archbishop Hunthausen" *Progress* 1 Oct. 1987, 10.

36 Hunthausen, Bill. Personal interview. Helena, Montana. 5 Aug. 2014.

37 Stergar, Dave. Personal interview. Helena, Montana. 6 Aug. 2014.

38 Hunthausen, Edna. Personal interview. Helena, Montana 17 Aug. 2011.

39 Stergar, Jean. Personal interview. Anaconda, Montana 27 Aug. 2011.

40 Miller, Carolyn. Personal interview. Helena, Montana. 6 Aug. 2014.

41 Walsh, Dick. Telephone interview and email correspondence. Polson, Montana. 23 Aug. 2014.

42 Walsh, Dick.

43 Morris, Jack. Personal interview. Portland, Oregon 5 July 2011.

44 Walsh, Dick. Telephone interview and email correspondence. Polson, Montana. 23 Aug. 2014.

45 Shea, Dan. Personal interview. Helena, Montana. 4 Aug. 2014.

46 Hunthausen, Tony. Personal interview. Helena, Montana. 4 Aug. 2014.

47 Hunthausen, Tony.

48 Hunthausen, Tony.

49 Hunthausen, Tony.

50 Morris, Patrick. *Anaconda Montana: In Changing Times*. Swan Publishing 2010, 9.

51 Morris, Patrick, 80.

52 Stergar, Dave. Personal interview. Helena, Montana. 6 Aug. 2014.

53 Hunthausen, Andy. Personal interview. Helena, Montana. 3 Aug. 2014.

54 Malone, Michael, Richard Roeder, and William Lang. *Montana: A History of Two Centuries*. Univ. of Washington Press 1990, 354.

55 Kohl, Martha. "The Butte-Anaconda National Historic Landmark" *Montana: The Magazine of Western History*, Winter 2006, 64-69.

56 Emmons, David. *The Butte Irish: Class and Ethnicity in an American Mining Town, 1875-1925*. Univ. of Illinois Press 1989, 95.

57 Emmons, David, 103.

58 Flaherty, Cornelia. *Go With Haste Into The Mountains: A History of the Diocese of Helena*. Falcon Publishing 1984, 69.

59 Flaherty, Cornelia, 73-74.

60 Flaherty, Cornelia, 161.

61 "Sixth Bishop Is Native Of Montana" *Montana Catholic Register*, Souvenir Edition 31 Aug. 1962, 7.

62 Hunthausen, Andy. Personal interview. Helena, Montana. 3 Aug. 2014.

63 Wilson, Cynthia and Rebecca Boren. 471.

64 Walsh, Dick. Telephone interview and email correspondence. Polson, Montana. 23 Aug. 2014.

65 Walsh, Dick.

66 Bugni, Guido. From original note cards for speech, delivered at Carroll College in Fall 1979. Notes were shared with me by Guido when we met in Helena in August 2014.

67 Semmens, John. "A Man Called 'Dutch': The Lasting Impact of Archbishop Raymond G. Hunthausen on Carroll College" Unpublished paper written for History Research Seminar 495, Carroll College 18 Dec. 2007, 1.

68 Semmens, John, 5.

69 Semmens, John, 5-6.

70 Semmens, John, 6.

71 Hunthausen, Raymond. "Coming to a Position on the Global Arms Race: A Personal Journey." 22 Feb. 1982. Mt. Angel Abbey, St. Benedict, Oregon. Catholic Archdiocese of Seattle Archives. 25.

72 Hunthausen, Raymond, 25.

73 "Archbishop Hunthausen Anniversary," *Progress* 30 May 1996, 14.

74 Oblinger, Joseph. *Fisher of Men*. Lifevest Publishing 2006, 23-25.

75 Oblinger, Joseph, 27.

76 Oblinger, Joseph, 29.

77 Hunthausen, Raymond. "Coming to a Position on the Global Arms Race: A Personal Journey," 26.

78 Flaherty, Cornelia, 161.

79 "Archbishop Hunthausen Anniversary," *Progress* 30 May 1996, 13.

80 "Archbishop Hunthausen Anniversary," 13-14.

81 Hunthausen, Tony. Personal interview. Helena, Montana. 4 Aug. 2014.

82 Walsh, Dick. Telephone interview and email correspondence. Polson, Montana. 23 Aug. 2014.

Chapter Nine

MONTANAN (AND VATICAN II BISHOP) FOR ALL SEASONS

Family and community bonds in Anaconda, studies and athletics at Carroll College, spirituality and vocational discernment at St. Edward's, and personal awakening to moral complexities in the context of World War II—these all shaped Raymond Hunthausen in the first quarter-century of his life. Ordained at the young age of twenty-five in the war-time accelerated seminary program, he then served at Carroll College in various roles before becoming the bishop of Helena in 1962. Family remained integral to him always. To better appreciate the character of the young man and how he approached life in those decades prior to his years as Seattle's archbishop, I sought out people who worked with him, folks he taught and coached, and members of the close-knit family that surrounded him and brought him much joy.

Dan Shea, like Ray Hunthausen, was born into a Catholic immigrant family in Anaconda. He knew Anaconda's "Goosetown" firsthand. He was ordained by Helena's Bishop Hunthausen in 1969. One day just a few years ago, Fr. Shea was traveling across part of Montana with the retired archbishop. As they drove from Helena to Bozeman, they got into a little humorous repartee. "Dutch, I have a bone to pick with you. I came and talked with you the day after ordination, and you appointed me a high school principal. There were other priests who had completed master's degrees and had experience, and yet you appointed me. I was not prepared for that job." Not defensively but ever so calmly Dutch queried, "Oh, is that right?" As a matter of fact, the superintendent of the diocesan Catholic schools at the time was Shea's mentor, and it was he who had recommended him for the post at Bozeman Rosary High, so the bishop's decision had not been arbitrary. But Shea certainly felt back then that he did not have the kind of training needed to take on the responsibilities thrust upon him. Dutch asked, "tell me, when did you get that assignment?" Shea replied, "I think it had to be the first day of June 1969." Dutch then inquired, "when did you have to report?" "I think it was the middle of July." "Oh, okay, so you had six weeks to get ready for the job?" When Shea confirmed this fact, Hunthausen had his closing argument ready. "Well, let me tell you a story. I was ordained in 1946 and I was first of all assigned to the cathedral. And I was up there and I was told, 'you will be teaching chemistry next week at the college.' I had a week to get ready. You had six weeks, what are you complaining about?" The pair had a hearty laugh.[1]

From the very beginning of his priestly life in 1946, a pattern began to emerge of Raymond Hunthausen being put in charge of one thing after another and having to find ways to step up. Prayer was a huge part of how he managed.

Fr. Jim Hogan, a retired priest of the Diocese of Helena living in Missoula, began his collegiate studies at Carroll College in 1953. Also a native of Anaconda and about thirteen years younger than Dutch, he first met Coach Hunthausen when he played basketball for him. Jim had been in Helena visiting his good friend in the early part of summer 2014 and they retold stories from their times together at Carroll and since. And as a result, Hogan's recollections were fresh when I met him in Missoula later that summer. It seems that in the early days, before the teams started using a bus, they would travel to games in a caravan, often just two or three cars.

> "When I was a freshman, we went on a road trip to Billings. It was in the middle of the winter, dead cold, fiercely cold, with lots of snow. So on the way there we started this game of 'ambushing' the other cars with snowball attacks. We'd get out, and they'd come by, and we'd let'em have it with snowballs. Hunthausen was driving. He never got into the snowball fights but he cooperated all the same. I remember another fellow was driving Fr. Topel's '36 Chevrolet. So we're coming back and it was even colder and we were on this side of Townsend, between Billings and Helena, and there was a long steep hill, and so we said to Dutch, 'pull over, pull over, here they come.' So he pulled off the side of the road. Joe Pat Sullivan was a senior. Jim Callahan was a year ahead of me, a sophomore, they were big guys, and so we jumped out of the car. Now Walt Romasko, driving the other car, sees us, so he floorboards that old '36 Chevy and he's just cruising up the hill and Joe Pat Sullivan grabs a big pile of snow and just throws it in the air. It had a big chunk of ice in it and it went right through the windshield."

The skill with which Hogan told the story made me feel like the whole team, and especially Romasko and Coach Hunthausen, were there with us for a re-dramatization. "Romasko could have killed us. He got the car stopped, got out, and stood there shaking his fist and yelling. He was a great big dude. What about Topel's '36 Chevy? I asked Dutch, 'so what'd you tell Topel?' And he says, 'well, I never said a word. I just got it fixed.'"[2]

Hogan had another tale from his days with Coach Hunthausen. They were in a post-1956–57 season tournament, which included Montana State in Bozeman,

Gonzaga in Spokane, and the College of Idaho. "No one had ever heard of him then, but Elgin Baylor was playing for Idaho. So, before the game Dutch says to Jim Callahan and me, 'there's this guy, Elgin Baylor, I want you two to double team him.' So we double-teamed him and the two of us held him to 45 points."[3] Not long after that, Baylor became a star player for the Los Angeles Lakers.

Coach Hunthausen was also Father Hunthausen. Fr. Topel had been Hogan's spiritual director, but when Topel was named bishop of Spokane, Hogan asked Hunthausen to take on the role. "That was great. We'd talk about spirituality every week." Like others in the Borromeo Club, a kind of pre-seminary program on the Carroll campus, Hogan would be assigned to St. Edward's Seminary in Seattle. But he did not stay there for long. "I wasn't too sure about this whole thing. I'd see guys who were lonely. So I decided to quit. So I came home and had a couple of sessions with Dutch. He said to me, 'try not to be pusillanimous, small-hearted.' He said, 'trust God, and if you feel called to the priesthood, trust that it won't be what you are afraid of.' In addition, he said, 'you don't have to live out your life as a priest the way others do, you can do it your own way." Hogan returned to the seminary. In the decades to follow, Hunthausen influenced him greatly. As priests, he said, "Dutch encouraged us to find time for spiritual reading. He urged us to make it something spiritually significant."[4]

He was a priest, teacher, and coach, always trying to balance commitments. Fr. Hunthausen taught and coached Dick Roche. From his home in Butte, Roche wrote to me in 2012. "He was my chemistry instructor and head football coach in 1956. One day he was checking each student in chemistry lab. He stops behind me, looks around and leans over to whisper in my ear, 'meet me in my office in ten minutes—the football films are in.'" Decades later, when Dick Roche was attending a Carroll College football game, he went up to the private box at half time intending to visit with the retired archbishop. "They said he just left by himself for a place some two hundred miles away to say Mass. He was 78 years old. That's the way he was—always trying to be wherever needed. He wanted to help out, mix with the common people. He had the ability to reach people, understand their situations and be a friend. For me, the characteristic I like best was making me feel like he was my friend—always had time for you."[5]

In December of 1955, the head of the Carroll chemistry department passed away and Hunthausen was appointed to take over. Again he had to step up and try to do his best. A few months earlier, August 4, 1955 to be exact, Fr. Hunthausen sent out a note to the Carroll College football team about plans for fall practice and hopes for the season. One thing seems clear; he was one conscientious coach-athlete.

> "As most of you know, our first game comes quickly—September 17th—against Ricks, a team which for the past several years has been

> one of our toughest opponents. Therefore, I would advise you to start getting in shape well before the day you make your appearance here. It will speed things along as well as make the going easier for you. This year let's not be content to say that we should have whipped Ricks; let's get down and do it! Victory must be prepared for long before the opening kickoff. It should be obvious that this advance practice period to be a success demands 100% attendance…don't let us down!"

And he added personal notes. For example, to Guido Bugni he typed a short message above the main lines he had typed to all the team. "Guids: How goes it? Good I hope. How much weight and speed have you picked up—we'll see when you arrive—I'll beat you in the 100. Say your prayers! Be seein' you soon. Father Hunt."[6] Coach Hunthausen brought to coaching the tenacious, gritty, and affirming energy he had displayed as a student-athlete.

Butte native Guido Bugni graduated from high school in 1953. Fr. Hunthausen came to Butte to recruit Bugni and, despite the fact that Guido was not home that day, he was able to convince Guido's parents to send their son to Carroll. Bugni:

> "So I went to Carroll in August of 1953. We started practice before school started. He had torn his Achilles tendon. So he coached us on crutches. I like to tell the story how now at Carroll they have a head football coach and he's got maybe three or four assistants. They have a recruiter. They have a trainer. They have a basketball coach and an assistant basketball coach. In his time he was all of those things. He was head football coach, he was the trainer, he recruited, and not only that, he taught two classes of chemistry."

As was normal for the priest faculty in those times, on weekends Fr. Hunthausen also went to small towns in the diocese to say Mass. "So we got our money's worth out of that guy."[7]

John Gagliardi was the coach at Carroll in the early 1950s before he left to take a job at St. John's in Collegeville, Minnesota. Hunthausen had been Gagliardi's assistant, so Gagliardi recommended him for the job as head football coach. As the story goes, Coach Gagliardi was walking up on the hilltop of the campus and looked down to the field and saw a guy punting the football. The fellow's punting skills were impressive. So Gagliardi came down to speak with the individual he assumed must be a Carroll student. "I was watching you punt. I wonder if you'd come out for football." And the guy replied, "I'm Fr. Hunthausen, I was just appointed to teach chemistry." Hunthausen could punt well over half the length of the field as could his brother Jack, according to Bugni. So Fr. Raymond Hunthausen came on as assistant coach. Gagliardi, who went on to become one of the winningest coaches in all of college football, returned to Carroll to visit and once wryly remarked, "You know, if I had stayed at Carroll I could be an archbishop."[8]

Guido kept telling me about Father and Coach Hunthausen. "I remember when he was the football coach; the field had rocks in it. He got a jeep from Army surplus and an old dump truck from Maronick Construction Company. We called it 'the Green Hornet' and we cleared the rocks. He planted grass on that football field on his hands and knees. He dug a ditch for the sprinkler system. He did all this when he was on crutches, he and Frank Sabados." Sabados, a friendly and colorful character, was a much beloved figure on the Carroll campus. He had struggled with alcohol.

> "All of Frank's fingers were cut off. He had gotten drunk one night and his hands were frozen, so they cut off his fingers. But he could do anything with those knobs. So he worked with Hunthausen to put in the sprinkler system. We called Hunthausen 'Coach' and 'Father'. I still call him Father or Coach. He did all this on crutches with his tendon torn. He and Sabados tapped into the city water main across Benton Avenue. They just made the connection, no permission asked in those days."[9]

Bugni described a day in the life of a Carroll student-athlete under the tutelage of Father and Coach Hunthausen:

> "We had football practice early, but even before that he would say Mass, at 6 a.m. Anyone could go who wanted to go, including some who were not Catholic, then we had practice, then breakfast. We had projects on the campus, like clearing the football field. He'd expect you to be in shape. He respected you as being smart enough to figure out what was going on, and it was really a pleasure to play for a guy like that. After he threw the crutches away, when the Achilles injury healed up, he'd run plays with us. He'd play every position and show you how to do it. We'd travel in different cars. Everybody wanted to ride with him because he was a fun guy."[10]

Late in the summer of 1954, "we went to Legendary Lodge where we practiced football for two weeks." Legendary Lodge, on Salmon Lake, some distance northwest of Helena, was originally built by William A. Clark, Jr. as a resort for the wealthy, but was obtained by Bishop Gilmore in 1950.[11]

> "The field where we practiced we called 'Hunthausen field' even then. One of the cabins was a chapel. We'd go to Mass, then breakfast, then practice, and then we'd do projects like taking pine needles out of the cracks between the shingles. We hauled wood to get ready for the

winter. Then we'd play in the one lane bowling alley where you had to set your own pins. We'd play ping pong, volleyball, go out on the lake by boat, water ski, and he would drive the boat. We practiced again in the afternoon. We sang in the evening. I played accordion."[12]

As we will see, Legendary Lodge would become dear to the whole Hunthausen clan.

Guido remembers seeing his coach during games "walking up and down the sidelines, with his collar on. He wore a hat, smoked a cigarette, and he was nervous but he was into it." Bugni, hired later by Hunthausen to teach chemistry, taught at Carroll for forty-one years.

> "We played our games at Vigilante Stadium, since the public high school had the only field in town at the time. He was just like one of the kids. But you respected him. You knew who he was, father and coach. After supper you could go up to his room. There were always several students up there, in St. Charles Hall, where he and the other priests lived. Hunthausen might say, 'let's go downtown to see a movie.' He was busy but he made time for us and for so many different needs."[13]

Carroll College pre-1960s was a closely disciplined campus community. But Hunthausen's prankster side came out in moments such as this tale from Guido:

> "Every once in a while the power would go out. There was a box up on the telephone pole and it would have a short. So all the lights would go off. The dean of men would say 'general quarters' so everyone could leave the building until they got the power back on. They could go downtown or wherever. A lot of kids would stay. There would be pandemonium, water fights and all. And there was this one guy, who had a flashlight under each arm and a water pistol in each hand, and he was hiding, and he was shooting at anybody who would go by. One person who went by was Fr. Paul Kirchen who taught German at Carroll, and the guy who was shooting at him was Fr. Hunthausen, assistant dean of students. Hunthausen had fun with everyone."

Well, almost everyone. It seems Fr. Kirchen was none too happy with the assistant dean of students in that moment, even though Kirchen and Hunthausen were close friends. "It was said of Kirchen, a serious fellow, that he was the only person who went to Germany and never had a beer."[14]

Hunthausen was appointed president of Carroll in 1957. "There are still people teaching there who Uncle Dutch hired," says nephew Andy. "He was their friend, not just their boss. Hank Burgess taught there forever." Burgess, who taught English Literature and was also from Anaconda, told Andy Hunthausen, "your uncle hired me on a handshake. I didn't have a contract or anything. It was your uncle's word." Andy Hunthausen took me around the campus in August 2014 as he told me about his uncle's legacy there. He certainly added to the buildings, but brick and mortar were not his most important gifts. "People wanted to work for him. He related in a way that was special. The whole time he was at Carroll you would have a difficult time knowing that he was the president of the college. He was always with the students. He was always trying to do things. He loved being with the students." The retired archbishop told a story, during a ceremony on campus in 2012 for the newly named Hunthausen Avenue. Andy says he talked about a hill that slopes down on the north side of the campus. Kids in the neighborhood were sledding nearby, long years ago, but into the street where it was dangerous at times. They were getting some complaints from people in the area. "So he met with the kids. He said to them, 'if we build a sledding hill over here will you stop using the street?' So he made the grassy hill into a sledding spot for the kids so sledding wouldn't be so dangerous anymore. He met with the kids and worked things out. It's still the best sledding in all of town."[15]

A distinguishing feature of Hunthausen was that the pupil of one of his eyes was smaller than the other, says Andy.

> "He was out there one day changing sprinklers and the pressure got him right in the eye and it never quite came back to normal after it healed. That happened in the 1950s. He put in sprinklers and he put in trees. There are trees all over the campus that he planted back then. It was more his presence and how he was, that is what is remembered in these examples. He did whatever needed to be done and he did it with people on campus."[16]

In the interview with John Semmens, Hunthausen described what it was like when Bishop Gilmore told him he would be teaching chemistry and math. "I burned a lot of midnight oil preparing for my classes," and "I also started to go to graduate schools." Each summer starting in 1947, he was studying either at St. Louis University, Catholic University, or Fordham. He then spent a full year at Notre Dame before receiving his Master of Science degree in organic chemistry. Hunthausen would have begun studies for a doctorate at Notre Dame but, when John Gagliardi moved to Collegeville, Fr. Hunthausen was invited to take on the role of athletic director. He was in charge of the football, basketball, baseball, track, and golf teams. He handled all that while also teaching chemistry. During the four years from 1953 through 1956, Semmens writes, "the Carroll College Fighting Saints, under his guidance, won an incredible eight conference championships." Tom Kelly, who played football for Hunthausen and later coached both football and basketball at Carroll, said Hunthausen "had the capacity to make the players feel good about themselves and consequently, that contributed to his effectiveness."[17]

When he was placed at the helm of Carroll he was only thirty-five. Guido Bugni told Semmens that one day U.S. Senate Majority Leader Mike Mansfield visited the campus, evidently unannounced. He wanted to meet with the president. Hunthausen' secretary, Ellen Ryan, could not find him. "He was outside mowing or raking the lawn," Bugni said, "and he comes in to see Mike Mansfield and he's not wearing his priestly garb or anything; he's wearing work clothes. I bet Mike got a kick out of that."[18] When I sat down with him for our interview in the summer of 2014, Tony Hunthausen talked about his brother's leadership at Carroll this way. "Someone would come to see the president. 'We can't find him.' 'Well, was he in his office? Well, go outside, he's probably out there helping someone put a tree up.' Sure enough, that's where he would be." Then of course, Tony told me, his older brother would say to the person who had come to see him, "okay, let's go back to the office." He was still able to do his work as president. "He was just that kind of a guy. If you needed help, he'd give it to you."[19]

Con Kelly grew up in Butte and was ordained a priest for the Diocese of Helena in 1958. His first assignment after ordination was to teach philosophy at Carroll. "There were about eighteen priests on the faculty then. During lunch in the priests' dining room, Hunthausen would just come in and say, 'I think I'll go skiing this afternoon.' Six or seven priests would invite themselves to go with him."[20] Of course, this continued when Dutch became a bishop. Like other priests in the Diocese of Helena, Jim Hogan used to ski with Dutch. One place they went to was Bridger Bowl near Bozeman. "I remember one day we were down there, great snow. No one else was with us. The two of us went over to an area and found powder snow. It was toward the end of the day. We got down to the bottom, and we said, 'woah man, that was the best thing ever!'"[21] As noted earlier in the book, this "I think I'm going to go skiing" custom he had of inviting others continued in his Seattle years with spontaneous ski trips up to Crystal Mountain near Mt. Rainier.

If Hunthausen knew how to recreate, he also knew how to be sensitive to painful realities in the world at large. In the early 1950s, war on the Korean Peninsula had been in his consciousness. "It was a very powerful distraction for me; I felt deep down, that we shouldn't be there…." Outside, he was teaching and coaching, but inside, he struggled. "It was the whole reality of death associated with war. It didn't make sense to me; it just didn't make sense as a way of resolving problems."[22] At this point in his life, issues of war and peace were not in the forefront of his awareness as they would be much later in Seattle. By the time John F. Kennedy had been elected as the first Catholic president in the nation's history, Hunthausen had been serving as Carroll's president for three years. During those years leading up to his appointment as the bishop of Helena in 1962, he reflected with students at Carroll about intercontinental ballistic missiles and the fact that ICBMs were going to be placed in silos in the Great Falls region of Montana. On a few occasions, he preached on the issue at the college. As with the Korean War earlier, and throughout the early decades of the Cold War era, Dutch was struggling internally to understand the magnitude of the tragedy and evil of war. His conscience would eventually, in Seattle, birth a prophetic voice.[23]

In the forties, fifties, and even into the sixties, before he entered the national and international spotlight, he made regional news for Carroll-related matters and for his church renewal initiatives during and just after Vatican II. Hunthausen's athletic record was newsworthy. Helena's newspaper, *The Independent Record*, announced in December 1966 that he had been selected for the National Association of Intercollegiate Athletics football Hall of Fame. He was inducted on December 10 in Tulsa, Oklahoma. "Bishop Hunthausen compiled an outstanding record as a football and basketball player at Carroll. He was captain of the football team which won Carroll's first Montana Collegiate Conference grid title in 1940. The team repeated in 1941 and was unbeaten."[24] The full character of Dutch Hunthausen draws together many features, including his outdoor spirit, youthful athleticism, and mature social change action. His athleticism and love of the outdoors did not stop. He kept fly-fishing, hiking, skiing, and golfing as long as his body would cooperate, well into his eighties. Small wonder he could not stay indoors in the Carroll College presidential office. He had to get out, move, take in the fresh air, change a sprinkler, and engage with the students.

In the autumn of 1979, Guido Bugni gave the address at a ceremony inducting Archbishop Hunthausen into Carroll College's Alumni Hall of Fame. During "his tenure at Carroll he taught general chemistry, organic chemistry and math; and he coached football, basketball, baseball, and track, and he served as athletic director; he was vocational director for the diocese and to prove his versatility he gained a reputation as one of the most popular deans of discipline, which in itself is quite a task." As president of Carroll he "transformed the campus from a one-building institution on top of the hill to a beautiful campus of five major buildings with a landscape of incredible beauty—most of which he did himself." He was, Bugni attested, a man for all seasons. He rolled up his sleeves. "If you wanted to see him when he was president you might have found him in the following places: working in his office, meditating in the chapel, mowing the lawn, directing some campus project, or wrestling with Tommy O'Halloran in the foyer of Borromeo Hall."[25]

BISHOP OF HELENA

Everyone expected that Bishop Gilmore would attend the first session of the Second Vatican Council, but while he was in San Francisco in early April 1962 for the installation of a new archbishop, he died suddenly during a dinner among fellow bishops.[26] Someone would have to be made bishop soon to prepare to go to Rome that autumn for the start of what would become a sea-change in Catholicism. In mid-July it was announced that Monsignor Hunthausen, who had been given that title in 1958, would be the new bishop. Cornelia Flaherty, in her history of the Helena Diocese, tells us that when the news broke about his appointment, Raymond Hunthausen was in Billings with his mother, so Mrs. Edna Hunthausen "had the joyous privilege of being the first to congratulate her son."[27] Hunthausen was the first Montana-born priest to become the bishop of Helena and was consecrated on August 30. In what was becoming a regular refrain marking his career, he was asked to step up yet again and take on a role for which he was not sure he was suited. "Becoming a bishop was the remotest thing from my mind," he said probably more than once. "I wanted to run away because I was sure I didn't have what it takes. Finally I said if God wants this, it'll have to be his doing. He'll have to make me big enough for the job."[28]

He was the newest and youngest of American bishops when the Second Vatican Council commenced that same autumn, 1962. The council involved matters of great seriousness for the future of the church and world. This man in his early-forties would be profoundly affected by the whole experience over the four sessions each fall through 1965, but he also had some lighthearted adventures that would make for humorous stories like sunshine moving across the full arc of his life. At Seattle University, on the 40th anniversary of Vatican II, he told the story about what happened when he and Bishops Topel of Spokane and Treinen of Boise were there together for the first session. Topel had arranged for a place they could stay:

> "And wouldn't you know, he had got us into a convent three miles away from St. Peter's. And when we got there, the question was how in the world are we going to get to St. Peter's? Now there were buses, as you remember from those days, all of the pictures of bishops in buses—dressed in their red regalia all over town and crowding the piazza at St. Peter's. Well, we, of course, didn't have any bus service. And so I checked around and I found a graduate student, a graduate priest from the United States that had a Volkswagen bug he wanted to sell. I remember buying it for $1,300. Besides Topel and Treinen, there was also a Bishop Hilary Hacker from Bismarck, and they said, 'That's great, as long as you do the driving!' So I did all the driving

> for that first session. Yeah, that's right! You think Seattle's bad. Now imagine this. Bishop Hacker about 6'2", Bishop Topel a little over six feet and Bishop Treinen about my size. The four of us in a bug! In these red cassocks. The council hadn't been in session very long when I was driving, making our way to the piazza of St. Peter's. We were right in front of what they used to call the Holy Office. We could see the colonnades of the square ahead of us. Busy, busy intersection. The policeman out front was waving traffic through. I was the last one to be waved through. And I was sort of sticking out. The bug was sticking out into the intersection more than I would like. So I edged up to the car in front of me and I touched the bumper. Holy smoke, the door of the car in front of me opened up, and this fellow comes dashing out and he looks down at the car and his hands are waving like this, and all of a sudden he looks into the Volkswagen. He just could not believe it. I can't gesture the way the Italians do. I can't do justice to it. But with that kind of helpless gesture, you know he got back into his car and drove away."[29]

Hunthausen told another tale, this one about George Speltz, who was newly ordained as the auxiliary bishop for Winona, Minnesota and was there for the second session in the fall of 1963:

> "George Speltz is a wonderful guy, but shy, retiring in a lot of ways. And he had his mind made up that he was going to record the opening talk by Paul VI, but he wondered how he might do this. 'Just take the tape recorder,' we said. 'Well,' he said, 'mine is a brand new one, and I have never really used it.' So we encouraged him, 'Just put it in your briefcase and take it in.' 'Won't the Swiss guard stop me?' 'No, they won't pay any attention to you at all.' And here we are at the opening session. We are in our miters and our copes and George has his briefcase. We hadn't seat assignments yet in the second session, so we were all sitting together about midway down on the bleachers way up high. I can still see it. Well, when it comes time for the Holy Father to speak, George reaches down inside his briefcase. You know, there are two buttons that you have got to push in order to record, and he hit only the play button. He had a demonstration tape in there and out comes a John Philip Sousa march. Everybody within earshot all turned and, of course, I looked the other direction. It must have been a year or two before George Speltz was even willing to look at a tape recorder again."[30]

On that occasion, at Seattle University forty years after Vatican II had been convened by John XXIII, retired Archbishop Hunthausen said it:

"…was a great time for the bishops of the world. I think any council would be, but certainly for the bishops of the United States. We got to know one another as we could never have gotten to know one another any other way. We saw one another frequently, not only in council halls, but in special gatherings arranged to bring us together. That lingered and it had its beneficial effect for us bishops after the council was over. Remember Cardinal John Deardon of Detroit was our chairperson of the United States Conference of Catholic Bishops…a marvelous gentleman, who certainly was touched deeply by the council. Because we knew one another, in those first years after the council, the discussion and the agenda was vital and lively. The agenda of the bishops these days pales compared to what we were talking about in those days."[31]

Pope John XXIII was an inspiring exemplar for many people across the world, and we know he became Dutch Hunthausen's model for ministry. Both were down-to-earth and warmhearted souls. At the special funeral Mass held in Helena in June 1963, Bishop Hunthausen mourned and celebrated Pope John.

"The deepest impact that our beloved deceased Pontiff made on the world as a whole was his great Christ-like love for his fellow men. It is indeed fitting that we should take time this evening to understand the meaning of this great example and should strive in the days ahead to emulate it. Is it not insignificant that in our day when men have been angered, puzzled and even made desperate by the dynamic power of the Gospel of hate that has swept the world in our century, God should send us one who would reveal to all of hate torn humanity the power of the Gospel of love. Pope John did this, not through learned treatises, or inspiring exhortations or even through new organizations. His influence was carried through the outpouring of love towards those who came into the circle of his geographically limited life in Rome…. It is most interesting to note that the world that was moved by his Christ-like love of men, is proclaiming him as the Pope of Peace. But there is not peace! The nations in fear muddle along in the uncertainty of an armed truce and humanity is haunted with the dread spectre of 'over kill' in our thermonuclear age. Yet somehow this great man is seen almost instinctively by men everywhere as a symbol of the peace for which men yearn and which Christ has promised. Long ago his great country man Dante had written, 'In His will is our peace.' The absence of peace in this world of ours is a reflection of the inner disorder in men's lives. What people felt intuitively, Pope John grasped fully. The peace of man can come only when the peace of God has been realized."[32]

In the talk Archbishop Hunthausen gave at Mt. Angel Seminary in 1982, when I first heard him, I was so taken by his message:

> "When I became a bishop and went off to the Second Vatican Council.... I remember those days in Rome, particularly when we debated the document on *The Church in the Modern World.* We talked about warfare and what the Church ought to say about warfare and the nuclear age. And as church in that document we made some pretty strong statements, but that is not what I want to refer to. I recall many evenings walking with my bishop friends...walking through the Square talking about the implications, the considerations that really as church, as people of the world we ought to take seriously relative to the nuclear age and what we could do about it, how we might in our own lives address what we were going to have to address ultimately. But again, that was conversation. It provided me opportunities to reflect and to pray about my own responsibility toward this issue. I went home after the Council and again, made no statements, little or nothing relative to the Vietnam War. Although on one or two occasions with the priests' senate in the Helena diocese we did together make a statement about the ICBMs that were being deployed in the plains area of Montana, protesting, trying to make our voices heard, to sensitize the people of Montana. But again, extremely conscious of the fact that to say anything that might be interpreted as disloyal or unpatriotic, I was not that willing to place myself in that position of jeopardy, to be somehow criticized or even taken seriously."[33]

Hunthausen moved confidently into ecumenism. Vatican II encouraged his ecumenical practice, which in turn put him in circles where colleagues across denominations would grapple with issues affecting the world as well as the church.

> "I heard at the Council a good bit of ecumenism, and it resonated with my own experience as a Christian. I grew up in Anaconda, Montana, which many people refer to as a Catholic city. But not really: it might be 40% Catholic and the rest Protestant. I do believe in that Montana community there was a great respect for church by all. We grew up with young people not of our own church. But still when we'd get to talk about churches and our freedom to go to a church, or a wedding or to a funeral, I still remember that caution, 'Oh no, you can't go to a Protestant church.' I just used to think, it doesn't make sense. After all, I play ball with that fellow whose mother was getting married. I don't think it came so much from my family but it was a kind of sense. It worked both ways. Well, listening to the Council and reflecting on

> it, I was liberated. Absolutely liberated. And when I came home… I remember being invited by the Montana Council of Churches in Boulder, Montana, to kind of a hotel and spa there. I was frightened to death. 'I'm completely comfortable with people of other churches,' I'm saying to myself. 'I'm going to have to go as a bishop. I'm going to have to go there and defend the faith!' This is what first crossed my mind. But I went…it was one of the greatest experiences of my life. I came to know men and women in a way that was so supportive of my own ministry. We were all looking for ways to get to God and to understand what was happening in our lives."[34]

Ecumenism figured into correspondence between Bishop Hunthausen and Bishop Marvin Stuart of The Methodist Church regional conference offices in Denver. Stuart wrote to Hunthausen in early April 1967, letting him know that the local Methodist pastor had said how supported they felt by the Catholic community and thanking Catholics for sharing facilities with a local congregation that had suffered a fire in their church. Bishop Hunthausen replied to Stuart:

> "Really, it is no great inconvenience for us to share Saints Cyril and Methodius Church in East Helena with your people. We are happy to do it. Father White told me recently that he has met many of you wonderful people that he might not have met otherwise. Methodius is not a common name in this part of the country. When mentioning our parish in East Helena radio announcers and newspaper articles often called it 'St. Cyril and Methodist Church'. Perhaps they were not too far wrong."[35]

He could relax listeners and bring out a light touch even as he waded into social justice issues. In one speech we can see his sense of humor and a growing sense of social justice. In May 1966, Bishop Hunthausen gave a talk to the crowd gathered for the Montana Beer Wholesalers Convention. He had credentials in their field and thought they might appreciate this.

> "Though I have never checked the family tree specifically, I am sure that between the Hunthausens and the Tuchscherers there has been a long line of men who dedicated their talents to the fine art of quenching properly man's thirst. But more to the point, I served my apprenticeship in your craft through many a summers' labor in the old Rocky Mountain Brewery…. Altogether too often your product has suffered from bad public image—being identified in the public mind with 'demon drink', the destroyer of man's happiness. A truer picture would reveal beer as the poor man's champagne, lifting up and refreshing the hewers of wood and the drawers of water in every

age as nothing else could, thus to soften the harshness of life. A fair appraisal of the role of beer in history would show, I am sure, that it has made a substantial contribution to jovial fellowship so necessary for man's social needs to flourish. What we really need is less emphasis on wine as the symbol of civilized living and more emphasis on beer as the common bond of all races. Instead of Belloc's now famous stanza 'Whenever I travel in a Catholic clime, There is always music and good wine; At least I have always found it so, Benedicamus Domino.' I would add, 'When you visit with gentlemen from far and near, There is always a spirit of friendly cheer; And more often than not it's sustained by beer, Too bad Belloc didn't find this goal, So the Lord could bless his body as well as his soul!' When the scrolls of history are unfolded the story of how to keep your head will most certainly be written by men of your distinguished profession."[36]

Sharing an "insider's" bond with the beer merchants, he asked them to envision their vocation of business to help foster economic justice.

> "As a priest I believe and teach that man lives not on bread alone but on every word that issues forth from the mouth of God. I am moved to my best efforts when I realize that to be a herald of that word gives dignity and meaning to my life's work. But I can never forget and it must not be forgotten that man does also live on bread and to say this is to cover the whole field of man as an economic being and to know that he can only develop his highest spiritual powers if his economic needs are satisfied. And so in a sense, you and I—I as priest and you as business men—we share a common vocation to bring to men all that is required for man to enjoy a truly human existence. It is no small achievement that men of business have supplied the foundation whereby man can satisfy his basic requirements. This is indeed a great vocation, an all essential contribution to the common good."

He put to them an aspiration for the future of their vocation. "The dominant theme of our social order is one of cooperation. Modern life has brought us closer and closer together. There is in every walk of life an increasing demand for interrelatedness.... The right of each to work only for his own selfish interests has passed away; indeed, it never really existed." He called for a cooperative effort in the business world. "The beloved Pope John, of great memory, asked the wealthy nations of the world to turn their attention to the needs of the suffering peoples of the underprivileged nations."[37] The real world dominant theme then, as now, may have been competition and corporate power expansion, but Bishop Hunthausen appealed to the better angels of the *brewmeisters*.

Earlier in the book we saw that, in Seattle, Hunthausen was a strong supporter of women, and helped try to move the church toward gender equality. In Helena, he was attuned to the changes taking place in the lives of women religious. Bishop Hunthausen spoke at St. Joseph Parish in Anaconda, on August 24, 1967, on the occasion of Sisters Profession of final vows.

> "Sisters today are trying to respond to the needs of the world in ways new and old. They are bringing the good news of salvation to people in the inner city, doomed to a life of perpetual poverty by the system in which they are caught. They are leaving the relative comfort of their convents and mingling with the poor, trying to discover their needs and problems, and to find a way to help them. They are becoming definitely involved with the men and women of today. Where there is a need for love, you will find the modern nun. It must be recognized, of course, that not all individual nuns, nor all communities have moved with the Church and caught this spirit of Vatican II. Ancient attitudes and customs are with difficulty changed. Of course, it is right that each religious congregation cherish its traditions and retain the spirit of its founder. However, this does not mean that there should be blind allegiance to the past. Some religious seem to forget that, almost without exception, the founders of religious communities were revolutionaries, innovators far ahead of their time."[38]

What later emerged so strongly in Seattle was well on its way in Hunthausen's style of leadership in Helena. Bishop Hunthausen made many moves to foster shared responsibility in the leadership of the church. The Priests' Senate began in 1966. Working collaboratively, Hunthausen and others created a Personnel Board in 1969. He encouraged the development of shared responsibility in each parish. He encouraged priests especially to make the shift in models of authority.[39] Hunthausen was with the priests for the Helena Clergy Assembly gathering at Carroll College on February 5, 1969. To his fellow priests he said:

> "None of us will deny, at least on the intellectual level, that the Holy Spirit is at work in the Church today. No greater proof need we than the fact of the Second Vatican Council. And yet, I fear we hesitate to accept the Presence of the Spirit in our every day dealings with men.... We live in turbulent times—times of change—times of confusion—times of fear—As men of our times, we must be open to the Spirit and listen to the prophetic voices around us—we must be men of change too—adapting ourselves, our lives, and our preaching to the needs of the people of today and tomorrow.... Let us be open to the voices around us, to the events that are happening, to the signs of the times

> and together in Christ and through the Holy Spirit plunge into the future with courage and determination."[40]

He had an attitude of openness to significant social change. On the eve of Thanksgiving 1973, he gave an address reflecting on the state of the world. This was a time of Watergate, unrest, and revolution.

> "If we define revolution as rapid, widespread, large-scale change in a short period of time, we can truly say that we all find ourselves in our various churches living in an age of revolution. This is also true of the world in which we live.... Because we are living in an age of revolution we find ourselves in crisis as a believing community.... We tend to be a little frightened by this.... We must not, however, let our fear stand in the way of our finding new forms to preach the person and the message of Jesus Christ to the people of God today.... The Christian Gospel tells us that man attains his happiness by responding with his whole being to the call of God, which call, according to St. John, is love. I believe that the call of the Gospel is to strive in every existential situation to recognize and love our neighbor in such a way that the Christian promotes the other and himself in an authentic inter-subjective relationship. I believe in doing this the Christian person responds to the call of God."[41]

He convened a diocesan pastoral council, a finance council, and other consultative and collegial bodies. He brought home Vatican II's call for liturgical renewal and catechesis.[42] He established liturgical, ecumenical, and family commissions, and later on a social development commission.[43] Robert Beaulieu, who was a priest serving in the Helena diocese, said Hunthausen brought a spirit of democracy to the church. "He expected us to be mature in applying Gospel principles to our jobs, and it gave the whole diocese a new sense of energy and life."[44]

Fr. Joseph Oblinger, the same age as Hunthausen, was serving as chancellor even before Hunthausen became bishop. Oblinger could offer some perspective on how the new bishop approached his office. "In Helena, having just taken part in Vatican II, his focus was more on implementing the vision of the council for the local church, our Guatemala Mission, a massive sociological study of the diocese, and the programs discerned from this study, and involvement in the Montana Association of Churches."[45] It was during Vatican II that Hunthausen met Bishop Angelico Melotto of Sololá, Guatemala. The country desperately needed priests. Hunthausen worked with the leadership of the Helena diocese and Bishop Melotto and his people in Guatemala to establish a mission there.[46] Bishop Topel in Spokane already had priests in Guatemala, a fact that helped Helena develop the Guatemala connection. Hunthausen's growing consciousness of global social issues had seeds in Sololá.[47]

Director of Guatemala Missions was among the several hats Oblinger wore as chancellor. "In the early spring of 1965, Bishop Hunthausen and myself flew to Guatemala to visit our men there and to see what progress they had made thus far in our new mission effort." They stopped over in Mexico City and toured the city, including a visit to the shrine of Our Lady of Guadalupe. In Guatemala City, they were met by Fathers John Ward and Jim Tackes, who had launched the mission effort in 1963. Oblinger and Hunthausen were both avid hikers, but Montana had not prepared them for the conditions they faced on a hike in Guatemala.

> "While in Santa Maria we were tricked into hiking the trail from Santa Maria to Santo Tomas. It's only seven miles we were told and all downhill. They didn't tell us about the heat and the humidity and the dry trail. I thought I would never make it all the way, mostly because of the humidity. We did eventually arrive there for some needed liquid refreshment and a welcome rest. Did we walk back? Not on your life!"[48]

Refreshment for the spirit, the Second Vatican Council was new and invigorating. Bishop Hunthausen then sat down with Frs. Jim Provost, Joe Oblinger, and Emmett Kelly, who was Dutch's administrative assistant, and others, including sisters and laity, and said, essentially, we are called to be church in a new way, let's find out what we can do in this diocese.[49] For the Vatican II 50th anniversary, the *National Catholic Reporter* included a reflection by retired Archbishop Hunthausen:

> "When I returned home to Montana, I set to work with the people of the Helena diocese—laypeople, priests and sisters—to implement the great vision. It didn't happen overnight, of course, but it happened quite quickly compared to the previous four centuries, in which the church experienced no appreciable change whatsoever. We priests were able to face the people as we prayed, to enjoy a closeness with them. The closeness signified that priests and people, although they had different roles and responsibilities, were first of all one people, one body of Christ. That was a major and momentous change. Praying the liturgy in language we could readily understand gave new meaning to our prayer. It let people know that it was their prayer too. Masses soon became joy-filled celebrations of a community with Christ at the center. Laypeople were no longer second-class citizens. Together with the hierarchy, they were—they are—the church. We formed a priests' senate—I was grateful to be able to share responsibility for leading the church. Priests quickly found their voice as they represented the

concerns and dreams of their brother priests and the people of their parishes. As laypeople quickly found their voices, it was marvelous to witness them awakening to and claiming their baptismal dignity. Except for the mundane, practical parish concerns, no one had ever consulted them before. Certainly not about their own faith life and their own hopes and dreams for the church. When they were asked, they quickly stepped forward. They were ready to exercise their baptismal priesthood."[50]

Fr. Jim Hogan was a young priest when Hunthausen was at Vatican II. "He used to come home and say, 'this is like going to bishops' school. I don't know what a bishop is but I'm learning.'" Hunthausen held workshops and invited progressive theologians to deliver addresses. He understood collegiality. Hunthausen's commitment to shared responsibility became especially significant in the context of what happened when many of the communities of women religious experienced the departure of nuns who had been teaching in the Catholic school system. Other teachers would have to be hired, and paid, whereas the sisters had long staffed the schools and kept the costs down substantially. So the diocese was under serious financial pressures with regard to the operation of its schools. In one case, Hogan recalls, there was a big debt at Helena Central Catholic High. Hunthausen empowered a lay commission to take leadership. The commission decided to close the entire Catholic school system in Helena. The larger drama affecting the Catholic parochial system, in the Diocese of Helena as in dioceses all over the country, was palpable and painful in the late 1960s and beyond.[51] Hunthausen accepted the commission's process and decision. "It was a really hectic time. The blame was put on the bishop and the priests. There was a lot of turmoil in the church then."[52]

There were many different tensions in the years coming out of the Second Vatican Council. It was, after all, the Sixties, perhaps one of the most turbulent periods of social and cultural change on record. "For many people the experience was a difficult one fraught with uncertainty and apprehension. Their Church, which had remained the same for so many generations, was now changing in so many ways some could not accept it.... In the early years following the Council," writes Cornelia Flaherty, "some people became alienated from the church because of the reform and renewal and others because it did not go far enough for them." In the Diocese of Helena, the tension in time gave way to revitalization, in no small part because Bishop Hunthausen "set out to make the documents and spirit of Vatican II a reality.... This was the thrust of his twelve-year administration of the Helena Diocese and the whole tone of his episcopacy."[53]

Decentralization was the mark of his tenure in Helena. Hunthausen made Vatican II's more egalitarian sentiments come alive. Fr. Jim Provost, who came on as chancellor in 1967, had played a pivotal role in helping Hunthausen implement many of the shared-authority ideas of Vatican II. Trained as a canon lawyer, Provost was able to help guide various innovations—creatively and carefully threading the ecclesiastical 'legal needle'—in governance and other aspects of the life of the church, such as liturgical renewal and issues around the laicization of priests.[54] Provost, who later taught at Catholic University and served as president of the Canon Law Society, pursued ideas ahead of their time, such as the election, rather than appointment, of bishops. The progressive thinking of Provost, like that of Hunthausen, did not curry Vatican favor, especially once John Paul II was pope.[55]

UNCLE DUTCHIE

To more fully understand the character of Raymond Hunthausen it is essential to be aware of his intimate family bonding that, like the family itself, extended across the generations. Family was not just formative background. It was vital throughout the arc of his life and provided him with a core experience of human relation, which greatly influenced how he approached the church and the world—as the human family. Beginning with the birth of his first nephew, Pat, son of Pat and Marie Walsh, in 1945, Fr. Raymond Hunthausen had a new role. The four Hunthausen siblings who married were all destined to have large families—Pat and Marie Walsh, twelve children; Tony and Harriet Hunthausen, nine; Art and Donna Hunthausen, eight; and John and Jean Stergar, nine. Dutch was a caring uncle, says his brother Tony. "It wasn't always easy, money wise. Dutch was always there when we needed help. He just seemed to be the fellow who would do anything for anybody if they needed that help. He was so lovable with the children. They loved him. That's why the kids all called him 'Uncle Dutchie'."[56]

Dutch's father died in Anaconda in 1957. Brother Tony says, "Dad was 65. He had heart problems and was diabetic. Dad did not have a way to treat it then like they do today. He passed away rather suddenly."[57] It was the same year that Fr. Raymond Hunthausen took on the role of running Carroll College. A few of the nieces and nephews were old enough to have gotten to know Grandpa Hunt. Kathleen, one of Tony and Harriet's daughters, remembers playing with her grandfather there in Anaconda. "We would gather at Grandma Hunt's. I remember Grandpa Hunt, crawling over his big belly as a little kid. It was like climbing over a mountain." That same affable way with the grandkids was passed on to Dutch's generation. Family gatherings were always important, then and ever since. "Dutch was always getting the family together, but Grandma Hunt was the one who did that in the early days. My mom and Aunt Donna and Aunt Jean and Aunt Marie would all get together, and they'd prepare all the food."[58]

Dutch taught his nieces and nephews how to row a boat. He taught them how to water ski. "He would take us on hikes. He loved to take us. 'Just one more switchback, just one more.' He would say this and carry little kids on his shoulders."[59] Of course there was more than just one more switchback, but Uncle Dutchie would rally their tenacity. Kathleen shared her angle on a story her father had told me about Christmas in East Helena.

> "My dad would put up green boughs outside and lights. We got our presents on Christmas Eve. So Santa is gonna come. But he won't come if we're there. So Dutch would take us for a ride. And we'd drive around and look at all the lights. I can't remember how many years in a row we did that. There was no such thing as seat belts, so we're all crawlin' around in the car, and he'd talk about the lights and we'd drive around and it seemed like hours of course because we wanted to get home. The signal was dad would put the lights back on outside, that meant Santa had been there. My parents were out there, as we drove up, saying, 'goodbye Rudolph,' and Dutch was just right there, loving it."[60]

When her uncle was installed as the new bishop of Helena, Kathleen was ten. She and her cousins were all dressed up in their finery. "It was at the reception. We'd get in the receiving line again and again, and we kiss his ring and he'd laugh. We just got such a kick out of it that Dutch was in this outfit as a bishop with a crosier and miter and all. We'd go play for a while and then get back in line and kiss his ring."[61]

Bill Hunthausen, also one of Tony and Harriet's kids, worked with his cousin Mark on the lawns at the chancery where his uncle the bishop and his grandma lived. It was at some point after Grandpa Hunt had died that Grandma Hunt moved from Anaconda to Helena, and in time her eldest son worked things out so she could live in an apartment on the second floor of the chancery, where he also had an apartment. Bill and Mark were working with Dutch, the bishop, on lawn projects. "One time, we still laugh about it, Dutch was trimming the hedge. He said to us, 'you guys gotta stand on that end while I lean over the hedge.'" They were on the back of the pickup on one end of a plank and he was out on the other end reaching to trim the hedge. "One time we kind of forgot. He fell into the hedge. 'You okay, Dutch?' 'Yes, I'm fine, what'd you boys do back there? You forgot your job.' We're all laughing. He wasn't hurt. He loved doing things with us." Dutch made little whistles out of willow saplings. "He'd cut it, loosen the bark, slide it off and cut the little whistle. He did this for the younger kids, each generation." That was at Legendary Lodge, and various nieces and nephews told me that same story. He made lots of whistles over the years for lots of family. And Bill and Mark were altar boys for Mass up on top of St. Mary's Peak outside of Stevensville in the Bitterroot Valley. Dutch would say Mass at the top of the peak. Everything they did, Bill says, was around the Eucharist. At all the family reunions, they started the day with Mass. "It was an experience of joy."[62]

Dutch taught them to fly fish and to hunt. Later in life, Dutch stopped hunting but kept up the fly fishing well into his retirement. Bill had a hunting story. "The first thing I ever shot at was a big bull elk, out of town not far, just a half hour drive. Dutch and Mark and I were there. It had a huge rack. Dutch was ready to shoot. 'Dutch,' I said, 'can I shoot at it?' Boom, the elk just reared up and took off. Dutch had never seen an elk there before." That was in the fall of 1967, when Bill was in the 8th grade. So the elk got away because an expert hunter gave a very young novice the opportunity to try. Bill was fourteen when he shot his first deer. He used a 308 lever action Winchester rifle. That rifle belonged to Uncle Dutch but later he gave it to Bill. Dutch gutted that first deer to show young Bill the technique. I asked Bill if there ever was any discussion or debate about the ethics of hunting. There was a seminarian, Steve Oreskovich, who was with them at Legendary Lodge once. Steve was a counselor there. "Steve and Uncle Dutch had a conversation about hunting. Steve raised questions. But," says Bill, "Dutch was comfortable hunting. He would never see a rifle to be used for any other purpose than hunting."[63]

Mark Hunthausen, the oldest of Art and Donna's children, was Bill's partner in those lawn duties at the chancery.

> "As a kid growing up around Dutch it was always just a lot of fun. He was as much a kid as we were and he always wanted us to be exposed to a lot of wonderful things about life. He always made it interesting. Uncle Dutch taught me how to mow the yard, how to drive, and how to ski. I remember how we went down to Bozeman to go skiing, some of us cousins, with Dutch and Jack. I can remember how they just got me in the line for the chair lift and then once I got off the chair lift it was like, Dutch just let me go. Then after the first fall he said, 'okay, this is how you're gonna do it if you don't want to fall anymore.'"[64]

Sarah Walsh, youngest child of Pat and Marie Walsh, told me a story she heard from Uncle Dutch about his experience when he was president of Carroll College. There was a professor or professor's wife at Carroll who spoke Italian and was from Italy, and Bishop Gilmore was preparing for the first session of Vatican II. So Gilmore was going to meet with them to learn about Italy and to pick up some Italian. "So he brought Dutch along with him. Dutch tells the story. 'I didn't pay any attention to what they were talking about. I was on the floor playing with their three year old son. I should have paid more attention.' Bishop Gilmore died, and Hunthausen was appointed bishop and had to prepare quickly to attend the first session of the Council."[65]

Dan Hunthausen, the youngest of Tony and Harriet's children, says at one point or another, probably all of the some 39 nieces and nephews of Dutch had the experience he had. "We would go to Dairy Queen for Dilly Bars. He would just come out and pick us up, when he was bishop here. He'd finish his day, call us up and come out and get us." Dan remembers the first time he was out trying to ski. "I was maybe 3 or 4. Dutch would put me on his shoulders, carry my skis, and he would hike up the entire hill. He did this with all of us at different times."[66] Paula Hunthausen, also one of Tony and Harriet's kids, remembers when Uncle Dutch would come to visit. "He would always lie down on the floor and we'd stand on his hands, and he'd lift us up over his knees. I remember when we'd go on trips with him. We'd be lying on the floor in those big cars, lying on the foot rests when seat belts were not all the rage. He had a Dionne Warwick cassette he would play. He would stop, pull in and buy Kentucky Fried Chicken, and we'd pull into a picnic place and have KFC."[67]

Legendary Lodge was special for the family and remains so. Dutch and Jack were part of it from the beginning. When they were young priests they had retreats up there. When he became bishop, Dutch wanted to find ways to share the place with the people of the diocese. So he transformed the place into a camp for kids. In 1965, the year Andy Hunthausen was born, the first kids' camp was held there. "Dutch made that happen," says Andy. Still, he was not at the helm of everything. "Grandma Hunt lived until I was a senior in high school." So Dutch made a lot happen, but she was definitely in charge. "You know, we talk about Dutch as the leader, the 'go to guy' in the family but when she was alive, it was kind of like, 'Ray, come over here.' She ran the show. He was always with the kids. So we'd be at Legendary Lodge and he was down at the lake with the kids and she's out on the porch of the lodge there, and she'd be yellin' to him, 'Now get the life jackets on the kids, Ray,' and he just kind of did what she told him." Andy was one of those kids. "Gosh, he was the Bishop of Helena, but she was still his mom and he was her son."[68]

Carolyn (Stergar) Miller remembers Dutch making those willow whistles at Legendary Lodge. "He would snap them, score them with his knife, carve out the whistling holes, and make them for everyone," she says.[69] Her cousin Dick Walsh describes the place. "Legendary Lodge is a Catholic Youth camp now and has been so since the late 60's. When Uncle Dutch became the bishop of Helena the Lodge was used mostly for priest retreats. Well it became the Hunthausen gathering place and in the early years before camps were used quite a bit in summers. With a few interruptions the Lodge has been the gathering for our Hunthausen family reunions every 2 years for the past 50 years." The family has grown over the years and Dick is one of the historians that keep the directory current. "The descendents of Anthony and Edna Hunthausen, including all spouses married into the family now tops 250 people. We get over 90% attending the reunion on a regular basis." There is a custom en route to Legendary Lodge. "When we come around the corner from Clearwater Junction towards Salmon Lake we still want to be the first to say, 'I see Dutchie's Lake'."[70]

Dick Walsh says Uncle Dutch understood the importance of family gatherings and felt both an obligation and opportunity to make them happen. "Dutch and Jack were often together and it was always an exciting time for all. They were the center of attention. You always knew that they just loved family and being around all the nieces and nephews. Dutch would entertain us with card games and tricks. I still can remember when he would push an object through the table or find a quarter in your ear."[71] Andy Hunthausen adds, "When Dutch came round he was like a magnet for the kids. We fished and hiked and did trips to Glacier and Yellowstone. He was the best uncle ever. We might spend the afternoon in Glacier and then the evening stay over at a parish in White Fish or Kalispell or Browning, towns close to the park. This is when he was bishop. He really did spend many great times with the nieces and nephews."[72]

Andy took me to see the place where Dutch lived above the chancery in an apartment; Grandma Hunt lived there in another apartment.

> "He always had family member college students staying there in the extra space as well. At the chancery the family often met for BBQ in the backyard. Dutch had a volleyball court and lawn darts for us to play. He took a huge blue spruce and cut out some of the branches so that it would be a climbing tree for the kids. He made a path up the tree so all the kids could climb. Dutch had a zip line for a while, from the upper patio outside his apartment running down to the lawn. It was a great place to be. Above the garage there was a storage area, filled with balls, games, and such. We called it 'Dutchie's house'. We would run full speed as we sprinted through the chapel, and we would drop and slide on one knee. You know, we had to genuflect, slide on one knee to touch the floor and then on we went at full clip. We had no idea why, but Grandma Hunt had told us to genuflect so we did. We were always having barbecue picnics there. The yard was full of laughter. We'd go to the chancery nearly every week for many years. The families would go over to Dutchie's house and Grandma Hunt was always there with cookies for us."

Dutchie's room was at the far north end of the second floor. Grandma Hunt's apartment was toward the middle, with the chapel in between the living room and the kitchen. Some years they would have Thanksgiving dinner downstairs in the big hall of the chancery offices.[73]

The chancery building was just to the west of the huge mansion. The bishop's mansion, located at the corner of Power and Harrison in upper west Helena, was originally built by a merchant named T.C. Power. Hunthausen did not feel comfortable there. Dick Walsh says, "Dutch just could not see the building space being wasted on him so sometime in the mid 60's he made the move to the apartment."[74] Kathleen recalls the bishop's mansion itself from the earliest years of her uncle's tenure as bishop.

> "They had a big dining room table and underneath it was a button beneath the carpet. The bishop could push the button and a bell would ring and the nuns would respond to see what he wanted. The whole idea was for the bishop to sit at the head of the table and push with his foot on the button. Dutch would not do this. We'd get down there and push it with our thumbs. We got the nuns all mixed up. We loved playing with it. He didn't want them fussing over him. He'd tell them, 'oh, don't worry about it, I'll just make myself a sandwich here.' The nuns took care of everything. He'd get up and want to fix his own mush. The nuns wanted to fix a big breakfast for him. He'd sneak down early in the morning and get his mush. He didn't want to be waited on. I remember the staircase. I remember there was a third floor and it had what seemed like a huge ballroom or hall. We'd play for hours in there. The place had a lot of ornate fancy stuff. Dutch was so uncomfortable there. He could not sleep at night. He moved out and gave it to the sisters and moved over across above the chancery."[75]

Dutch did not have a family of his own, he had "all of us," says Andy. And "he was the guy that brought us all together." He was never comfortable with wearing his status.

> "He was not looking for attention, or accolades or recognition for what he was doing. He just lived the way he thought he was supposed to live. That is how he was in the community as well. People knew him as Dutch. Dutch did not like wearing the garb. He didn't look forward to ceremonies where he had to dress up in the entire garb as a bishop. He would prefer to just get up there in a simple robe with all the other priests. I think that speaks to who he was."[76]

Whenever any of the families needed help or support, he was always there, says Andy.

> "My parents were living on one salary with nine children. Dutch helped in different ways. He was a big part of making higher education

> a norm in our extended family. He helped a lot of family get into their first car or home. The Tuchscherer side passed some family money on to Dutch. He used that money as a source to help people in the family who needed help over the years. He was always generous and giving in many ways. He would hand down skis or golf clubs to a niece or nephew that was next in line or that still needed a pair or a set. Dutch would always be giving things away. People often gave him gifts and he would just as often pass them on to the family."[77]

Dick Walsh shared an example of his uncle's care for people.

> "Just a few days ago I was visiting with a friend, Dannette Sullivan, who was the registrar at Carroll when Dutch was bishop. Dannette also was registrar of Seattle University until a few years ago. She is like family in so many ways. She graduated with my sister Edna Cahill as well as our current Bishop George Thomas in the early 70's. The story she told was a great one to understand the compassion that Dutch has. An Anaconda classmate of Dutch's with 3 children and an absent husband was unable to see any way to provide a college education to her children. Dutch called her and stated that he needed her to move to Helena and work for Carroll. By being an employee of the college her children could attend Carroll tuition free."[78]

What could seem like a family's hagiography of Uncle Dutch is really not intended to paint him as extraordinary. He was just a regular guy who cared deeply, they all say. It is his down-to-earth character that stands out. One time he was involved both in contributing to the mischief of his nephews and then in helping resolve the predicament they got into. Dick Walsh:

> "I remember the apple story very well as I was one of the nephews involved. Dutch was at our house on Henry Street near Carroll and told the story of when he was young in Anaconda and he and his buddies would throw apples at passing cars. Well, we carried it too far for sure as my brother Tom and I along with our cousin Paul Hunthausen proceeded to pick some apples and throw at the cars on Euclid Avenue. It was not too long before a man came down the sidewalk and jumped the fence at our hiding location and we all scrambled. I was old enough to know better at 17 or 18 years old at the time. We ran to the house and then around the house twice with the man in pursuit. Paul and I made it in the back door but Tom was caught at the door. Well Dutch was there to the rescue pretty quick and took the man away from the house to discuss the situation. The man was quite upset and using some foul language. I can only imagine

what Dutch had to say to calm the situation down. It was a lesson learned for us kids for sure."[79]

Dutch always loved to tell stories, even if on that occasion he ought not to have shared it with his rambunctious nephews when lots of apples lay in waiting. Dutch told Dick another story, this one recalled in late summer of 2014 after he had just turned 93, a story Dick had never heard. "When Dutch was the bishop of Helena he received a call from his sister-in-law, Harriet Hunthausen. She had received a call from the Catholic elementary school because her daughter Paula was sick and needed to be picked up. Harriet said she could not think of anyone else to call. Dutch said he would go pick her up. Dutch went to the school to pick her up and noticed that another niece in the same class, Lynn Hunthausen, was near the back of the class and kind of crying. The teacher asked if she was sick and she said she no, but wanted to go with Dutchie too."[80]

MONTANA FAMILY BOND

Eight years into his post as Seattle's archbishop there was a big loss in the family. The "General" died. Hunthausen gave the homily on April 15, 1983 at "Ma's Resurrection Liturgy." "I don't have to tell you this is the way she would have wanted it—to be surrounded by her family and friends…." This loving testimony by a son for his mother lends insight into his own character:

> "Obedient son that I would like to be, I've been wondering what my mother's wish for me might be as the homilist, at this her funeral Mass. Two things are certain—she would say, 'I don't want you to say very much about me and *above all* be brief!' And I can hear myself protesting, 'But, Ma, that's an impossible task.' Her response would be 'Well try!' Again I would object, 'But, Ma…and she would stop me in full flight and say, 'Never mind, just try.' That expression 'never mind' is so characteristic of our mother and I think I could say it's behind the choice of the readings, which we have just heard. Readings which say to us, do not be anxious about your life—trust in God—look first to his kingdom—I called you by name—I love you. Because I always understood in my mother's 'never mind' all of those notions. For her it really meant 'don't worry about it—do your best—that's all anyone can do.' But being of a very practical spirituality that also meant don't waste time—get busy about it…. I remember how curious it is that we come to be introduced to God, and one of my most poignant introductions was through St. Anthony. One morning, in my early life, we were anxiously and in a hurried fashion trying to get downtown and we couldn't find one of my sister Marie's shoes (you mothers know how

> that is…you never lose two you only lose one) and as we were hunting around the bedroom she said 'look under the dresser'. The dresser went almost to the floor and I said it couldn't be there. She said, 'Never mind, look' and I don't have to tell you it was there! That's a simple story but there's so many other things, like when there was lightning and thunder outside and we kids would run home and plead with her to light a blessed candle—not any candle, but a blessed candle. There was a sense of prayer and a sense of comfort—a feeling that God was there and it was portrayed by what she said and how she lived. How she urged us to go to Mass during Lent (she went with us), every morning during May and other significant times during the liturgical year. But most of all, I believe our mother's faith was displayed in the way she gave herself to other people, especially the family. Her sons and daughters were her pride and joy (and grandchildren). We refer to our mother, playfully, as the "General" because she watched over us not in any overbearing fashion, always respecting us—who we were as individuals and I don't have to tell you that we loved her for that—deeply loved her for that. She urged us to have family reunions, parties and picnics and in the last days of her life she made that very clear that that was to continue after she left—knowing that love for one another—a sense of community—a sense of family—is absolutely essential if we are to live out the Christian message…."[81]

Raymond Hunthausen approached his work as a bishop, in Helena and in Seattle, with his experience of a deeply bonded family at the center of his ministry. He appreciated the faith community as a family where all could work together and share responsibilities, and with this attitude he envisioned the world as the human family. How he related to his own family was intrinsic to how he bonded with common humanity as a priest, bishop, and prophet.

ENDNOTES

1 Shea, Dan. Personal interview. Helena, Montana 4 Aug. 2014.

2 Hogan, Jim. Personal interview. Missoula, Montana 7 Aug. 2014.

3 Hogan, Jim.

4 Hogan, Jim.

5 Roche, Dick. Personal correspondence. Butte, Montana. 12 Oct. 2012.

6 From personal files of Guido Bugni. Helena, Montana.

7 Bugni, Guido. Personal interview. Helena, Montana 5 Aug. 2014.

8 Bugni, Guido.

9 Bugni, Guido.

10 Bugni, Guido.

11 Flaherty, Cornelia. *Go With Haste Into The Mountain: A History of the Diocese of Helena.* Falcon Publishing 1984, 149

12 Bugni, Guido. Personal interview. Helena, Montana 5 Aug. 2014.

13 Bugni, Guido.

14 Bugni, Guido.

15 Hunthausen, Andy. Personal interview. Helena, Montana 3 Aug. 2014.

16 Hunthausen, Andy.

17 Semmens, John. "A Man Called 'Dutch': The Lasting Impact of Archbishop Raymond G. Hunthausen on Carroll College" Unpublished paper written for History Research Seminar 495, Carroll College 18 Dec. 2007, 7. Semmens quotes Kelly from article by Cindy Wooden, "Faith, family and friends continue to guide Archbishop Hunthausen" *Progress* 1 Oct. 1987.

18 Semmens, John, 18.

19 Hunthausen, Tony. Personal interview. Helena, Montana 4 Aug. 2014.

20 Kelly, Cornelius Joseph "Con". Telephone interview. Missoula, Montana 21 Aug. 2014.

21 Hogan, Jim. Personal interview. Missoula, Montana 7 Aug. 2014.

22 Hunthausen, Raymond. "It Comes From Faith." 2.

23 Hunthausen, Raymond. Personal interview. Seattle, Washington 16 Dec. 1988.

24 "Bishop Hunthausen Chose for NAIA Hall of Fame" *Independent Record.* Helena, Montana. 2 Dec. 1966, 1.

25 Bugni, Guido. Personal notes for address at induction of Archbishop Hunthausen into Carroll College Alumni Hall of Fame. 13 Oct. 1979. Guido Bugni personal file. Helena, Montana.

26 Flaherty, Cornelia, 150.

27 Flaherty, Cornelia, 161-162.

28 Wilson, Cynthia and Rebecca Boren. "The Peace Bishop" in *Washingtonians: A Biographical Portrait of the State.* David Brewster and David Burge, eds. Sasquatch Books 1989, 473.

29 Hunthausen, Raymond. "We Need A Miracle—Expect One: Reminiscences on Vatican II and My Life as a Bishop" Carroll Magazine Summer 2008, reprint of article from *Seattle Theology and Ministry Review*, Vol. 3 (2003).

30 Hunthausen, Raymond.

31 Hunthausen, Raymond.

32 Hunthausen, Raymond. Homily at special funeral Mass of Pope John XXIII. June 1963. Diocese of Helena Archives.

33 Hunthausen, Raymond. "Coming to a Position on the Global Arms Race: A Personal Journey" Mt. Angel Seminary, St. Benedict, Oregon. 22 Feb. 1982. Archdiocese of Seattle Archives.

34 Hunthausen, Raymond. "We Need A Miracle—Expect One: Reminiscences on Vatican II and My Life as a Bishop" Carroll Magazine Summer 2008.

35 Correspondence between Bishops Marvin Stuart and Raymond Hunthausen. 6 and 15 Apr. 1967. Diocese of Helena Archives.

36 Hunthausen, Raymond. Talk delivered to the Montana Beer Wholesalers Convention. 13 May 1966. Diocese of Helena Archives.

37 Hunthausen, Raymond.

38 Hunthausen, Raymond. "Do We Need The New Nun?" Address at Sisters Profession (final vows). St. Joseph, Anaconda, Montana. 24 Aug. 1967. Diocese of Helena Archives.

39 Flaherty, Cornelia, 173.

40 Hunthausen, Raymond. Remarks at Helena Clergy Assembly, Carroll College. 5 Feb. 1969. Diocese of Helena Archives.

41 Hunthausen, Raymond. Address on eve of Thanksgiving, 1973. Diocese of Helena Archives.

42 Thomas, George. "Hunthausen Jubilee Homily" Helena, Montana. 30 Aug. 2012. Diocese of Helena Archives.

43 Clark, Paul. "New Seattle Archbishop is a 'people prelate' *Progress*, Souvenir edition. Seattle, Washington. 23 May 1975, 7.

44 Wilson, Cynthia and Rebecca Boren. "The Peace Bishop" in *Washingtonians: A Biographical Portrait of the State*. David Brewster and David Burge, eds. Sasquatch Books 1989, 477.

45 Oblinger, Joseph. Email correspondence. 31 July 2012.

46 Flaherty, Cornelia, 163.

47 Oblinger, Joseph. Telephone interview. Bozeman, Montana 25 Aug. 2012.

48 Oblinger, Joseph. *Fisher of Men*. Lifevest Publishing 2006, 50.

49 Tucker, Jim and Lorraine. Personal interview. Helena, Montana 5 Aug. 2014.

50 Hunthausen, Raymond. "A bishop receives 'on-the-job training'" *National Catholic Reporter*, special edition for 50th anniversary of Vatican II "A church reborn" 11 Oct. 2012, 35-36

51 Flaherty, Cornelia, 178-179.

52 Hogan, Jim. Personal interview. Missoula, Montana 7 Aug. 2014.

53 Flaherty, Cornelia, 162-163.

54 This was the case of Michael Miles. See *Love Is Always* by Michael Miles. William Morrow and Company 1986.

55 Kelly, Con. Telephone interview. Missoula, Montana 11 Sept. 2014.

56 Hunthausen, Tony. Personal interview. Helena, Montana 4 Aug. 2014.

57 Hunthausen, Tony.

58 Hunthausen, Kathleen. Personal interview. Helena, Montana 4 Aug. 2014.

59 Hunthausen, Kathleen.

60 Hunthausen, Kathleen.

61 Hunthausen, Kathleen.

62 Hunthausen, Bill. Personal interview. Helena, Montana 5 Aug. 2014.

63 Hunthausen, Bill.

64 Hunthausen, Mark. Personal interview. Helena, Montana 2 Aug. 2014.

65 Walsh, Sarah. Personal interview. Helena, Montana 2 Aug. 2014.

66 Hunthausen, Dan. Personal interview. Helena, Montana 3 Aug. 2014.

67 Hunthausen, Paula. Personal interview. Helena, Montana 3 Aug. 2014.

68 Hunthausen, Andy. Personal interview. Helena, Montana 3 Aug. 2014.

69 Miller, Carolyn (Stergar). Personal interview. Helena, Montana 5 Aug. 2014.

70 Walsh, Dick. Telephone interview and email correspondence. Polson and East Helena, Montana. Aug. 2014.

71 Walsh, Dick.

72 Hunthausen, Andy. Personal interview. Helena, Montana 3 Aug. 2014.

73 Hunthausen, Andy.

74 Walsh, Dick. Telephone interview and email correspondence. Polson and East Helena, Montana. Aug. 2014.

75 Hunthausen, Kathleen. Personal interview. Helena, Montana 4 Aug. 2014.

76 Hunthausen, Andy. Personal interview. Helena, Montana 3 Aug. 2014.

77 Hunthausen, Andy.

78 Walsh, Dick. Telephone interview and email correspondence. Polson and East Helena, Montana. Aug. 2014.

79 Walsh, Dick.

80 Walsh, Dick.

81 Hunthausen, Raymond. Homily at "Ma's Resurrection Liturgy" Helena, Montana 15 April 1983. Personal files of Denny Hunthausen.

Chapter Ten

THE CHARACTER OF HUNTHAUSEN'S CALL

In the late 1980s, tensions between Rome and Seattle were finally subsiding. Yet those tensions still required emotional outlets. One way Dutch dealt with life in rough patches was to look for levity and grace in prayer and in a good story. There was a beautiful large wooden rocker in his Seattle chancery office and it was being used to hold some of his documents and papers. That rocking chair was about to cause trouble—and make for a droll tale to share during his sunset years. Dutch was walking toward the rocker to pick up a document and by misstep catapulted the top of the chair right smack to his mouth, busting out a tooth. He described it as similar to taking a blow from a boxer. It nearly knocked him out. Coadjutor Archbishop Murphy took him to the emergency room. The doctor wanted to put stitches in but Dutch asked if there was any alternative. The physician advised that *if* he could keep his mouth still for a few days it would probably heal alright. Now it turns out Dutch had some speaking engagement that evening, so he told Murphy he would have to come with him and take his place at the podium. Murphy, with his Irish wit, told a series of jokes, making it almost impossible for Hunthausen to keep his mouth still.[1]

Dick Walsh, who related the rocking chair tale, attests that, for the remainder of life, his uncle had a retainer holding that tooth in place. Humor served him well in those final years in Seattle and afterward, as it always had. This final chapter traces the culmination of Hunthausen's life journey and explores the larger meaning of his life. Raymond Hunthausen's call to his country and church may speak to us now and to future generations. To the degree that he embodied prophetic conscience and courage, these were primarily channeled through his character or, to put it another way, through the habits of his heart. His genuine character is what gave his prophetic words power and made him such a disarming spirit. The character of the man seems to be the key. Episodes yet to share from his sunset years, some happy and some sad, can help us ponder the implications of his life story.

Hunthausen once reflected on the concept of character and its relationship to the formation of conscience. "What needs to be brought out is that each of us has a value system imbedded deeply within us that is the fruit of a lifetime of living, experiencing, reacting, reading, worshiping, understanding, judging and deciding."

His character emerged in a close-knit family, in interpersonal relations with people from many walks of life and worldviews, in the great outdoors of Montana and the Pacific Northwest, and in his Catholic faith in conversation with people of other faith traditions. "In a religious person that value system and the depth to which it is internalized depends upon the extent to which that person has been immersed in the life and values of his/her religious tradition." Hunthausen lived out his faith in the ecumenical spirit conveyed in Vatican II's *Pastoral Constitution on the Church in the Modern World*. He tried to attune himself to the joys and hopes as well as the griefs and anxieties of the people of this earth, especially the poor or those afflicted in any way, for these too would be his joys and hopes, his griefs and anxieties. In keeping with those opening lines of the *Pastoral Constitution, Gaudium et Spes*, joys and hopes, griefs and anxieties, nothing genuinely human could fail to raise an echo in his heart.[2] When he spoke about the influence of a faith tradition on character and conscience, his own story made the words more meaningful. "The more a person experiences the values of a tradition by living amidst people who cherish those values, the more a person worships in that tradition, the more a person studies and reflects on the tradition, the more a person tries to live a whole life in obedience to the God that the tradition mediates, the more that person will be marked to the depths of his or her being by the richness of the tradition."[3]

Raymond Hunthausen was empowered by the richness of his Catholic tradition, including the "people of God" spirit of Vatican II, and encumbered by the conduct of some of those in the church who suppressed him, and also by his own internalized oppression linked to his official place in a patriarchal structure. With all of this and its ambiguity, he made his way into a deeply personal call to Christian nonviolence. Nonviolence as a call of conscience challenging himself, his nation, and his religion, came to the fore during the Seattle years. He made nonviolence into a way of life, with implications for public policy, as earlier chapters have documented, but also for his personal practice. "Trying to live this way has caused us to become more humble and gentle toward others, and more reliant on God and the spirit for the effects we want to see in ourselves, in others and in our world. Hopefully we have been becoming more and more what we are trying to create." His path was as much about inner peace as outer peace:

> "I am convinced it is not only what we do, but even more what we and the others we touch become that will change the world. That is the very definition of nonviolence.... We commit ourselves, our best critical and creative powers, our resources and time to witnessing in behalf of our neighbors, in discipleship and fellowship with Jesus who shows us the way. In the end we are called to lay down our lives for our friends, little by little until completely."[4]

He made prayer the core of his life. "My openness to reflect, to allow God to touch me with that sense of love—that happens only by a willingness to step away from the noise of our lives and to find some time to do that, so that when we come back into the mainstream we come back with something that has been supplied by the Lord." He drew from deep wellsprings. "We can't let the well run dry; we really have to be willing to try at least to struggle with the issues of life as they touch us through the Gospel."[5] Personal prayer was a regular practice for Dutch. "I don't have to go without prayer very many days to know things aren't right in my life.... I'm not saying, (as I would want to), 'Lord, point me in the right direction and help me to do the right thing. Keep me close to you so that what I do is really yours.'" He reflected on his own life and his need for divine guidance. "What is needed is wisdom and I don't have it. It's an issue of making oneself vulnerable. No one ever is totally, but I believe that we can't even try except through prayer. We need a growing appreciation that this is who Jesus is, the vulnerable one, and that's what is expected of us if we're to be disciples."[6]

At one point during the Vatican's "storm over Seattle" he participated in a retreat given by the well known Franciscan, Fr. Richard Rohr. At that retreat, Rohr shared a book by James Finley. *Merton's Palace of Nowhere: A Search for God through Awareness of the True Self* became a meditation guide that Hunthausen could rely upon during the long ordeal with the Vatican. I once asked Hunthausen about this book. One key notion in *Merton's Palace of Nowhere* was surrender.[7] One passage, originally found in Merton's *Contemplative Prayer*, was especially poignant for Hunthausen: "The deepest prayer at its nub is a perpetual surrender to God...all meditation and specific acts of prayer might be seen as preparations and purification to ready us for this never ending yielding."[8] Merton asks us to realize that God may turn out to be other than we have pictured God to be. In that case, "whole layers of what I have known myself to be should dissolve away and an utterly unpredictable encounter should take place?"[9] So we need to surrender in prayer our whole being to God. Let God love us, for God loves and accepts us just as we are—which is almost certainly different from how we see ourselves. This notion of God's unconditional acceptance—and our ever-yielding acceptance of God's acceptance—permeates another book of importance for Hunthausen. *As Bread That Is Broken*, by the Dutch Jesuit Peter G. van Breemen, includes a line Hunthausen found to be the crux of his own outlook. "Faith is to discover that there is only oneness: God is the deepest Ground of my being."[10]

Hunthausen's grounding in the Catholic tradition pointed toward a universal vision—a truly catholic (small "c") view. He tried to live as a universal spirit. Like Socrates in the world of Plato's dialogues, facing people such as Thrasymachus, who insisted that justice is whatever those who have power say that it is, he tried to be a just person in an unjust society—and in an unjust church. He joined others in trying to help transform both his society and his religion—to overcome the systemic injustices of both. He loved his country. He loved his church. His story really is one about the inner and outer quest for peace and justice. He was an authentic religious leader who engaged us in powerfully inspiring ways, most importantly doing so by his way of being as much as by anything he said. So to understand the meaning of his story we must try to appreciate how his personal spirituality shaped his public religion. His way of being was integral. The surface expressed a depth of being within. In his retirement years, Hunthausen would lead retreats for diverse groups. One of his favorite books was Anthony de Mello's *Awareness*. A key to wisdom in life was to be found in the practice of detachment.[11] Anthony de Mello writes, "What is a loving heart? A loving heart is sensitive to the *whole* of life, to *all* persons; a loving heart doesn't harden itself to any person or thing."[12] So ultimately our attachments, including narrow notions of what God is, who we are, or who is important to us, all these must give way to a detached spirit—so that we can embrace all. Hence the *catholic* in Hunthausen's open and yet deeply rooted *Catholicism*. If there is a path to a universal it seems it can only be found, paradoxically, in each particular person's unique walk. Hunthausen's walk, or hike—"just one or two more switchbacks," as he loved to say on those Montana mountain treks with his nieces and nephews—still had adventures ahead.

SEATTLE TRANSITION

In June 1991, Hunthausen announced he was going to retire. "It's my own decision made after long and prayerful deliberation. No one was asking me to retire." He felt that it would not be fair to his successor, Thomas Murphy, then serving as his coadjutor archbishop by Vatican arrangement, if he stayed on longer.[13] With priests for their annual gathering at Ocean Shores on the Long Beach peninsula in southwestern Washington, opening a brief talk with prayer, he broke the news to them. Many things were just developing, plans being made in the archdiocese, and it would not be fair to stay on. The *Seattle Post-Intelligencer* reported that the news came as a surprise to most. "Only a few family members and colleagues were warned of Archbishop Raymond Hunthausen's startling announcement: The quiet but gutsy Roman Catholic leader will retire Aug. 21, his 70th birthday." Erven Park, chairman of Roman Catholic Laity for Truth and an incessant Hunthausen critic, said of the archbishop's decision, "I think it's long overdue.... We're looking for nothing more than a leader who follows the supreme authority, which is the Vatican." Church historian Martin Marty, with a broader sense of history, thought Hunthausen's stature would only grow. "Many of the things he stood for have become taken for granted today: the futility of nuclear war and the need to give priority to social needs instead of being the world's policeman," Marty said. "He will be well-remembered and in a few years, when the passions of the mid-'80s are cooled, he will have a very positive profile in American Catholic history."[14] His profile was already positive among most of the priests at the retreat in Ocean Shores. "When he made the announcement, it was like being hit in the stomach," said Fr. Horacio Yanez, then serving at a parish in Bellevue. The priests of the archdiocese made a collective statement in the archdiocesan newspaper honoring Archbishop Hunthausen and his 16 years in Seattle as a time when "the vision of the Second Vatican Council took root in our parishes and faith communities." A *National Catholic Reporter* story captured the range of feelings across the region: "Stunned Catholics in the Seattle archdiocese reacted to controversial Archbishop Raymond G. Hunthausen's surprise retirement announcement last month with mixed feelings of shock, disbelief, sadness and—for some—relief."[15]

One thing that came across very clearly in the tributes paid to him was the breadth of his social justice concerns and the fact that for him justice meant participation—giving agency to people. In March 1990, he had announced that plans for an all-male training program for the permanent diaconate would be suspended. Behind this decision was his long-held commitment to gender equality. He got pushback from vocal critics on this issue, as on so many. In May 1990, some 20 conservative Catholics were at the chancery office protesting Hunthausen's decision.[16]

Another legacy was the creation of the Multicultural Ministry Services office.[17] Esther Lucero Miner was appointed as the founding director in 1985, and served in that role until 1992. As a member of the cabinet, she hired people to coordinate ethnic clusters, including Asian and Pacific Islanders, Native Americans, Latinos, and African-Americans. "Social justice concerns were of paramount concern. In the ethnic communities we had quarterly gatherings of all the people from across these communities."[18] Archbishop Hunthausen and staff pursued many social justice concerns during his Seattle years. They were deeply engaged in homelessness and affordable housing issues. The Archdiocesan Housing Authority was formed in 1981, and developed during Hunthausen's tenure, for the provision of services and in solidarity with grassroots groups advocating for social justice.[19] The point was not that he did everything himself. The tributes made it clear that his role had always been to empower people to achieve various accomplishments.

The *Seattle Post-Intelligencer*'s Sunday, June 23, 1991 paper expressed what the editorial board believed to be a central feature of Hunthausen's character:

> "What do you say about a churchman who day in and day out was selfless in service to others? Whether it was his determined and very public opposition to nuclear war or his heartfelt ministry to society's rejects, the archbishop never sought to advance himself above the issue. Hunthausen's legacy here can be documented by his many good works. He practiced moral courage in opposing nuclear holocaust. He

demonstrated Christian compassion by ministering to the poor and the sick, especially those with AIDS. Hunthausen spent money with other churches and synagogues to combat hatred and bigotry, to build low-income housing, to buy food for the hungry. He worked with his brother bishops in Washington to provide legal aid to migrant workers at risk of being railroaded by the government or ripped off by sinister immigration lawyers. These are the monuments Hunthausen leaves behind, as well as his gift of humility, which is his true legacy here. We will remember the man of God for the day he went to help clean the filthy apartment of a fellow not quite capable of caring for himself. There was the archbishop, dressed in work clothes, on his hands and knees wiping up the floor in the bathroom, no robes or bishop's miter to suggest the trappings of his office."[20]

Right through to the completion of his Seattle tenure, Hunthausen kept up his passionate call for peace and justice on a global scale. He spoke in Hing Hay Park in Seattle on Sunday, June 3, 1990, joining with civic leaders and other members of the community to memorialize the students and others who faced fierce repression in Beijing's Tiananmen Square one year earlier:

> "The relative security and freedom in which we live gives us all the greater responsibility to care for the human rights of our sisters and brothers everywhere. We are responsible to act on our privilege to participate in our political life, to petition our government to demand that the students who participated in the demonstrations in Tiananmen Square be freed, and that the abuse of their human rights cease. Further, it is our responsibility to demand that the government which claims to represent us cease to support those who violate human rights anywhere, be those violators in Beijing or San Salvador. We have all heard that the price of liberty is eternal vigilance. The moral price of our freedom is our eternal vigilance for the human rights of all our sisters and brothers everywhere."[21]

He raised his voice against U.S. plans for the war in the Persian Gulf. This was in early January 1991. At a rally held in Olympia, Hunthausen spoke of "the spirit of wisdom" and challenged Americans to act against starting the war. If we fail to act, he warned, "we will have surrendered our citizenship. We will have placed in jeopardy our democratic process. Most especially, we will have failed the essential moral test because we will have failed all those whose lives hang in the balance."[22] In early January 1991, on the steps of the statehouse in Olympia, he told about 2,000 people gathered there for the peace rally: "We must speak out now, before it is too late. We must speak out now, while we can still draw back from a war whose only foreseeable consequence is massive destruction."[23] January

14, 1991 was a paradigmatic moment in the ecumenical and interfaith movement in Seattle. With 30,000 people this was the largest march in the country at the time. The march was from St. James Cathedral to St. Mark's Episcopal Cathedral, two miles. Archbishop Hunthausen, Rev. William Cate and Rev. Loren Arnett, and others walked together leading the march. It was just on the eve of U.S. bombing in Iraq.[24]

In the early spring of 1991, Archbishop Hunthausen returned to Tacoma's Pacific Lutheran University where one decade earlier he had delivered the compelling "Faith and Disarmament" speech. He asked questions in 1991 that may haunt us more than ever today: "Have we become dependent on our military might for our national security and our national identity? Or can we build an identity rooted in justice and peace for all?" He asked what kind of power would inform and guide the United States in the years ahead, and he denounced power that seeks to dominate and control. "This is the power whose security required the construction of thousands of nuclear weapons. This is the power whose penchant for control sent a half million armed men and women to the desert and set them in motion.... The power of this world prefers propaganda to truth...." He announced power of another kind. "Truth affects people.... It moves our inner being. It allows us to claim our actions as our own. Truth sets us free...." He made a particular call to those who, across denominations, shared his faith as Christians.

> "I believe that we Christians are called to conscientiously object to maintaining the world's largest military establishment. Why? Because I believe that it destroys the capacity of government to seek and promote the common good.... It seems to me we've never truly been able to have both guns and butter. If we continue to opt for guns, I fear two dire consequences. First: We will neglect pressing domestic problems such as poverty, crime, pollution, homelessness and unemployment. Isolation and alienation will increase; our social life will become sadder and meaner. Second: Opting for guns tempts us to use them. Weapons we built to deter nuclear attack were pressed into service in the Gulf. I fear that the weapons with which we won a quick and seemingly painless war will make going to war again all too easy."

What could we do? "The struggle for the soul of the United States, our soul as a nation, will occur in the coming struggle over how our government will spend our money. The church must join in this struggle."[25]

Hunthausen's strong stand against U.S. war making and war machinery was a problem for certain people in various establishment positions, both regionally and nationally. In early May 1991, The *Seattle Post-Intelligencer* reported that the regents of Pacific Lutheran University voted down a nomination of Archbishop Hunthausen for an honorary doctorate award. Jane Hadley, the *Post-Intelligencer* reporter, noted that several faculty members believed the rejection was politically motivated. Robert Stivers, then serving as chair of PLU's religion department, thought that "one of the big issues was (Hunthausen's) refusal to pay taxes." By coincidence, the meeting at which the regents had a majority vote against the nomination was held on Tax Day, April 15. Hadley did ask the chairman of the board of regents, Rev. David Wold, to explain the regents' decision. "Some feel that (Hunthausen) is a marvelous example of the faith of the church. Some equally devout persons see those same actions in a very different way. Those kinds of impressions and opinions were present in the voting, I presume," Wold told her.[26]

"Walk in the Light," held on summer solstice, June 21, 1991, saw over 1,000 people marching though the streets of Seattle for the purpose of celebrating life and calling for the creation of a world without war. It took place on the heels of the first Persian Gulf War. Archbishop Hunthausen spoke. "Light has always had great spiritual influence," he said. "Light in St. John's Gospel is invoked as a symbol of Jesus Himself. The truth is that love that Jesus lived out. Our truth is the life we live." He asked people to listen to each other no matter what might be their stand on the war, to uncover intolerances. As John Iwasaki reported, along with many pastors, politicians, union leaders, veterans, and minority leaders, Hunthausen tied colorful cloths together to represent an interconnected world.[27]

Hunthausen walked his life for justice and peace in the world and in the church. After he stepped down, he continued that walk, but not as a public figure. On Sunday, August 12, 1991, he told parishioners at a farewell Mass held at St. James Cathedral: "I've had some difficult days during my time as archbishop. But I have never felt abandoned." He lived the Beatitudes, said Fr. Ryan to the congregation. He was a peacemaker and he was persecuted. At the close of the liturgy, Ryan embraced Hunthausen and said, "Thank you, archbishop, for being our brother and our friend."[28] That same Sunday, in the evening hour, an interfaith prayer service to honor him took place at St. James. Angelo Bruscas, writing for the *Seattle Post-Intelligencer*, covered the event. Many lauded his witness. Sr. Barbara Matteson, president of the Dominican Sisters of Edmonds, said: "Raymond, your name for us means peace throughout the land."[29] And among those from various faith traditions who paid him tribute came these words from Rabbi Norman Hirsh from Temple Beth Am in Seattle: "You have been a model of what a religious leader should be." At the prayer service, Hunthausen asked the standing-room only crowd a series of questions:

> "Are we a church that includes gays, welcomes the divorced and separated, offers equal opportunity to women? Have we really taken a preferential option for the poor? Are our doors sincerely open to the least of our brothers and sisters? If charity begins at home, let's look at

> our own house. Are we good stewards of what God has given us? How do we treat our former priests and religious? How willing are we to dialogue with those troubled by what we teach or how we act?"

The prayer service was followed by an outdoor reception—with ice cream and joviality. Hunthausen was wearing a straw hat and receiving a thousand hugs.[30]

At the farewell celebration Archbishop Hunthausen voiced his gratitude. "You have made these years as Archbishop of Seattle wonderful for me, years of personal joy and great spiritual growth." There were just too many people to thank. "I think of the kindness and concern given to me by so many people of this city and state without reference to any boundaries. I think of the generous support of the Catholic community for my ministry and a myriad of good works." He spoke of all the people with whom he had walked the streets or stood in some crowded hearing room, of the people in the offices of the church, of the leaders of communities of faith in the state and his fellow bishops in the Northwest, the country, and throughout the world. "I think of the priests of this archdiocese. Your integrity and loyalty have given me real peace. I call you my family. And there is, finally, my family—brothers, sisters, nieces, nephews—you have been a constant and dear home, a source of nurture and regeneration." They had all come together that evening to join him "to mark an important change in my life and in our mutual relationships." Change, he said:

> "...has been a constant presence in the lives we have shared. We naturally resist change. Change at the very least breaks down that with which we have become comfortable. Sometimes change shakes us to our roots. We lose order and stability. We find ourselves without safe harbor, lost and confused. In our human experience, change and fear entwine. But change is essential to growth. Change is a matter of the spirit."

He cited a passage from the Gospel of John, where Jesus tells Nicodemus to be willing to sail on the winds of change. "The wind blows about at will, You hear the sound it makes, But do not know where it comes from or where it goes, So it is with everyone begotten of the Spirit." He recollected his own journey with change as a constant companion. The church he knew as a boy, a church that gave him a clear and solid framework for being and also gave him "a place of secure position and established purpose," underwent great change when he went to the Second Vatican Council.[31]

> "When I went to Rome, a different church revealed itself. What we saw when we came together in the heat and excitement of Rome in August, in the endless prayers and discussions, in the confusion of our many languages was simply ourselves as church. We saw, for the first time, the diversity and unity of the human family expressed

> as church. As the Council unfolded, the meaning of this revelation became clear. Great change had been taking place beneath our feet. Our diversity made conformity to rigid structures and formulations not only destructive but impossible."

This change at the Second Vatican Council had everything to do with a realization about a different way of experiencing unity. "Unity from above was false. We needed to rediscover and renew the unity that came from within. And there it was. At the deepest point we all share the divine image, reflected both in our unique personhood and our radical need to be together in community. The Council became a great dialogue on human community and the human person." Vatican II was not so much the opening of the church to the modern world, he said, but rather "the opening of the church to the human person in the modern world. In embracing modern humanity, the church actually set itself up for confrontation with the modern world."[32]

WHY FIVE YEARS EARLY?

His decision to retire at age seventy, given that the normal (and mandatory) retirement age for a bishop is seventy-five, deserves to be examined. Some people on the inside have shared their understandings of what happened, offering further insights into Hunthausen's character.

Fr. Michael McDermott, a key administrator with the archbishop in Seattle, believed Hunthausen came to the conclusion that he should step down because he could see that things were going in a different direction with Archbishop Murphy. Hunthausen had spoken powerfully at the bishops' national meeting back in late 1986, and the Vatican shifted to a different arrangement after that:

> "He retired because he did not want to stand in the way. He could, but he did not, want to use his authority to tell Murphy to cool it. It would not be Hunthausen's way to do that. His story, his life, speaks louder than his words. Fr. Jim Eblen once said to Archbishop Hunthausen, 'you know that you have ruined the church here in Seattle.' Archbishop Hunthausen said, 'what do you mean?' Eblen answered, 'well, you've trusted us as mature people and it will be a long time before we experience it again.'"[33]

This fundamental orientation of love and care in Hunthausen's character is key, thinks McDermott. He cared for the church:

> "That's why he didn't want to make a confrontation. He wanted to make a statement about things. So when his income was garnished, he did not fight it, he just asked me to cooperate with the IRS. He just paid it. So, in every realm, he said, while this thing with Rome is very disheartening, I am not going to confront them. He said that the unity of the church

was more important than anything else. I remember Hunthausen telling me this when he was going through it. He would state his position, he would accept the decision, but he would not fight it in the way that others have fought it. He would not rally people around him either to claim that this is wrong, this is unjust. He got people around him to help him articulate his sense of the situation. So he could talk and share his view. But you see, he talked to the bishops. He didn't call reporters together and say, 'this is unjust'. He talked to his brother bishops and said to them, 'would you look at this and help me understand if this is the right thing that our church should be doing' and the bishops came back to him and said, 'No, there's something wrong here. Let's go to Rome and see if we can get some mediation here.' That is what the commission was about. And that's why, after a few years with Archbishop Murphy he stepped back. If Hunthausen had been the bishop here and had been left alone he would have continued on. But because he could see that Archbishop Murphy had a different agenda and the idea was to begin a five year plan at the time, Hunthausen said 'this cannot be my plan, it has to be his plan. I am going to step back.' He stepped back for the good of the church, something perhaps like Pope Benedict did, and though there is an analogy here of sorts there is also a lot of irony in comparing the two examples."[34]

Fr. Ryan, the archbishop's right hand person through so much of what happened in Seattle, described Hunthausen as a man truly rooted in the Gospel and open to the Spirit. He listened to the Spirit to find guidance about the decision whether to stay or move on. He did this in every dimension of his journey, Ryan felt:

> "He always believed that the Spirit is alive and active and that we have to listen and learn, and only in prayerful discernment does that happen. So he has done that prayerful discernment in his life time. Whenever he would tell you that he would pray about that, whatever it was, these were not just words, he meant it. I think he was always just one of the most solid down to earth wholesome holy Montana natives who lived a balanced and inspired, inspiring life. It was always there. But I think that when he became a bishop in 1962, he only knew one model of being a bishop, the model of Joseph Michael Gilmore, then bishop of Helena. I am sure that is why when he found out he was going to be called to be a bishop he said, 'well, I guess I am going to be one of those.' But a few months later he was in Rome, the Council opened, and as he has already said, he got his on the job training to be a bishop via these four sessions of Vatican II. I think that crystallized for him what the church was and what it wasn't, what bishops were and what they weren't, what

> the church's role vis á vis the wider world was and what it wasn't, all those currents that ran through the Council. He came back from that convinced, as he told me many times, 'I thought I knew what it meant to be a bishop.' This is when he was being questioned. And you know, he never said it spitefully, not like, 'how can they dare come after me.' He would just say it wistfully, 'I thought I knew what it meant to be a bishop, I thought that is what I learned, and I have always tried to live that out,' and it had to do with being a man of prayer, of man of the Gospel, a man who listens to the entire church, who honors the spirit who is alive in the entire church, not just in the top of the hierarchical pyramid. He believed that the church should be in dialogue with the world, that it can learn from the world, that it can teach the world. And he believed that the church needs to be prophetic and not simply to blend into the landscape. Those currents that were so strong in Vatican II that shaped and formed him, I think that he was just humanly speaking very receptive to them, his family, just as a person, I think he was an ideal receptacle for that, it found a home in him."[35]

When Donald Wuerl was moved back to Pittsburgh and became the bishop there, and Archbishop Thomas Murphy was installed as the coadjutor on July 13, 1987, there was an expectation that he would be taking over before too long, since he was designated as coadjutor. It was a year later that Hunthausen confided with Fr. John Heagle his pastoral concern. Fr. Heagle and Sr. Fran Ferder began TARA (Therapy and Renewal Associates) in Seattle in 1985, taught at Seattle University, and worked with Archbishop Hunthausen and the Archdiocese of Seattle in providing counseling services and theological and psychological guidance for diverse constituencies in the church. "On the weekend of September 16-18, 1988, Fran Ferder and I led the retreat for the Archdiocesan permanent deacons and their wives at St Mary's Retreat Center near Toledo, Washington. Dutch came down and joined the community for lunch, and he asked if we might go for a walk before the closing liturgy." Hunthausen and Heagle went for a walk there by the retreat center. Hunthausen said he was agonizing about Archbishop Murphy. He said he wanted him to be the coadjutor and to share leadership, but for five years? "I don't know if I should tell him, 'look Tom, I'm going to be here for five more years, get used to it,' or should I just resign?" So Heagle said, "Archbishop, you're asking me?" He said, "Well, I'd like your opinion." Then Heagle said, "Well, that's a no brainer. I want you to stay on. So if you are looking for objectivity, you are asking the wrong person. I'm not going to give you an objective perspective. I'm going to give you what I think the archdiocese needs." Hunthausen said, "Well, let me think about this."[36]

When it was time to celebrate the closing liturgy of the retreat, the archbishop said that the crosier, the miter, and other vestments were in the trunk of his car. "I asked him if he wanted me to bring in those things. He said, 'no, leave them in the trunk. I just want to be a priest.' The permanent deacons wanted him to dress up." So John went out to the car to get the garb and crosier. "You could tell Hunthausen was uncomfortable getting all dressed up. I still remember unpacking his crosier in the sacristy and Dutch saying something like: 'I'm not sure how this thing comes together'—which, of course, Fran and I took as a more profound commentary on the unfolding crisis that he was facing at the time."

On February 5, 1991, Dutch came to Therapy and Renewal Associates at 8:30 in the morning, and spent an hour with Heagle.

> "He brought two letters, one a letter of resignation to the Vatican, the other a letter to Archbishop Murphy informing him that he intended to move ahead with the next five years as the Archbishop until his required retirement age of 75. He asked me, with his disarming honesty, which letter I thought he ought to sign. I, of course said, once again, 'Archbishop, you know I can't give you an objective answer to that question. So, tear up the letter to the Vatican and sign the one to Murph!' We both laughed and then spent the rest of the hour exploring the pros and cons. Hunty was clearly struggling in his depths with what was best for the people of the Archdiocese, as well as how to serve the Gospel with integrity. It was a moving and poignant conversation. During the following months most of us in the archdiocese were under the impression that Dutch had opted to stay on and move forward. But on the Saturday night before priest days in June 1991, I clearly remember that Dutch called me and told me that he wanted me to know that he would be telling the priests of his decision to resign on his 70th birthday (August 21, 1991). Fran and I were teaching at Seattle University, so I couldn't go to priest days, but I recall feeling heartbroken, sad, and angry—all at the same time."[37]

When it was clear he was leaving, Heagle said to him:

> "You know, Archbishop, you're resigning five years early. Do you plan to remain active? He said, 'no, I might give a retreat or two, but I'm not going to be active in the public eye. I'm not going to keep a high profile at all. I'm going to try to go deep into reflection and prayer and be with my family.' I did not ask him, well, why are you going to do that, because he seemed pretty committed to it. I said to him, 'well, I understand and I respect your decision even though I think it's going to be a great loss to the wider church and to the human community not to hear your voice.'"

Heagle told me:

> "One of the things I came to understand about Dutch is that he was a very humble man. But it wasn't just humility. There was also a trace of shyness in him. He just did not seek the public spotlight. I remember one time we were going back to the chancery office, there were all these people outside picketing him. Right-wing Catholics, carrying signs, saying 'take our Red Archbishop', an obvious reference to the notion that they thought he was a communist, and they were saying the rosary, and I said to him, 'do you want to go in the back door.' He said, 'no, no, I want to ask these people to pray for me.' The cameras were rolling. I said, 'well okay, you're the archbishop.' So he went up and asked them to pray for him, and of course the TV cameras were on. And I said, 'well, Archbishop, I know what you'll be doing tonight, you will probably be watching yourself on television.' And he said, 'no I won't do that. If the Mariners were playing I might watch them. But tonight I'm just going to go to bed. This isn't news to me.'"

Heagle believes Hunthausen may have felt that when he decided to resign he had caused enough trouble for the church, and that it was time for him to step back. "It was as though he was saying, 'I've been a source of conflict in ways that I didn't anticipate, and I have no regrets. But now I have resigned. I've walked the road, stood my ground, and tried to speak the truth of the gospel. It's over.'"[38]

Hunthausen's coat of arms, when he became bishop of Helena, depicted a large dog running in front of an ancient stone castle. That coat of arms reads *Fiat Voluntas Tuas,* which translates as "Thy will be done."[39] He tried in Seattle, and before and after his time there, to live that motto. When Hunthausen was preparing for his transition from Helena to Seattle in the spring of 1975, he was in Browning, Montana and was honored by the Blackfeet tribe. Sr. Edna Hunthausen, his sibling, worked with the Blackfeet for much of her career and was given the name "Holy Bird Woman" or "Sings in the Air" by the Blackfeet. Her brother was bestowed the name "Holy Traveler" and was made an honorary member of the Blackfeet tribe.[40] So a holy traveler who would strive to do God's will was destined to journey to Seattle and to what would become the home of Trident. He could not have known the half of what all was in store for him. Then, sixteen years later, it was time to travel back home to Montana. His sister Edna, when she met with me in Helena in later summer 2011, described her brother as not being a political person. It was just not in his character to engage in political strategy. "He cares about the poor, the common good. He was always grounded and never bitter," she said. "He is deeply forgiving." When she would be angry over what happened in Seattle, he would forgive and ask her to be forgiving of the people who went after him. "He taught me how to forgive many times. He is very peaceful. He is Gospel-centered."[41] After he resigned in 1991, he maintained strong ties in Seattle and even resided there for various periods of time, especially in the first years after he retired. But his center of gravity was back home close to family and wild outdoor Montana.

HOLY TRAVELER HEADS HOME

In the summer of 2014, Hunthausen talked about retirement: "You know, I retired when I was seventy. I wasn't sure how I would feel about it." He'd enjoyed it so much more than he thought he would.[42] This Holy Traveler was on his skis whenever he could get up on the snow-covered slopes. All of the Hunthausen, Stergar, and Walsh kin could be with him much more now. Nephew Denny Hunthausen described his passion for downhill skiing. "Once he got retired he would ski anywhere around the state, wherever there was a group of us skiing. But mostly he skied outside Anaconda at Discovery Basin, right across from Georgetown Lake. He had an affinity for that area, he loved it. He'd get a season pass. He had skied very close to there as a young man."[43] One of his favorite expressions was "Powder River!" to celebrate remarkable skiing conditions and also to unite family energy out there together. "Powder River!" is a shout you can expect to hear whenever any of the family are together up on the slopes. "When we would see each other on the lift," says Dick Walsh, "we would yell 'Powder River' and we still do it today. Dutch was a great athlete. He was better than most on the hill. He was competitive at sports. He lived life to the fullest."[44]

When he was a bishop, Hunthausen would do horseback trips with fellow bishops into the Bob Marshall Wilderness Area in Montana. He would go to numerous places to be in the great outdoors. There is a place that was truly special to Dutch. Denny described this spot:

> "Moose Lake lies at 6,000 ft elevation on the edge of the Anaconda-Pintler Wilderness Area. The area has exceptional hiking and fishing—two things Dutch loved to do all his life. And it's close to Anaconda where he grew up. There are a number of small, remote lakes among five or so peaks over 10,000 ft. Because of its elevation, weather can change quickly. Summers are very nice but the dependable weather is relatively short. It's even been known to freeze and snow in July or August. Dutch began to go there when still a seminarian in the 40's. He helped develop it—he and others building the second cabin and other improvements. Uncle Jack went up there in the early years as well. The two original cabins were quite primitive with no electricity or in-door plumbing. In the 90's after Dutch retired, he had a third, more modern cabin built so he and family could be spend more time there and do so more comfortably. It's simple but has the typical modern conveniences of indoor plumbing, heating, electricity

and a large outdoor deck. For Dutch, Moose is a place that he really enjoyed as a younger man and was only able to enjoy occasionally during his working years. Since retiring he's figured out how to spend a lot more time there again. For a number of years, he and Jack (sometimes with other family tag-a-longs) would go to Moose Lake as early in the spring as they could and return as late in the summer/fall as possible. That often meant they'd encounter snow on first and last trips. They would typically spend a few days to two weeks on each visit. Dutch enjoyed maintaining, repairing or improving the property and grounds wherever he spent time and Moose was no exception."

(The kin often refer to it as just "Moose," not Moose Lake, as in "Have you been up to Moose lately?"). He continues that Dutch

"…was always active—recreating (he would organize a hike every day), doing maintenance or repairing something or reading, but rarely, if ever, just lounging. He's a consummate outdoorsman who would share much about nature and the outdoors on our hikes. Mass was celebrated every day and meals were always communal—in preparation, enjoyment and cleanup. During and following meals is when we'd sit and share stories of the day or Dutch and Jack shared recollections of Moose adventures from times past—fishing trips to the remote lakes, encounters with wildlife, and always lots of laughter. He and Jack would swim and bathe in the lake at some point every day. The kids (and some adults) would be swimming and playing around the dock and the lake often during the day but we would always try to be there when Dutch and Jack went to the lake/dock (down a trail, just a few hundred feet from the cabin) so we could play and have fun with them. Whereas Legendary Lodge holds more memories with Dutch and the many nieces and nephews as kids, Moose was something we nieces and nephews experienced more as adults. It's a place the grand nieces and nephews have spent a good deal of time with Dutch."[45]

In the early 1990s, Tony Hunthausen wired the new cabin at Moose. "We worked pretty hard on that cabin project. We had fun up there working and watching it grow."[46] Bill remembers that Dutch had just gotten a titanium knee replacement that spring of 1992. That summer Dutch, Tony (Bill's dad), Uncle Jack, and others all built the new cabin. "A beautiful mountain peak can be seen from there. Moose Lake is spring-fed. It was part of the diocese for years. He and Jack bought it at some point when Dutch was in Seattle. Dutch never hunted later on when he retired. He enjoyed the serenity of Moose Lake. You could walk down a trail by the lake. You could see Mt. Warren, looking southeast."[47]

He lived for most of that time upon retirement with his sister Marie down the street from his brother Tony's in East Helena. They would all get together and invite Jack and celebrate Mass every day, or certainly every week. And so that is how they would start the day. He did quite a bit in those early years of retirement relieving pastors around the diocese who needed a break, a vacation, or other personal leave time. So he was able to retain a lot of the things he most enjoyed about parish pastoral life—getting to know the people, celebrating liturgy with them, reconnecting—but with no committees, no meetings, no administrative or personnel matters. He gathered with family often, whether traveling to Anaconda, Butte, or Billings, following nieces and nephews, grand nieces and nephews, with their sports, to every family event, with each part of the family. Denny remembers one time thinking, "let's go to Moose Lake, and there they were, Dutch and Jack, setting on the deck, enjoying the sunshine, and they would sit on lawn chairs half way in the water and watch the kids play. They loved to do that. Uncle Dutch would get up and throw a ball."[48]

He brought his spirituality into the great outdoors, which in turn nurtured his faith. For years, Dutch regularly went up to the top of Mt. Helena to the west of town, starting when he was the bishop of Helena. He would celebrate Mass up there. And he would take the family to St. Mary's Peak, just out of Stevensville, south of Missoula. He lived close to the earth. Andy says, "conversations with Uncle Dutch were not so much about philosophy but simply about being thoughtful in your life. It was less intellectual and more about the simplicity of it all. He showed us by how he lived. He spent time praying every day."[49]

Tony told me, "my brother Dutch never worked in a parish. He came to teach at Carroll and never worked in a parish his whole life. So Dutch would go to the parishes to help out when he got back from Seattle and retired. We, many of us siblings, Marie, myself and Harriet, would have daily Mass here in our house, or at Marie's or over at the home of Art and Donna in Sun Haven."[50] Dick Walsh asked Dutch once about his priestly life and if he ever wanted to be a parish priest.

> "He said he always assumed he would be a parish priest. In retirement he made himself available to local priests to be a substitute priest when they were on vacation or unable to say Mass. He clearly enjoyed that as well as hearing confessions. He did this regularly at the East Helena parish up to just a few years ago. For many years the seven elders along with spouses would take trips. Some of them were planned around retreats Dutch was involved with. Many were to sunny places and trips that otherwise would not have happened without Dutch."[51]

Victoria Ries, one of the leaders in Seattle with whom Hunthausen practiced the empowering model of shared responsibility, recalled how after he retired he did a retreat for the North Seattle deanery. "It was a half day retreat. He was nervous. He said he had not prepared. He said he was living with his sibling, and he said that his sibling whistled and that was annoying. He was extemporaneous about the ordinary challenges of daily life. As to the retreat, it did not matter what he said, we just wanted to be in his presence. He would be a superb spiritual director." If she could sit down with him now, she would ask him how he prays.

> "What is your experience of God at this point in your life? With all of your life experience, how do you pray? He lives in the world with all of its challenges and yet he is a very peaceful person, a very centered person. His wholeness was so clear. When you were in his presence you knew you were in the presence of a holy and centered person. He was centered and solid, but he was not perfect. People felt his simple holiness. He was also very much in the outdoors, athletic, engaged physically in the world and at the same time deeply spiritual. They were not two different realms for him. They formed his wholeness."[52]

Eventually, of course, his athletic energies diminished. He was up at Whitefish, beside Glacier National Park, skiing in his early eighties. He told the story of his last ski trip, as recalled by niece Kathleen. "I was coming down and I fell. And I couldn't get up. I was looking at the scenery. The sun was out, it was so beautiful. I just sat there in the snow. These two young kids came along and they said, 'are you alright, do you need some help?' And I said, 'yea, could you help please.' It was there that I decided, you know, I think my skiing days are over. I don't think I'll go out anymore."[53] But he hiked, golfed, and fished for many more years. In fact, his golfing habit and the pace at which he played the game reveals another side of his personality. Dutch could be impatient, his niece Sarah says. "I'm not a golfer, but I did try to golf with him once. Everyone warned me, you better keep it going. Come on, let's move it. I think he has a side that is kind of impatient."[54]

The family has known much happiness, yet has experienced challenges and tragedies that can touch families across the world in one way or another. Tony and Harriet's daughter Kathleen tells a poignant story. Kathleen was eventually divorced from her first husband. Then she met Ken, fell in love, and they decided to get married.

> "I'll never forget, when I asked Dutch and Jack if they would do the wedding, and they said, 'sure.' Well, just about five days before our wedding, Ken was diagnosed with terminal cancer. We didn't tell anybody because he didn't want to ruin the wedding. He asked me, 'do you still want to marry me?' and I said, 'of course.' So all my family was there, all my siblings. They all came, that was on July 8, 2000. It was a beautiful wedding. Five days later Ken was in the hospital. He had a large tumor and it had to be removed. And he died about

> ten months after we were married. You know, when he was really sick, I called Dutch and I said, 'you know, it won't be too long, and I was wondering if you and Jack would do the funeral,' and he said, 'absolutely.' In less than a year span of time they married us and then they buried him. And every one of my siblings came back for the funeral. My sister from Ohio, my brother from California. You know, when there was a tragedy, a sadness, something difficult, Dutch and Jack were always there."[55]

Dutch and his brother Jack were very close and they lived together in their final years.

Grief struck again just a week or so after the family reunion at Legendary Lodge in 2006. Sarah Walsh-Kelly's fourteen year old son, Patrick, died suddenly. "It was a tragedy beyond belief and will always be a big loss. The Helena cathedral was overfilled and people gathered outside for the service," says her brother Dick.[56] Young Patty was out boating at Gate of the Mountains north of Helena. It turns out he had a heart defect that had never been detected. It was a Friday in mid-July when he died. Sarah shared with me about this great loss. "I remember Dutch and my mom came up to the hospital. My son had died. There was nothing to say. They were just present. Jack did the vigil, and Dutch did the homily the next day for the funeral. It was a beautiful homily, simple, not explaining anything away."[57]

Homily for Patty:

> "None of us lives for oneself and no one dies for oneself, St. Paul tells us—another way of saying that we don't go to God alone. We go as a family, a neighborhood, a parish, a community.... Patty touched us with his spirit of kindness and his gentle way. We give thanks to God for him—The Blessing he has been. We will miss him more than we can say.... It's at moments like this that we are reminded all too poignantly that not too far beneath the surface all of us live with a great deal of fear and anxiety. The media constantly holds before us war and terrorism; then there are the everyday fears; the fear of losing our jobs; the fear of losing our health; the fear of losing our life's savings; the fear of another war; the fear of accidents; the fear of misfortune coming to our husbands, our wives, our parents, our children; the fear of being rejected, being unwanted; the fear of some people, as they move into old age, of being left alone without friends or family or loved ones. And finally, of course, there is the fear of loss: the loss of our faculties, the loss of our hearing, our sight, the loss of our sanity, the loss of our loved ones, and the loss that we call death. Even after we suffer these losses, particularly the loss that comes through death, then there are other fears that creep in, fears we don't always

> express: the fear of losing control. The fear of coming to terms with our feelings of anger, like holy Job, in the Old Testament, had against God. Why can't God prevent young people from dying, or people from having cancer, or war or pestilence or hunger or famine, and all the other ills we suffer? We want to shake our fist at God and say, 'Well, it was all right until it hit home.'... When we are faced with this great anxiety called death, we don't know whether to run the whole gamut of acceptance to anger, to disbelief, to hurt, to bewilderment, because after all, in death we always lose a person, a loved one. But we have to remember that we never lose our relationship to God. We still have someone who says, 'It's okay, it's all right.' That someone is God: God present in his word, in the Spirit, and in the church... You know well enough why we sing 'Alleluia' as we enter the church. We sing that 'Alleluia' because through our tears we believe that God has made it 'all right' for Patty, who has died. We wear the white vestments and put out colorful flowers, not because we're insensitive to human grief, but it's our limited way of saying, 'Now, now, it will be all right.'... And finally, we're at this Mass where bread shall be taken, and wine brought up and changed into the body and blood of Christ, and broken and crushed and given, because today Jesus is still saying, 'This is my body given for you. This is my blood, shed for you—and for Patty who has died.' And this, above all, is our greatest assurance that God pats us on the head and says, 'It's all right.' So we go back to the altar in a moment with that double stream of feeling: human grief and loss, a sense of bewilderment, facing death so squarely and closely. But above all, I hope, with a deeper sense of faith. Faith that God gives us in our collective selves and this ancient liturgy. And faith in the promises that God made, the pat on the head, the allaying of our fears, the uplifting of our hopes, the forgiveness of our anger, the strengthening of our faith, and the promise that through Jesus, as our liturgy says, life is never ended but merely changed. And so for Patty, as for us, 'it's all right.'"

People after Patrick's funeral told Sarah that the homily changed their lives. "I just remember feeling so lucky to be from this family and to have those elders there."[58] Sarah's father had passed away in 1991, and she had lost her oldest brother in 1975. This sense of being fortunate to have "those elders there" and all the family across the generations that could be there was truly deep-felt.

THE SEX-ABUSE CRISIS

The past came back to haunt Catholicism, especially in the first decade of the new millennium. Victims called for accountability. This was happening across the nation. It became a global crisis. The grave injustice of sexual abuse of minors was hardly limited to the Catholic Church. But it did have significance in Seattle. At the time of his deposition in 2009, Hunthausen became one of the highest ranking members of the hierarchy to be called to testify in a case. Sarah Walsh recalled when Uncle Dutch was deposed in Seattle. "You could just tell it was heartache for him. You could just see it in his face and it was heartache for the rest of us."[59] The sex-abuse crisis is an enormous issue in the Catholic Church, and it is a complex and multi-faceted reality, and therefore there will be no attempt here to cover such breadth. Instead, the focus will be on a couple of cases and some background that shed light on how Hunthausen approached the issue.

On Monday, May 18, 2009, retired Archbishop Raymond G. Hunthausen testified in King County Superior Court in Seattle. According to the Associated Press story, the case involved an abuser priest, Fr. Patrick G. O'Donnell, who in 1976 was transferred from Spokane to Seattle. The question posed to Hunthausen that day in the courtroom was whether he—and others in positions of responsibility with him at the Seattle Archdiocese—knew back then about O'Donnell's abusive history. From the testimony and cross-examination it was clear that Hunthausen let O'Donnell come from Spokane to Seattle without properly vetting him. Hunthausen agreed that he ought to have done more to look into O'Donnell's background. "It was a breach on my part," he testified. "It's hard to acknowledge that now. It hurts me." Patrick O'Donnell, one week earlier in court, had taken the witness stand and admitted that he had committed acts of sexual abuse against many victims—as many as 30 or more—over the course of time when he was in Spokane serving as a priest, and then while he was in the Seattle Archdiocese from 1976 to 1978, serving at St. Paul Church in Rainier Beach.[60]

It turns out that O'Donnell had been sent to Seattle for deviancy treatment because he had molested adolescent boys in Spokane. Hunthausen, however, said he was never told the real reason. The Archbishop and his staff assumed O'Donnell was in Seattle to work on a doctorate in education at the University of Washington and viewed him as a priest in good standing. But on what basis? Hunthausen testified that he and his staff had not sought more background on O'Donnell because Hunthausen so deeply trusted his close friend, Bishop Bernard Topel, who was Spokane's bishop at the time. "The assumption was that he was a priest in good standing because of my relationship with Bishop Topel," Hunthausen said. "Your best friend sent a pedophile to your diocese without telling you anything?" was the question posed by a victim's lawyer Michael Pfau. Hunthausen replied, "that's what it amounts to." But O'Donnell was "one of Spokane's most dangerous sex offenders?" Pfau asked. "Yes," Hunthausen replied, "that's why it hurts so much. I definitely feel that he should have told me. I have struggled with why." When the judge relayed to the archbishop a question from a juror asking if Topel, who died in 1986, had ever told Hunthausen that he was aware of O'Donnell's abusive history in the Spokane Diocese, the archbishop answered that Topel had not.[61]

Hunthausen acknowledged that under his leadership the Archdiocese of Seattle had not properly vetted O'Donnell before he came to work in a parish. He had put his trust in Topel, his close friend and spiritual mentor. The previous week, attorneys for the plaintiffs in the case had called Rev. Michael G. Ryan to the stand. During Hunthausen's early years in Seattle, Ryan had served on the personnel board that made assignments of priests for parish posts. Attorney Pfau wanted to know why there was only one very brief written archdiocesan record, a note in the personnel board minutes, about O'Donnell. According to the *Seattle Times*, Ryan "attributed the lack of written records in part to then-Seattle Archbishop Raymond Hunthausen's style, which he described as more pastoral and less by-the-book."[62]

Both Sr. Carol Ann McMullen and Fr. Jack Walmsley, who served in priest personnel leadership roles, remember Hunthausen telling them about the key meeting of U.S. bishops at St. John's in Collegeville, Minnesota in 1985. Hunthausen called a group together, including Fr. Ryan, Sr. McMullen, Fr. Walmsley, Fr. John Heagle, Sr. Fran Ferder, and others. Heagle recalls:

> "He brought in some 30 files and told the group we needed to do something about it. He wanted us to look at the files closely. At Collegeville, Ray Mouton, an attorney from Lafayette, Louisiana, where the first big story came out, and a psychologist priest. Fr. Michael Peterson, head of the St. Luke's Institute near Baltimore, and Fr. Thomas Doyle, a Dominican canon lawyer, all really got Hunthausen's attention. He took the message from the Collegeville meeting very seriously. The group kept meeting and he asked us to develop a vision, policy and protocols for how the archdiocese should respond to the problem. He wanted the approach to have three dimensions, legal, moral, and pastoral. If there was clear legal proof, he wanted perpetrators reported to the civil authorities. And in moral terms, even if a case could not be legally proven, he wanted us to evaluate moral guilt. And on a pastoral level, even if there was not legal or moral proof, we needed to reach out to people because pastorally speaking this was our first responsibility. He was willing to provide aid, to provide archdiocesan funds for people even in cases that were not proven. He wanted to help people in their anguish and their sense of betrayal."

Walmsley noted how humanly pained Hunthausen was that people could abuse little ones. Hunthausen was passionate about doing the right thing. He did not vilify the priests. He had great compassion for the children and their families. He wished he had known the severity of the problem sooner than Collegeville.[63]

Nonetheless, Hunthausen's management of the sex abuse matter was not without some serious problems even after 1985, as in the case of Fr. James McGreal. As Timothy Egan of the *New York Times* reported in mid-June 1988, Hunthausen wrote a letter to the people of the Archdiocese of Seattle identifying McGreal as a pedophile. Hunthausen realized that the church had made serious mistakes in this case as in others. He asked priests in parishes all across the archdiocese to read his letter at the Sunday liturgies on May 29, 1988. McGreal had been in 12 different parishes in the archdiocese since his ordination decades earlier, and was sent to St. Theresa's Parish in Federal Way in 1987 without parishioners being informed about his background. In Hunthausen's letter he acknowledged "the struggles we have faced concerning Fr. Jim McGreal, who has undergone extensive treatment for a sexual disorder, eventually identified as pedophilia. I am writing in hopes this situation, as painful as it is, will serve as an opportunity to break the cycle of silence that perpetuates abuse in the human family." Fr. Joe Kramis, the pastor at St. Theresa's, had kept the McGreal background confidential because both he and Hunthausen and key archdiocesan staff felt confident that he did not pose a threat; he was undergoing treatment and was being supervised by Kramis. In retrospect, a year later, Kramis said he wished he had told the parish council about McGreal's background. "A year ago, when I welcomed him into my rectory, I was convinced confidentiality was the best way to go. Now, I would tell the parish council."[64]

In late July 2002, the *Seattle Post-Intelligencer* reported that a lawsuit was being filed by eight more men, accusing the Archdiocese of Seattle of leaving them vulnerable to McGreal. By that time it was the fourth lawsuit dealing with McGreal's predatory conduct in various parishes and schools, including St. Catherine's in Seattle and St. Michael's in Olympia. "The lawsuit says that parents of two of the plaintiffs reported the alleged abuse to the archdiocese in the 1970s, while McGreal was at St. Catherine. One of them met personally with Archbishop Raymond Hunthausen, according to the complaint."[65]

There were numerous other cases in the archdiocese involving other priests. Hunthausen's compassion was primarily focused on the abused children, but included care and concern for priests. There were cases in the Helena Diocese during Hunthausen's tenure there as well.[66] Compassion for a priest could mean less than firm action to ensure that no child would ever be in harm's way. John Heagle told me about the case of McGreal.

"He had been in a parish in Renton. Things got very heated and intense in the meeting with the people of the parish. We went out to all the parishes that wanted us to do hearings. We learned that we had been mistaken in being secretive. We had to be transparent. For cxamplc, whcn Fr. Joc Kramis was pastor at St. Theresa's in Federal Way, he was so compassionate. Fr. Jim McGreal was there. It was a very painful time. The people of the parish were not told that he was there. We were on a learning curve, and we had to learn fast. And we had to change that. Hunthausen was not permissive regarding clergy sex abuse, but he was compassionate."[67]

The serious problem of pedophilia is certainly not confined to the Catholic Church—in Seattle, Helena, or any place across the globe. Yet a serious and perhaps systemic pedophilia problem was plaguing the church. It was the courage of victims and their families, the diligent work of lawyers, the reparative impact of lawsuits and the tenacity of investigative journalism that brought to light so many sad stories of child molestation. And certainly it seems clear that in the context of Raymond Hunthausen's role in all of this over the years he made efforts to grow on that "learning curve" Heagle spoke about. It would be unfair to judge him entirely by the expectations and knowledge base that we have available to us on the issue at the present time. On the other hand, it appears that in this area of his ministry, he did not take action as early and as forthrightly as he could have, and it also appears clear that he has acknowledged the pain such hesitancy and priest-to-priest compassion has caused to those who have been abused.

Over a decade into his retirement, Hunthausen was asked about the sex abuse crisis. "There is a lot of suffering and sadness on the part of the whole church," he said. "It's fair to say the church is in agony over that. The victims, the perpetrators, all Catholics—we feel stunned." And he was asked about his overall career as a church leader in Montana and Washington. "There's no point in looking back at what I'd do differently," he said. "I feel confident that under the circumstances of my life, I made the best choices I could. God led me where I eventually ended up, and I have peace in that from beginning to end."[68]

SUNSET OF A RELUCTANT PROPHET

In Helena in October 2012, Hunthausen said: "My longest assignment has been retirement. I never expected that."[69]

He would often be in prayer, reading, in quiet time, say his nieces and nephews. "Every day he prays at Mass that Pope Benedict will find peace in his retirement." He never showed any animosity or anger toward Pope Benedict, they say. "He prays for him in the prayers of the faithful, that Pope Benedict in his retirement will find peace and joy," says niece Kathleen, a family nurse practitioner with experience working with elderly, who heard Dutch say once or twice late in his life journey, "my body just doesn't work like it used to."[70] One time, nephew Denny went to visit his uncles Dutch and Jack in Helena late in their lives. They'd had Mass at the kitchen table, at some point both had fallen down, and they could not get up. They were just there on their backs laughing. It was a classic moment; the two of them so often together in those years, each facing the diminishment of the body—with humor. After Hunthausen had a debilitating stroke in the summer of 2013 and could not get around on his own at all anymore, he was asked how he was coping. He said, "Well, I just sit in my chair and let God love me."[71]

Dutch made his peace with those who had led the Vatican's effort to suppress him in Seattle. Tony says that his brother Dutch never said much about the Seattle-Rome conflict:

> "He never opened up a conversation with a feeling of anger. He never said, 'why is this happening to me?' I personally think he was right in his thinking about the military and all. He was right regarding the nation and in the issues of the church. He doesn't talk too much about all this. We've never gotten down to a real 'dig it out' meeting. He never asked us to get behind him, he just assumed we were."[72]

He never came back and made the Seattle conflict an issue. "He was going through a lot," Tony said, "but he did not discuss it or let on." Nephew Bill once wrote to him during the tough times to express his support. What Bill saw in him then he saw in his uncle in the final years as well. "Dutch's relationship with Jesus Christ is absolutely real. He doesn't preach about it, he just lives it. He never did once talk badly about the church. He never shared remarks about what the Vatican was doing to him. He just lived through it and prayed. The joy comes out in him. Even right now, he can do very little on his own physically, and he is still full of joy. It is his personal relation to the Lord."[73]

Sarah was in Washington, D.C. in 2006. She just happened to go to St. Matthew's Cathedral, and it turned out, by coincidence, to be the first Mass of the newly installed Archbishop of Washington, Donald Wuerl. After the Mass, Wuerl was greeting people.

> "I had met him just once in Seattle. I wanted to introduce myself, so I got in the line. I told him I was Sarah, one of Archbishop Hunthausen's nieces. He said, 'you are, well, how is Dutch?' He had wonderful things to say about Dutch, and he had talked to him not that long before. Even a person who I assume had opposing views on some things, he still really likes Dutch. And I remember coming back and telling Dutch about seeing Wuerl, and Dutch not having any animosity."[74]

Why had Archbishop Hunthausen not spoken up more during his retirement? According to Sarah, he did not want the attention focused on himself. Also, had he left Seattle and been outspoken about so many issues, this would have made it difficult for the bishop there in Seattle after him. The biggest reason for his relative quiet, however, is that Dutch just loved the church. "You know, the church is just like a person, we all have our issues, we all have our warts, and we thank God, we're mostly good."[75] Andy, reflecting on his uncle in these final years of life, felt Dutch was consistent. "It's been the same all the way through. He ends his speeches, talks, and correspondence with 'His joy, His peace, His love.' He is a humble guy who, when he came back from Seattle, said, 'I don't want to be in the public life so much as before.' In day to day life he wakes up every day, probably just like before, says his morning prayer and has lived like this always." Andy never once saw anger in his uncle. With regard to the situation in Seattle when it was happening and since:

> "…he saw it as 'I have to approach all this as Jesus would and do what the Gospel tells us about how we have to be in the world and how we have to be an example for others.' When he talked about the human family and the threats to the human family, it was a simple approach. When he'd come back here while all the troubles were going on, he would never mention it with our family. We'd sit around the porch or wherever at night. He would not say a word about what was going on in Seattle."[76]

Andy said that if he had taken every engagement offered to him, Dutch would have been all over the world. "I'm no longer in that position. I want to respect those who come after me and their space and position. I've spoken. You know where I am on all this." Dutch took a different role in retirement. He did spiritual retreats. When he first became a priest he imagined being a parish priest in western Montana. So when he came back, he heard lots of confessions, filled in for other priests, and did retreats in various places. He did occasional public events on special anniversaries of Vatican II or for Carroll College.[77]

In 2001, there was a party in Seattle to honor Hunthausen's turning 80. Fr. Michael Ryan shared what happened at that birthday celebration.

> "I thought it was very vintage Hunthausen that the story he chose to tell his friends at the end of the Mass—he didn't give the homily at the Mass, he just spoke at the end—was a story recalling how in 1988, I think it was, the Pope called all the archbishops of the country to Rome for a meeting. During an early session they were given a chance to share their hopes and concerns. The Pope met with them and listened to them in a formalized setting, which is typical of those Roman meetings. At the end of the session they crowded into the aisle as the Pope was walking out."

Ryan continued, and Hunthausen "told us how the Pope came over to him, put his arm around his shoulder and said, 'I'm very glad you came.'" Ryan felt that Hunthausen always tried to be a unifier. "He never wanted himself to be perceived as at odds with the Pope, or our local Church with Rome. And I think he wanted the people in that room (at the party the other night) to be reminded of our communion with the larger Church."[78]

Sr. Louise Dumont, a member of the Sisters of St. Joseph of Peace who was active in Concerned Catholics, believes Hunthausen was ultimately obedient to the church power structure. She expressed a little disappointment. She once wrote to him when he retired, telling him that he could speak out on issues that were not right. But he was a son of the church and loyalty to it was a priority. Later on, when they saw each other in person, he told her he had gotten her letter. He just did not want to speak about what he had gone through. He led retreats, for example at the Palisades in Federal Way, with women religious of the Seattle Archdiocese during the first decade of the new century.[79]

In the perspective of Dumont's colleague, Sr. Kathleen Pruitt, Dutch Hunthausen was:

> "...guileless, humble, a true son of the church in its best sense. He was deeply hurt by the church he loved so much. He had deep compassionate conviction. He learned from many, willing to sit at the feet of others and learn. Always he had this deep sense of compassion, very little false self and ego. He was a man of deep deep faith. He opened the space for others to be prophetic voices. He was not an exclusivist; God is not the property of the church. He had a sense of God much bigger than the walls of Rome."

The central ego was the eye of God, deep faith, and a mystery that Hunthausen did not know. His prophetic witness, she thinks, was not in the prophetic stance of publicly criticizing the church, the institution that he loved to the end. His prophetic witness was that of the importance of the little people. This was not a dramatic witness. In those public moments around war and peace, he did speak prophetic words:

> "He opened space so that others could be prophetic. He was so approachable. This was his down to earth, holy humble way. Very central to his story is this fact that in some ways he was a very private person thrust into a very public role, pushed even further by people like Jim and Shelley Douglass and others. He was thrust as a reluctant prophet into the war and peace arena and he became a lightning rod in other areas as well. He was a man who prayed. Out of that place he touched people. He moved among people as one of us, not aloof

> from us. He would step out of line, so to speak, to greet people. This touched the marrow of the human soul. The God of mystery was made real among people, and he expressed this."[80]

Fr. Michael Ryan thought Hunthausen was reluctant in a certain sense. "He was reluctant to be in the limelight, I don't think he was reluctant to speak the truth. I never saw fear. Not in any way, whether it was with the Vatican and the people who were making life difficult for him, he didn't fear them. He did his best to understand them." So was this deep humility?

> "Yes, he never liked the limelight. Some people thought he was after grandstanding, but they couldn't have been wider from the mark. I never saw fear. The word just doesn't come to my mind. I don't think I have ever even asked myself, was he fearful about the role of the prophet. Of course he would be the last one to call himself a prophet. But he believed the church should be prophetic and I think if you really pushed him on it I think he would say, 'well, I guess I did some things that qualify there' but I think he would be very slow to do that, you know, it is just not who he was. I think he was prophetic in the church, I think he was, in the way he governed the church, in the way he envisioned the church and enabled the church to be all it could be."[81]

I asked Ryan if Hunthausen was a prophet who both announces and denounces.

> "I think he would stop short of denouncing, his own sense of loyalty, I guess this is the right word. He would never say, 'I have it right, they have it wrong.' I think the most he would ever say is, 'I thought I had it right and I thought I understood what it meant to be a bishop.' And today he would say, 'I just can't understand, I do not understand the direction they are going, why they are doing what they are doing' but he wouldn't get up in the public to say that because that would ratchet it to another level, and I think, first of all, when he was bishop it would have been too divisive, it was very difficult, his role was to unify, and he was torn that way, it was always painful for him, that his conscience led him to take positions that in fact did divide or at least cause people to separate. He was there to unify. It was a tension, of course, and I think to have gone the extra step—it was one thing to critique the government, as he did on the whole civil sphere there, but for him to do a similar critique of the church would have been a step too far for him. He was raised in the church, you know, shaped and formed in so many different ways, deep down he must have thought, 'I'm not going to put myself over and against this thing, I'll question, I'll wonder, I'll express my thought and my perplexity in safe places with people I can really trust

about my dissatisfaction with things, but I'm not going to stand up and tack my theses to the door there,' to use the Martin Luther reference."[82]

Ryan used to tell Hunthausen, even after Hunthausen had retired,

> "You should go to those bishops' meetings, you need to speak up, they need to hear you, you have a point and you have nothing to lose. I think he had just had it. I think there was a certain amount of disillusionment, where would it go, he was tired of it, bone tired of it, really. You see, that is the hard thing, I used to say, your voice is needed there. He just chose to drop off that whole part of life. I still have to ask why, I don't know, I think to some degree he said, more than one time, 'I'm so glad my mother didn't have to witness all of this.' He was close to his mom, she lived with him for years when he was in Helena. I think he was basically saying that she would have found this whole matter so troubling because the church was important to her and here is her son with all this. I don't think he thought that she would be anything other than supportive of him but I think he thought that she would have found it very troubling and he was glad that she didn't have to go through that. I think there is that thing, you know, 'I am a son of the church in the best sense of that word, it has formed and shaped me, and my mom and my whole family, I'm glad she did not have to deal with that.'"[83]

What did Fr. Michael McDermott believe to be at the heart of the story?

> "Hunthausen was definitely a man of prayer and faith, a faithful disciple of the Lord. Nothing else makes sense, in my mind, unless you know that. He was definitely as bishop of the church in the best expression of this role. Clearly he was a person of his time and that means the Second Vatican Council. And so those qualities of shared responsibility and collegiality, of care for people, these were definitely there in his way. He was a person who both respected us as adults and challenged us as adults to be our very best. And that means not only for church people but for others. He did that in his ecumenical relationships and in his wider world relationships. I do not think that he consciously set out to make this his pattern. I think you see this in retrospect. It just came out of those deepest values. He was not somebody who was apart; he was somebody always with people—with the church, with other religions, and with the world."[84]

Fr. John Heagle believed that during his years of retirement, Dutch consciously chose not to dwell on all that he had endured with the Vatican investigation.

> "It was an enormously painful experience for him. He had no idea that there was so much behind-the-scenes political intrigue in the institutional church. He loved the church as the people of God, but he felt let down by its institutional leaders. He certainly did not anticipate being betrayed by the very institution to which he had committed his life. Hunthausen was fully invested in the church. He believed in it; he was steeped in it. He was a genuine theological moderate like Oscar Romero before he became archbishop of San Salvador. In the end, I believe that Dutch—in his usual resilient spirit—chose not to focus on his personal pain but on the gospel vision that had sustained his life and ministry."[85]

Fr. Jim Hogan, one of Hunthausen's old friends in Missoula, told Dutch a story when he was over in Helena visiting around 2012. "You know, Dutch, I'm so disturbed by what they did to you. Did you ever hear what Jim Provost said about that?" When Dutch answered, "no," Hogan continued.

> "Jim Provost told me some years ago that he learned from some friends that he had in the Vatican, and he had a lot, that the Reagan administration was very disturbed by what you were doing with the Trident missiles, with all the things you were doing. And Reagan's people went to see John Paul II, and said that if Rome would silence you they would establish diplomatic relations with the Vatican. And lo and behold, they silenced you and they established diplomatic relations."

And Hunthausen said, "Ah, I don't think they would do that." Hunthausen never wanted to be critical. It's one of his strengths, part of his nonviolent approach to life, but also a weakness. "He ought to have spoken up more on this."[86]

Another one of Hunthausen's good friends in Missoula, Con Kelly, shared two stories from Dutch's sunset years:

> "Dutch and his brother Jack were playing golf with my wife and myself here in Missoula a few years ago. Both were very good golfers, even at their advanced ages. During the course of play, Dutch asked, almost out of the blue, 'Do you know why the Jews had to wander for forty years in the desert?' To my response that I didn't know, he smiled slyly and said: 'They had an all-male leadership that was unwilling to ask for directions.' The second story related to a visit I had with him in the sacristy of a local church after a liturgy at which he had presided. The liturgy celebrated 100 years of ministry in the diocese by the Blessed Virgin Mary sisters. In keeping with the celebration, the homily/address was presented by the president of the congregation, who, as it turned out, was a native of the diocese of Helena. BVM congregational offices are in

> Dubuque, Iowa. Immediately after we shared our personal greetings, he referenced his satisfaction with the just-completed liturgy by remarking how he appreciated the homily/address by saying something like, 'that is a marvelous example of what we are lacking.'"[87]

Jesus touched the raw nerve of the power system, and Hunthausen did the same. Hunthausen's story resembles classic stories in various religious traditions across time and space. Consider how his story reminds us of other stories of other persons and other situations we have heard about. The themes are found in all of these stories, war and peace, injustice and justice, selfishness and compassion, religious oppression and religious liberation. This has been a chronicle of conscience, courage, and character. This book has chronicled Hunthausen's inner and outer quest for peace. In 1989, I asked him if he saw himself as prophetic. "I do not see myself as prophetic. What I have done I have done as common sense. I simply set out to live in the spirit, to implement the Vatican II mandate as a bishop."[88] Could a bishop in the Roman Catholic Church be prophetic and remain a bishop for long? Hunthausen never made a habit of consciously taking prophetic stands. He saw himself, as Ryan said, as reluctant. In an interview with Michael Gallagher in 1988, he explained it this way. "Every time I go over to Ground Zero and take part in one of those demonstrations, every time I see some of my friends cross the line and get arrested, I say why can't I do that." He struggled with the challenges of being a public figure facing all the responsibilities of speaking truth to power.

> "I don't want to be in this situation. I'd like to slip into seclusion somewhere so that I could take up my comfortable prayer life and let someone who could do it a lot better than I take up this responsibility. But, again, I see my reluctance as part of the growth process. Something would be wrong if I were comfortable. If I got comfortable in anything the Lord wanted me to do, then I'd have to start worrying."[89]

A lad from Anaconda, Montana, grew up, and in the course of a lifetime, just trying to be a good disciple of Jesus, got into a fair amount of trouble. He became a prophetic-minded Roman Catholic archbishop, one who shared authority and responsibility, who envisioned and enacted nonviolence, called for unilateral nuclear disarmament, practiced conscientious war tax resistance by redirecting a percentage of his tax to a peace fund, and, to be sure, disturbed some power elites of his church and his country.

When I met with him in June 1989, he spoke about faith in this way. "What does not change is one's conviction of God's love in our life." God accepts us as we are, not as we should be. The key, he told me, is to grasp the totality of the life of Jesus. It is the way of life lived by Jesus that we should strive to follow. "It all comes down to what it means to be a follower of Christ." God's acceptance of us as we are provides us with an infinite well of faith from which we can draw in the midst of our own shortcomings, to deepen our commitment to follow Jesus.[90] Hunthausen tried to follow in the footsteps of Jesus. "It would be the life of Jesus that I look at. How he himself responded to injustice.... I think if we look at the New Testament and the life of Jesus, it certainly tells us to love our enemies and to do good to those who hate us."[91] What did Hunthausen mean when he said that Jesus has called us to the vow of nonviolence? "My strongest feeling about it is to look at the life of Jesus, to see the totality of his life." We must open up to forgiveness.

> "It takes a great deal for someone to say that violence stops here. It won't stop unless there is a fundamental willingness to forgive. In my own reflection on this I have found it tremendously valuable to just know that the Lord has forgiven me so much, and to say 'yes' to it. I try to be aware of my own shortcomings, my faults and failures, and how over my life I have been unworthy of forgiveness, if you will. But I know, I just know the goodness of God and that I am immediately forgiven if I accept this forgiveness."[92]

Hunthausen believed we are all called to holiness and this is the way to human happiness.

> "If we're going to live a holy life, if we're going to live a truly human life, this is the only way it's going to happen. We give ourselves away; we live for the life of the other. That is what love is all about. That has touched me. Yes, it's a command, but properly understood it's a lot more than that. It's the Lord trying to tell us who we are. To live a happy life—this is how you do it."[93]

Hunthausen tried to pattern his life not so much after an abstract ideal, as after the life and character of Jesus. Breemen's *As Bread That Is Broken*, a profoundly influential book for Hunthausen, captures this well: "The ideal, then, is not a state of perfection to be reached but fidelity to God's love.... We are centered on a Person, not on an ideal."[94]

How did Hunthausen think about the relationship between spirituality and social and political action for justice and peace? "I do believe that if one is striving to grow in intimacy with the Lord, in other words to develop a spiritual life, that person will be almost forced to speak to the politics of the time. If justice issues are involved, and it seems to me that that's almost a synonym for politics, one will feel obligated to speak, to bring about just and healthy developments in the life of people." We are called by God to love God with our whole heart and our neighbor as ourselves. "We do that in love, which means that we can't avoid touching the political scene."[95]

For the 40th anniversary of Vatican II, at Seattle University, in 2002, Archbishop Hunthausen reflected on how the council:

> "helped us take real responsibility for our lives and our decision making. It was not enough simply to do what we were told. Before the council, something or somebody out there had to take the responsibility, someone else had to take the blame for what might go wrong in our lives. That's not enough, nor is it sufficient to say, 'I'll do whatever I want to do.' That is totally contrary to what the Gospel is about and what Jesus has come to teach us. The harder way is to make an effort in prayer to examine what the church is saying on an issue, if it be a church issue. Open ourselves to the Spirit to discern the Spirit. And then, even though you know it might be difficult, arrive at a decision that is truly ours."

He asked his listeners there in Seattle that day to "examine our motivation and to do that under the influence of the Spirit—always, always the Spirit. Today we need to pray for the Spirit in our life, in our church and in our world." He reflected on something he read in Anthony de Mello's *Contact with God*.

> "He makes the observation: the church of our time is in crisis. That is not always a bad thing. Crisis is an opportunity to say, 'Yeah, it's okay to grow, to grow up and become mature and examine one's life, to work at it, to become better people.' There is chaos only if the Spirit isn't hovering over it. So what we really need in our church and our world today is an inpouring of the Spirit, an inpouring of the Spirit, to become people of the Spirit and to recognize as did the first disciples that the Spirit is always there in our lives, that as Jesus told his disciples you need to wait for the coming of the Spirit."

And he prepared to conclude his talk:

> "We have a hard time waiting. But to devote ourselves to prayer is to ask for insight. To remain as individuals and people gathered in prayer and in parishes and wherever else, to seek the assistance of the Spirit. We cannot make the Spirit happen. The Spirit is gift. But we need to have a sense of anticipation. We need a miracle. Expect one. Expect one, be people of hope. Always, because God is in our midst. There isn't any question about that. And over and over again we continue to pray, as honestly and as profoundly as we can, that the Spirit will touch our lives and touch our world.... Ask yourself, 'When last did I ask for the Spirit in my life and in my work and in the church?' It is there to help us all, more than ever before to understand what Vatican

II was about because I have no doubt in my mind that Vatican II has a lot yet to be lived."[96]

In 2012, for the 50th anniversary of the beginning of the Second Vatican Council, Hunthausen expressed his indelible experience of the Spirit at work.

> "I have the strongest conviction that the Second Vatican Council has been and continues to be an incredible grace in the life of the church. I also believe that the council is not locked up in documents but is alive through the Spirit, who is always doing something new in the church. For that reason, the church—the whole people of God—needs to be listening and learning. Otherwise, we will miss the Spirit's voice and that would be a great sin indeed.
>
> I have to acknowledge that much of the early excitement and energy the council ignited have cooled. For that reason, I find myself returning to John XXIII and his great vision for a 'new Pentecost' for the church. We have made significant strides, but we—as Christians—still remain on the Lenten side of Easter and Pentecost.
>
> We need to keep praying the prayer John XXIII composed for the council, the prayer that I prayed each day, along with my brother bishops during those years of grace and hope: We stand before you, Holy Spirit, conscious of our sinfulness, but aware that we gather in your name. Come to us, remain with us, and enlighten our hearts. Give us light and strength to know your will, to make it our own, and to live it in our lives. Guide us by your wisdom, support us by your power.... You desire justice for all; enable us to uphold the rights of others; do not allow us to be misled by ignorance or corrupted by fear or favor.... As we gather in your name, may we temper justice with love, so that all our discussions and reflections may be pleasing to you, and earn the reward promised to good and faithful servants."[97]

Dutch, well into the twilight, once said to one of his nieces, "One of these days when I die God's going to say to me, why did you guys make such a big fuss over me?" Uncle Dutch said, "I'm sure it's very simple and we just can't figure it out." Then he added, "I'm sure I'm gonna go, wow, okay I get it. Why are we making it so difficult?"[98]

ENDNOTES

1 Walsh, Dick. Email correspondence from Helena, Montana, late August 2014.

2 The lines read, translated into English: "The joys and the hopes, the griefs and the anxieties of the men of this age, especially those who are poor or in any way afflicted, these too are the joys

and hopes, the griefs and anxieties of the followers of Christ. Indeed, nothing genuinely human fails to raise an echo in their hearts." *Gaudium Et Spes, Pastoral Constitution on the Church in the Modern World*, see in David O'Brien and Thomas Shannon, eds. *Catholic Social Thought: The Documentary Heritage*. Orbis 1992, 166.

3 Hunthausen, Raymond. "How Conscience is Informed in the Making of Moral Decisions." Speech delivered at Plymouth Congregational Church, Seattle 9 Oct. 1983. Archdiocese of Seattle Archives.

4 Hunthausen, Raymond. Ground Zero and Sanctuary Anniversary Speech 21 Nov. 1987. Archdiocese of Seattle Archives.

5 "It Comes From Faith." Interview with Raymond Hunthausen. *Ground Zero*. Summer 1987, 3.

6 "It Comes From Faith."

7 Hunthausen, Raymond. Personal interview, Seattle, Washington 22 June 1989.

8 Finley, James. Quoting from Merton's book, *Contemplative Prayer. See Merton's Palace of Nowhere: A Search for God through Awareness of the True Self.* Ave Maria Press, 1978, 143.

9 Finley, James. Quoting Merton, 143.

10 Breemen, Peter van G. *As Bread That Is Broken*. Dimension Books, 1974, 9.

11 Burns, Jim. Personal interview. Edmonds, Washington 17 Sept. 2012.

12 De Mello, Anthony. *Awareness: The Perils and Opportunities of Reality*. Doubleday 1990, 140.

13 "Archbishop Hunthausen, Whose Views Sparked Controversy, Announces Retirement" Associated Press 18 June 1991. *Lexisnexis.com*. Web. 6 Aug. 2012.

14 Maier, Scott. "Hunthausen To Retire Early; Catholics Divided; Backers Sorrowful, Critics Delighted" *Seattle Post-Intelligencer* 19 June 1991, A1.

15 Wolcott, John. "Catholics stunned by Seattle Archbishop Hunthausen's decision to leave his post" *National Catholic Reporter* 5 July 1991, 1,6.

16 Bruscas, Angelo. "Group Protests Hunthausen Policies" *Seattle Post-Intelligencer* 19 May 1990, A8.

17 Fleck, Mary Anne. "'Everybody's archbishop' build justice" *Progress* 1 Aug. 1991, 21-22.

18 Miner, Esther Lucero. Personal interview. Seattle, Washington 12 Dec. 2012.

19 Fleck, Mary Anne. "'Everybody's archbishop' build justice" *Progress* 1 Aug. 1991, 22.

20 "Hunthausen's Legacy The Gift of Humility" Editorial, *Seattle Post-Intelligencer* 23 June 1991, D2.

21 Hunthausen, Raymond. Talk at Hing Hay Park, Seattle. 3 June 1990. Personal Files of Don Hopps.

22 Connelly, Joel. "Hunthausen Calls For Vocal Stand Against Starting War" *Seattle Post-Intelligencer* 10 Jan. 1991, A2.

23 Penhale, Ed. "2,000 Rally For Peace In Mideast; 'Fresh' Ideas Needed For Policy On Gulf, Say Governor, Archbishop" *Seattle Post-Intelligencer* 11 Jan. 1991, A4.

24 Ramos, Michael. Personal interview. Seattle, Washington 12 Dec. 2012.

25 Hunthausen, Raymond. "Faith and Truth in a Decade of Power". *Ground Zero*. Spring 1991, 2,4.

26 Hadley, Jane. "PLU Vetoes Degree For Hunthausen; He Was Nominated For Honorary Doctorate" *Seattle Post-Intelligencer* 8 May 1991, B1.

27 Iwasaki, John. "A Walk To End All Wars; Marchers Remember Those Killed In Gulf, Call For World Peace" *Seattle Post-Intelligencer* 22 June 1991, B1.

28 Werner, Larry. "Hunthausen Draws Faithful To Final Masses; Peacemaking Posture Praised" *Seattle Post-Intelligencer* 12 Aug. 1991,B1.

29 Bruscas, Angelo. "Farewell To A Man Of Peace; Hunthausen Praised, Blessed At Service" *Seattle Post-Intelligencer* 13 Aug. 1991,B3.

30 Ostrom, Carol. "Hunthausen steps down at warm farewell" *Seattle Times* 13 Aug. 1991.

31 Hunthausen, Raymond. Address at Celebration. 12 Aug. 1991 Seattle, Washington. Personal Files of Don Hopps.

32 Hunthausen, Raymond.

33 McDermott, Michael. Personal interview. Tacoma, Washington 14 Dec. 2012.

34 McDermott, Michael. Personal interview. Tacoma, Washington 25 Mar. 2013.

35 Ryan, Michael. Personal interview. Seattle, Washington 2 Dec. 2011.

36 Heagle, John. Personal interview. Gleneden Beach, Oregon 16 Mar. 2013.

37 Heagle, John.

38 Heagle, John.

39 Semmens, John. "A Man Called 'Dutch': The Lasting Impact of Archbishop Raymond G. Hunthausen on Carroll College" Unpublished paper written for History Research Seminar 495, Carroll College 18 Dec. 2007, 22-23. See *Montana Catholic Register*. 31 Aug. 1962.

40 Hunthausen, Edna. Personal interview. Helena, Montana 17 Aug. 2011. Also see Cornelia Flaherty's *Go With Haste Into The Mountains* Catholic Diocese of Helena 1984, 183.

41 Hunthausen, Edna. Personal interview. Helena, Montana 17 Aug. 2011.

42 Hunthausen, Mark and Pam. Personal interview. Helena, Montana 2 Aug. 2014.

43 Hunthausen, Denny. Personal interview. Tacoma, Washington 25 Mar. 2013.

44 Walsh, Dick. Email correspondence from Helena, Montana, late August and September 2014.

45 Hunthausen, Denny. Email correspondence from Tacoma, Washington, 5 April 2014.

46 Hunthausen, Tony. Personal interview. Helena, Montana 4 Aug. 2014.

47 Hunthausen, Bill. Personal interview. Helena, Montana 5 Aug. 2014.

48 Hunthausen, Denny. Personal interview. Tacoma, Washington 25 Mar. 2013.

49 Hunthausen, Andy. Personal interview. Helena, Montana 3 Aug. 2014.

50 Hunthausen, Tony. Personal interview. Helena, Montana 4 Aug. 2014.

51 Walsh, Dick. Email correspondence from Helena, Montana, late August and September 2014.

52 Ries, Victoria. Personal interview. Seattle, Washington 10 Dec. 2012.

53 Hunthausen, Kathleen. Personal interview. Helena, Montana 4 Aug. 2014.

54 Walsh, Sarah. Personal interview. Helena, Montana 2 Aug. 2014.

55 Hunthausen, Kathleen. Personal interview. Helena, Montana 4 Aug. 2014.

56 Walsh, Dick. Email correspondence from Helena, Montana, late August and September 2014.

57 Walsh, Sarah. Personal interview. Helena, Montana 2 Aug. 2014.

58 Walsh, Sarah. Sarah shared a copy of the homily with me when we met that evening.

59 Walsh, Sarah.

60 Klass, Tim. "Archbishop faced controversy before sex abuse case" Associated Press 19 May 2009. *Lexisnexis.com*. Web. 6 Aug. 2012.

61 Klass, Tim.

62 Tu, Janet. "Archdiocese defends vetting former priest" *Seattle Times* 14 May 2009.

63 Heagle, John. Personal interview. Gleneden Beach, Oregon 16 Mar. 2013. Also personal interviews with Carol Ann McMullen Edmonds, Washington 8 Dec. 2012 and Jack Walmsley West Seattle 8 Dec. 2012.

64 Egan, Timothy. "Molestation of Child by Priest Stirring Furor and Anguish in Seattle Church" *New York Times* 12 June 1988 Global Issues in Context. Web 9 Aug. 2012.

65 Ho, Vanessa. "Eight More Men File Suit Against Seattle Archdiocese" *Seattle Post-Intelligencer* 25 July 2002, B4.

66 "Montana Catholic diocese files bankruptcy to settle sex abuse claims" *Los Angeles Times*. *LAtimes.com* 31 Jan. 2014.

67 Heagle, John. Personal interview. Gleneden Beach, Oregon 16 Mar. 2013.

68 Kidston, Martin. "Hunthausen looks back" *Independent Record.* Helena, Montana. 22 Feb. 2003, 1,11.

69 In unpublished piece by Marilyn Veomett (sister of Dave Jaeger), "A Day with Dutch" Oct. 2012.

70 Hunthausen, Kathleen. Personal interview. Helena, Montana 4 Aug. 2014.

71 Shea, Dan. Personal interview. Helena, Montana 4 Aug. 2014.

72 Hunthausen, Tony. Personal interview. Helena, Montana 4 Aug. 2014.

73 Hunthausen, Bill. Personal interview. Helena, Montana 5 Aug. 2014.

74 Walsh, Sarah. Personal interview. Helena, Montana 2 Aug. 2014.

75 Walsh, Sarah.

76 Hunthausen, Andy. Personal interview. Helena, Montana 3 Aug. 2014.

77 Hunthausen, Andy.

78 Schilling, 328.

79 Dumont, Louise. Personal interview. Seattle, Washington 10 Dec. 2012.

80 Pruitt, Kathleen. Personal interview. Seattle, Washington 3 Dec. 2011.

81 Ryan, Michael. Personal interview, Seattle, Washington 2 Dec 2011.

82 Ryan, Michael.

83 Ryan, Michael.

84 McDermott, Michael. Personal interview. Tacoma, Washington 25 Mar. 2013.

85 Heagle, John. Personal interview. Gleneden Beach, Oregon 16 Mar. 2013.

86 Hogan, Jim. Personal interview. Missoula, Montana 7 Aug. 2014.

87 Kelly, Cornelius (Con) Joseph. Telephone interview and email correspondence. Missoula, Montana 21 Aug. 2014. Con Kelly was enormously helpful in reviewing Part III with me, and likewise served as an excellent editing partner chapter by chapter throughout the book.

88 Hunthausen, Raymond. Personal interview. Seattle, Washington 22 June 1989.

89 Hunthausen, Raymond. Interview by Michael Gallagher 9 Apr. 1988.

90 Hunthausen, Raymond. Personal interview. Seattle, Washington 22 June 1989.

91 Hunthausen, Raymond. Personal interview, Seattle, Washington 16 Sept. 1988.

92 "It Comes From Faith."

93 "It Comes From Faith."

94 Breeman, 101.

95 "It Comes From Faith."

96 Hunthausen, Raymond. "We Need A Miracle—Expect One: Reminiscences on Vatican II and My Life as a Bishop" *Carroll Magazine* Summer 2008, reprint of article from Seattle Theology and Ministry Review, Vol. 3 (2003).

97 Hunthausen, Raymond. "A bishop receives 'on-the-job training'" *National Catholic Reporter*, special edition for 50th anniversary of Vatican II "A church reborn" 11 Oct. 2012, 35-36

98 Miller, Carolyn (Stergar). Personal interview. Helena, Montana 6 Aug. 2014.

CONCLUSION

> "In our human experience, change and fear entwine. But change is essential for growth. Change is a matter of the spirit."—Raymond G. Hunthausen

The sociological imagination, wrote C. Wright Mills, "enables us to grasp history and biography and the relations between the two within society." Mills understood how this imagination could help us "range from the most impersonal and remote transformations to the most intimate features of the human self" in order to understand the relations between the two.[1] By using this approach, painting his character on a large canvas of religious and societal complexities, we have come to see the significance of Archbishop Hunthausen's witness for justice and peace.

Dutch Hunthausen was a religious leader grounded in practices of faith, hope, and love. He was fortunate to have experienced an upbringing conducive to his positive disposition. As son, brother, uncle, and great uncle, Dutch Hunthausen enjoyed the gift of a loving family. Others have not always been so fortunate. Raymond Hunthausen was aware of this painful reality around him. The affability so evident in his good-natured character did not mean that he blithely ignored the injustices committed against human beings. Nor did he fail to see the impact that hubris was having on the planet. In this regard, Dutch Hunthausen had an environmental ethic that arose from his deep sense of nature. He cherished the great outdoors. Archbishop Hunthausen could experience the sacred in nature.[2] On many a hike he would celebrate Mass with family and friends on mountain tops.

If one were to view his life through a skiing metaphor, it could be said that he loved the journey. Yet he faced some formidable obstacles. Some of those obstacles, alas, were not natural. They were put in his path by contrary forces in his religion and in his society that did not want to hear his prophetic message.

Hunthausen did not hold bitterness toward those who made his journey an ordeal. He focused on the good of the community—the religious, as well as the national—not on his own plight. He believed that forgiveness and healing could arise from shared membership in communities striving for authentic memory. His ecumenical and interfaith spirit gave evidence of this, as did his inclusive spirit with people in various communities too long marginalized and disenfranchised. As a classic representative character, he called on both his nation and his church to become communities of fuller memory. This call could be a personal one to each of us as well, for it was Hunthausen's personal impact on people, one-to-one, that was perhaps his greatest charisma. As Robert Bellah and colleagues observed in *Habits of the Heart*, a community of memory can help its participants foster the courage to remember not only suffering endured, but also suffering inflicted. A faith tradition, or a nation, when it is a living tradition open to healthy argument and honest exchange can be just such a community of memory.

> "The stories that make up a tradition contain conceptions of character, of what a good person is like, and of the virtues that define such character. But the stories are not all exemplary, not all about success and achievements. A genuine community of memory will also tell painful stories of shared suffering that sometimes creates deeper identities than success.... And if the community is completely honest, it will remember stories not only of suffering received but of suffering inflicted—dangerous memories, for they call the community to alter ancient evils."[3]

To remember what has been forgotten—for a nation, a religion, or a person—takes courage. We have to uncover shards that have been left in forgotten ruins. In some ruins, as in the sad history of the church sex-abuse crisis, the stories have been kept hidden deliberately. To truly become a community of memory, we must see how the pieces fit together and thereby come to see what the whole story really means. Hunthausen's whole story would not be fairly told if it became mere hagiography. Like many others in positions of leadership, as a bishop in Helena and as an archbishop in Seattle, he could have done more to address the church sex-abuse patterns. Hunthausen was part of an institutional system that failed to hold perpetrators accountable, even though he made some efforts in Seattle to change the system.

He was as human as any of us and had room to grow. As suggested in this book, he was caught in a labyrinth built of both suppression and loyalty. Yet, Raymond Hunthausen was inspired on the path of conscience and courage by an inner call of faith and by people engaged conscientiously in the struggle to become a religious as well as a civic community of memory and hope. He, in turn, called his church and his country to conscience. He never gave up hope in the capacity for positive personal and collective change. He affirmed, in his commitment to communal action, what the authors of *Habits of the Heart* have written: "The communities of memory that tie us to the past also turn us toward the future as communities of hope. They carry a context of meaning that can allow us to connect our aspirations for ourselves and those closest to us with the aspirations of a larger whole and see our own efforts as being, in part, contributions to a common good."[4]

Hunthausen's most compelling authority was to be found in the humility so characteristic of his leadership. This is the authority-power paradox so vital to understanding the meaning of his witness. He never sought power and authority, if power and authority are understood as control and domination. As a matter of fact, he confronted and challenged this very paradigm of power and authority in his nation and in his church. He was more explicitly prophetic and direct in calling his nation to turn away from such a dominating power paradigm. He might have been better served had he been just as forthright in calling his religion on the same account. Yet he never stopped cultivating an ethos of shared responsibility with the people. This remained true even when the powers in the Vatican, in a choice moment that exemplified Rome's "centralization of power" paradigm, told him he had lost all credibility because he lacked the necessary firmness to govern—that is, to govern "from above," as Rome in that era wanted its bishops to do. Today, with Pope Francis, the tide has turned, but it was a very different See when Raymond Hunthausen tried to share power and authority rather than guard them.

Raymond Hunthausen's call to his country and church could endure in several ways, all traced in the pages of this book. In his spiritual practice—both personal and communal—he could invite us to center our lives in prayer and contemplation. These habits of the heart are so needed in a time when materialism, distraction, and even the sirens of nihilism call too many people away from their better character. Through his sense of humor, athletic outdoor ethic, and gift of storytelling—both with family and the wider community—he offers us a model of an embodied and down-to-earth way of living. At times some of us get caught up in disembodied theoretical discourse, forgetting the wisdom that awaits our discovery until we engage our whole beings as we are and where we are. I am reminded of what happened once in the late 1980s. I had asked Archbishop Hunthausen to explain to me his theology of peace. Right after that interview had ended, as I learned many years later, he asked his theological adviser, "So, do I have a theology of peace?" I was so focused on trying to fathom his approach to peace on an intellectual and theological plane. Hunthausen's real theology of peace was to be discovered in how he lived it. The habits of his heart and mind were his path of peace. Peace came alive in the mimetic and mythic expressions of his life, not simply in the theoretic. As cultural anthropologists have shown us, religion was dance and story before it was ever theology and dogma. Dutch Hunthausen's ubiquitous sense of play, humor, and story invite us into a more intrinsically meaningful way of living.[5]

One way Hunthausen's message may hopefully endure comes from his model of church, how he lived it and shared it. As we have seen, it was so different from the hierarchical and controlling model of governance employed to thwart him and the Vatican II spirit of collaboration he exemplified. Here he calls us to a path we are seeing anew in the ways of Pope Francis, a sign of hope for change Dutch

Hunthausen must be celebrating. He calls us to live with respect and full equality with people, regardless of their gender or sexual orientation. His welcoming example in this area remains a challenge to the leadership of the institutional church, even though here again we see indications of the same deeply respectful spirit in Pope Francis. Raymond Hunthausen made a concerted effort to welcome gays and lesbians and to overcome gender inequality in the church. That work remains as important now as ever.

We come full circle to what remains the single most significant call Hunthausen made to his nation, "Faith and Disarmament." That call relates to all of the other calls for change he made, for indeed Rev. Martin Luther King was right when, in his famous Letter from Birmingham Jail, he reminded a nation that "an injustice anywhere is a threat to justice everywhere." Likewise, Hunthausen could see the inextricable relationships that tie together myriad concerns for justice and peace. It was his June 1981 "Faith and Disarmament" call and his subsequent civil disobedience actions, that played a catalytic role in so much of the church turmoil he was to be put through. We remember that it was people from the Ground Zero Center for Nonviolent Action who helped Hunthausen move deep into the issues which would concentrate his mind as he pondered the nearby reality of Trident as a massive first-strike nuclear weapons system.

According to the dedicated people who today continue the research, reflection, and peaceful resistance work at the Ground Zero Center for Nonviolent Action next to the Bangor base on the Hood Canal, the U.S. nuclear enterprise:

> "...is a self-feeding monster that lost its reason for existing with the fall of the Berlin Wall. Now, two and a half decades after the end of the Cold War, the U.S. has been completely rebuilding the infrastructure that researches, builds and maintains the nation's nuclear weapons. Beyond that, plans are in motion to build new delivery platforms for all three legs of the nation's nuclear triad—sea, land, and air. Chief among these is Trident. Over the next three decades this will cost the U.S. upwards of $1 trillion dollars. A new generation of Trident ballistic missile submarines will cost (according to the Congressional Budget Office) approximately $100 billion just to build, and will increase the proliferation of nuclear weapons and accelerate a new arms race (including a nuclear submarine arms race). Our nation is squandering our human and financial treasure on the very tools of humanity's demise. We stand at a new crossroads, one that is very reminiscent of the period when Hunthausen delivered his 1981 speech."[6]

Picture a pie chart of worldwide military spending. The United States takes up nearly half of the pie. That massive spending has not simply produced a humongous arsenal. The *use* of U.S. military force has been pervasive. Think of its use in the world in the aftermath of 9/11, but also recall the years when Archbishop Hunthausen was in Seattle. From 1975-1991, the U.S. applied military force in places including Angola, El Salvador, Afghanistan, Nicaragua, Lebanon, Grenada, Iran, Libya, Panama, Kuwait, and Iraq. Chalmers Johnson, in a sobering trilogy—*Blowback*, *The Sorrows of Empire*, and *Nemesis*—documented the reach of American militarism as it still stands today with well over 700 bases throughout the world.[7]

Raymond Hunthausen, with soft-spoken eloquence, called out to his country:

> "Propaganda and a particular way of life have clothed us to death. To relinquish our hold on global destruction feels like risking everything, and it is risking everything—but in a direction opposite to the way in which we now risk everything. Nuclear arms protect privilege and exploitation. Giving them up would mean our having to give up economic power over other peoples. Peace and justice go together. On the path we now follow, our economic policies toward other countries require nuclear weapons. Giving up the weapons would mean giving up more than our means of global terror. It would mean giving up the reason for such terror—our privileged place in the world."

Hunthausen asked a question in that era which each of us could ask today:

> "How can such a process, of taking up the cross of nonviolence, happen in a country where our government seems paralyzed by arms corporations? In a country where many of the citizens, perhaps most of the citizens, are numbed into passivity by the very magnitude and complexity of the issue.... Clearly some action is demanded—some form of nonviolent resistance."[8]

Raymond Hunthausen listened to a disarming spirit alive in others, acted on what he heard, and became a disarming spirit himself. We could catch the same spirit. To turn away from the hubris of empire and the idols of false security, as a nation, we will need the social power of nonviolence. We will need collective conscience, courage, and character. Still, as made evident by the life of a man called Dutch, it is in part up to each of us to draw from our individual wellsprings of conscience, to muster our unique courage, and to write with the integrity of our own lives the next chapter of our personal character.

ENDNOTES

1 Mills, C. Wright. *The Sociological Imagination*. Oxford University Press. 1959 (40th anniv. edition, 2000), 6-7.

2 Unlike some of the bishops who, when they reviewed the early draft of the international pastoral letter on the Columbia River, did not accept the language of "the sacramental commons" for fear

that nature would be confused with the official sacraments; see Catholic Bishops of the Region. *The Columbia River Watershed: Caring for Creation and the Common Good. An International Pastoral Letter.* 8 Jan. 2001. Columbia River Project. Seattle, Washington.

3 Bellah, Robert, Richard Madsen, William Sullivan, Ann Swidler, and Steven Tipton. *Habits of the Heart: Individualism and Commitment in American Life*, 153

4 Bellah, 153.

5 For a discussion of the mimetic, mythic (or narrative), and theoretic, see Robert Bellah's masterpiece, *Religion In Human Evolution: From the Paleolithic to the Axial Age*. Belnap Press of Harvard University 2011.

6 Eiger, Leonard. Ground Zero Center for Nonviolent Action. Correspondence with the author, 11 Nov. 2014, Veterans Day.

7 In addition to the excellent trilogy by Chalmers Johnson, see also *American Society: How It Really Works,* by Erik Olin Wright and Joel Rogers. W.W. Norton & Company 2011, Chapter 20, "Militarism and Empire".

8 See chapter one, citing from Archbishop Hunthausen's "Faith and Disarmament" address at the Pacific Northwest Lutheran Synod, Tacoma, Washington, June 12, 1981.

RAYMOND G. HUNTHAUSEN

A Brief Chronology

- Born in Anaconda, Montana, August 21, 1921
- Oldest of seven children of Anthony Hunthausen and Edna Tuchscherer, grew up in Anaconda, 1921–1939
- Carroll College student athlete, Helena, Montana, 1939–1943
- Theology student at St. Edward's Seminary, Kenmore, Washington, 1943–1946
- Ordained a Catholic priest, Anaconda, Montana, 1946
- Graduate studies at Notre Dame, and then chemistry teacher and coach of various sports at Carroll College, 1946–1957
- President of Carroll College, 1957–1962
- Bishop of Helena, 1962–1975 (Attended each session of the Second Vatican Council, 1962–1965)
- Archbishop of Seattle, 1975–1991
- Began many efforts to listen to the people, to engage in ecumenical work, and to transform the church (just as he had in Helena), 1975
- Met Jim Douglass and began to ponder the meaning of Trident and Bangor base, 1976
- Pastoral letter on the role of women in the church, 1980
- "Faith and Disarmament" Speech, June 12, 1981
- Verbal attack on Hunthausen by U.S. Navy Secretary John Lehman, March 1982
- Opened St. James Cathedral to Dignity (gay and lesbian Catholic community), September 1983
- Vatican's Apostolic Visitation in Seattle, November 1983
- Confidential letter to Hunthausen from Cardinal Ratzinger, September 1985
- Key areas of Archbishop Hunthausen's official authority taken away by Rome, 1986
- Making his case to his brother bishops, Washington, D.C., November 1986

- Apostolic Commission (Cardinal Bernardin et. al.) completes its oversight of Seattle, 1989.
- Archbishop Hunthausen resigns, August 1991
- After retirement at age 70, returns to Montana to be near family and the good earth. He leads retreats while traveling about the Helena diocese to perform liturgies and pastoral acts.
- He spent the last years of his life in shared residence with his brother, Father Jack Hunthausen.
- Died in Helena, Montana, July 22, 2018

HUNTHAUSEN, WALSH, & STERGAR FAMILY TREE

The Archbishop was preceded in death by his parents Anthony and Edna Hunthausen, sister Marie Walsh, brother Art Hunthausen, sisters-in-law Harriett and Donna Hunthausen, brothers-in-law Pat Walsh and John Stergar, nephews Pat, Ed, and Jack Walsh, Ray Hunthausen, and great-nephew Patrick Kelly. He is survived by his brothers Tony and Fr. John (Jack) Hunthausen, both of Helena; and his sisters, Sister Edna Hunthausen, of the Sisters of Charity of Leavenworth, KS, and Jean Stergar of Anaconda, 34 nieces and nephews, 101 great nieces and nephews, and 64 great-great nieces and nephews.

Last Name	First Name	Middle	Birthdate	Current City	Current State	Death
Children of Anthony Hunthausen and Edna Tuchscherer						
Hunthausen	Raymond "Dutch"	Gehardt	August 21, 1921	Heaven		July 22, 2018
Walsh	Marie	Frances	January 14, 1923	Heaven		September 22, 2016
Hunthausen	Anthony "Tony"	Adam	January 25, 1926	E. Helena	MT	
Hunthausen	John "Jack"	Frederick	July 25, 1927	Helena	MT	
Hunthausen	Edna	Ruth	May 13, 1929	Helena	MT	
Hunthausen	Arthur "Art"	Robert	February 12, 1931	Heaven		October 23, 2010
Stergar	Jean	Ann	November 5, 1934	Anaconda	MT	

Last Name	First Name	Middle	Birthdate	Current City	Current State	Death
Marie and Pat Walsh Family						
Walsh	Patrick "Pat"	Francis	October 30, 1945	Heaven		July 22, 1975
Walsh	Raymond "Ray"	Eugene	October 24, 1946	Kingwood	TX	
Hardy	Joan	Marie	October 12, 1948	Billings	MT	
Cahill	Edna	Ruth	November 30, 1949	Billings	MT	
Stevenson	Michelle		December 11, 1950	Anaconda	MT	
McCutcheon	Colleen	Ann	January 17, 1952	Helena	MT	
Walsh	John "Jackie"	Anthony	June 1, 1953	Heaven		December 27, 1958
Ciez	Mary	Margaret	October 14, 1954	Ronan	MT	
Walsh	Richard "Dick"	James	December 31, 1955	E. Helena	MT	
Walsh	Thomas "Tom"	Joseph	July 1, 1959	Missoula	MT	
Walsh	Edward "Eddie"	Paul	December 9, 1961	Heaven		November 26, 1982
Walsh	Sarah	Jean	May 17, 1965	Helena	MT	
Tony and Harriet Hunthausen Family						
Hunthausen	Anthony "Tony"	Gerard	February 4, 1951	Westminster	CA	
Hunthausen	Kathleen "Tads"	Ann	June 7, 1952	Helena	MT	
Hunthausen	William "Bill"	Arthur	May 17, 1954	Helena	MT	
Cristiani	Mary	Teresa	July 8, 1956	Dublin	OH	
Hunthausen	Dennis "Denny"	Joseph	June 6, 1959	Fircrest	WA	
Hunthausen	Paula	Jean	January 26, 1961	Great Falls	MT	
Hunthausen	Andrew "Andy"	John	February 9, 1965	Helena	MT	
Hunthausen	John	Michael	July 8, 1968	Luxembourg		
Hunthausen	Daniel "Dan"	James	August 3, 1970	Helena	MT	

Last Name	First Name	Middle	Birthdate	Current City	Current State	Death
Art and Donna Hunthausen Family						
Hunthausen	Arthur "Mark"	Mark	November 19, 1955	Helena	MT	
Hart	Kimberly "Kim"	Ann	November 19, 1956	Olympia	WA	
Hunthausen	Paul	Joseph	January 19, 1959	Helena	MT	
Smigaj	Lynn	Marie	August 4, 1961	Helena	MT	
Hunthausen	Raymond "Ray"	Gerhardt	November 29, 1962	Heaven		June 4, 2010
Ternes	Mary	Carol	May 5, 1964	Helena	MT	
Kalbfleisch	Lisa	Renee	September 13, 1965	Whitefish	MT	
Lavin	Amy		September 5, 1969	Kalispell	MT	
Jean and John Stergar Family						
Stergar	Cindy	Jeanne	June 17, 1956	Butte	MT	
Stergar	John "Jay"	Joseph	September 1, 1957	Anaconda	MT	
Stergar-Stone	Mary	Helen	October 18, 1958	Milwaukie	OR	
Stergar	Laurie	Ann	September 16, 1959	Billings	MT	
Miller	Carolyn	Dianne	October 28, 1960	Helena	MT	
Lacey	Joan	Marie	January 6, 1963	Port Orchard	WA	
Stergar	David	Anthony	March 14, 1967	Helena	MT	
Shipman	Kathryn "Kathy"	Joan	October 17, 1969	Dillon	MT	
Stergar	James "Jim"	Gerard	April 18, 1971	Billings	MT	

*Special thanks to Dick Walsh for this family tree

MAP OF SEATTLE ARCHDIOCESE

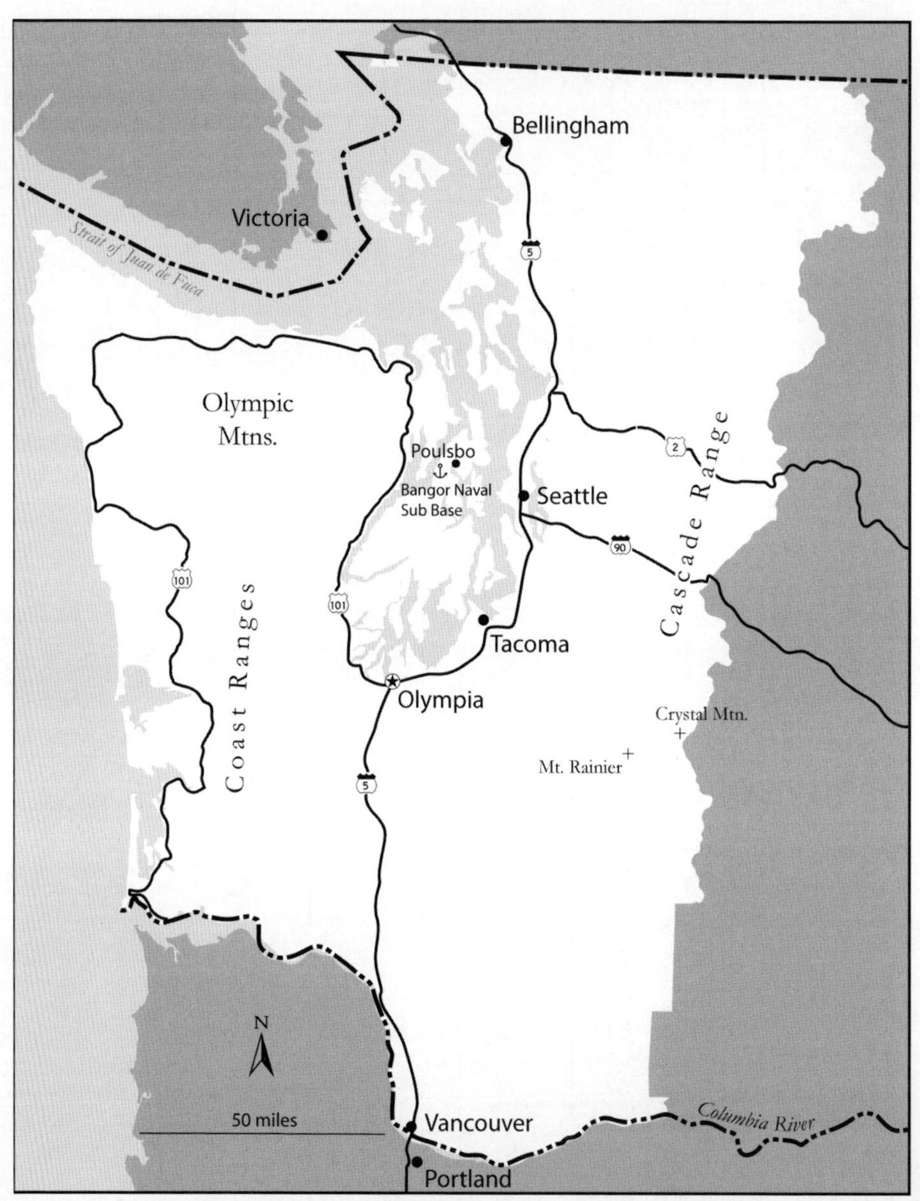

MAP OF HELENA DIOCESE

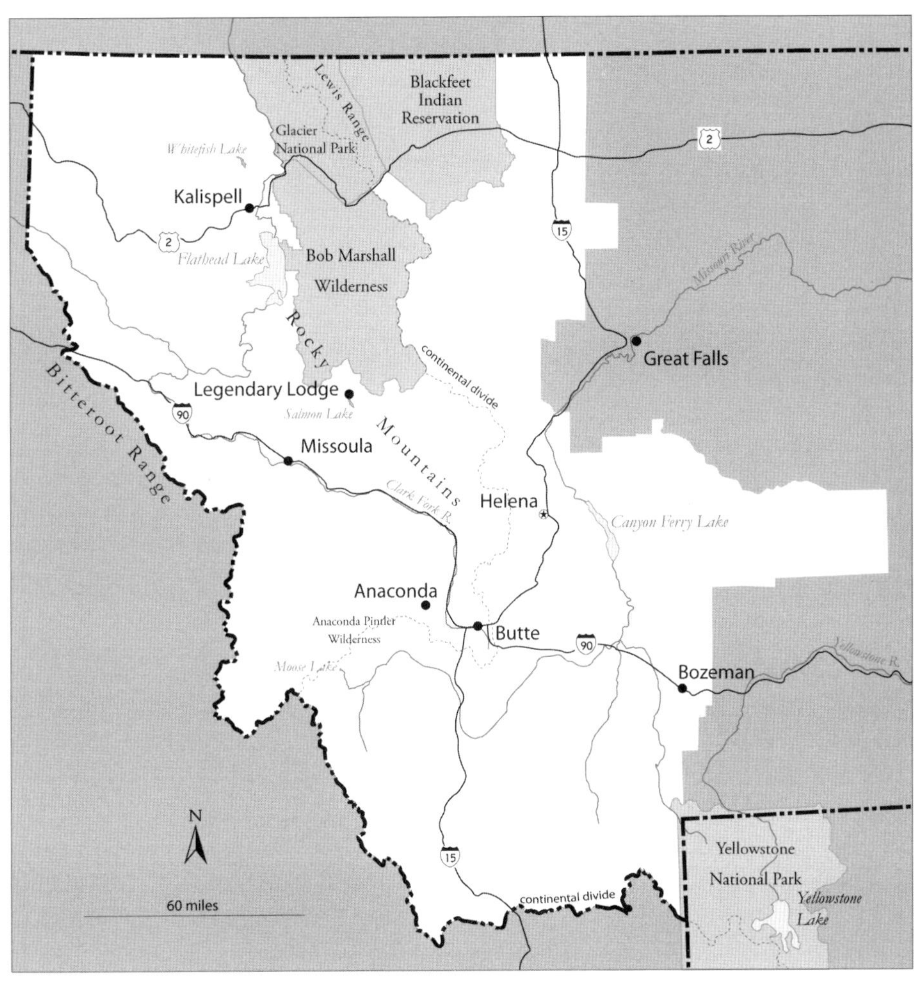

STATE OF MONTANA

Governor's Proclamation

I hereby order all flags flown in the State of Montana to be flown at half-staff on Friday, July 27th, 2018 to honor the memory of Archbishop Raymond G. Hunthausen, who passed away on July 22nd, 2018.

Archbishop Raymond G. Hunthausen "Dutch" was a born and raised Montanan, Anaconda native, teacher, coach, Carroll College President, Bishop of the Diocese of Helena, Archbishop of Seattle, the last remaining American Bishop to participate in the Second Vatican Council, and a devoted leader to all people. Dutch leaves behind a legacy as a seeker of peace and a fighter for social justice, conservationism, service to the poor, and human rights for migrant families. His work, his struggles, and his achievements are shared by all who knew him and through the cultural and religious divides he sought to heal.
We honor his life as a true Montanan and a true servant of God.

Dated this 26th day of July 2018.

STEVE BULLOCK
Governor

POSTSCRIPT FOR
A Disarming Spirit

As I pen this brief postscript, it is the morning after learning that Raymond "Dutch" Hunthausen had passed away. With his death on Sunday afternoon, July 22, 2018, his life journey brought him within one month of what would have been his 97th birthday, the 21st of August. During the last years of his life, he grounded his integrity, and accepted his frailty and fragility, with a vigorous and seasoned spirituality.

As I learned all through the process of working on this book, it is Dutch's spirit which disarms us. I tried to convey the conscience and courage which guided this humble giant. Yet his conscience and courage were guided by his character, and his character in turn was guided by what he believed to be a spirit of unconditional love at the heart of the cosmos.

I have tried to capture the essence of his true character. If I have done so it is because of all the people along the way, many cited in this book, who have shared their experiences knowing him. Even his fierce critics have, perhaps unwittingly in some cases, helped us to better appreciate the nobility and tenacity of his witness for peace and justice.

In the present moment—as we reflect on how our own personal lives relate to large social history and to the social forces and injustices all around us—what could be more important that to look for guidance in how to become a better person, to shape a better society, and to foster a better religion? Dutch Hunthausen, who loved the great natural outdoors AND walked the metaphorical path of prophetic peace, can be a guide on a long and demanding mountain trail. We can hear him speaking to us in a gentle voice: "Our security is in a loving, caring God. We must dismantle our weapons of terror and place our reliance on God."

INDEX

D

E

F

G

O

P

R

S

T

U

V

W